BRITISH COLUMBIA HANDBOOK

SECOND EDITION

BRITISH COLUMBIA HANDBOOK

SECOND EDITION

JANE KING

MOON
PUBLICATIONS INC.

Please send all comments, corrections, additions, amendments, and critiques to:

JANE KING
c/o MOON PUBLICATIONS
722 WALL STREET
CHICO, CA 95928 U.S.A.

BRITISH COLUMBIA HANDBOOK

Published by
Moon Publications Inc.
722 Wall Street
Chico, California 95928 U.S.A.
tel. (916) 345-5473

PRINTING HISTORY
1st edition—June 1989
2nd edition—August 1992

Printed by
Colorcraft Ltd., Hong Kong

Library of Congress Cataloging in Publication Data
King, Jane, 1956-
British Columbia Handbook / Jane King
p. cm.
Includes bibliographical references and index
ISBN 0-918373-77-8: $13.95
1. British Columbia—Guidebooks. I. Title
F1087.K56 1992
917.1104'4—dc20 92-6035
CIP

Printed in Hong Kong

All photos by Jane and Bruce King unless otherwise noted.

Cover photo: Jane King

WARNING: Nothing in this book is intended to be used for navigation. Mariners are advised to consult official sailing directions and nautical charts.

CONTENTS

MAPS

MAP SYMBOLS

MAIN HIGHWAY
SECONDARY ROAD
UNPAVED ROAD
FOOT TRAIL
HIGHWAY ROUTE NUMBER
INTERNATIONAL BOUNDARY
PROVINCE BOUNDARY
OTHER BOUNDARY

ALL MAPS ARE ORIENTED WITH NORTH AT THE TOP UNLESS OTHERWISE INDICATED

LARGE CITY
TOWN OR DISTRICT
SMALL TOWN
MOUNTAIN
POINT OF INTEREST

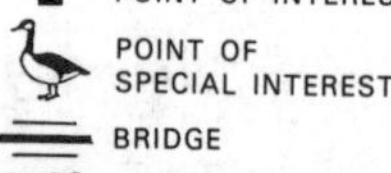

BRIDGE

WATER

PARK

SKI AREA

SCENIC HWY.
FERRY ROUTE

PASS

N.P. = NATIONAL PARK
P.P. = PROVINCIAL PARK
C.G. = CAMPGROUND

ABBREVIATIONS

C.G.—campground
d—double
4WD—four-wheel drive
HP—horsepower
HQ—headquarters
I.—island
Is.—islands
km—kilometer
km/h—kilometers per hour
OW—one-way
no.—number
p.o.—post office
pp—per person
RCMP—Royal Canadian Mounted Police
RR—railroad
RT—roundtrip
RV—recreational vehicle
s—single
t—triple
tel.—telephone number

ACKNOWLEDGEMENTS

A heartfelt thank you goes out to all the people who helped create *British Columbia Handbook:* to the friendly British Columbians who took me into their homes and made me a part of their families; to those who willingly shared their knowledge of B.C. and their insight; to all the well-trained staff of Travel InfoCentres and National Parks throughout British Columbia; and to all those who encouraged me to go to the end of the road, track, or rainbow to find a treasure I could share with those that follow.

In particular I would like to thank the following InfoCentre, Chamber of Commerce, and Park staff who greatly assisted in the update of each chapter: Elvira Quarin (Vancouver), Vi Mayer (Clearwater), Nancy Hagel (Kamloops), Victoria Charal (Banff/Lake Louise), Bobbie Phillips (Terrace), Wendy Magee (Squamish), Kris Nielsen (Fort St. James), the staff at Vanderhoof, Miriam Winston (Port Hardy), Jill Hamacher (Kimberley), Raquel Jue (Sechelt), Barb Cooper (Comox Valley), the staff at Fort St. John, Sandy Ross (Golden), Jack Hooper (Prince George), Geri Britton (Smithers), Maggie McDowell (Jasper National Park), Jacqui Hunter (Yoho National Park), Janette Gelzinis (Nelson), Keith Webb (Mt. Revelstoke and Glacier national parks), Nancy Panton and L. Edwards (Pacific National Park), Candice Brown and Judith Lowe (Salmon Arm), L.W. Biggemann (Parksville), Angie Neary (Nanaimo), P. Cavanaugh (Banff National Park), the staff at Powell River, the staff at Mt. Robson, Janice Wardle (Quesnel), Fiona Morgenthaler (Trail), Ellen Corea (Dawson Creek), Tammy Thompson (Duncan), Carol Riehl (Fernie), Dallas Mathiason (Campbell River), Susannah Khan (Revelstoke), Nikki Laine-Mayor (Tofino), Beverley Hoffman (Vernon), Lydia Mangell (Castlegar), Leah Gray (Cranbrook), the staff at Stewart, Julia Ferguson (Prince Rupert), Joy La Fortune (Queen Charlotte Islands), the staff at the Tourism Association of Vancouver I., Dawna Moon (Williams Lake), Kathy Buchowsky (Penticton), Julie (Kelowna), Heather E. Day (Victoria), Rick Rhynolds (Clinton), Inge Wilson (Hope), Julie Gaudet (Nakusp), the staff at Jasper National Park, the staff at Whistler, Sherry Kirkvold (Ministry of Lands and Parks), Ken Fisher (Kootenay National Park), Tanya Pelly (Princeton), and Maryann Rumney (Port Alberni). Also a big thank you to all the readers who took the time to share interesting tidbits of info and updated material with all of us. Keep writing!

Without the zany, hardworking, fun-loving bunch at Moon Publications, this book would be just a passing thought and a bunch of memories from previous visits. Many thanks to Managing Editor Beth Rhudy, Senior Editor Taran March (friend . . . with cookie drawer!), Mark Arends, with Bob Race, Brian Bardwell, Dave Hurst, Nancy Kennedy, Carey Wilson, Asha Johnson, Donna Galassi, Rick Johnson, and all the rest of the Moon staff—couldn't do it without you.

Extra big hugs go to my husband, Bruce, and our two-year-old bundle of joy and enthusiasm, Rachael. Thanks for the support and encouragement, patience, and all the laughs. Also hugs to the rest of the Kings, the Longs, Robert Crouch in Vancouver, and my friends in the U.S. and Australia for putting up with me when I'm on the road, glued to my computer screen, or otherwise temporarily out of touch.

IS THIS BOOK OUT OF DATE?

We strived to produce the most well-researched and up-to-date travel guide to British Columbia available. But! Accommodations and restaurants come and go, others change hands, new attractions spring up out of nowhere, prices go up, taxes are introduced—and your concerned travel writer loses considerable sleep over it all! You can help. If you discover some wonderful off-the-beaten-track attractions, outdoor delights, new places to stay and eat, or if you have info you'd like to share, or find inaccuracies or map errors, please scribble your comments into your copy of *British Columbia Handbook* and send us a synopsis when you get home. If you can improve a map, add a map of your own, or have artwork, good-quality color slides, or black-and-white prints that you'd like to see in the next edition, send them too.

We need your input. If we use your artwork or photos, Moon Publications will own the publication rights, but you'll be mentioned in the credits and receive a free copy of the book. Moon Publications is not responsible for unsolicited manuscripts, photos, or artwork, and cannot undertake to return them unless return postage is sent—so please keep copies. All your comments or ideas on how to make *British Columbia Handbook* better are welcomed, so grab this opportunity to get something off your chest and write to:

Jane King
c/o Moon Publications Inc.
722 Wall St. Chico
CA 95928 U.S.A.

LOUISE FOOTE

INTRODUCTION

British Columbia, westernmost province of Canada, covers 952,263 square kilometers of spectacular mountains, glaciers, plains, river valleys, lakes, coastline, and islands. That's an awe-inspiring 95 million hectares of land and fresh water to explore from all angles. Third-largest province in Canada and larger than all U.S. states other than Alaska, British Columbia is also 2½ times as large as Japan and four times larger than Great Britain. If you're touring the entire province, it takes almost three months to drive all the major roads—much vaster than most first-time visitors expect!

Long, and relatively narrow and rectangular, British Columbia lies between the 49th and 60th parallels. To the south are the neighboring U.S. states of Washington, Idaho, and Montana, to the northwest, Alaska, and due west the Pacific Ocean (and distant Japan). To the east is the Canadian province of Alberta, and to the north the provinces of Northwest Territories and the Yukon. Within British Columbia's boundaries lies some of the most magnificent scenery on the planet.

The largest city is **Vancouver,** a splendid conglomeration of old and new architectural marvels, parks, gardens, and beaches lying along the sheltered shores of Burrard Inlet in the southwestern corner of the province. The provincial capital is old-world Victoria, jauntily perched at the southeastern tip of nearby Vancouver I., just across the Strait of Georgia from Vancouver—an intriguing mixture of old English architecture, customs, and traditions, along with modern attractions, cosmopolitan restaurants, and an infectious joie de vivre.

THE LAND

Mountains

British Columbia occupies part of the mountainous terrain that runs down the entire western margin of the Americas, its landscape offering endless variety and enough ooh-and-aah scenery to keep even the most jaded jet-setter in awe. It lies mainly in the **Cordilleran Region,** composed of Precambrian to Cenozoic sedimentary, igneous, and metamorphic rocks which have become mountain ranges, deep intermountain troughs, and wide plateaus. The landscape is dominated by three parallel mountain ranges running north-south and a series of parallel valleys. Along the west coast is the steep **Coastal Range** containing the tallest peaks in the province. The eastern border is made up of the mighty **Rocky Mountains,** a continuous ridge of glaciated peaks. In between lie the **Cassiar Mountains** to the north and **Columbia Mountains** (made up of the Purcell, Selkirk, and Monashee ranges) to the south, and a series of rolling plateaus dotted with lakes and riddled by rivers and streams. The tallest mountain in British Columbia is 4,663-meter **Fairweather Mountain** (sixth-highest in Canada) in the **St. Elias Mountains** on the Alaskan border. In the far northeast corner are the lowlands, part of the **Great Interior Plains.**

Waterways

The province has more than its share of lakes, rivers, and streams—two million hectares of freshwater surfaces. The **Rocky Mountain Trench** contains the headwaters of the **Kootenay, Columbia, Fraser, Peace,** and **Liard** rivers. The longest river is the **Columbia** (fifth longest in Canada), which runs for 2,000 km through B.C. and Washington. A number of large islands, **Vancouver I.** (largest and closest to the mainland) and the **Queen Charlotte Is.,** and many other smaller islands lie along the deeply indented coastline, effectively protecting the mainland from much of the wind- and wave-battering action of the Pacific.

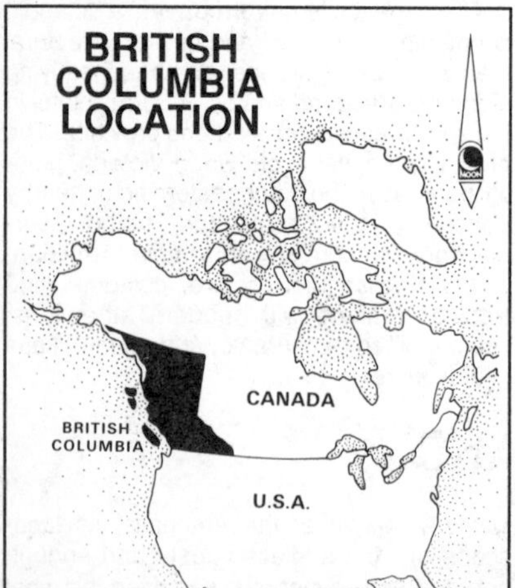

Parks

Within the province some of the most outstanding scenic delights, wildlife reserves, or places of historic interest are protected as national, provincial, or historic parks. They range in size from less than one to over a million hectares, providing almost unlimited recreational activities. The six national parks are: **Kootenay** and **Yoho** in the Rocky Mountain region, **Glacier** and **Mount Revelstoke** in High Country, **Pacific Rim** on the west coast of Vancouver I., and the newest, **South Moresby National Park** on the Queen Charlotte Islands.

Most of the national parks provide campgrounds where the maximum stay is two weeks (on a first-come, first-served basis; no reservations). Some are primitive campsites where access is only on foot (usually located near hiking trails), some are for tents only, others for tents and RVs, and some for RVs only. Most campgrounds don't have trailer hook-ups, though many do provide sewage disposal stations. Expect a level tent and parking spot, a picnic table, a fireplace or fire grill, and drinking water and toilets nearby. Some have toilet blocks, some have hot showers (rare) and kitchen shelters. In winter many campgrounds remain open, providing pit toilets and fireplaces only. Expect to pay $9-16 per night in summer, depending on the facilities provided. Please leave your campsite cleaner than you found it.

British Columbia boasts an amazing 336 provincial parks. All but the wilderness parks have a few facilities such as pit toilets and/or

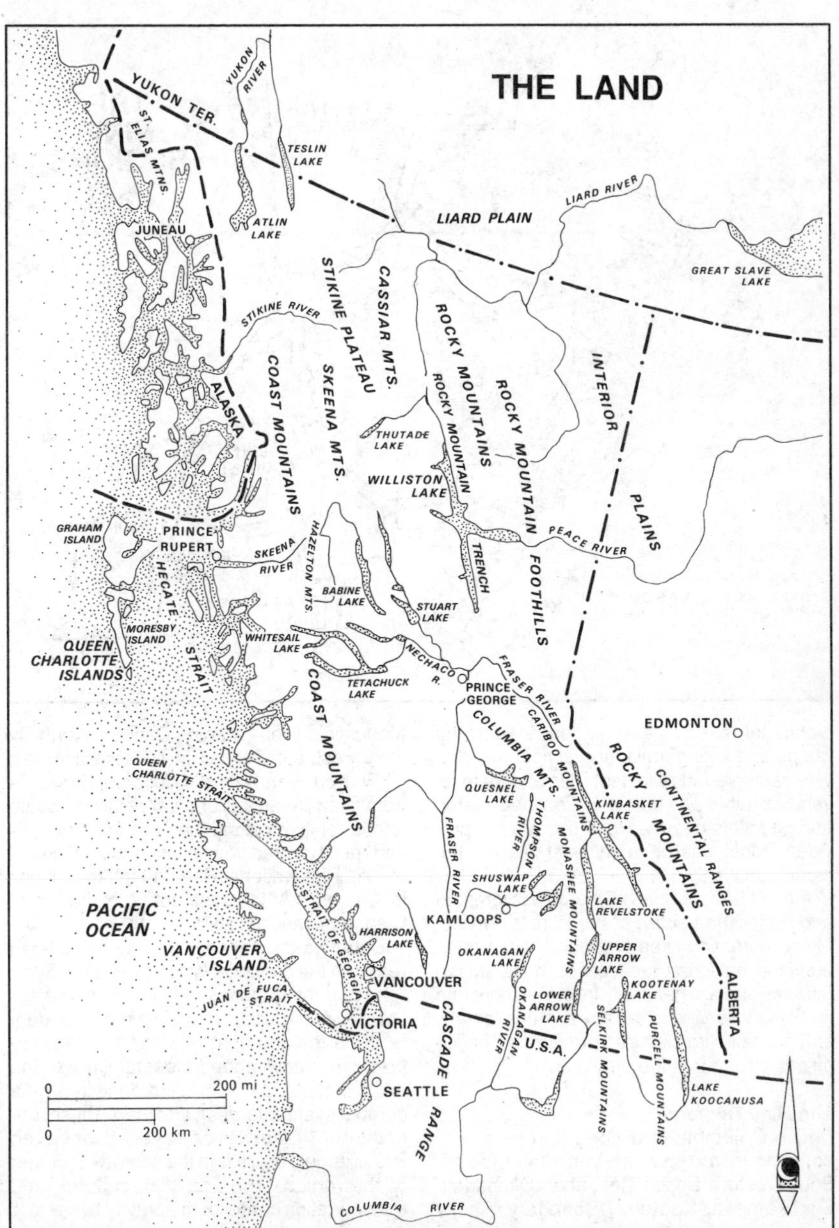
THE LAND
YUKON TER.
YUKON RIVER
ST. ELIAS MTNS.
TESLIN LAKE
ATLIN LAKE
JUNEAU
LIARD PLAIN
LIARD RIVER
GREAT SLAVE LAKE
STIKINE PLATEAU
CASSIAR MTS.
ROCKY MOUNTAINS
ROCKY MOUNTAIN TRENCH
ROCKY MOUNTAIN FOOTHILLS
INTERIOR PLAINS
STIKINE RIVER
ALASKA
COAST MOUNTAINS
SKEENA MTS.
THUTADE LAKE
WILLISTON LAKE
PEACE RIVER
GRAHAM ISLAND
PRINCE RUPERT
SKEENA RIVER
HAZELTON MTS.
HECATE STRAIT
BABINE LAKE
STUART LAKE
MORESBY ISLAND
QUEEN CHARLOTTE ISLANDS
WHITESAIL LAKE
NECHACO R.
TETACHUCK LAKE
PRINCE GEORGE
FRASER RIVER
CARIBOO MOUNTAINS
COLUMBIA MTS.
EDMONTON
ROCKY MOUNTAINS
CONTINENTAL RANGES
QUEEN CHARLOTTE STRAIT
QUESNEL LAKE
THOMPSON RIVER
KINBASKET LAKE
MONASHEE MOUNTAINS
FRASER RIVER
SHUSWAP LAKE
KAMLOOPS
LAKE REVELSTOKE
PACIFIC OCEAN
STRAIT OF GEORGIA
HARRISON LAKE
OKANAGAN LAKE
UPPER ARROW LAKE
VANCOUVER ISLAND
VANCOUVER
KOOTENAY LAKE
ALBERTA
JUAN DE FUCA STRAIT
VICTORIA
CASCADE RANGE
LOWER ARROW LAKE
OKANAGAN RIVER
U.S.A.
SELKIRK MOUNTAINS
PURCELL MOUNTAINS
LAKE KOOCANUSA
SEATTLE
0
200 mi
0
200 km
COLUMBIA RIVER
MOON

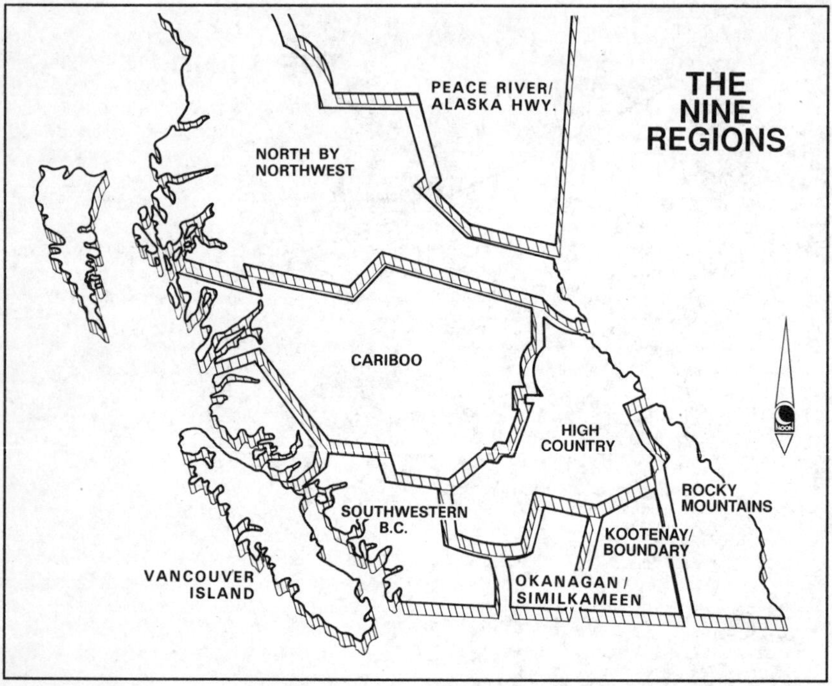

picnic tables, some have boat-launching ramps and hiking trails, and almost half provide campgrounds with tent sites and room for vehicles, table and fireplace, firewood, water, and pit toilets nearby. Hook-ups are not provided. Most charge a minimal fee for the night, usually $6-13.

Almost 85% of British Columbia is forested and under the control of the Forest Service. Many recreation sites or grounds have been provided on forest land; these have limited facilities and are generally free. Get more info on Forest Service sites, forest roads, safety, and possible fire closure from Forest Service offices throughout the province.

The Nine Regions

British Columbia is divided into nine economic/tourism regions—Vancouver Island, Southwestern British Columbia, Okanagan/ Similkameen, Kootenay/Boundary, Rocky Mountains, High Country, Cariboo, North By Northwest, and Peace River/Alaska Highway.

Vancouver Island's topography varies from fairly flat agricultural valleys in the south to coastal fiords along the east, from the rugged, rain-battered west coast and beaches of Pacific Rim National Park to high mountains in the north. At the southern tip of the island lies the provincial capital, **Victoria.**

Southwestern B.C. is the most populated region in the province, with more than 1.5 million residents (approximately 53% of the entire provincial population). Within its boundary is found the southern end of the steep, impressive, snowcapped Coastal Range, the mainland island coast (interconnected by a number of small ferries), and the flat, lush, agricultural Fraser River Valley. **Vancouver,** B.C.'s largest city, sits in the southwest corner of the region—the financial, cultural, and transportation center of the province.

Warm, dry **Okanagan/Similkameen** is often described as the heartland of B.C.: enormous transparent lakes with sandy beaches and resorts, endless fruit orchards and vineyards, rolling ranchlands, and several large cities catering to all the vacationers that flock here from colder climates in search of a tan.

Mountainous and forested **Kootenay/Boundary** is in the southeast corner of the province, offering large lakes, snowcapped peaks, and deep, lush valleys. With a history of gold and silver mining in the last century, picturesque communities and ghost towns line the lake shores and snuggle in the mountains, and a number of parks protect some of the best scenery. Economically the residents rely on mining, smelting, forestry, hydroelectric power generation, and tourism.

The **Rocky Mountains** region has some of the best scenery in the world. It's hard to beat majestic rocky peaks, alpine meadows splattered with wildflowers, sky-blue glaciers and turquoise lakes, rollicking rivers and emerald-green valleys, abundant wildlife, and cities either surrounded by or facing the mountains. It also contains splendid Kootenay and Yoho national parks, and access to the outstanding scenery of Alberta's Banff and Jasper national parks. You'd be hard-pressed to find a landscape more beautiful!

To the northwest lies **High Country,** known for its two national parks, Glacier and Mount Revelstoke, and its wide variety of terrain and climate. Travel through Glacier National Park, seeing large, impressive glaciers, waterfalls, and plenty of mist and rain, then continue into the dry, crisp, rolling ranch lands and desert heat or cold of the Kamloops (main city) and Cache Creek areas.

More dry, rolling grasslands, prairies, forests, and enormous cattle ranches separated by kilometers of well-kept log fences are found within the **Cariboo** region. Its main cities are Williams Lake and Quesnel.

North of the Cariboo lies the vast **North By Northwest** region, which sprawls from Alberta clear across the province to the Pacific Ocean. In the east are the Rocky Mountains and spectacular parks. In the center sits the large city of Prince George, the economic, cultural, and transportation hub of the north. From Prince George west, the Yellowhead Hwy. meanders through one forested and snowcapped range after another, following several vast rivers all the way to the coast. On the west coast sprawls the city of Prince Rupert, another vital transportation center for those traveling south to Vancouver I., north to Alaska, or west to the mountainous, heavily forested, wind-battered and mysterious islands of the Queen Charlottes (where Canada's newest national park has been established on South Moresby Island). Branching off the Yellowhead Hwy. is a road leading north to the Stewart-Cassiar region, an isolated, sparsely populated wilderness of high mountains, many glaciers, waterfalls, forests, and parks, that stretches all the way to the Yukon.

The most northeasterly region is **Peace River/Alaska Hwy.,** bordering both Alberta in the east and the Northwest Territories in the north. Only two percent of British Columbia's population lives here. Within the region is an enormous reservoir and several dams, the rugged peaks of the Rocky Mountain Foothills between Prince George and Dawson Creek, both flat and gently rolling prairie land from Dawson Creek to Fort St. John (the largest city), and forested and mountainous country with spectacular wilderness parks in the far north. Economically the region's resources are as varied as its terrain—oil and natural gas production, mining, farming, hydroelectric power generation, forestry, transportation, and tourism.

CLIMATE

Precipitation in British Columbia is strongly influenced by the lay of the land and the waft of the wind—resulting in an astonishing variation in rainfall from place to place. For example, **Kamloops** in the sheltered Thompson River Valley in south-central B.C. receives only 25 centimeters of rain per year, whereas the west coast of **Vancouver I.** averages an annual total of 274 centimeters. Quite a difference! The **Insular Mountains** and the western side of the **Coast Range** are very wet areas (keep your raincoat and umbrella handy), separated by a drier coastal trough. East of the Coast Range lies the **Interior Plateau,** a relatively dry area (suntan lotion and hat country), bordered by the wet windward side of the **Rocky Mountains.** Location on the windward or lee sides of the mountains also greatly influences rainfall, with the windward side usually copping most of the downpour.

A topography of such great variation also radically affects the general temperatures, which vary according to elevation, latitude, slope aspect, and inland or coastal location. The **coastal zone** is influenced by Polar Maritime air which makes cool and relatively dry summers and mild, wet winters. Most of **Interior B.C.** is influenced by both continental and maritime air, resulting in colder, relatively dry winters and hot, dry summers. In the **northeast,** the main influences are Polar Continental and Arctic air masses. Winters are extremely cold, with plenty of snow, and summers are short, cool, and wet. In general, no matter what season you visit British Columbia, take clothing to suit a variety of temperatures (layers of clothes are most appropriate) and always have a windbreaker and raincoat handy.

FLORA

Two colors jump to mind when you say "British Columbia"; invariably they are green and blue. Just about everywhere you travel in B.C., you see trees, trees, and more trees; much of the rest of the landscape is covered by water. The only differences are the types of tree in each geographic and climatic region. On the Queen Charlotte Is., the west coast and central Vancouver I., and the west coast of the mainland, **western hemlock** predominates—Queen Charlotte rainforest is thickly covered in spongy pale-green moss—along with **coastal Douglas fir;** in the alpine areas are **subalpine mountain hemlock.** In the south-central interior you find a mixture of **interior Douglas fir, ponderosa pine,** and **subalpine Engelmann spruce;** in the central interior **Cariboo aspen, lodgepole pine,** and **subalpine Engelmann spruce;** then in the northern interior, **sub-boreal spruce, subalpine Engelmann spruce, birch,** and **willow.** Farther southeast lie forests of **interior western hemlock** and **subalpine Engelmann spruce.** Up in the northeast the landscape is carpeted in **spruce, birch, willow,** and **boreal white** and **black spruce.** The official tree of British Columbia is the **western red cedar**—a valuable resource for the province.

In summer, British Columbia turns on a really magnificent floral display. Wildflowers of every color of the rainbow pop up on the roadsides—white and yellow daisies, purple lupines, pale- and dark-pink wild roses, blood-red Indian paintbrush, orange and black lilies, red and white clover, yellow buttercups, to name but a handful—and if you venture off the beaten track and up into the alpine meadows the floral beauty is hard to believe. Pick up a wildflower guide at local bookshops, or if you're in a national park, ask at HQ if they have a brochure on wildflower recognition—most do. British Columbia's official floral emblem is the **Pacific dogwood,** a small tree (6-12 meters in height) sporting dark green leaves and huge clusters of green-tinged, cream-colored flowers in spring (April to June), bright foliage and red berries in autumn. The tree is a protected plant in British Columbia, and it is a punishable offense to pick or destroy it.

FAUNA

British Columbia is one of the best provinces in Canada to see wildlife—the great diversity of environment provides habitat and breeding grounds for more species—and more *unique* species—of birds and mammals here than in any other province or territory in the country. You're also more likely to encounter wildlife without trying, because the far-flung cities and towns have wilderness backyards—in fact, drivers need to be prepared to take sudden avoidance measures when a moose, elk, or deer suddenly decides to play chicken.

Within provincial boundaries live 112 species of mammals (74 exclusively in B.C.), including 25% of the world's grizzly bears, 60% of the mountain goats, 75% of the Stone sheep, 50% of the trumpeter swans and blue grouse, and 25% of the bald eagles. The Lower Mainland (where the most people live) is a migration stop for the million-odd birds that travel the Pacific flyway—with the largest population of waterfowl wintering in Boundary Bay near Vancouver. View beautiful Canada and snow geese, trumpeter and whistling swans, and all kinds of ducks. British Columbia's official bird is the often-cheeky, vibrant blue- and black-colored **Steller's jay,** found throughout the Province.

Offshore B.C. is also a wildlife enthusiast's delight: thousands of Pacific gray whales cruise the coast twice a year; killer and humpback whales, porpoises, and dolphins can be seen frolicking in coastal waters; and colonies of seals and sea lions can be viewed by boat or kayak. Many an angler experiences "real" fishing for the first time in B.C.—five species of Pacific salmon, rainbow, brown, and cutthroat trout, steelhead, Dolly Varden, grayling, and plenty of others—happily returning to the province again and again for a life sentence of standing in hip waders, fly rod in hand, hat covered with assorted flies!

If you're lucky enough to encounter wildlife, keep a safe distance, particularly if young ones are present (the protective mother will not be far away)—and never harass or feed wild animals. Also resist the temptation to get an award-winning close-up shot (at these moments a telephoto lens is an invaluable piece of equipment)—wild animals are unpredictable. When hiking in the backcountry ask local park or forest service staff about the likelihood of encountering wildlife along your planned route, and heed their advice. Often it's a good idea to take a noisemaker—a few rocks in a soft-drink can or a bell—or let out a loud yell every now and again to let wildlife know you're coming. They usually leave you alone. However, you may encounter the odd inquisitive black bear, fearless grizzly, or sudden cougar—all of which need to be left well alone. If a bear rears up, or growls with ears back, move slowly behind a tree or rock, or stand your ground and stay still. If an attack seems inevitable, drop to the ground in a hunched-up position, covering your neck, and play dead. Do not run (a bear can outrun a human quite easily). The national parks hand out brochures on bears—read them! Also keep all food in airtight containers, locked in a vehicle or strung from a high tree branch far from your tent. Tasty food odors openly invite wildlife to your area, like ringing a dinner gong and yelling "Food's on!" For more info, write to the Wildlife Branch, Ministry of Environment and Parks, Parliament Buildings, Victoria, B.C. V8V 1X5.

HISTORY

EXPLORATION AND COLONIZATION

By Sea

Only 200 years ago the northwest coast of North America was one of the least explored areas in the world. Its geography presented some mighty natural barriers to penetration from either the east (the formidable Rocky Mountains) or the west (kilometers of ocean away from other land masses). In the second half of the 18th century curiosity and a common desire to discover rich natural resources lured Russian, Spanish, British, and American explorers and fur traders to the new and challenging land. The ship of Mexican **Juan Perez** was the first vessel to explore the coastline and trade with the Indians, in 1774. He was quickly followed by Spaniard **Bodega y Quadra** who took possession of the coast of Alaska for Spain. England's **James Cook** arrived in 1778 to spend some time at **Nootka,** trading with the Indians while he overhauled his ship. Cook received a number of luxuriant, soft sea otter furs which he later sold at a huge profit in China. This news spawned a fur-trading rush that began in 1785 and resulted in ship after ship loaded with iron, brass, copper, muskets, cloth, jewelry, and rum calling in along the coast for the next 25 years. The Indians were eager to obtain the foreign goods, but they were no pushovers when it came to driving a hard bargain. In return, the traders received furs which they took directly to China to trade for silk, tea, spices, ginger, and other luxuries. In 1789, Spain established a settlement at **Nootka,** but after ongoing problems with the British (who also claimed the area), Quadra gave up possession of the settlement to **Captain George Vancouver** in 1793.

By Land

In the meantime, adventurous North West Company fur traders were crossing the Rockies and trying to find waterways to the coast. The first white man to reach the coast via the Peace, Fraser, and West Road rivers was **Alexander Mackenzie** in 1793—you can still see the rock in the Dean Channel (off Bella Coola) where he inscribed "Alex Mackenzie from Canada by land 22nd July 1793." He was followed by other famous explorers—Simon Fraser, who followed the Fraser River to the sea in 1808, and David Thompson, who followed the Columbia River to its mouth in 1811; today their names grace everything from rivers to modern motels. In the early years of the 19th century, trading posts were established by the North West Company in New Caledonia (the name Simon Fraser gave to the northern interior) and then were taken over by Hudson's Bay Company after amalgamation with the North West Company in 1821.

The Indian Response

The fur trade brought prosperity to Indian society, which was organized around wealth, possessions, and potlatches. The Company had no interest in interfering with the Indians and, in general, treated them fairly. This early contact with the white man resulted in expanded trade patterns, increased commerce between coastal and interior tribes, and a peak in west coast art and crafts (chiefs required more carved head gear, masks, costumes, feast dishes, etc., for the number of ceremonial occasions that came with increasing wealth). However, it also caused an abandonment of traditional sites and the clustering of tribes around the forts (for trading and protection); in addition, muskets, alcohol, and disease (especially smallpox) were introduced, all of which took their toll. Only when white colonists arrived, intent on taking land (and many years later Christian church lobbies insisting on the banning of potlatches) did major conflicts arise between Indians and whites—conflicts regarding land ownership that have continued to this day.

Vancouver Island

The Imperial Government decided in 1849 that Vancouver I. should be colonized to confirm British sovereignty in the area and forestall any American expansion. Though they mostly left the island in the hands of the Hudson's Bay Company, **Richard Blanshard** was sent out from England to become its first governor. **James Douglas,** Chief Factor of the Company, had always been in control; when Blanshard soon resigned, Douglas became Governor of Vancouver I. in 1851. His main concerns were to maintain law and order and to purchase ownership rights to the land from the Indians, setting aside what he considered were adequate reserves for Indian use. He made treaties with the tribes in which the land became the "entire property of the white people forever." In return, Indians retained use of their village sites and enclosed fields, and could hunt and fish on unoccupied lands, and each family was paid a pitiful compensation. In 1852, coal was discovered near Nanaimo (English miners were imported to develop the deposits), and enormous timber stands along the Alberni Canal were used for spars. Several large farms were developed by the Puget Sound Agricultural Association (a subsidiary of Hudson's Bay Company) in the Victoria region. By the 1850s, the town of Victoria, with its moderate climate and good soil for growing an abundance of vegetables and flowers, had already developed into an agreeable settlement.

LAW AND ORDER, THEN GOLD!

Firsts

In 1856 the first parliament west of the Great Lakes was elected, and Dr. J.S. Helmcken (you can still see his house in Victoria) became Speaker. Only two years later this still relatively unexplored and quiet part of the world was turned upside down with the first whispers of "gold" on the mainland along the banks of the Fraser River. As the news spread, miners (mostly Americans) arrived by the shipload at Victoria, increasing its size from a community of several hundred to one of more than 5,000. Fur trading faded as gold-mining jumped to the forefront. Realizing that enormous wealth could be buried on the mainland, the British Government quickly responded by creating the mainland colony, British Columbia, in 1858. Governor James Douglas of Vancouver I. also became governor of B.C., giving up his Hudson's Bay Company position to serve both colonies; in 1866 the two colonies were combined into one.

Cariboo Gold

The Cariboo Gold Rush, in which large quantities of gold were discovered and miners quickly made their fortune, resulted in the construction (1861-65) of the famous Cariboo Road, opening up British Columbia's interior from Yale to Barkerville—one of the richest and wildest gold towns in North America. These were the years of mule trains, stagecoaches, roadhouses, overnight gold towns, and **Judge Begbie,** an effective chief of law and order (and a colorful character who demanded respect) during a time when law and order might as easily have been nonexistent. Another group that made its way to the Cariboo was the **Overlanders.** With carts, horses, and oxen, a large horde of settlers left Ontario and Quebec in summer 1862 to travel over the vast plains and Rockies via Yellowhead Pass. One detachment rafted down the Fraser, the other down the North Thompson, both arriving in Kamloops in autumn that same year. Some still went to the Cariboo, but others headed for the coast, having had more than their fill of adventure on the trip across.

Rapid Development

The Cariboo Road, one of the north country's greatest feats of engineering prior to the building of the Canadian Pacific Railway, was completed in 1865. Also, in the early 1860s, other trails opened up the province, including the Hope-Princeton and Dewdney trails into the Kootenays, which led to settlement in its eastern parts. Salmon canning was also developed in the 1860s, and several canneries on both the lower Fraser and Skeena rivers (you can still see one of the old canneries near Prince Rupert today) had the world market in their pockets. After the retirement of Governor Douglas in 1864, the Colonial Office in London appointed a governor for each colony—Arthur Edward Kennedy for Victoria and Frederick Seymour for New Westminster, the short-term capital of mainland B.C.

It wasn't until 1862 that Burrard Inlet (where Vancouver now stands) sprang onto the map with the building of a small lumber mill on the north shore. The tall, large, straight trees became much in demand, and more lumber mills started up, developing a healthy export market in only a few years. Farmers began to move into the area, and by the end of the 1860s a small town had been established. "Gassy Jack" Deighton started a very popular saloon on the south shores of Burrard Inlet near a lumber camp, and for some time the settlement was locally called Gastown. Once the townsite had been surveyed in 1870, the name was changed to Granville, and then in 1886 the town was officially called Vancouver, in honor of Captain George Vancouver. At this time, New Westminster was the official capital of the colony of British Columbia—much to the concern and disbelief of Vancouver Islanders who strongly believed Victoria should have retained the position. Two years later the capital reverted to Victoria—and the seat of government has remained there ever since.

Confederation

The next big issue to concern British Columbia was confederation. The eastern colonies had become one large dominion, and B.C. residents were invited to join. After much public debate and discussions between London, Victoria, and Ottawa (London and Ottawa wanted B.C. to join to assist in counterbalancing the mighty U.S. power to the south), the southwesternmost colony entered the Confederation as the Province of British Columbia in July 1871—with the provision that the B.C. coast be connected to the east by railway. Aside from many roads being built during the 1870s, it was the completion of the railway in 1885 that opened up B.C. to the rest of the continent. Other railways followed, steamships plied the lakes and rivers, more roads were built, and industries including logging, mining, farming, salmon fishing, and tourism started to develop. Within the last century B. C. roads to major multilane highways, from horses to ferries, and from gold-mining to sportfishing. It still attracts backcountry hikers, mountain climbers, and explorers: some to tread where Simon Fraser trod centuries before, some in search of new and uncharted wilderness—plenty is left!

ECONOMY AND GOVERNMENT

British Columbia's economy has relied on resource-based activities for as long as man has lived in the province, starting with hunting and fishing by the native Indians, then the mass slaughter of sea otters and the cutting of timber when whites arrived on the scene. Luckily, the province has many natural resources: timber, minerals, petroleum, natural gas, and coal; plenty of water for hydroelectric power; abundant wildlife; and a superb physical environment which attracts outdoor enthusiasts and visitors from around the world. Reforestation, fishing and hunting seasons and limits, a freeze on changing the use of agricultural land, and the restraining of hydroelectric development to protect salmon runs are just some of the measures that have been adopted to protect these resources. But the ongoing battle between concerned conservationists and profit-motivated developers continues.

Timber Resources

More than half of British Columbia is forested. Forty-three million hectares contain about 50% of the marketable wood in Canada (about 25% of the North American inventory); most of it is coniferous softwood (fir, hemlock, spruce, and pine). Along the coast the hemlock species is dominant; in the interior are forests of spruce and lodgepole pine. Douglas fir, balsam, and western red cedar are the other most valuable commercial trees. The B.C. government owns 94% of the forest land, private companies own five percent, and the national government owns the remaining one percent. The provincial forest resource has been divided into units called timber supply areas and tree farm licenses, and harvesting in these units is delegated to private operators under a number of licensing agreements. Forestry has been the mainstay of the economy in this century; however, pressures on the industry have been steadily increasing as the demand grows to preserve the forests for wildlife, recreation, and a resource for following generations.

Mining

Mining for metals (copper, gold, zinc, silver, molybdenum, lead, and others), industrial minerals (sulphur, asbestos, limestone, gypsum, and others), structural materials (sand, gravel, dimension stone, and cement), coal (most of it exported to Japan and other Asian markets), and drilling for petroleum and natural gas in northeastern B.C. make up another major part of the economy.

Tourism

Tourism has rapidly climbed the list of importance (now the second-largest industry and the province's largest employer) as more people become aware of the national, provincial, historic, and regional parks scattered throughout the province, the outstanding scenery, and the bountiful outdoor recreational activities available year-round in this world-class destination.

Agriculture

Cultivated land is sparse in mountainous B.C. (only four percent is arable), and agriculture is diverse. Dairy farming predominates in the lower Fraser Valley, southeast Vancouver I., and north Okanagan-Shuswap areas; cattle farms are mainly found in the Cariboo, Chilcotin, Kamloops, Okanagan, and Kootenay regions; orchard crops and grapes grow in the Okanagan, while berries flourish in the lower Fraser Valley; poultry farms, vegetables, bulbs, and ornamental shrubs are found near Vancouver and Victoria; and Peace River Country is the grain basket of B.C., with a mixture of livestock and crop farming. Agriculture provides an estimated 55-60% of the food required for British Columbia's needs.

Fishing

Commercial fish farming has also taken off, producing oysters, five species of salmon (the most valuable crop), and trout. Commercial fishing, one of B.C.'s principal industries, concentrates on salmon, herring, halibut, cod, and sole. Canned and fresh fish are exported to markets all over the world—the province is considered the most productive fishing region in Canada. Japan is the largest export market, followed by the European Common Market countries (excluding the U.K.), the U.S., and the United Kingdom.

Recreational salt- and freshwater sportfishing for salmon, steelhead, and trout is also very popular. More than 255 licensed freshwater angling guides scattered throughout the province eagerly await the arrival of both resident and nonresident fishing enthusiasts to share their expertise (for a price) and a few of their fish!

Industry

In manufacturing the leaders have always been the sawmill and pulp and paper industries, but others such as the fabric, clothing, sports and recreational equipment, and outdoor furniture industries are now becoming prominent.

The film industry is also developing, as more and more Hollywood production companies discover the beauty of B.C., its film studio facilities, on-site production crews, support services, and the favorable exhange rate.

Energy And Transportation

In the energy field, British Columbia has vast resources, including hydroelectric potential (plenty of precipitation and steep land—the perfect combo), natural gas, and coal.

Transportation is another important segment of the economy, providing ports that are

Logging trucks—you see them everywhere.

open year-round, deep-sea international shipping lanes, log-towing vessels, specialized freight and passenger steamers, and all the required facilities. The U.S. and Japan are B.C.'s main export and import trading partners.

Government

Canada is a constitutional monarchy. Its system of government is based on England's, and the British monarch is also King or Queen of Canada. However, because it's an independent nation, the British monarchy and government have no control over the political affairs of Canada. An appointed **governor general** based in Ottawa represents the Crown, as does a **lieutenant governor** in each province—both roles are mainly ceremonial, but their **royal assent** is required to make any bill passed by Cabinet into law. Elected representatives debate and enact laws affecting their constituents. The head of the federal government is the **prime minister,** the head of provincial government is the **premier,** and the **speaker** is elected at the first session of each Parliament to make sure parliamentary rules are followed. A bill goes through three grueling sessions in the legislature—a reading, a debate, and a second reading. When all the fine print has been given the royal nod, the bill then becomes a law.

In the B.C. legislature, the lieutenant governor is at the top of the ladder; under him are the members of the **Legislative Assembly** (elected for a period of up to five years, though an election for a new assembly can be called at any time by the lieutenant governor or on the advice of the premier). In the Legislative Assembly are the premier, the cabinet ministers and backbenchers, the **leader of the official opposition,** other parties, and independent members. Elections must be held every five years. All Canadian citizens and B.C. residents (providing they've lived in the province for at least six months) 19 years old and over can vote.

The two main parties are the **Social Credit** (tends to advocate free enterprise and government restraint), and the **New Democratic Party** (for moderate socialism and government economic and social involvement). After an election, the leader of the majority party becomes provincial premier and forms a government, selecting elected members of his/her party to head a variety of government ministries; these politicians make up the **Executive Council** or **Cabinet.** The Leader of the Official Opposition and members form a check system by questioning government policies and actions and presenting alternatives.

Some of the responsibilities of the Legislature include administration of justice, property and civil rights, municipal government, crown lands, forests, water resources, and education. The laws of B.C. are administered by the cabinet, premier, and lieutenant governor, and interpreted by a **judiciary** made up of the Supreme Court of B.C., Court of Appeal, and County or Provincial Courts.

PEOPLE

Indian

The coast and interior valleys of B.C. were first occupied by native people some time after the last ice age. Prior to "discovery" by whites, Canada's West Coast supported several Indian populations: the Kwakiutl, Bella Coola, Nootka, Haida, and Tlingit Indians. These coastal bands lived comfortably off the land and the sea, hunting deer, beaver, bear, and sea otters, and fishing for salmon, cod, halibut, and edible kelp. The interior bands were more nomadic and depended heavily on hunting. The Indians built huge 90-meter-long huts and 20-meter-long dugout canoes, and developed a distinctive and highly decorative arts style featuring animals, mythical creatures, and oddly shaped human forms believed to be supernatural ancestors. West Coast Indian society was based on the private property and material wealth of each chief and his tribe, displayed to others during potlatches.

At ceremonial potlatches, held in honor of a special event such as marriage, puberty, death, or the raising of a totem pole, the wealth of a tribe became obvious when the chief gave away enormous quantities of gifts to his guests—the nobler the guest, the better the gift. Platters beaten from native placer ore and painted with the owner's crest were broken during memorial potlatches. A platter's value increased with each change of ownership—reassembled, it carried the most value. Individually named, and attaining renown, these plates were also used as part of marriage payments. The potlatch exchange was accompanied by much feasting, speechmaking, dancing, and entertainment, all of which could last many days. Stories performed by hosts garbed in elaborate costumes and masks educated, entertained, and affirmed each clan's historical continuity. However, when white settlers arrived and demanded land, villages and sites used by each local band were marked off as reserves, and the Indians were expected to live there. Urged by a strong church lobby which considered potlatches heathen affairs, the government banned potlatching in 1884—the ban lasted until 1951. During this time the costumes, masks, songs, dances, ritual items, and oratory began to disappear. These two factors, plus the influence of guns, alcohol, and disease introduced by whites, started the breakdown of Indian society.

Today the Indian peoples of the north Pacific coast have adopted the technology and the ways of the European, though they still remain a distinct group, contributing to and enriching the culture of British Columbia. A social barrier still exists between the Indian and non-Indian. Much of the traditional social organization is gone, and many of the old obligations (based on kinship and heredity) have changed or disappeared (e.g., the chief is now elected), and yet many of the handicrafts and traditional woodworking continue.

White Man

When B.C. became a province of Canada in 1871, its population was only 36,000—27,000 of them Indians. With the completion of the Canadian Pacific Railway in 1885, immigration years of the early 20th century, and the effects of WW II followed by rapid industrial development, the provincial population rapidly grew. Between 1951 and 1971 it doubled. Today 3,131,700 people live in British Columbia, most of them in southwestern B.C. (more than a third in the metropolitan area of Vancouver) and southern Vancouver Island. Overall this works out at a density of only three persons per square kilometer!

But Where Do You Come From, Dahling?

British Columbia is a young province, with almost 40% of its population under the age of 40. Most British Columbians are of British origin (51% have British ancestry, another six percent claim some British background), followed by those of German, Chinese, and French descent. To really get the British feeling, just spend some time in Victoria—a city that has retained its original English customs and traditions from days gone by. Native peoples form a large minority (the Indian population is becoming less Indian over the generations due to intermixture), followed by a large variety of ethnic groups and combinations.

Language

The main language spoken throughout the province is English, though almost six percent of the population also speaks French, Canada's second official language. All government information, labels, packages, etc., are written in both English and French throughout Canada. The Indians of British Columbia fall into 10 major ethnic groups by language: Nootka (W. Vancouver I.), Coast Salish (southwest B.C.), Interior Salish (southern interior), Kootenay (in the Kootenay region), Athabascan (in the central and northeast regions), Bella Coola and Northern Kwakiutl (along the central west coast), Tsimshian (in the northwest), Haida (on the Queen Charlotte Is.), and Inland Tlingit (in the far northwest corner of the province). However, most Indians still speak English more than their mother tongue.

ARTS AND CRAFTS

Totem Poles

Traveling through British Columbia you can't help but notice, then admire, all the totem poles that decorate the landscape. Unfortunately, many have been snatched up by museums and personal collectors from around the world. The only two factors that all types of totem poles have in common is that they're made of red (occasionally yellow) cedar, and erected as validation of a public record or documentation of an important event. Five types of poles are believed to have evolved in the following order: house posts (an integral part of the house structure), mortuary (erected as a chief's or shaman's grave post, often with the bones or ashes in a box at the top), memorial (commemorating special events), frontal (a memorial or heraldic pole), and shame poles. None of them is an object of worship; each tells a story or history of a person's clan or family. The figures on the pole either represent a mythical character or a zoomorphic clan symbol.

Totem poles are the most splendid form of mortuary art among northwest coast natives. Small wooden sculptures were also used in grave houses or as figures on which mortuary boxes were placed, or placed on top of poles. With European contact came the usual commercialization. The native Indians' monumental art was miniaturized—even the most flexible airlines, for example, frown at a full-size totem pole being carried on as hand luggage! Today, miniatures by well-known artists are prized collectors' possessions.

With the renewed interest in this symbol of West Coast Canadian life, many of the decaying original totem poles are being moved into provincial museums where they can be preserved. Their replacements are newly carved replicas, and they're often commissioned for new exterior displays. However, you can still admire authentic (but carefully restored) totems at a number of villages along the Yellowhead Hwy., at Alert Bay (Cormorant I.), Stanley Park in Vancouver, the University of Vancouver, the Provincial Museum in Victoria, and on the southern Queen Charlotte Islands.

Cedar Skills

The Indians of the northwest coast made just about everything they needed out of cedar: houses, canoes (hollowed out from tree trunks), boxes and containers (from steam-bent and joined wood), totem poles, masks, baskets, costumes, fish hooks, clubs, spears, bows and arrows—you name it! Their well-constructed houses were either long and rectangular with a roof sloping down to lower back walls, or square, the interior often divided by hanging mats. The interior main framework lasted for years, and the outside shell or covering could be easily removed. Canoes varied in shape and size according to the tribe. The northern tribes built canoes with a raised bow and stern which both projected out over the water; the southern tribes designed canoes with a vertical stern and projecting bow. They varied from two to 23 meters in length and could carry from several to 60 men or more! You can still see the large ones in museums, or on ceremonial occasions, beautifully painted with geometric designs, with superbly crafted paddles and bailers, slipping silently through the water.

Art And Crafts

Indian artistry tends to fall into one of two categories: "art" such as wood carving and painting, argillite carving, jade and silverwork, and totem restoration (all generally attended to by the men); and "handicrafts" such as basketry, weaving, beadwork, skinwork, sewing, and knitting (generally created by the women). Today, all of these arts and crafts contribute significantly to Indian income.

Woodcarving and painting are probably the most recognized artforms of the northwest coast Indians. Throughout B.C.—in museums, people's homes, outdoors, and of course in all the shops—you can see brightly colored totems, canoes, paddles, fantastic masks, and ceremonial rattles, feast dishes, bowls, and spoons. Fabulous designs, many featuring animals or mythical legends, are also painstakingly painted in bright primary colors on paper. You can buy limited-edition, high-quality prints of these paintings at many Indian craft outlets (good collection at the museum in Prince Rupert). They are more reasonable in cost than carvings, yet just as stunning when effectively framed.

Look out for decorative cedar-root (fairly rare) and cedar-bark baskets (still made on the west coast of Vancouver I.), spruce-root baskets (Queen Charlotte Is.), beaded and fringed moccasins, jackets, vests, and gloves (available at most Indian craft outlets), and beautiful, functional, birch-bark baskets (as you travel the Yellowhead Hwy. from Prince George to Prince Rupert, you can often find these around the Hazelton area). All outdoorspersons should at least consider forking out for a heavy, water-resistant, raw sheep's wool sweater. They're generally white or gray with a black design. Much in demand because they're so warm, they're good in the rain, rugged, and they last longer than one lifetime. One of the best places to get your hands on an original fair-dinkum sweater is the Cowichan Valley on Vancouver I., although you can also find them in the Fraser Valley from Vancouver to Lytton and in Indian craft outlets. (Expect to pay around $90-160 for the real thing, more in tourist shops.)

Carved argillite (black slate) miniature totem poles, brooches, ashtrays, etc., highly decorated with geometric and animal designs, are exclusively created by the Haida on the Queen Charlotte Islands—they were first developed specifically for early "tourists" when the sea otter trade declined. You can find argillite carvings in Skidegate on the Queen Charlottes (the argillite comes from a quarry near Skidegate and can only be used by the Skidegate band) and in craft shops in Prince Rupert, Victoria, and Vancouver. With the rebirth in popularity of primitive art, argillite carvings are once again in demand. Silverwork is also popular—some of the best is created by Haida Indians—by Bill Reid, Haida artist of Vancouver, in particular. The conventional geometric designs are old, yet the finished article is modern. Another popular artform is that of jade jewelry—see it in the Lillooet and Lytton areas.

FESTIVALS AND EVENTS

British Columbia seems to have at least one festival or event going on somewhere in the province every day of the year! To make sure you don't miss anything when you're in the province, stop by one of the multitude of Travel InfoCentres at the beginning of your trip and pick up a current *Arts And Entertainment* brochure produced by the Ministry of Tourism, then stock up on brochures on local events as you travel. Many of the most popular festivals are held during summer, B.C.'s peak visitor season, but special events and artistic performances can be attended year-round. Many towns hold winter events featuring zany happenings such as snow golf, bed races on ice, and anything they can come up with that's good for a laugh!

Vancouver Island

In Victoria in July and Aug., several plays are presented during the **Victoria Repertory Festival** at the Belfrey Theatre. In June/July there's **Folkfest,** and the **Jazz Festival,** and in July/Aug. **Victoria International Festival** at McPherson Playhouse and various other locations. As you travel up the island, **Chor-**

fest (a weekend of choral music) is held at Port Alberni and a **Bluegrass Festival** is held at Coombs, both in May. In Duncan in May/June, the **B.C. Festival of the Arts** is a five-festival occasion. Ganges, Salt Spring I., also has its **Festival of Arts** in July, and in July/Aug. Nanaimo puts on the very popular **Shakespeare Plus.**

July is a very busy month: Courtenay also has a music festival, **Summer Music From Courtenay;** Ucluelet and Tofino celebrate their **Pacific Rim Summer Festival;** Coombs has a **Bluegrass Festival;** and the walls of Chemainus are the main focus during the **Chemainus Festival of Murals.** In Aug., attend the artistic **Filberg Festival** (juried craft show) at Comox, or kick up your heels at the **Hornby Midsummer Festival** on Hornby Island.

Southwestern B.C.
In May, start off the season with the **Vancouver Children's Festival** at Vanier Park in Vancouver; in June the **Du Maurier International Jazz Festival** in Vancouver; in July, **Canada Day** celebrations at scattered locations, the **Sea Festival** and **Vancouver Folk Festival,** both in Vancouver, and the **White Rock Sandcastle Competition** at White Rock Beach; in Aug. **Abbotsford International Airshow** at Abbotsford.

Okanagan And The Kootenays
In the Okanagan, the major summertime events are the **Penticton Peach Festival** at Penticton in late July, the **Kelowna International Festival of the Arts** in Kelowna in Sept., and in late Sept./early Oct. the delicious **Okanagan Wine Festival**, which is held throughout the valley.

In the Kootenays, Castlegar celebrates Sunfest and Cranbrook has its Sam Steele Days in June. In July, Kimberley attracts a mass of accordion players and appreciators to the Annual International Old-Time Accordion Championships. Rossland gets into the event action with Rossland Golden City Days in September.

Cariboo And The North
In the Cariboo, children have lots of the fun during June at the **South Cariboo Children's Festival** at 100 Mile House, and at the **Children's Festival** at Williams Lake. In July the **Country Bluegrass Festival** is held on the Indian Grounds in Kamloops, and the city also celebrates **Sunfest**, with tons of beach events. If you're up north in summer, Prince Rupert has a **Fine Arts Festival** in May, and in June Dawson Creek is thoroughly entertained during **Tentertainment.** Prince Rupert also celebrates **Seafest** in June with a multitude of zany water-based events, and Chetwynd has its annual **Peace Country Bluegrass Music Festival.** Also in June, Smithers gets into the folk music action with a **Midsummer Festival,** and at Burns Lake in July crowds of camping country-music fans gather to enjoy the **Bluegrass and Western Swing Music Festival** on the Darter Ranch. Dawson Creek celebrates **Mile 0 Days** in July, and in Aug. there's **Simon Fraser Days** in Prince George and the **International Airshow** at Vanderhoof to attend. Busy, busy, busy!

Holidays
British Columbia celebrates 10 statutory holidays, but this doesn't mean the province closes down on these days! Most businesses do close, but you can always find some restaurants, pubs, and a few stores selling basic necessities open. In general you can still get around by public transportation (though local bus networks won't be running). Be aware of the holiday dates and stock up the day before: 1 Jan. is New Year's Day; in late March or early April is Good Friday; on the 24 May weekend (or closest Mon.) Victoria closes for Victoria Day, and on 1 July, Canada Day is celebrated by just about everyone; 1 Aug. is B.C. Day; the first Mon. in Sept. is Labor Day; in early Oct. it's Thanksgiving; on 11 Nov. Remembrance Day; 25 Dec. is Christmas Day and 26 Dec. Boxing Day. Happy holidays!

THE GREAT OUTDOORS

NAME YOUR GAME!

The great outdoors: British Columbia certainly has it. With more than 5,800 square km of unspoiled land, spectacular scenery around every bend, several national parks, hundreds of provincial parks, and abundant wildlife, it's an outdoorsperson's fantasy come true. Hiking; mountain climbing; lake, river, and ice fishing; hunting; boating; canoeing; whitewater rafting; scuba diving, downhill and cross-country skiing—it's all here. All you need is a love of nature at its finest, the time to appreciate it, the gear to make the most of it, and a camera and plenty of film.

For specific recreation information, contact the Ministry of Lands and Parks at 800 Johnson St., Victoria, B.C. V8V 1X4; tel. (604) 387-4330.

Hiking

Just about everywhere you go in British Columbia you find good hiking opportunities—from short, easy walks in city and regional parks to long, strenuous hikes in wilderness parks. Provincial parks contain some of the most outstanding scenery and wildlife, crystal-clear lakes and rivers, and established trails that are generally well maintained and easy to follow. The national parks in the Rocky Mountains are great places to hike. Short trails lead to natural features of interest such as waterfalls, lakes, rock formations, and viewpoints; the longer trails wander high into alpine meadows tangled with wildflowers, past turquoise lakes, and up into snow-dusted peaks for breathtaking views. Alpine huts are provided at regular intervals along wilderness trails. To get the most out of a hiking trip, peruse the hiking section of major bookstores—many books have been written on British Columbian hiking trails.

Before setting off on a long hike, study the trailguides and a topographical map of the area to plan your trip. Leave details of your intentions with a relative or friend. It's best to travel in a small group in the backcountry in case anyone needs help, but if you're on your own, stick to frequently used trails. Carry dried fruit, high-energy snacks, water, a tent, a flashlight, insect repellent, first-aid supplies with a snakebite kit and poison-oak ointment, and wind- and waterproof clothes. Wear comfortable hiking boots, layers of clothes (strip off as you get hot and replace clothing as you cool down to avoid hypothermia sneaking up on you later), and take it easy the first few days. It takes most people a few days to adjust from everyday life to hiking in the wilderness!

Fishing

Both fresh- and saltwater fishing for coho, chinook, and pink salmon are excellent in the protected ocean waterways between Vancouver I. and the mainland. And almost all the lakes, rivers, and streams in British Columbia can produce salmon, trout (in particular rainbow), kokanee, and Dolly Varden. The Vancouver I. communities of Campbell River, Duncan, Courtenay, and Port Alberni are popular fishing destinations. Winter brings the ice fishermen out to try their luck from late Nov. to March, in the lakes around Kamloops, Williams Lake, and Prince George, catching a steelhead in the Thompson River, cutthroat trout in the lower Fraser, and spring salmon around Vancouver Island.

Fishing-license prices vary according to your age and where you're from: there are differing prices for B.C. residents 16-64 years old, B.C. residents 65 and over, other Canadians 16 years and over, and aliens 16 years and over. A Canadian resident adult license, good for one year, is $20.33, for nonresidents $28.89. A Kootenay Lake rainbow trout license is $4.28 per tag, with a limit of five tags pp. A resident steelhead license is $18.19, for nonresidents it's $44.94. All prices include GST. A resident tidal-water sportfishing license is $35 for adults and seniors, under 16 free, and it's good for one year. Nonresident licenses are $17.50 for five days, $14 for four days, $10.50 for three days, $7 for two days, or $3.50 for one day, plus an extra $3 for a chinook stamp (allowing you to keep it if you catch one). When fish-tagging programs are on, you may be required to make a note of the date, location, and method of capture, or to record statistical info on particular types of fish on the back of your license. Read the current rules and regulations.

The latest issues of *Freshwater Fishing Regulations Synopsis, Saltwater Fishing Adventures,* and *British Columbia Tidal Water Sport Fishing Guide* are all packed with useful information, photo or illustration identification of everything fishy, and tips on where to go. The *Sport Fishing Guide* is particularly informative and makes interesting reading even for the not-remotely-interested non-angler. All pamphlets are free and are usually available at Travel InfoCentres or at sporting stores. For detailed freshwater fishing info and regulations, write to the **Fish and Wildlife Branch,** Ministry of Environment, Parliament Buildings, Victoria, B.C. V8V 1X5. For saltwater fishing info contact the Ministry of Fisheries and Oceans at tel. (604) 363-3252.

If you're on a hurried fishing trip, want to cash in on the knowledge of a local guide, need to hire a boat and gear, or are only interested in catching that trophy fish for the living room wall, B.C. has many, many guides, tours, lodges (from rustic to exclusive and luxurious), and packages to suit everyone. Expect to pay anything from $30 an hour or $100-300 a day for a guide to several thousand dollars for several days at a luxury lodge with all meals and fishing expertise included—the kind of place where you can catch your fish and eat it too.

Canoeing And Kayaking

B.C. has so many lakes and rivers suitable for canoeing and kayaking it's hard to know where to begin. The first necessity is a good topographical map—preferably one with rapids, falls, obstacles, and portages marked. Topographical maps for B.C. may be purchased for a nominal fee from **Maps B.C.,** Room 110, 553 Superior St., Victoria, B.C. V8V 1X4; tel. (604) 387-1441. Or contact your nearest Canadian map dealer and request the excellent *Maps and Wilderness Canoeing* map (MCR 107). It's an index to the map series of the National Topographical System (each of these costs several dollars), and it has good wilderness canoeing planning tips on the back. You can also order aerial photos (several dollars each plus a handling charge) of your route by sending a topographical map with your area of interest marked on it and details on what features you'd like to see (i.e., water features) to **National Air Photo Library,** 615 Booth St., Ottawa, Ontario, K1A 0E9.

For info on canoe routes, courses, and clubs, write to the **Outdoor Recreation Council of B.C.,** Suite 334, 1367 West Broadway, Vancouver, B.C. V6H 4A9 (tel. 604-737-3058) and the **Canadian Recreational Canoeing Association,** 1029 Hyde Park Rd., Suite 5, Hyde Park, Ontario, N0M 1Z0 (tel. 519-473-2109). Handy telephone numbers for recorded weather info are 656-3978 in Victoria, 376-3044 in Kamloops.

One of the most popular canoe routes is in **Bowron Lake Park,** a 116-km circuit through a chain of lakes in the Cariboo Mountains (see "Bowron Lake Park" under "Cariboo," p. 289). This route attracts canoeists and kayakers in search of a wilderness experience (no facilities en route, but plenty of fellow canoeists in summer). *The Bowron Lakes* guidebook (Heritage) tells you how to prepare for your five- to seven-day wilderness journey. Before setting off down an unknown river, know the grades and your capabilities—most of the guidebooks on canoeing in B.C. contain grades and all the pertinent details.

An international standard has been adopted for classifying the difficulty of rivers and rapids: Grade one is easy and suitable for novices; Grade two is fairly easy, with rapids of medium difficulty and occasional obstacles, and suitable for intermediate paddlers; Grade three is of medium difficulty, with numerous, high, irregular waves, obstacles necessitating maneuvering experience, advance scouting required, and canoes will take on water, suitable for expert paddlers in open canoes; Grade four is difficult with long rapids, powerful irregular waves, dangerous obstacles, boiling eddies, and difficult passages, not suitable for open canoes; Grade five is very difficult, with long, violent rapids almost without interruption, lots of obstacles, big drops, a steep gradient, and obviously not suitable for open canoes; Grade six is extraordinarily difficult—you could say suicidal!

Boating

British Columbia's 27,000 km of coastline, in particular the sheltered, island-dotted Strait of Georgia between Vancouver I. and the mainland, is a boatie's paradise. Along it are sheltered coves, sandy beaches, beautiful marine parks, and facilities specifically designed for boaters (many only accessible by water). One of the most beautiful marine parks is **Desolation Sound,** north of Powell River—locals claim it's one of the world's best cruising grounds. Many of the enormous freshwater lakes inland are also excellent places for boating.

For the entire rundown on amenities and facilities, pick up a copy of the invaluable *Pacific Yachting Cruising Services Directory,* put out by *Pacific Yachting* magazine, which covers coastal British Columbia and the American San Juan Islands. In it are lists of boat builders/repairers, charters/schools, charts/maps, haul-out facilities, marinas and resorts for each coastal region, sail makers, water taxis, and yacht clubs, along with an abundance of other useful information. If you can't find one in InfoCentres, write to Special Interest Publications, Division of Maclean Hunter, Suite 202, 1132 Hamilton St., Vancouver, B.C. V6B 2S2. For more detailed info on boating in B.C., and for info on vessel entry points and customs regulations, write to **BC Parks,** 800 Johnson St., Victoria, B.C. V8V 1X4; tel. (604) 387-3940.

To get weather info in Vancouver call Marine Weather at (604) 270-7411; in Victoria call Marine Weather at (604) 656-2714/7515; at Port Hardy the Weather Office at (604) 949-6559; the Terrace Weather Office can be reached at (604) 635-3224. A network of continuous weather broadcasts on VHF-FM can be heard along the coast. Forecasts and amended forecasts are usually preceded by a synopsis, giving the broad weather picture. Wind directions are true, not magnetic. Wind speeds are given in knots, and are sustained unless identified as gusts or squalls. Less than 12-knot winds are classified as light, moderate winds are 12-19 knots, and strong winds are 20-34 knots. Small-craft warnings are issued between April and Nov. for Georgia, Juan de Fuca, Johnstone, and Queen Charlotte straits, and year-round for gale-, storm-, and hurricane-force winds for all coastal waters. Before setting off, learn how to survive in cold water, what to do if someone suffers from hypothermia, and what are considered the best flotation devices from the free *Cold Water Survival* brochure put out by the Canadian Red Cross Society—knowing what to do in an emergency could save someone's life.

Whitewater Rafting

Many of B.C.'s wild rivers provide an unforgettable experience and long-remembered adrenaline rush for whitewater rafters. The most popular rivers are the Fraser, Thompson, Chilliwack, and Lillooet rivers (all in the southwest), the Chilko, Chilcotin, and Fraser rivers (in Cariboo-Chilcotin country), and the Kootenay River (in the Rocky Mountains). As you travel through these regions, brochures advertising the various trips and prices are invariably found at all the Travel InfoCentres—and in many places, large billboards lead you off the main highway toward the rafting company office. Most range from a several-hour scenic cruise or a mind-boggling trip down a series of rapids to overnight or several-day rafting adventures. Expect to pay from $40 pp for the shortest trips. Companies are required to provide life jackets, and many also provide or rent wetsuits (worth the extra cost). Some provide crash helmets—a very good idea in case you get unexpectedly ejected into a rock-laden rapid!

Scuba Diving

The best time to appreciate the cold, clear waters along British Columbia's coastline is winter, when you can expect up to 40 meters visibility; diverse marinelife; sponges; anemones; soft corals; china, vermillion, and canary rockfish; rock scallops; cukes; and plenty of shipwrecks. First of all, get your hands on the British Columbia diver's bible, *141 Dives in The Protected Waters of Washington and British Columbia* by Betty Pratt-Johnson (*Diver* magazine is another good source of local information, and in its scuba directory are lists of retail stores, resorts, charter boats, and other services). Then head for Vancouver, where a quick flip through the telephone directory lets you know that scuba diving is alive and well in this community. A host of scuba shops has everything you need, plus they're excellent sources of info on all the best spots along Georgia Strait and can usually tell you who is chartering what, and when.

The most popular dive sites are off the Gulf Is., Nanaimo, Campbell River, Telegraph Cove, Port Hardy, and Powell River (the scuba-diving capital of Canada). Don't miss a visit to Beach Gardens Diving Resort, Powell River, which caters specifically to divers; tel. (604) 485-6267. Many of the coastal communities along Vancouver I. and the Sunshine Coast provide dive shops with gear rentals and air tanks, and many can put you in touch with a charter diving boat and/or guide.

Hunting

Bear, moose, elk, bighorn sheep, and deer are all hunted in British Columbia, and waterfowl (particularly abundant around the Fort St. James, Cranbrook, Prince George, and Lac la Hache areas) are also popular game birds. Nonresidents hunting big game must be accompanied by a licensed B.C. guide, and at the end of the hunt get a completed form of declaration from the guide. A nonresident of B.C., who is a resident of Canada may go with a B.C. resident instead of hiring a guide, provided the resident is a Canadian citizen and has the required permit from the Regional Office of the Ministry of Environment and Parks of the area in which hunting is intended. Applications for the permits need to be submitted at least one month before hunting. You don't need to hire a guide if you're hunting small game and/or game birds.

Again the licenses depend on whether you're a B.C. resident, a Canadian resident from another province, or an alien nonresident. A nonresident Canadian license is $49.22 adult, $7.49 junior; a nonresident alien license is $155.15 adult, $7.49 junior. To hunt in the Fraser Valley Special Area it's an extra $10.70, to hunt in the Gulf Is. Special Area it's an extra $2.14, and to hunt Canadian migratory game birds you have to get another permit (available only at the post office). To hunt black bear, caribou, cougar, deer, elk, grizzly bear, moose, mountain goat, mountain sheep, or wolf you need to pay another fee (anything from $26.75 to $535) for a big-game license, on top of the basic license fee above. Nonresident hunting licenses are only available from the Ministry of Environment, Fish and Wildlife Information, 780 Blanshard St., Victoria, B.C. V8V 1X5 (they can be obtained by mail); tel. (604) 387-9737. Before hunting, be sure to read the latest *British Columbian Hunting and Trapping Regulations Synopsis* put out by the Ministry of Lands and Parks.

Cycling

Cycling in B.C. can be a very rewarding experience, allowing time to stop and appreciate the flowers—and the flowers are *everywhere* in summer—and all the wildlife and scenery along the highway that can easily be overlooked at high speeds. Some of the most popular areas for cycling trips are the Gulf Is. between Vancouver I. and the mainland (quiet, laid-back, loads of sunshine, rural scenery, and lots of artists), the east coast of Vancouver I. (following the sea past lazy beaches and bustling towns), the Kootenays (forest-clad mountains, deep lakes, curious old gold- and silver-mining communities, and ghost towns—good mountain-bike country), and the Rockies (outstanding mountain sce-

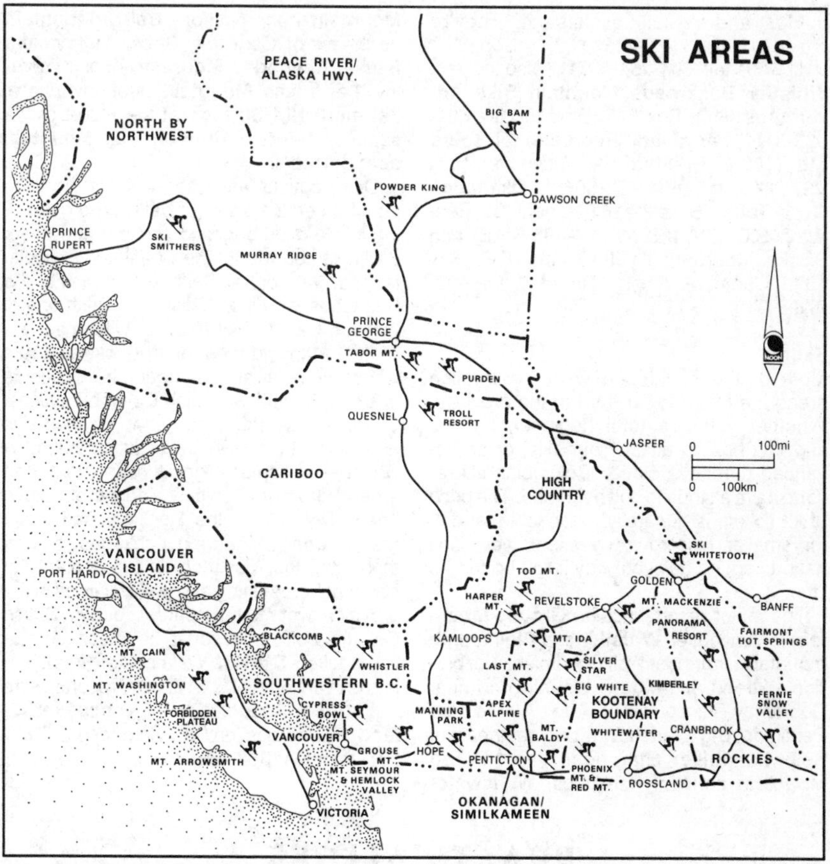

SKI AREAS

nery second to none, abundant wildlife often right beside the highways, hot springs, and hiking trails). Rocky Mountain routes suit the intermediate to advanced cyclist.

For info on touring, racing, books, bicycle routes, or clubs, contact the **Bicycling Association of B.C.** at (604) 332-1367 West Broadway, Vancouver, B.C. V6H 4A9, tel. (604) 737-3034 or (604) 731-7433 (Bicycle Hotline), the **Outdoor Recreation Council of B.C.** (same address as Bicycling Assoc.), tel. (604) 737-3058, or the **B.C. Safety Council** at (604) 877-1221. The Outdoor Recreation Council also publishes a series of maps which cover much of British Columbia—these maps can by bought directly from the council or at many sporting goods stores and bookstores. Several bicycle companies in the province offer bicycle trips and tours. **Benno's Adventure Tours** offers eight-day trips through B.C. and the Canadian Rockies, with bus lifts between the most spectacular sections (3/1975 Maple St., Vancouver, B.C. V6J 3S9, tel. 604-738-5105); **Kootenay Mountain Bike Tours** provides four- to six-day tours through the Kootenay region, with guides and vehicle assistance. They're based in Nelson (P.O. Box 867, Nelson, B.C. V1L 6A5, tel. 604-354-4371). Also contact **Whistler Backroads Mountain Bike Adventures** (P.O. Box 643, Whistler, tel. 604-923-3111), **Aardvark Recreational Tours Ltd.** (203-888 Burrard St., Vancouver, B.C. V6Z 1X9, tel. 604-431-8066), **Okanagan Cycle Tours** (Suite 2-516 Papineau St., Penticton, B.C. V2A 4X6, tel. 604-493-BIKE), and **Rocky Mountain Cycle Tours** (P.O. Box 1978, Canmore, Alberta T0L 0M0, tel. 403-678-6770).

Skiing

Most of the developed winter recreation areas are in the lower third of the province. Whether you're a total beginner, not yet knowing how to attach your skis, or an advanced daredevil, British Columbian ski resorts have a slope to suit everyone. The price of lift tickets is generally reasonable, and at the smaller, lesser-known resorts, you don't have to spend half your day lining up for the lifts.

The major resorts include **Grouse Mountain** in Vancouver, **Whistler** and **Blackcomb** mountains northeast of Squamish, **Forbidden Plateau** and **Mount Washington** near Courtenay (Vancouver I.), **Apex Alpine** near Penticton, **Big White Mountain** southeast of Kelowna, **Silver Star** near Vernon, **Tod Mountain** north of Kamloops, **Whitewater Mountain** near Nelson, **Baldy Mountain** northeast of Osoyoos, **Snow Valley** near Fernie, **Kimberley Mountain** near Kimberley, **Panorama Mountain** near Invermere, **Fairmont Hot Springs** at the resort of the same name, and **Hudson Bay Mountain** near Smithers.

Other options are also available: if you're an intermediate skier (or better), go heli-skiing in the mind-boggling scenery and deep, untracked powder of the Coast and Chilcotin ranges, the central Cariboo Mountains, the Bugaboos, and the Rockies, or catch one of the Sno-Cats to high-country wilderness ski areas. Many lodges offer package tours which can be arranged through travel agents or through Tourism British Columbia offices. Cross-country skiers can strap on their skis and blaze their own trails just about anywhere—particularly good skiing is found around the communities along the Yellowhead Hwy. and in the Rockies. And many resorts offer ski-touring packages, guided trips, etc., too. For more info and plenty of free brochures listing all the ski facilities in the province, write to the nearest Tourism British Columbia office. Request the latest information-packed *Ski With Us!* booklet (free). For info on Vancouver I. ski hills and resorts, write to **Tourism Association of Vancouver Island,** 302/45 Bastion Sq., Victoria, B.C. V8W 1J1, tel. (604) 382-1665.

PRACTICALITIES

GETTING THERE

By Air

In today's topsy-turvy world of air travel—the hub system, competition, inflation, astronomic fares, bomb scares, lost luggage, and late flights—the first step in getting to B.C. is to find yourself a travel agent who takes the time to call around, does some research to get you the best fare, and helps you take advantage of any special offers or promotional deals. The next best attack is to call the airlines in person (in the U.S. most have toll-free information numbers) and compare fares (ask if they have any specials), then look in the travel sections of major newspapers (often on a Sun.), where budget fares and package deals are frequently advertised.

The farther in advance you buy your ticket, the lower the cost (APEX fares—pay for your ticket 14-28 days in advance), but expect a number of potentially nasty restrictions on the cheaper fares, such as the latest non-changeable, nonrefundable, 100% penalty tickets. Traveling in the off-season always saves you money, and if you can go for a number of months, try to pick dates that are out of the high-season period (summer in B.C.) at both ends. Student travel offices (or agents on campus) offer better fares for students, and some also provide cheaper- than-normal fares for nonstudents. All flights vary tremendously in price according to the time of year and the specials the airlines are currently running. To give a very rough idea of costs: at the least expensive end of the scale you could expect to pay $228 (APEX) to $273 RT (regular fare) from San Francisco to Vancouver; at the most expensive end of the scale, Sydney (Australia) to Vancouver standard fares range from $2,039 RT in low season to $2,400 RT in high season. You can get much better deals if you can pay for your ticket in advance, and airline specials can halve these fares.

Major airlines throughout the world provide regular service to Vancouver International Airport, British Columbia's main gateway and Canada's second-busiest airport. The following airlines provide service: **Air Canada, Air China, Air New Zealand, American Airlines, British Airways, Canadian Airlines, Cathay Pacific, Continental, Delta Airlines, Japan Air Lines, KLM Royal Dutch, Korean Air, Lufthansa, Qantas, Singapore Airlines,** and **United Airlines.** Several smaller airlines and charter services also operate from Vancouver Airport.

Vancouver International Airport's information and reservation number is (604) 276-6101. The airport is a 25-minute drive south of city center; make your first stop the info booth on level three. (See "Vancouver" for more details.)

By Sea

One of the most pleasurable ways to get your first view of British Columbia is by boat. Many American visitors catch one of the car ferries over from Port Angeles, Anacortes, or Seattle, Washington. **Black Ball Transport** provides scheduled ferry service daily from Port Angeles to Victoria. For a current schedule and fares, call the Port Angeles office at (206) 457-4491 or the Victoria office at (604) 386-2202. **Washington State Ferries** runs daily scheduled service from Anacortes to Sidney (Vancouver I.) via the San Juan Islands—a very popular route with cyclists. For a current schedule and fares, call (206) 464-6400 (recorded message), or toll-free within Washington (800) 542-7052/0810. Bicycles are loaded first—cyclists should wait near the head of the dock and, when on board, secure bikes in the space provided. Most ferry routes are very busy during weekday commuter periods and on sunny weekends.

From Seattle you can hop on the speedy **Victoria Clipper** (foot passengers only) to Victoria (tel. 206-448-5000 or 443-2560 in Seattle, 604-382-8100 in Victoria). Regular B.C. Ferries connect Vancouver and Victoria (see "Getting Around," below); their main office is at 1112 Fort St., Victoria.

From Alaska, catch one of the **Alaska State Ferries** down the spectacular Inside Passage from Skagway, stopping at a number of southern Alaskan ports of call en route, to Prince Rupert, B.C. (see "Prince Rupert," under "North By Northwest," for all the details); make reservations as far ahead as possible to avoid disappointment. From Prince Rupert **B.C. Ferries** continues south to Port Hardy at the top of Vancouver Island (see "Prince Rupert" and "Port Hardy" sections for more details). Check-in is two to three hours ahead of sailing depending on your destination—ask when you book.

Traveling by ferry is relaxing and a great way to see some of B.C.'s spectacular coastline. However, make your reservations for the Inside Passage as far ahead as possible—at least several months ahead in summer—to avoid disappointment. You can't just turn up and get on without reservations (though it's relatively easy for foot passengers), particularly if you have an oversize vehicle. If you're doing the Inside Passage from Port Hardy to Skagway, reservations must be made separately with both the B.C. Ferry and Alaska State Ferry companies. Supply your name, full address, telephone number, the number of persons traveling (and ages under 12

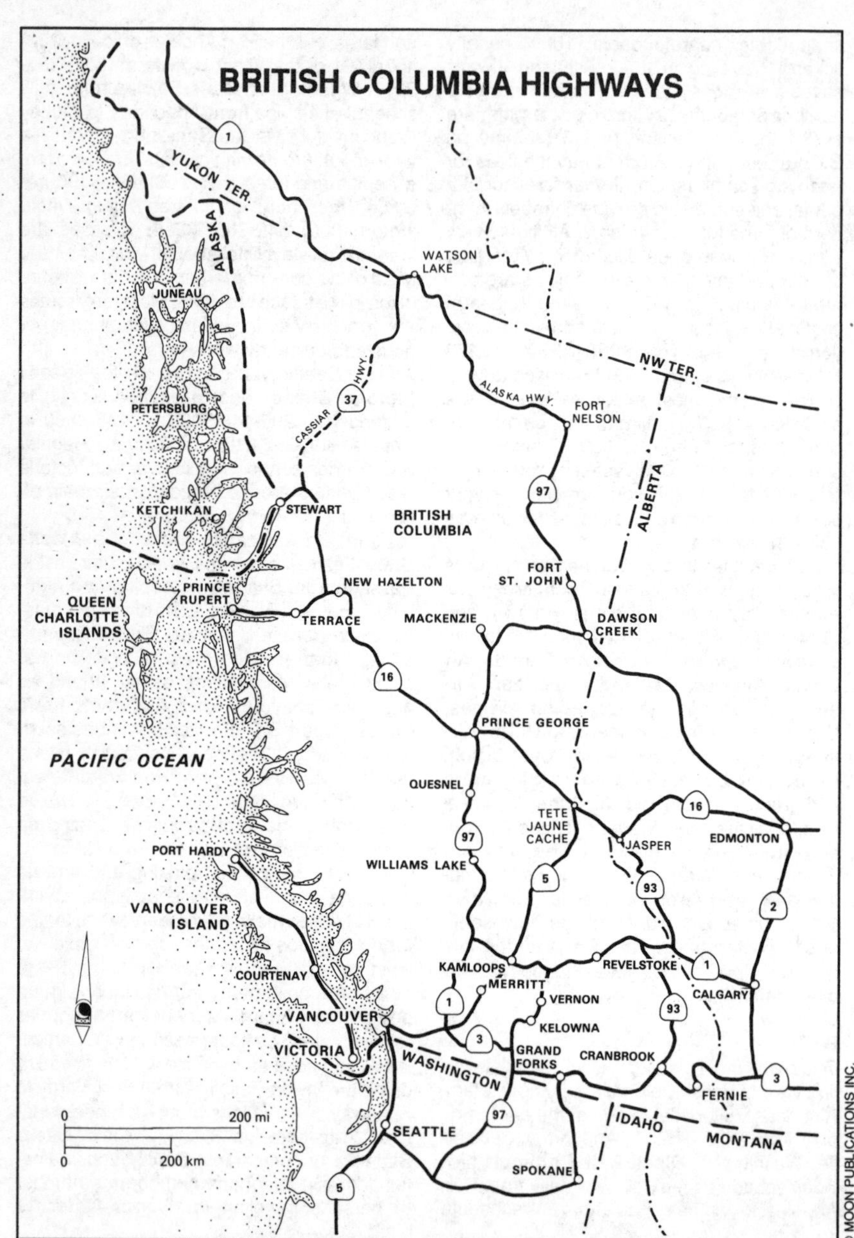
BRITISH COLUMBIA HIGHWAYS
YUKON TER.
ALASKA
WATSON LAKE
JUNEAU
NW TER.
CASSIAR HWY.
ALASKA HWY.
FORT NELSON
PETERSBURG
ALBERTA
KETCHIKAN
STEWART
BRITISH COLUMBIA
FORT ST. JOHN
NEW HAZELTON
PRINCE RUPERT
QUEEN CHARLOTTE ISLANDS
TERRACE
MACKENZIE
DAWSON CREEK
PRINCE GEORGE
PACIFIC OCEAN
QUESNEL
TETE JAUNE CACHE
JASPER
EDMONTON
PORT HARDY
WILLIAMS LAKE
VANCOUVER ISLAND
KAMLOOPS
REVELSTOKE
COURTENAY
MERRITT
VERNON
CALGARY
VANCOUVER
KELOWNA
VICTORIA
GRAND FORKS
CRANBROOK
WASHINGTON
FERNIE
IDAHO
MONTANA
SEATTLE
SPOKANE
0
200 mi
0
200 km
1
37
97
16
5
93
2
3

years), type of vehicle, vehicle length, height of vehicle if it exceeds six feet eight inches, if you're towing a trailer the length of vehicle and trailer, cabin requirements, and preferred dates of travel, with alternate dates if possible. Vehicle check-in time is from one to three hours before sailing. The **B.C. Ferries Reservation Centre** is open daily 0700-2200 at tel. (604) 669-1211 (Vancouver), tel. (604) 386-3431 (Victoria), and tel. (206) 441-6865 (Seattle). Or write to B.C. Ferries, 1112 Fort St., Victoria, B.C., V8V 4V2. For info and reservations on the **Alaska Marine Highway System,** phone (907) 465-3941 (in Canada) or (800) 642-0066 (within the U.S. and Alaska), or write to Alaska Marine Highway System, Pouch R, Juneau, AK 99811-2505.

By Land

British Columbia has a well-maintained road and highway network, though in winter heavy snowfalls may result in some temporary road closures. To avoid delays around Vancouver I., the lower mainland, and major southern routes call 1-660-9775 for an up-to-date road condition report.

By bus, **Greyhound Lines** services Canada and the U.S. The company offers Trans-Canada Highway Service from Toronto, Winnipeg, Regina, and Calgary to Vancouver, a Southern Trans-Canada Route from Calgary to Cranbrook and Vancouver, and a Yellowhead Route from Winnipeg, Saskatoon, and Edmonton to Vancouver. From the thousands of depots throughout the U.S., you can go just about anywhere you desire. Reservations are not necessary—just turn up when you want to go, buy your ticket, and kick back for the long journey north. As long as you use your ticket within 30 days, you can stop over wherever the bus stops and stay as long as you want. When calling for info, ask if they have any special deals—sometimes they offer excursion fares to certain destinations that save you money if you buy a RT ticket, other times they offer good prices if you buy your ticket a month in advance. Get current schedules and fares from your travel agent, or call the nearest Greyhound Bus depot. In Vancouver, Greyhound is at 150 Dunsmuir St., tel. (604) 683-8133. For info in Spanish within the U.S. call (800) 531-5332.

GETTING AROUND

The best way to get around British Columbia is via your own vehicle—be it a car, RV, motorbike, or a bicycle if you have plenty of time. It's easy to get around by bus and train, but you can't get off the beaten track and, let's face it, that's exactly where most of British Columbia is! It's also easy to get around by air (all the larger airports have scheduled intra-provincial flights, and many of the smaller ones have air charter services), but this is one heck of an expensive way to not see the scenery (close-up is best!), and if it's a dull day you'll only see B.C. clouds.

Vancouver International Airport is serviced by the following domestic airlines: **Air B.C.** (tel. 604-273-2464), **Air Canada** (tel. 604-688-5515), **Time Air** (tel. 604-682-1411), and **Canadian Airlines International** (tel. 604-665-4400). Victoria International Airport is serviced by the following domestic airlines: **Air Canada** (tel. 604-382-9242 or 800-663-3721), **Canadian Airlines International** (tel. 604-382-6111), **Time Air** (tel. 604-388-6711 or 800-663-3502), and **Air B.C.** (tel. 604-382-9242 or 800-663-0522). If you're going to fly around, take a floatplane—for fun!

Car rental (and RV rental) is also pricey if you're planning on staying awhile—from $45 a day for an almost-new economy car, plus around 10-15 cents a kilometer, but the first 100 or so are "free!" Gas is around 57 cents a liter. You can easily rent a car from major and not-so-major car rental companies in all the cities in B.C. (scan the yellow pages, call and compare), and many have airport offices also. Cheaper used cars are available from only $19.95 a day plus 10 cents a km (insurance is an optional extra) from Rent-A-Wreck (offices all over B.C.); call toll-free in Canada (800) 268-1430 for more info and reservations. If you're spending some time in B.C. and don't have a vehicle, it's really a lot less expensive to buy an old bomb of a car that still has a bit of life left in it for $500-1,000 in the U.S. or Canada (less expensive in the U.S.), drive up, then sell it at the end of your trip. Check on current registration and insurance regulations when you buy—you may need paper proof when you cross the border.

By Ferry

From **Tsawwassen,** 30 km south of Vancouver, to **Swartz Bay,** 32 km north of Victoria, **B.C. Ferries** sails through the Gulf Islands, taking one hour and 35 minutes, departing hourly in summer and every two hours the rest of the year; reservations are necessary at least a few days ahead if you're going to stop at any of the Gulfs but not taken for the Vancouver to Victoria route—in summer it can be a madhouse! Sample fares: adult passenger $5.25, car and driver $24. For mainland/Vancouver I. 24-hour recorded schedule information, call (604) 685-1021 (Vancouver) or tel. (604) 656-0757 (Victoria). See the **Victoria** and **Vancouver** transportation sections for more details.

Ferries also connect Tsawwassen to **Nanaimo** (Vancouver Is.), the **Southern Gulf Is.** to one another and to Vancouver Is., the **Northern Gulf Is.** (Texada, Hornby, and Denman) to **Comox** (Vancouver I.) and **Powell River** (mainland), Northern Gulf Is. (Quadra and Cortes) to **Campbell River** (Vancouver I.), and **Sointula** and **Alert Bay** to **Port NcNeill** (Vancouver I.). They also interconnect the **Sunshine Coast** (Horseshoe Bay to Langdale, then Earls Cove to Saltery Bay); seven to nine sailings a day depending on the time of year. See the Sunshine Coast section for more details.

B.C. Ferries connects **Prince Rupert** and **Port Hardy** at the top of Vancouver I. year-round. From the end of May through Sept. the ferry goes every other day, from Oct. through April once a week, and during May twice a week. Sample fares: adult passenger $80 OW, car and driver $245, motor home or camper and driver $330 (the cheapest cabins are noisy and claustrophobic—you'll probably sleep just as well in a chair!). All vehicle traffic on the Inside Passage route must be reserved well in advance, and unless you're camping hotel/motel reservations are strongly recommended in summer for both Port Hardy and Prince Rupert. For info on all routes and vehicle reservations for the Inside Passage, Mainland/Gulf Is., and Queen Charlotte Is., call 669-1211 in Vancouver (0700-2200 daily). See both the Prince Rupert and Port Hardy transportation sections for more details.

For the Prince Rupert to the **Queen Charlotte Is.** route, vehicle reservations are strongly advised in summer. Check-in is one hour before sailing. The ferries run four to five times a week from each port during summer, and three times a week from each port Oct. through May. Sample fares: adult passenger $16, car and driver $77. See the Prince Rupert and Queen Charlotte Is. sections for more details.

By Bus

British Columbia by bus is a snap. Just about all the cities have local bus companies providing transportation in town, and many that also cover their local region—check the transportation sections of each individual chapter for more details. **Greyhound Lines** operates daily bus services to just about anywhere in B.C., and you don't need to make reservations—just buy your ticket and go. All scheduled services are nonsmoking. The bus depot in Vancouver is at 150 Dunsmuir St., tel. (604) 662-3222 or 683-8133. See each individual chapter for bus depot locations and telephone numbers.

Pacific Coach Lines provides coach service between Victoria and Vancouver city centers via the ferry (3½ hours), and service between Victoria and Vancouver Airport (3½ hours). The Vancouver depot is at 150 Dunsmuir St. (at Beatty); for a current schedule and fares call (604) 662-8074. The Victoria depot is at 700 Douglas St. (corner of Belleville), tel. (604) 385-4411. **Maverick Coach Lines** serves the Sunshine Coast, Squamish, Whistler, Pemberton, and Vancouver to Nanaimo and other Vancouver I. connections. Also offering a variety of bus tours, Maverick is based at 1375 Vernon Dr., Vancouver, tel. (604) 255-1171. For scheduled bus info in Vancouver call (604) 662-

8051, Nanaimo (604) 753-4371, Squamish (604) 898-3914, Whistler (604) 932-5031, Pemberton (604) 894-6818, Gibsons (604) 886-7742, Sechelt (604) 885-2217, Pender Harbour (604) 883-9327, or Powell River (604) 485-5030.

Getting around **Vancouver I.** by bus is easy with **Island Coach Lines,** also based at the Victoria bus depot (710 Douglas St.), open Mon.-Fri. 0830-1600—pick up a current schedule (changed regularly). Connecting coach service is provided from Port Hardy to the B.C. Ferry terminal, from Port Alberni to Ucluelet and Tofino. Outside the Victoria depot are luggage lockers, $2 for 24 hours. For general info call (604) 385-4411.

B.C. Transit info can be obtained at the following numbers: Victoria (604) 382-6161, Vancouver (604) 261-5100, West Vancouver (604) 985-7777, and Nanaimo (604) 390-4531.

By Train

British Columbia Railway, commonly called **B.C. Rail,** provides daily service from North Vancouver to Prince George via Howe Sound and Lillooet; reservations required beyond Lillooet. To get to the B.C. Rail Station at 1311 West 1st St., catch a bus from the Vancouver bus depot at 150 Dunsmuir St. or take the SeaBus across to Lonsdale Quay and pick up the bus from there. Bicycles are carried (for a fee) on the train if there's enough space; canoes are not permitted. B.C. Rail also operates the **Royal Hudson Steam Train,** an antique steam engine which travels between North Vancouver and Squamish. For info and reservations call (604) 984-5246 in North Vancouver, departures and arrivals (604) 984-5264. For general info on all B.C. Rail services, call (604) 631-3500.

VIA Rail provides daily service through Prince George west to Prince Rupert or east to Jasper and on to Winnipeg. For recorded arrival and departure info (updated daily) call (604) 669-3050. For reservations call toll-free in British Columbia (800) 561-8630. See individual chapters for more details. Points north of Prince George are serviced by bus.

ENTRY REQUIREMENTS

Stamps Of Approval

All overseas visitors (other than U.S. citizens or residents) must have a valid passport and may need visas or visitor permits according to their country of residence—and the international politics being played behind the scenes. At present, visas are not required by residents of the U.S., Commonwealth countries, or Western European countries. Check with your travel agent on the latest visa and permit requirements a few months before you travel—it can take several months to get what you need—or contact the nearest Canadian Embassy, High Commissioner, or

BOB MARSHALL

Consulate in your country. **United States citizens and residents** need only have some form of identification proving their citizenship and residency, such as a birth certificate or voter's registration card, a driver's license with photo (not always enough on its own, it never hurts to carry your passport as well), an alien card (essential for aliens to reenter the U.S.), etc. Anyone wishing to work or study in Canada must obtain employment or student authorization before entering—contact the nearest Canadian Embassy or Consulate General, then apply at a port of entry (you may need job clearance and a medical exam).

Americans may take out $400 worth of household and personal items duty-free, if they've been in Canada for more than 48 hours, $25 worth if they were in Canada for less than 48 hours (see "Goods and Services Tax," below). Duty-free exemptions differ country to county; get the details at any duty-free shop.

Goods And Services Tax

On 1 Jan. 1991 Canada initiated a seven-percent goods and services tax (GST) on the purchase price of many goods and services sold in Canada. However, this will be rebated to nonresident visitors on short-term accommodation and most consumer goods bought and taken home (services and retail purchases over $100) upon application at duty-free shops (now also called Visitor Rebate Centres) when exiting the country. Note: Keep all receipts and vouchers that prove GST was paid on goods and services bought or consumed, and include them with the claim.

A rebate can be claimed any time within one year from the date the goods and/or accommodations were purchased. To claim the rebate either lodge a completed GST rebate form at any duty-free shop or mail it to Revenue Canada, Customs and Excise, Visitors' Rebate Program, Ottawa, Ontario, K1A 1J5. For more info call toll-free from anywhere in Canada at (800) 66VISIT, from outside Canada at (616) 991-3346. Up to $500 can be rebated on the spot at Canadian duty-free shops, but claims of more than $500 must by processed by mail through Revenue Canada, and rebates are made in Canadian funds.

If a visitor to Canada arranges for the seller to ship a purchase directly from Canada to another country, GST is not applicable to the purchase price, therefore a rebate cannot be claimed. Departing visitors can make tax-free purchases at the duty-free shop at airports or border crossings.

Items not included in the GST rebate program include: gifts left in Canada, meals and restaurant charges, camping and trailer park fees, services such as dry cleaning and shoe repair, alcoholic beverages, tobacco, automotive fuels, groceries, agricultural and fish products, prescription drugs and medical devices, and used goods that tend to increase in value (paintings, jewelry, rare books, coins).

Write To . . .

More details and info on work permits can be obtained by writing to the Immigration Division, Canada Employment and Immigration Commission, Ottawa. General info on just about everything can be obtained from the **Ministry of Tourism, Recreation, and Culture,** Parliament Buildings, Victoria, B.C. V8V 1X4; in the **U.S.** from the same office at Box C-34971, Seattle, WA 98124-1971, or 100 Bush St., Suite 400, San Francisco, CA 94104 (tel. 415-981-4780), or 3400 Wilshire Blvd. no. 34 Arcade Level, Ambassador Hotel, Los Angeles, CA 90010 (tel. 213-380-9171); in the **U.K.** from 1 Regent St., London, England SW1Y 4NS (tel. 01-930-6857).

Booze, Pets, And Plants

You can take reasonable quantities of clothes, personal effects, up to 50 cigars and 200 cigarettes, one kilogram of tobacco, up to 1.1 liters of spirits or wine, food (a two-day supply), oil, and gas (normal tank capacity) over the border into Canada before duty is applied. Pets from the U.S. can travel in Canada providing they have all the necessary documentation: dogs and cats must be over three months old and have a rabies

WHAT TO TAKE

Essential Papers
passport or birth certificate (and alien card if you're a U.S. resident)
traveler's checks
airline tickets
driver's license
bus pass
youth hostel card
student ID
automobile association membership card
British Columbia Handbook

Clothing And Toiletries
shirts/T-shirts
at least one warm sweater—several in winter
shorts
jeans or pants
socks—including wool
wind- and waterproof jacket or coat
down vest
wool hat
long winter underwear in winter
swimsuit
dressy outfit and shoes or sandals
tennis shoes
hiking boots
thongs for campground showers
toiletries
shower cap
hair dryer
cosmetics

Camping Gear
tent and rain fly
waterproof gel
sleeping pad
sleeping bag
YH sleeping sheet and pillow case
stove
cooking equipment
lightweight plate, bowl, and mug
utensils
Swiss Army knife with can and bottle opener and corkscrew
a sharp fillet knife
matches
flashlight
candle
salt and sugar in waterproof containers
toilet paper
towel
laundry soap powder in a plastic bag
extra plastic bags
first-aid kit with aspirin (or substitute), Band-Aids, poison oak remedy, and antibiotic cream
sewing kit

certificate with date of vaccination; birds can be brought in only if they have not been mixing with other birds (parrots need an export permit because they're on the endangered species list). Leave your plants at home! They need plant health certificates and advance authority to import them—lots of paperwork hassles.

No-nos
Taking **revolvers, pistols,** and **fully automatic firearms** into Canada is prohibited; those wishing to hunt or carry firearms must get a license, and all guns must be declared at the border. National parks also forbid the entry of guns unless they're dismantled or the muzzle is securely wrapped and the gun is in

a case and kept completely out of sight. If you hunt at home and carry ammunition in your vehicle, be sure to clean out your entire vehicle thoroughly before crossing the border. You can, however, take boats, canoes, kayaks, your fishing gear, cameras and film, and other sporting equipment into B.C. You're also not allowed to take up goods for sale or goods for persons without declaring them and possibly paying duty.

Boats And Planes

If you're going to be entering B.C. by private boat, contact Customs in advance for a list of ports of entry that have Customs facilities, and request their hours of operation. After cruising in, you must report to Customs and go through all the mandatory paperwork and questioning. If you're entering by private aircraft, land at an airport with Customs clearance and report there immediately to complete all the usual documentation. In an unforeseen emergency landing report to the nearest Customs office or RCMP. Write to Transport Canada, AISP/A, Ottawa, Ontario K1A 0N8, for the handy publication Air Tourist Information Canada (TP771E). For the invaluable *Ministry of Transportation and Highways Air Facilities Map* (info on 374 land and water aerodromes and useful aeronautical info for trip planning), write to the British Columbia Aviation Council, Esso Avitat Building, 303-5360 Airport Rd., South Richmond, B.C. V7B 1B4, or call them at (604) 278-9330. The council is an organization promoting the development of aviation—members can assist you in planning a safe and enjoyable flight through their spectacular province.

MONEY

Canadian currency is based on dollars and cents—all prices quoted in this guidebook are in **Canadian** dollars unless otherwise noted. Prices listed may or may not include the goods and services tax (seven percent) according to business preference; always ask if tax is extra when you're given a quote. The safest way to carry money is in the form of U.S. traveler's checks from a reputable and well-known U.S. company such as American Express, Visa, or Bank of America (easiest to cash), cashing only the amount you need when you need it at a bank (better exchange rates) or foreign currency exchange outlet. It's also a good idea to start off with a couple of traveler's checks in Canadian dollars so that you're never caught without *some* money if you don't make it to a bank on time. International currency exchange services are located at Vancouver International Airport and at the Douglas (White Rock) border-crossing point.

HEALTH

British Columbia is a healthy place. To visit, you don't need vaccinations, boosters, or other horrible needles, and you can drink the water from the faucet (though it's always wise to boil backcountry water to be on the safe side) and eat the food without worry. When in backcountry areas, be aware of poison oak (which causes itchy open blisters and sores a short time after contact) and keep your eyes peeled for rattlesnakes—taking along a snakebite kit and ointment for poison oak is not a bad idea. If you bathe in hot springs, keep your head above water and *do not* let the water enter your nose, ears, or mouth—the *Giardia lamblia* parasite thrives in hot water and can cause meningitis and other nasty complications.

The big concern of AIDS and other venereal and needle-sharing-communicated diseases is the same as anywhere in the world today. Take exactly the same precautions you would at home—know your partners well, use condoms, and don't share needles.

It's a good idea to get health insurance or some form of coverage before heading to Canada if you're going to be there for a while, but check that your plan covers foreign services. In-hospital charges vary from hospital to hospital, but can start at around $900 a day, and some facilities impose an extra 30% surcharge for nonresidents! Some Canadian companies offer coverage specifically aimed at visitors; for an example, write to Hospital Medical Care, Box 1012 West Georgia St., Vancouver, B.C. V6E 2Y2, for their brochure, or call them at (604) 684-0666. If you're on medication take adequate supplies with you, and get a prescription from your doctor to cover the time you will be away. You may not be able to get a prescription made up at Canadian pharmacies without visiting a Canadian doctor, so don't wait till you've almost run out. If you wear glasses or contact lenses, ask your optometrist for a spare prescription in case you break or lose your lenses, and stock up on your usual cleaning supplies.

If you need the services of an ambulance, call the telephone number listed on the inside front cover of the local directory, and if you're unsure of your whereabouts ask the operator for assistance. All the cities and most of the large towns have local hospitals—look in each individual chapter for locations and telephone numbers. Be aware that some of B.C.'s highways snake for many kilometers through high mountain pass wilderness areas—if you or your passengers can't handle elevation well, read a good topographical map before you set off—particularly for the Rockies where highways reach 1,146-1,774 meters. For info on traveling in B.C. for the physically handicapped, write to the Canadian Paraplegic Association, 780 Southwest Marine Dr., Vancouver, B.C. V6P 5Y7, or phone (604) 324-3611.

ACCOMMODATIONS

Campgrounds

All the national parks and many of the provincial parks provide campgrounds. Most have tent sites, camper or RV sites (don't count on hookups, but many places have sewer drops), picnic tables, fire grates (with wood generally provided), fresh drinking water, and pit toilets. Some of the national park campgrounds have flush toilets and hot showers. Prices range $5-15 per night depending on facilities and services. All campgrounds are open during the summer peak months, and many stay open year-round, although you can expect only pit toilets in midwinter. Forest campgrounds are usually free.

Private campgrounds and RV parks are found throughout the province. Recommendations are listed in each chapter under "Accommodations." Pick up the invaluable Automobile Association guides to campgrounds for full listings, and the free *Accommodations* booklet put out by Ministry of Tourism, Recreation, and Culture, available at all Travel InfoCentres.

Youth Hostels

British Columbian youth hostels are like YHs around the world. All provide separate dorms and washroom facilities for men and women (occasionally family rooms), most have fully equipped kitchens and common rooms. You provide your own sleeping bag, linen, towel, etc. Prices are $10-12.50 per night. The main YH hostels are located in Vancouver, Victoria, and Whistler. To use the hostels you must be a YH member—join at one of the hostels or write for info to the **Canadian Hostelling Association,** 1515 Discovery St., Vancouver, B.C. V6R 4K5, tel. (604) 224-7111. The Victoria office is at 516 Yates St., Victoria, B.C. V8W 1K8, tel. (604) 385-4511. Anyone of any age can join. Mini-hostels also offer budget accommodation in private homes or small commercial hotels with breakfast included; you generally need to provide your own sleeping bag and gear. These come and go. Request a current list of mini-hostels at any of the YHs—prices range $8-13 per

TODD CLARK

night, plus some add a surcharge for those who are not YH members.

Bed And Breakfast

Throughout B.C. many places offer bed-and-breakfast accommodations—a great way to meet British Columbians. Stop in at Travel InfoCentres for lists of guesthouses and bed-and-breakfast homes; prices generally range $35-50 s, $40-80 d. Many bed-and-breakfast agencies (especially in the Vancouver and Victoria areas) list a number of homes to suit whatever you desire: city homes, rural homes, homes with sea views, or farms where you can join in the activities. Call and let them find the right place for you, but be sure to also let them know what price you're prepared to pay. Brochures from the various agencies can be picked up at Travel InfoCentres throughout B.C., or write to the **British Columbia Bed and Breakfast Association** at 810 West Broadway Ave., P.O. Box 593, Vancouver, B.C. V5Z 4E2.

Motels And Hotels

The best guide to motels and hotels is the free *Accommodations* booklet put out by the province, available at all Travel InfoCentres. In it are listed hotels, motor hotels, motels, lodges, and resorts, that have been approved by the Ministry of Tourism. Prices start at around $25 s, $30 d and go all the way up! Aside from accommodation info, the booklet has all sorts of info on B.C. in the first few pages. The *AA Accommodations Guide* is another handy book to lug around.

FOOD

British Columbia is not world-renowned for its culinary delights. Canadian food is similar to American food—in general, bland and not very interesting. You can get everything from burgers, hot dogs, ready-made sandwiches, and chicken-in-a-box to gourmet continental cuisine at the best restaurants in the large cities. Vancouver is the best place to eat—with a wide variety of ethnic foods along with the usual Canadiana and a complete range of prices to suit all. Victoria also has its share of good restaurants, but gets the reputation for serving predominantly British food in as British an atmosphere as you could imagine outside of Britain. The pubs are fun to visit—scarf down a cold pork pie or two, tomatoes, cheddar cheese, pâté, and a hunk of bread with your Guinness. Do try some salmon or fresh seafood when you're on the coast, or go out and get yourself a trout or salmon from one of the many lakes—a squeeze of lemon, a frying pan and camp stove, and you'll have one of the best meals on your trip! For restaurant suggestions, see the "Food" section of each chapter.

PRACTICAL INFORMATION

Help!

The **RCMP** (Royal Canadian Mounted Police) are often contacted to send urgent messages to people on vacation. If your name is listed in a newspaper, on TV or radio, or at the Travel InfoCentres, contact the nearest RCMP office for the message. See individual chapters for the location of the local RCMP and its telephone number. If you notice a **forest fire,** please rush to the nearest phone and dial 0 and ask for Zenith 5555, the free province-wide forest-fire-reporting number.

Services

The **area code** for the entire province of British Columbia is 604.

Canadian **postage stamps** must be used on all mail posted in Canada. First-class letters and postcards within Canada are 40 cents, to the U.S. 46 cents, to foreign destinations 80 cents—more if the letter is heavier, etc. You can buy stamps at post offices, automatic vending machines, most hotel lobbies, railway stations, airports, bus terminals, and at many retail outlets and some newsstands. Visitors can have their mail sent to them c/o General Delivery, Main P.O., City, Province, and postal code. The post office will hold the mail for 15 days, then return it to the sender.

Electrical voltage in B.C. is 120 volts, same as the United States. British Columbia is on the **metric system,** though you still hear everyone talking in pounds and ounces, miles, and miles per hour! See the Metric Conversion Chart in the back of this book to put things into the perspective *you* recognize!

Shops throughout B.C. are generally open weekdays 0900-1700, Sat. 0900-1700, many with extended hours, and some are open 24 hours a day. Major malls stay open all weekends. If you're in a city or large town, you can always find a store open for essentials, and restaurants and fast-food outlets. In small towns and villages, don't count on stores being open—stock up ahead. Most **banks** are only open 1000-1500 on weekdays (some stay open longer hours)—don't get caught out on weekends. **Tipping** charges are not usually added to your bill—you are expected to add a tip of 15% to the total amount for waiters and waitresses, barbers and hairdressers, taxi drivers, etc. Bellhops, doormen, and porters generally receive $1 per item of baggage.

Driving in B.C.

United States and International driver's licenses are valid in Canada. Safety belts are mandatory, as are motorcycle safety helmets, and an infant car seat is required for children weighing up to nine kilograms (20 pounds). A child car seat is recommended for nonresident children from 9-18 kilograms (20-40 pounds) and required for residents! Before you venture off into the wilds, ask your vehicle insurance company for the pale-yellow Canadian nonresident interprovincial motor-vehicle liability insurance card—what a mouthful! You may also be asked to prove vehicle ownership, so carry your vehicle registration form. If you're involved in an accident with a B.C. vehicle, contact the nearest Insurance Corporation of British Columbia (ICBC) office (Vancouver tel. 661-2800, Victoria tel. 383-1111). If you're a member of an automobile association, take your card—the Canadian AA provides full services to members of associated associations, including free maps, travel info, itineraries, excellent tour books, road and weather conditions, accommodation reservations, and travel agency and emergency road services on presentation of a valid, current AA membership card. For more info write to the British Columbia Automobile Association at 999 West Broadway Ave., Vancouver, B.C. V5Z 1K5, tel. (604) 732-3911. Note: drinking and driving (.08%) in B.C. can get you imprisonment of up to five years for a first offense, plus your license will be removed for at least 12 months.

LOUISE FOOTE

VICTORIA

INTRODUCTION

Victoria, elegant capital of the province of British Columbia, welcomes visitors to "banana-belt" Vancouver I. with a mild climate, friendly people, and a distinct holiday atmosphere somewhat unusual for a capital city. Standing proudly at the southern tip of Vancouver I., with its colorful 140-year history of fur trading, gold mining, and seafaring, Victoria is a fashionable city projecting an intriguing mixture of images, old and new. Well-preserved century-old buildings line inner-city streets, ancient totem poles sprout from shady parks, restored historic areas house trendy shops, offices, and exotic restaurants, double-decker buses and horse-drawn carriages compete for summer trade, and the residents keep alive the original traditions and old-world atmosphere that attract visitors searching, half a world away, for a bit of merry old England. Click into vacation mode in Victoria and you'll be in the right frame of mind to experience the rest of the island.

Early Days

Vancouver I. first became recognized as an island in 1792 when Capt. George Vancouver explored and charted the hazardous island-dotted waters of Johnstone Strait, between the Queen Charlotte Strait in the north and the Strait of Georgia in the south. Little did he realize at the time that he'd just discovered the largest North American island in the Pacific—an island that delighted him with its natural beauty and serene climate.

Many Indian communities lived around Vancouver Island's shoreline when Vancouver first made his discovery and continued to do so without many changes in lifestyle for almost another 50 years. White explorers and fur traders representing companies from both the West Coast of the mainland and as far away as the East Coast were the first to recognize the potential value of the island. Hudson's Bay Company became the most dominant, establishing control over the entire

VICTORIA CITY CENTER

1. Ogden Point Cruise Ship Terminal
2. Fisherman's Wharf Park
3. Washington ferry terminal
4. Royal London Wax Museum
5. Pacific Undersea Gardens
6. The James Bay Inn
7. Parliament Buildings
8. Helmcken House
9. Thunderbird Park
10. Crystal Garden
11. Royal B.C. Museum
12. bus depot
13. Empress Hotel
14. Miniature World
15. The Victoria Clipper
16. Tourism Victoria Travel Information Centre
17. Maritime Museum
18. Bastion Square
19. youth hostel
20. post office
21. Chinatown
22. Centennial Square
23. public library
24. YWCA
25. Cherry Bank Hotel
26. Christ Church Cathedral
27. Collectors Car Museum
28. Craigmyle Guest House
29. Craigdarroch Castle
30. Government House
31. Art Gallery of Greater Victoria

island as well as the mainland territory of "Columbia." Needing to firmly establish British presence on the northwest coast, in 1843 the company chose the southern tip of the island as the location for a new fort, naming it after Queen Victoria. In 1849 Vancouver I. became a Crown colony, administered by the Hudson's Bay Company, and gradually the land around the fort was opened up by groups of British settlers brought to Fort Victoria by its subsidiary Puget Sound Agricultural Company. Several large company farms were developed, and Esquimalt Harbour became a major port for the British Pacific Fleet.

In the late 1850s gold strikes on the mainland Thompson and Fraser rivers brought hundreds of gold miners into Victoria, the region's only port and source of supplies. Overnight, Victoria became a classic boomtown, but with a distinctly British flavor; most of the company men, early settlers, and military personnel firmly maintained their homeland traditions and celebrations. Even after the gold rush ended several years later, Victoria remained an energetic bastion of military, economic, and political activity and in 1866 became capital of the new British Columbia.

And Now

Many people view the city for the first time from the Inner Harbour, entering by boat the way people have for almost 150 years. On rounding Laurel Point, Victoria sparkles into view: quiet residential suburbs; manicured lawns and flower gardens; Inner Harbour busy with ferries, fishing and tour boats, and seaplanes; and striking inner-city architecture. Easygoing Victorians (pop. 64,800), understandably proud of their city, lure visitors from around the world and, despite the pressures that go with city life, still find the time for a stroll along the waterfront, a round of golf, or a typically English high tea.

Victoria is a two-season city, very dependent on tourism. High season is May through Oct. and low season falls in winter when the weather can be less appealing. In spring, the city jumps to life and shakes out the welcome mat, and enormous baskets of daffodils and other blooming bulbs are hung from all the downtown lampposts, watered several times a week by a tank truck and tall hose.

Summer is the time to enjoy the hustle and bustle of a city full of visitors, with activities designed to meet all needs, desires, and higher budgets. If you prefer a more laid-back atmosphere, don't mind the possibility of rain and nippy sea breezes, and like meeting relaxed locals enjoying their few months of peace and quiet, take advantage of the lower prices, grab your windbreaker and brolly, and discover Victoria in the off-season.

SIGHTS

INNER CITY

Victoria has so many attractions, both free and commercial, that if you want to see *everything* give yourself a few extra days. The best way to get to know this beautiful city is on foot. All the downtown attractions are within a short walk of each other, the more remote easily reached by bus. In summer you have the added option of seeing Victoria by horse-drawn carriage or on a variety of tours by bus, coach, minivan, boat, horseback, bicycle, limo, you name it! But if you still feel the need to have a car readily available, there's plenty of parking if you know where to look (see below).

The best place to start your discovery of this city is the **Tourism Victoria Travel Information Centre,** 812 Wharf St. at the waterfront, tel. 382-2127; open daily. Pick up a free city map dotted with attractions, a handy *Parking Guide* brochure if you have a car, and the assorted free publications and newspapers. Then head down to the waterfront marina several pounds heavier!

Initially this area was part of the harbor, and the impressive Empress Hotel stands on what was once an area of deep, oozing mud flats prior to the construction of the massive stone causeway that now forms the marina. Walk along the lower level, then up the steps in the middle to come face to face with an unamused Capt. Cook, prime local target for low-range bird drops, longing to stroll across to the Empress for a shampoo, blow-dry, and large-brimmed disposable hat. The statue commemorates his first recorded landing, in 1778, on what was later to become known as British Columbia.

Empress Hotel

The pompous, ivy-covered Empress Hotel (main entrance on Government St.) was designed in 1908 by the well-known architect Francis Rattenbury, who also designed the Parliament Buildings, CPR Terminal (wax museum), and Crystal Garden. It's worthwhile walking through the hotel lobby to gaze—head back, mouth ajar—at the interior razzle-dazzle, hobnob with the guests, practice your Japanese, and watch people watching people partake in a traditional afternoon tea (see p. 49). Browse through the conservatory and gift shops, drool over the menus of the various restaurants, see what tours are available, and exchange currency if you're desperate (banks give a better exchange rate).

If you happen to be called Gulliver, or you have several whining children hanging on your shirttail, **Miniature World,** one of Victoria's many commercial attractions, could be right up your alley. Located on the north side of the Empress Hotel on Humboldt St., tel. 385-9731; open daily, adult $6, student $5. Vintage car enthusiasts may want to continue up Humboldt to 813 Douglas St. to view 42 vintage cars along with auto paraphernalia in the **Collectors Car Museum;** open daily (tel. 382-7180), adult $5, senior or student $4, child $2, family $14.

Parliament Buildings

Satisfy your lust for governmental, historic, and architectural knowledge all in one go by taking a free tour of the Provincial Legislative Buildings. These prominent buildings were designed by Francis Rattenbury and completed in 1897. The exterior is British Columbia Haddington I. stone, and if you walk around the buildings you'll no doubt spot many a stern or gruesome face staring down from the stonework. On either side of the main entrance stand statues of Sir James Douglas, who chose the location of Victoria, and Sir Matthew Baillie Begbie, in charge of law and order during the gold-rush period. Atop the copper-covered dome stands a gilded statue of Capt. George Vancouver, first navigator to sail around Vancouver Island. In summer free guided tours (available in at least six languages) are provided many times a day, in winter less frequently on weekdays only. The time of each tour changes daily according to the goings-on inside; call the Travel Information Centre, tel. 382-2127, for current times.

Be sure to return for another visit after dark when the Parliament Buildings are outlined in lights and the Empress Hotel is floodlit. If you like taking spectacular reflection photos, take a tripod or fast film down to the marina. Occasionally, locals grumble about the cost of lighting these buildings and they're plunged into darkness, but when the officials get just as many complaints they're relit, in a never-ending cycle!

More Harborfront Attractions

Oodles of ways to trim bulging wallets confront you in Victoria, some excellent, some routine. Continuing along the waterfront on Belleville St., across the road from the Parliament Buildings is the former CPR Steam-

The Parliament Buildings, outlined by 3,333 lights, are spectacular at night.

ship Terminal, now **The Royal London Wax Museum.** This building, completed in 1924, was also designed by Francis Rattenbury and has been called a "Temple to Neptune" (Neptune's head decorates several pillars). The museum features more than 180 wax figures direct from London; open daily 0930-1700, admission adult $5.25, senior or student $4.50, child $2.50. **Pacific Undersea Gardens,** on the water beside the wax museum, boasts more than 5,000 marine specimens in their natural habitat, performing scuba divers, and Armstrong the giant octopus; open daily 1000-1700, adult $5, senior $4, child $2.50.

Laurel Point

For an enjoyable short walk from downtown, continue along Belleville St. from the old steamship terminal, passing a conglomeration of modern hotels, the Washington ferry terminal, and some intriguing architecture dating back to the late 19th century. A path leads down through a shady park then hugs the waterfront, passing more hotels with good views of Inner Harbour, to the end of Laurel Point. If you're feeling really energetic, continue to **Fisherman's Wharf Park** and the crowded marina, round Ogden Point, pass a pond crowded with waterfowl, bypass the steps down to **Fonyo Beach,** zero in on the **Mile Zero** sign at the beginning of the Trans-Canada Hwy., and end up at popular Beacon Hill Park.

Beacon Hill Park

This large, hilly city park, a lush, sea-edged oasis of grass and flowers, also boasts cliffs with spectacular views of Juan De Fuca Strait and the distant Olympic Mountains on a clear day. Add a handful of rocky points to scramble on and many protected pebble-and-sand beaches and you've found yourself a perfect spot to sit and indulge your senses. Catch a sea breeze (along with numerous hang gliders, sailboarders, and kite-fliers) and gaze at all the strolling, cycling, dog-walking, and pram-pushing Victorians passing by. On a bright sunny day you'll swear that most of Victoria is there too. Within easy walking distance from downtown, the park can also be reached by bus number five. For a tidbit of history, walk through the park to rocky Finlayson Point. Once the site of an ancient fortified Indian village, between 1878 and 1892 two enormous guns protected the point against an expected but unrealized Russian invasion.

Horse Power

Horses have been clip-clopping through Victoria's streets for as long as the oldest locals can remember. In fact, between 1903 and 1987 more than four million passengers en-

a relaxing way to tour Victoria

BILL MARSHALL

joyed this popular Victorian sightseeing tradition. In 1980, with a stable of 40 draft horses and nine carriages, the **Tally-Ho Horse-Drawn Sightseeing Co.** was born. The tours operate between the first week of May and the end of Sept., starting in front of the Parliament Buildings across from the wax museum (tel. 479-1113). Tune in an informative commentary while you plod at a relaxing pace through picturesque Beacon Hill Park, along seaside Dallas Rd., to return downtown through the Old City with its typically English cottages and heritage homes. The tours run every 15-20 minutes May-Sept. with extended hours from mid-June to the end of August (0900-1900); adult $9, student $5.50, child under 12 $4.50, child on lap free, family $25.

Several other horse-drawn carriage tours also operate from the carriage stand on the corner of Belleville and Menzies streets.

The Royal British Columbia Museum

British Columbia's Natural and Human History Museum—easily one of the best museums in North America—is a must-see attraction for even the most jadedly museum-averse. All the displays are extraordinarily true to life, complete with appropriate sounds and smells. Come face to face with an ice-age woolly mammoth, stroll through a coastal forest full of tweeting birds and deer, along a seashore or tidal marsh, and descend into the open ocean (a very real trip not recommended for claustrophobics!). Take a tour through time via the time capsules. Walk along a turn-of-the-century street. Experience the hands-on exhibits of industrialization, the gold rush, and the exploration of B.C. by land and sea. An Archaeology Gallery, First Peoples Gallery, Totem Pole and Art Gallery, and Kwakiutl Indian Bighouse complete the tour. The museum is at 675 Belleville St., tel. 387-3701, open daily in summer 0930-1900, winter 1000-1730; admission adult $5, student $3, child $2, family $10, plus GST. The gift shop has an excellent collection of books on Canadiana, birds, animals, history, and native Indian art and culture, along with postcards and tourist paraphernalia. Next door, the tearoom is always crowded with visitors renewing energy for the next attraction on their lists.

Plant appreciators should stop for a moment in front of the museum and note the **Native Plant Garden.** Another interesting piece of architecture, a stone's throw from the museum, is the **Carillon Tower.** A centennial gift from B.C.'s Dutch community, the steps lead up to bells ranging from 20 to 1,900 pounds and a keyboard and foot pedals that can be played automatically or by hand and foot.

Thunderbird Park

Behind the Provincial Museum, on the corner of Belleville and Douglas, lies Thunderbird Park, a small green spot chockablock with authentic totem poles intricately carved by northwest coastal Indians. Walk through the park to historic **Helmcken House,** tucked away behind the museum. It was built by Dr. J. S. Helmcken, pioneer surgeon and legislator, who arrived in Victoria in 1850 and aided negotiating the union of British Columbia with Canada in 1870. It's the oldest house in Victoria still standing on its original site in its original condition. Explore the interior and see the doctor's gruesome surgical equipment (you'll appreciate modern medical technology); adult $3, senior or student $2, child $1. If you're also going to visit Craigflower Farm, Craigflower Schoolhouse, and Carr House, ask for the four-site pass for adult $6.50, senior or student $4.50, otherwise you'll pay the same admission at each historic site.

The Crystal Garden

Designed by Francis Rattenbury and built by Percy James, the Crystal Garden was opened in 1925 as the largest saltwater pool in the British Empire. With tearooms, ballrooms, and a promenade, it was the venue for flower shows, craft shows, and big-band dancing, along with swimming, of course. In 1971 it was closed due to rising maintenance costs then bought by the provincial government and turned into a conservatory. Surrounded by lush greenery and flowering plants, visitors are ear-assaulted by fabulous parrots, cockatoos, and an enormous variety of exotic birds from South America, New Guinea, and Australia. The Garden also contains a waterfall and a series of pools where coral-colored flamingos strut their stuff; a room full of iguanas, monkeys, squirrels, wallabies, and marmosets; and peeking out of the lush undergrowth are a number of wood carvings from New Guinea. Sip afternoon tea on the humid upper floor, close your eyes, and you'll swear you're in the tropics! Located behind the Empress Hotel at 713 Douglas St., tel. 381-1213, open daily 1000-2100; admission adult $6, senior or child $4, with the added option of English tea 1415-1615 (extra).

Christ Church Cathedral
On Quadra at Courtney, Christ Church Cathedral is the episcopal seat of the Bishop of the Diocese of B.C. Built in 13th-century Gothic style, it is one of Canada's largest churches. Open 0830-1730 weekdays and 0730-2030 Sun. for self-guided tours, the Cathedral also sponsors free choral recitals at 1600 on Sat. July-August. The park next to the cathedral is a shady haven to rest weary feet, and the gravestones make fascinating reading.

Rockland
From Christ Church Cathedral, walk up Rockland Ave. through the historic Rockland district, passing stately mansions and colorful gardens on tree-lined streets. Turn left on Moss St. and you come to the 1889 Spencer Mansion and its modern wing that together make up the **Art Gallery of Greater Victoria.** It contains Canada's finest collection of Japanese art, a range of contemporary art, and a variety of traveling exhibits, along with a Japanese garden with Shinto shrine. Refresh yourself in the tearoom and buy hand-crafted jewelry, pottery, glass, art books, and reproductions in the Gallery Shop. At 1040 Moss St., tel. 384-4101, open Mon.-Sat. 1000-1700, Thurs. 1000-2100, and Sun. 1300-1700; admission adult $4, senior or student $2, free on Thurs. 1700-2100. Continue up Rockland Ave. to **Government House** on the right. The green velvet lawns and picture-perfect flower gardens are open to the public throughout the year.

Craigdarroch Castle
A short walk from the art gallery (bus no. 11 Uplands or 14 University from downtown) along Rockland and left on Joan Cres. brings you to the baronial mansion known as Craigdarroch Castle. Completed in 1890 by Robert

Craigdarroch Castle

Dunsmuir, a wealthy Victorian industrialist and politician, it's certainly an architectural masterpiece. For all the nitty-gritties, tour the mansion with volunteer guides who really know their Dunsmuir, or admire at your leisure all the polished wood, stained-glass windows, and period furnishings, and the great city views from upstairs. At 1050 Joan Cres., tel. 592-5323, open daily 1000-1630 in winter and 0900-1900 in summer; admission adult $5, senior or student $4, child under 12 by donation.

Old Town

To experience the oldest section of Victoria, start in **Centennial Square** between Government and Douglas streets and Pandora Ave. and Fisgard Street. Many buildings from the 1880s and '90s still stand here, refurbished in recent times for all to appreciate—don't miss Victoria City Hall (fronts Douglas St.), built in 1878, and the imposing Greek-style building of the Hudson's Bay Company. Continue down Fisgard St. into colorful **Chinatown,** one of the oldest and most prosperous Chinatowns in Canada, a delicious place to breathe in the aroma of authentic oriental food wafting from the many restaurants (isn't it time to eat again?!). Chinese prospectors and laborers first brought exotic spices, plants, and a love of intricate architecture and bright colors to Victoria in the 19th century. Poke through dark little shops along Fisgard St. where you can still find everything from fragile paper lanterns and embroidered silks to gingerroot and imported canned fruit and vegies, then cruise Fan Tan Alley, the center of the opium trade in the 1800s. Walk south along Store St. and Wharf St. to Bastion Square.

Bastion Square

Several blocks north of the city center, this cobblestone square and bustling pedestrian walkway with its old gas lamps is lined with decorative architecture dating from the 1860s to 1890s. This was the original site chosen by James Douglas in 1843 for Fort Victoria, the Hudson's Bay Company trading post. Today these restored buildings house trendy restaurants, cafes, nightclubs (Harpo's is one of Victoria's most popular), and fashionable offices. Give your feet a break at the Wharf St. end—a good place to sit, people-watch, and reload your camera for another magnificent harbor view. At the other end is the **Maritime Museum of British Columbia**, which traces Victoria's seafaring history through displays of dugout canoes, model ships, Royal Navy charts, figureheads, photographs, naval uniforms, bells, and much more. It's open Sept.-May 0930-1630, June 0900-1830, July-Aug. 0900-2030; adult $5, senior $3, student $1, under six free. Ahoy!

Finish the tour of Old Town by walking back to the city center along Wharf St., where Hudson's Bay Company furs were loaded onto ships bound for England, gold seekers arrived in search of their fortune, and shopkeepers first established businesses. Cross to the waterfront side of the street to view the marina from the lookout (by the government info sign) where you can see the original mooring rings for the bygone Hudson's Bay Company ships.

Life In The Fast Lane

Tours, tours, and more tours. By bus, boat, horse, train, and plane, to name but a few! Summer in Victoria means you can attraction-visit, cocktail-cruise, fish, whalewatch, straddle Vancouver atop the Parliament Buildings—do just about anything your little heart desires. In winter the pace is decidedly more sedate and you may actually have to track down a tour through the Information Centre.

For the personal touch, a small group, and a price that won't break the bank, locals recommend Sterling Tours. Their individualized tours will take you wherever you want to go; average price is $35 per adult, however it naturally depends on what you're doing. If you're looking for a tour with a particular theme (statues, gardens, miniatures, etc.), they'll try to arrange it; call 380-3959 (or in North America 800-565-8687) for more information.

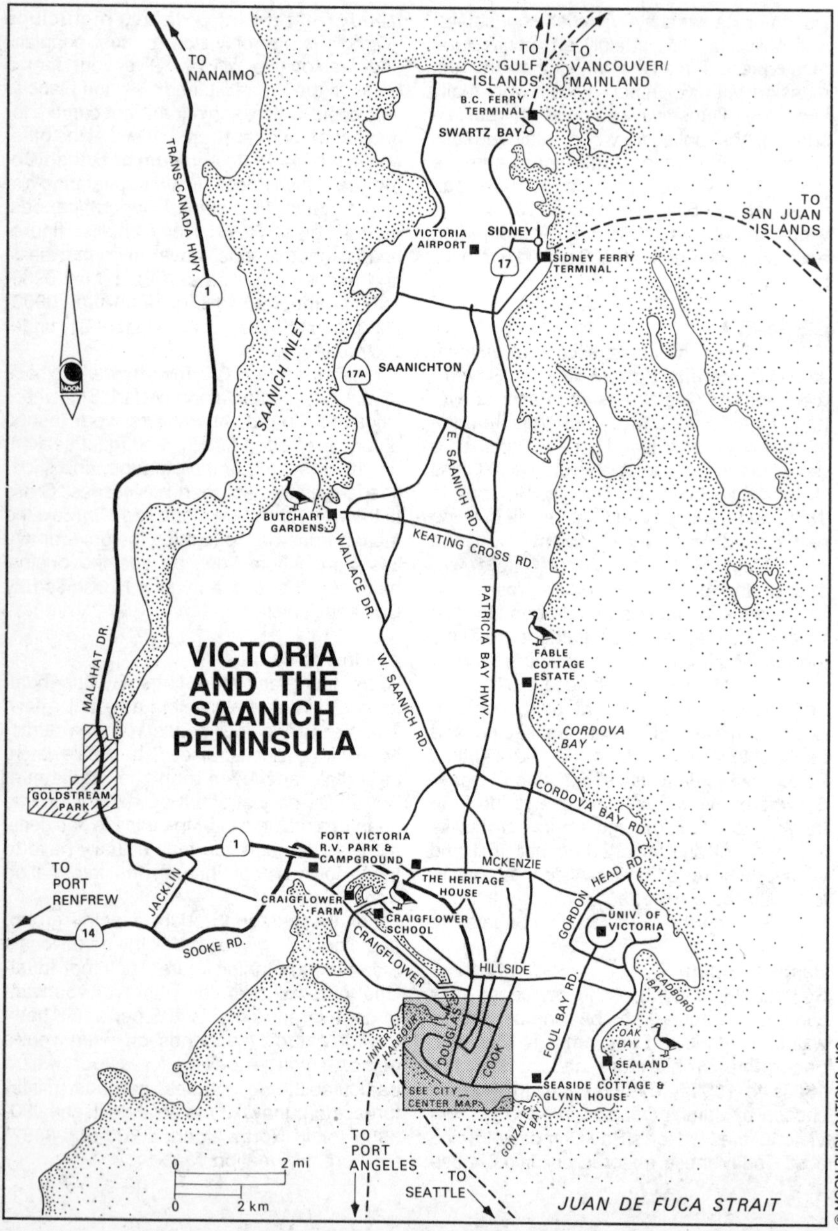

VICTORIA AND THE SAANICH PENINSULA

TO NANAIMO
TRANS-CANADA HWY.
1
TO GULF ISLANDS
TO VANCOUVER/ MAINLAND
B.C. FERRY TERMINAL
SWARTZ BAY
TO SAN JUAN ISLANDS
SIDNEY
VICTORIA AIRPORT
17
SIDNEY FERRY TERMINAL
SAANICH INLET
17A
SAANICHTON
E. SAANICH RD.
BUTCHART GARDENS
KEATING CROSS RD.
WALLACE DR.
PATRICIA BAY HWY.
FABLE COTTAGE ESTATE
W. SAANICH RD.
MALAHAT DR.
CORDOVA BAY
GOLDSTREAM PARK
CORDOVA BAY RD.
1
FORT VICTORIA R.V. PARK & CAMPGROUND
MCKENZIE
GORDON HEAD RD.
TO PORT RENFREW
JACKLIN
CRAIGFLOWER FARM
THE HERITAGE HOUSE
CRAIGFLOWER SCHOOL
UNIV. OF VICTORIA
14
SOOKE RD.
CRAIGFLOWER
HILLSIDE
FOUL BAY RD.
CADBORO BAY
INNER HARBOUR
DOUGLAS
COOK
OAK BAY
SEALAND
SEE CITY CENTER MAP
SEASIDE COTTAGE & GLYNN HOUSE
GONZALES BAY
TO PORT ANGELES
TO SEATTLE
0 2 mi
0 2 km
JUAN DE FUCA STRAIT

ON THE NORTH SIDE

Marine Drive
Take Dallas Rd. from downtown to the oceanfront following the blue Scenic Drive signs. This route takes you through quiet residential areas, past small pebble beaches covered in driftwood, and into the ritzy mansion area where the residents have manicured gardens, sea views, and reportedly live "behind the tweed curtain," because they are "so British." Continue through the velvet greens of Victoria Golf Club on **Gonzales Point,** stopping at **Sealand** (see below) and the **Royal Victoria Yacht Club** at Cadboro Bay. The route borders the east side of the **University of Victoria,** passes **Fable Cottage Estate** (guided tours of the cottage and gardens from 0900 in season, adult $7.50, senior $6.50, student $4, child five to 12 $3) at Cordova Bay, then meets Patricia Bay Highway (Hwy. 17). Head south for the city center, or north toward famous **Butchart Gardens** (see below), the airport, Sidney, and the terminal at the tip of the Saanich Peninsula where ferries depart for the beautiful Gulf Is. and Vancouver.

Sealand
Descend "three fathoms beneath the Pacific" into a room lined with enormous aquariums crammed with fish of all kinds, waving sea urchins, corals and sponges, starfish, and enormous octopi, and another large tank swirling with seals (great underwater views of these graceful mammals). Outside, four separate pools contain harbor and fur seals, sea lions, baby seals in a "nursery pool," and three powerful killer whales. Performances are continuous (prepare to get wet if you stand too close to the whale pool—it's an awfully small pool for such large, magnificent creatures). After the shows, browse through the gift shop, dabble your hands in a pool full of sea urchins, or reenter the submarine grotto. At 1327 Beach Dr., Oak Bay, tel. 598-3373, open 1000-1700; adult $6.50, child $2.75 (includes GST).

Butchart Gardens
These well-known gardens on Tod Inlet, approximately 20 km up the Saanich Peninsula from Victoria, grew from an ugly, abandoned, limestone quarry. A Canadian cement pioneer, Butchart built a mansion near the quarries. He and his wife, world travelers, collected rare and exotic shrubs, trees, and plants, which they replanted, starting in 1904, in a number of formal gardens to beautify the quarry. Interspersed with concrete footpaths, small bridges, waterfalls, ponds, and fountains, the gardens now contain more than 5,000 varieties of flowers—and they swear that 35,000 new bulbs and more than 100 new roses are tested in the extensive nurseries every year. Many a gardener would give both hands to be able to work in these gardens. Go there in spring, summer, or early autumn to treat your eyes and nose to one heckuva sensual experience. In winter, when little is blooming and the entire landscape is green, the basic design of the gardens can best be appreciated—and if you get some kind of facetious joy from watching people work while you play, you'll enjoy lounging in the midst of innumerable teams of gardeners mowing, weeding, checking out the tourists, transplanting, and reorganizing like crazy.

Take Hwy. 17 north to the Brentwood-Butchart Gardens turnoff, turn left on Keating Crossroad and follow the signs, or catch a no. 74 or 75 bus from downtown. Many guided tours also include the gardens. At 800 Benvenuto Dr., Brentwood Bay, tel. 652-5256 (recorded info) or 652-4422, the gardens are open every day of the year from 0900, closing at 2100 in summer (illuminated from mid-May through Sept.), 1700 in winter. In summer, visit the gardens early in the evening when you can appreciate both the daylight and after-dark illumination effects. Admission in summer is adult $9.50, student $5, child $1 (much lower admissions in winter). There's also a gift shop specializing in, you guessed it, floral items, and several tearooms and restaurants.

ON THE WEST SIDE

Living History

On the west side of Victoria (heading for Sooke) are several historic sites (take Craigflower bus no. 14 from the corner of Yates and Douglas streets). **Point Ellice House,** on Pleasant St. just before the Point Ellice Bridge, was built in 1861. Check out the original Victorian artifacts cluttering every nook and cranny, and the 19th-century garden. It's open 1000-1700 in summer; admission adult $3.25, senior or student $2.25, child $1.25, family $7.50 (including GST). Ask about the four-site pass.

Continue along Craigflower Rd., right on Admirals Rd., to come to **Craigflower Farm.** From 1853-56 Kenneth McKenzie built this house with native materials for the Puget Sound Agricultural Co., a subsidiary of the Hudson's Bay Company. The employment of colonists by Craigflower Farm and three other farms helped in the transition of the area from a fur-trade camp to a permanent settlement on the northwest coast. The manor was the center of social life for Victorian residents and the navy officers from Esquimalt. Step into your time machine, dial in 1860, and enter the house to discover furniture, lace bedspreads, bedwarmers, cooking pots, books, and all sorts of things that belonged to the original family. An appropriately dressed guide lets you in on all the family secrets—how the family kept their food refrigerated without a refrigerator, cooked without a microwave, and kept the entire house (minus the nanny's room) warm in winter. See all the glamorous and hideous wallpaper designs that were "in" throughout the years, and much more. Admission adult $3.25, senior or student $2.25, child $1.25, family $7.50 (ask about the four-site pass).

Cross Gorge Waterway and you come to **Craigflower Schoolhouse** on the right which was built in 1854-55 from lumber obtained from a steam-powered sawmill at Craigflower Farm. The men employed to build it were notoriously drunk, the evidence quite obvious when you tour the interior (note the sloping doorframes and tilted fireplace!). The one schoolroom served children from the farm and nearby district, and the upper floor provided living quarters for the teacher's family and his student boarders. Oldest surviving schoolhouse in Canada, it operated 1855-1911. Since 1931 it has served as a museum. Open daily 1000-1700; admission adult $3.25, senior or student $2.25, child $1.25, family $7.50 (ask about the four-site pass).

Anne Hathaway's Cottage

Still craving a bit of England and not yet burned out on commercial attractions? Visit this replica of Anne Hathaway's original cottage in Stratford-upon-Avon. Authentically furnished with 16th-century antiques, it's open for tours daily 0900-2200 in summer, 1000-1700 the rest of the year. Located at 429 Lampson St. (tel. 388-4353), catch bus no. 24 Munro from downtown and return on 24 Colville; admission adults $5, senior or child $3. Next to the cottage is the **Olde English Inn** and a series of Tudor-style buildings that make up an English village. If you feel like splurging, the food at the Inn is excellent and oh so English. For an even bigger splurge, suffer through the night in one of the large, antique-furnished rooms with draped four-poster beds so high you need a stool to clamber up, fireplace, and all the mod cons.

SOOKE TO PORT RENFREW

If you have your own transportation and a day to spend exploring the southwest coast of Vancouver I., take one of several main routes leading west out of the city, then Hwy. 14 toward Sooke (Regional Transit buses also operate to Sooke). So many beautiful parks and beaches (excellent camping) line this route you'll swear you've seen all the hiking enthusiasts, tent owners, and tanned bodies a city can produce—on a sunny weekend at the parks closest to the city, expect to experience Victoria's very own madding crowd!

The first place to stop is **Sooke,** a logging, fishing, and farming center known for its good salmon fishing, about 34 km from Victoria. **Sooke Regional Museum and Travel Info-Centre** lies just beyond Sooke River Bridge on the corner of Sooke and Phillips roads; open daily May through Sept. 1000-1800, Oct. through April 1000-1700. Sooke is the last town along the route, so fill up on detailed info on the west coast, picnic supplies, and gas. The road from Sooke takes you past gray pebbly beaches scattered with shells and driftwood, past **Gordon's Beach** and **French Beach Provincial Park** (about 20 km from Sooke). Wander down through the trees to the ocean to watch Pacific breakers crashing up the beach, and keep an eye open for killer and gray whales. It's a great place for a windswept walk, picnic, or camping on the grass behind the beach (pit toilets provided); $8 plus GST per night. An info board at the park entrance has articles on many of the beaches and interest spots along the route to Port Renfrew and the plants and wildlife in the area, and fairly detailed maps.

The main road winds up and down forested hills for another 12 km or so, passing regular logging evidence and signposted forest trails to sandy beaches. When you emerge at the small logging town of **Jordan River,** known for its good surf, stop for a burger, fries, or seafood sandwich at **Shakies,** a popular hamburger stand on the far side of the river. The Jordan River General Store is only open a couple of hours in the morning and a couple in the afternoon.

Continue west for another four km or so to **China Beach Provincial Park,** where a 15-minute walk through rainforest leads to a sandy beach (watch for black bears—only an hour or so from the big city!). A few kilometers down the road the pavement ends, but it's good gravel all the way to Port Renfrew. Pass trails to **Mystic Beach** and **Sombrio Beach** and continue on to **Port Renfrew,** a small logging settlement about 107 km from Victoria, gateway to the **West Coast Trail.** This 72-km trail is for experienced, well-equipped hikers only, taking seven to eight days to reach Bamfield (see p. 73). Follow the signs to **Botanical Beach,** a fascinating tidal-pool area where all sorts of marinelife is exposed at low tide along the scoured-out sandstone cliffs. The road to the beach is rough and can be unpassable in winter.

If you don't want to return along the same route, and you're eventually heading north up the island, consider taking the gravel road from Port Renfrew to **Lake Cowichan** (see p. 48). It's usually in good condition, but find out from locals the present conditions and whether there's active logging in the area—logging trucks don't give way, *you* do! Make sure you have enough gas, and drive with your headlights on so the trucks see you from a good distance.

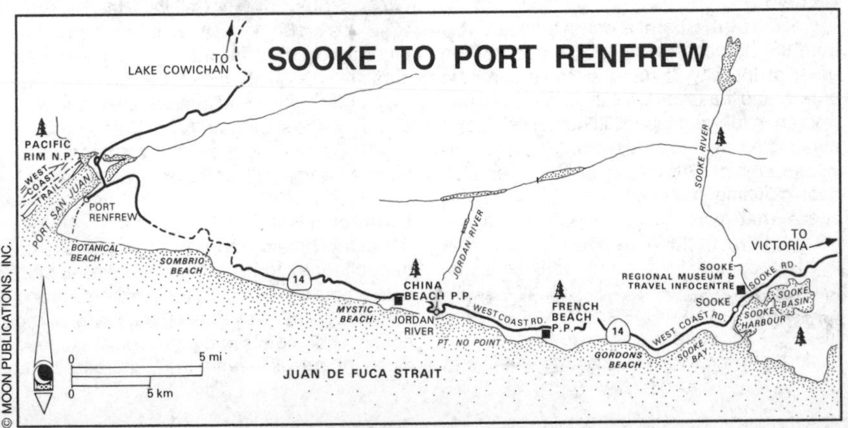

PRACTICALITIES

ACCOMMODATIONS

Rates vary depending on the season for most accommodations in Victoria, and all are subject to a seven-percent goods and services tax (introduced in 1991). Before you start looking, pick up the excellent Accommodations publication put out by the Ministry of Tourism, free at any InfoCentre in B.C. It lists all the accommodations approved by the Ministry throughout the province, with current high-season rates and page after page of useful fine print about B.C., updated every year.

Budget tight? Finding a room may be a challenge, especially May through September. Lodgings with the same reasonable rates year-round, such as the YH and YWCA, generally operate first-come, first-bedded—expect them to be full in summer unless you're lucky. The best way to be prepared for summer is to have a tent and your own transportation, then head for the provincial parks. In winter finding a room is relatively easy, and the off-season rates are, on the whole, very reasonable, allowing even those counting every penny to stay in historic bed and breakfasts and nicer hotels.

Hostels

Victoria Youth Hostel is only a stone's throw from the harbor, several blocks north of the heart of the city. It has the usual separate dorms and bathroom facilities for men and women, a fully equipped kitchen, plus a large meeting room, a lounge, a library, travel services, an informative bulletin board, an outdoor camping store, and an outgoing manager. What more do you need? To make a reservation, send a deposit for the first night—recommended during peak seasons. Located at 516 Yates St., tel. 385-4511; $12.50 per night for members, $17.50 nonmembers. If you're traveling up the island or exploring the rest of B.C., ask for the list of mini-hostels at the office. These are not YHA hostels but private homes or small commercial hotels offering low-budget accommodation geared toward the hosteller at various locations throughout the province.

For single women, one of the best places to stay is the Victoria YM-YWCA Women's Residence, 880 Courtney St., only a couple of blocks from downtown. For women only, it provides small, clean rooms with shared bathrooms. No cooking facilities but there's a good cafe on the ground floor, usually crowded at lunchtime with locals taking classes at the Y. The rates are $26 s, $39 d including GST (weekly rates available May-Sept.), with the use of a TV lounge and the swimming pool during coed recreational swims. Reservations can be made between 0830 and 2000 at 386-7511, or after hours at 389-9280.

From May through Aug., **University Housing And Conference Services** provides single and shared rooms with shared bathrooms, a communal lounge, coin-operated washers and dryers, and free guest parking on the University of Victoria Campus (Sinclair at Finnerty Road). Rooms are from $25 s, $37 twin, and include linen and towels and a full breakfast. For more info, call 721-8396.

Another private hostel to try is **Selkirk Guest House** at 934 Selkirk Ave., tel. 389-1213. It's a 15-minute bus ride from city center, but your bed for the night will be in an attractive historic home on the Gorge Waterway, and couples and families are made welcome by hosts Lyn and Norm Jackson. Cost is $10 pp per night for YH members, $15 nonmembers. Call for transportation details.

Downtown Hotels

So many hotels and motels are scattered throughout Victoria that the best way to start is to scan the *Accommodations* booklet and compare rates. November-Feb. many of the hotels and motels provide rooms at good discount prices—even the Empress Hotel

The Cherry Bank Hotel is a fun place to stay.

gets into the competitive action! Check all the accommodations brochures at the Information Centre, in which special rates are often advertised. A couple of good-value places are listed below.

Cherry Bank Hotel is centrally located on a quiet street with plenty of private parking. Aside from a choice of rooms in either the original or new wings, there's a bar and Trivial Pursuit Lounge, and a restaurant known for excellent ribs (see "Food," below). The rooms have shared or private bath ($5 extra), but no TV or phone; high-season rates are $34.50-59.50 s, $41-66 d and include an excellent cooked breakfast served 0800-1000. Located at 825 Burdett St. between Blanshard and Quadra streets, tel. 385-5380.

James Bay Inn is a good place to stay, within easy walking distance of all city attractions and Beacon Hill Park. Some rooms have private bath and color TV, and the popular pastel pub downstairs serves unusually fattening breakfasts and creative Continental cuisine. Located at 270 Government St., tel. 384-7151; $29-37 s, $44-60 d, $48-72 twin, off-season rates available.

Motels

Victoria also has plenty of motels, from inexpensive to "that much?" Refer to the *Accomodations* booklet for the complete picture. One of the newer motels is located between the B.C. Ferry Terminal at Swartz Bay, the U.S. Ferry Terminal at Sidney, and the city of Victoria, on Hwy. 17. **Western 66 Motel** has a large variety of affordable rooms, free movies, free local phone calls, complimentary coffee in the lobby each morning to get you going, and a family restaurant on the premises. Rates start at $37.90 s, $50.55 d ($55.15 queen), $55.15 twin (all rates include GST). No pets. At 2401 Nt. Newton Cross Rd., Saanichton, B.C. V0S 1M0, tel. 652-4464.

Bed And Breakfasts

Victoria's bed and breakfasts are even more abundant than tour operators in the height of the season! Prices range from reasonable to outrageous. Check the brochures at the Info-Center, but if you're looking for something specific you may want to call the various B&B agencies listed in the front section of *Accommodations*. However, you can't go wrong staying at one of the personally selected places below!

The Heritage House, a beautiful 1910 mansion surrounded by trees and gardens, is located in a quiet residential area near Portage Inlet, northwest of city center. Run by friendly owners Mike and Marlene Gilbert, Heritage House provides guests with a choice of several appealing rooms (one with a view of Portage Inlet from a private veranda, another furnished in antiques), two shared bathrooms, a large communal living room, and a cooked breakfast in the elegant dining room. It's very busy in summer (book ahead or try your luck), but quieter Nov.-April, when a 15% discount is offered. Rooms $50-75 s, $60-75 d; 3808 Heritage Lane, tel.

479-0892. The lane is not shown on any Victoria maps. From city center, take Douglas St. to Burnside Rd. east and turn left. Immediately after crossing the Trans-Canada Highway, turn left, still on Burnside Rd., and continue past Grange Road. The next lane on the right is Heritage Lane. By bus, catch no. 22 Burnside and get off at the Grange Rd. stop, opposite the school.

Seaside Cottage stands on a bluff overlooking beautiful Gonzales Bay, southeast of city center along the scenic marine drive. With a fantastic view of the beach below (hardy souls swim there in summer!), the Captain's Room (can sleep four) has its own veranda, bathroom, and private entrance; $45-95 d (depending on season). The Mate's Room is similar; $45-55. All rates include a cooked breakfast and every seventh day is free. Run by friendly Elisabeth and Lorne Doyle, at 157 Robertson St., tel. 595-1047. A bus stop on the corner of Ross and Robertson makes access easy, and shops, banks, and restaurants are nearby.

Glyn House, across the street from Seaside Cottage, a three-minute walk from Gonzales Beach, also provides a bed and breakfast in a vintage 1912 home. The rooms have period furnishings and collectibles and private bathrooms; $55 s, $75 d (high season) including a full breakfast, and very reasonable off-season rates are available on application. Located at 154 Robertson St., tel. 598-0064.

Craigmyle Guest House is a beautiful old home full of character, comfortable furnishings, and lots of original stained-glass windows, in the quiet residential area of Rockland. It's within walking distance of the city and stands directly in front of Craigdarroch Castle. Singles, doubles, family suites (all with bathrooms), a comfy living room with TV, a bright sunny dining area, and friendly owners Jim and Kathy Pace make it a real home away from home. It's located at 1037 Craigdarroch Rd., tel. 595-5411, and can be reached by buses 11 or 14 to the corner of Fort St. and Joan Cres.; rates start at $50 s, $65-85 d, $80 twin, and include a hot breakfast. Book ahead in summer.

Campgrounds

The nearest campground to Victoria is **Fort Victoria RV Park and Campground,** six km northwest on Hwy. 1A at 340 Island Hwy., tel. 479-8112, with campsites, hookups, salmon-fishing charters, free showers, laundry facilities; during the summer sites cost $13.50-18.50 for two, electricity $2, sewer $2.

One of the most beautiful provincial parks where camping is permitted is **Goldstream Provincial Park,** 19 km northwest on Trans-Canada Hwy. 1. All sorts of recreational activities are in the area, plus good hiking trails, free hot showers, but limited facilities in winter; tentsites from $13 plus GST per night. You won't believe you're only minutes outside a city of 65,000! If you're coming from, or heading for, the ferry terminal at the tip of the Saanich Peninsula, **McDonald Provincial Park** is 32 km north of the city. Limited facilities, no showers; campsites from $8 plus GST per night. There are also numerous provincial parks with good beaches where camping is permitted along the highway to Port Renfrew (see Sooke to Port Renfrew, p. 44).

FOOD AND ENTERTAINMENT

Light Meals

If you're staying at a B&B, you're probably already getting some of the best breakfasts in town. Otherwise you can get the usual at all the family restaurants around the city. The cafe on the lower floor of the YWCA serves a hot breakfast for $3, sandwiches under $3, hamburgers up to $5, but it can be difficult to find a seat if you get there between classes; the entrance to the Y is at the top end of Courtney Street. One of the best places for lunch, dinner, or in-between snacks is Sam's Deli, on the corner of Government and Humboldt streets (tel. 382-8424), just across from the Information Centre. Try the delicious "Ploughman's Lunch"—sourdough bread, cheese, pâté, fruit, and a bowl of tastebud-tingling homemade soup for $5. Creating excellent inexpensive sandwiches ($3.65-5), soups (from $2.25) and salads, cakes, juices (try the raw apple juice), and a variety of coffee drinks, they're open seven days a week in winter 0730-1900, in summer Mon.-Thurs. 0730-2100, Fri. 0730-2200, Sat. 0800-2200, Sun. 1000-2030, and you can sit in- or outside.

Eugene's Snack Bar at 731 Fort St. has good Greek lunches and La Petite Colombe at 604 Broughton St. is popular with locals for French food—lunch is affordable. If you want a quick meal, head for fully renovated Harbour Centre on Government St., where you'll find the International Food Fair: cheapie Chinese, Mexican, vegetarian, pizza, hamburgers, stuffed potatoes, and salads. For a more formal sit-down lunch and an excuse to eat in the Empress Hotel, the Bengal Lounge serves meals Mon.-Sat. 1130- 1830; prices range from $4 for soup to $9 for open sandwiches, $9-12 for main courses. Try the tasty curry special for $10.50. The Empress's less formal Garden Cafe serves light meals daily 1000-2200.

Afternoon Tea

Afternoon tea is served just about everywhere in Victoria—it's a local tradition. The one at the **Empress Hotel** is a snooty affair in the main lobby (dress code enforced—no jeans, shorts, tennis shoes, etc.), but keep in mind that you're taking part in one of the oldest Victorian rituals. It's so popular with tourists that reservations are necessary for the 1300, 1430, and 1600 sittings. Sample English honey crumpets, homemade scones with cream and jam, sandwiches, Empress cakes, and an Empress blend tea for $15.95 pp.

For a less formal English tea, try the **Olde English Inn** next to Anne Hathaway's Cottage at 429 Lampson Street. A light afternoon tea (black-currant scones with cream and jam and a pot of tea) is $2.95, or gorge yourself on the lot *and* sample English sherry trifle and Scottish shortbread, served by a buxom wench in Elizabethan costume, for $8.50. Breakfast, lunch ($7-8), and typically English dinners ($14-17) are also served in the restaurant.

Pub Meals

Toad In The Hole pub at Burnside West and the corner of Harriett Rd. has a jovial pub atmosphere, fireplace (cozy in winter), and a large local attendance. Good meals, good prices (ask about the specials of the day) in the $6-12 range, and friendly service. **The Keg** on Wharf and Fort streets has steak and seafood dishes, $9-16, less for lunch, featuring a hot and cold salad bar. **Swan's Pub** at 505 Pandora St. brews their own beer, serves delicious food, and is probably one of the most popular spots in town. **Six Mile Pub** in Colwood is also popular for its excellent meals at good prices, lunch or dinner, and is always busy—can get a little rowdy in the evenings. Highly recommended by locals is **Spinnakers Brew Pub,** at 308 Catherine St., where they brew their own beer.

Restaurants

One of the most popular restaurants for Italian food, homemade bread, big half or full meals, great desserts, and loads of atmosphere is Pagliacci's at 1011 Broad Street. Small, always busy, featuring a three-piece jazz band every night, it attracts a lively local crowd and it's easy to meet people while you inevitably wait for a table. Herald Street Caffe on Herald St. is also good, with a menu comparable to Pagliacci's but more extensive. A good place to go for Greek food and live entertainment (nightly in summer, weekends in winter) is Periklis Greek Restaurant at 531 Yates St., across from the YH. Main courses range $10-15, and almost anything can be happening on the floor—from exotic belly dancers and impromptu, crazy Greek dancing to a roomful of people doing knee-bends with souvlakis balanced on their noses!

The restaurant at the Cherry Bank Hotel, **Gay '90s Spare Rib House,** has plenty to see and do while you wait for your ribs, seafood, or chicken. The room, usually filled with visitors in their 50s and 60s, springs to life as the honky-tonk piano player starts pounding out one old-fashioned tune after another. The air fills with voices, hands clap, feet tap, tables and chairs jive, even the mounted duck, pheasant, and mountain lion spring down from their corners to bop to the beat. The food is excellent (ribs get bibs!); main courses are $12-19 and come with salad, potato, vegetable, and garlic bread. Early-bird specials run weekdays 1700-1800 and Sun. 1630-1730. On Burdett St., open Mon.-Thurs. 1700-2100, Fri. and Sat. 1700-2200, Sun. 1630-2100.

White Spot restaurants always have good food, high-calorie desserts, and won't empty your wallet; 710 Caledonia Street. **Smitty's Pancake House** on Douglas St. opposite Courtney is open until 2400 daily.

Go On, Splurge!

Two local favorites for dressing up and traveling for a splashy night out on the town are **Sooke Harbour House,** perched atop a seaside bluff in Sooke, featuring seafood so fresh that it may take its last breath on your plate, along with other rave-review cuisine (telephone first to see if they're open before you drive out there), and **The Deep Cove Chalet** in Sidney, for delicious food and loads of atmosphere. Take your credit card. Take two credit cards to the **Empress Dining Room.** Expect five or six different courses, each with a glass of appropriate wine; $24.50 pp for food, $22.50 pp for wine, for an approximate total of $47 pp for a "complete dining experience." Kick up your heels on the dance floor on Fri. and Sat. nights, sit back and take in a live pianist Mon. through Thurs. nights. There's a dress code, and reservations should be made in advance, tel. 384-8111.

Entertainment

Something fun is always going on in Victoria: theater, concerts, dancing to live music, movies, or a game of cricket or lawn bowling. As usual, ask at the Information Centre for your particular good-time pursuit, or pick up the various free newspapers which advertise the local merriment, in particular *Monday* (published on Thursday) and *Cut To: The Lower Island's Entertainment Monthly.*

For live music, check out **Harpo's Cabaret** at the Wharf St. end of Bastion Square, tel. 385-5333. They put on all kinds of bands, often blues and jazz, and it's a particularly well-known singles hot spot (cover charge). **The Forge** in the Strathcona Hotel, on the corner of Courtney and Douglas streets, tel. 383-7137, also bops to live rock 'n' roll six days a week (cover charges are the norm). **Big Bad Johns,** also in the Strathcona Hotel, is described as a hillbilly bar (with plenty of peanuts in the shell and rubber chickens!). For live country and western music (and home-cooked meals) try **Esquimalt Inn** at 856 Esquimalt Rd., tel. 382-7161. **Pier 42** attracts the 25-55 group with its canned music, European flavor, and club atmosphere; at 1605 Sotre St. and Pandora, tel. 381-7437. **Sweetwaters,** on Wharf St. just past Harpo's, plays taped music.

For live theater head for **McPherson Playhouse** at 3 Centennial Sq. (corner of Pandora Ave. and Government St.) or **Royal Theatre** at 805 Broughton Street. For more info and tickets call 386-6121. For movies head for **Towne Cinema** at 808 Douglas St., tel. 382-5922.

Local celebrations: in May, Jaycee Fair and Parade, Swiftsure Race, Victoria Days, Oak Bay Tea Party; in June-July, Folkfest, Victoria International Festival, Canada Day Celebrations; in Aug., Victoria Air Show at the International Airport, SunFest; in Sept., Classic Boat Festival, Fringe Festival; in Oct., the Royal Victoria Marathon, British Fortnight; in Dec., First Night (a New Year's Eve Carnival). For all the details, stop by the Information Centre.

INFORMATION AND SERVICES

The **Tourism Victoria Travel Information Centre** is located at 812 Wharf St., tel. 382-2127, or reservations tel. 382-1131 or (800) 663-3883; open seven days 0900-1700. The friendly personnel have most of the answers. They book accommodations, tours and charters, restaurants, entertainment, transportation, all at no extra cost, and sell local bus passes and map books with detailed area-by-area maps. Browse through the enormous selection of brochures covering all the commercial attractions, tours, accommodations, restaurants, and a variety of transportation modes and schedules. Also collect the free *Accommodations* publication and pick up the free local news and entertainment papers—the best way to find out what's happening in Victoria while you're in town.

The main **p.o.** is on the corner of Government and Yates. The entrance to the **Greater Victoria Public Library** is on Blanshard and Courtney. **The Ministry of Lands and Parks** is on Johnstone St., tel. 387-4330. To **exchange currency,** head for one of the many banks around town, open Mon.-Fri., or Conference Centre Currency Exchange at 724 Douglas St. (immediately behind the Empress Hotel), open seven days a week. **Pharmacies** are located at 1222 Douglas St., tel. 384-0544, and 649 Fort St., tel. 384-1195. **Victoria Laundry Ltd.** is located at 731 Fisgard St., tel. 384-7751.

Victoria is a shopper's delight. Most shops and all major department stores are generally open Mon.-Sat. 0930-1730, and stay open for late-night shopping to 2100 on Thurs. and Fri. nights. Some are also open on Sun. 1100-1700. Shopping arcades, plazas, and specialty shops are found throughout Victoria—for typically Canadian (Cowichan sweaters are expensive but last a lifetime) or very British gifts, browse along Government Street.

Public restrooms are located in the Inner Harbour Causeway (by the Information Centre on Wharf St.), the Johnson St. Parkade at 750 Johnson St., the Centennial Sq. Parkade at 600 Fisgard St., Beacon Hill Park, and all major department stores.

GETTING THERE

By Water

Many people arrive in Victoria by ferry from Port Angeles, Seattle, or Anacortes, Washington, or from Vancouver. If you're a foot passenger buy your ticket at least 10 minutes prior to sailing, and if you're taking a vehicle allow a lot longer—cars start lining up an hour before sailing, maybe two in high season. **Pacific Coach Lines** operates a connecting service between Vancouver, the B.C. Ferry terminals at Tsawwassen and Swartz Bay, and Victoria. In summer the coaches run hourly 0545-2045, in winter bi-hourly, arriving at the Victoria Bus Depot at 700 Douglas St. (corner of Belleville), downtown Victoria; $19.70 OW or $39.40 RT Vancouver to Victoria including ferry. For current schedule call 385-4411 (Victoria) or 681-1161 (Vancouver). If you take the ferry over independently, you can catch a **B.C. Regional Transit** bus from the Swartz Bay ferry terminal to downtown for only $1.25 OW; for more info call 382-6161 daily to 2230.

From **Port Angeles,** while awaiting the ferry, be sure to collect the two free newspapers, *Victoria Vancouver Island Visitor* and *B.C. Big Island* from the terminal. The crossing of Juan De Fuca Strait on the MV *Coho* takes just over 1½ hours. Two crossings are made daily each way, four daily crossings in the peak summer months (advance reservations are not accepted—phone a day or so before your planned departure for estimated waiting times); OW fares start at adult passenger US$6, child passenger US$3, car or van or motorhome and driver US$24, bicycles US$2.75, motorcycle and driver US$14.50 (prices subject to change). Checks and credit cards are not accepted. Call **Black Ball Transport Inc.** at (206) 457-4491 in Port Angeles or 386-2202 in Victoria.

From **Anacortes** and the **San Juan Islands** the crossing takes approximately three hours. For current schedules and fares, call **Washington State Ferries** at (206) 464-6400 Seattle, or toll free within Washington at (800) 542-7052, 381-1551 Victoria, or 656-1531 Sidney.

A speedy way to get between Seattle (Pier 69) and Victoria (Inner Harbour) is by the jet-propelled catamaran, ***Victoria Clipper.*** Whisking you from the U.S. to Canada in about 2½ hours (foot passengers only), the rates are adult US$49 OW, $79 RT, child $24.50-49 OW, $39.50-69 RT (depending on age) during high season (May 1 to Sept. 13). Low-season (Sept. 14 to April 30) fares also available; tel. (206) 448-5000 in Seattle, 382-8100 in Victoria (based at 1000 Wharf Street).

From **Vancouver,** for all the current mainland-to-Vancouver I. schedules, including the Vancouver (Tsawwassen)-to-Victoria (Swartz Bay) route (the most direct and the one used by Vancouver-Victoria buses), call the 24-hour prerecorded **British Columbia Ferry Corporation** info line at 685-1021 in Vancouver, (206) 441-6865 in Seattle, or 656-0757 in Victoria. Up to eight sailings a day embark in winter, up to 17 in summer, each taking about 1½ hours; book ahead if you're taking a vehicle across during the high season. It can also be busy on weekends and holidays year-round. One-way fares start at adult $5.75, bicycle and rider $8, motorcycle and driver $15, car and driver $24.50, motorhome or camper and driver from $30.25 (goes by length and height). Foot passengers need to purchase tickets at least 10 minutes before sailing. In Victoria, the British Columbia Ferry Corp. office is at 1112 Fort St., tel. 656-0757.

By Air

Victoria International Airport is approximately 20 km north of the city on Hwy. 17. The terminal building has a bar/lounge, cafe, and various rental car agencies. The P.B.M. Airporter bus to the city (with stops at major hotels) costs around adult $10, seniors and children $8, family $25. A taxi costs approximately $35-40 per car (maximum five) to downtown. The airlines represented in Victoria are: **Air B.C.,** tel. 388-5151 or (800) 663-0522 within B.C.; **Canadian Airlines,** 615 Broughton St., tel. 382-6111; **Lake Union Air,** tel. (800) 663-3502; **Helijet Airways,** tel. 382-6222.

GETTING AROUND

By Bus

Most of the inner-city attractions can be reached on foot. However, Victoria has an excellent bus network and it's easy to jump on and off and get everywhere you want to go. Pick up a *Victoria Regional Transit System Rider's Guide* and a *Victoria By Bus* brochure, both free from the Information Centre. All the info you need to know, including detailed schedules, bus fares (one zone $1.25 adult, 85 cents child; two zones $1.75 adult, $1.25 child), and day-pass info ($4 adult, $3 child, good on all city routes) is contained in these self-explanatory handouts. Or call 382-6161 Mon.-Fri. 0630-2230, Sat. 0700-2230, Sun. and holidays 0800-2230. You can also pick up bus info at Transit Information kiosks at the downtown Public Library, Harbour Square Mall (buy bus passes at the post office here), CanWest Shopping Centre, Victoria City Hall, Tillicum Mall, and the B.C. Transit office at 520 Gorge Rd. East. Bus passes can also be bought at the Information Centre. Be sure to have the exact fare ($1.25) on all buses—the drivers do not carry change.

By Car

Pick up the handy *Parking Guide* brochure at the Information Centre—it shows many of the parking areas closest to inner-city attractions and the meter rates. Also look for the cheap parking along the harborfront, opposite the Harbour Square Shopping Mall and Port's Restaurant, where daytime meters charge 75 cents for two hours in one section and $1.50 for five hours in another.

Rentals

Call around and compare prices for cars—some lesser-known agencies advertise cheaper daily rates than others, but the cars are often used, old, large, and less economical and usually must be returned to Victoria. Renting by the week is better, and you often get a number of kilometers free. Always check if there's an added drop-off fee if you don't want to return the car to Victoria—there usually is, and the farther up the island you go, the higher the fee. For a used car in the low season, rates start around $19.95 a day plus 10 cents/km and gas, and go up to around $119 a week with a kilometer limit so high that you're unlikely to use them up—unless you're researching a book! Insurance is usually an optional extra. Prices are adjusted according to the season in the same way attractions and accommodations reflect the number of visitors in town. A relatively new small economy car rents for around $44.95 a day plus 15 cents/km, or $195 a week (with up to 1,400 km free).

Auto rentals: **Budget,** 757 Douglas St., tel. 388-5525 (also check **Budget Used Rentals,** within shouting distance on the same street); **Hertz,** 901 Douglas St., tel. 656-2312; **Tilden,** 767 Douglas St., tel. 386-1213; **Rent-A-Wreck,** tel. 384-5343; **Ada Rent A Used Car,** 752 Caledonia St., tel. 388-6230; **Thrifty,** 455 Belleville St., tel. 592-5994.

For **bicycle rental,** contact **Sports Rent,** 3084 Blanshard St., tel. 385-7368; **Harbour Scooter Rentals,** 1223 Wharf, tel. 385-2314 (summer only); **Explore Victoria,** 1007 Langley, tel. 381-2453; **James Bay Bicycle,** 1A-507 Simcoe, tel. 381-7615; **Oak Bay Bicycle,** 1968 Oak Bay Ave., tel. 598-4111; or **Budget Cycle-Time,** 727 Courtenay, tel. 388-4442. Expect to pay from around $4 an hour, $16 per day. Shop around!

By Taxi

Taxis operate on a meter system and, after the initial flag charge of $1.50, charge around $1 per kilometer. Call **Blue Bird Cabs** at tel. 382-4235; **C & C Taxi** at tel. 383-1121; **Empress Taxi** at tel. 381-2222; or **Victoria Taxi** at tel. 383-7111.

MAJOR ROUTES OUT OF VICTORIA

By Road And Bus

The main routes out of Victoria are Hwy. 1 to the rest of Vancouver I., Hwy. 14 west to Port Renfrew, and Hwy. 17 north up the Saanich Peninsula to Sidney and Swartz Bay. **Island Coach Lines** serves all of Vancouver Island. For current schedules, stop in at the Victoria Depot, 710 Douglas St. at the corner of Belleville St., tel. 385-4411. A ticket from Victoria to Nanaimo runs around $13.65 OW, to Campbell River $31.20, from Campbell River to Port Alberni $17.55 OW (connect with **Orient Stage Lines Ltd.** to Ucluelet $13 OW and Tofino $14 OW), Victoria to Port Hardy $70 OW to connect with ferries to Prince Rupert. They also operate service to Vancouver about eight times a day, $19.70 OW, direct to Vancouver Airport on the 0800 and 1000 route. Storage lockers are located outside the depot and cost $2 for 24 hours.

Pacific Coach Lines also operates service to the B.C. Ferry Terminal at Swartz Bay and various Vancouver I. cities (Victoria to Nanaimo is $13.65 OW, to Port Hardy is $56.60 OW); for schedules and fares, stop by the Victoria Terminal at 700 Douglas St., tel. 385-4411.

By Train

VIA Rail operates weekday passenger E & N Rail service between Victoria and Courtenay, with stops at all major towns, leaving Victoria at 0815, arriving at Courtenay at 1245, departing Courtenay at 1315, and returning to Victoria at 1745 the same day; $28.89 OW to Courtenay or $57.78 RT. Make reservations at (800) 665-8630 as far ahead as possible in summer, and buy your ticket the day before departure. This route is so scenic that many make the train trip a one-day RT excursion. For more info, stop in at 450 Pandora Ave. or call 383-4324.

By Air

The following airlines service Vancouver I. and the mainland: **Air B.C.,** tel. 382-9242 or 388-5151; **Air Canada,** tel. 382-9242; **Canadian Airlines,** tel. 382-6111; **Time Air,** tel. 388-6711 or at airports through Canadian Airlines International, tel. 382-6111.

LOUISE FOOTE

THE REST OF VANCOUVER ISLAND

INTRODUCTION

Surrounded by Queen Charlotte Strait to the north, Juan de Fuca Strait to the south, the island-dotted Strait of Georgia to the east, and the Pacific Ocean to the west, Vancouver I., largest in North America's Pacific, stretches for more than 450 superb kilometers along the west coast of mainland British Columbia. A magnificent chain of rugged snow-capped mountains (part of the Insular Mountain Range), sprinkled with lakes and rivers and pierced by a number of deep inlets, effectively divides the island into two distinct sides: dense, rain-drenched forest and remote surf-and-wind-battered shores on the west, and well-populated, sheltered, beach-fringed lowlands on the east. At the northern and southern tips lie large regions of low, rolling hills.

Much of Vancouver I. is carpeted in dense forests of Douglas fir, western red cedar, and hemlock. In fact, wherever you go you see green: dark green trees (and more trees, and more trees), bright green grass, green-clad mountains, deep-green lakes, and many visitors to this beautiful island green with envy! The climate, stabilized by the Pacific Ocean and warmed by the Japanese current, can be quite different from north to south, east to west—the west side of the island receives the ample share of rain. It never really gets too hot or too cold, but be prepared for a cloudburst, especially in winter, and on days when you're grumbling about the weather, keep in mind that it's the rain that makes this island so lush—and so green.

BUT I'VE ONLY GOT A WEEK!

For scenery buffs, wildlife enthusiasts, and outdoor appreciators (good hiking, fishing, skiing, diving, kayaking, whalewatching, boating, birdwatching, and much more), or those intrigued by northwest American Indian art and culture, this island delivers! However, if you don't have a few months or so to experience it all, it's wise to decide what kind of scenery and activities you desire before you start to explore. Vancouver I. is a lot bigger than most first-time visitors expect.

Fancy some island-hopping? Take Hwy. 17 up the Saanich Peninsula to Swartz Bay, jump on a B.C. Ferry, and cruise the scenic Gulf Islands. For sandy beaches, resorts, and old logging, mining, and fishing towns that now base their existence to a large degree on tourism, take Hwys. 1 then 19 hugging the east coast of Vancouver I. all the way to Campbell River. If you're in search of "oooh" and "aaah" mountain scenery, picture-perfect fishing villages, and driftwood-littered sand for as far as you can see, Hwy. 4 leads you to the relatively untamed west coast and Pacific Rim, the island's solitary national park. Branching inland off Hwy. 19, Hwy. 28 cuts through the outdoorsy world of enormous Strathcona Provincial Park to Gold River.

North of Campbell River lies a surprisingly large area mostly untouched by civilization—in fact, today you can still find maps of the island that fizzle out above Campbell River. Does life exist farther north? Anything to see or do? Can birds fly? Travel kilometer after kilometer along Hwy. 19 through impressive mountain scenery where the road itself, rest areas at all the very best views, and some unfortunate stretches of clear-cutting are the only human signatures on the landscape. Avail yourself of excellent camping spots, hiking trails, lakes perfect for canoeing and fishing, and more than a smattering of northwest American Indian art and culture along the way. At the end lies Port Hardy, largest community in the north and the terminal for ferries to Prince Rupert and Alaska. Unique Telegraph Cove, a boardwalk village known for its fishing and whalewatching activities; and intriguing Alert Bay on Cormorant I. are definitely worthwhile side trips on your way to the top.

Island-hopping

In the Gulf of Georgia between Vancouver I. and mainland B.C. snuggle hundreds of protected islands, marine parks, and tiny islets of all shapes and sizes, named by 18th-century Spanish and British explorers, most uninhabited and accessible only by private boat. Called the Gulf Is., they're a northern continuation of the San Juan I. group that starts in Puget Sound. The southern Gulf Is.—Saltspring, Pender, Mayne, Saturna, and Galiano—are populated and easily reached by B.C. Ferries from both Vancouver I. and Vancouver. Their mild, mellow, almost-Mediterranean climate, beautiful pastoral scenery, and prolific marinelife (sea lions, bald eagles, harbor seals, killer whales, blue herons, cormorants, diving ducks) seem to attract creative people in search of life in the slow lane. However these appealing qualities have also lured swarms of hikers, campers, cyclists, canoeists, fishermen, beachcombers, island-hoppers, and art lovers looking for an artist's studio bargain, particularly in summer—if you want an island to yourself, grab a boat and head north! Bronzed boaters, cruising from one provincial marine park or full-facility marina to the next, claim the crystal-clear waters and sheltered bays make the Gulf Is. one of the finest cruising regions in the world!

Jump on a ferry and visit a few islands in one day, or take a vehicle over and spend several weeks exploring all the islands from top to toe (in summer the ferries can be jam-packed and you may have to wait in line if you're taking a car). If you plan on seeing them all, check the ferry schedules and do the circle tour, stopping at Nanaimo, Chemainus, Sidney, and Victoria on Vancouver I., as well as the Gulf Islands. If you're catching the B.C. Ferry from Tsawwassen to the Gulf

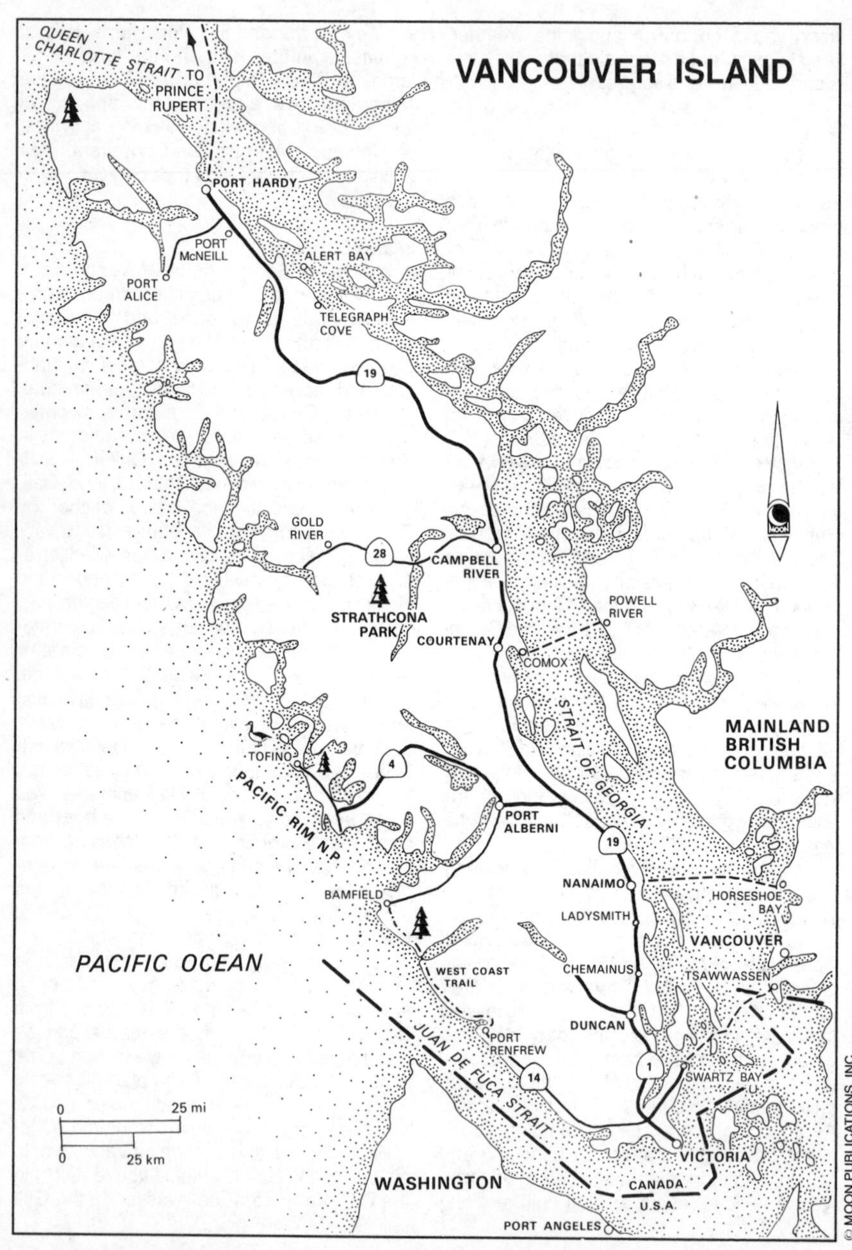
VANCOUVER ISLAND
QUEEN CHARLOTTE STRAIT
TO PRINCE RUPERT
PORT HARDY
PORT McNEILL
PORT ALICE
ALERT BAY
TELEGRAPH COVE
19
GOLD RIVER
28
CAMPBELL RIVER
STRATHCONA PARK
POWELL RIVER
COURTENAY
COMOX
STRAIT OF GEORGIA
MAINLAND BRITISH COLUMBIA
TOFINO
4
PACIFIC RIM N.P.
PORT ALBERNI
19
NANAIMO
HORSESHOE BAY
BAMFIELD
LADYSMITH
VANCOUVER
PACIFIC OCEAN
WEST COAST TRAIL
CHEMAINUS
TSAWWASSEN
DUNCAN
PORT RENFREW
JUAN DE FUCA STRAIT
1
SWARTZ BAY
14
0
25 mi
0
25 km
VICTORIA
WASHINGTON
CANADA
U.S.A.
PORT ANGELES
MOON

Is. you need to make reservations (Vancouver, tel. 669-1211; Victoria, tel. 386-3431; Saltspring I., tel. 537-9921; Outer Gulf Is., tel. 629-3215; Nanaimo, tel. 753-1261). From Swartz Bay, Crofton (an InfoCentre is located near the ferry dock), Chemainus, and Nanaimo no reservations are necessary. All ferries take private vehicles, motorcycles, and bicycles. Keep in mind that some of the islands are large, and if you don't have your own transportation you'll only see the ferry terminal area or have to fork out for a taxi (available on some islands) to see the rest. You'll find plenty of campsites in provincial parks (in summer grab a campsite by mid-afternoon; no reservations), bed-and-breakfast lodgings, resorts, and hotels (see *Accommodations* booklet, and book ahead in winter, well in advance in summer!), and pubs, coffee shops, and restaurants.

Before you head for the islands, get the complete rundown from the InfoCentre in downtown Victoria, the Saanich Peninsula InfoCentre on Hwy. 17 near the Swartz Bay Ferry Terminal, or Tourism Vancouver Island, 302-45 Bastion Sq., Victoria; tel. 382-3551. For every detail, refer to *The Gulf Islands Explorer—The Complete Guide*, published by Gray's Publishing Ltd., Box 2160, Sidney, available in most good bookstores.

Victoria To Duncan

This section of Hwy. 1 is fast and efficient, whizzing rubber traffic to Duncan in 30 minutes (45 if highway construction is going on), unless a choice is made to meander off the beaten track. Before you leave Victoria, pick up a handy *Provincial Parks of Vancouver I.* brochure, which has an excellent map and descriptions of attractions and facilities of each of the too-numerous-to-mention provincial parks in this neck of the woods. If you're not scampering up the island at breakneck speed, stop at **Goldstream Provincial Park** and consider hiking the many trails (from five minutes to more than one hour OW) along creeks, up Mt. Finlayson for ocean and island views, or to the top of Niagara Falls. It's one of the best parks near Victoria for camping (see p. 48) and there's always something going on: in May capture the flowering dogwood trees on film; in summer join others on guided nature walks with a park naturalist; in Nov. witness all the coho and chum salmon churning up the Goldstream River to spawn and die where they were born four years before.

Still in a leisurely mood? Take a short detour along the coastal road between **Bamberton** and **Mill Bay** (a car ferry runs many times a day across to Brentwood Bay on the Saanich Peninsula; $6.50 per car, $2.25 per adult, $1 per child) for quiet shady streets and water views. At the end of May or in early June each year the Mill Bay community kicks up its heels by sponsoring continuous music, dancing, and entertainment during the three-day **Country Music Festival** at Kerry Park Arena. Just north of Mill Bay is the road to **Shawnigan Lake** and two provincial parks, one on either side of the lake, and the logging road (restricted access if there's active logging) to **Port Renfrew** (see p. 45).

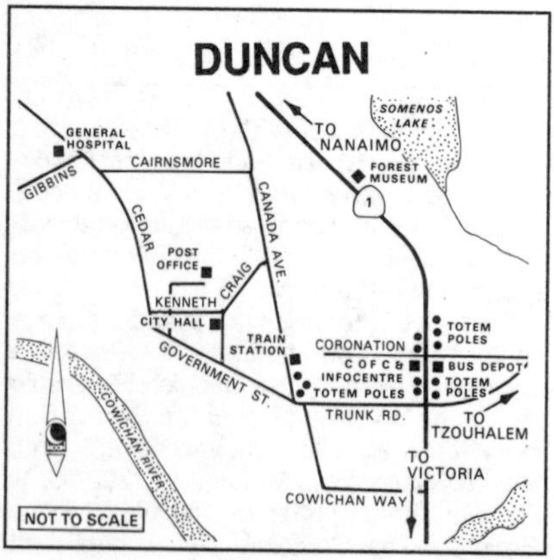

DUNCAN

Duncan, self-proclaimed "City of Totems" at the junction of Hwys. 1 and 18, is a small city serving the surrounding farming and forestry communities of the Cowichan Valley. It's a good place to appreciate more than 30 intricate and colorful totem poles by native carvers, many from the local Cowichan band. Most of the poles stand along the main highway near the InfoCentre, or beside the railway station in the old section of town. Others are found by City Hall, and inside local businesses scattered throughout town.

Stop at **Duncan Information Centre and Cowichan Chamber of Commerce** on the main highway by Coronation St. for the complete rundown on this area, including hiking, fishing, and camping info for nearby Lake Cowichan, and for a map showing the location of all Duncan's totem poles; open in winter Mon.-Fri. 0900-1700, in summer 0800-1800. If you're thinking about doing the **West Coast Trail** from Port Renfrew to Bamfield, don't miss the detailed wall map of the entire trail (see p. 77).

Local Highlights

Aside from all the totem poles, Duncan's main attractions are **The Glass Castle** (a home built from glass bottles, medieval miniature golf course, and haunted mansion, open Feb. through Oct.) on the main highway south of Duncan, **Native Heritage Centre** for a taste of the arts, crafts, legends, and traditions of Northwest Coast Natives at 200 Cowichan Way, and "the world's largest hockey stick" from Expo '87 impaled on Cowichan Community Centre (many cities bid on this item after Expo and, to local delight, Duncan won). Duncan also has several museums worth a visit. Don't miss the excellent forest museum (see below) one km north of town, the restored Station Museum on Canada Ave. (open in summer Mon.-Sat. 1100-1600, admission free), and collect a brochure and tour map of the 1,000-square-km Ecomuseum Heritage Region (a "museum without walls" where the natural and human heritage of the area is being preserved, protected, and shared) from the Information Centre.

Follow the signs off the main highway to City Centre for a quick wander around the renovated "old town" (free two-hour parking by the old railway station on Canada Ave.). Start your totem pole hunt here or just wander down the streets opposite the railway station to appreciate some of the pleasing older architecture such as City Hall (corner of Kenneth and Craig streets). Two distinctly different native carvings stand side by side behind City Hall—an American Indian carving, and a New Zealand Maori carving donated by Duncan's sister city, Kaikohe.

If you wander into Duncan in July you may find yourself in the middle of a bed race, baby contest, pet show, bands and parades. Don't worry, you're not hallucinating—it's the annual **Cowichan Summer Festival**—in full swing! Duncan also hosts an **Island Folk Festival** in July.

If you find there's a lot more to do in Duncan than you originally thought, consider staying the night at one of the local guesthouses providing bed and breakfast. It's a great way to meet locals. An updated list of B&Bs is available at the Information Centre. Feeling peckish? Most of the locals crowd into always-busy **Arbutus Cafe** on the corner of Kenneth and Jubilee streets. They concoct the best shrimp salad in this corner of the world for $5.75 (half) or $6.95 (for the hungry), sandwiches for $4-5.50, hamburgers for $3.50-5.50, and specialty pies for $2.95. Or try almost-as-busy **White Hart Tea Shoppe** on Station Street.

If you've been looking for an invaluable Vancouver I. souvenir, or a gift that will really excite, look no further! Cowichan Indian sweaters, hand-knitted from 100% wool in natural colors and great designs, are so warm, water repellent, and durable that locals claim they're passed down from one generation to the next, and to the next. . . . They're not cheap ($90 and up), but they obviously last at least one lifetime, and they're made right in this valley. To see a large selection, visit **Hill's Indian Crafts** and **Big Foot Trading Post,** both on the main highway about one mile south of Duncan—they buy directly from Native knitters. Before you buy, compare prices at the **Modeste Mill** (on the south side of the Cowichan River turn east at Boys Rd., then right on Mission Rd. to Modeste). Another Native art gallery well worth visiting is the **Arts of The Swaqwun Gallery** featuring Salish masks, miniature totem poles, baskets, jewelry, prints, and paddles, at 80 Trunk Road.

The Duncan area's star attraction is the excellent **British Columbia Forest Museum Park,** one km north of town on the main highway. Catch a ride on the old steam train and puff back in time through a farmstead, a logging camp, and the forest, and over Somenos Lake, visiting a forest museum, a working sawmill, a restored planer mill, a blacksmith's shop, a variety of forestry and lumber displays, films, demos, and much more. It's also a pleasant place to wander through shady glades of trees (most identified) or over to the pond where a gaggle of friendly geese await a tasty morsel. Locals come prepared for the day with healthy picnic baskets in hand. It's open daily May-Sept. 0930-1800; admission adult $4.50, senior $3.50, student $3.50, child $2.50.

THE COWICHAN RIVER AND LAKE COWICHAN

Don a good pair of walking shoes, grab your swimsuit, sleeping bag, fishing pole, and frying pan, and head for the well-maintained, 31-km footpath along scenic **Cowichan**

River that skirts Skutz Falls and ends at Lake Cowichan. Eagles and hawks soar overhead, clear swimming holes invite quick dips, and catching a trout for dinner is a real possibility (some areas are reserved for fly-fishing only). The trail starts at the end of Robertson Rd. (on the south side of the river) in Glenora, runs along the south bank of the river to the falls, then crosses the river by suspension footbridge to the intersection of Mayo and Riverbottom roads. You can also continue following the river path all the way to the lake. Prearrange your return transportation or be prepared to walk back. Pick up a detailed map of the Cowichan Footpath for only $1.95, with info on the routes, camping, and fishing in the area from Duncan Information Centre. If you fancy a bit of comfort at the end of the day, call the riverside **Sahtlam Lodge and Cabins** and inquire about their tent bedrooms (from $50 d), lodge rooms (from $65-75 d), or cabins (from $70-100 d); at 5720 Riverbottom Rd. West, tel. 748-7738.

Continue north along the main highway to the Hwy. 18 turnoff to **Lake Cowichan** (called *Kaatza,* "The Big Lake," by local Indians). This 32-km-long lake, about 31 km from Duncan along a paved road, is the largest freshwater body on Vancouver I., a popular spot for canoeing, water-skiing, swimming, and hiking in the wilderness around the lake. The lake's best claim to fame is its good fishing. The lake and river are well stocked with steelhead, rainbow, brown, and cutthroat trout, and kokanee, or landlocked coho salmon, and locals modestly consider it the "Fly-fishing Capital of the World!" But before your fishing pole starts to quiver with too much anticipation, check with a local sporting-goods store—the fishing can be incredibly good, or equally bad, depending on the season, the weather, and a number of other factors.

Partially paved and good logging roads encircle the lake (75 km RT), and boat-launching facilities and excellent campsites are found at regular intervals along the lakeshore; minimal or no facilities but very popular year-round with locals, and free. **Gordon Bay Provincial Park** on the south side of the lake has hot showers and restroom facilities, and there are plenty of hotels, motels, beach cottages, etc. along the river or in the lakefront communities of **Cowichan Lake, Mesachie Lake, Honeymoon Bay, Caycuse,** and **Youbou.** The village of Cowichan Lake has a Tourist InfoCentre open mid-June-Sept., tel. 749-4141.

DUNCAN TO NANAIMO

Chemainus

The next place well worth a visit on your way north is the small town of Chemainus, billing itself as "The Little Town That Did." Did what, you may well ask? Well, Chemainus has always been a sleepy little milltown (its first sawmill dates back to 1862)—that is, until MacMillan Bloedel shut down the antiquated mill that employed 400 people in 1982. In 1983 they built a modern mill on the old site, employing only 155 people, specializing in rough Douglas fir and hemlock sales to Japan, Western Europe, Australia, and to remanufacturing plants in B.C. (tours are available in summer). Chemainiacs did not want their town to die. Needing tourists, they hired local artists to cover many of the town's plain walls with fantastic larger-than-life murals depicting the town's history and culture. The result was outstanding. The town received the prestigious "First Place Award" in the New York 1983 downtown revitalization competition for its efforts. It's definitely The Little Town That Did survive—and go on to better things.

Follow the signs to Chemainus from Hwy. 1 and start at the InfoCentre (closed in winter) on the main road where you'll see the first enormous mural of a street scene. If you're in a vehicle, stash it here and explore the rest of Chemainus on foot, following the yellow footprints into town. Murals are everywhere! Walk down to shady waterfront **Heritage Park,** passing a mural info booth (open in summer), where there's a small replica of the waterwheel that powered the original sawmill in 1862, and a detailed map of the town.

Then wander down through the park to "old town" and the small museum on Maple Street. Daily guided tours around town are also available for $2 per person.

The ferry to **Thetis** and **Kuper Is.** leaves from Chemainus: car and driver $9 RT, motorcycle and driver $5.65, passengers adult $2.25, child $1.

If you're continuing north from Chemainus, take the scenic route out of town instead of backtracking to the main highway, for views of snowcapped, tree-covered mountains to the far west, agricultural land dotted with small farmhouses, and occasional glimpses of the water through the trees before emerging once more on the coast for great views of the Gulf Islands.

Ladysmith

Ladysmith's main claim to fame is its location straddling the 49th Parallel, the invisible boundary line separating Canada from the U.S. After much bargaining, Canada got to keep all of Vancouver I. despite the 49th Parallel chopping the island in two. Ladysmith was originally designed as a dormitory and recreation town for the Nanaimo coal miners; today this pretty little waterfront town is home to foresters and commercial fishermen. If you appreciate old-style architecture, wander through town to see many of the original buildings still in use. The **Travel Information Centre** on the main highway and the **Arboretum** behind it are worth a visit.

For good food and more than a bit of atmosphere, locals recommend a stop at the **Crow and Gate,** on Yellow Point Rd. about 19 km north of Ladysmith. It's a typical English pub where you can sit inside by the fireplace or outside with the ducks and tuck into bangers and mash, steak and kidney pie, or roast beef and Yorkshire pud, and wash everything down with a glass of ale or cider. Open for lunch and dinner Mon.-Saturday.

Petroglyph Provincial Park

Don't miss this small park, off the main highway on the right several km south of Nanaimo. Park in the lot and stroll up the trail through woods to the petroglyphs (Indian rock carvings). Petroglyphs occur throughout B.C. and are quite common along its coastal waterways—made with stone tools, they recorded important ceremonies and events. The designs in this park, perhaps carved thousands of years ago, are believed to represent human beings, animals (real and supernatural), bottom fish, and rare depictions of sea wolves, mythical creatures part wolf and part killer whale. Sadly this park has not escaped modern petroglyphs by vandals—please stay on the trail. For more info on rock art sites in the Nanaimo area, contact the Centennial Museum in Nanaimo.

NANAIMO

"Harbour City," "Hub City," and "Bathtub Capital Of The World," warm, sheltered Nanaimo (pronounced Nan-NYE-mo by residents though you may hear several versions as you travel around) sprawls lazily up and down the hilly coastal terrain between sparkling Nanaimo Harbour and Mt. Benson. Aside from all its impressive subtitles, this city also boasts "the finest climate in Canada" due to its mild winters and warm, dry summers—and if you don't believe it, locals will quickly point out the row of flourishing palm trees growing along the main highway as you enter the city from the north!

Five Indian bands lived here (the name Nanaimo is a derivative from the Salish Indian word *Sney-Ny-Mous,* or "Meeting Place"), and it was they who innocently showed dull, black rocks to Hudson's Bay employees in 1852. For most of the next century, huge quantities of coal were exported from the many mines in the area until oil-fueled ships replaced the coal burners, and most of the mines were closed in 1949. Surprisingly, there are no visible traces of the mining boom left in Nanaimo, aside from a museum (built on top of the most productive mine) accurately depicting those times, and

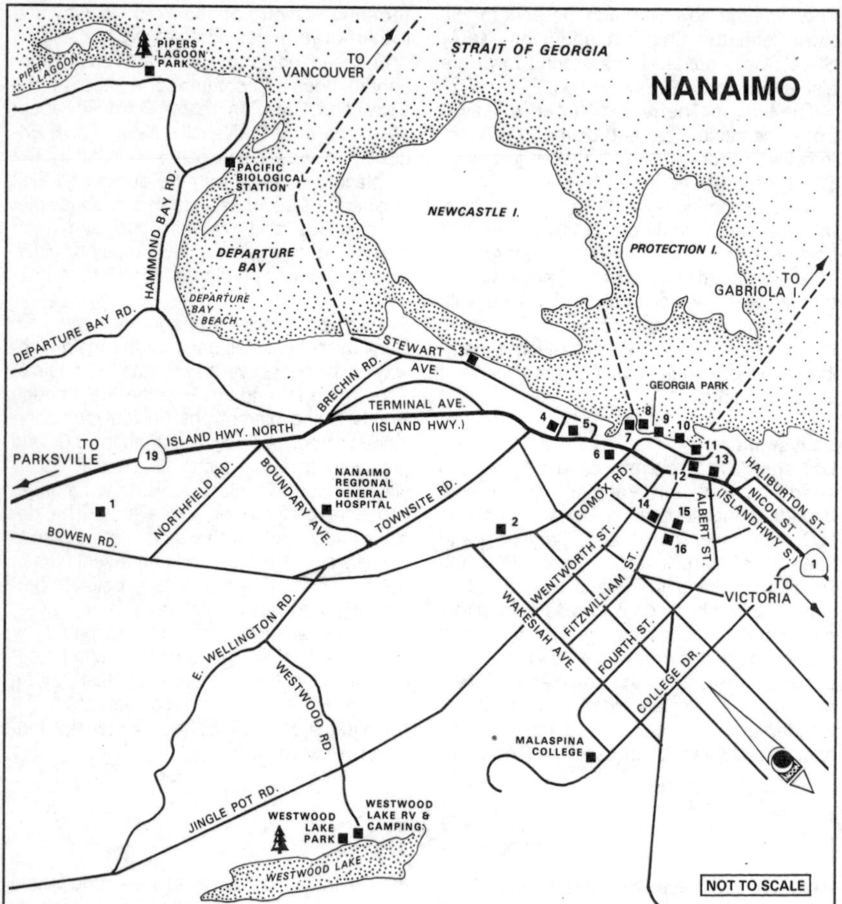

NANAIMO

NOT TO SCALE

1. Beban Park Complex
2. Bowen Park Complex
3. Bluenose Chowder House
4. tourist information
5. White Spot Restaurant
6. bus depot
7. Maffeo-Sutton Park
8. Swy-A-Lana Marine Park
9. post office
10. Seaplane Terminal & Lighthouse Bistro & Pub
11. Hudson's Bay Company Museum
12. Coast Bastion Inn
13. Centennial Museum
14. library
15. R.C.M.P.
16. E&N Rail Station

a sturdy fort (now a museum) built in 1853 in case of Indian attack. Nanaimo was officially incorporated in 1874, which makes it the third-oldest town in the province. When the coal mines closed, forestry and fishing became mainstays of the city. Today Nanaimo is a major deep-sea shipping port and the terminus of the B.C. Ferries' Departure Bay-to-Horseshoe Bay route (hence the term "Hub City"). Along with forestry and fishing, an enthusiastic tourism industry actively encourages all sorts of festivals and activities to attract visitors, such as the popular annual bathtub race to Vancouver.

ATTRACTIONS

Waterfront Walk

To get an initial feeling for this harbor city, start at **Maffeo-Sutton Park** where the ferry for Newcastle I. (see p. 65) departs (plenty of parking beside the Civic Arena building). Walk right along the waterfront gardens for views of the marina to the north and Nanaimo Harbour, then over the man-made lagoon and natural tide pool, full of all sorts of sealife if you look closely, to **Swy-A-Lana Marine Park.** Continue along the waterfront and up to **Georgia Park** where two totem poles and a Squamish dugout canoe stand, then back down to the water and along the walkway to the **Seaplane Terminal** and **Lighthouse Bistro and Pub.** Aside from outstanding harbor views and nonstop seaplane and boating action, the delectable food and drinks (see p. 66), comfortable surroundings, and friendly atmosphere may bring on an attack of total relaxation and utter content. If you can drag yourself up, out, and onward, continue past the busy marina and up the stairs to . . .

The Bastion

At the junction of Bastion and Front streets, overlooking the harbor, stands the Bastion, a well-protected fort built in 1853 by French-Canadian axemen for the Hudson's Bay Company to protect employees and their families against Indian attack. Originally used as a company office, a defense arsenal, and a storage area for extra supplies, today it's the **Hudson's Bay Company Museum,** open in summer 1000-1700; small admission charge. For the benefit of tourists, a group of local university students dressed in appropriate gunnery uniforms, led by a piper, parades down Bastion St. daily at noon in summer to the Bastion and fires the three cannons out over the water. It's the only ceremonial cannon firing west of Ontario, and quite a spectacle! For a good vantage point, be there early.

the Lighthouse Bistro and Pub

Centennial Museum
In Piper Park, just across Front St. from the Bastion and up the stairs, is the Centennial Museum, well worth a visit. Walk around the outside to appreciate harbor, city, and mountain views, and the replica petroglyphs of animals, humans, and spiritual creatures. Then allow at least an for hour wandering through the two floors of displays featuring life in early Nanaimo, its geology, early native people, pioneers, and coal-mining days (with a realistic coal mine from the 1850s). Don't miss the impressive Indian carvings by James Dick. The displays are changed regularly so there's always something new to see. At 100 Cameron Rd.; open in winter Tues.-Sat. 0900-1600, in summer Mon.-Fri. 0900-1800, Sat. and Sun. 1000-1800; admission is free.

The downtown area has been rejuvenated, but the old buildings, with all their character, still stand.

Old Town
From the museum, walk down Cameron Rd. toward city center, heading for Commercial St., focus of Nanaimo's revitalization project. The cobblestone-surfaced street is lined with old-fashioned lamps and beautifully restored buildings (the fronts are done in a heritage theme), now housing fashionable boutiques specializing in the latest in trendy attire.

Step Right Up And Take A Tour
The obvious way to appreciate the harbor aspect of Nanaimo is by boat. Wander down to the marina below the Bastion and browse through the fishing and sightseeing charter boats, or call in at the InfoCentre and ask for a list of the local guides and charters, plus current prices. The *Bastion City* operates 2½-hour narrated cruises of the harbor and adjacent islands, and during the cruise, depending on the time of year, you may well spot sea lions (especially in March and early April when they come into the harbor to feed on abundant shoals of herring), seals, bald eagles, killer whales, blue herons, and cormorants; adult $20, senior $18, child $11, early spring specials. For more info and reservations phone 753-2852, or call in at the InfoCentre (tel. 754-8474).

Several free guided tours are operated during the summer (some in winter on special request), but most necessitate a small group: **Morrell Wildlife Sanctuary**, tel. 753-5811; **Beeyard Tour** at Malaspina College, tel. 754-3245; **St. Jean's Custom Cannery,** tel. 754-2185; **MacMillan Bloedel Harmac** (two-hour tours, slacks and shoes required), tel. 722-3211; **Pacific Biological Station** for an intro to aquaculture, fish farming, fish diseases, and shellfish culture (daily in summer by appointment, tel. 756-7049 or 756-7000). For more details on all these tours, call in at the Tourism Nanaimo InfoCentre at 266 Bryden St., tel. 754-8474.

Parks
Locals claim there are more parks than people in the Nanaimo area. It's almost true! Many parks lie within the city limits or close by, along with four freshwater lakes—two for

boaters and two for canoes, kayaks, and sailboards.

For a breezy walk along a grassy spit, wildflowers, and never-a-dull-moment bird-watching, head for coastal **Piper's Lagoon Park,** off Hammond Bay Rd., north of city center. On a clear day it's a great spot for views of mainland B.C. across the Strait of Georgia, and when the wind's howling, colorful sailboarders chase each other across the water. **Departure Bay,** between the city and the park, is another well-patronized sailboarding area, and in summer the beach swarms with teenagers, boom boxes in hand.

Looking for a bit of wilderness not far from the city, some canoeing or kayaking, or maybe a campsite? Head for large **Westwood Lake Park** with its crystal-clear waters and resident Canada geese—tame enough to snatch food from fingers and flap back to the lake. It's off Westwood Rd., due west of the city (from the main highway turn west on Wentworth St. which becomes Jingle Pot Rd., then left on Westwood). No gas boats are allowed here, though it was the venue for the Canadian National Waterskiing Championships in 1987 (also see "Accommodations and Food").

Offshore Islands

Newcastle I. Provincial Marine Park, an unspoiled island park attracting lots of local families on nature outings, has 20 km of developed trails, beaches, plenty of resident wildlife (deer, raccoon, rabbits, beaver, and birds), camping (see "Accommodations and Food," below), and the **Pavilion Visitor Centre, Museum, and Restaurant,** where salmon barbecues, concerts, and other special events are held from May to September. Run by the Parks Dept., only caretakers permanently reside on the island. Get there by ferry from the wharf at Maffeo-Sutton Park; in summer daily on the hour 1000-1900 (late sailings on Fri. and Sat. nights during peak period), adult $3.50, senior or child $2.25, bicycle $1 RT. For camping info, call 754-5499; for Pavilion info, call 753-1931; for ferry info, call 753-5141.

Gabriola I., the most northerly of the southern Gulf Is., is home to about 2,000 people; many are artists and craftsmen. With its beaches, abundant wildlife, two provincial parks, unusual Malaspina Galleries (huge caves carved out of the sandstone by wind and water), beachcombing and scuba diving, petroglyphs, and relative lack of congestion, it attracts those escaping the madding crowd (unless the crowd also goes over on the ferry). The ferry makes up to 17 trips a day, except on dangerous-cargo Wednesdays, and it's only a 20-minute ride, $2 RT from downtown Nanaimo. The island makes a good day-trip, but if you want to stay longer some of the resorts provide campsites, and bed-and-breakfast lodging is plentiful.

A Dangle On The Wild Side

Nanaimo has added another first to its multiple list of local attractions—North America's first **Bungy Jumping Park.** Yes, it's true: people flock from afar to have their ankles tied and connected to "Bungy Bridge" by a long elastic rope. Next they dive head first 140 feet down almost to the surface of Nanaimo River, rebound for another fall . . . or two . . . or three, until momentum dissipates. To receive this thrill of a lifetime (many jumpers say the natural adrenalin rush beats any drug known to man, and it's just as addictive) you have to part with $95 (plus tax), and if you have any cash left over, you'll find must-have T-shirts, hats, posters, videos, stickers, and other souvenirs to prove to the world that you really did it. This is also a thoroughly entertaining spectator sport, with good viewing areas and plenty of parking provided. The Bungy Zone is located 13 km south of the Departure Bay Ferry Terminal in Nanaimo, and open seven days a week. Be sure to make a reservation if you're taking the leap; it's so popular that bookings are essential, tel. 753-5867. For more info write to Bungy Zone, 149 Wallace St., Nanaimo, B.C. V9R 5B2.

NANAIMO PRACTICALITIES

ACCOMMODATIONS AND FOOD

Campgrounds

Nanaimo has many campgrounds within 10 km of city center. See listings in the *Accommodations* booklet or the brochures in the InfoCentre. **Westwood Lake RV Camping and Cabins** is right on the edge of beautiful Westwood Lake, providing the venue for all sorts of outdoorsy activities as well as campsites, full and partial hookups, showers, laundromat, and store. Open year-round; campsite $10-14 d, cabin $35-40 s or d, and off-season rates. Located at 380 Westwood Rd., due west of city center, tel. 753-3922. Oceanfront **Newcastle I. Provincial Marine Park** is also open all year and provides tentsites for $8 per night. No showers, limited facilities in winter; tel. 754-5499. Get there by ferry from Maffeo-Sutton Park (see "Off-Shore Islands," above).

If sunny or shady lakeside campsites on an operating beef ranch grab your fancy, head north of town toward Rutherford Shopping Centre (Ruth Rd.), turning left on Mostar Rd. then right on Biggs Road. **Brannen Lake Campsites** provides hiking trails, hayrides, sani station, store, dryers, washrooms, and full hookups on 30 acres along Brannen Lake, tel. 756-0404; from $10-12 per vehicle per night.

Mini-hostel

A mini-hostel and campground is operated year-round by Verdun Thomson at 1660 Cedar Rd. (next to the bakery), seven km south of Nanaimo (right off Hwy. 1 heading north), tel. 722-2251. It's near a good swimming and fishing river, and there's a recreation room with pool tables, table tennis and TV, a fully equipped kitchen, and laundry facilities ($2.50); $12 pp for YH members only, campsites $5 pp per night. Free pick-up at Island Bus Depot 1800-2100, and daily drop-off at 0815.

The **Nicol Street Mini Hostel** operates from May 1 to Sept. 1, providing hostel-style accommodations, campsites, kitchen, laundry, TV room, and bicycle rentals. At 65 Nicol St. (three blocks from the train station, seven from the bus depot), tel. 753-1188; $12 a night for YH members, $14 nonmembers, or $6 pp for a tent site (register 1600-2200).

Bed And Breakfasts, Motels, And Hotels

Many homes provide bed and breakfast, starting from $30 s, $43 d. Most offer good views, nearby activities, and substantial breakfasts, and they're a great way to meet locals. For a listing of those currently available and a variety of brochures, call in at the Info Centre. Nanaimo also has a large number of motels and hotels—most line the highway as you enter and leave the city. Expect to pay anything from $28-35 s, $32-38 d in the least expensive motels to $118-128 s and $128-138 d at the grand **Coast Bastion Inn,** a full-service downtown hotel with harbor and city views from every room; 11 Bastion St., tel. 753-6601. Nanaimo has a number of first-class hotels. For a waterfront view of Long Lake and a private balcony in park-like surroundings, check out the rooms at **Long Lake Inn.** It's at 4700 North Island Hwy., tel. 758-1144; guest rooms are $59-69 s or d Sept.-May, $79 June-Aug., kitchen units and deluxe apartments also available. For a full listing of the local motels and hotels, refer to the *Accommodations* booklet.

Eating Out

Aside from a wonderful harbor view and exciting seaplane action, **Lighthouse Bistro** in the Seaplane Terminal on the waterfront (below the Bastion) serves excellent seafood chowder with delicious bread, tasty appetizers, assorted salads, burgers, sandwiches, and croissants, pasta dishes, and good daily specials. Anyone with a sweet tooth? Wrap your lips around a Nanaimo Bar made at a local bakery (**Scotch Bakery,** 87 Commercial St.), featured at the bistro and worth every delicious cent! Dinners range $12-18. Open daily 1100-2300, and 1100-1600 on weekends for a great brunch. **Lighthouse Pub,** upstairs, is always busy, has daily drink specials, and shows movies on Sundays; open Sun.-Thurs. 1100-2400, Fri. and Sat. 1100-0100.

Another good place to go for excellent seafood is **The Bluenose Chowder House** at 1340 Stewart Avenue. Locals rave about the clam chowder with garlic bread, chowder topped with shrimp, or plain old fish and chips, and again, you get terrific views whether you eat inside or out on the deck in summer. Open Mon.-Sat. 1100-2000, Fri. and Sat. to 2100, closed Mondays. For reliably good food, large servings, high-calorie, delectable desserts, and family prices ($5-12), head for crowded **White Spot Family Restaurants**—the Nanaimo Spot is on the north side of the city at 130 North Terminal Ave. (near InfoCentre); open daily 0630-2400. Another local recommendation for some of the best Mexican food north of Mexico is **Gina's Mexican Cafe** at 47 Skinner St., behind the courthouse; open Mon.-Fri. 1100-2100, weekends 1600-2100.

Ahoy me hearty! A spot well known for its tasty nautical food, plenty of seagoing atmosphere, and good entertainment on Fri. and Sat. nights (May-Sept.) is the **Dinghy Dock Floating Marine Pub.** It's the only "floating pub" on the west coast, reached by a 10-minute ferry ride to Protection I., and open daily 1100-2200, later on weekends. The ferry leaves Nanaimo Boat Basin hourly 0910-2210, from Protection hourly 0900-2200. For pub info call 753-2373, for ferry info call 753-8244.

ENTERTAINMENT

For lovers of the arts Nanaimo is quite the cultural center. In July and Aug., professional theater is put on every night during the **Nanaimo Festival.** Original Canadian plays, musicals, and comedies, as well as the plays of William Shakespeare, are performed in contemporary settings by world-renowned actors. It's been called "the Stratford of western Canada." For a brochure of scheduled events stop by the InfoCentre, call the Nanaimo Festival Office at 754-7587, or phone the College Theatre Box Office at 755-8700 to see what summer shows are playing. For more live theater, investigate performances by the **Nanaimo Theatre Group** on Rosstown Rd. and comedies by the **After Eight Dinner Theatre Company** at the Tally-Ho Island Inn.

The **Madrona Exposition Centre** at Malaspina College displays works of art, science, and technology from Canada and around the world, and at the gift shop you can buy arts and crafts by local and B.C. artists. The center is open Mon.-Fri. 0930-1700, Mon.-Thurs. 1900-2100, weekends 1200-1600; at 900 Fifth St., tel. 755-8790.

Nanaimo has its share of movie theaters, and pubs featuring live entertainment (see the local paper for all the details), but if you're feeling energetic and need to burn off a Nanaimo Bar or two, head for **Beban Park Recreation Centre** at 2300 Bowen Rd. on the west side of the city. A dry sauna and a wet dip in the heated public swimming pool (call 758-1177 for sessions) will cost you a measly $1.65 adult, 90 cents child; admission to the ice-skating rink is $2.90 adult including skate rental, $1.75 child (call 758-1177 for schedule).

July is a particularly entertaining month to be in Nanaimo. Aside from the ongoing **Nanaimo Festival and Salmon Festival** (fishing derby, salmon barbecues, live entertainment, dances, craft and food stalls) at Swy-A-Lana Lagoon Park by Vancouver Island's "largest carved salmon," the utterly zany Bathtub Week draws worldwide attention when hundreds of entrants from as far away as Australia compete in the annual **International Bathtub Race** on the third Sun. in July. Imagine yourself in a one-man bathtub stuck to a flat planing board and powered by a small outboard motor, slapping across 54 km of choppy waves between Nanaimo Harbour and Vancouver's Kitsilano Beach, escorted by hundreds of boats of the more regular variety loaded with people just waiting for you to sink! Every bathtubber wins a prize—a golden plug for entering, a small trophy for making it to the other side of the strait, and a silver plunger for the first tub to sink! You can also see the "world's largest motorized bathtub," the Spirit of Nanaimo, in action, promoting Nanaimo's bathtub-racing-capital image.

In Sept. Nanaimo is full of men in kilts, wee lassies, and the sound of bagpipes and drums as the city fills with Scots from the whole of Vancouver I. to take part in the annual **Scottish Highland Games.** Expect to see colorful musical opening and closing ceremonies, bagpipe competitions, highland dancing, sheepdog trials, caber toss, and other heavy field events.

INFORMATION AND SERVICES

Nanaimo Tourist and Convention Bureau on the north side of town at 266 Bryden St. (corner of Bryden and the main highway north), tel. 754-8474, is open Mon.-Fri. 0900-1700 throughout the year, and 0800-2000 seven days a week from the first of May throughout summer. They can supply you with more info on Nanaimo (and the rest of the island) than you could possibly need—be sure to pick up the free city map. In summer the Cassidy Bureau, another InfoCentre, opens on the main highway at the south end of Nanaimo, and there's also an InfoCentre in the Bastion Museum.

Nanaimo Regional General Hospital is at 1200 Dufferin Cres., tel. 754-2121 (call this number for all medical, dental, and optical emergencies after normal business hours). **Ambulance,** tel. 758-8181. If you need a **pharmacy** head for Pharmasave in the Beaufort Centre across from Nanaimo General Hospital, open seven days a week 0900-2200, holidays 1300-2200, tel. 753-6655. **RCM Police,** 303 Prideaux St., tel. 753-2212. The **p.o.** is on Front St.; open Mon.-Fri. 0830-1700. **Huckleberry Books,** across the road from the p.o., is open Mon.-Sat. 0900-1700 and they buy, sell, and trade books. If you're looking for **shopping malls,** one after another lines the main highway on the north side of the city.

TRANSPORTATION

By Land

Island Coach Lines depot is at the rear of the Tally-Ho Island Inn, on the corner of Terminal Ave. and Comox Rd., tel. 753-4371; open daily 0600-2115. Coach to Port Alberni is $9.75 OW, to Campbell River $17.55, to Port Hardy $56.40, to Victoria $13.65. The **local bus depot** is located on Front St. in the Gordon St. Arcade adjacent to the Coast Bastion Hotel. For car rental rates call **Budget** at 754-7368 or **Rent-A-Wreck** at 753-6461. If you want to explore the waterways by boat, call **Row Boat Rentals** for car-top boats from $30 a day. The office is at 507 Stewart Ave., tel. 753-6301.

By Water

B.C. Ferries sails from Departure Bay to Horseshoe Bay (one hour and 35 minutes) on the mainland, just north of Vancouver, eight to twelve times a day (extra sailings on holidays). No reservations; adult $5.25 OW, child $2.25, bicycle and rider $7.50, motorcycle and driver $14.50, car and driver $24 (more for taller or longer vehicles and cars pulling trailers). The ferry from Nanaimo to Tsawwassen, Vancouver (two hours), leaves four times a day year-round, eight times during summer season; same fares as the Horseshoe Bay ferry. The ferry to Gabriola I. leaves from downtown Nanaimo, and the ferry to Newcastle I. leaves from Maffeo-Sutton Park (see "Off-shore Islands," p. 65).

By Air

Nanaimo Airport, off the main highway on the south side of town, is serviced by a number of airlines flying to Vancouver I. cities and Vancouver. Car rental is also available at the airport. Alternatively, regular flights to the mainland are also available on scheduled seaplane flights. Stop in at the Port of Nanaimo's Seaplane Terminal at the downtown waterfront for Thunderbird Air's and Tyee Airways' current schedules and prices, and for lists of all the charter possibilities.

PARKSVILLE

Life's A Beach

If your idea of heaven is a long, sandy beach, sitting on a log watching waves splinter on the rocks, or lying semi-comatose in the sun, dabbling a hot limb in the warm, shallow waters of Georgia Strait—with motels, resorts, campsites, and everything you could possibly need within a stone's throw—Parksville, 37 km north of Nanaimo, is where you'll find it. In winter you can swoosh down the slopes of 1,820-meter Mt. Arrowsmith early in the morning, work up an appetite with a stroll along Parksville Beach, catch a fish for lunch, play a round of golf in the late afternoon along with the large local retirement community, and finally let your muscles unknot in a motel Jacuzzi before your head hits the pillow that night.

The coastline from Parksville to Qualicum Beach is fringed with golden sand; to the west lie impressive mountains, dusted with snow in winter, and within a 1½-hour drive from the coast along Hwy. 4 are an assortment of rivers, waterfalls, lakes, and provincial parks. For swimmers who prefer tepid bath-temperature water, Parksville Beach claims "the warmest water in the whole of Canada." When the tide goes out along this stretch of the coast, it leaves a couple of kilometers of sand exposed. When the water returns, *voila,*—sand-heated ecstasy!

Rathtrevor Beach Provincial Park

This 348-hectare park, three km south of Parksville, is one of the main local attractions, featuring a fine 2,000-meter sandy beach, a wooded upland area, nature trails (get details at the Visitor Centre), and birdwatching action that's particularly good in early spring when seabirds swoop in for an annual feast on herring. Plenty of campsites are available, but in summer it's necessary to line up early in the morning to stake your claim. As most people come here for the beaches, you can usually find campsites and fewer people (though no showers) inland at the next closest provincial parks, **Englishman River Falls** (13 km west, off Hwy. 4) or **Little Qualicum Falls** (24 km west). If crowds bring on an acute attack of claustrophobia, avoid Rathtrevor Park *and* this stretch of the coast in July and Aug., when fun-in-the-sun seekers flock by the thousands to this part of the island. Head west!

More Information

For detailed info on this particular stretch of the east coast, stop in at the **Parksville and District Chamber of Commerce Info-Centre**—follow the signs from the highway along Dorcas Point Road. You can load yourself down with kilos of free reading material and maps; open in winter weekdays 0900-1700, in summer all week 0900-2000, tel. 248-3613.

HIGHWAY 4—LOTS TO SEE, LOTS TO DO

Highway 4 is well worth traveling just for the scenery—and on top of that there's a multitude of worthwhile places to visit along the way. Provided by nature, the highlights are free. To get the most out of this route, allow at least a couple of days, have your own transportation, stock up on film, and pull off at all the signposted attractions and rest areas along the highway to Pacific Rim National Park. Check out the availability of accommodations along the way while you're in Port Alberni (in summer it can be difficult to find a place to stay along the entire west coast unless you've made reservations).

Island Coachlines (Parksville, tel. 248-5332) goes from Nanaimo to Port Alberni ($9.75 OW) several times a day, stopping in Parksville en route, and connecting once a day with **Orient Stage Lines** (tel. 723-6924) to Ucluelet ($13 OW) and Tofino ($14 OW); check current schedule and fares.

PARKSVILLE TO PORT ALBERNI

Highway Highlights

This stretch of Hwy. 4, in the shadow of Mt. Arrowsmith, is the highest road pass (370 meters) on Vancouver I.—if you're traveling in a small, gutless rental car, you'll notice the climb. The first place to stop is **Englishman's Falls Provincial Park,** signposted about three km west of Parksville and another nine off the highway along Errington Road. Englishman River, known for its excellent cutthroat, rainbow trout, and steelhead fishing, cascades down from high Beaufort Range snowfields in a series of beautiful waterfalls. Within the park you'll find a picnic area, easy hiking trails to both upper and lower falls, crystal-clear swimming holes, and plenty of campsites ($8 per night; no showers) amongst tall cedar trees and lush ferns—it's a popular spot year-round.

Coombs is the next intriguing stop along the main road. What you may notice is the row of old-fashioned country stores, plenty of parking, and plenty of vehicles filling those parking spots. Cast your eyes toward the grass-covered roof of Old Country Market,

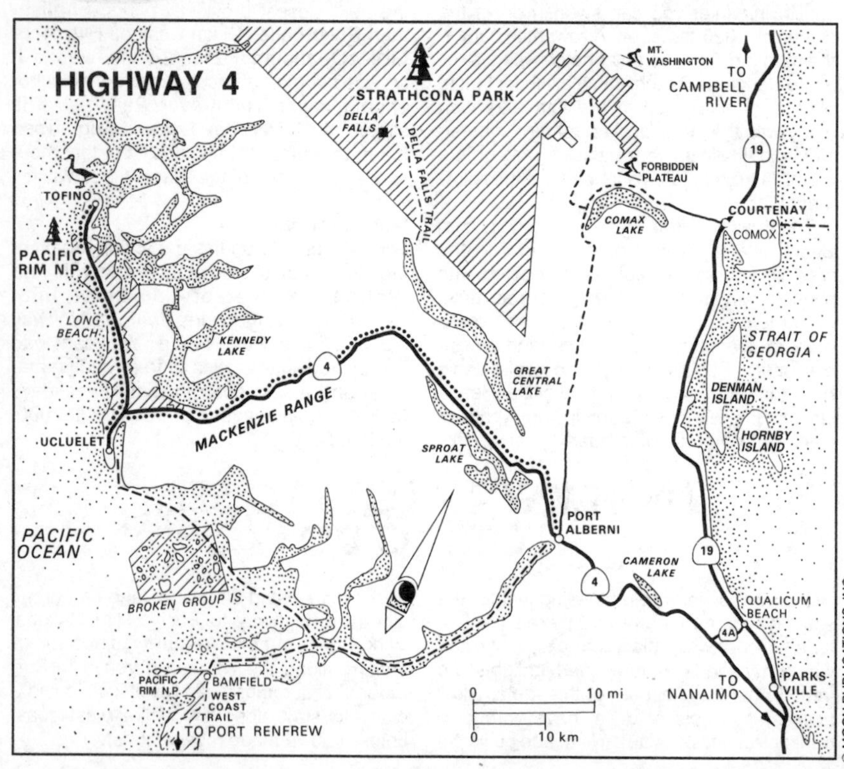

where several goats can be seen contentedly grazing, seemingly oblivious to amused, camera-clicking visitors. The shops sell everthing from pottery planters, jewelry, and assorted knickknacks to cram in spare corners of your vehicle to tasty snacks and cool drinks. Coombs is also home to 1,000 free-flying butterflies at **Butterfly World,** a rodeo ground, and a campground with sites from $12 per night.

Continuing along the highway, anglers may want to pull off and take the 7½-km gravel road signposted to **Little Qualicum Hatchery** where the focus is on chum, steelhead, trout, and chinook salmon. **Little Qualicum Falls Provincial Park** is the next place to definitely stop, about 20 km from Parksville, where a deliciously fragrant forest trail leads you down to a series of plummeting waterfalls (don't forget your camera). Take your fishing pole along the riverside trail and catch a trout, stop for an exhilarating dip in one of the icy emerald pools, and stay the night in a sheltered campsite near the river ($8 per night; no showers).

At the west end of large, deep-green, trout-filled **Cameron Lake** the highway enters a magnificent area of giant trees that meet overhead in a dense green canopy. You can enjoy a lot of the forest from your vehicle, but don't! Stop, take a short walk to get the old circulation going, and at the same time appreciate **MacMillan Provincial Park** (no camping). A 10-minute riverside trail leads you through majestic **Cathedral Grove,** an area of 200- to 600-year-old skyscraper Douglas firs that grow 45-70 meters high and up to 1½ meters wide—breathe in the cool, damp aroma and feast your eyes on the greenery. A small InfoCentre is open in summer at Cathedral Grove.

To the southeast of MacMillan Park at Alberni Summit is the road leading to **Mt. Arrowsmith Regional Park** and **Mt. Arrowsmith Ski Hill** (27 km off Hwy. 4, about a 1½-hour drive from the east coast, but to get to the top you need a 4WD vehicle or good winter tires and chains). Find out from Port Alberni Chamber of Commerce if the ski hill is open before you drive up there. In summer, choose from several trails to the summit—the main **Mt. Arrowsmith Trail** is relatively easy, starts at the Cameron Lake picnic site, and takes six to nine hours to hike. From Alberni Summit Hwy. 4 meanders on through magnificent mountain scenery, passing numerous roadside waterfalls before dropping down to the town of Port Alberni.

PORT ALBERNI

If you hit Port Alberni on a cloudy day, you won't know what you're missing—unless the sky lifts! Beautiful tree-mantled mountains (snowcapped in winter) suddenly appear, and Alberni Inlet and the Somass River turn a stunning deep blue. Situated at the head of the island's longest inlet (40 km), Port Alberni is a fairly large industrial town (stock up on all supplies here) centered around the forestry industry, with three mills—lumber, specialty lumber, and pulp and paper—the main sources of income. The mills belch evil-smelling steam ("the smell of money," bantered a local) into the atmosphere, but residents categorically state that you get used to the odor (at its worst in winter when trapped under low clouds)—either that or your sense of smell disintegrates with time! The town is also a port for pulp and lumber freighters, deep-sea vessels, and fishing boats, and has a well-earned reputation for excellent salmon fishing, luring anglers by the thousands each year.

First Stop

There's a lot to see and do in the immediate area, both indoors and out. If you don't want to miss anything, start your exploration of the area by following the "question marks" from the main highway to the **Alberni Valley Chamber of Commerce,** and pick up both a city map and a map of the surrounding area. Going to do the **West Coast Trail?** Note the detailed wall map of the entire trail—the staff is more than willing to spend time discussing all the trail smiles and trials with potential hikers (see p.77).

If you'd like to get to the bottom of fabulous **Della Falls** in Strathcona Provincial Park, highest waterfall in North America, ask for the trail description handout and map. The 440-meter falls can only be reached by canoe or boat from Great Central Lake (north of Port Alberni) and hiking trail, taking about five to seven days RT, or by seaplane. Canoeists can request canoe routes for the whole of Vancouver I., showing length, width, grade, time, distance to the nearest community and camping areas.

The center also has a list of easy hikes in the Port Alberni area, along with handy info sheets listing all the accommodations and restaurants around town. Located on the main highway as you enter town from the east (look for the impressive carved wood sign welcoming you to Port Alberni in front); open daily in summer 0800-2000, in winter 0900-1700, tel. 724-6535.

Alberni Harbour Quay

Follow the signs from downtown to brightly decorated Alberni Harbour Quay, at the foot of Argyle St., to climb the Clock Tower for excellent views of the inlet, marina, and paper mill, browse the Forestry Visitor Centre (an entertaining spot for kids too) and gift shops, sample seafood fresh off the boat, take a short waterfront ride from mill to mill on a steam engine (summer weekends only; adult $2, child $1), visit the small InfoCentre and the Forestry Visitor Centre, or hire a charter boat for fishing, diving, or cruising.

Head For The Sea

If visiting the west coast by water sounds more appealing than by road, the best way to get there is aboard the vintage Scottish coaster, MV *Lady Rose,* leaving Port Alberni first thing in the morning for an unforgettable cruise down Alberni Inlet into Barkley Sound. The boat, berthed at Alberni Harbour Quay, slips through the deep-blue water between tree-covered, stream-riddled mountains, delivering mail, cargo, and passengers to solitary cabins, dropping eager canoeists and kayakers off at the Broken Group Is. (part of Pacific Rim National Park), depositing whale-watchers and hikers at Bamfield and, in summer, tourists at Ucluelet. Depending on the time of year, killer and gray whales, seals, sea lions, porpoises, river otters, bald eagles, and all sorts of seabirds join you on your trip through magnificent Barkley Sound. Day-trips to Ucluelet run Mon., Wed., Fri. (summer only), and take 4½ hours, $16 OW, $32 RT. Breakfast and lunch are available in the onboard coffee shop.

Some of the best diving on North America's Pacific coast is reputedly found around the Broken Group Is. in Barkley Sound—air and equipment are available in town. If you have a canoe, kayak, or scuba-diving gear (all can be hired), prearrange a pick-up date and time and catch a ride to the islands on the same *Lady Rose* (three hours, $16 OW, $32 RT); very popular in summer—book well ahead. For another excellent day-trip, take the boat to the picturesque village of Bamfield, northern head of the West Coast Trail, to meet up with prearranged whalewatching boats in winter (end of Feb., early March), or hike the 77-km trail to Port Renfrew; the boat runs year-round on Tues., Thurs., and Sat., and takes four hours via Kildonan (three hours on Sun., summer only); $15 OW, $30 RT. Get breakfast or lunch on board. In summer the *Lady Rose* does a roaring business—book as far ahead as possible.

Sailboarding

If you just happen to have your sailboard along, and ripping across an inlet, colors flying, appeals to your senses or lack of sense, head for **China Creek Marina** (tel. 723-9812) farther down the inlet, about 14 km south of Port Alberni. In summer, the water up-inlet is warm, while at the mouth of the inlet it's cold, resulting in some thermal wind activity. At about 1300 each day, the wind comes up, the boats come in, and the sailboarders go out! This area is quite notorious for excellent windsurfing activity.

History And Forestry

Find out more about the origins of the infamous West Coast Trail, see a collection of native Indian artifacts, or tinker with a variety of operating motorized machines from the forestry industry at the **Alberni Valley Museum** on Tenth Ave. and Wallace St.; open daily 1000-1700, to 2100 on Thurs., admission free.

Ever wonder what goes on in a pulp and paper mill? You'll be able to tell others after taking a 1½-hour tour of the **Alberni Pulp and Paper Division** at 1030 weekdays, at 4000 Stamp Ave., tel. 723-2161. **Alberni Pacific Sawmill** also offers a 1½-hour tour when the mill is operating, departing from the personnel office at 2500 1st Ave. on weekdays at 0830 (slacks and good walking shoes required); tel. 724-6511. **Somass Division Sawmill,** tel. 724-7474, also offers a tour 0830-1000 on Tues. and Thursdays. **Woods Tours** depart daily from the Forestry Visitors Centre at Alberni Harbour Quay and last from 1300 to 1530; for more details call 724-7888. All the tours are free. During provincial **Forestry Week** in May, lots of the trucks and heavy equipment used in local forestry activities are brought in from the boonies, cleaned up and polished, and proudly paraded through downtown.

Oh For A Salmon

Attention frustrated anglers! If you don't know this area, yet dream about catching a salmon so big it could pull two waterskiers, run—don't walk—to **Port Alberni Marina** at 5104 River Rd. (tel. 723-8022). The owners, local fishing guides, have put together all kinds of printed info on local fishing (just ask), know all the best spots, how to catch 'em—in fact, all you need to know about fishing but were embarrassed to ask. Open daily in summer dawn to dusk, in winter 0900-1700, for guide hire, salmon charters (six-hour morning charters are $300 for two, $330 for three; four-hour afternoon charters are $200 for two, $220 for three, sharing a guide and boat), boat rentals (from $14 per hour plus gas or $75 per day plus gas), rod rentals ($10 pp per day), sportfishing/accommodations packages in Alberni Inlet and Barkley Sound, freshwater drifting for steelhead and salmon on the Stamp River, day moorage, and all the necessary bait and tackle. At **Clutesi Haven Marina** in the same neck of the inlet are 250 boat berths, public restrooms, and hot showers.

The annual **Port Alberni Salmon Festival** fishing derby each Labour Day weekend (first Mon. in Sept.) draws anglers from afar in the hopes of winning the $20,000 first prize for largest salmon. A multitude of salmon-eaters converge for the three-day salmon barbecue, and crowds of fishing enthusiasts gather to watch thousands of pounds of salmon being weighed in over the weekend at Clutesi Marina.

West Coast Trail

This rugged 77-km trail in Pacific Rim National Park is most easily reached by the MV *Lady Rose, West Coast Busline,* or by private vehicle from Port Alberni. For the entire rundown, visit the InfoCentre in Port Alberni, Pacific Rim National Park InfoCentre inside the park boundary on Hwy. 4, and see p. 77 for more details.

Accommodations

Whether you're in search of a tentsite with water views, cozy bed and breakfast, or luxurious motel room, Port Alberni has something to suit. Furthermore, if you're going on to the west coast during high season and haven't made any reservations in advance, there's a good chance you'll be back here for the night! As usual, refer to the *Accommodations* booklet for complete descriptions and rates of most places in town. For a comprehensive list of campgrounds in the area, and a list of those currently offering B&B (places quickly come and go), call in at the InfoCentre.

China Creek Park Marina And Campground is particularly comfortable, 15 km south of town on Alberni Inlet, tel. 723-9812. Not only do you get a choice of open or wooded sites with all the facilities a camper needs ($8-15 per site), but there's also a marina to wander along, sailboard rental, great views of the inlet from a sandy log-strewn beach, and lots of bald eagles for company. Or try **Junction,** just down the road from the Chamber of Commerce; grassy, wooded tent and trailer sites for $10-

12 per night, picnic area, coin-op showers (75 cents), and laundry.

If you like meeting locals wherever you travel, try this B&B. Mrs. Eileen Anderson, a lively and fascinating world traveler, offers a self-contained room with twin beds, bathroom, own entrance, and use of a small patio down the side of her house, at 5847 River Rd. (the main highway west). It's a couple of blocks west of town, directly across from the Somass River (good swimming in summer), has off-street parking, and is on the main bus route to Ucluelet. A cooked breakfast is included in the daily rate of $30 s, $40 d; call ahead at 723-3617. For a list of other B&Bs currently operating, call in at the Chamber of Commerce.

PORT ALBERNI TO UCLUELET

This stretch of the highway is best driven either early in the morning or late in the afternoon when the light is perfect for photos. Fill up with gas in Port Alberni, and have plenty of film on hand or a video camera charged up and ready for action. The next 100 km to Ucluelet or 125 km to Tofino, the road meanders through unspoiled mountain wilderness, and you won't find a gas station or store for at least a couple of hours. If you're going straight to Tofino, avoid doing the last hairy coastal section in the dark—when the signs say 30-km/h corners, they mean 30-km/h corners, or slower! By bus, **Island Coach Lines** runs a daily service between Port Alberni and Ucluelet ($13 OW) and Tofino ($14 OW).

No Water Shortage Here!

Keen trout and salmon anglers, campers, photographers, and seaplane enthusiasts will enjoy large **Sproat Lake** (look out for the turnoff to the left before the lake). It's a hive of activity in summer when the clear water lures swimmers, anglers, canoeists, waterskiers, and campers who stay in **Sproat Lake Provincial Park.** Providing there isn't a fire, you can also see the largest water bombers in the world parked here—the Martin Mars "Flying Tankers" that carry up to 6,000 gallons of water and are used to douse forest fires (they can also be toured—make arrangements through the Tanker Base). **Robertson Creek Hatchery,** about 18 km from Port Alberni and another seven km on Great Central Rd., is the source of millions of juvenile chinook and coho salmon and steelhead trout annually released into the Stamp-Somass river system, the primary spawning grounds for gigantic Alberni Inlet salmon. Open daily 0930-1630; tel. 723-3837.

First-place Images

The main highway continues to follow the northern side of long, narrow, mountain-backed Sproat Lake, passing one glorious reflection view after another. Even though you *know* your first shot will win first prize at the fair back home, try to resist the urge to snap every beautiful scene you see—although it's hard to believe, the farther you travel along the lake, the better the views and reflections get. The same follows for the splendid, snowcapped mountain scenery of the blue-tinted **Mackenzie Range.** The only scars on the landscape along this highway are those areas that have been logged. The forests in the Port Alberni area (several spots along this highway) have supplied logs for the lumber industry since the early 1900s. Whiz through the logged areas, but stop at every rest area between Port Alberni and the west coast and you'll see all the very best views.

North Or South?

Ninety-one km from Port Alberni, Hwy. 4 splits, leading eight km south to Ucluelet, or 34 km north to Tofino passing the **Long Beach** section of Pacific Rim National Park most of the way. If your idea of the good life involves kicking back, relaxing, surrounding yourself by stunning scenery (mountains, lakes, rivers, rainforest, and sandy beaches all within easy reach of one another) and abundant wildlife, with all kinds of outdoorsy activities available year-round, be warned—you may unexpectedly find the sensible side of your brain taking over, moving your not-so-reluctant bod to this wet but beautiful paradise! If you've got plenty of time to explore the

fishing boats at Ucluelet

west coast, visit Ucluelet first, then meander up through Pacific Rim National Park to Tofino at the northern end of the road.

Ucluelet

This small port (pronounced Yoo-CLOO-let, meaning "People With a Safe Landing Place") on the northern edge of Barkley Sound was first established centuries ago as a fishing village by the Nu-chal-nulth Indians. During the last century or so the village has also been a fur sealers' trading post and a logging and sawmill community, but fishing (with its resident fishing fleet and several fish-processing plants) remains the steady mainstay. Today Ucluelet is obviously benefitting from the tourism industry, billing itself as the "Whalewatching Capital" and netting a good share of all the west coast visitors—along with great numbers of Pacific salmon as they head for their spawning grounds.

In winter Ucluelet is relatively quiet. When the weather warms up it lures hordes of anglers to participate in the always-good fishing for salmon, halibut, and cod in Barkley Sound; deep-sea fishermen; divers to the nearby Broken Group Is.; whalewatchers (early spring, and again in late Autumn); and wildlife enthusiasts who cruise the shorelines in search of the abundant sea creatures that have made the west coast either a migration resting spot or a permanent home. Ucluelet has a variety of accommodations (see the *Accommodations* booklet), many lining Peninsula Rd., the main road into town. It also has a handful of restaurants serving, you guessed it, fresh seafood. If you're looking for a quick lunch, try the **Block and Cleaver Deli** on the main road for made-to-order sandwiches.

PACIFIC RIM NATIONAL PARK

Long Beach, the Broken Group Is., and the West Coast Trail are the three separate, distinctly different areas that together make up Pacific Rim National Park. To see all three units, you need at least two weeks (one week to do the trail), a willingess to travel by road, water, and foot, and a spirit of adventure. Long Beach, an 11-km stretch of surf-swept, driftwood-strewn sand, is easily reached by car or bus along winding Hwy. 4; the Broken Group Is., more than 100 islands and islets in Barkley Sound, are reached by passenger-freight or charter boat from Port Alberni, Ucluelet, or Bamfield; and the trailhead for the West Coast Trail, a rugged 77-km hike between Bamfield and Port Renfrew, is reached by water or road from Port Alberni.

Pacific Rim National Park is a heavy rainfall area (300 centimeters per year) and the weather can only be described as extremely changeable. It can be cold, windy, and wet in the morning, yet warm and dry in the afternoon—always carry extra clothes and raingear while exploring the park. In summer (high season) the average temperature is 14° C, and dense morning fog usually clears in the afternoon. In winter the average temperature is six degrees C and the park experiences a good proportion of its annual rainfall. In spring you can expect 10° C days, six-de-

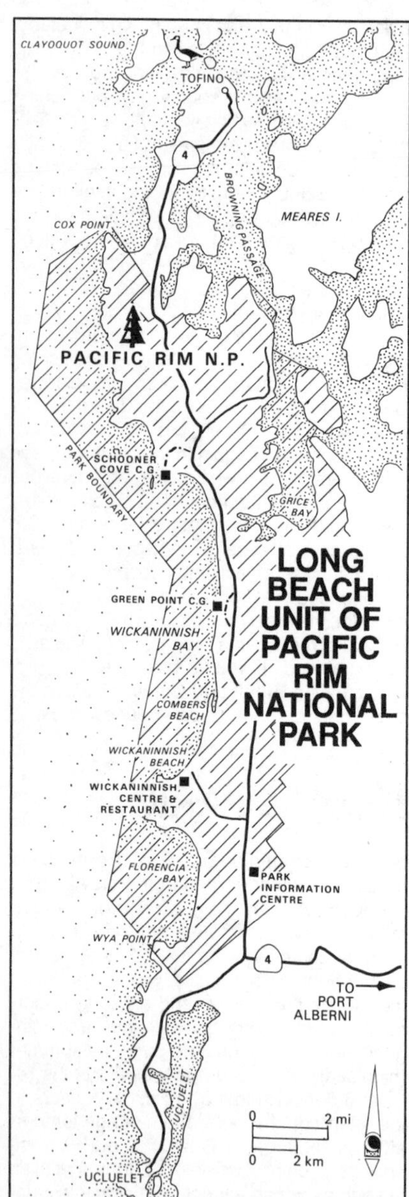

gree C days in autumn. For the latest weather forecast, call 726-4212.

LONG BEACH

Imagine rocky headlands and more than 11 km of hard-packed white sand covered in twisted driftwood, shells, and the occasional Japanese glass fishing float, backed by dense rainforest and the high snowcapped peaks of the Mackenzie Range. Offshore lie surf-battered craggy islands and islets, home sweet home to a myriad of marinelife.

Long Beach is a popular spot year-round. Whalewatchers arrive in spring to get glimpses of migrating gray whales from the beach or close-up views from charter boats (best seen mid-March to mid-April, though occasionally in Feb. and June). When the weather warms up, Long Beach attracts swimmers, surfers, beachcombers, clam diggers, and anglers. Thousands of migrating Canada geese, pintails, mallards, and black brants converge in this area during Oct. and Nov. to harvest the ripe pickings from the vast tidal mud flats of **Grice Bay** on the other side of the peninsula. In winter hikers dress for the harsh elements and walk the surf-pounded beach in search of treasures, admiring the ocean's fury during the many ferocious storms.

The ocean off western Canada reputedly has more species of marine animals than any other temperate coast—and one of the best places to see all these creatures is the tidal zone and offshore islands. Respect the wildlife, keep your distance, and don't feed any wild animals. They are unpredictable—getting too close could be dangerous to your health. Collecting marinelife, flowers, or plantlife is also forbidden within the park.

Eight well-maintained beach, headland, and woodland trails, each one to two km in length, keep hikers happy exploring rock arches, blowholes, tidal pools, and the rainforest; a guide to the trails is included with the orientation map provided at the Long Beach Information Centre. Other popular park activities include canoeing, kayaking, boating, surfing, sailboarding, birdwatching, sea lion watching, surf fishing, and golfing at Grice Bay. For a wonderful view of the peninsula and far out to sea, head for the lookout atop **Radar Hill.**

Camping Out

The best camping spot (though crowded in summer) along the west coast is at **Green Point** on a beautiful bluff above the beach with drive-in sites, washrooms, picnic tables, and firewood provided, but no showers or hookups; open year-round, fee $12.75 per site per night, $5 per night self-registration from Thanksgiving to Easter. This campground is full every day throughout July and August. It is operated on a number system. Go to the campground kiosk to obtain your number. Each numbered sheet will indicate a specified time to return. At the indicated time you are either issued a site or issued a lower number for the following day; the average wait is one to two days.

The other campground is more primitive, situated at the northern end of the beach at **Schooner Cove,** a 1.2-km hike from the parking lot. Open seasonally, fresh water and outhouses provided, find your own driftwood; $6 per tent from mid-May to mid-September. Winter camping is not advised because extreme tides submerge the camping area. The closest commercial campgrounds are in Ucluelet and Tofino.

BROKEN GROUP ISLANDS

These 100 or so islands, originally the site of Indian villages, then some of the first trading posts on the coast, lie in the mouth of Barkley Sound and are now populated only by occasional campers. The rough waters and reefs around them, combined with heavy morning fog, have claimed more than 50 vessels in the last century, but the sheltered lagoons at **Gibraltar, Jacques,** and **Hand Is.** offer protection and good boating conditions. Boaters should buy Marine Chart 3670 from Canadian Hydrographic Service, Chart Sales and Distribution Office, Institute of Ocean Services, 9860 W. Saanich Rd., Box 6000, Sidney, B.C. V8L 4B2; $8. The chart has detailed navigational info on the islands and park, and a handy description of campsite facilities.

The islands can be reached by boat or seaplane from Port Alberni (see "Head for the Sea," p. 72), Ucluelet, or Bamfield. They provide an excellent playground for canoeists and kayakers, some fine coho and chinook fishing, and scuba diving around barnacle-encrusted wrecks, but if you plan on camping on the islands, note that fresh water is scarce (see the park brochure for drinking water locations). Keep an eye open for Pacific gray whales in the sound, harbor seals in the islands' sheltered lagoons, resident bald eagles, and cormorants.

THE WEST COAST TRAIL

Steps From The Past

The magnificent West Coast Trail starts at Pachena Bay, five km south of Bamfield on the southeast side of Barkley Sound, and meanders a total of 77 km along the untamed shoreline of the west coast to Port Renfrew. This stretch of the coast, the southernmost section of Pacific Rim National Park, was nicknamed "Graveyard of the Pacific" due to the great number of shipwrecks that occurred along here. After the SS *Valencia* ran aground in 1906 and most of the passengers and crew drowned or died from exposure (38

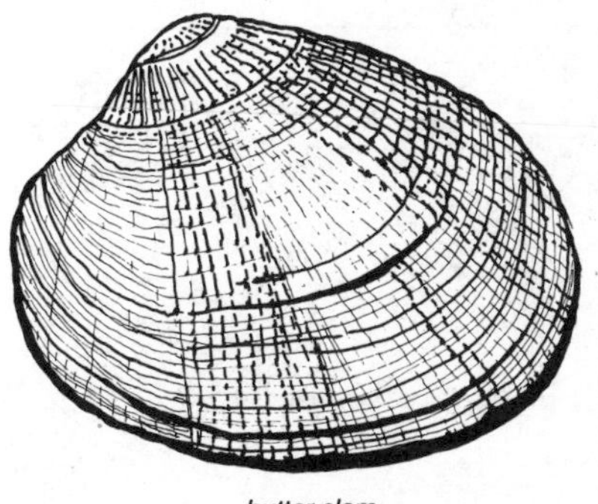

LOUISE FOOTE

butter clam

survived), the Canadian government constructed a lifesaving trail to help future survivors penetrate the dense coastal forest. It followed a rugged telegraph route, connecting lighthouses and towns toward Victoria, and was kept open by telegraph linesmen and lighthouse keepers. It's the same trail today, and if you're not an experienced, well-equipped hiker, it can be just as treacherous.

The Challenge

The northernmost section of the route from Bamfield to Pachena Lighthouse (11 km) takes only a couple of hours and is the easiest part—many who don't tackle the entire trail do this section RT. For the next six to eight days you follow a rough route wandering along beaches (don't get trapped by the tide), atop steep cliffs and slippery banks, fording rivers by rope, suspension bridge, or hand-pulled cable cars, climbing down sandstone cliffs by ladder, crossing slippery boardwalks, muddy slopes, bogs, and deep gullies, balancing on fallen logs. But for all your efforts you're rewarded with panoramic views of sand and sea, dense lush rainforest, sandstone cliffs with waterfalls cascading straight down into deep pools in the sand, all kinds of wildlife—gray whales, eagles, sea lions, seals, and a variety of seabirds—with the constant roar and hiss of the Pacific surf pummeling the sand.

The trail is a high-season summer experience: you have to go between mid-May and the beginning of Oct., when the weather is generally accommodating and the trail is patrolled by park wardens. There are two major water crossings necessitating ferry service—one at the Gordon River outside of Port Renfrew (contact Norm Smith, Port Renfrew at 647-5430; price varies $5-9 pp), and another midway along the trail across Nitinat Narrows, the treacherous mouth of tidal Nitinat Lake (park-sponsored ferry operates 12 May to 30 Sept., 0900-1700, seven days a week; $5 pp). These crossings cannot be made without the ferry services provided by contractors. July is generally the driest month, but be prepared for rain, strong winds, thick fog, and muddy trail conditions even then. Those that have completed the trail describe it as exhilaratingly challenging, incredibly beautiful, and very satisfying—and many come back to do it again.

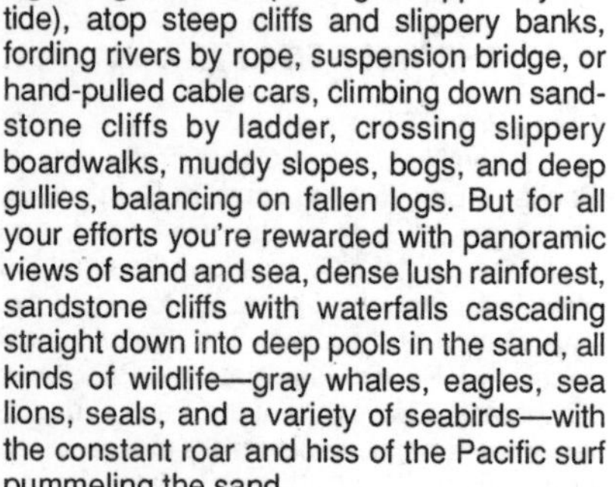

Stamina And Equipment

For visitors planning a trip to the West Coast Trail, Pacific Rim National Park provides a mail-out information package specific to this unit of the park. Contact the Superintendent, Pacific Rim National Park, Box 280, Ucluelet, B.C. V0R 3A0. The recommended topographic map *West Coat Trail, Pacific Rim National Park-Port Renfrew to Bamfield* ($5.59 B.C. residents, $7.49 other Canadian residents, $9 outside Canada includes taxes, shipping and handling) is an absolute must for hiking the trail. It's available from: Province of B.C., Map Production, Surveys and Mapping Branch, Ministry of Environment, 553 Superior St., Victoria, B.C. V8V 1X4, or call 387-1441. However, please note that the above map and Tofino tide tables are not available as a mail-out from the park, but are available at the two trailhead information centers at Pachena Bay and Port Renfrew.

Canadian Tide Tables can be purchased at most marine and sporting-goods outlets in the Pacific Rim region, or write for Volume Six (use the "Tofino" section) from Canadian Hydrographic Service, Chart Sales and Distributors, Box 6000, 9860 West Saanich Rd., Sidney, B.C. V8L 4B2; $6.78 B.C. residents, $6.42 rest of Canada, $6 outside of Canada which includes taxes and shipping.

Reference books for trail preparation include *Pacific Rim Explorer* by Bruce Obee (Whitecap Books, North Vancouver), *West Coast Trail and Nitinat Lakes* (Sierra Club, Victoria), and *Blisters and Bliss* by David Foster and Wayne Aikens (Cloudcap Books, Seattle).

Go with at least two other people, and travel as light as possible. Experts recommend you wear comfortable hiking boots, take a stove, a small axe, at least 15 meters of strong light rope, head-to-toe waterproof gear (keep your spare clothes and sleeping bag in a plastic bag), a small amount of fire starter for an emergency, suntan lotion, insect repellent, a first-aid kit (for cuts, burns, sprains, and blisters), and waterproof matches. Also take enough cash to pay for boat crossings (allow at least $15 OW) and transportation at the end of the trail (reservations required). Tell someone responsible when you're going, when you should be back, and the number in your party. Burn or pack out any garbage.

Transportation

To get to the northern end of the trail from Port Alberni, catch the MV *Lady Rose* on Tues., Thurs., or Sat. ($15 OW) to the boardwalk fishing village of Bamfield (shops, motel, cottages, and a luxurious inn), or catch a Western Bus Lines (Port Alberni) Ltd. bus from the depot at 4521 10th Ave., Port Alberni (tel. 723-3341). At Bamfield the bus departs from the Tides and Trails Cafe (tel. 728-3491). Plane charter is also an option through Car Aviation (tel. 723-3255).

At the Port Renfrew end of the trail there's the San Juan River to cross (ferry for a fee), then only a pub and grocery store. For bus service between Port Renfrew and Victoria (reservations required), contact West Coast Trail-Port Renfrew Connector through Knight Limousine Service Ltd., 3297 Douglas St., Victoria, tel. 383-7311 or 361-9080. Alternatively you can hitchhike (tedious but possible) the 70 km or so back to Sooke (see "Sooke To Port Renfrew," p. 44), then take a bus another 30 km to Victoria. Double-check the latest transportation modes for both ends with the Information Centre.

PARK PRACTICALITIES

Information And Services

Before you explore any areas of the park, stop in at the **Information Centre,** two km north of the Hwy. 4 and Ucluelet/Tofino Hwy. junction, just inside the park boundary. A number of exhibits and displays, and of course lots of info, will help you enjoy your stay; open mid-March to mid-June 1000-1800, late June, July, and Aug. 0800-2000, Sept. to mid-Oct. 1000-1800, tel. 726-4212. In the off-season, phone 726-7721. For preliminary contact, write to Pacific Rim National Park, Box 280, Ucluelet, B.C. V0R 3A0.

The **Wickaninnish Centre** at Long Beach is the place to learn about the natural and human history of the park and the open ocean through a variety of exhibits, spectacular hand-painted murals, and films; open mid-March to Thanksgiving, tel. 726-4212. Audiovisual presentations, naturalist programs, and outdoor events run mid-June-Sept.—get details at the Information Centre and park bulletin boards.

No stores or gas stations are within park boundaries, but supplies and gas are available in Ucluelet and Tofino. Tired of peanut butter sandwiches and want a real meal? Try the **Wickaninnish Restaurant** at Long Beach adjacent to the Wickaninnish Centre, open mid-March to the end of Oct., where a great ocean view is served along with your meal. Another place to try is the clubhouse restaurant at **Long Beach Golf Course.** The next closest restaurants are in Tofino and Ucluelet.

TOFINO

At the western terminus of the Trans-Canada Hwy. on the southern edge of sheltered Clayoquot Sound, surrounded by forest-covered islands, lies the small, picturesque fishing village and port of Tofino. Serving the several hundred people who live along the secluded shores of the Sound, it's also a source of supplies for the annual influx of visitors to Pacific Rim National Park just to the south. In winter Tofino is a quiet and friendly community with a population of fewer than 1,000. In summer the population swells to several times that size and the village springs to life—fishing boats pick up supplies and deposit salmon, cod, prawns, crabs, halibut, and other delicacies of the sea, and cruising, whale-watching, and fishing boats, along with seaplanes, do a roaring business introducing visitors to the natural wonders of the west coast.

Tofino started out as a native Clayoquot Indian village. It was one of the first points in Canada to be visited by Capt. Cook and was named in 1792 after Don de Vincent Tofino, a hydrographer with a Spanish expedition. Aside from contact with fur traders and whalers, the entire district remained basically unchanged for almost 100 years. Today's Tofino is a bustling fishing village, just beginning to see some of the financial benefits of tourism. However, due to a large number of aware residents who like Tofino exactly the way it is, it's unlikely that high-rise hotels or fast-food chains will ever spoil this peaceful coastal paradise.

Get To Know Tofino

The best way to get a feel for Tofino is to wander around on foot—it's small and it won't take you long to find everything there is to see and do. Walk down to each of the docks to see fishing boats, charter boats, seaplanes, fishing tackle, and crab pots, to watch fresh fish of every description being unloaded, and to find out what charter boats are going where.

And the best way to experience all the marinelife is to take a nature cruise along the coast and around the islands—sea lions and puffins sun themselves on offshore rocks, dolphins and harbor seals frolic in the bays and inlets, gray whales and killer whales cruise the shoreline, and majestic bald eagles gracefully swoop around in the sky or perch in the tops of trees. Whalewatching is one of the most popular activities along the west coast. The migration route of the great gray whale passes close to the coast—they can be seen from the shore as they cruise, dive, surface, and spout. Their feeding grounds are about 30 km up the coast at **Maquinna Marine Park,** accessible by a 20-minute boat trip or an even shorter seaplane flight from Tofino. During the spring migration and some feeding periods, gray whales are also frequently sighted in Tofino's calm inland waters around **Meares Island.** Several companies offer whalewatching cruises daily March-Oct. (average $35 adult, $20 child)—check out the various docks and compare trips and prices.

Tofino Marina

Hot Springs

Pamper yourself and take a boat or seaplane to **Hotsprings Cove,** the only hot springs on Vancouver Island. Water bubbles out of the ground at a temperature of 189° F, tumbles over a cliff, down through a series of pools (each large enough for two or three people), then into the sea. Lobsterize yourself silly in the first pool, or go for the ultimate in hot/cold torture by immersing yourself in the last pool, where breathtakingly refreshing ocean waves (at high tide) slap you back into reality; get there by a 45-minute to one-hour boat ride from Tofino (leaves the 1st St. Dock in the morning and returns in the afternoon; $40 RT), then follow the short trail (30 minutes) through lush rainforest to the springs. You can also take a scenic 15-minute flight to the hot springs by seaplane ($67 pp RT, minimum three persons); for more info call **Tofino Air Lines,** based at the First St. Dock, tel. 725-4454.

Fishing For Fun

If you love to fish but don't have your own gear, charter a boat or take a guided fishing trip for salmon or cod, head for one of the freshwater lakes and try for trout, or hop on a seaplane and fish in your own private inlet—the opportunities are endless! Just wander down to each of the docks and check out all the options. In Feb. the herring season starts and the area hums with fishing-boat activity. Rod and Betsy Buhtz at **Tofino Swell Lodge** run fishing and diving charters, along with whalewatching trips, for $60-120 per hour depending on the activities, fishing gear provided; tel. 725-3274.

Sun, Sand, And Solitude

If you fancy a long walk along a fabulous stretch of white sand looking for shells (and if you're lucky, a Japanese glass fishing float), like to sit on craggy rocks watching the waves disintegrate into white spray, or just want a piece of sand all your own to work on your tan, head for **Chesterman's Beach** just south of Tofino. At low tide you can walk all the way out to **Frank I.** to watch the surf pound the exposed side while the tide creeps in and cuts you off from civilization for a few hours. The turnoff (not marked) to Chesterman's Beach is on the right just past the Dolphin Motel as you leave Tofino—follow the road until you come to a parking lot on the left, then take the one-minute trail to the beach. The road eventually rejoins the main highway.

Hiking Trails

Many good hiking trails cover the Tofino area. For an unforgettable walk through dense lush rainforest, catch the boat from Weigh West Marina for a 15-minute cruise to **Meares I.** ($12 pp), then follow the Tribal Park trails—the basic loop takes about 2½ hours at a leisurely pace. To arrange your hike phone 725-3277. For more hiking suggestions, call in at the Travel InfoCentre downtown.

Eagle Aerie Gallery

For outdoor scenes with clean lines and brilliant colors integrated with native Indian designs, don't miss visiting this unique gallery, featuring the excellent paintings, prints, and sculpture of Roy Henry Vickers, a well-known and highly respected B.C. artist. Browse through the gallery, watch the video on the artist, and if you fall for one of the most popular paintings but can't afford it, you can buy it in card or poster form. The gallery itself is built on the theme of a West Coast Indian longhouse, with a carved and painted exterior and interior totem poles. You can't miss it on the main road across from the InfoCentre, next to the Loft Restaurant; open in winter 0900-1700, in summer 0900-2000.

Accommodations

The best camping (crowded in summer) is back at **Green Point** in Pacific Rim National Park (see p. 77), however several resorts provide beachfront campsites. An assortment of motels lie along the highway between the park and Tofino and as you enter the village. For a full listing, refer to the *Accommodations* booklet.

If you're looking for a comfy room, use of a fully equipped kitchen and living room (complete with stereo, TV, and mounted telescope), and incredible views of Tofino Inlet, tree-covered Meares I., and distant snow-capped mountains, head straight for **Tofino Swell Lodge.** Nothing beats that first cup of complimentary coffee, bowl of cereal, or toast and honey as you watch the sunrise from the veranda, bubbling hot tub, barbecue area, or private jetty. You can also go on a fishing or diving charter (see "Fishing For Fun," above) or go crabbing. To see a Dungeness crab close up, just look in the clear water under the dock. The rooms range $40-68 s, $45-69 d or triple. Located at 341 Olsen Rd., off the main highway to the right as you enter Tofino. For more info or reservations (necessary in the high season though you can also turn up and try your luck), write to Rod and Betsy Buhtz, Box 160, Tofino, B.C. V0R 2Z0; tel. 725-3274.

Food And Entertainment

Tofino has grocery stores, fish and seafood stores, bakeries, and quite a variety of cafes and restaurants (most of them serve seafood so fresh it could swim or crawl off your plate)—ask the locals for their recommendations. At friendly **Weigh West Pub** (Weigh West Marina) off the main road you can savor delicious clam chowder and garlic toast for $4.95, seafood or steak dinners for around $10, or nachos with a Canadian beer while you feast your eyes on the colorful marina view below; open daily for lunch and dinner. **The Loft** on the main highway is open daily f0700-2200 in summer, from 1130 in winter, for lunch ($4-8) and dinner ($10-25). Specializing in West Coast seafood, they serve everything from sandwiches to salmon—popular with locals at any time of day. Crab lovers head for the **Crab Bar** at 601 Campbell Street. It's licensed, open for lunch and dinner, and it specializes in fresh local crab, but you can't make a reservation at this one. **The Schooner,** oldest restaurant in Tofino, opens in summer serving excellent seafood on the expensive side ($12-30, reservations recommended); on the main highway across the road from the Loft.

In spring and summer (occasionally in winter) the small-town local theater, **Clayoquot Sound Community Theatre,** on the main road near 3rd St. puts on good-quality productions on Thurs., Fri., and Sat. nights; for reservations and info call 725-3947. Tofino and Ucluelet join together each spring to put on the annual **Pacific Rim Whale Festival,** which features "Whales in the Park Week" (shows and special events) in Pacific Rim National Park, a native song and dance festival, crab races, plays at the local theater, dances, concerts, and a multitude of events and activities in celebration of the gray whale spring migration. It usually happens mid-March to mid-April (around spring break). To receive a Pacific Rim Whale Festival Package (calendar of events, whalewatching info, charter info, and accommodation brochures), write to Box 129, Tofino, B.C. V0R 2Z0, or tel. 725-3414.

Services And Transportation

The **Travel InfoCentre** is on the main highway, downtown, open in summer (chamber of commerce tel. 725-3414). The **p.o., Tofino General Hospital** (tel. 725-3212; ambulance tel. 1-756-1243), and a **laundromat** are all on Campbell Street. The **RCMP** is on Campbell St. and Third, tel. 725-3242.

The **Orient Stage Lines** bus from Port Alberni arrives in Tofino once a day at 1410 and leaves at 1600 for Ucluelet and Port Alberni ($14 OW, $13 from Ucluelet). The parcel van (limited passenger space) makes the same trip once a day on weekdays only, arriving in Tofino at 0940 and leaving at 1000. For the current schedule and reservations call 723-6924. **Tofino Air Lines,** based at the First St. Wharf, provides a variety of scenic flights (you pay by the hour; from $90) and charters in their floatplanes, but no scheduled flights. For more info stop by the wharf office or call 725-4454.

As you leave Tofino, look for the sign that sums up the good-time holiday feeling this area projects so well—"Hope you had a whale of a good time!"

QUALICUM BEACH TO COURTENAY

Qualicum Beach

This small beach community is generally quieter than Parksville (11 km south), but it shares the same golden sands of Georgia Strait and attracts the same droves of beach-goers, sun worshippers, anglers, and golfers on summer vacation. The beachfront highway through town is lined with motels, resorts, and RV parks. For the complete rundown on this stretch of the coast, stop in at the Travel InfoCentre on the waterfront side of the highway.

The attractive downtown area, locally known as "the Village," is off the main highway and up a steep hill to the west. If you appreciate high-quality arts and crafts, detour off the main drag at this point and head for **The Old Schoolhouse Gallery and Art Centre.** In this beautifully restored 1912 building you'll find almost all the arts represented—wander through the gallery, then visit the working artist studios below to see woodcarving, printmaking, pottery, weaving, painting, and fabric art. Each studio has a viewing window—and the artists don't seem to mind nameless faces peering at them through the glass while they create! Don't miss a stop at the gallery shop where all kinds of original handcrafted treasures are more than likely to lure a couple of dollars out of your wallet. It's located at 122 Fern Rd. West, tel. 752-6133.

Big Qualicum River Hatchery

Yep, another hatchery! This one has assorted tanks, a river-level viewing room, maps, and trails. It was originally built to increase the not-so-hot survival rate of salmon and steelhead in the area. The best months to visit are Oct. and Nov. when you can see spawning salmon madly flinging themselves up the fish ladders; April is the best month to watch steelhead.

Denman Island

Island-hoppers can catch the Denman I. ferry for a 10-minute trip across Baynes Sound to this quiet rural island with its beaches, fishing, boating, scuba diving, provincial park, artisan community, and turn-of-the-century heritage buildings downtown, only a short walk from the ferry. It's a good place to take your bicycle or canoe (or you can rent them on the island). Beachfront camping can be found on both sides of the island, and B&Bs abound. From Denman I. you can also catch another ferry across to smaller Hornby Island. The Denman I. ferry departs hourly from Buckley Bay.

THE COMOX VALLEY

The three communities of Cumberland, Courtenay (on the main highway north), and Comox lie in the beautiful Comox Valley, nestled between Georgia Strait and the high snowcapped mountains to the west. Welcome to the "Recreational Capital of Canada"—beaches, excellent downhill and cross-country skiing at two ski resorts, fishing, golf, and camping—and yet another "Salmon Capital of the World" (Vancouver I. must have more salmon capitals than any other place *in the world!).*

B.C. Ferries operates a car ferry from Comox to Powell River on the mainland, allowing mainlanders easy access to mid-island ski fields and beaches and saving North Vancouver I. visitors from having to backtrack down to Nanaimo or Victoria. The ferry leaves from Little River Terminal, Comox, four times a day for the 1¼-hour crossing to Powell River Terminal. A current schedule and fares are posted at each terminal. For more info call Little River Terminal at 339-3310.

Courtenay

Largest community in the valley (population almost 10,000) and a commercial and cultural center (the annual summer music festival is a big hit) for local farming, logging, fishing, and retirement communities, Courtenay was named after Capt. George Courtenay, who led the original surveying expedition of the area (1848). As you enter Courtenay from the south, you pass all sorts of restaurants along the main highway, the **InfoCentre** at 2040 Cliffe Ave., and motel after motel. Keep going and you come to the pleasing downtown area with its cobbled streets, old-fashioned lamps, and brick planters full of flowers—a good place to shop. Cross the bridge to the totem-pole-flanked entrance to **Lewis Park** to view the confluence of the Puntledge and Tsolum Rivers as they become the Courtenay River, the shortest tidal river—yep, in the world. In summer the southern entrance to Courtenay, starting at the InfoCentre, is flanked with flowers for a couple of kilometers—locally referred to as "The Mile Of Flowers," brainchild of pioneer Kath Kirk. Today the annual planting is a community event sponsored by the local Rotary Club.

Mount Washington Ski Park

Aside from the area's main outdoor activities—skiing and hiking in Strathcona Provincial Park, and fishing—the main local attraction is the **Courtenay and District Museum and Archives** at 360 Cliffe Ave., housed in the Native Sons Of Canada Hall. Built in 1928, this building is one of the largest vertical-log cabins in the world. Step back in time to visually relive the history of the Comox Valley from prehistoric times (starting with a fossil collection) to the present day through a series of realistic dioramas, or check out the replica of an Indian bighouse containing many Native artifacts and items, some formerly belonging to prominent chiefs. And if you're a doll collector, you'll be fascinated with the large collection. Finish up in the gift shop, well stocked with local arts and crafts. The museum is open daily May through Aug. 1000-1630, in winter Tues.-Sat. 1000-1630, admission by donation; tel. 334-3611.

The Comox Valley Travel InfoCentre on the main highway as you enter town from the south (2040 Cliffe Ave., tel. 334-3234), is the place to go for all the nitty-gritty on the entire Comox Valley; open in summer daily 0800-2000, in winter daily 0830-1630. In the small park behind the buildings are public restrooms.

Super Salmon

The best fishing for salmon in this area is generally from mid-May to the end of June for bluebacks (coho under seven pounds), then surface fishing or "bucktailing" picks up again in Sept. when the northern coho run through the Strait of Georgia. Fish from the beach, or hire a guide from the Comox Valley Fishing Guides Association, which usually provides everything from boat and equipment to lures, bait, and refreshments. Get the names of guides and their rates at the InfoCentre.

Comox

In the small community of Comox, six km east of Courtenay, **Filberg Heritage Lodge and Park** on Comox Ave. is worth a visit. Wander through the beautifully landscaped nine-acre grounds (open dawn to dusk year round) that stretch along the harbor waterfront and the herb garden above the teahouse, tour the lodge (dating to 1929; open daily in summer 1100-1700, admission $1), visit with a variety of farm animals at the "hands-on farm," then savor lunch or afternoon tea in the Filberg Teahouse. In early Aug. the **Filberg Festival,** a major four-day event in this area, features unique arts and crafts from the best of the province's craftspeople, gourmet food, and free entertainment. It usually takes place during the first week of August, open daily 1100-2000; admission adult $3, child $1. To get to Filberg Lodge from Courtenay turn east toward Comox, then continue east on Comox Ave. through town until you come to the entrance to Filberg Estate (corner of Filberg Road).

HIT THE SLOPES

If you're making your way up the island in the off-season, you may be surprised on reaching the Comox Valley to find all the least-expensive motels and a good proportion of the fanciest hotels fully booked, with local restaurants and pubs doing a roaring trade. Off-season for the rest of Vancouver I. is high season here, when hordes of energetic skiers from the island and the mainland come to plant their poles on the nearby slopes of Mt. Washington and Forbidden Plateau.

Forbidden Plateau

In Strathcona Provincial Park, Forbidden Plateau, Vancouver I.'s original ski area, is best described as a family resort. You'll find a wide variety of terrains, fabulous views, a day lodge and ski school, and a chair, three T-bars, a rope tow, and a beginner's handletow. The name "Forbidden" comes from an old Native Indian legend: the village of Comox was threatened by Cowichan warriors many moons ago, so the Comox men sent their women and children up the mountain to be out of harm's way. When the flap was over, the men went up to collect their families but they had disappeared without a trace—and were never seen again. Not knowing how or why the party disappeared off the face of the planet, the mountain became for the Comox a fearful and forbidden place. But judging by the number of skiers and hikers who have explored Forbidden Plateau each year and returned to tell the tale, the legend has been put to rest.

Forbidden is a 30-minute drive from Courtenay (snow tires required, carry chains), open Fri., Sat., and Sun. 0900-1600, and every day during Christmas and Easter breaks. Downhill skiers pay $23 per day adult, $20 youth, $13 junior; cross-country skiers pay $6 per day which covers the chairlift to the beginning of the advanced trails; snowboard rentals are $24 per day. Ski lessons and rentals are available at the Lodge. For ski reports phone 338-1919; for more details on the resort, swing by the office at 2050 Cliffe Ave. or phone 334-4744. Get to Forbidden via public transportation from Courtenay; for details phone 334-2544.

In summer Forbidden Plateau is a great hiking area. Even couch potatoes can enjoy the views of the Comox Glacier, the open slopes, the Valley, the Strait of Georgia, and the distant mainland mountains by hopping on the year-round Forbidden chairlift. Summertime operating hours are Mon.-Sun. 1100-1600; same day return ride adult $6, child $4, mountain bike and rider all-day pass $12. Mountain Restaurant and Legend Lounge are open in summer 1000-1700; a buffet lunch put on every Sun. costs only $7.95.

Mt. Washington

Mt. Washington (1,609 meters), outside Strathcona Provincial Park, boasts the largest annual snowfall of all ski areas in the province, steep slopes in the downhill area, and some of the best cross-country skiing in the Pacific Northwest—30 km of triple-trackset trails through Paradise Meadows (with a name like Paradise Meadows, how can you resist?) and the more challenging hills of West Meadows. The facilities include a fully serviced alpine village, two double chairs, two triple chairs, and a beginner handletow.

The ski resort is a 32-km, 45-minute drive from Courtenay (snow tires required; carry chains) up a paved then well-maintained dirt road. Downhill skiing costs adult $29 per day, 13-18 years $26, child $18, senior $18 (very reasonable weekly and season rates too), cross-country $7 per day. Rentals and lessons are available at the Alpine Lodge, which also houses a cafe, a ski shop, and ski repair facilities. For the ski report call 338-1515. Get there via HiLo Ski Bus from Courtenay, which departs Economy Inn at 0730 daily during ski season and returns from the mountain at 1600; make reservations at 334-2544 before 2000 the night before. Or catch the Ski Bus operated by Forest Bus Tours, leaving every Sat., Sun. and Tues. from their parking lot across from the Mohawk and Sunset Lanes; get the schedule and make reservations at 248-4525 (Parksville) or Nanaimo (tel. 754-3454).

In summer you can hike or bike to your heart's content in this area. Catch the summer chairlift up. It operates on weekends starting at the end of June, daily from the end of July to early Sept., then weekends again during September, from 1100-1700; call **Mt. Washington Mile High Adventures** for details and current chair rates, tel. 338-1386.

COURTENAY TO CAMPBELL RIVER

The highway between Courtenay and Campbell River is lined with sandy beaches, rocky shores, waterfront parks, lush agricultural areas, RV parks, campgrounds, resorts, and plenty of motels, with the occasional signposted stop of historic interest. If you're looking for an enjoyable place to pitch a tent, follow the signs to **Miracle Beach Provincial Park,** about 19 km off the main highway, halfway to Campbell River. The wooded campground provides plenty of campsites in the trees, and the sandy beach, good swimming, fishing, and a variety of nature trails should keep everyone happy. Look for porpoise and hair seals at the mouth of Black Creek, killer whales in the Strait, black-tailed deer, black bear, and raccoons in the park, and seabirds and crabs along the shoreline; in summer take a nature walk with a park naturalist, participate in a clam bake or barbecue, or watch demos and films at the Miracle Beach Nature House; on the expensive side at $12 per night, but definitely worth it for all the activities.

As you approach Campbell River from the south, scan the treetops for winged action. This area is frequented by a large number of magnificent bald eagles—the white-headed eagles are mature, the brown ones immature. They like to perch in the very top branches (preferably of dead trees, or branches with less foliage), sit in twos or threes on offshore rocks, or skim the beaches and water in search of tasty morsels. Park off the highway, take your binoculars, tripod, and telephoto lens down to the beach, pull up a rock, and wait—if you're lucky, you'll agree, it's a birdwatcher's paradise.

1

2

1. a Banff National Park scene (Jane King); **2.** scene near Cassiar Highway (Bill Weir)

1. young bighorn sheep at the top of the gondola, Banff (Bruce King);
2. Columbian ground squirrel (Jane King); **3**. elk in velvet (Bruce King);
4. mallards in Stanley Park (Jane King); **5**. elk along Highway 93 (Jane King)

CAMPBELL RIVER

When Capt. George Vancouver landed on nearby Quadra I. in 1792, he found six seasonal Indian villages in the Campbell River area, on land densely carpeted in Douglas firs and cedar trees. In time the loggers arrived, paving the way for settlers who initially made Quadra I. their home. In the 1890s, sportsmen, led by natives in dugout canoes, recognized the salmon potential of this area with glee (rumor has it there were days when you could just about cross Discovery Passage on foot atop the salmon!), and in 1904 a hotel designed to accommodate loggers and tourists was built in what is now downtown Campbell River.

Today this scenic resort town of nearly 17,000, "The Salmon Capital of the World" (the most likely candidate for the "reel" title), stretches along Discovery Passage on both sides of the river, facing tree-covered Quadra I. and the magnificent snowcapped mountains of mainland British Columbia. Why is the fishing so hot? Georgia Strait ends just south of Campbell River, and Discovery Passage begins, suddenly narrowing to only two km in width between Vancouver and Quadra Islands. This incredibly narrow channel causes some of the strongest tides on the B.C. coast, attracts bait fish (and salmon to hunt them, and anglers to hunt *them),* and also forces the thousands of migrating salmon to concentrate off Campbell River, much to every fisherman's delight.

The highway as you enter town from the south, lined with motels, hotels, resorts, and restaurants, gives a rather touristy first impression—but don't let that put you off. It's a scenic spot to kick back and relax, make a base for jaunts into Strathcona Park, or go fishing, fishing, fishing. More than 60% of all visitors to Campbell River come here to catch a salmon in Discovery Strait. Fishing is the subject most commonly discussed, and if you don't have a pole and tackle, some good tales to tell, or at least a willingness to listen to some pretty fishy stories, you'll stand out like a fish out of water!

ATTRACTIONS

Campbell River Saltwater Fishing Pier
The best place to absorb some of the local atmosphere is on this pier. Opened in July

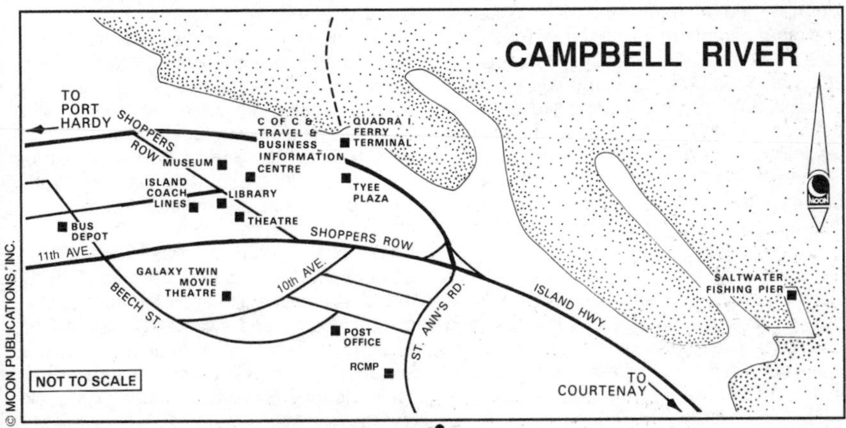

1987, it's 180 meters long and 6.6 meters wide, projects out over deep water and strong tides, and is fun to walk on whether you're into fishing or not. The benches and protected shelters on the pier allow proper appreciation of the marina, strait, mainland mountains, and fishing action even on wet and windy days. The pier also has built-in rod holders, colorful signs describing the fish you're likely to catch, and fish cleaning stations for when you do. Anglers of all sizes and ages spin cast for salmon, bottomfish, and the occasional steelhead from the pier, hauling them up in nets on long ropes. To fish you need a license or a season's pass (prices vary); stroll along the pier for free. Rod rentals are also available at the pier for $2 per hour, $5 per half-day, $10 per day, and you can buy a variety of snacks and drinks while you wait for the fish that won't be getting away.

Campbell River And District Museum And Archives

In the same building as the **Chamber of Commerce InfoCentre** (Tyee Plaza), this small museum is well worth a visit. Learn about Campbell River's early beginnings from photos and interesting written snippets, then feast your eyes on mystical Indian artifacts, masks, exciting artwork, baskets, woven articles, carved-wood boxes, colorful button blankets, petroglyphs, and totem poles. Finish up in the gift shop where you can buy stunning Indian prints, masks, postcards, and other paraphernalia. It's open Tues.-Sat. 1000-1600 April-Dec., daily 1000-1600 in summer, Tues.-Sat. 1300-1600 Jan.-March; admission $1.07. In the courtyard between the museum and chamber of commerce is a magnificent Kwakiutl thunderbird, carved by Sam Henderson in 1962. Scan the notice boards at the entrance for info on local activities and ferry schedules.

Outdoor Action

Salmon are pursued year-round in this area, but May-Oct. is peak season. Steelhead and freshwater cutthroat trout can also be caught year-round in the many freshwater lakes and rivers in the area, but the peak season for steelhead is Jan. through April, for freshwater trout March-May. Start your research for fishing guides, equipment, or the best spots to try for that shimmering salmon in the Chamber of Commerce Travel InfoCentre. Choose from hundreds of brochures, or ask advice from the exuberant young staff—they'll point you in the right direction. The next best thing to do to find out where the fishing's hot and where it's not is to wander out on the saltwater pier and chat up a local fishing enthusiast.

If you're going for the big one between July 15 and Sept. 15, you may want to look into the requirements necessary to qualify for **Tyee Club** membership. This exclusive club, famous among anglers around the world, has been dedicated to upholding the traditional methods of sportfishing since 1924. You have to preregister your intent to fish under its rules, troll from a rowboat in the mouth of the Campbell River without using a motor, use a rod between six and nine feet, an artificial lure, a line not more than 20 pounds pretested breaking weight, and then catch a trophy-sized tyee (chinook over 14 kilograms); for more info, call the club at 287-2724.

For all sorts of outdoor activities, browse through the brochures in the InfoCentre, or give **Island Pacific Adventures** a call at 923-3952. They specialize in fishing and scuba diving.

Quadra Island

A 15-minute ferry ride takes you to this historical spot where you can visit the **Kwakiutl Museum** in Cape Mudge Village and see potlatch regalia and exciting tribal ceremonial costumes and masks (open summer Mon.-Sat. 1000-1630, Sun. 1200-1630, winter Tues.-Sat. 1200-1630). Wander over to the park across from the museum to see petroglyphs, hike the trails along the coast or up **Chinese Mountain** for great views of the island, canoe and fish the freshwater lakes, rent a boat and tackle and fish the coastline, or beachcomb and swim at **Rebecca Spit Provincial Park.** Finish yourself off with a luxurious stay at one of the fancy resorts or fishing lodges (see *Accommodations* booklet). The car ferry leaves from the Campbell River waterfront, just across from Tyee Plaza, about once an hour every day; schedule and fares are posted at the terminal (see "Transportation," below).

PRACTICALITIES

Accommodations

As Campbell River is a resort, every kind of accommodation you could possibly want is here, from campgrounds and RV parks to luxury hotels and exclusive fishing lodges. Refer to the *Accommodations* booklet, and call in at the InfoCentre for the useful handout "Campbell River and District Accommodation Guide," which lists all the details and prices.

Several RV parks are located along the main highway. These two are several km south of town, both overlooking Discovery Passage and providing level grassed sites, sewer, water, and electrical hookups, and all the usual facilities. **Lighthouse RV Park** is at 356 South Island Hwy., tel. 287-9914; $15-17 d. **Little Rock RV Park** is at 854 South Island Hwy., tel. 923-1057; $13-15 d.

For a motel with reasonable prices, try the **Super 8 Motel** at 340 South Island Hwy., tel. 286-6622. The rooms are large (wheelchair accessible), have more furniture than usual, and feature a water-and-mountain view of Discovery Strait and Quadra I. that's refreshing to wake up to; from $50 s, $54 d, $60 triple, including complimentary coffee. Toll-free reservations can be made in B.C. at (800) 843-1991.

Food

You can't go far in Campbell River without seeing a cafe or restaurant. The Tyee Plaza has several family-style restaurants worth trying, some with a view of the Quadra I. ferry coming and going across the strait (the docking process is fascinating on a stormy day when the wind is howling—restaurant patrons make bets on whether it will dock first try). **Mr. Mike's,** another family-style chain restaurant (also in the Plaza) serves burgers from $3.50, salad bar for $6 ($3 with a meal), fish dinners from $4.50, steaks from $6-12; open Sun.-Thurs. 1130-2100, Fri. and Sat. 1130-2130. For a light meal or a snack break between attractions, try for a seat at **The Coffee Shop** in the plaza—it's always crowded; open Mon.-Sat. 0800-1730, Fri. 0800-1900.

For good self-serve pub food, head for **The Willows Neighbourhood Pub** at 521 Rockland Rd. (off the main highway at the south end of town), tel. 923-8311. Open for lunch Mon.-Fri. 1130-1400, weekends 1200-1430, for dinner Sun.-Thurs. 1730-1930 and weekends 1730-2000. Barbecue Day, on Sun. 1730-1930, features steak, prawns, and salad bar for $13.95 pp. The Willows also has a beer and wine store. For much of the same fare, try **Royal Coachman Neighbourhood Pub** at 84 Dogwood St., tel. 286-0231, which also has a beer and wine store. It's an English-style country pub with an enclosed outdoor garden, serving fresh seafood. Lunch ranges $3.50-6, dinner $6.50-19. Open daily 1100-2400.

For good Greek food or tasty pizza, head for **White Tower Pizza, Steak, and Lobster** at 1920 Island Hwy., tel. 287-9011. They specialize in tangy Greek dishes ($9-16); a large combo pizza (more than enough for two) sets you back $13-16. Takeout, free delivery, and half portions are also available. Open Mon.-Thurs. 1600-0100, Fri. and Sat. 1600-0200, Sun. 1600-2200.

For fast-food restaurants, cruise Island Hwy. through town and you can't miss McDonald's, Dairy Queen, Kentucky Fried Chicken, and all the others. If you're looking for a nice place to dress up and go for a night on the town with your credit card, ask at the InfoCentre for their handout *Campbell River and District Restaurants Guide* which lists all the places to eat, the type of food served, the hours, and the price range.

Entertainment

At the end of an outdoorsy day in Campbell River, most visitors are too pooped to party. However, the locals whoop it up at the pubs, at **Peoples** off Ironwood St. (live rock 'n' roll), or **McFarr's Lounge** at the Anchor Inn on

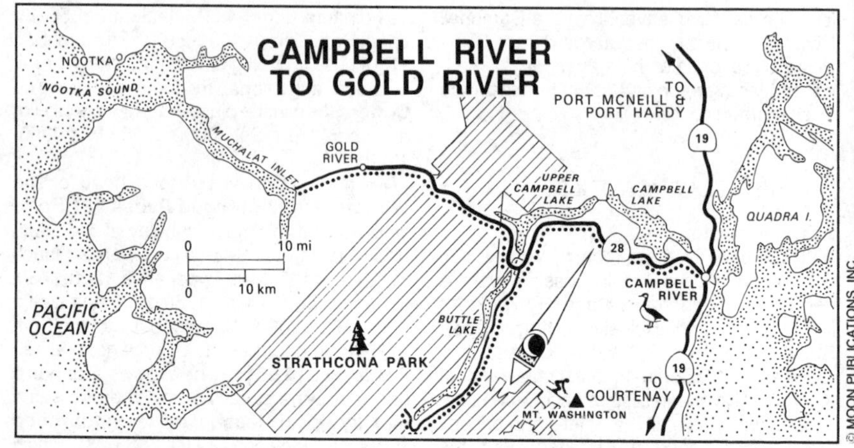

South Island Highway. (DJ and canned music; dress code). For symphony recitals, plays, operas, and live bands, the **Tidemark Centre** at 1220 Shopper's Row is the place to go—get a schedule of upcoming events at the InfoCentre. Movies are shown at the **Galaxy Twin** on 10th Avenue.

Information And Services

The **Chamber of Commerce Travel and Business InfoCentre** is one of the best InfoCentres on the island. Aside from tons of brochures, free tourist papers, and info on both the local area and Vancouver I. in general, the knowledgeable staff can answer just about any question on the area you could think up. It's open in summer every day from 0800- 2000, in winter Mon.-Fri. 0900-1700.

Aside from the **hospital** on 2nd Ave. and Birch St. and the **RCMP** at 908 Alder St. (tel. 286-6221), everything you need can be found in **Tyee Plaza**—banks, supermarkets, restaurants, etc. **Words and Music** in the middle of the plaza buys, sells, and trades fiction and Canadiana; open seven days a week to 1730, to 2100 on Friday. Next door is the **Campbell River Laundromat;** open every day 0800-2200, Sat. 0800-1800. The main **p.o.** is downtown, but there's also a branch in the back of **Island Images** gift shop at the south end of the plaza. If you're still in the mall mood, another to browse is **Ironwood Mall** on Ironwood Road. It's open Mon.-Thurs. 0900-1730, Fri. 0900-2100, and weekends 1000-1700.

Transportation

Island Coachlines runs daily north to Port Hardy ($38-85 OW, four hours), departing from behind the Royal Bank on Cedar St., tel. 287-7151. Some coaches connect with B.C. Ferries to Prince Rupert. Check the schedules carefully—they change season to season. Get around town by **Campbell River Bus Service,** departing from Tyee Plaza via Shopper's Row. Pick up a schedule in the InfoCentre or call 287-RIDE; adult $1, child 75 cents (have exact fare ready). The ferry to **Quadra I.** leaves from the dock across from Tyee Plaza daily, at least once an hour 0640-2330, with extra sailings on Fri. and Sat. nights. It leaves Quathiaski Cove at Quadra I. every hour 0615-2300. Buy your ticket at the vehicular entrance before boarding the ferry; car and driver $8, motorcycle and driver $5, adult walk-on $2.50, child half fare. No vehicles or passengers are carried on Tues. when dangerous cargo is aboard. **Budget Rent-A-Car** has an office on the main highway in the building at the north end of Tyee Plaza and another at the airport. The airport, serviced by several airlines, is off Erickson

Rd. on the south side of town, about a 20-minute drive from town center.

HIGHWAY 28

Passing from the east coast through the northern section of magnificent **Strathcona Provincial Park** to the west coast, Hwy. 28 is another island road worth traveling for the scenery alone. The central north section of the island is mountainous, heavily treed, dotted with lakes, riddled with rivers and waterfalls, and almost completely unsettled—only logging roads and logged slopes provide telltale signs that people have carved a route through the dense forests. It's quite a relief after the heavily populated southeastern fringe of the island!

The first place to stop is **Elk Falls Provincial Park,** six km northwest of Campbell River. Follow beautiful forest trails to waterfalls, swim, fish, and stay the night (April-Oct.) in a wooded campsite; $8 per night (no showers). Not far beyond the park, the highway passes Campbell Lake, Upper Campbell Lake, and **Strathcona Park Lodge and Outdoor Recreation Centre** before splitting to follow the east shore of Buttle Lake in Strathcona Park, a popular place with anglers, canoeists, and hikers.

Strathcona Provincial Park

British Columbia's oldest and Vancouver I.'s largest park, Strathcona preserves a vast tract of wilderness (231,000 hectares) in the northern center of Vancouver Island. Within the park lies **Golden Hinde** (2,220 meters) west of Buttle Lake, highest peak on the island; **Della Falls** drops 440 meters in three cascades in the southern section of the park, one of the world's highest waterfalls; and a 1,000-year-old, 93-meter-high Douglas fir stands on the Puntledge River in the south corner, the tallest known tree in the province. With a buildup like that, how could you miss exploring some of this park?! The valleys are carpeted in Douglas fir and western red cedar, the high slopes with wildflowers—lupine, Indian paintbrush, moss campion, and kinnikinnick. Watch out for roaming deer, wolverine, cougar, wolf, the island's last herd of elk, and all kinds of birds.

To get a taste of some of Strathcona's beauty, you only have to drive along Hwy. 28 to Gold River. To get into the park, take the turnoff halfway between Campbell River and Gold River. Follow the eastern shore of **Buttle Lake** to the end of the road. Many well-marked nature walks and hiking trails of varying distances lead off Hwy. 28 or the road by Buttle Lake. Park HQ (summer only) and two campgrounds with water, toilets, and firewood provided are located on Buttle Lake. For the complete rundown on the park and a map, pick up a park brochure at any InfoCentre, and if you're hiking the longer trails or attempting a cross-country route (not marked and only suitable for experienced, well-equipped hikers), buy topographic maps (sheets 92F/5, F/6, F/11, F/12, and F/13) from MAPS BC, Ministry of Environment and Parks, Parliament Buildings, Victoria, B.C. V8V 1X5. *Hiking Trails III, Central and North Vancouver Island,* published by the Outdoor Club of Victoria, has additional info on the hiking trails and cross-country routes in the park. Campbell River Travel InfoCentre also has all the details.

The only commercial facilities in this area are at **Strathcona Park Lodge and Outdoor Education Centre** on Campbell Lake near the Buttle Lake entrance (outside park boundaries). At the resort you can camp near the beach and use the bathhouse, sauna, and recreational facilities for $14-16 per vehicle per night, or stay in hostel-type accommodations (you'll need your own sleeping bag) with the use of a kitchen for $12 pp. Apartments with kitchens or one- to three-bedroom cottages range $52-85 s, $65-90 d or t, or you can rent an entire chalet that sleeps 20! They also serve breakfast, lunch, and dinner buffet-style in the dining room, rent all kinds of recreational gear, hire out instructors or guides, and organize wilderness adventure packages covering just about every outdoor sport you can think of. For more info write to Box 2160, Campbell River, B.C. V9W 5C9, or phone 286-8206.

Gold River
This town, at the western edge of Strathcona Provincial Park between the Gold and Geber rivers, was built in 1965 to house employees of a pulp mill, and was the first all-electric town in Canada. Today it has a hotel, restaurants, stores, gas stations, and banking facilities. Continue to the end of Hwy. 28 and take a tour of beautiful **Nootka Sound** on the MV *Uchuck III,* a converted WW II minesweeper. It runs several days a week year-round to settlements along Nootka Sound, dropping off supplies and passengers, ocean canoeists and kayakers. In summer you can take a trip back in time by visiting **Friendly Cove,** where Capt. James Cook and his men first landed and made contact with the Indians in 1778, and where negotiations occurred in 1792 between Vancouver and Bodega y Quadra over possession of Nootka Sound territory; adult $35 RT, child $17.50. Or take an overnight cruise to **Tahsis** or **Esperanza** for adult $45 RT, child $22.50, or **Kyuquot** for adult $50, child $25. Before planning on any of these cruises, check the current schedule in Campbell River or Gold River, and make reservations at 283-2325 (in B.C., tel. 800-663-1915).

NORTHERN VANCOUVER ISLAND

CAMPBELL RIVER TO TELEGRAPH COVE

Highway 19, covering the 238 km between Campbell River and Port Hardy, is a good, fast road with plenty of straight stretches so you don't have to poke along behind, or get tailgated by, the relatively little traffic you run across for very long. Passing through kilometer after kilometer of relatively untouched mountain, forest, and lake wilderness, with only logged hillsides to remind you of the ugliness man can produce with such ease, it's almost as though you've entered another world, or at least another island. Stop at all the frequent rest areas for the very best views of deep-blue mountains, white peaks, sparkling rivers and lakes (excellent reflection shots on a still day), and cascading waterfalls.

Faces And Food
Aside from innumerable photo stops, the first place to take a break is **The Valley of a Thousand Faces** at the junction (turn left) to the small logging and farming community of Sayward, about 67 km north of Campbell River. This used to be a rather remarkable park where more than 1,000 faces beautifully painted on cedar slabs hung from the trees. Though the park is now closed, the artist's gallery is still open to visitors. Feeling a bit peckish again? Take the road toward Sayward, stopping at **The Cablehouse Cafe,** housed in a unique steel-frame building made entirely from used logging cables. The food is reputedly worth the stop (closes at 2000 in winter). In summer the **Link and Pin Museum** opens next door, featuring artifacts from the valley's pioneering days.

Nimpkish Valley
Continuing north, the highway is one moment flanked by steep snowcapped mountains and gorgeous lakes, the next by bleak, desolate logged areas—the only human scars on a landscape of much natural beauty. In the Nimpkish Valley you pass the turnoff to **Mt. Cain Ski Area,** the closest downhill spot to Port Hardy (community operated, two T-bars, good for beginners) and **Schoen Lake Park. Hoomac Lake,** providing great reflection shots on a still day, has two forest trails leading off from the rest area. See the info board for an extremely detailed map of northern Vancouver I., showing the location of all the lakes, trails, logging roads, and campgrounds. The campsites are always situated in attractive forested areas or by beaches or boat-launching facilities and provided free of charge on a first-come, first-served basis. Each campsite has a parking and picnic spot,

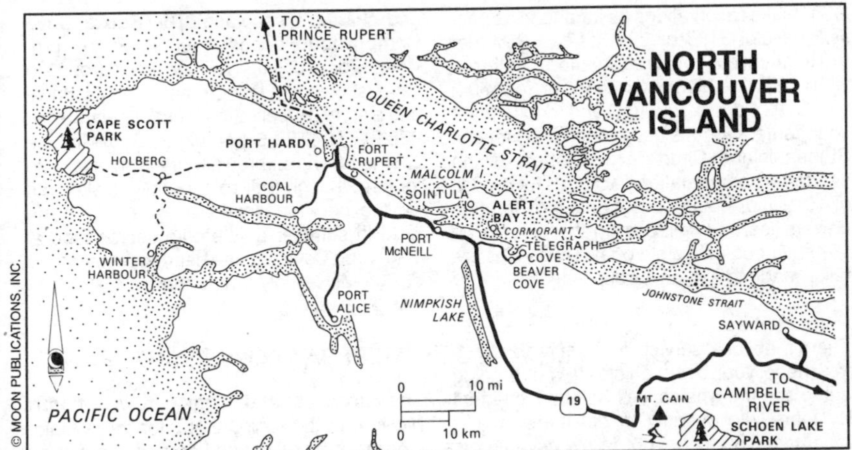

firepit, firewood, and garbage pick-up, and nearby you'll find pit toilets and a lake or stream for water.

TELEGRAPH COVE

For coastal scenery, abundant photo opportunities, fishing, diving, canoeing, and whalewatching in summer, take the turnoff, 53 km south of Port Hardy, to Beaver and Telegraph coves. The paved/gravel road takes you past a serene inlet to **Beaver Cove,** a log-sorting and -grooming facility where small boats arrange huge logs into booms for transport to coastal sawmills. At the end of the road lies the delightful village of Telegraph Cove, one of the last existing boardwalk communities on the east coast.

Built around a deep sheltered harbor, many of the Telegraph Cove cabins and homes stand on stilts and pilings raised above the water, linked by a boardwalk. Only 23 people permanently reside here, but the population swells enormously during late spring and summer when whalewatching, diving, and fishing charters do a roaring trade, canoeists and kayakers arrive to paddle 20 km down Johnstone Strait to Robson Bight, and the campground opens for the season. Walk along the boardwalk passing cabins, a small store selling groceries, fishing tackle and licenses, bait, gas, oil, and souvenirs, a gift store, a p.o., and **Stubbs I. Charters,** *the* place to go for whalewatching cruises and diving charters; the office is open five days a week 0900-1100, and Sat. 0900-1100, but over summer daily 0800-1600 and from July to early Sept. till 2200.

Whalewatching

Friendly Bill and Donna MacKay, two forerunners of the formation of **Robson Bight** as an ecological reserve to protect killer whale habitat, are part-owners of Stubbs Island Charters. They know everything known to date about killer whales. In summer Johnstone Strait is a playground for these magnificent, intelligent mammals; they come to Robson Bight to rub on the gravel beaches near the mouth of the Tsitka River. Jump on the *Lukwa* which departs daily from late June to early Oct. at 0900, for a day cruise. The experienced crew takes you out to see the whales in their natural habitat, to hear their mysterious and beautiful sounds through the underwater hydrophone, returning around 1400. Between mid-July and Labor Day they offer a second trip each day departing at 1500, returning around 2000. The cost of the cruise includes a hearty homemade meal; $60 adult, $54 senior or child (2-12), including

GST. Make reservations as far ahead as possible at 928-3185 or 928-3117 (a 25% deposit secures your reservation), toll-free within B.C. at (800) 665-3066, or fax (604) 928-3102; dress warmly, and don't forget your camera for this experience of a lifetime. Stubbs Island Charters also offers diving charter/accommodation packages for groups of 10 or more, and educational trips through universities and colleges on the *Gikumi,* an 18-meter coastal freight boat. These trips are tailor-made to suit any group.

Practicalities

There's no bus service to Telegraph Cove. You need your own vehicle. If you're going out to see the whales, call Stubbs I. charters for more info on how to get there, or get together with a couple of fellow adventurers and charter a seaplane! The **Bauza Cove Campground** opens in summer and provides wooded sites a short walk from the cove, showers, a laundromat, a boat launch, and a store. Reservations recommended, tel. 928-3131; $12-16 per night. Some of the cabins on the boardwalk are also available for hire, though they're generally booked out for the peak season—ask, you may be in luck! In summer a little cafe serves food at Telegraph Cove, but the nearest restaurant is at Port McNeill, 27 km northeast.

ALERT BAY, CORMORANT ISLAND

The small coastal logging town of **Port McNeill** is the regional HQ for three major logging companies and home of "the world's

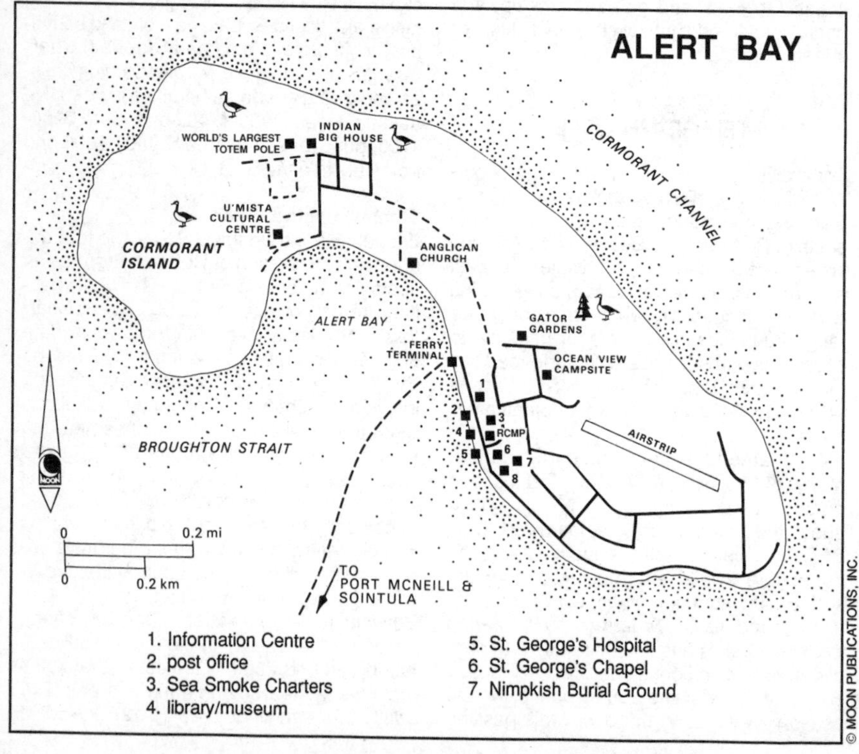

Nimpkish burial grounds

largest burl" on the main highway one mile north of town at the entrance to MacMillan Bloedel's logging company office—you can't miss it! The town is also the jumping-off point for Cormorant and Malcolm islands. If you have a day or more to spare, don't miss a visit to fascinating Alert Bay, a village of dual cultures where the population of 1,300 is 50% native, 50% white. A car ferry makes the 40-minute trip from Port McNeill many times a day (twice a day crowded with teenagers who attend high school at Port McNeill); adult walk-on $2.75 RT. For the current schedule phone 956-4533. Go prepared to stay longer than a day if you enjoy picturesque fishing villages and friendly people and have an interest in Indian art and culture.

A Busy Bay

Alert Bay has plenty of history. Since its discovery by Capt. Vancouver in the late 1700s, it's been a supply stop for fur traders and gold miners on their way to Alaska, a place for ships to take on water, and home base to an entire fishing fleet. Today the village is one of the major fishing and marine service centers in the region, with two fish-processing and -packing plants. Half the island is owned by Kwakiutl Indians—many visitors come to Alert Bay to appreciate their powerful art. Tourism, as another source of income, is being actively encouraged.

Attractions

All the numerous attractions on the island can be reached on foot—by bicycle is even better! Start your tour at the **Information Centre** on the waterfront (turn right when you leave the ferry); open in summer daily 0900-1700, in winter on weekdays 0900-1700. Wander through the village to appreciate turn-of-the-century buildings along the waterfront, and the colorful expressive memorial totems decorating **Nimpkish Burial Ground.** If you're interested in the history of the village and the Northwest coast, browse the displays in the Alert Bay Museum; open Mon.-Wed. 1900-2100, Fri. and Sat. 1330-1600.

For an outstanding introduction to the fascinating culture and heritage of North Island Native Kwakiutl Indians, do not leave this island without visiting the **U'Mista Cultural Centre.** It was built to house a ceremonial potlach collection confiscated by the Federal Government after the 1921 ban on potlatches and contains masks from the potlatch collection and prehistoric to modern Kwakiutl art and artifacts. Take a guided tour through the center for all the details, then wander at leisure past the photos and colorful displays to watch the two award-winning films produced by the center—one explaining the origins and meaning of the potlatch, the other called *The Box of Treasures*. The center is also used to teach local children the Indian language, culture, song, and dance. If you're lucky you'll see a group of tiny children dressed in ceremonial costume dancing with much concentration to the beat of the drum. The center is open throughout the summer Mon.-Fri. 0900-1700, Sat. 1200-1700, closed weekends in winter, tel. 974-5403; admission adult $2.40, senior $1.60, child 80 cents.

Other must-sees are the **Indian Bighouse, World's Largest Totem Pole** (the only way to photograph this is on your back!) and the historic century-old **Anglican Church.** Take a boardwalk stroll through the intriguing ecological area called **Gator Gardens** to see cedar, hemlock, and pine trees draped in old man's beard (a high-protein moss that can be boiled and eaten), salal, ghostly black-water swamps full of drowned white-barked cedar trees, and lots of ravens, bald eagles, and other birds. Gator Gardens is the kind of place where you wouldn't be too surprised to find an alligator suddenly surge out of the oil-black water, slither onto the boardwalk, and snap off your toes! Admission to this worthwhile attraction is free. If you're still looking for something to do, consider a whalewatching cruise (June-Sept.) with **Sea Smoke Sailing Charters** (tel. 974-5225); adult $65, child (5-14) $55.

Practicalities

Stay at **Oceanview Camping and Trailer Park** overlooking Johnstone Strait for $12 per night (all services and hot showers included), less for tenters, or at one of the two waterfront hotels from $40-45 s to $45-50 d. There are a couple of cafes and restaurants—ask locals for recommendations. Alert Bay has its own 39-bed **St. George's Hospital** on the main road. If you need a cab, call **Forty K Taxi** at 974-5525, or **T'Lisla** at 974-5577.

OUTDOOR RECREATION

The northernmost section of Vancouver I. seems to offer just about every outdoor recreational activity you can think of. Using Port Hardy as a base, you can take remote logging roads (restricted use during active logging) into the wilderness to discover your own virgin lakes and rivers (where fishing provides many an exciting moment). Visit **Coal Harbour,** a former whaling and air force center, **Holberg,** gateway to remote and totally undeveloped **Cape Scott Provincial Park** at the tip of the island, and the tiny fishing and logging community of **Winter Harbour.** For a 40-minute drive through beautiful forest and lake scenery, take the road off Hwy. 19 about halfway between Port McNeill and Port Hardy to **Port Alice,** a quiet logging and pulp-mill village on the edge of **Neroutsos Inlet.** It's a good place to go for fishing, scuba diving, boating, mountain climbing, camping, and caving. **Devil's Bath and Eternal Fountain,** reputedly one of the best caving areas in the North Island, lies close by; get all the details from the village info office, or InfoCentres in Port Hardy and Port McNeill. Despite a peaceful facade, Port Alice has all the facilities you need, plus one you hopefully won't need—a hospital with 24-hour emergency service.

If you have a reliable vehicle and you're feeling adventurous, get *way* off the beaten track by taking a 75-km winding logging road from Port Alice over the mountains to **Side Bay** and beautiful **Klaskino Inlet** on the west coast. A well-marked trail leads to a beach, or an eight-hour hike takes you to **Lawn Point.** Before attempting to drive or hike in this area, get a detailed map of all the logging roads from MacMillan Bloedel Ltd. (available at the InfoCentre and the museum in Port Hardy) or stop in at Western Forest Products' office at Port McNeill—without a detailed map, it's easy to get lost.

PORT HARDY

Port Hardy lies along sheltered Hardy Bay on the edge of Queen Charlotte Strait. It's the largest community in North Vancouver I., and the terminal for ferry traffic sailing the Inside Passage to Prince Rupert (on mainland B.C.) and Alaska. It's also a good base from which to explore the wild and untamed northern tip of the island, fish for salmon in the sheltered waters of "King Coho Country," or go diving, caving, or whalewatching.

Sights

As you enter the Port Hardy area, take the scenic route to town via Hardy Bay Road: past several original chainsaw wood carvings (look for the magnificent bear family outside **Jessie's Gifts and Gallery** and the eagle outside **Glen Lyon Inn,** both by Terry McKinnon), along the edge of peaceful Hardy Bay, past **Port Hardy Marina,** before entering downtown via Market Street. Call in at the **Chamber of Commerce Tourist Information** building on Market St. (across from Hastings) where the energetic staff will happily fill you in on everything there is to see and do in Port Hardy and the entire area. Collect maps (if you want to get off the beaten track, pick up the detailed logging road maps) and brochures, and you're ready to explore!

One of the most enjoyable things to do in town, starting at the InfoCentre, is to stroll along the **seawalk** to **Tsulquate Park** to appreciate Indian carvings, and beachcomb if the tide is out. A large number of bald eagles have addresses in Port Hardy, and if you're lucky you'll see them swooping about in the neighborhood. Along the way you'll see another chainsaw wood carving at **Watchman's Bay,** welcoming you to Port Hardy with representations of the fishing, logging, and mining industries that support the town, and **Carrot Park** with its unusual "Mile Zero Trans Carrot" sculpture. For years the residents of North Vancouver I. pleaded for a link with the populated south, a paved road across the 100 miles of wilderness that became known as the "Incredible Gap." Throughout the years various governments made promises and "dangled the carrot" but never came through with the money required to complete the task. Eventually north islanders launched a massive "Carrot Campaign," using every means to spread the word of their plight—until it became an item on national radio and TV. The government relented and they got "the rest of the carrot."

Another interesting place to spend a little time is the small **Port Hardy Museum and Archives** on Market St. across from Shipley Street. Browse through a variety of North Island artifacts and an old photograph collection, finishing up in the gift shop where you can buy T-shirts with Indian designs, silver jewelry, crafts by local artists, books, and postcards. In summer on Wed. evenings they put on films and talks. The museum is open Tues. through Sat. 1200-1630, tel. 949-8143; admission by donation.

To see some carvers in action, call in at the InfoCentre and check if it's okay to go out to **Fort Rupert Indian Village** and see **The Copper Maker,** Calvin Hunt and his family. They do spectacular northwest coast Native carvings, masks, bowls, totem poles, paintings, prints, and silver jewelry (much of their work is on display in museums worldwide), and you can buy pieces from their gallery. To get there, take the Island Hwy. south, then turn left on Byng Rd. toward the airport. Turn left on Beaver Harbour Rd., then take your first right and look for the Fort Rupert Big House at the entrance to the reserve. The Copper Maker is at 112 Copper Way.

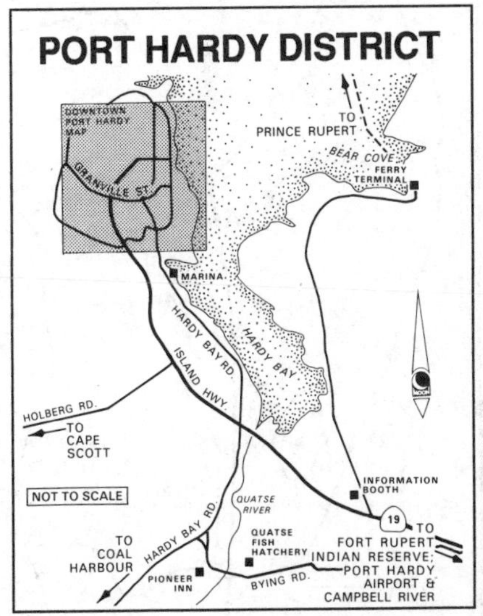

Outdoor Activities

If you like salmon, visit the **Quatse River Hatchery** to observe the incubation and rearing facilities for pink, chum, and coho salmon, and steelhead. It's located in the middle of a regional park on the scenic Quatse River, open weekdays 0800-1600, with nature trails and a campground (see below) nearby. The good fishing on the river attracts droves of fishermen year-round. In summer the campground is very busy, and the talk revolves around, you guessed it, river conditions, bait, weather, "It was a *monster* of a fish. . . ."

Of course this isn't the only place to go—chat with any of the fishermen and you'll hear about favorite spots all over the North Island. So much ocean and so many lakes and rivers surround Port Hardy, providing opportunities

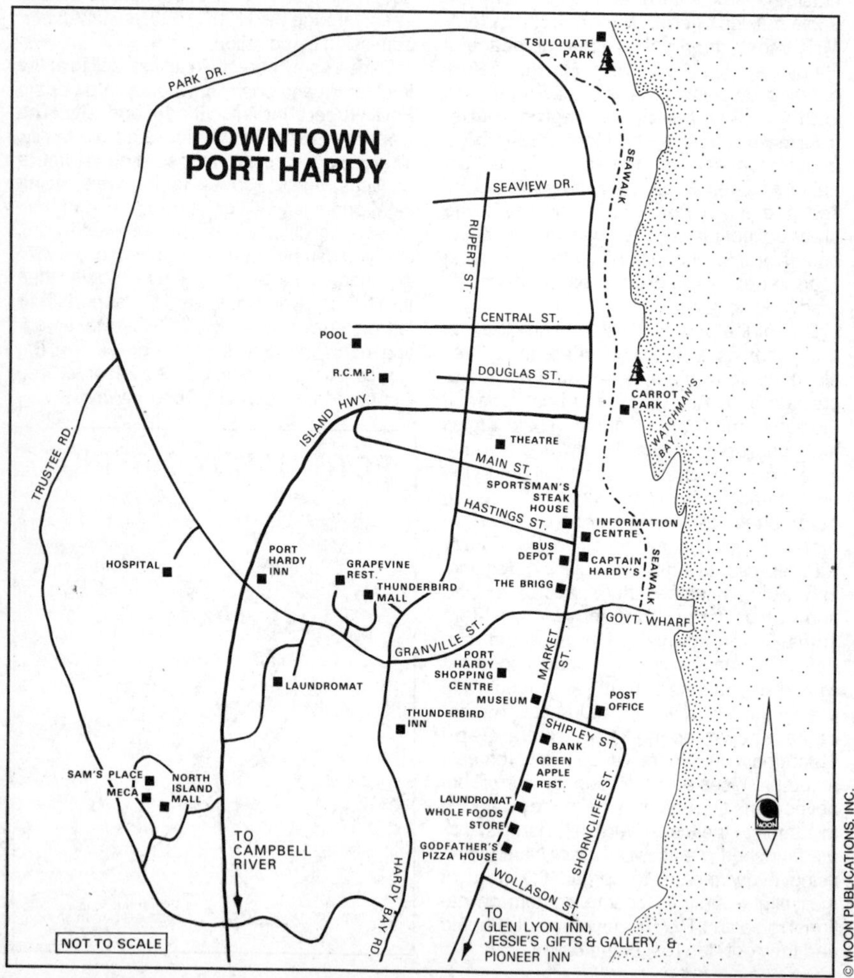

for saltwater and freshwater fishing, that you probably won't know where to start. So just start at the local sporting-goods store on Market St., or take a fishing charter—info available at the InfoCentre. And where there's good fishing, there's also good canoeing, kayaking, swimming, and scuba diving. Get the latest on diving charter operators, equipment rental, etc., at the InfoCentre.

Accommodations

Port Hardy has everything from campgrounds to luxury hotels (refer to the *Accommodations* booklet for complete listings). However, it can be difficult to find a bed on the night between ferry arrival and ferry departure. Advance motel reservations will save you some grief if you don't have a tent.

The closest campground to the terminal is **Wildwoods Campsite,** about three km along Bear Cove Rd. (on Forestry Rd., tel. 949-6753; $10 per night), but the best one for tents and natural surroundings is **Quatse River Campground,** one km south of town next to the salmon hatchery, providing endless fishing opportunities—catch a fish for every meal! Shady sites, showers, laundromat; $12 per night. Located off Hwy. 19 on old Hwy. 1 (take Hardy Bay Rd. out of town, cross Hwy. 19, continue to the totem pole and turn left); tel. 949-2395.

Pioneer Inn, also just across from the hatchery, has reasonable rates (very reasonable off-season rates, and you can rent the room by the week to save even more) and an excellent coffee shop, licensed restaurant, and laundromat on the premises; $44 s, $50 d, tel. 949-7271. If you're willing to pay for water views, try the **Glen Lyon Inn** at 6435 Hardy Bay Rd., tel. 949-7115. Large well-equipped rooms, great views, and a very good dining room on the premises; $50-55 s, $60-65 d, $68-73 t.

Food And Entertainment

Port Hardy does not have a lot to offer in variety of dining—wander around town and you'll soon see what there is. In the off-season the town is slightly comatose. For delicious breakfasts so huge that a two-meter logger would have difficulty finishing the hash browns, and fresh hot cinnamon rolls the size of Paul Bunyan's fist, head for **The Roadhouse Çoffee Shop** by Pioneer Inn (across from Quatse Fish Hatchery). For excellent lunches and dinners (try the chef salad with house dressing), go to the licensed dining room at the Glen Lyon Inn on Hardy Bay Road. If you're in luck, you'll see bald eagles feeding right outside the window! For more of a flashy affair and an excuse to dress up a little, try **The Brigg** for seafood and salad bar on Market St., or **Sportsman's Steak House** for steak, seafood, and salad bar ($9-30), also on Market Street. For entertainment, see what's playing at the **movie theatre** on Main St., try the public **swimming pool** off Island Hwy. by the municipal offices, or go to one of the bigger hotels for some drinking, dining, and entertainment.

Information And Services

The **Port Hardy and District Chamber of Commerce InfoCentre** is at 7250 Market St., tel. 949-7043 or 949-7622. Open year-round: Oct.-May on weekdays 0900-1700, June-Sept. daily 0800-2030.

The local **hospital** is on Douglas St. off Park Dr., tel. 949-6161. For a **doctor** call the clinic at 949-6514; an **ambulance** tel. 949-7224; for a **dentist,** call 949-9441 or 949-7153. **The RCMP** is off Rupert St., tel. 949-6335. For an excellent selection of Native arts and crafts, paintings, jewelry, scarves, carved bowls, masks, you name it, go straight to **Jessie's Gifts and Gallery** on Hardy Bay Rd. near the Island Hwy.; open in winter Mon.-Sat. 1030-1730, in summer daily 1030-1730.

Transportation

B.C. Ferries runs the spectacular trip up the Inside Passage to Prince Rupert every other day in summer at 0730, arriving in Prince Rupert at 2230; walk-on $80 OW, vehicle from $165 OW. Reservations are required—make them as far ahead as possible if you're taking a vehicle. In winter the ferry leaves once a week at 1600 with a stop at Bella Bella. Pick up a brochure and current schedule at the Port Hardy InfoCentre. If you're

Port Hardy marina

planning ahead (very wise if you're going in summer), call B.C. Ferries at (604) 669-1211 (Vancouver) and ask the operator to mail the latest schedule, fares, and reservation information.

The local **bus and taxi depot** is on Market St. at the corner of Hastings St., base for **North Island Transportation Services.** Head here for all your transportation needs—they arrange transportation to the ferry terminal (a limo costs $4 pp) and airport and take reservations for bus travel down the island with **Island Coach Lines.** The coaches coincide with ferries from Prince Rupert. Port Hardy to Campbell River by coach is $38.85 OW, to Nanaimo $56.40, and to Victoria (about 10 hours) around $70.05 OW, including GST. The office is open daily 0800-1800, tel. 949-6300.

CAPE SCOTT PROVINCIAL PARK

Cape Scott Provincial Park lies at the northernmost tip of Vancouver I., 15,070 hectares of untouched rugged coastal wilderness. It's the place to go if you really want to get away from everything—and everyone. Rugged trails, suitable for experienced hikers and outdoorsmen, lead through dense forests of cedar, pine, hemlock, and fir to 23 km of beautiful sandy beaches and rocky promontories and headlands.

To get to the park boundary, you have to follow 60 km or so of logging roads (remember that logging trucks always have the right of way), then hike in. The trail to **Cape Scott Lighthouse** takes about eight hours of pretty level walking—but you need stout footwear. One of the most popular trails takes only 45 minutes to walk to beautiful **San Josef Bay** (the locals affectionately call it "San Jo") at the southern boundary of the park. Before setting off for the park, pick up the park brochure at the InfoCentre, and detailed logging road maps for the area. Be well-equipped for unpredictable weather, even in midsummer. Enjoy!

LOUISE FOOTE

VANCOUVER

INTRODUCTION

Let your mind fill with the images of dramatic, deep-blue, snowcapped mountains rising vertically from a city's backyard, a mighty river slicing through its southern perimeter. Inner-city century-old buildings and steel and mirrored-glass skyscrapers facing the sheltered shores of a large wide inlet. Manicured suburbs perching along the edge of the Pacific Ocean, fringed by golden sandy beaches. Lush tree-filled parks and brilliant flower gardens overflowing with color. Flocks of striking Canada geese overhead, noisily honking to one another as they fly toward the setting sun.

Where else can you savor all this beauty as you don skis and swoosh down a steep mountain, bake on a beach, race across the harbor on a sailing boat, quietly stroll through a city park discovering ducks and polar bears, tantalize your taste buds at a fine restaurant, then whoop it up into the wee hours—*all in one day?* The answer: Vancouver—an alluring and unforgettable city. On the list with the best of them!

Carved Out Of The Wilderness

Today it's difficult to imagine the seemingly impenetrable forested wilderness that Capt. George Vancouver saw in 1792 when he cruised through the Strait of Georgia in search of a northwest passage to the Orient. Or the land that Simon Fraser, a fur trader and overland explorer for the North West Company, found in 1808 when he reached the Pacific via a river that was later named after him. A Hudson's Bay Company fur-trading post at Fort Langley, 48 km east of present-day Vancouver on the Fraser River, was the first attempt at settlement in 1827. But it wasn't until the discovery of gold up the Fraser in the late 1850s that settlement really began in the Lower Mainland. The town of New Westminster (just southeast of present-day Vancouver) became the first capital of

Vancouver city center lies along the sheltered shores of Burrard Inlet.

British Columbia in 1866. Two years later Victoria became the new capital.

With the establishment and subsequent failure of a brickworks ("Bricks? Why on earth make bricks when we've got all these trees?" said the Woodcutters' Union spokesman) on the south side of Burrard Inlet in 1862, followed by the successful establishment of sawmills and related logging and lumber industries, several boom towns were carved out of the wilderness. The first was the town of Granville (now downtown Vancouver) which the original settlers called Gastown after one of its earliest residents, notorious saloon owner "Gassy Jack" Deighton. In 1886 Granville became the City of Vancouver, but not long after, an out-of-control clearing fire roared through the timber city, burning just about everything to the ground. With true pioneering spirit Vancouver was rebuilt at lightning speed, and the following year, with the arrival of the first transcontinental train at Coal Harbour, it became the West Coast terminus for the Canadian Pacific Railway. Today, metropolitan Vancouver is Canada's third-largest city with a population of 420,000 (over 1.4 million in the Greater Vancouver Regional District), and the largest port on the West Coast of Canada; its 27 specialized terminals handle more tonnage than any other port in Canada.

Let's Explore!

Downtown Vancouver, almost surrounded by water, is an intriguing mixture of concrete, steel, polished granite and mirrored-glass skyscrapers, a number of architectural marvels, modern sculptures, old-fashioned fountains, and beautiful old buildings decorated with plaster unicorns, fish, and other designs from an age gone by. Yet, in the midst of the cityscape, there's a feeling of space. Look to the end of almost any of the streets bustling with people and traffic to catch glimpses of sparkling water and snow-dusted peaks. Look up to see mountains and clouds reflected in high-rise towers. And don't be surprised to find yourself joining other out-of-towner congregations at intersections, gazing and pointing, mouths ajar, at unexpectedly delightful views of sea and sky, or at pairs of Canada geese gracefully gliding through the maze of buildings (as though someone had just yelled "Are the geese ready? All right. And . . . Action!"), honking to one another only a few meters above the crowds.

Vancouver residents are fashion-conscious, sophisticated, fun-loving, friendly, and helpful—especially if you ask for it. Watch and you'll see people of all nationalities walking, jogging, cycling, driving, or waiting in bus shelters, pocket radios or tape players in hand, headphones in place. Listen and you'll hear a melodious assortment of languages and accents from around the world. It's an exciting place to be, yet a relatively safe place to wander, even on your own at night.

Whether you approach by land, sea, or air, view this gleaming mountain- and sea-dominated city for the first time on a beautiful sunny day and you're bound to fall for Vancouver in a big way. See it on a dull, dreary day when the clouds are low and Vancouver's backyard mountains are hidden and you may come away with a slightly less enthusiastic picture—you'll have experienced the "permagray," as residents are quick to point out with a laugh. But don't let the weather get you down—nobody else does! It doesn't really matter whether it rains or shines; nothing can dampen the outdoorsy atmosphere that pervades this city. Explore Vancouver and you'll discover all kinds of indoor and outdoor attractions, activities, good hiking and skiing in nearby provincial parks, and an abundance of lush greenery, manicured gardens, and rhododendrons everywhere you go. Allow a little extra time to soak up some of the city atmosphere. Savor the aromas of just-brewed coffee and freshly baked bread wafting from cosmopolitan sidewalk cafes, feast your eyes at the corner flower stands, join in the bustle at seaside markets, and relax in tree-shaded squares where the main pastime is people-watching.

SIGHTS

The Gentle Approach

If you're approaching the city from the south, don't know exactly where you're going, and are not quite ready to fight the traffic (or the abuse when you drive up one-way streets the wrong way), turn off Hwy. 99 immediately after the Oak St. Bridge and follow signs to Marine Drive. This meandering scenic route to city center is longer, quieter (but busy on weekends), and allows ample opportunities to pull off and consider a map.

Along Marine Dr. are trendy apartment blocks and condos, elaborate mansions with full-time gardeners, an assortment of golf, polo, and country clubs, then **Marine Drive Foreshore Park.** Around the tip of **Point Grey** you'll pass numerous entrances to the modern architecture and tree- and rhododendron-covered campus of the **University of British Columbia,** oldest and largest public university in the province. Within its grounds lie the **Botanical, Rose,** and **Nitobe Japanese gardens,** and the excellent **Museum of Anthropology** (see "Museums," below), all well worth a visit.

Once you reach the large parking lots and groomed sands of **Spanish Banks** and lush **Jericho Park,** the view—of West Vancouver and the steep snowcapped mountains across English Bay, the peninsula oasis of **Stanley Park,** and the cluster of central-city skyscrapers to the east—is nothing short of spectacular.

Where Marine Dr. meets 4th Ave. (the YH is a stone's throw from here), turn left. At Macdonald turn left, then right on Cornwall which takes you over Burrard Bridge into the city center. Still want to meander? Make a worthwhile stop at **Vanier Park,** home of **Vancouver Museum,** the **Planetarium,** and the **Maritime Museum.** From Macdonald turn right on Pt. Grey Rd., then left on Arbutus St. keeping Kitsilano and Hadden Parks on your left until you reach Vanier Park. After this stop it's a case of studying your map, taking a deep breath, then hopping across Burrard Bridge to find yourself smack in the middle of cosmopolitan Vancouver, with all its hustle and bustle, traffic, one-way streets, and metered parking.

Views, Views, Views

Aside from the excellent city views featured along Marine Dr., Vancouver has oodles of other viewpoints, many from the north side (see "North Vancouver" and "West Vancouver," below). But when you're downtown, head for tiny **Portal Park** on West Hastings

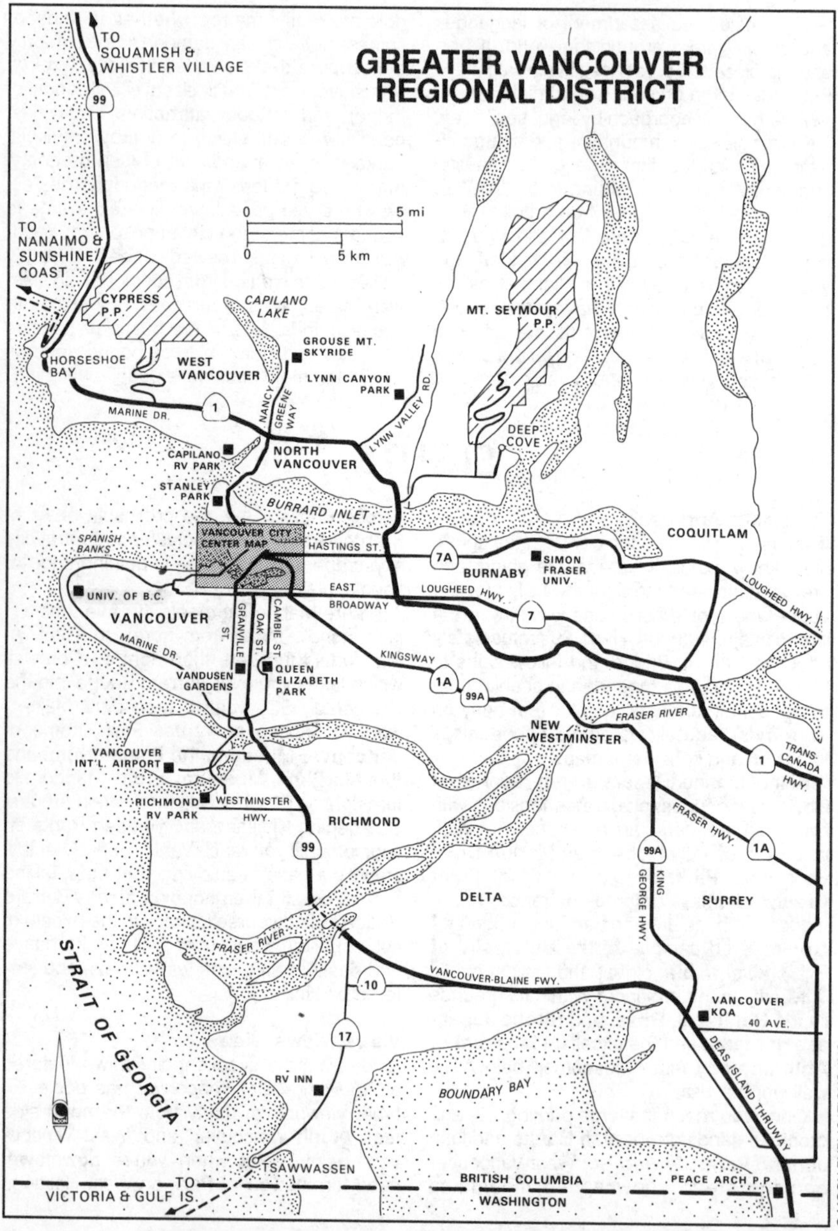

GREATER VANCOUVER REGIONAL DISTRICT

TO SQUAMISH & WHISTLER VILLAGE
99
0 5 mi
0 5 km
TO NANAIMO & SUNSHINE COAST
CYPRESS P.P.
CAPILANO LAKE
MT. SEYMOUR P.P.
HORSESHOE BAY
WEST VANCOUVER
GROUSE MT. SKYRIDE
LYNN CANYON PARK
LYNN VALLEY RD.
NANCY GREENE WAY
MARINE DR.
1
DEEP COVE
CAPILANO RV PARK
NORTH VANCOUVER
STANLEY PARK
BURRARD INLET
COQUITLAM
SPANISH BANKS
VANCOUVER CITY CENTER MAP
HASTINGS ST.
7A
SIMON FRASER UNIV.
BURNABY
LOUGHEED HWY.
UNIV. OF B.C.
EAST BROADWAY
LOUGHEED HWY.
7
VANCOUVER
GRANVILLE ST.
OAK ST.
CAMBIE ST.
MARINE DR.
KINGSWAY
VANDUSEN GARDENS
QUEEN ELIZABETH PARK
1A
99A
FRASER RIVER
NEW WESTMINSTER
TRANS-CANADA HWY.
1
VANCOUVER INT'L. AIRPORT
RICHMOND RV PARK
WESTMINSTER HWY.
RICHMOND
FRASER HWY.
1A
99
99A
KING GEORGE HWY.
DELTA
SURREY
STRAIT OF GEORGIA
FRASER RIVER
VANCOUVER-BLAINE FWY.
10
VANCOUVER KOA
40 AVE.
17
DEAS ISLAND THRUWAY
RV INN
BOUNDARY BAY
TSAWWASSEN
TO VICTORIA & GULF IS.
BRITISH COLUMBIA
WASHINGTON
PEACE ARCH P.P.

St., built over the top of the Sky Train Terminal. Sit beside the rhododendron and azalea bushes and absorb the view of Canada Place to the east, (see "Canada Place," below), Burrard Inlet, and North Vancouver on the far side of the water. The best time to head here is just before sunset when the sparkling white "sails" of Canada Place turn a soft, glowing pink—but expect to share the park with couples who are decidedly more interested in one another! For more great views of the port of Vancouver, walk the promenades of Canada Place and the seawall (or take the scenic drive by car or bus) around beautiful Stanley Park (see "Parks and Gardens," below).

For immediate orientation and a 360-degree bird's-eye view, catch the high-speed, stomach-sinking glass elevator up the outside of 40-story **Harbour Centre** to the enclosed **Observation Deck,** 167 meters above sea level. The elevator ride costs adult $5.35, senior or child (no children under six) $3.75 and includes a 15-minute multimedia screen presentation of Vancouver's highlights. At 555 West Hastings St. (near Richards St.; entrance from Mall Level), tel. 689-0421, open every day 0830-2230 in summer, 1000-1800 in winter. After visiting Harbour Centre you may want to visit Gastown (see below), a couple of short blocks away.

DOWNTOWN

Get Rid Of That Car!

Parking downtown is a major headache unless you know where all the parking lots are (as the residents do—expect them to be full) and are prepared to pay, or have a pocketful of quarters and don't mind feeding the meter every couple of hours. If you have a vehicle, stash it at your motel, at the YMCA, or in one of the downtown hotels' private lots, and walk. Or park it in one of the suburban "Park and Ride" lots (ask at any InfoCentre for the closest lot, or refer to the detailed Transit Guide map that comes with your Explorer Pass) and use the excellent public transportation network.

Robson Street Razzle-dazzle

If you like to shop in trendy boutiques, sample European delicacies, and sip cappuccinos at sidewalk cafes as you watch the crowds go by, saunter along colorful and exciting Robson St., also known as **Robsonstrasse** because the neighborhood was, at one time, predominantly German. At no. 1610 (the west end) is **Robson Public Market,** an impressive glass-atrium-topped building filled with meat, seafood, cheese, dairy products, fruit and vegies, nuts, flowers, craft vendors, fresh fruit juice and salad bars, and an upper-level international food fair (see p. 120). To get there catch bus three, which runs west along Robson St. from Granville Mall. Between the market and Burrard St. is the trendy Robsonstrasse shopping area, and at the east end you'll find **Vancouver Public Library** on the corner of Burrard.

Continue east along Robson to **Robson Square,** between Hornby and Howe streets, a large complex with indoor and outdoor restaurants, attractive tree-shaded squares and fountains, and in winter a skating rink. Across the street is the imposing classic courthouse, designed by Francis Rattenbury in 1911 (he also designed the Parliament Buildings and several other masterpieces in Victoria), which now houses **Vancouver Art Gallery** (main entrance on Hornby Street). On a sunny day during lunch hour the steps of the gallery crawl with partly bared business bodies soaking up rays, shoppers meeting for a chat, and visitors taking a seat in the heat to rest their sight-seeing feet. The gallery houses a large Emily Carr collection (a renowned B.C. artist), the work of other Canadian and international artists, and a children's gallery and puts on lecture series, guided tours, films, and concerts. It's open seven days a week; admission $4.25 adult (free admission Thurs. evening), $2.50 student or senior. Find out current hours by phoning 682-5621. The gift shop has a wide selection of art books, beautiful jewelry, and gifts, and the always-crowded gallery cafe is open daily 0600-1800, later on Thurs. nights.

VANCOUVER CITY CENTER

1. English Bay Café
2. Quilicum West Coast Indian Restaurant
3. Stanley Rentals
4. harbor ferries
5. Pharmasave and post office
6. Robson Public Market
7. Yangtze Mandarin Restaurant
8. railway yards
9. Drugmart and post office
10. Joe Fortes Seafood and Chop House
11. Royal Centre Mall
12. Monte Cristo
13. Le Crocodile
14. Bananas California Restaurant
15. White Spot Restaurant
16. YMCA
17. St. Paul's Hospital
18. Vancouver Aquatic Center
19. Vancouver Museum and Planetarium
20. Maritime Museum
21. Granville Island Market
22. Arts Club
23. Emily Carr College of Art and Design
24. Granville Island Hotel
25. Vancouver Scooter Shooter
26. Robson Square
27. Vancouver Public Library
28. Vancouver Art Gallery
29. Hotel Vancouver
30. YWCA
31. Tourism InfoCentre
32. Pan Pacific Vancouver Hotel
33. CN IMAX Theatre
34. Sky Train SeaBus Terminal
35. steam-powered clock
36. Old Spaghetti Factory and Brother's Restaurant
37. Maple Tree Square
38. Chinese Cultural Centre and Dr. Sun Yat-sen Classical Chinese Garden
39. post office/main branch
40. Queen Elizabeth Theatre
41. Greyhound Bus Depot
42. Sky Train/Stadium Station
43. Expo Theatre
44. BC Enterprise Centre
45. Science World
46. Sky Train/Main St. Station
47. VIA Railway Station

Canada Place

The stunning architectural curiosity with the billowing white teflon-coated "sails" on Burrard Inlet—the one that looks like it may weigh up anchor and cruise off into the sunset at any given moment—is Canada Place, Vancouver's impressive trade and convention center and cruise-ship docking facility at the foot of Burrard Street. It was built for Expo86 as the Canada Pavilion, but now houses Vancouver's Trade and Convention Centre, the luxurious Pan Pacific Hotel (the glass marvel with domed top), restaurants, shops, the CN IMAX Theatre at the far end, and a cruise-ship terminal which can berth up to five ships at one time. Start your self-guided tour at the InfoCenter at the front of the hotel (ask for a map), then allow at least an hour to wander through this impressive complex. For a free guided tour, call 688-8687. Don't miss walking the outside promenade (three city blocks in length) for splendid views of the harbor, North Vancouver, the Coast Mountains, and docked cruise ships. To get to Canada Place by public transportation, catch the Sky Train to Waterfront Station and walk west along Cordova—you can't miss it!

Gastown

If it's one of those permagray days, head for Gastown, the oldest section of Vancouver. The brightly painted restored buildings date from 1886 (before and after the great fire that demolished the city), old gas lamps line the tree-lined red cobblestone streets, and the galleries, restaurants, and overabundance of gift and souvenir shops along Water St. will make you forget the weather. Start at Maple Tree Square (junction of Water, Carrall, Powell, and Alexander streets) by the robust statue of **Gassy Jack,** the city's first saloon-owner, after whom Gastown was nicknamed, then saunter along Water St. (before 1100 to miss the crowds) to the world's first **steam-powered clock** on the corner of Cambie Street. Scottish lads and lassies won't want to miss the **House of McLaren** at 125-131 Water St. for the best of imported Scottish goods and candy from the mother country. For good meals, try **Brother's** or **The Old Spaghetti Factory,** both on Water St. (see "Food," below). To get to Gastown catch the Sky Train to Waterfront Station and walk east along Cordova to Water St., or catch bus no. 50 north from Granville Mall.

A LITTLE FARTHER OUT

Chinatown

Second-largest Chinese community in North America and one of the largest outside Asia, Vancouver's Chinatown is an exciting place any time of year. It's especially lively during a Chinese festival or holiday when the place hums with thronging masses following the ferocious dancing dragon, avoiding exploding crackers, sampling tasty tidbits from outside stalls, and pounding feet to the beat of the drums. It lies several blocks south of Gastown, along Pender St. from Carrall to Gore streets. Browse through intriguing stores selling everything from ginseng to windchimes, soy sauce to teapots, enormous bags of dried mushrooms and unrecognizable shriveled things to delicate paper fans. Admire the architecture, pagoda-roofed telephone booths, and painted signs. Eat in one of the multitude of restaurants. At the east end you can munch on genuine Cantonese-style cuisine, or wander appropriately west to sample tamer Chinese-Canadian dishes.

The **Chinese Cultural Centre** on Pender sponsors an assortment of exhibitions and displays varying from bonsai to watercolor paintings, and admission varies according to what's going on. Gardening enthusiasts won't want to miss the peaceful and harmoniously designed **Dr. Sun Yat-sen Classical Chinese Garden** to see the limestone rockeries, waterfall and tranquil pools, and variety of beautiful trees and plants hidden away behind tall walls at the back of the Cultural Centre. The garden, first authentic classical Chinese garden built outside China, was designed and built by artisans from the Chinese city of Suzhou, recognized for its green-thumbed residents and the gardens they produce. At 578 Carrall St., tel. 689-7133, open daily from 1000; admission $3.50 adult,

$2.50 student or senior. To get to Chinatown catch bus no. 22 north on Burrard St.—you'll know when you're there!

Science World

The impressive, 17-story, gleaming geodesic sphere that looks like a giant silver golf ball poised at the east end of False Creek on the southeast side of city center was **Expo Centre** during Expo86. Then, it housed info on the Expo theme, restaurants, shops, and two theaters (one an Omnimax, largest in the world). Today it's a Vancouver landmark and the home of Science World—a museum providing changing exhibitions that "introduce the world of science to the young and the young at heart," always featuring lots of hands-on displays, and an Omnimax film theater. Open daily 1000-1700, and on Sat. 1000-2100; $11 adult, $7.50 child, to Science World only (no film admission) $7 adult. Find out what's currently on by calling 687-7832. Located at 1455 Quebec St. at the west end of Terminal Ave., there's lots of parking available, but the easiest way to get there is via Sky Train to the Main St. Station, then walking across the street.

B.C. Place Stadium

Another Vancouver landmark, this 60,000-seat stadium with giant video screen and all-weather dome is the largest air-supported domed stadium in the world and the first covered stadium in the country. It's also the home of the B.C. Lions, one of the top Canadian Football League teams. For info on upcoming games, call the B.C. Lions office at 588-5466. The stadium is also the location for major shows, concerts, and other big events; for coming events call 661-7373. Located at 777 Pacific Blvd. in South Vancouver, tel. 681-3664. The easiest way to get there is by Sky Train to Stadium Station, or by buses 15 or 17 on Burrard.

Gregarious Granville Island

This refurbished, jazzed-up island, connected to the south side of city center by Granville Bridge, used to be the dowdy center of Vancouver's marine-based industries, but is now *the* place to go on a bright sunny day—allow at least several hours or an entire afternoon for this hive of activity (wear comfy shoes). Aside from just walking around the island looking at the marina, all the gift shops, the restaurants, and the theaters, don't miss the two galleries at the **Emily Carr College of Art and Design** and the **Kids Only Market.** One of the most entertaining places to browse is the colorful **Granville Island Public Market.** The market is open Tues.-Sun. 0900-1800 (Mondays as well in summer) and inside you'll find all kinds of things to eat, from fresh fruit and vegies to prepared ready-to-go meals and drinks, along with unique jewelry and crafts, potted plants, and cut flowers. Grab a tasty bite or a complete meal and take it out onto the wharf to enjoy all the False Creek harbor activity—in summer the water teems with sailing boats, small ferries, and barges, and if you want to participate in all the surface action yourself, rent your own rowboat, kayak, or windsurfer right there!

Start out at the island **Information Centre** at 1592 Johnson St., open daily 0900-1800. To get to the island take a False Creek no. 50 bus from Howe St. to the stop under Granville Bridge at the entrance to the island ($1.25 OW; ask the driver where to get off), or the Granville Island bus from downtown. An alternative route is via one of the fleet of False Creek ferries from Vanier Park (see below). Car parking on the island is monstrous, at best, especially on weekends when locals do their fresh-produce shopping. Unless you enjoy spending most of your time driving around the parking lot with skyrocketing blood pressure, take the bus or the ferry.

False Creek By Ferry

Jump aboard one of the small **False Creek Ferries** just for fun! It's an inexpensive way to see a portion of False Creek harbor. The boats run so regularly between Granville I. and **Vancouver Aquatic Centre** at Sunset Beach ($1 OW), and **Vanier Park** ($2 OW from the island), you can spend as little or as much time as you want exploring each place. At the Vancouver Aquatic Centre (1050

It's lots of fun putt-putting about False Creek by ferry—and inexpensive too.

Beach Ave., tel. 665-3424) swim in the large indoor pool ($2.70 adult) or work out in the fitness center ($3.20 adult), soak up some rays outside on the grassy banks, or explore the Sunset Beach area. At Vanier Park, visit the Marine Museum and nearby Vancouver Museum and Planetarium, but allow at least several hours to see both complexes (see "Museums," below). Return to the island for dinner and some theater entertainment to end a perfect day, but if you came by bus or ferry, check the schedules—the buses usually stop around 2400.

The West End

Pretty, park-fringed **English Bay Beach** is part of the section of Vancouver the locals call the West End. The golden sands, tree-shaded grass roadsides, and sidewalks are popular places to find poodle walkers, joggers, cyclists, and sun worshippers. Behind the beach lie upper-echelon condos and apartment blocks, homes with tidy gardens up quiet back streets, and trendy cafes and restaurants. Go on a Sunday to find large numbers of Vancouverites congregating there for brunch and an afternoon stroll along the bay. The more energetic head for the north end of the beach to walk the Seawall Promenade that runs right around the edge of magnificent Stanley Park—great views, nice beaches (all Vancouver's beaches lie along English Bay), and lots to see and do (see "Parks And Gardens," below).

MUSEUMS

Vancouver has many intriguing museums and galleries, large and small, general and specialized, scattered throughout—it could take you several weeks to see them all. For a comprehensive list, and methods of transportation to each, refer to the *Discover Vancouver On Transit* guidebook that comes with your Explorer Pass (pick one up at any InfoCentre or 7-Eleven store).

University Of British Columbia Museum Of Anthropology

If your interests include the first-class arts and crafts of the north Pacific coast Indian, the UBC Museum should be at the top of your list. Wander through the ultramodern concrete and glass building designed by innovative Canadian architect Arthur Erickson to view ancient majestic totem poles and intricate carvings, fabulous displays of jewelry, ceremonial masks, baskets, and a huge cedar carving depicting the legend of the raven and first humans. In the research area's visible storage gallery pull out drawer after drawer of thought-provoking objects. Allow at least a couple of hours here. At 6393

Northwest Marine Dr. (tel. 822-3825), the museum is open Tues. 1100-2100, Wed.-Sun. 1100-1700; admission $4 adult, $2 students and senior citizens, free admission on Tuesdays. If you have your own vehicle, go armed with a fistful of quarters and park in the lot beside the museum (watch for the sign), or get there by bus no. 10 from Granville Mall.

After exploring the interior, take a short stroll along the deliciously scented woodland path (left side of museum) to the back of the building to see a number of contemporary totem poles with descriptive plaques, and the reconstruction of a Haida village. Then cross Marine Dr. and follow the sign to the serene **Nitobe Memorial Gardens,** a traditional Japanese garden of shrubs and miniatures, only a short on-campus walk away. The entire campus is well worth exploring if you have the time—perfectly kept grounds overlooking Georgia Strait, rose gardens, beaches, theater, and aquatic center open to the public (for info on campus activities, call 822-3131), and lots of natural treed areas. In spring the air is thick with the perfume of lilacs.

Vancouver Museum

The history of the Lower Mainland from pre-Cambrian to modern times is brought to life in this museum—museum maniacs should allow a couple of hours here. Start in the West Coast Archaeology Gallery, then continue through the West Coast Culture Gallery with its ravishing masks, highly patterned woven blankets, and fine baskets you'd love to take home, and on into the Discovery and Settlement Gallery featuring British Columbia's exploration by land and sea. Browse through the forestry and milltown displays and the metropolis of Vancouver, ending up in the gallery of changing exhibitions where you never know what you'll find. A self-serve restaurant, overlooking the park, and a gift shop are also located within the complex. The museum is at 1100 Chestnut St. in Vanier Park, tel. 736-7736, open Tues.-Sun. 1000-1700, in summer (May-Sept.) daily 1000-1700; admission $5 adult, $2.50 child, free on Tuesdays. If you're also visiting the Maritime Museum (see below), buy tickets for both and save $1. To get there catch bus no. 22 on Burrard and get off after Burrard Bridge at the Cornwall and Chestnut St. stop, or catch a ferry from Granville I. or the Aquatic Centre at Sunset Beach to Vanier Park. If you have a vehicle there's plenty of free parking.

Above the museum is the **H.R. MacMillan Planetarium.** Galaxy-gaze at 1430 and 2000 Tues.-Sun., additional shows at 1300 and 1600 on weekends and holidays; admission $4.50 pp. One of the most popular events at the Planetarium is the laser rock music show Tues.-Sun. nights at 2130, with additional shows at 2245 on Fri. and Sat. nights; $6 pp—buy your ticket in advance to avoid disappointment. Call the info line at 736-3656 to hear what's happening. Next to the museum is the **Gordon Southam Observatory,** open Fri., Sat., and Sun. 1200-1700 and 1900-2300 when the skies are clear; admission is free.

Vancouver Maritime Museum And *St. Roch*

Shiver me timbers! Everything a seafaring person could wish to know about British Columbia's big drink—from its first sea explorers and their vessels to today's oceangoing adventurers, modern fishing boats, and fancy ships—is all in this museum. The historic RCMP vessel St. Roch, first patrol vessel to circumnavigate the Northwest Passage and now a National Historic Site, is dry-docked within the building, and admission includes a tour. If you sailed up in your own vessel, moor it at Heritage Harbour right behind the museum. Located at 1905 Ogden Ave. (the end of Cypress Ave.) in Vanier Park, a five-minute stroll from Vancouver Museum, it's open daily 1000-1700, in summer 1000-1800; admission adult $4, child, student, or senior citizen $2.50. If you buy a ticket to both the Maritime complex and Vancouver Museum, admission is $6 adult, $2.75 child. Get there by car, bus no. 22 from Burrard St., or ferry from Granville Island. Anchors aweigh!

PARKS AND GARDENS

Stanley Park

Beautiful Stanley Park, a lush 405-hectare tree- and garden-carpeted peninsula jutting out into Burrard Inlet, is a sight for sore eyes in any weather—an enormous peaceful oasis sandwiched between city center's skyscrapers and commotion, and North Vancouver at the other end of Lion's Gate Bridge. It was named after Lord Stanley, Canada's governor general 1888-93, who had the foresight to preserve the peninsula as a park "for all time."

Walk the 10-km **Seawall Promenade** or cycle or drive the perimeter via **Scenic Drive,** drinking in water and city views and stopping at the Lost Lagoon Bird Sanctuary, totem poles, nine o'clock gun, *Girl in Wetsuit* statue, SS *Empress of Japan* figurehead, and Pauline Johnson Memorial, to finish up in the Teahouse Restaurant. Saunter along many of the peaceful, forested trails that crisscross the park or along the edge of Lost Lagoon to appreciate the resident waterfowl—mallards, Canada geese, and swans abound amongst the yellow-iris-edged shoreline, and in spring fluffy ducklings and goslings are everywhere. Don't miss the **zoo** where you can see everything from cheeky river otters that really put

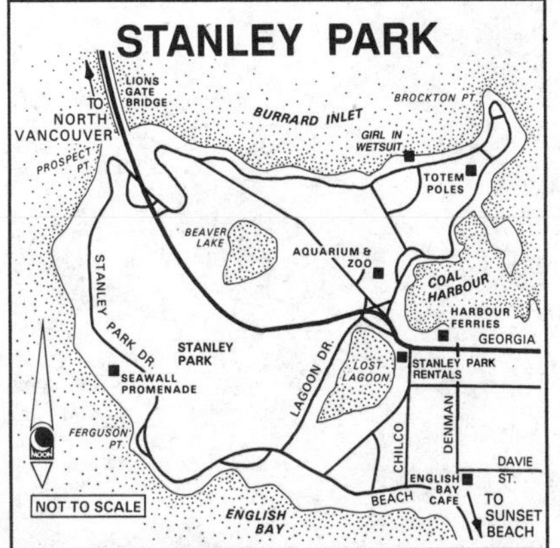

Canada goose in Stanley Park

on a show to lethargic polar bears panting in the sun (open daily 1000-1700; admission free), and **Vancouver Aquarium** which contains more than 8,000 aquatic animals from around the world (open 19 March to 17 June 1000-1800; admission adult $8, child $7). On the weekends or during bouts of permablue weather, the zoo and aquarium are good places to meet locals.

If you have a vehicle, finding a place to park can be difficult in summer, especially in the areas closest to the zoo and aquarium. Enjoy walking? Park in the lagoon area and take a brisk 15-minute lakeshore walk to the zoo—along with most of Vancouver's population, especially on a sunny weekend. The best way to see the park aside from walking every inch is to bicycle around it. If you don't have two wheels, no worries, you can easily rent from one of several outfits. **Stanley Park Rentals** is located near the entrance to the park at 676 Chilco St., tel. 681-5581. They rent one-, three-, and five-speeds (starting at $5 per hour), cruisers, tandems, and 21-speed mountain bikes (from $7 an hour); open in winter 0900-1800 and summer 0800-2100. The bus system also operates within Stanley Park on summer weekends (end of April-Oct.). To get to the entrance any day of the week, catch bus no. 19 on Pender. On good weather weekends and holidays (no service on rainy days) transfer onto bus no. 52 Stanley Park Loop—get on and off at all the stops; a free transfer from the last bus, but $1.25 adult, 60 cents student, senior, or child if you only take this bus ride.

Queen Elizabeth Park
On the south side of Vancouver, Queen Elizabeth Park is a 53-hectare gardener's paradise of sweeping lawns, trees, and flowering shrubs, formal flower gardens, and masses of rhododendrons (a vivid spectacle in May and June). An added bonus is the magnificent view of Vancouver and the Coastal Mountains from the top of 152-meter **Little Mountain,** highest spot in the city. Admission to the park is free. Stroll through the large, circular, domed **Bloedel Conservatory** to appreciate an exotic profusion of flowering plants, multihued resident parrots and tiny birds thriving in this temperature-controlled, humid tropical jungle; open daily 0900-1700, admission $2.80 adult, $1.40 students and senior citizens. A cafeteria, open 0930-1800, and **The Quarry House Restaurant** also lie within park grounds; located between East 33rd Ave. (entrance) and Cambie in South Vancouver, it's open daily. To get there take bus no. 15 south on Burrard.

Vandusen Botanical Gardens
These 22-hectare gardens in South Vancouver are the city's answer to Victoria's Butchart Gardens, but on a smaller scale. Feast your eyes on over 1,000 varieties of rhododendrons (the display in the parking lot alone is spectacular in May), roses, all kinds of botanical rarities, an Elizabethan hedge maze, and children's garden with hedges trimmed into animal shapes. The gardens are on 37th Ave. (entrance) and Oak St., open daily in summer 1000 to dusk, in winter 1000-1600; admission $4.25 adult, $2.15 students and senior citizens. Also within the complex are a gift shop selling cards, perfumes, soaps, potpourri, and all kinds of gifts with a flower theme, and popular **Sprinklers Restaurant.** The light and airy decor, picture windows, and view of the gardens bring the outside inside. It's open 1130-1500 (reasonable prices) and 1730-2200 (more expensive; people tend to dress for the occasion), weekend brunch 1030-1500; reservations recommended. To get there take bus no. 17 on Burrard.

TOURS

If you don't have a lot of time to explore Vancouver on your own, consider one of the many tours available—they'll maximize your time and get you to the highlights with minimum stress. To find out all that's available and the prices, and to make bookings, go to any of the Tourist InfoCentres.

Gray Line Of Vancouver's wide variety of tours start at around $32 adult, $15 child, as well as day-trips to Victoria on Vancouver

Bloedel Conservatory in Queen Elizabeth Park

Island. Drop by their office at 108-900 West Georgia St., or call 681-8687. **Landsea Tours** also conducts tours of Vancouver (and Victoria) starting at $28 adult, $15 child; 2596 Pandora St., tel. 255-7272. **Pacific Coachlines** runs a number of Vancouver tours. Tour number one gives you a brief introduction to the city for adult $19.25, senior $17.15, child half adult fare. The number-two tour is 3½ hours; adult $30, senior $26.75, child half. The third tour roams the North Shore in just under five hours; adult $40.65, senior $37.45. The fourth tour is a combination of numbers one and three, takes all day, and costs adult $53.50, senior $48.15. All tours depart from the Vancouver Bus Depot at 150 Dunsmuir St. (also pickup at selected hotels; tel. 662-7575 for times). The morning tours leave at 0930, and afternoon tours at 1345.

From June to Sept. take a **Harbour Ferries** 1½-hour tour of Vancouver's bustling harbor on the paddle wheeler MV *Constitution* from the north foot of Denman St.; $18 adult or $23.50 (with lunch), $15 child. For more info, phone 687-9558.

NORTH VANCOUVER

To explore the many outdoor attractions and activities in North Van (one of the most active port areas in Vancouver) and West Van, cross Lions Gate Bridge from the north end of Stanley Park, or Second Narrows Bridge from Burnaby, catch a bus, or take the SeaBus from city center to Lonsdale Terminal on the north side of Burrard Inlet. Several provincial and regional parks provide the outdoor adventurer with fabulous mountain, canyon, and river scenery, plenty of hiking trails over varied terrain, and some excellent downhill and cross-country skiing. If you go over to the north side by ferry, connecting bus service will get you to most of the sights.

Lonsdale Quay Market

One of the most entertaining ways to get to North Van from downtown Vancouver is by SeaBus (adult $1.25, child 55 cents RT, or $1.75 and 90 cents in rush hour; see p. 128), and when you get there, one of the liveliest North Van attractions is right next to the SeaBus Terminal—**Lonsdale Quay Market.** It's an excellent place to watch people watching people. Locals come here to stock up on fresh fruit and vegies, fish, meats, bread, flowers, and plants, to meet friends over a coffee, or to take time out from shopping with a quick bite to eat, a cool drink, and a stunning harbor view from one of many in- or outdoor tables. Aside from all the fresh produce and food booths on the ground floor, gift shops and boutiques offer an endless array of shopping possibilities on the second floor, and on the third is the entrance to **Lonsdale Quay Hotel** (see p. 119) and **Tug's Cafe Bar** (a trendy nightclub and bistro). At the SeaBus Terminal and Bus Depot is a handy info booth where it's easy to find out exactly how to catch public transportation to just about anywhere you want to go on the north side.

Capilano Suspension Bridge And Park

Capilano Park in North Vancouver was first opened in 1899 with a remarkable wood and hemp bridge spanning 137 meters across the canyon. Today, several bridges later, the deep canyon is spanned by a wood and wire suspension bridge a fearsome 70 meters above the Capilano River. Allow 30 minutes to explore the park, cross the bridge (billed as one of the many "eighth wonders of the world"), walk the nature trails on the other side of the bridge, view the totem-pole carvers in action in summer, and browse the requisite gift shop. Open daily in summer 0830-2030 (illuminated in the evening), winter 0900-1700; adult admission $5.50, senior $4, student with ID $3, child $1. (Also see "Lynn Canyon Park," below.) To get there by car, cross Lions Gate Bridge to Marine Dr., turn left on Capilano Rd. and continue to no. 3735 on your left. By bus: catch no. 246 Highlands west on Georgia Street. In summer take the SeaBus to Lonsdale Quay, then bus no. 236.

Capilano Salmon Hatchery

If you've always wanted to know more about the miraculous life cycle of a salmon, or want some reel facts to back up your fish stories, visit this hatchery on the Capilano River, the first fish farm in the province. Along with educational displays and nature exhibits, you can see what the fish see from an underwater point of view. From July through Oct. magnificent adult coho and chinook salmon fight their way upriver to the hatchery. At 4500 Capilano Park Rd.; admission is free. Get there by car, bus, or SeaBus and bus (see "Capilano Park," above). A little farther north is **Cleveland Dam** (Capilano Rd. becomes Nancy Greene Way) which was built in 1954 and resulted in the formation of Capilano Lake—Vancouver's main drinking water supply. Good hiking trails in this northern section of Capilano Canyon Park.

Grouse Mountain

You don't have to be a ski bum or bunny to enjoy Grouse Mountain. For an excellent view of the inner city, Stanley Park, the bay, and North Vancouver, continue up Nancy Greene Way following signs to Grouse Mt., then hop on the **Skyride Gondola** for an almost vertical eight-minute ride up the 1,250-meter peak to the ski area. The gondola runs year-round, departing in summer every 15 minutes weekdays 1000-2100, weekends and holidays 0900-2100; adult $12.75, senior citizen $10.50, child $6.50. At the top are paved paths, mountain meadows, nature trails, and hiking access to the rugged West Coast Range. In July the World Invitational Hang Gliding Championship takes to the air from these slopes and in summer you can often watch hang gliding demos. In winter, skiers can choose from beginner to advanced runs, with the added magic of nighttime illumination. World Cup Ski Racing is held here in March.

For a bit of extra excitement when you get to the top, get a bird's-eye view of Vancouver with a **Grouse Mountain Helicopter Tour.** The five-minute tour costs $30 pp and the 10-minute $55 pp, lifting off daily from 1100 to sunset, weather permitting. For more info call 525-1484. Grab a bite to eat at the **Mountain Bistro** and drink in some high-elevation sunshine along with the view on the outdoor deck (open daily 1100-2400), or enjoy dinner in the fancy **Grouse Nest Restaurant** (free Skyride ticket up with dinner reservations), open daily 1700-2130, or view a film in the **IMAX Theatre.** Access to Grouse Mountain is at 6400 Nancy Greene Way, tel. 984-0661. To get there by car go to the end of Nancy Greene Way; by bus, take no. 246 Highlands west on Georgia St. to Edgemont Village, then no. 232 Queens to Grouse Mountain.

Lynn Canyon Park

The suspension bridge in this park, though much shorter and lower than Capilano Bridge, is just as exciting, has fewer visitors, and is free. It crosses the impressive tree-edged Lynn Canyon 80 meters above Lynn Creek and its waterfalls, and gives access to a number of trailheads (the various hiking trails range from 15 minutes to 1½ hours OW). Also visit **Lynn Canyon Ecology Centre** where displays, models, and free slide shows and films explore plant and animal ecology; open 1000-1700, admission free. A concession stand sells snacks and hamburgers. To get there by car, take the Lynn Valley Rd. exit off the freeway and look out for signs, then right on Peters Road. By bus, take the SeaBus to Lonsdale Quay, then bus 228 or 229.

Mount Seymour Provincial Park

By car or bike (if you enjoy long, torturous hill climbs), take Mt. Seymour Parkway off Hwy. 1/99, then turn up Mt. Seymour Rd. (about a 30-minute drive from city center) to enter the 3,508-hectare semi-wilderness of Mt. Seymour—closest provincial park to Vancouver. In winter go for the excellent downhill and cross-country skiing, and snowshoeing. Year-round go for the outstanding views of Vancouver, short trails and day-hikes, and mountaineering. The 12-km drive through stands of timber (some trees over 2,000 years old) from the park entrance to the base of the alpine area (1,006 meters) is a good trip for the views alone. At the top is **Mount Seymour Cafe** (open in summer weekdays 1000-1600, weekends 0900-1700), an Info-Centre, ski rentals, restrooms, hiking trails (one takes you up to the 1,453-meter summit of Mt. Seymour for an outstanding panoramic view), and a summer **chairlift** to alpine meadows. The chairlift operates only in July and Aug 1100-1700 daily, and on weekends in Sept. and Oct., weather permitting. For more info call 986-3444.

If you continue along Mount Seymour Parkway instead of turning up toward the park, you end up in the scenic little village of **Deep Cove** on the west shore of Indian Arm (northeast end of Burrard Inlet)—an excellent spot to take a picnic to the waterfront park and watch the fishing and pleasure boats coming and going in the bay, and maybe to swim, scuba dive, or go water-skiing (you'll need your own gear). If you're there in the evening, try the bistro bar (reasonable) or the **Savoury** restaurant (more expensive) on Gallant.

WEST VANCOUVER

Cypress Provincial Park

This is another park to visit for magnificent views of Georgia Strait (separating Vancouver I. from the mainland)—and if you have industrial-strength binoculars and a vivid imagination, maybe you'll spot *Say-noth-kai,* the two-headed sea serpent of Salish Indian legend, believed to inhabit the strait. On a clear day you can also make out the snow-capped cone of Mt. Baker, one of a row of Pacific coast volcanoes, to the southeast. In summer hike along well-marked trails, spread out a picnic in a mountain meadow full of wildflowers, or ride the **chairlift** (July- Sept.) to the top of Black Mountain (1,220 meters).

In winter head up to Cypress Bowl for plenty of downhill skiing thrills (1,700 vertical feet and 18 runs) and 26 km of scenic groomed cross-country trails (call 926-5612 Mon.-Fri. 0900-1630 for more info and current rates). Relax on the licensed sundeck or replenish your calories in the restaurant. In winter during school holidays, a bus departs from White Rock, Delta, Richmond, and Vancouver and runs up to Cypress Bowl—book at least one day in advance at 926-8644. To find out if any events are happening in the park, call the Fun Line at 926-6007.

Horseshoe Bay

A pretty little residential area appreciated by visitors coming and going on B.C. ferries to Vancouver I. or the Sunshine Coast, Horseshoe Bay has plenty to see and do while you wait for the ferry. If you and your trusty vehicle are catching one of the ferries, buy your ticket at the car booth, move your mobile into the lineup, then explore the town. Several restaurants, a bakery, supermarket, pub, and a couple of good delis cater to the hungry and thirsty. A stroll along the waterfront marina taking in the beauty of the harbor (don't forget your camera) is a good way to cool your heels and dwindle away some waiting time.

ACCOMMODATIONS

Whether you're looking for a tent or RV site, hostel, bed-and-breakfast guesthouse, motel, or luxury hotel, Vancouver has accommodations to suit your every whim, and all budgets. The best places to get all the accommodation info in one shot are the Travel InfoCentres, located along all the main routes into Vancouver, and at the main Vancouver Travel InfoCentre, Pavilion Plaza, Four Bentall Centre, 1055 Dunsmuir St., tel. 683-2000 (see p. 125). Collect accommodation listings for Vancouver and the entire province, and choose from a good selection of brochures provided by owners; the staff will make bookings, too. And if you haven't already, pick up the free *Accommodations* guide put out by the Ministry of Tourism. If you show up in late spring or summer without reservations, you may find all the best places, and definitely all the most reasonable, booked for the season. If you know where you want to stay in advance, make reservations as far ahead as possible.

CAMPGROUNDS

There are no campgrounds in the city center, but a limited number are found in suburbs along the major approach routes. Before trekking out to any of them from the city, check with the nearest InfoCentre to make sure they still exist, and then get directions.

Provincial Parks

Many provincial parks in southwestern B.C. provide campsites (overnight fee $6-8) or wilderness walk-in camping areas, but at the favorite parks, you need to grab your spot early in the day or you'll miss out (they don't take reservations). The established campsites have a picnic table, a fireplace and wood, a source of fresh water, and a pit or flush toilet; some put on ranger-guided nature walks and lectures in summer. For more info on South Coast Region B.C. Parks, call 929-1291.

In **Mt. Seymour Provincial Park,** 15 km northeast of downtown in North Vancouver, alpine camping is allowed north of Brockton Pt.—check first with park personnel at headquarters just up the road on the right from the entrance. In **Cypress Provincial Park,** 12 km northwest of downtown in West Vancouver, wilderness camping is permitted above the ski areas and along the Howe Sound Crest Trail (no open fires; take a stove).

Commercial Campgrounds

The closest campground to inner-city attractions is **Capilano Mobile Park.** It has a good location on the north side: just across the Lions Gate Bridge from Stanley Park, next to the Capilano River (salmon run in July and Sept.), across the road from **Park Royal Shopping Centre,** and a 10-minute drive from Horseshoe Bay (B.C. Ferry Terminal). However it's only suitable for vehicle camping and RVs (limited spots for tents), and it's crowded in summer. Advance reservations are required (prepayment by money order) for July and August. If you want a tentsite, call ahead and ask if they have any grassy areas left. A site ranges $18-28 d per night with electricity, water, and sewer included, $3 each additional person; $5 deposit for washroom key, free showers, coin-op laundry. Located at 295 Tomahawk Ave., North Vancouver (direct access from Hwy. 1/99), tel. 987-4722. To get there from city center, cross Lions Gate Bridge and turn right on Marine Dr., right on Capilano Rd., right on Welch St.; from Hwy. 1/99 in West Van, exit south on Taylor Way toward the shopping center and turn left over the Capilano River.

The closest campground suitable for both tents and vehicles is the large **Richmond RV Park and Campground** in Richmond, a 20-minute drive south of the city (a 10-minute walk from a main bus route to downtown). Immediately across the road from the park is the Fraser River. The dyke that protects the road from flooding has an eight-km footpath that runs along the North Arm of the Fraser and is extremely popular with local walkers, joggers, dog-exercisers, cyclists, and seaplane and jet enthusiasts (the seaplane terminal is within sight, and the campground is just off the final flight path for Vancouver International Airport). Grassy banks and strategic benches encourage quiet reflection on a bright sunny day. A tentsite with no hookups starts at $13, $17-20 RV site with hookups (sewer additional $3). Free showers, coin-op laundry, games room. Located at 6200 River Rd. (corner Hollybridge Rd.), Richmond, tel. 270-7878.

If you're coming or going from Tsawwassen Ferry Terminal, **Park Canada RV Inns** (next to **Splashdown Park** waterslides) on Hwy. 17 is convenient for ferry traffic (a 30-minute drive south of city center), but crammed with RVs in summer (open 1 April to 31 October). Heated pool, store, laundromat, lounge, free showers; $12-18 for two, additional persons $1-2. To get there follow signs to Victoria Ferry on Hwy. 17 and take the 52nd St. exit; tel. 943-5811.

If you're coming into Vancouver from the south through Surrey, the **Vancouver KOA** is popular for its grassy tent area and large pull-through RV area with hookups. Heated pool, coin-op laundry, store, recreation room, miniature golf, bicycles for rent, bus passes for sale, city bus stop nearby; $16.50-22.50 per family, additional persons $2. Located at 14601 40th Ave. (take King George Hwy. exit off Hwy. 99; turn right on 40th), Surrey, tel. 594-6156.

HOSTELS

Vancouver has several inexpensive hostels downtown—most in the more run-down areas of the city where you wouldn't choose to hang out at night, particularly on your own. For listings of budget hostels and hotels, scan the info board and use the free phone in the Greyhound Bus Station. However, it's wise to check out the rooms, bathroom facilities, and residents before you commit yourself over the phone.

Vancouver Youth Hostel

For a scenic and safe location, particularly for women traveling alone, Vancouver Youth Hostel is by far the best. It's not downtown (30 minutes by bus; stop nearby), but it's right across the road from beautiful Jericho Park, Beach, and Marina. The area is very popular with cyclists (wheels far outnumber legs in summer). Inside the huge white building with snazzy blue trim are separate dorms for men and women, rooms for couples and families, a living area with TV, kitchen, cafeteria (open

Vancouver Youth Hostel has a great beach and park location, but it's a fair way from the city center.

for breakfast and dinner, good food, reasonable prices), handy info board (the place to look if you need a ride, want to buy or sell a bicycle, meet up with friends, etc.), lockers (don't leave valuables in cars), left-luggage service for $3 a bag per week, and limited free parking. It costs YH members $12.50 per night, nonmembers $17.50, and family rooms are available if previously reserved (at last a week ahead). Reservations recommended; maximum stay three consecutive nights. Located at 1515 Discovery St., just down the road from the intersection of Northwest Marine Dr. and West 4th Ave., Pt. Grey; tel. 224-3208.

GOOD VALUE HOTELS

YMCA Hotel

If you're looking for a small, clean room and don't object to sharing bathroom facilities (separate for men and women), the YMCA Hotel has a good downtown location, only two blocks from busy Robson St. and all the restaurants and nightlife. No cooking facilities, but the cafe is open daily from breakfast to 1600. Coin-op laundry, TV rental, weight room, racquetball, sauna, and two lap pools. Supervised (daytime only) parking up the alley beside the Y for 75 cents overnight or two hours during the day, or $3.75 for 24 hours. Rooms for men, women, and couples. Single rooms from $30, $50 twin (plus $4 key deposit), linen provided, and weekly rates are available. At 955 Burrard St. across from B.C. Hydro, tel. 681-0221.

YWCA Hotel

The modern high-rise YWCA Hotel also has a good downtown location and provides rooms for women, couples, or families, with shared or private bathrooms. TV lounge, kitchen, and laundry facilities on each floor. Swimming pool and fitness center (women only). From $38-43 s, $49-55 twin, $55-65 d, including linen, and weekly rates are available. No private parking facilities. At 580 Burrard St., tel. 662-8188.

University Of British Columbia Conference Centre

Summer housing is available at UBC (Pt. Grey, 16 km southwest of city center; on city bus route) during the May-Aug. vacation (plus a limited number of rooms are also available during the school year). Plenty of single rooms with shared bathrooms, and one- or two-bedroom suites or studio suites with private bathrooms and kitchenettes. Restaurant close by, with swimming pool, sauna, whirlpool, tennis and fitness center on campus, $18-47 s, $63 d, $36-80 twin; kitchen $5. Contact UBC Conference Centre, 5961 Student Union Blvd.; tel. 228-2963.

Simon Fraser University Housing And Conference Services

If you don't mind being about 20 km southeast of downtown Vancouver, and like the idea of an inexpensive room on a hilltop campus known for its modern architecture and excellent city views from Burnaby Mt., contact S.F.U., Rm. 212, McTaggart-Cowan Mall, Burnaby, tel. 291-4201. Single or twin fully furnished rooms with shared bathrooms are available during the May-Aug. vacation, and the room rate of $18-26 s, $37 d, includes a continental breakfast. Lounges on each floor, coin-op laundry, and recreational facilities are on campus. Free campus tours are available in July and Aug., hourly 1030-1530; Sept.-June by appointment only. The university is located between highways 7 and 7A in Burnaby. To get there by bus, catch no. 10 or 14 on Granville Mall (ask the driver to tell you where to get off, and get a transfer ticket), then transfer to bus no. 135.

Kingston Hotel

A small downtown hotel with continental atmosphere, the Kingston has rooms with shared bathroom facilities and some rooms with private baths, plus a sauna, laundry facilities, TV rental, and guest parking. Rates start at $33-48 s, $38-60 d, $55-70 twin, and include breakfast; weekly and off-season rates are also available. It's near the bus depot and Robson St., at 757 Richards St., tel. 684-9024.

2

3

1. The Skeena River can be admired from the Yellowhead Highway most of the way between Terrace and Prince Rupert. (Jane King); 2. Tangle Creek, Jasper National Park (Jane King); 3. Takakkaw Falls, Yoho National Park (Province of British Columbia) (Jane KIng)

1. ox-eye daisy (Jane King); **2**. clematis (Jane King); **3.** Indian paintbrush *(Castilleja spp.)* (Jane King); **4.** lily pads on Portal Lake, Mt. Robson Provincial Park (Jane King); **5**. A carpet of wildflowers lines the road to Prince George Airport in summer (Jane King); **6**. a purple profusion of blooms in Princeton (Jane King)

BED AND BREAKFAST GUESTHOUSES

If you want to meet locals, and prefer the idea of staying in someone's home rather than an impersonal hotel room, stay in a B&B. There are so many in the greater metropolitan area (they sprouted all over Vancouver just before Expo), you can find just about whatever you're looking for—a heritage home, a modern townhouse, a rural farmhouse, a hammock in a backyard. Some have private bath, others shared facilities, some with swimming pools and saunas, others on the beach or close to city attractions. Expect to pay at least $30-65 s, $45-105 d, which includes a hearty breakfast.

Most B&Bs belong to an association or agency. To quickly locate one in your area of choice at a price you can afford, refer to the *Accommodations* guide for a complete list (in the backmatter of the booklet, not under "Vancouver") of agencies with a description of the type of homes they represent, the facilities, and the prices they charge. When you call, state exactly what you want, e.g., private bath. Also drop by an InfoCentre. They have brochures put out by private owners that may grab your attention.

MOTELS AND TOP-OF-THE-LINE HOTELS

The range and price of motels and hotels throughout Vancouver vary enormously. The most reasonably priced motels are located along Kingsway (Hwy. 1A/99A, the section between Boundary Rd. and Main St.) approaching the city center from the south; from $38 s, $50 d. If you're looking for luxury, there's plenty from which to choose. All the hotels have the facilities you'd expect, plus most have outstanding views—of the city, harbor, or both. Refer to the *Accommodations* guide for listings in each area and the prices. In summer, go to the Travel InfoCentre to find out what's available. Unless you've made reservations, you may not be able to stay at your first few choices. Everyone books ahead if they can.

Granville Island Hotel attracts a trendy, fun-loving, jet-setter crowd looking for action. Located on Granville I., just south of city center overlooking False Creek, most of the rooms have water views. Jacuzzi, sauna, restaurant, lounge, pub (always crowded in the evenings), disco, and valet parking. Theater entertainment, restaurants, art galleries, shops, and a public market are all located on the island. Rooms run $115-125 s, $130-140 d, $150-170 twin, each additional person $15. If you object to loud, pounding music till 0200, be sure to ask for a room far from the disco! At 1253 Johnston St., tel. 683-7373.

Looking for old-world elegance? The copper-roofed **Hotel Vancouver** is one of the downtown landmarks—you can't help but notice the odd-shaped green roof, the gargoyles, and classic gothic "chateau"-style architecture of this grand old lady. Inside are restaurants, comfortable lounge, indoor pool, saunas, weight room, health facilities, 24-hour room service, ample parking, and plenty of staff to attend to your every whim. Rooms run $160-280 s, $185-305 d or twin. Centrally located at 900 West Georgia St., tel. 684-3131.

For all the mod cons and unbeatable city and harbor views, the sparkling **Pan Pacific Vancouver Hotel** perched on the edge of Burrard Inlet at Canada Place has everything. Pool, saunas, racquetball courts, health club, restaurants, lounge, shops, 24-hour room service, and valet parking. Rooms run $109-225 s, $129-265 d or twin, and off-season rates are available. Located at 300-999 Canada Place, tel. 662-8111.

If you want to stay on the north side of Burrard Inlet, consider **Lonsdale Quay Hotel** above lively Lonsdale Quay Market in North Vancouver. Rooms range $102.50-122.50 s, $122.50-145 d, $127.50-140 twin, depending on the view. Restaurants, fitness center, sauna and whirlpool, nightclub with entertainment, shops, and covered parking. Good location beside the SeaBus Terminal, only 12 minutes to downtown by water. At 123 Carrie Cates Ct., North Vancouver, tel. 986-6111.

OTHER PRACTICALITIES

FOOD

Markets

When your stomach is rumbling and you don't have the time or the inclination to sit in a restaurant, head for public markets, where you can feast your eyes and satisfy your pangs without breaking the bank. **Robson Public Market** at 1610 Robson St. (west end) is open seven days a week (underground parking at the rear) 0900-2100, tel. 682-2733. You can buy fresh fruit and vegies (or make a selection from a salad bar stand).

All kinds of tasty delicacies are to be found at Robson Public Market.

Try the meat, seafood (pick your own live Dungeness crab out of the tank if you can handle it), plus pasta, all kinds of baked, deli, and dairy goods, freshly squeezed fruit juices (even "live juice"), bulk spices and herbs, wines, fresh flowers, and the list goes on. Or head upstairs to gorge yourself on hamburgers, pastries, sandwiches, or teriyaki meat dishes—eat there (pull up a chair and watch the lower level positively swarm with activity) or get something tasty to go. Hungry yet?

Granville Island Market on Granville I., just south of city center, is another excellent place to get all kinds of dishes to go, or the place to shop for everything you need to concoct your own culinary feast. Eat inside or out by the marina. Parking is horrific—take the bus or ferry, and a large shopping bag.

Good-deal Restaurants

For an enormous selection of cafes and restaurants with flavors from around the world, just stroll along **Robson Street.** Pick from French, Italian, Chinese, Portuguese, Japanese, Vietnamese, Indian, Mexican, California-style American—tastebud cravings for the exotic and the international can all be satisfied within several blocks!

In **The Cellar** (downstairs) at 745 Thurlow St., you'll find a California-style Mexican restaurant, a steak and seafood restaurant, and two Japanese restaurants. **Las Margaritas** (tel. 669-5877) is open for lunch (around $8) and dinner ($10-12) and boasts "mild or wild, we can add all the octane you wish"—it's true! The south-of-the-border decor—white stucco walls, colorful blankets, Mexican hats, tile floor and tile-topped tables—add to the overall flavor. It's a good place to go on a rainy day (or any day for that matter) to give your taste buds a buzz (try the fajitas with hot salsa and chips for $10), throw back a couple of margaritas, and pretend you're in Mexico. You don't have to pretend you're in The Cellar in the dark but cozy, wood and brick surroundings of **The Keg** steakhouse (tel. 685-4388). It's open weekdays for lunch and dinner, weekends for dinner only, and it's usually crowded in the evenings. A small serving from the salad bar starts at $3.50 with meals or $6.99 with soup and a main dish, steak and seafood dishes are $9-12 with good daily lunch specials for $5.99, dinner runs around $9-25 and you won't leave feeling hungry.

Hamburger gourmets will appreciate **Red Robin Restaurant** on the corner of Thurlow and Alberni streets (upstairs). Choose from a large variety of burgers, tasty sandwiches, salads, and a selection of main entrees, or wet your whistle with one of many exotic concoctions available at the elegant bar. Head for a window seat and do a bit of street watching or mountain gazing between gulps. Expect to pay from around $10 for a main course and drink. It's open Mon.-Fri. 1100-2300, Sat. 1100-0100, and Sun. 1100-2300. The **Food Fair** below Red Robin offers cheap Chinese, fish and chips, deli and bakery goods to eat at the tables provided or to go.

Monte Cristo, a bakery and restaurant on the corner of Robson and Thurlow streets (tel. 682-2131), is always crowded, and once you've sampled one of their freshly baked croissants or pastries, you'll understand why. Breakfast specials are served until 1000, lunch is reasonable ($6-8), dinner is a little more expensive ($10-15). Eat in, or outside at one of the sidewalk tables in summer and watch the world go by—very cosmopolitan. Häagen-Dazs fanatics congregate at the takeout window in the evenings for an enormous ice-cream cone for less than two bucks. It's open Mon.-Sat. 0800-1300 and Sun. 0800-2400.

Joe Fortes Seafood and Chop House at 777 Thurlow St., between Robson and Alberni streets (tel. 669-1940), specializes in "the freshest seafood in the area." Named after one of Vancouver's best-loved heroes, a swimming coach at English Bay who saved many lives, it's open Mon.-Fri. from 1130 for lunch ($8-11), Sun. brunch from 1000, and dinner ($15-26) Mon.-Thurs. 1730-2300, Fri. 1700-2400, Sat. 1730-2400, and Sun. 1730-2230—feast your eyes on the wall murals while you wait for the perpetual crowd ahead of you to be seated.

Gastown Gourmet

When you're in Gastown, try **Brother's Restaurant** at One Water St. (tel. 689-9124). In monastery-like surroundings of wood, brick, stained glass, chandeliers (no swinging allowed), and monkish murals, you can enjoy delicious soups (try the Boston clam chowder), salads, sandwiches, or a variety of dishes ($8-14) seriously served by waiters appropriately dressed in monk attire (with accompanying congregational sing-alongs and laser entertainment!); open Mon.-Thurs. 1130-2200, Fri. and Sat. 1130-2400, and Sun. 1130-2100.

The Old Spaghetti Factory at 53 Water St. (tel. 684-1288) is another local favorite because you get plenty of tasty food for your six bucks. As you might gather, pasta and spaghetti dishes are strongly featured on the menu, and while you wait, you can hop on and off the 1910 cablecar parked center stage. Opens daily at 1130, till 2300 Mon.-Thurs., till 2330 Fri. and Sat., and till 2200 on Sunday. Expect to pay around $6-8 for lunch, $7-12 for dinner.

Canadian Family-style

White Spot Restaurants are reliable (white) spots for Canadian cuisine (sandwiches, salads, burgers, complete dinners) at reasonable prices. There are many in Vancouver (open Sun.-Thurs. 0630-2300, Fri. and Sat. 0630-2330) and they're always crowded with locals at any time of the day or evening. The one on Robson St. (near the corner of Burrard, upstairs) seats you in bright comfy surroundings with a view of the imposing copper-roofed Hotel Vancouver and bustling street below, or outside amongst the greenery on the Sunspot Terrace. Main courses are $5-10, lighter fare is $4-7, and delectable desserts (the fresh strawberry pie's worth every calorie) are around $3. If you're in North Van, try the White Spot on Lonsdale between 22nd and 23rd streets.

Trendy And Healthy

Bananas California Restaurant at 1044 Robson St. (tel. 682-2411) is one of the in places to go. It's the kind of place where you can sit in the cool gray and pink decor and watch the beautiful people, or have a good laugh at all the banana art on the walls—Moby Banana, King Banana VIII, Sir Gala-banana, Laurel and Banana, dirty old banana, etc. They present delicious healthy food with nouvelle elegance—which means servings are small. Go before 1100 to avoid the lunchtime crowds. Several egg concoctions ($3.50-6) are on the menu till noon (weekends and holidays till 1400), and they have salads ($3.50-7) and a variety of main dishes ($6-16). Guess what the garnish is? Open Mon.-Fri. 1000-2200, Sat. 1000-2400, Sun. 1000-2200.

Another well-recommended restaurant is **Woodlands Natural Cuisine** at 2582 W. Broadway (at Trafalgar upstairs), tel. 733-5411. Serving vegetarian, Indian, and Asian dishes, expect to pay $4.50-9 a plate; average $7-8. It's open seven days a week, 0700-2200 weekdays, 0800-2200 weekends and holidays.

Chinese Cuisine

You can't go wrong in Chinatown—just look for the restaurants that are the most crowded with locals. For the most authentic cuisine, head to the east-end restaurants. (At the west end the food seems to have been appropriately Westernized.) Outside of Chinatown, **Yangtze Mandarin Restaurant** at 1542 Robson St. (between Cordova and Nicola streets; tel. 687-7142) is recommended by locals for its excellent authentic dishes. Open seven days for lunch and dinner; average main course $8, dinner for two with several dishes is around $20.

Another good place to go for quick authentic Chinese cuisine (eat in or take out) is **Bill Kee Restaurant** at Eight West Broadway and the corner of Ontario St., tel. 879-3222 or 874-8522 (delivery from 1800 within three km). It's open Sun.-Thurs. 1030-0200, Fri. and Sat. 1030-0300. The decor isn't fancy but the food is good, plentiful, and averages $7-10 per meal (at lunch one dish is around $5, at dinner around $8) including bottomless glasses of hot Chinese tea.

Northwest Coast Native Indian

If you have a hankering to try some authentic American Indian food—smoked oolichans, bannock bread, seaweed and wild rice, watercress salad, smoked salmon, seafood or caribou barbecued over an alderwood fire, or perhaps a potlatch platter for two—head for **Quilicum West Coast Indian Restaurant** at 1724 Davie St., tel. 681-7044; open seven days from 1700 (last seating is at 2130) and reservations are essential. Expect to pay $14-20 for main dishes, or have the set potlatch menu for two that allows you to sample a variety of the delicacies for $43.95-54. Take your credit card, and enjoy the native artwork!

Frightfully French, Darling

Another small, intimate, in place to go for excellent French food (culinary experts gave it the double thumbs up, and local patrons are equally enthusiastic) is **Le Crocodile** on Thurlow St. near Robson. It's open Mon.-Thurs. 1200-1400 and 1800-2200, on Fri. and Sat. 1800-2230, and reservations are essential. Expect to pay $14-19 for à la carte dishes.

Weekend Brunch Favorite

English Bay Cafe is a popular local hangout at 1795 Beach Ave. (corner of Denman, tel. 669-2225), English Bay, any day of the week, but it does a roaring trade on weekends. They serve up good food (the house specialty is tasty *tapas*) at reasonable prices, along with a beach and bay view. It's open for lunch Mon.-Fri. 1130-1400 ($6-12), dinner 1800-2300 (in winter) and 1700-2400 (in summer; $11-24), and Sun. brunch 1000-1430 ($6-12). The bistro downstairs is open daily 1130-2330 ($6-12).

West Vancouver

On the northwest side of the bay, try **Salmon House On The Hill Restaurant** for delicious food (the specialty is barbecued salmon cooked over an open alderwood pit). The intriguing decor includes all forms of northwest coast Indian arts and crafts (nothing beats an entire dugout canoe suspended above your head for suspense), and a great view of West Van, Stanley Park, and downtown. A rhododendron garden borders the front of the building—a stunning floral display in May. Enjoy drinks and appetizers ($5-8) or afternoon tea and dessert ($4-5—their "Chocolate Paradise" is sinfully delicious!) in the bistro bar, or a full meal in the adjoining restaurant; lunch averages $9-12, a main course at dinner averages $15-20. Expect to pay at least $50 for two; make reservations unless you plan on eating at 1700 or after 2200. Located at 2229 Folkstone Way, West Van (from Upper Levels Hwy. take the 21st St. exit to Folkstone Way, then follow the signs); open Mon.-Sat. 1130-1430, dinner Sun.-Thurs. 1700-2200, Fri. and Sat. 1700-2300, and for Sun. brunch 1100-1430, tel. 926-3212.

ENTERTAINMENT

There's never a dull moment in Vancouver. For complete listings of all that's happening around the city, pick up the free *Georgia Straight* (out once a week), the *West Ender* (once a week; 25 cents), and the two daily newspapers, the *Province* and the *Vancouver Sun*.

Theater

Vancouver has theaters all over the city—for professional plays, amateur plays, comedy, and "instant" theater. See what's on in the papers, or drop in at the Travel InfoCentre (see "Information," below).

Back Alley Theatre at 751 Thurlow St. puts on a variety of shows on weeknights (from $8 pp). The highly entertaining **Theatresports** has shows on Fri. nights at 2000 and 2300 and Sat. nights at 1900, 2100, and 2300 (from $11 adult, $9 student, line up at least 30 minutes in advance if you haven't reserved a ticket). Two teams of actors compete against one another to win the approval of the audience, taking suggestions from the audience and putting on a number of instant plays. The resulting live theater is never the same twice and can be sidesplittingly hilarious, and because both the actors' and the audience's reactions are spontaneous you never know what to expect (if you don't want to actively participate, sit in the back!). For more info and reservations, call 688-7013.

The Arts Club always has excellent theater productions at their three locations. You're bound to find something you like playing at the **Arts Club Theatre Granville Island** on Johnston or the **Arts Club Review** next door, both on Granville I., or the **Arts Club Theatre** on Seymour St.; make reservations ahead at 687-1644, Mon.-Sat. 0930-1500 and pick up your tickets at the door 30 minutes prior to showtime. In the **Queen Elizabeth Theatre** at 630 Hamilton and Georgia St., the city's largest theater, you can see plays, concerts, dance, opera, and music recitals, and it sponsors out-of-town guest artists. The **Vancouver East Cultural Centre** at 1895 Venables creates a wide variety of live entertainment—many original and experimental works. **Robson Square Conference Centre** at 800 Robson St. has a theater where you can attend films, concerts, readings, fashion shows, and other events. Pick up a free *Calendar of Events* at the Travel InfoCentre.

Comedy Punchlines Theatre next to the Old Spaghetti Factory at 15 Water St. in Gastown presents "the best" in stand-up comedy at 2130 and 2330 on weekends, amateur night on Mon. at 2130; $8.50 pp. For more info call 684-3015. **Yuk Yuk's** at 1238 Davie St. has comedy nights Wed.-Saturday. Wednesday is amateur night at 2100, $3 pp; the Thurs. performance is at 2100, $6 pp; and on Fri. and Sat. nights it's at 2100 and 2330, $9 pp; call for reservations at 687-5233.

Music

The **Queen Elizabeth Theatre** at 630 Hamilton St. is a major venue for music recitals and opera performances; call 665-3050 to see what's coming up. For cut-price QE tickets call **Front Row Centre** at 683-2017 on the day of the performance. The **Vancouver**

East Cultural Centre at 1895 Venables is worth looking into for musical events, as are the two **Universities**—there's usually something happening in their theatres. The **Orpheum Theatre** on Granville St. stages pop, classical, and symphony concerts. For info call the box office events number, 280-4444.

For live jazz, call the **Hot Jazz Society** at 873-4131 to see who's playing at 2120 Main St.; cover charge $3-5. For rock, blues, folk, jazz, and pop music (and a good sushi bar, according to locals), try the trendy **Soft Rock Cafe** at 1935 West 4th Ave., tel. 736-8480; cover charge varies according to who's playing. For live bands, dancing, video, and piano lounge, head for **Town Pump** at 66 Water St., tel. 683-6695; cover charge varies for live band entertainment.

Movies

To find out what's playing at all the cinemas around town and their locations, refer to the daily newspapers. The **CN IMAX Theatre** at the far end of Canada Place provides spectacular movie entertainment. Ever wondered exactly how it feels to soar through the sky with a family of Canada geese, to roar down the Colorado River on a raft, or to blast off into space in a rocket? You'll experience it here. Attend a matinee or evening show (reservations neccessary ahead of time) in this impressive theater with its enormous curved screen and resulting special effects. Prices vary: $6.15-6.50 adult, $5.10-5.35 senior or student, $4.05-4.30 child, and a double show is $9.10 adult, $8.05 senior or student, $6.40 child; buy tickets at the theater box office, or phone 280-4444 for reservations. For more info and showtimes, phone 682-4629. Allow time (5-10 minutes) to walk the length of Canada Place to get to the theater!

Pubs

Ever since "Gassy Jack" Deighton set up the first instant pub (two barrels, a plank, and a barrel of whiskey) on the shores of the area that became known as Gastown, Vancouver has had its watering holes. Ask any local the name of a favorite and you'll get quite a number to try. One of the most popular neighborhood pubs is the small but always lively **Stamp's Landing** at 610 Stamp's Landing, False Creek, tel. 879-0821. Aside from beer and liquor, you can get delicious tasty snacks to keep you going, listen to live music on weekends, and appreciate a harbor view sunset. **Blarney Stone** at 215 Carrall St., tel. 687-4322, is another lively one, with lots of impromptu rowdy Irish sing-alongs.

Queens Cross Neighbourhood Pub on Upper Lonsdale at the corner of Queens Rd., North Van, tel. 980-7715, is a favorite local hangout for lunch, after-work drinks, conversation, and tasty appetizers and meals for $4.75-8. Try the Mediterranean Platter for $6.95 or the fajitas for $5.95-7.95—they're great! It's open seven days a week 1100-2400 (Sat. open at 1000), and the gourmet brunches (Sat. 1000-1300 and Sun. 1100-1400) gather a good crowd. Another North Van favorite is the **Rusty Gull** on Lower Lonsdale, tel. 988-5585. Many pubs have live entertainment, especially on Fri. and Sat. nights.

Events

In May don't miss the **Vancouver Children's Festival** at Vanier Park; it's a kid's paradise. Even if you're not into photography, you'll take away dozens of snapshots—with all the face painting, costumes, and fancy hat competitions you may find yourself running up to total strangers and begging to get their faces on film. Buy tickets in advance for the special events (plays, puppetry, mime, sing-alongs, story-telling, etc.), but the rest of the fun and frivolity is free. A fun (and less congested) way to get there is by ferry from Granville I. or the Aquatic Centre at Sunset Beach. For more info call 687-7697.

In late June/early July Vancouver taps its feet to the beat of the annual **Du Maurier International Jazz Festival**—a more-than-one-week event that shouldn't be missed by any serious (or not-so-serious) jazz lover. Musicians (more than 500 of them!) from countries around the world gather to perform traditional and contemporary jazz at various venues around the city. Get your tickets early; if you want to go to a number of events, buy a jazz pass from ticket outlets. The jazz hotline is 682-0706 (or write to Coastal Jazz and Blues Society, 435 West Hastings St., Vancouver, B.C. V6B 1L4).

Also in July each year, Jericho Beach Park becomes the focus for folk music appreciators from near and far when the **Vancouver Folk Music Festival** springs to life for a long weekend. During the festival you'll hear wonderful music and storytelling, see dance performances and live theater. If you plan on attending the entire weekend, buy tickets in advance from outlets and you get the quantity discount. For all the details, write to Vancouver Folk Music Festival, 3271 Main St., Vancouver, B.C. V5V 3M6, or phone 879-2931. Note that there are no camping facilities at the park, but the YH is a stone's throw away—make reservations early. Parking is also extremely limited; take the 4th Ave. bus to rid yourself of excess hassles.

Another hilarious mid-July event that brings Vancouverites out to the beach in force is the weekend **Vancouver Sea Festival** in July. You can expect parades, fireworks, salmon barbecues, and concerts, and the remaining competitors of the internationally famous, zany **Bathtub Race** from Nanaimo (Vancouver I.) to limp into Vancouver (Kitsilano Beach) to the delight of the crowd. For more info call 684-3378, or write to Vancouver Sea Festival, 213-900 West Georgia St., Vancouver, B.C. V6C 2W6.

Vancouver International Film Festival is held at the end of Sept. through early Oct. each year and features the very best movies from the Pacific Rim, Canada, Great Britain, Russia, and more than 35 other countries at several theaters. For more details call 685-0260.

INFORMATION

As you enter Vancouver from any direction, look out for **Travel InfoCentres** and stop! They're invaluable sources of info on Vancouver and the entire province. Collect a free city map and an *Accommodations* guide put out by the Ministry of Tourism, and pick the brains of the personnel. The main **Vancouver Travel InfoCentre** is at Pavilion Plaza, Four Bentall Centre, 1055 Dunsmuir St., tel. 683-2000, reservations tel. 683-2772. The specially trained staff provides free maps, brochures, and public transportation schedules, books sightseeing tours, makes accommodations reservations, and sells the invaluable B.C. Transit DayPass (adult $3, child and senior $1.50), along with postcards, stamps, and film. The InfoCentre is open seven days a week from May to early Sept. 0830-1730, closed on Sun. the rest of the year. An info kiosk is also located at the corner of Granville and Georgia streets, and there's another in Stanley Park in summer.

If you approach Vancouver from the south, the first InfoCentre is at the border (look out for it on the right). If you miss it, no need for panic, there are several more. The next one is the **Delta Chamber of Commerce and Travel InfoCentre** (take the Delta exit and follow the signs), and the one after that is the **Richmond Visitor's InfoCentre** to the right immediately after the George Massey Tunnel crossing the Fraser River (parking provided). If you're approaching the city from the east, stop at the **Coquitlam Travel InfoCentre.**

Coming from the northeast, the main **North Vancouver Travel InfoCentre** is at 131 E. 2nd St., tel. 987-4488; open daily in summer, weekdays in winter. There are also two info booths in North Vancouver open daily in the summer, at the junction of Capilano Rd. and Marine Dr., and at Lonsdale Quay by the SeaBus Terminal and Bus Depot. If you arrive by ferry at **Tsawwassen,** stop at the info booth two km from the Ferry Terminal (open only in summer). For fly-in visitors to **Vancouver International Airport,** an information booth is located on Level Three.

Don't want to take your vehicle into the city center? Locate the handy "Park and Ride" lots (these were created during Expo86 to lessen inner-city congestion and parking problems) on the city map you get at InfoCentres; park your vehicle for free and catch a bus into the city center.

SHOPPING AND SERVICES

Shops, And More Shops

Vancouver has shopping centers, malls, and specialty stores everywhere—especially along Robson St., and along Granville Mall in the city center. Before you set out, call in at the Travel InfoCentre (1055 Dunsmuir St.) and ask for their free *Shopping Guide*—aside from listings of all the department stores and specialty shops you're likely to want to visit, it contains two very handy fold-out maps of Downtown Vancouver (with all the shops and malls marked on) and Greater Vancouver.

For a unique market, exclusive shops, and an arts and crafts gallery, head for Granville Island. Stunning native art, jewelry, carvings, weaving, and original paintings can be bought at **Wickaninnish Gallery,** Suite 14, 1666 Johnston St., Granville I., tel. 681-1057. For over 190 shops, three department stores, and services all in one scenic location, take the Lions Gate Bridge to West Vancouver and the **Park Royal Shopping Centre.** It's open seven days a week, till 2100 on Thurs. and Fri. nights, and Sun. 1200-1700, at Marine Dr. and Taylor Way, tel. 922-3211.

Hospitals

For emergencies or health needs, contact: **Vancouver General Hospital,** 855 West 12th Ave., tel. 875-4000; **St. Paul's Hospital,** 1081 Burrard St., tel. 682-2344; **Lions Gate Hospital,** 239 East 13th St., tel. 988-3131; or **Children's Hospital,** 4480 Oak St., tel. 875-2345. **Seymour Medical Clinic,** 1530 West 7th Ave., tel. 731-2151, is open 24 hours. For a **doctor,** call one of the hospitals and ask their advice, or call 683-2474. For **emergency dental help,** call 946-9526 or the 24-hour clinic at Burnaby, tel. 524-3674. **Royal Canadian Mounted Police,** tel. 264-3111 (East Division HQ).

General

If you see your name on the "Tourist Alert" list posted at InfoCentres or in newspapers, at provincial campgrounds, and on ferries, or hear it on the radio or TV, contact the nearest Royal Canadian Mounted Police office or the local police. This excellent service is provided so that tourists can be contacted in an emergency.

Telephone: For **police** or **ambulance** call 911. Local calls on pay phones cost 25 cents. For local directory assistance, phone 411. For long-distance calls, dial 1, then area code, then number. The area code for the entire province of B.C. is 604.

Vancouver Main Post Office is at 349 West Georgia St., tel. 662-5725 (open Sat.). **Postal Station A** at 508 West Hastings St. and **Bentall Centre** at 595 Burrard St. are also open on Saturdays. Subbranches are located in some drugstores—ask a local for the nearest. The **American Express Office** is at 1040 West Georgia St., tel. 669-2813. **Vancouver Public Library** is at 750 Burrard St., tel. 665-2280.

TRANSPORTATION

LOCAL

If you have a car, parking it downtown can be a big hassle—you need to be armed with quarters and lots of patience. Parking spots are free only on Sun. and holidays. The best and easiest way to explore Vancouver is by using the excellent public transportation system. Whether you catch a bus, Sky Train, or SeaBus, all the OW fares are the same ($1.25 off-peak for one-, two-, or three-zone travel; in rush hour $1.25 for one zone, $1.75 for two zones, and $2.50 for three zones). Rush hour is before 0930 and 1500-1830 weekdays.

If you're sightseeing using the public transporation network, the most economical way is to buy a $3 DayPass, which allows you to jump on and off all day long (weekdays from 0930, weekends and holidays all day) for the one low price. You can buy the DayPass at any 7-Eleven or Safeway store, and at Sky Train stations—the bus drivers do not carry the DayPasses. Pick up a copy of the invaluable *Discover Vancouver On Transit* guidebook at any InfoCentre, or buy a detailed Transit Guide map of all transit routes at 7-Eleven stores, TicketMaster outlets, and locations where you see the red, white, and blue FareDealer sign. Any schedule or fare questions? Call Transit Information at 261-5000 any day 0630-2330.

By Bus

You can get just about anywhere you want to go by bus. Have the exact fare ready to deposit in the fare box at the front of the bus, and ask for a transfer if you're continuing your journey on another bus (transfers are valid for 90 minutes of travel in one direction), or show your DayPass to the driver (then you don't need a transfer). The coin-collecting devices are clearly marked "Please do not feed me $1 notes," so you'll need to travel with a pocketful of $1 coins or small change. The drivers do not carry change.

Visit Stanley Park on Sun. in summer and you can jump on and off the bus at all the stops around the park for free. Some of Vancouver's attractions have free admission days, so read up on the places you want to see ahead of time and plan accordingly.

Sky Train is a fast, efficient, and entertaining way to see some of Vancouver.

By Sky Train

The rapid-transit computer-operated Sky Train is fun to ride even if you don't want to go where it's going! Take a roundtrip. It runs on 35 km of elevated rail (good views) connecting downtown Vancouver with New Westminster in 27 minutes (terminating at Surrey), stopping at 15 stations (three of the four city-center stations are underground, but clearly marked at each street entrance) along the route. Sky Train leaves the waterfront Mon.-Fri. at 0550 and runs to 0115, Sat. 0650-0115, Sun. and holidays 0850-2415. It departs New Westminster weekdays 0520 and runs till 2445, Sat. 0620-2445, Sun. and holidays 0820-2345. Buy your ticket at the station, or use your DayPass. Bicycles are not permitted onboard.

By SeaBus

The SeaBus Terminal is worth seeing whether you're catching the ferry or not. In 1887, Vancouver became the western terminus for Canada's first transcontinental railway, and in 1914 this impressive marble and brick CP Rail Terminal was opened. Today it houses the Vancouver SeaBus Terminus, a bakery, coffee shops, a travel agency, and restrooms. The SeaBus, a harbor passenger ferry, whisks you from the downtown waterfront across Burrard Inlet to Lonsdale Quay, North Vancouver, in 12 enjoyable minutes; bicycles permitted on Sun. and holidays for an extra fare. Once you reach the north side, B.C. Transit buses take you just about anywhere you want to go. In summer look for the handy info kiosk between the SeaBus Terminal and Bus Depot in North Vancouver—the staff will tell you exactly where to go!

By Car

You have a big choice when it comes to picking a vehicle-rental agency in Vancouver, and all have a wide range of vehicles, prices, and deals. Some throw in extras such as "coupon books" giving you discounts or free admission to attractions, discounts at certain restaurants, etc., but look closely at the coupon book. There's usually a catch, e.g., buy two meals, get discount off one, or discount off family admission—really useful when you're by yourself! Look in the yellow pages for a full listing of all the car-, camper-, and motorhome-rental agencies.

The least expensive place to try is **Rent-A-Wreck** at 180 West Georgia St., tel. 688-0001. Obviously you're not getting a new car, and it may be a gas-guzzler, but the rates are usually lower than others; $20-32.95 a day for basic compact cars, plus 15 cents a kilometer but the first 150 km are free. In the high season it's best to reserve a vehicle a week in advance because the turnover is high. If you want one of the least expensive rentals, show up at the beginning of the week—by Thurs. or Fri. they're all gone for the weekend.

The following agencies have downtown and airport branches (most branches operate independently and their rates fluctuate according to available vehicles and demand); expect to pay at least $31-45 per day plus 15 cents per kilometer, with the first 100-200 km free. In general it's cheaper to rent by the week, and cheaper still by the month. Try: **Avis Rent-a-Car** at 757 Hornby St., tel. 682-1621 (airport 273-4577); **Budget Rent-a-Car** at 450 West Georgia St., tel. 685-0536 (toll-free airport number within Canada, 800-268-8900); **Dominion U-Drive,** 901 Seymour St., tel. 689-0550 (airport 278-7196); **Hertz Rent-a-Car** at 666 Seymour St., tel. 688-2411 (airport 279-5411); or **Tilden Rent-a-Car,** 1140 Alberni St., tel. 685-6111 (airport 273-3121).

By Bicycle

For a full listing of rental agencies look in the yellow pages. **Stanley Park Rentals** at 676 Chilco St. (entrance to Stanley Park) rents three- and five-speeds (from $5 per hour), cruisers, tandems (from $9 an hour), and mountain bikes (from $7 an hour). For current rates, call 681-5581. They're open in summer 0800-2100, in winter 0900-1800.

By Taxi

Look in the yellow pages for full listings of taxi companies in Greater Vancouver Regional District, or call **Yellow Cabs** (initial flag charge $1.90, plus $1.18 per km) at 681-1111, **McLure's** at 731-9211, or **Black Top** at 731-1111.

Handicapped Services
Handydart, an excellent wheelchair-accessible bus service, is provided for handicapped travelers by B.C. Transit, allowing door-to-door service for about the same price you'd pay on regular buses, but you need to book in advance at 430-2692 or call the general info line at 264-5000.

Another excellent service is provided for travelers with wheelchairs by **Vancouver Taxi,** tel. 255-5111. The taxi cabs have been redesigned to accommodate a wheelchair, yet the fares are the same as regular taxis; $1.18 a kilometer.

LONG DISTANCE

By Bus
The **Greyhound Bus Depot** at 150 Dunsmuir St. has all the info on bus routes and schedules throughout B.C.; tel. 662-3222. You can't make reservations—just buy your ticket and go. Sample OW fares from Vancouver to: Kamloops $36.22, Penticton $36.92, Banff $83.46, Jasper $78.81, Prince George $72.65, Prince Rupert $142.10, Whitehorse $253, Calgary $84.53, and Cranbrook $75.54. The only excursion ticket offered at present is to Whitehorse—$152 and good for 15 days. All fares include GST. Always ask if they have any excursion tickets to your destination of choice. Major credit cards are accepted.

Maverick Coach Lines in the same depot runs bus service to Vancouver I. (Nanaimo $15.80 OW); the Sunshine Coast (Gibsons $11.50, Sechelt $14.40, Powell River $23.25); and Squamish ($6.70), Whistler ($12.85), and Pemberton ($19.90). For more info call 662-8051. These fares are for adults, OW; fares are less for seniors and children.

Within the depot are lockers, a gift shop, a baggage room (open 0800-2400), a newsstand, and a coffee shop. If you've just arrived and want hostel or budget hotel accommodations, check the info board and use the free telephone in the terminal.

Pacific Coach Lines runs bus service to Victoria, with a shuttle service from Vancouver International Airport; call 662-8074 for more information. **Perimeter Transportation** provides bus service from Vancouver International Airport to Whistler and Blackcomb; for airport bus info call 273-9023, for info on the Whistler Express call 266-5386.

the Greyhound Bus Station

By Train

The **VIA Rail Station** is at 1150 Station St., behind the Sky Train station at Science World. In the station is a cafeteria (open 0530-1630 weekdays, 0530-1330 weekends), baggage check-in, info, and a newsstand. VIA runs passenger trains from Vancouver to Kamloops, Banff, Jasper, Calgary, and on to eastern Canada. Pick up a train schedule in the station (the station closes at 1700). For more info call 669-3050, or toll-free within B.C. at (800) 561-8630.

B.C. Rail provides a very scenic daily service from North Vancouver to Squamish, Whistler ($13.50; free shuttle bus to and from the Village during ski season), Pemberton, Lillooet ($28), and several trains a week to Clinton, 100 Mile House, Williams Lake ($52), Quesnel ($59), and Prince George ($71.50). These fares are OW and include GST. The station is at 1311 West First St., North Vancouver. Call for current fares and schedules at 984-5246.

By Ferry

Tsawwassen Ferry Terminal, 30 km south of Vancouver, is the place to catch ferries to the southern Gulf Is. and Swartz Bay, 32 km north of Victoria on Vancouver Island, and to Nanaimo on the island. From downtown by car, follow 17 south to the terminal—in summer it gets quite crazy with traffic. The ferries run about once an hour in high season (June to Sept. 0700-2200), about once every two hours (0700-2100) the rest of the year. You can't make reservations on the Vancouver I. Ferry (they operate on a first-there, first-on system), so expect a bit of a wait (usually not more than an hour or two) in summer, particularly if you have an oversized vehicle. A comforting thought while you wait: the greater the demand, the more ferries are put into service. Mainland to Vancouver I. costs $18.75 per vehicle (under seven foot) plus $5.25 per adult, $2.25 child. For the Gulf Islands (limited vehicle space) it's always necessary to make vehicle reservations—at least a few days ahead in summer. No waiting or reservations necessary for walk-on and cycling passengers.

To get from the ferry terminal into the city, catch a 640 bus to Ladner Exchange (ask the driver for a transfer ticket), then catch a Vancouver bus (601) to downtown; $1.25-2.50 depending on the time of day. To get to Vancouver International Airport from the ferry terminal, catch a 640 bus to Ladner Exchange, then a 601 to Massey Exchange, then a 404 or 405 to the airport.

Horseshoe Bay Ferry Terminal, a 10-minute drive west of West Vancouver, is the place to go for daily ferries to Nanaimo on Vancouver I., Bowen I., and up the Sunshine Coast. If Departure Bay, Nanaimo, is your destination, be prepared for a wait in summer (busy from May on), as you can't make reservations and it's first-there, first-on boarding (line up at least one hour before sailing time); $18.75 OW per vehicle and driver, $5.25 adult walk-ons, child $2.25.

The scenic Horseshoe Bay to Langdale (mainland Sunshine Coast) and Egmont to Saltry Bay crossings cost $24 RT per vehicle and driver (includes both crossings); the ferries make several crossings a day, timed so that you can catch the first ferry, leisurely drive up the coast, then catch the second. Buy your ticket at the car booth, park your vehicle in the lineup, then explore Horseshoe Bay while you wait for boarding. If you're doing the circle route (Sunshine Coast, Vancouver I., Vancouver), the Powell River-Comox crossing will cost you another $24 OW for vehicle and driver.

By Air

Vancouver International Airport is a 25-minute drive south of Vancouver city center. In the three-level airport terminal are coffee shops and restaurants, car rental agencies, currency exchange, newsstands, gift shops, and a duty-free shop. For quick airport orientation, check the info boards located in the center of each floor. For detailed info, brochures, bus schedules, and taxi fares, head up to the level three **information booth.**

Public transit buses, the Express Bus, and taxis all serve the airport. To get downtown by public transit, catch bus no. 100 **Midway Connector** from level three and get off at

70th St. and Granville, then take bus no. 21 Vancouver to downtown; $1.25 OW. If you're in a hurry, catch the Express Bus which leaves every half hour from level two for downtown and the North Shore; $8.25 OW. If you're staying at the Airport Inn, Delta River Inn, Richmond Inn, Skyline Hotel, or Bluebay Hotel, your bus leaves from level one. Taxis cost around $22 OW from the airport to city center. Need a bus to the parking lots? Catch it from levels one or three. **Perimeter Transportation** at 8695 Barnard St., tel. 273-0071, provides Airport Express bus service from the airport to downtown Vancouver hotels and the Greyhound Bus Depot; adult $8.25 OW or $14 RT, child $6.50 OW or $13 RT.

If you fly out of Vancouver Airport on an international flight, don't swap all your money at the currency exchange booth or spend your last few dollars in the duty-free shop because you need a whopping $40 to cover departure tax! On domestic flights the tax is eight percent of your ticket price, or $19, whichever is cheaper.

LOUISE FOOTE

LOUISE FOOTE

SOUTHWESTERN BRITISH COLUMBIA

INTRODUCTION

Once you've reluctantly decided to drag yourself away from Vancouver, another choice lurks in the wings: which of the five major routes to take to escape the city and get off the beaten track. While mulling this one over, keep in mind that wherever you go in B.C., magnificent scenery and an abundance of outdoor activities await. Disappointments in these two areas don't occur! But for those desiring anything *but* an action-packed vacation, ample places throughout the province in summer require only the bare necessities—a beach towel, a deck chair, a loaded cooler, suntan lotion, a good book, a fishing rod, and as much ambition as a polar bear would have in the tropics.

Believe it or not, all the routes out of Vancouver promise all of the above, and if you don't have wheels, you can still easily get to wherever you're going by bus, train, or ferry (see "Long Distance," p. 129). Even hitchhiking from the outskirts of the city is fairly easy if you look clean, friendly, and at least willing to walk all the way if you have to. Holding up a creative, easy-to-read sign stating your anticipated destination, i.e. "HOPE! Any hope?," usually shortens the wait.

Once you've decided where you're going, only the weather can throw a spanner in the works. No matter the season, expect some rain (then you'll probably get less than you expected), and take four-season basics so you're equipped for whatever Mother Nature throws your way.

OH, THE CHOICES!

Bays, Beaches, And Sunshine
A vehicle ferry from Horseshoe Bay (west of West Vancouver) to Langdale, then Hwy. 101 to Earls Cove and a second ferry to Saltery

Bay, followed by more Hwy. 101, takes you northwest up the Strait of Georgia along the **Sunshine Coast.** Passing fishing villages and seaside towns that swell with visitors in summer, good beaches, road access to a large number of provincial parks and sea access to an abundance of marine parks, you come to the town of Powell River—a good day-trip if you start out early. At Powell River you can either catch the Comox ferry to "the island" (mainlander jargon for Vancouver I.) and return to the mainland south of Vancouver without backtracking, or continue north up Hwy. 101 to the fishing village of Lund, where the road ends but a host of marine activities on and in Desolation Sound begin.

Mountain Mecca

Spectacular Hwy. 99, the aptly named "Sea To Sky Highway," leads you northeast out of Vancouver along the edge of island-dotted Howe Sound, past numerous provincial parks, to the year-round mountain resort of **Whistler.** In this area you can expect excellent cross-country and alpine skiing (usually still good in late spring), hiking, canoeing, windsurfing, mountain biking, and abundant photo ops, or continue (in summer) via a paved and gravel road that zigzags over steep snow-topped mountains to the historic gold town of **Lillooet** on the border of the Cariboo and Thompson Country. Again, no backtracking is needed, though it's not a good idea to take a trailer or motorhome over the gravel mountain road—getting stuck on one of the zigs or zags could take the smile right out of your vacation.

Raging Rivers And Lazy Lakes

From Vancouver there are two ways to head east—either whizzing along fast Trans-Canada Hwy. 1 on the south side of the wide Fraser River, or meandering along slower Hwy. 7 on the north side of the river. Both routes take you through the lush, fertile, and obviously agricultural Fraser Valley to the warm, lake-dotted Okanagan/Similkameen region (where in summer you're bound to meet some of a vast number of vacationing Canadian families), or into the rolling ranchland, river, and desert landscapes of **High Country.**

Victoria, The U.S. Border, Or Bust

The southern route out of Vancouver, Hwy. 99, takes you past **Vancouver International Airport** and **Tsawwassen** where you can hop on a ferry for Swartz Bay and the provincial capital of Victoria at the southern tip of Vancouver I., or continue straight down to the U.S. border (but go back, you're heading the wrong way!).

A One-day Steam Train And Ferry Escapade

If you're visiting Vancouver between May and Sept., only have a day to spare, and want to get out of the city for a quick taste of unsurpassed British Columbian scenery, this is the way to do it. Board the restored antique steam train, the **Royal Hudson,** at the B.C. Rail Station in North Vancouver to chug in style and comfort (viewing the scenery through picture windows) to Squamish at the head of Howe Sound. For train info contact B.C. Rail at 631-3500. Then take the MV *Brittania* back to Vancouver (north foot of Denman Street). The train/boat combo makes a wonderfully scenic 6½-hour day-trip, or take the train in both directions for a slightly shorter trip. For ferry info call Harbour Ferries at 687-9558 (or 800-663-1500 within B.C.) for current schedule, fare information, and bookings.

THE SUNSHINE COAST

INTRODUCTION

The 150-km Sunshine Coast lies along the northeast shores of the Strait of Georgia between Howe Sound in the south and Desolation Sound in the north. It's a rare bit of sun-drenched B.C. coastline well worth visiting whether you just need a day-trip from Vancouver, plan to do the "circle route" to Vancouver I. and back, or are looking for an ultimate vacation destination. Bordered by countless bays and inlets, broad sandy beaches, quiet lagoons, rugged headlands, provincial parks, and lush fir forests backed by the snowcapped mountains of the Coast Range, the Sunshine Coast is accessible by a twisty road with delightful glimpses of wilderness islands in the Strait of Georgia and two short ferry rides. In the summer expect to share the delight with masses of Sunday drivers, cyclists, and camper vans; meet anglers, scuba divers, boaters, beachcombers, and hikers just about everywhere you stop.

As you cruise up this stretch of the coastline, where settlement began in the late 19th century, notice the odd assortment of place names given to the inlets, bays, and seaside villages and towns—names left by Coast Salish Indians and Spanish and British navigators. The local economy is based on forestry, fishing (locals proudly claim that this area is undoubtedly one of the finest sportfishing areas in B.C.), and a rapidly growing tourism industry—every summer the coastal population swells by 25%. Boasting the mildest climate in Canada, the Sunshine Coast has moderately warm summers and mild winters,

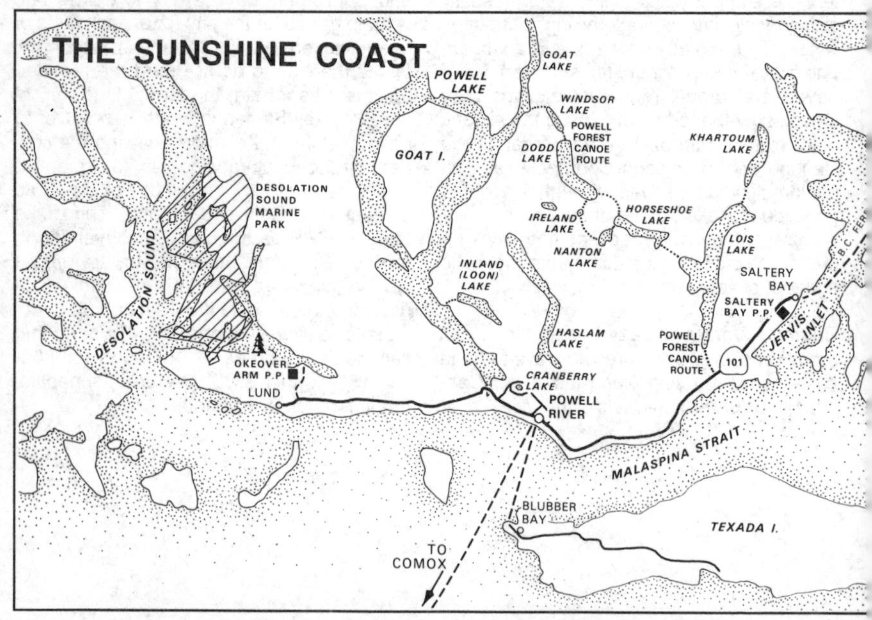

with only 94 centimeters of rain a year and 2,400 hours of UV light—a few more hours than Victoria, the so-called provincial hot spot. Browse through arts and crafts or antique shops, drink up the tranquil atmosphere and meet mellow locals, laze on a beach, or actively participate in many outdoor recreations.

Boaters can cruise into a number of beautiful marine parks (most are accessible only by boat) providing sheltered anchorage and campsites amongst some of the most magnificent scenery along the West Coast, or anchor at sheltered fishing-village marinas with all the mod cons. Would-be boaters can rent charter boats or catered charters, or even learn to sail while they tour the coast.

Looking for a scenic campsite? Nab some terra firma at one of the many provincial or regional parks along the Sunshine Coast, or at a private campground—there's one in just about every town. In the provincial parks each campsite has a parking spot, a tent site, a picnic table, a fireplace with wood provided, pit toilets, and fresh water nearby (showers available at Porpoise Bay), but no hookups. The maximum stay is 14 days, no reservations are taken, and most are full throughout summer—make camp early in the day; $6-13 per night is charged from early spring through fall. The least-crowded time to enjoy the parks is from Sept. through May. If you prefer to escape the crowds, undeveloped walk-in or canoe-in campsites can also be readily found along the Powell Forest Canoe Route near Powell River (see p. 138), and isolated marine-park campsites are available to the visiting boating community.

Getting There

The best way to appreciate the coast is by private vehicle—car, bicycle, or boat—so you can meander at your own pace and stop frequently. Take the 35-minute vehicle ferry ride from Horseshoe Bay to Langdale, then Hwy. 101 to Egmont, the 50-minute ferry ride to Saltery Bay, then continue along the highway to Powell River and

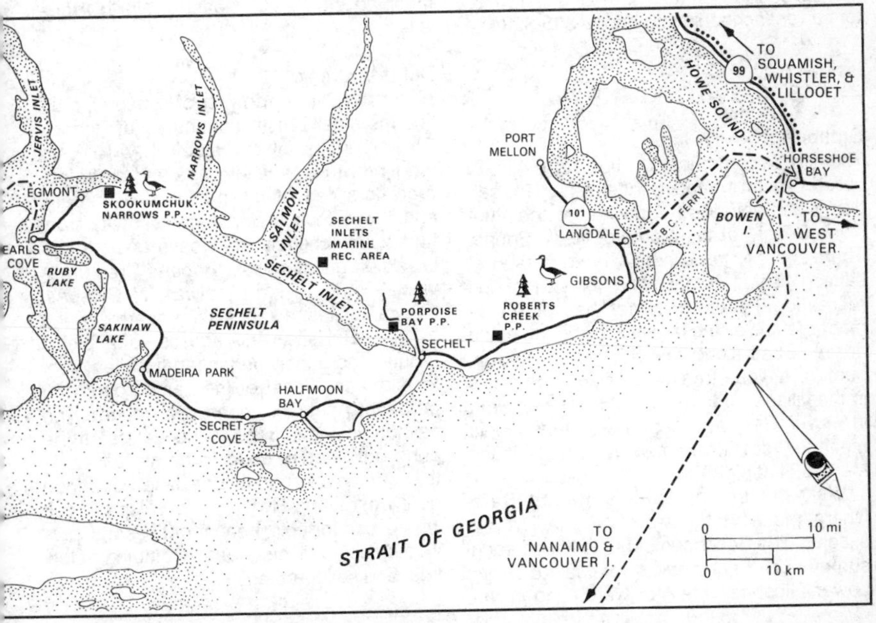

Lund. The one-way fare (includes both ferries) is adult $5.25, child $2.25, car and driver $24. For more info call B.C. Ferries at 685-1021 (24 hours) or B.C. Ferries Saltery Bay Terminal at 487-9333. At Powell River you can catch a vehicle ferry over to Texada I., or to Comox/Courtenay on Vancouver I.; 1¼ hours and $24 OW per vehicle and driver. For more info call B.C. Ferries Westview Terminal at 485-2943. On all the above ferries no reservations are taken—it's strictly first there, first on. If you don't have wheels, call **Maverick Coach Lines** at 255-1171 for their Sunshine Coast schedule (Vancouver to Gibsons is $11.50 adult OW, to Sechelt $14.40, and to Powell River $23.25), or pick up a schedule at the Greyhound Bus Depot, 150 Dunsmuir St., Vancouver, or call toll-free within B.C. for more bus info (24 hours) at (800) 972-6301. The **Sunshine Coast Transit System** operates two minibuses providing regular service between Gibsons/Langdale and Sechelt (adult $1, senior and child 90 cents OW), and limited service to Halfmoon Bay and Redroofs; for current schedule info phone 885-3234.

STOPS ALONG THE WAY

Gibsons

The hillside community of Gibsons, originally called Gibson's Landing after a pioneer settler, is the self-billed "Gateway to the Sunshine Coast," at the mouth of Howe Sound. There's plenty to do here. Try your hand at salmon fishing, windsurfing, or sailing; the recreational marine center has plenty of moorage and all the facilities a seafarer could desire. Stroll along the picturesque harbor, hunt for antique treasures or arts and crafts in the village, or take the **Gibsons Seawalk** in Lower Gibson, a 10-minute, very scenic meander from Government Wharf to Gibsons Marina (lit at night).

Visit the set of **Molly's Reach Cafe** where much of the weekly Canadian TV sitcom, "The Beachcombers," is filmed each summer. The set's on Lower Marine Dr. in Lower Gibsons, open for wandering in the afternoon after filming is finished for the day, with guided tours available. The **Elphinstone Pioneer Museum** on Winn Rd. downtown has some intriguing pioneer and Coastal Salish Indian displays, and it's a veritable shell-collector's paradise, containing what must be one of the largest collections (25,000!) on the planet. Finish off your day in one of the restaurants, savoring saucy seafood so fresh it may swim a couple of laps around your plate. In Aug. locals celebrate their annual **Sea Cavalcade** (various water sporting events, a swimming race from nearby Keats I. to Gibsons, a parade, and fireworks) and perhaps participate in the two salmon derbies. Get more info on the immediate area and the entire Sunshine Coast at the **Gibsons Travel InfoCentre** on Lower Marine Dr. and Gower Pt. Rd., tel. 886-2325; open daily.

At historic **Gower Pt.,** four km southwest of Gibsons, a cairn marks the first place on this stretch of the coast that Capt. George Vancouver visited in 1792 when he was mapping the Pacific Coast of North America.

Roberts Creek

About nine km northwest of Gibsons you'll find the small artistic community of Roberts Creek (take the lower road off Hwy. 101). It's the kind of place where arts-and-crafts appreciators can often snatch up a bargain, and those looking for a home away from home can choose from several bed-and-breakfast guesthouses. Roberts Creek Provincial Park, 14 km northwest of Gibsons, has campsites, a sani station nearby, hiking trails, waterfalls, and access to a picnic ground and pebbly beach (an excellent spot to relax) southeast of the campground ($8 per night April-Oct., open year-round). The salmon fishing is good in the waters off the park, but boaters need to be skilled along this stretch of rugged coastline. Continue northwest along Hwy. 101 to Wilson Creek where comfortable beachfront resorts provide camping, fishing, beachcombing at low tide, and sailboarding.

Sechelt

The Indian cultural and coastal service center of **Sechelt,** perched on the isthmus of the Sechelt Peninsula between Sechelt Inlet (humming with seaplane activity) and the Strait of Georgia, is supported by logging, fishing, and summer tourism. Stop here to appreciate the local Sechelt Band's totem poles, masks, fine woven cedar-bark baskets, and shell and jade jewelry, and to cruise the craft shops, beachcomb, hike trails to waterfalls and caves, scuba dive, sailboard, or set up camp in one of the many campgrounds. Local Sechelt festivities include **Timber Days** in May, and the annual Sechelt Indian Band **War Canoe Races** in July. For more info visit the **Sechelt Travel InfoCentre** at 5509 Shornecliffe Ave. downtown, tel. 885-3100; open daily mid-June to mid-Sept., weekdays the rest of the year, tel. 885-3100.

Porpoise Bay Provincial Park is four km northeast of Sechelt via East Porpoise Bay Rd. (Tillicum Bay Rd.). It has open grassy areas amongst fir and cedar forest, a broad sheltered sandy beach (safe swimming but no lifeguard) on the eastern shore of Sechelt Inlet (catch spring salmon from the beach May-Aug.), and a picnic area and campground (toilets and showers; $12 per night April-Oct.; open year-round). Several hiking trails connect the campground with the beach and day-use area, and a woodland trail leads to and along the banks of Angus Creek, a tree-lined chum and coho salmon spawning waterway in fall. The park is a handy base for kayakers and canoeists exploring Sechelt, Salmon, and Narrows inlets, and Sechelt Inlets Provincial Marine Recreation Area. Porpoise Bay is noted for good sportfishing; oysters and clams cling along the inlet northwest of the park. Nearby rivers (you need a boat for some) could provide you with a coho salmon or steelhead trout for dinner, and lakes and streams on the nearby Sechelt Peninsula contain cutthroat trout and kokanee.

Pender Harbour

Along the shores of Pender Harbour lie the villages of **Madeira Park, Garden Bay,** and **Irvines Landing.** Boaters and sportfishing enthusiasts seem to enjoy exploring this stretch of the coast, but good freshwater fishing can also be found in nearby lakes. **Ruby** and **Sakinaw lakes** between Madeira Park and Earl's Cove are reportedly a trout fisherman's delight in season. Canoeists head for the chain of eight lakes between Garden Bay and Egmont, fishing for cutthroat trout with success if they explore the lakes May through October.

Pender Harbour is also killer whale, or orca, habitat—unfortunately one of the main sources of whales for aquariums throughout the world. These highly intelligent gentle giants travel in packs of up to 100. Feeding on the salmon found year-round in these waters, they grow up to nine meters long, weighing as much as eight tons. Keep your eyes on the water and your camera ready to capture their triangular-shaped dorsal fins slicing through the water. For more info on this strip of the coast, contact **Pender Harbour/Madeira Park Travel InfoCentre** at 883-2561.

Egmont

Before reaching Earls Cove, stop for a must-see highlight. Turn off to Egmont to hike the four-km trail from the parking lot to **Narrows** and **Roland Points** in **Skookumchuck Narrows Provincial Park.** Allow about one hour OW; the path is good, but gets too rough for strollers—be prepared to carry little ones much of the way. The park (no camping) lies along the western edge of 400-meter-wide, rock-strewn Skookumchuck Narrows (Skookumchuk means "Turbulent Water" or "Rapid Torrent" in Chinook) between Jervis and Sechelt inlets where the tides of three inlets roar through a narrow passage four times a day. The resulting rapids and eddies boisterously boil and bubble to create fierce-looking whirlpools—fascinating to see when your feet are firmly planted on *terra firma,* but very dangerous for inexperienced boaters unfamiliar with the tides. It's a particularly amazing spectacle during extreme tides in spring when the rapids may reach as high as five meters and the water whooshes past at 20 km an hour. You'll also see abundant marine creatures in tidal pools—it's a fascinating spot. Take a picnic lunch, pull up a rock, and enjoy the view! At **Earls Bay Cove,** catch the ferry to picturesque Saltery Bay (50 minutes).

Saltery Bay

Seaside **Saltery Bay Provincial Park,** on the north shore of Jervis Inlet just west of Saltery Bay (named for the fish saltery that was located nearby in the early 1900s), has campsites ($8 per night March-Sept., open year-round) and a sani station, picnic and day-use areas, a nice beach, a boat-launching ramp, and good offshore salmon fishing from April through late fall. A couple of swimming beaches (no lifeguards) are connected to the campground by a trail, and the shoreline of Saltery Bay is also a popular spot for scuba and skin diving. Keep your eyes glued to Jervis Bay and you may see seals, sea lions, porpoises, and whales, and the dorsal fins of killer whales.

POWELL RIVER

Situated between Jervis Inlet and Desolation Sound along the edge of Malaspina Strait about 135 km from Vancouver, Powell River is almost surrounded by water. The town was originally named in 1885 after Dr. Israel Powell, Superintendent of Indian Affairs for B.C., who led the movement that brought B.C. into confederation with Canada in 1871. During the early years of the 20th century, logging of the tall and slender local trees began in the forests around Lois, Horseshoe, and Nanton lakes, producing exceptionally fine flagpoles that were exported to the rest of the world. In 1912, Powell River became the first newsprint manufacturer of western Canada (check out the photos, displays, and artifacts in the Powell River Historic Museum).

Today the city is a thriving fishing resort, has one of the largest pulp and paper mill complexes in the world, and provides abundant opportunities for outdoor activities. Try your hand at sportfishing for salmon (good year-round) or lake fishing for trout, scuba diving, sailing, ocean or lake canoeing or kayaking, wilderness hiking, or beachcombing. The city successfully lures swarms of visitors from all necks of the woods, particularly in summer, to get into the "great outdoors," or to pull up their own piece of seaside sand and just stay put.

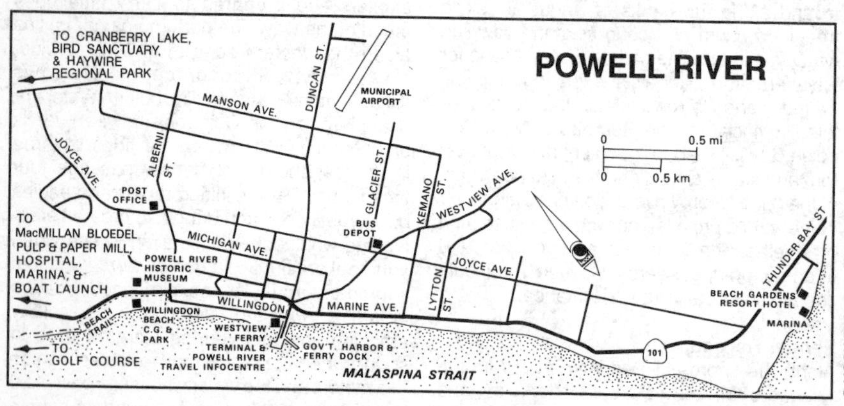

TREES, FLAGPOLES, AND PAPER

Downtown Attractions

One of the best ways to explore Powell River is on foot, armed with the ***Heritage Walk*** brochure (available at the Travel InfoCentre or museum). The first commercial building was the original 30-room **Powell River Hotel,** completed in 1911. Most of the buildings you'll see in "old town" Powell River were built between 1911 and 1939, and the homes were built between 1911 and 1916—quite an intriguing architectural variety.

After meandering around town and getting a feel for the place, wander back in time by visiting the excellent **Powell River Historic Museum** across the road from Willingdon Beach (watch for the sign) on Marine Ave., tel. 485-2222. Peruse the vast collection of photographs (third-largest archives in the province) and displays to find out about this seashore community, and to see what the area was like before the town was established. Also see well-preserved artifacts, and native carvings and baskets—even sand from around the world. It's open daily 1000-1800 in summer (May-Aug.), Mon.-Fri. 1000-1700 the rest of the year, with the exception of December; admission $1 adult, 50 cents child.

If touring paper mills is more your bag, don't miss visiting the **MacMillan Bloedel Powell River Division,** one of the largest pulp and paper mill complexes in the world. The first roll of newsprint manufactured in western Canada was produced here in 1912. The log-storage pond, formed by a breakwater made of 10 anchored cement ships chained together, is one of Powell River's exotic sights. Mill tours are available from May/June to Aug./Sept. on weekdays at 0900, 1000, 1300, and 1400 (allow two hours). Arrive at the main gate at 6270 Yew St. at least 10 minutes prior to the tour, and wear closed footwear. Children under 12 cannot go along. For more details call 483-3722.

Kids going crazy? Need an entertaining time-out? Take them to the **Petting Farm** where *they* can meet all sorts of resident animals and *you* can shop for farm products, meats, organic vegies, and country crafts. It's part of Mountain Ash Farm on Nassichuk Rd., tel. 487-9340; open Sat.-Thurs. 1200-1700, admission adult $2, child $1. To get there from the main coast road, turn right at Zilliashy, cross Keely Creek Rd., then turn left on Nassichuk (the farm is on the right side of the road).

Hikes For All

Around the Powell River district are short walks along sandy or pebbly ocean beaches and along the edge of the local golf course, trails into the **Cranberry Lake Bird Sanctuary** to see resident eagles, swans, geese, ducks, and a variety of migratory birds, and difficult wilderness hikes through rainforest into high alpine country. Or hike one of the many abandoned logging roads up mountainsides for spectacular unobstructed alpine views.

One of the most popular short local trails is the 20-minute hike up 182-meter **Mt. Valentine,** northeast of Powell River, to a viewpoint for a stunning panoramic view of Malaspina Strait and the Strait of Georgia. Access is from the end of Crown Street. Another beautiful trail takes you right around **Inland (Loon) Lake,** north of Powell River between Powell and Haslam lakes. The wheelchair-accessible trail is 13 km long, approachable from either end, has bridges and boardwalks over swampy areas, picnic sites at regular intervals, and two campsites (and another island campsite accessible only by canoe). For more trail suggestions, call in at the InfoCentre.

GET WET!

Underwater Action

Whether you like to be in, on, or under the water, you'll find some kind of aquatic enticement if you stay in Powell River longer than 10 minutes. Internationally known as the "Diving Capital Of Canada," the Strait of Georgia provides divers with exceptionally clear (up to 30-meter) warm water and more than 100 exciting dives mapped by local experts. All the inlets and offshore islands provide a large variety of excellent dive sites, accessible from shore or by boat. Expect an abundance of colorful marinelife, some of it unique, and protected marine sanctuaries (artifacts and marinelife must not be removed), underwater cliffs covered in sponges, shipwrecks, the Saltery Bay mermaid (first underwater statue in Canada), giant octopi (up to 50 kilograms), wolf eels, tubeworms, sea anemones, nudibranch, sea stars, crabs, yellow and white sponge, and tunicates. Seals can by seen year-round, sea lions Nov.-April. The diving is excellent in the cooler months, with best visibility in winter. Get detailed info from local guides or drop by **Emerald Sea Diving Adventures** at 4675 Marine Ave., a PADI, ACUC, and CMAS store providing diving instruction, D.A.N. oxygen first-aid instruction, personal underwater videos, air, rentals, guiding, repairs, and charters; tel. 485-7637.

A-lure-ing Fish

Powell River, with ocean on the west and lakes on the east, is a fishing fantasy come true! Locals claim that the waters produce "one of the highest salmon-per-angler/per-trip success rates in the Strait." Saltwater fishing for chinook (or spring) salmon is good year-round, but particularly good in autumn and midwinter. By late summer, some of the smart (or lucky) salmon weigh over 30 pounds—then they're called tyee, and you'll notice many a proud angler on the dock struggling to hold up his or her fish at just the right angle while beaming for the camera. Coho salmon usually arrive around April/ May. Sport anglers also pursue red snapper, perch, flatfish, ling cod, and rock fish. Bring your own boat (launching ramps are free) or charter one with or without a guide and equipment. Dangle a line from the wharf, docks, or breakwaters, or hurl it out from the shore; a saltwater fishing license is required.

Good cutthroat trout can be found in more than a dozen accessible (most by logging road) freshwater lakes, many are stocked with rainbow trout and kokanee salmon, and in a couple you can also catch Dolly Varden. Note that you need separate fishing licenses for freshwater and saltwater fishing. Government harbors, a private marina, and several float-moorages cater to avid boaters visiting the area. Get more detailed info, the rundown on fishing regulations, and appropriate licenses from local tackle stores. Try **Marine Traders,** at 6791 Wharf St., tel. 485-4624, or **Taw's Gun & Cycle,** at 4597 Marine Ave., tel. 485-2555. Collect your *Freshwater* and *Saltwater Fishing Regulations Synopsis* at the Visitor's InfoCentre. For 24-hour sportfishing info call toll-free within B.C., (800) 663-9333.

Got A Canoe?

The sheltered Sunshine Coast provides plenty of opportunities for good lake and ocean canoeing or kayaking. Rent a canoe for $4/ hour, $20/day, $95/week (six or seven days) from **Nellie's Canoe Rentals** at the Edgehill Store at 5206 Manson Ave., or call 483-3909. It's wise to get hold of a tide and current schedule before your paddle hits water. Ocean tides can work with you, or rapidly sweep you out into areas you had no inkling to explore—places so dangerous and unpredictable you might think you've entered the Twilight Zone! Be prepared, and especially don't take ominous-looking weather too lightly—don't even take fair weather for granted!

The most well-known inland canoeing action in this area centers on the 57-km semicircular **Powell Forest Canoe Route** developed by Powell River District Forest Service in the early 1980s. It starts south of Powell River at **Lois Lake** and connects 12 lakes with eight km of well-established portage trails, bridged creeks, and swamps, to finish at the headwaters of Powell Lake near the MacMillan Bloedel mill. Along the trail you'll find handy canoe resting racks at four- to five-minute intervals, and regular campsites (most of them only accessible to canoeists and hikers). The entire route takes up to a week; best traveled between April and Oct. when good weather is anticipated.

The Canoe Route is a great way to get away from it all, to surround yourself by tree-covered lowlands and rugged mountain peaks while you slip through fjord-like lakes. Take side trips and you can extend the water distance to more than 150 km, or just do one or two sections of the trail at a time—all the major lakes have road access. The longest paddle is 28½ km along Powell Lake at the end of the route, but you can also arrange pickup at Haywire Bay on Powell Lake or at Inland Lake to avoid part of the long haul home. The three-lake route, starting at Lois Lake and paddling in a northeast direction across Louis and Khartoum lakes, is a 14-km trip taking one to two days. Carry a tent and stay at one of the many Forest Service recreation sites and camping areas along the route, and don't forget your fishing rod and tackle. All the lakes are stocked with cutthroat trout, and some have rainbow trout and kokanee salmon (freshwater fishing license required).

To get to the Canoe Route departure point, turn off Hwy. 101 about 20 km southeast of Powell River on the Branch 41 logging road just south of the Eagle River Bridge (about two km south of Lang Bay) and follow the signs to the Lois Lake departure point. As with any logging road, check if active logging is going on and the hours that it's safe to travel at 485-9831 or 485-4701—if you meet a loaded logging truck there's usually nowhere for you to go but a ditch or heaven (if you're lucky), or hell (if you're not). Collect a map and brochure describing the route in detail and find out present water levels and campfire regulations at the Powell River District Forest Service office at 7077 Duncan St., tel. 485-9831, or visit the InfoCentre at 6807 Wharf St. (open weekends), tel. 485-4701.

PRACTICALITIES

Accommodations

Campers find more than 20 provincial and regional parks and private campgrounds in the area. For a downtown location (and hospitable manager), stay at **Willingdon Beach Municipal Campground** on Marine Ave., tel. 485-2242. You'll find sheltered campsites along the beach (very popular), washrooms with free hot showers, laundromat, and full hookups; basic tent sites go for $9.10-11.24 per vehicle per night, powered sites $13.91 (stay three days and it's only $11.50 a night), full hookups from $14.44 (less for seniors). Canoeists find **Haywire Bay Regional Park** handy. It's at the end of the Powell Forest Canoe Route on Powell Lake, seven km north of town, has hot showers, a sandy beach, and a boat launch, and you can rent a canoe if you didn't bring one. Accessible by logging road or lake, for directions call 483-3231; $8 per vehicle.

Tired of your tent and want some oceanside comfort? Try **Beach Gardens Resort Hotel** on the edge of Malaspina Strait at the east end of town, where rooms with marina views range $46-115 s, $46-125 d, and for an extra $8 you can also get your own kitchen. Facilities include indoor swimming pool, sauna, tennis courts, restaurant with lunchtime smorgasbord buffets, neighborhood pub, and a marina with boat rentals and divers' air—a great place to meet fellow scuba enthusiasts and maybe find a diving partner; at 7074 Westminster Ave., tel. 485-6267.

Food

For light meals try **Beverly Anne's Cafe** at 4715 Marine Ave. near Willingdon Beach, or **Dutch Sandwich Shop** at 4480 Willingdon Ave. near the Westview ferry terminal. For good Chinese fare, try **The Oriental** on the corner of Wharf and Westview; dishes from $5.50. For more elegant dining with a great view of the comings and goings of the Vancouver I. ferry, check out **The Seahouse,** a restaurant in a heritage house at 4448 Marine Ave., tel. 485-9151. Open for lunch from 1130, dinner from 1630, brunch and dinner on Sundays serving delicious seafood fresh from local waters, salads, and meat dishes; take your credit card. Or visit **Chanterelles** for seafood, **Viva Restaurant** for family dining and a variety of cuisines, or **Shinglemill Pub and Bistro** overlooking Powell Lake. Another popular place for seafood and fine cuisine is the **Beach Gardens Resort Hotel** with outdoor tables overlooking Malaspina Strait. Sample their lunch buffet, salad bar, or bistro, or go for the formal sit-down dinner; at 7074 Westminster Ave., call 485-6267 for reservations.

Information

The **Powell River Travel InfoCentre** is at 6807 Wharf St. by the Westview Ferry Terminal, tel. 485-4701; open weekdays 0900-1700, daily to 2100 in summer. In an emergency, call the **hospital** (north end of Marine Ave. on Arbutus Ave. near the paper mill) at tel. 483-3211, **ambulance** tel. 485-4211, **police** tel. 485-6255, **Coast Guard** tel. 485-7511, **marine or aircraft distress** tel. (800) 742-1313. Continuing on from Powell River, catch the ferry over to **Texada I.** to see its limestone quarries and secluded sandy beaches, or to collect "flower rocks"; put up your tent at **Harwood Point Regional Park.** Catch the B.C. Ferry to Comox/Courtenay on Vancouver I.; 1½ hours and $24 OW per vehicle and driver, adult $5.25, child $2.25, bicycle and rider $7.50. For more info call **B.C. Ferries Westview Terminal** at tel. 485-2943. The **bus terminal,** on the corner of Joyce Ave. and Glacier St., can be reached at tel. 485-5030. **Powell River Municipal Airport** is north of town, off Dunedin St.; commuter service to Vancouver.

NORTH OF POWELL RIVER

About 19 km north of Powell River, eight km east of Lund, on the east side of Malaspina Peninsula lies **Okeover Arm Provincial Park.** This small, rustic waterfront and forested park has only a few undeveloped campsites (free), a pit toilet, and a boat-launching ramp, but it's a nifty spot to camp if you're into canoeing or kayaking. The warm, sheltered waters of Okeover Arm provide the perfect environment for all kinds of prolific marinelife (and lots of oyster farms). Access is via Malaspina Rd., off Hwy. 101 south of Lund.

Lund, a tiny fishing village on a secluded harbor backed by the magnificent peaks of the Coast Mountains, 28 km north of Powell River, is the gateway to beautiful **Desolation Sound** at the north end of Hwy. 101 (charter boats available). Here you'll discover a marina bustling with activity, **Lund Breakwater Inn, General Store, gift shop, RV Trailer Park**, and **Carvers Studio and Coffee House**—excellent baked goods and delicious coffee.

Desolation Sound Marine Park is the largest marine park in B.C., covering 8,256 hectares of Gifford Peninsula, the adjacent waters of Desolation Sound, and a number of offshore islands. There's no road access and it's totally undeveloped—a wilderness-seeker's paradise. The area was named by Capt. Vancouver after his visit in 1792—he was obviously unimpressed, as the name implies! Today the warm waters teeming with marinelife provide the opportunity for all sorts of marine activities and adventures, attracting boaters, canoeists, and anglers.

SEA TO SKY COUNTRY

The spectacular, aptly named Sea To Sky Highway (Hwy. 99) from Horseshoe Bay to Whistler is a stretch of road that shouldn't be missed—even if the sky has just opened up and you notice locals building arks. With the almost-vertical tree-covered **Coast Mountains** on the right and the railway tracks and island-dotted **Howe Sound** on the left, this cliff-hugging highway precariously clings to the mountainside as it winds through a dramatic glacier-carved landscape created during the last ice age.

The weather certainly affects what you see and how you feel about this part of Southwestern B.C. On sunny days everything seems to be bright blue, emerald green, and sparkling clean; only water trickling down the roadside cliffs gives you the clue that it rains a bit around here. On the other hand, after a string of dull drizzly days, impressive waterfalls, one after another, plummet down those same cliffs right beside you (good car-washing potential) to abruptly disappear underneath the highway, and the scenery merges into a magnificent multi-shaded blue and gray blur as you whiz up into the mountains. Along the road expect some tight corners, narrow stretches, and enough traffic to keep your toes a-tapping between the accelerator and the brake—a real workout if you're on a bicycle. Be aware of potential hazards in bad weather (washouts can occur), and if you want to go slowly to absorb everthing, use the slow-lane pullouts to avoid sending hurried locals into a state of near-frenzy.

Public Transportation Options

Access to this part of Southwestern B.C. is also made easy by various modes of public transportation. By coach: call **Maverick Coach Lines** at 662-8051 in Vancouver, 898-3914 in Squamish, or 932-5031 in Whistler Village. By train: call **B.C. Rail** at 631-3500 in North Vancouver, 898-2420 in Squamish, 932-4003 in Whistler Village (the station is on Lake Placid Road). B.C. Rail operates daily service from Vancouver through Southwestern B.C. (ask for their Day-Tripper schedule and fares to Squamish and Whistler) all the way to Prince George. They also run special day excursions, such as the Lillooet Cariboo Excursion which includes three meals, deluxe seating with bar service available, and a guided bus tour of Lillooet and museum visit. For departure dates, current fares, and reservations call 631-3500 or drop by the B.C. Rail Passenger Station at 1311 West 1st St., North Vancouver.

Between mid-May and the end of Sept., there's also the antique steam train day-trip option (for all the details call B.C. Rail at 631-3500), or jump aboard the majestic MV *Brittania* to Squamish at the head of Howe Sound. (Call **Harbour Ferries** in Vancouver at 687-9558.) In summer you can take the steam train one way and the boat back, or vice versa.

HIGHWAY HIGHLIGHTS

Porteau Cove Provincial Park

On the east shore of Howe Sound, Porteau Cove provides boat-launching and scuba-diving facilities (reportedly some of the best diving on this part of the coast), an ecology info center, good swimming and fishing, picnic tables, and a waterfront campground for tents and RVs ($13 per site per night Mar.-Oct., but open year-round). This particular area of the Sound also gets strong winds, but no waves, providing perfect windsurfing conditions.

Brittania Beach

Small Brittania Beach is worth a stop to visit the **B.C. Museum of Mining.** In the early 1930s the Brittania Beach Mine was the largest producer of copper in the British Empire, producing more than 600 million kilograms.

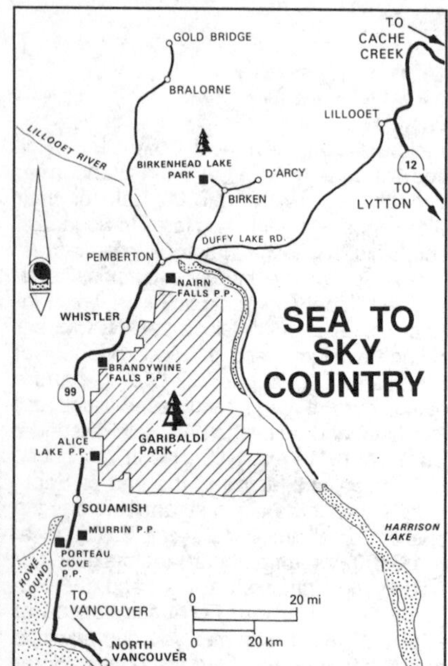

Today it's not operating as a working mine, but as a working museum. Ever wondered what it's like to slave away underground? Here's your chance to don a hard hat and raincoat, hop on an electric train, and travel under a mountain, without even getting your hands dirty! See the techniques of mining through a variety of fully functional equipment, demos, and displays, then take a step into the past in the museum where hundreds of photos and artifacts tell the story of the mine. There is also a gift shop, a restaurant, and a gold-panning pool; open mid-May to Sept. daily 1000-1600, to 1700 on weekends, admission adult $7, senior $5, student $4, child under five free, family $22. For more info, call 896-2233.

Pleasurable Parks

Straddling the highway, **Murrin Provincial Park** is one of many coastal parks providing good boating, fishing, swimming, and walking trails, but with an added bonus—steep cliffs that attract novice and intermediate rock climbers. Picnic tables; no campsites. The next spot to stop along the highway is **Shannon Falls Provincial Park** to see spectacular 335-meter Shannon Falls from the platform viewpoint at the base. Have a picnic or hike a few trails; no camping, but just down the highway is the **Klahanie Campground,** restaurant, and climbing shop.

Squamish

A town of 12,000, natural deep-water port, and "nuclear-weapons-free zone," Squamish has a stunning location at the head of Howe Sound, surrounded by snowcapped mountains. Its location gives true meaning to the well-coined phrase "Sea To Sky Country" applied to this area. The name Squamish is a Coast Salish Indian word meaning "Mother of the Wind"—obviously, since the beginning of Squamish time, the town has been getting the same stiff breezes in all seasons that delight today's sailors and sailboarders. The town is also the gateway to the Whistler recreation corridor, and the beginning of the Nugget Route to Lillooet.

The first white settlers made their home in the valley in 1888, logging the local giant cedar and fir trees for a living. Squamish quickly became a logging town, and then a railroad town; at one time it was the southern terminus for the Pacific Great Eastern, until the line was extended to Vancouver in 1956. Today lumber is still the lifeblood of the area—see the dumping and booming of logs along the **Mamquam Blind Channel** on the east side of town, ready for towing to southern mills. It's also a service center for a growing number of visitors arriving via the steam train and/or boat day-trip from Vancouver, or outdoor recreationalists en route to Whistler. Experienced climbers also flock to Squamish to conquer "The Chief," 762-meter **Stawamus Chief,** the second-largest granite monolith in the British Commonwealth, after the Rock of Gibraltar.

Other attractions include **Squamish Valley Museum** in a heritage house on 2nd Ave. (open Wed.-Sun.), the **Indian Cultural Centre, Government Dock,** sightseeing flights with exciting glacier landings (daily during summer, reservations recommended; call Squamish Municipal Airport at 898-9016 for fares), an 18-hole golf course, fishing, horse riding, bald-eagle watching in the Squamish Valley in autumn and winter, a great number of wilderness hiking trails ranging from six- to 32-km RT routes (get details and maps at the InfoCentre), and excellent cross-country skiing in nearby Garibaldi Park.

Early in Aug., Squamish is mobbed by loggers from around the world who congregate here to participate or compete in the annual **Squamish Days World Championship Logging Show.** Don't be too surprised to see people racing up or hanging from trees, rolling logs, and throwing axes in early August! For the less competitive try an RV rally, Truck Loggers Rodeo, sports races, dances, pageants, parades—you name it! For detailed info on Squamish, local provincial parks, and Whistler, follow the signs from the highway to the **Squamish Chamber of Commerce Travel InfoCentre** at 37950 Cleveland Ave., tel. 892-9244; restrooms and telephone. Open daily in summer 0900-1700, in winter Mon.-Fri. 0900-1600.

Garibaldi Provincial Park

This beautiful park covers 195,000 hectares of pristine alpine wilderness, only 64 km from Vancouver in the heart of Sea To Sky Country. Dominated by the snow-covered Coast Mountain Range, in particular 2,678-meter **Mt. Garibaldi** (named in 1860 after Giuseppe Garibaldi, a 19th-century Italian soldier and statesman), other park features include 2,315-meter **Black Tusk Mt., the Gargoyles** (eroded rock formations reached by a trail from the park's southern entrance), and the 1½-km-long **Barrier** lava flow above the west side of **Garibaldi Lake.**

Keeping in mind that Garibaldi is a true wilderness park, with no road access except to the park boundary, explore the park in summer (late July through early Sept. is best) to find fabulous hiking through high meadows crowded with wildflowers (a spectacle in late summer), forests of fir, red cedar, hemlock, and balsam, bright blue lakes, jagged volcanic peaks and lava flows, extinct cinder cones, and huge glaciers. If you're in the right spot at the right time (or the wrong spot at the right time, depending on your outlook), you may see black and grizzly bears, mountain goats, and deer, along with lots of marmots, chipmunks, squirrels, and birds. In winter the park is thickly blanketed in snow, luring experienced cross-country skiers from Nov. to mid-June. Snow can linger well into July in fact, and the higher peaks are permanently mantled.

To reach Garibaldi, you have to drive in on one of five entrance roads off Hwy. 99 which lead you to access points into the most popular areas of the park, **Diamond Head, Black Tusk/Garibaldi Lake, Cheakamus Lake, Singing Pass,** and **Wedgemount Lake,** and then hike developed trail systems. All the access roads are clearly marked on Hwy. 99 between Squamish and Pemberton. Aside from the five most popular areas, the rest of the park is untouched wilderness, only explored by mountaineers and experienced cross-country skiers.

If you want to camp in the park, tent sites and pit toilets are located at Diamond Head at **Red Heather Campground,** six km from the parking lot, and **Elfin Lakes Campground,** 11.2 km from the lot; at Black Tusk/ Garibaldi Lake at **Taylor Meadows** and the west end of the lake (small fee in summer; no campfires so take a stove); at **Cheakamus Lake** at the west end of the lake and at the end of the trail; at **Singing Pass** at the northwest end of the lake; and at **Wedgemount Lake** at the northwest end of the lake.

Before you enter the park pick up a *Garibaldi Provincial Park* brochure, put out by B.C. Parks, from any InfoCentre. If you plan on getting off the beaten track, write for the following maps (nominal fee for each): a contour map (scale 1:100,000) of Garibaldi Provincial Park from the Outdoor Recreation Council, 1200 Hornby St., Vancouver, B.C. V6Z 2E2, and the NTS Sheet 92G/09 map from MAPS BC, Ministry of Lands and Parks, Parliament Buildings, Victoria, B.C. V8V 1X5. For more specific info, contact the Garibaldi/Sunshine Coast District Office, Alice Lake Provincial Park, Brackendale, or call 898-3678.

Alice Lake Provincial Park

Alice Lake, surrounded by open grassy areas, dense forests, and the impressive snow-covered peaks of the Coast Mountain Range, is particularly good for canoeing, swimming, and fishing for small rainbow and cutthroat trout. In winter cross-country skiers can explore a variety of (summer hiking) trails. Have a picnic at one of the tables, wander along the self-guided nature trail, and stay the night in the campground (pit toilets); open all year, $13 per site per night March-October.

Brandywine Falls Provincial Park

If you like waterfalls, stop at this park to follow the 300-meter, five-minute trail starting from the parking lot. It's the kind of trail that excites all your senses—magnificent frosty peaks high above, dense lush forest on either side, a fast, deep river roaring along on one side, the pungent aroma and cushiness of crushed pine needles beneath your feet. The trail takes you to a viewing platform to see 66-meter **Brandywine Falls** plummet down a vertical lava cliff into a massive swirling plunge pool, then roar down a forest-edged river into a lake—most magnificent early in summer. The falls were named in the early part of this century when they were the subject of a wager by two railroad surveyors guessing their height, the winner to receive bottles of, you guessed it, tequila and a six-pack! From the trail to the falls you can also branch off on another trail that leads to **Swim Lake** (400 meter) and **Calcheak Trail** (four km). Aside from hiking, the park is also a good spot for swimming and fishing. A campground near Hwy. 99 provides gravel campsites; May-Oct. the overnight fee is $8 per night, seniors $4, maximum stay 14 days.

WHISTLER AND VICINITY

Magnificent, steep, snow-dusted peaks, dense green forests, transparent lakes, sparkling rivers, and a cosmopolitan village providing all the services you could possibly need right in the middle of it all—welcome to Whistler. With abundant snow from Nov. to May, and two major ski mountains within a short walking distance from one another, locals and snow addicts from afar say Whistler is one of the finest ski areas in the country. Some go on, with little prompting, to categorically state it's one of the premier resorts in North America. It got its intriguing name in the mid-1960s from two sources: the whistling sound that the wind makes as it blows down through Fitzsimmons Pass between Whistler and Blackcomb Mountains, and the high-pitched whistle made by the large number of communicating hoary marmots (animals, not of the party variety) that make this area their home.

Despite its reputation for excellent skiing, it's not just one of those places to think about when a nip is in the air, the leaves start to fall, and your ski equipment jumps out of the closet. There's also plenty to do in spring and summer. You'll be so busy hiking on a good network of alpine trails, mountain biking, fishing in nearby lakes, canoeing or kayaking, river rafting, windsurfing, horse riding, or golfing, you may wonder what all the skiing fuss is about—unless you're going for the summer skiing on Blackcomb Mountain!

Whistler demands to be seen in good weather. On a gray day when the mountains are blanketed in low clouds, you can't tell how beautiful the area is. Spend another day, a week, however long it takes for the clouds to lift, *et voila,* Whistler is transformed. You'll probably spend at least the next couple of hours madly running around trying to capture everything you see on film, like I did!

The town, only 87 km from Vancouver, stretches from the "Whistler Welcomes You" sign (by **Whistler Archives and Museum,** tel. 932-2019, and the entrance to **Cheakamus Lake trail**) to north of **Green Lake. Whistler Village** nestles in the shadow of **Blackcomb Mountain.** On entering the resort from the south, look for the sign to the

Travel InfoCentre on the right. It's on Lake Placid Rd., opposite the Husky Gas Station, in Whistler Creek (a local name for this area); open daily, hours vary throughout the year. The map of the Garibaldi-Whistler area outside the center is very handy for orientation; inside collect detailed info on all the local skiing and outdoor recreational activities, accommodations, restaurants, and services in the area.

A WINTER WONDERLAND

Downhill Skiing

The two mountains, **Whistler** and **Blackcomb,** are known internationally for their long, long runs—two of the longest vertical drops in North America—and some of the most picturesque cross-country skiing in Canada. The season, weather and snow permitting, is Nov.-May, though summer skiing continues on Blackcomb June-Sept. (see "Summer Action," below).

Whistler Mt. has a top elevation of 2,176 meters, and 85 ski runs—the longest, from Peak to the bottom of Olympic, is eight km. To get up the mountain choose from gondolas, T-bars, tows, and a variety of chairlifts. Twenty-five percent of the runs are suitable for beginners, 55% for intermediate skiers, and 20% for experts. **Blackcomb Mt.** has a top elevation of 2,284 meters, a base elevation of 675 meters, a vertical drop of 1,609 meters (or 5,280 feet, the longest vertical drop in North America). On this mountain are 85 runs—the longest run from the top of 7th Heaven to the bottom of Cruiser is eight km. Get up this mountain by express quad chairs, double and triple chairlifts, T-bar, or handle tow. Twenty percent is suitable for

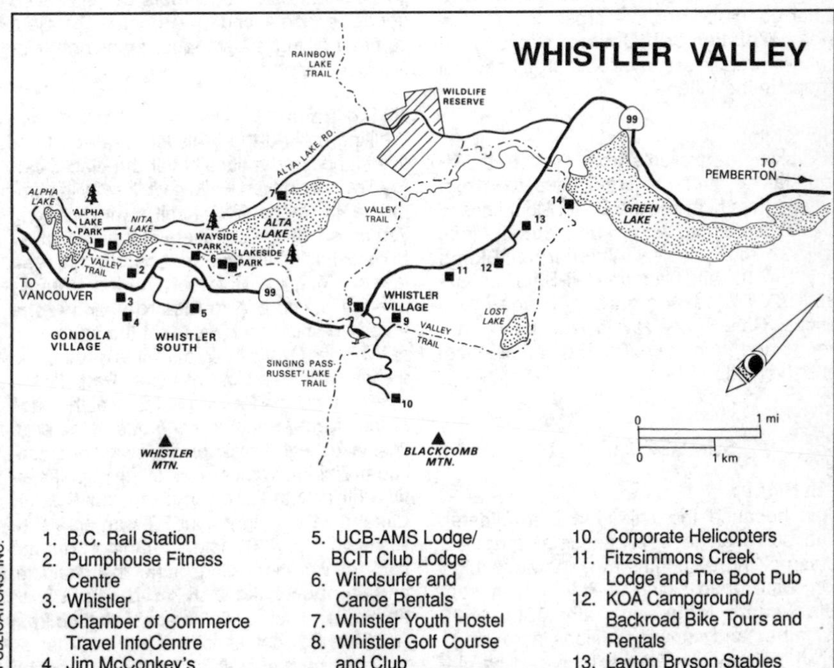

beginners, 55% for intermediate skiers, and 25% for experts. There are also ski schools and racing programs, and ski rental, equipment, and clothing shops in the Village. Downhill ski, boot, and pole rentals are available. Snowboarding is permitted on both Blackcomb and Whistler.

Cross-country Skiing

The cross-country skier is also in his or her element with hectares of groomed trails through snow-covered wilderness, many starting at Whistler Village. **Valley Trail,** a paved walk/bikeway in summer that runs the length of the valley (see "Summer Action," below) becomes a very popular cross-country ski trail in winter. **Lost Lake Park,** just northeast of the Village, has a variety of trails (15 km track-set) suitable for everyone through to advanced skiers, with a log warming hut at Lost Lake. Another good spot for free cross-country skiing is **Whistler Golf Course.** Cross-country ski rentals are available from several shops in the Village.

Heli-skiing

Heli-skiing is available from **Tyax Heli-Skiing,** taking strong intermediates to expert adventurers high into the Coast Mountains to ski fields of unbroken powder; for more info, call 932-7007. Also call **Whistler Heli Skiing** at 932-4105, and **Canada Heli-Sport** at 932-3512/2070, to compare packages and prices. Rates generally include transportation to and from the helipad, gourmet lunch, and the guide.

SUMMER ACTION

Get High!

Just because the calendar, thermometer, and sun's angle say it's summer doesn't mean skiing is months away. June-Oct. go for some good skiing in 7th Heaven from Blackcomb Mountain daily 0800-1500 (weather and snow conditions permitting), on the Horstman Glacier (serviced by glacier T-bars), or brush up your style at a summer ski camp; for more info, call 932-3141.

You can also get high into the mountains for excellent alpine hiking (guided naturalist walking tours are also available), or go for a snack or meal with a wonderful view, even if you have no intention of skiing. Take the two fun **summer chairlifts** up Blackcomb, watching from the upper chair as the skiers swoosh down the slopes below you; they operate daily 0800-1630. Even if it's a beautiful spring or summer day down in the Village, take a warm wind- and waterproof coat and wear hiking boots—tennis shoes just don't make the grade at the top. The restaurant (open in summer for lunch to 1400) is expensive but has excellent views of Whistler Village far below. The less expensive self-serve cafeteria (open until 1530 in summer) in the same building has soup, salad bar, hamburgers ($4-6), baked goods, and hot and cold drinks. Excellent summer hiking is also up for grabs on Whistler Mountain.

Hiking Trails

Walking around the Whistler area you'll notice signposted trails all over the place. **Valley Trail** is a paved walkway/bikeway in summer, a cross-country ski trail in winter, taking you on an almost complete tour of the valley from Whistler Village to **Lost** and **Green lakes,** along the **River of Golden Dreams** and the golf course, to **Alta, Nita,** and **Alpha lakes,** to finish on Hwy. 99 at the south end of Whistler (or vice versa). If you'd rather do a short walk, head for **Lost Lake Park** via the 1½-km trail from Parking Lot East at the back of the village. Saunter along one of the prettiest lakes in the area, picnic, swim, or cross-country ski in winter. Two other popular alpine hiking trails are **Singing Pass-Russet Lake,** a 21-km eight-hour RT with an elevation gain of 1,400 meters, starting from the back of Whistler Village near the chairlifts, and **Rainbow Lake,** a 16-km six-hour RT with an elevation gain of 850 meters, starting from Alta Lake Rd., not far north of the youth hostel.

Some of the best alpine hiking can be reached by the summer chairlift up Blackcomb Mt. and on Whistler Mt., but if you plan on hiking above the snow line, stay off glaciers unless you are equipped and experienced in glacier travel, be aware of potential avalanche areas, select routes that follow ridges and valley bottoms, windward sides of ridges, and tree-covered slopes, and avoid cornices or lee slopes. Experts recommend carrying an ice axe and self-arrest mechanism.

A Two-wheeler's Paradise

This area is a perfect place to take a bicycle or mountain bike—but if you'd like to ride most or all of the trails in the valley, plan on staying for months. Many of the locals have abandoned their cars for bikes that, in some cases, are definitely worth more than their cars! You can see them scooting along **Valley Trail,** a paved walk/bikeway that links the entire valley and appears to be the resident bicyclists' freeway. Another popular place for mountain bikers is beautiful **Lost Lake Park** on the east side of Whistler, where the trails are marked with signs telling cross-country skiers how easy or difficult they are—the same applies to mountain bike trails. Even experienced mountain bikers will find challenging routes along unmarked horse trails here.

If you didn't bring a bike, not to worry—they're for rent. Or perhaps a guided bicycle tour of the local area sounds appealing—it's not a bad idea to have a guide at first. For all the details, tours, and current rates, contact **Whistler Backroads Mountain Bike Adventures** at 932-3111; **Team McConkey** at 932-2311; **Sea To Sky Cycling** at 938-1233; or **Sports West Bike Tours** at 932-4484. Whistler resort is host to several major mountain-bike racing events each summer; find out more at the InfoCentre.

Take To The Water

Looking for a high-elevation tan and sand? Head for the public beaches at **Wayside** and **Lakeside parks** along the shores of **Alta Lake**—watching all the sailboarders whipping across the water or beginners repeatedly taking a plunge is a good source of summer entertainment. Wayside Park at the south end of the lake has a beach, a canoe launch, an offshore pontoon, a grassy area with picnic tables (no camping), pit toilets, and hiking/biking trails. **Whistler Outdoor Adventure Company** at Lakeside Park (signposted off the highway) rents canoes for $10 an hour or $40 per half day, mountain bikes for $7 an hour, $18 per half day, or $25 for a full day. They also do a variety of adventure tours (each includes transportation) to suit just about everyone: a two-hour river-rafting trip from $49 pp; a two-hour horseback-riding trip for $48 pp; and in winter they offer cross-country, heli-ski, and snowshoe adventures. To reserve a spot, call 932-3389.

For a little whitewater excitement, try river rafting with **Whistler River Adventures.** They provide a variety of guided scenic and whitewater tours between the end of May and early Sept. ranging from half-day to three-day trips, starting around $55 pp which includes lunch. For more info, call 932-3532. Also phone **Whistler Outdoor Experience Company** at 932-6623 for their latest offerings (rafting, horseback riding, etc.) and rates.

Horseback Riding

Follow the highway one mile north of Whistler Village, turn off at Mons Rd. by the KOA sign, then branch left to the **Layton Bryson Stables** to enjoy a one-hour trail ride for $20 pp, a three-hour ride for $50 pp, an evening barbecue (on request), a hayride, an overnight pack trip with gourmet campfire cooking, a fishing or hunting trip, or an entire holiday on horseback. For more info, dial 932-6623. Also contact **Whistler Outdoor Experience Company** for details and rates at 932-6623.

The Bird's-eye View

Nothing beats enjoying the spectacular Coast Mountain Range—its majestic peaks, glaciers, icy-blue lakes, and lush mountain meadows—from an unforgettable vantage point high in the sky. Flights start at $49 pp for a 25-minute flight (minimum four people) in a floatplane from Green Lake with **Whis-**

tler Air, tel. 932-6615 (they also provide scenic fly-in fishing trips, and charter service). Or if a helicopter ride is more appealing, it will cost you from $69 pp plus GST for a 20-minute flight with **Corporate Helicopters,** tel. 932-3512 (they also provide heli-skiing and heli-picnic packages). Or go for a one-day heli-hike with a gourmet mountain-top lunch provided, June-Oct., with **Whistler Heli-Hiking,** tel. 932-4105. Prices start at $325 pp for two people, $250 pp for three to four people, and $200 pp for five.

Anyone For A Game Of Golf?
The **Whistler Golf Course,** between Alta Lake and Whistler Village on the left side of the highway as you head toward Lillooet, is an 18-hole par-72 championship course designed by Arnold Palmer. Call for current rates and make bookings at 932-4544. If miniature golf is more your style, head for **Whistler Wonderland** in the Conference Centre.

More Outdoor Adventure?
Several companies in Whistler specialize in outdoor adventures—call around and see what grabs your fancy. For guided fishing, contact **Whistler Backcountry Adventures** at 938-4267 or **Whistler Fishing Guides** at 932-4267. For fly-in fishing call **Whistler Air** and charter your own specialized expedition to backcountry and otherwise inaccessible lakes at 932-6615. **Parawest Paragliding** at 932-7052 provides year-round paragliding thrills. For mountaineering excitement, give **The Escape Route** a call at 938-3338.

ACCOMMODATIONS

Whistler's accommodations range from a YH and KOA to guest cabins and luxury resort hotels. It's just a matter of selecting one to suit your budget, and location preference (skiers may want to be right in Whistler Village or by the Gondola Base in Whistler Creek so they can stroll out their door, strap on their skis, and go for elevation). For a full listing, call in at the InfoCentre. If you know ahead of time that you're going to be staying several days in Whistler, call the central reservation service at 932-4222, or toll-free (within Canada and U.S.) at (800) 759-1015, or in Vancouver at 685-3650, and ask for their package rates. Most hotels and lodges offer package rates for both winter (peak) and summer (slightly less expensive) seasons.

Whistler Youth Hostel
This youth hostel right on the western shores of Alta Lake (laps the back of the building) has possibly one of the best views in the province. Meet people from around the world in the communal kitchen, dining area, and big, cozy living area where you can delight in the view of the lake and the mountains without moving one of your tired muscles! It's understandably popular year-round; members $12.50 per night, non-members $17.50. Call ahead to see if there's room at 932-5492. From town, it's quite a hike with a heavy pack. If you're driving into Whistler from the south, take Alta Lake Rd. to the left off Hwy. 99 and continue until the road parallels Alta Lake. Look for the sign on the lake side of the road, park your car in the lot, then follow the sign down over the railway tracks to the hostel; open daily 1600-1000. If you don't already have a list of mini-hostels throughout B.C., ask for one here (at InfoCentres you have to specifically ask for hostel accommodation).

Whistler KOA Campground
A couple of kilometers north of Whistler Village, turn right off the highway at Mons Rd. and continue straight ahead. This campground has relaxed, friendly owners; a large number of shady creekside tent and vehicle sites; free hot showers; a communal lounge with wood stove, TV, Jenny the resident cat, laundromat, hot tub, sauna, public telephone, skating pond, bicycle and skate rental, propane; a store with basic groceries, supplies, books, and postcards; and lots of free brochures on things to do in this neck of the mountains. It's open all year; rates are $16 tent or vehicle site plus $2 for electricity

1. reflections from Highway 29, south of Chetwynd (Jane King);
2. beaver lodging along the road to Wapta Falls (Jane King); **3.** Toomuk Creek from the Marble Canyon Trail, Kootenay National Park (Jane King)

1

2

4

5

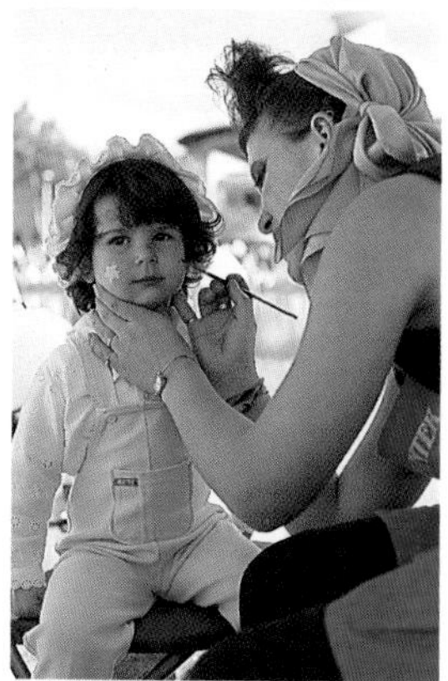

1. horse packer at Fort St. James National Historic Park (Jane King); **2.** Cycling in northern British Columbia (Bill Weir); **3.** Carol, one of the owners of Whitewater Inn, and Pouncer the cat (Jane King); **4.** artist working in 'Ksan Indian Village (Jane King); **5.** Victoria Day festivities in Chinatown (Jane King); **6.** face painting at the Children's Festival, Vanier Park (Jane King)

in summer, $5 in winter, $2 sewer, $2-3 each extra adult; tel. 932-5181. Need somewhere to eat? Check out the sample menus on the wall in the lounge, then ask the owner for her advice.

Budget Accommodations

Some of the lodges have dormitory accommodations or private rooms available. They generally also provide guests with the use of a kitchen, a living or common room with fireplace, laundry facilities, a games room, ski lockers, a ski-tuning room (you need your own tools), a sauna and/or Jacuzzi. Provide your own bedding and towels (sometimes available at a small extra charge). Get more details and find out if they have any space by calling **BCIT Club Lodge** (Nordic Estates) at 932-4660, **Fireside Lodge** (Nordic Estates) at 932-4545, **UBC-AMS Lodge** (Nordic Estates) at 932-6604, or **Tyrol Ski Club Cabin** (midweek only) at 932-5588.

Hotels, Lodges, Pensions

Accommodations in Whistler range from reasonable to outrageous, with facilities to match! In summer most places are a little less expensive. For the complete rundown on all that's available, call in at the InfoCentre at Whistler South. They have full listings of all the rooms in the resort, their facilities, and prices. Or call the Whistler Resort Association at 932-3928, reservations tel. 932-4222. Pensions (Whistler has several) provide homey surroundings and a full hearty breakfast for around $49-99 s, $59-129 d.

Fitzsimmons Creek Lodge has clean comfortable rooms and is one of the most reasonable lodges in the area. Soak in the sauna, relax in front of the open fire, or go for a pub meal (1700-2200) and a rip-roaring evening in **The Boot Pub** ("first and friendliest pub in Whistler"), all without leaving your home away from home. Rooms start at $45-85 s or d in summer, $65 in winter; at 7124 Nancy Green Dr., White Gold Estates (north of the Village on the right side of the highway), tel. 932-3338.

FOOD AND ENTERTAINMENT

In a growing on-the-move resort like Whistler, restaurants and entertainment spots come and go, but you can always find out what's happening by asking the locals, picking up the *Whistler Question* weekly newspaper and the color supplement, *Whistler This Week,* put out by the *Citizen* newspaper, and by calling in at the InfoCentre. Or just follow your nose and ears! In the slow months between winter and summer seasons (particularly Oct. and May), some of the restaurants and entertainment spots close or reduce hours, but according to locals, there's always something going on!

Good Food, Good Prices, Good Fun

Whistler's vast number of restaurants cater to all budgets, tastes, and cravings. **Jimmy D's** (tel. 932-4451) in the Whistler Fairways Hotel has, according to local advice, the largest and tastiest hamburgers in town, and the prices are also reasonable.

For steaks, seafood, salad bar, fresh hot bread, and plenty of food at a reasonable price, **The Keg** is a sure thing. It's always busy, open from 1700, at the Whistler Village Inn, Sundial Place, tel. 932-5151. **Boston Pizza** serves up pasta, ribs, pub fare, as well as pizza, at the Gateways in Whistler Creek, tel. 932-7070. For more of a splurge, sample the seafood, pasta, and continental cuisine at **Florentyna's.** It's at 2129 Lake Placid Rd., Whistler Creek. Make reservations at 932-4424.

Après-ski, Après-anything

In summer (June 15-Sept.) the streets of Whistler Village come alive with all sorts of walking, talking, singing, and dancing street entertainment—wander through the Village and join in the fun. The hottest night spot in town is **Tommy Africa's** (tel. 932-6090), downstairs at Gateway Dr. in the Village. Very popular with the younger crowd, it pumps out high-volume reggae music that "permeates the village." Throughout the year you can usually find live evening entertainment at **Buffalo Bill's** (tel. 932-5211) in the Timberline Lodge off Golfer's Approach, at the **Longhorn Pub** (tel. 932-5999) in the Carleton Lodge off Mountain Square, and at **Umberto's Lounge** and **Rim Rock Cafe** on weekends. The **Savage Beagle Club** (tel. 932-4540) on Skier's Approach has disco. The **Boot Pub** (tel. 932-4246) in Fitzsimmons Lodge and **Planter's Lounge** occasionally provide live entertainment.

Movies are shown twice an evening at **The Rainbow Theatre** in the Conference Centre at Whistler Village; call 932-2422 to see what's playing. If working out after a hard day's workout is more your idea of entertainment, the **Pumphouse Fitness Centre** has weight training and fitness classes, a weight room, a swimming pool, and racquetball and tennis courts; daily, monthly, or yearly rates. It's across the highway from the Gondola base at Whistler South; for more info, call 932-1984.

Local sporting events of all types go on throughout the year—from major ski competitions to mountain-biking races. For a list, contact Whistler Resort Association, Box 1400, Whistler, B.C. V0N 1B0, tel. 932-3928, or drop by the InfoCentre.

Wet-day Entertainment

Rain or drizzle holding you back? Head for **Whistler Public Library** behind the emergency clinic (tel. 932-5564), or **Whistler Museum and Archives** on Hwy. 99, about seven km south of Whistler Village. **Whistler Wonderland** in the Conference Centre provides miniature golf and video arcade games.

INFORMATION AND SERVICES

On entering the ski resort from the south, look for the sign on the right to the **Travel InfoCentre** on Lake Placid Road. A map outside the center shows in detail the Garibaldi Whistler area with trails (length and elevation change), downhill and cross-country ski areas, overnight shelters, vehicle and tent camping spots, fishing, hiking, picnic spots, canoe or kayak portage, sani stations, etc. The center is open daily, but the hours change throughout the year. In summer an info booth opens on the right side of Village Gate Boulevard, the main road leading into Whistler Village. Within the Village are all the services any visitor could possibly need—just ask around or pick up the free *Whistler Journal*, which has a detailed map of the village. The InfoCentre also has good maps and plenty of free literature.

Handy Emergency Numbers

For an **ambulance,** call 932-4233; **police,** tel. 932-3044; **Whistler Emergency Clinic,** tel. 932-4911; **dentist,** tel. 932-3677 or tel. 938-1550.

TRANSPORTATION

Getting There

Take Hwy. 99, the Sea To Sky Highway, less than a two-hour drive from downtown Vancouver. Catch a **Maverick Coach Lines** bus (tel. 255-1171) from downtown Vancouver, or if you're coming directly from Vancouver International Airport, catch a **Perimeter Transportation** bus all the way to Whistler (reservations, tel. 261-2299). **B.C. Rail** runs daily train service from North Vancouver; for more transportation info and reservations, call 932-4222. **Whistler Air** does charter flights to wherever you want to go; tel. 932-6615 (collect from Vancouver) for current schedule and reservations.

Getting Around

Once you're in Whistler, getting around is pretty easy—if you're staying in the Village, everything you need is within easy walking distance, or get around on **B.C. Transit** buses. If you're staying farther out, i.e., the YH, and you don't have a vehicle or bicycle (easily rented from several outfits; see "A Two-wheeler's Paradise," above), hitchhiking is relatively easy. Locals claim that it's particularly easy (and fairly safe) to get a ride if you are carrying skis or look like a liftee going to work! The other alternatives are to call **Whistler Taxi** at 932-5455, **Sea To Sky Taxi** at 932-3333, or **Alliance Taxi** at 932-3399.

Rainbow Budget Rentals is on Hwy. 99 at the north end of Whistler, tel. 932-1236/6601. For **Avis Rent-a-Car** toll-free reservations, dial (800) 268-2310. **Budget Rent-a-Car** is in the Cornerstone Building next to the A&W Restaurant in Whistler Village. If you want a spectacular bird's-eye view of the area or to see glaciers close-up, call **Alpine Adventure Tours** at 932-2705 for info on their variety of tours; from $45 pp for 20 minutes, $55 pp for 30 minutes, and $75 pp for glacier landings. Also call **Mountain Adventure Whistler** for info on their tours, tel. 932-4594.

THE GOLD NUGGET ROUTE

The route from Whistler to Lillooet is best traveled in good weather—the scenery is so spectacular that you don't want to miss *anything*. See white-topped peaks all around you and heavy-duty glacier-colored rivers, and if you have the time, stop at provincial parks along the way for always-good scenery and outdoor activities. **Nairn Falls Provincial Park** on the banks of Green River has a wooded trail leading to a waterfall. It's worth a stop to see the falls, or to stay overnight at the campground; open April-Oct., $8 per site per night from May to October.

Pemberton

A small logging town and distribution center surrounded by mountains, trees, lakes, and rivers (reputedly providing excellent fishing), Pemberton sits in the fertile Pemberton Valley, best known for its "certified disease-free potatoes." Locals affectionately call the area "Spud Valley." It's only a short distance south of the Lillooet River, a main transportation route to the Cariboo during the gold rush days of the 1860s. Today's visitors mostly leave their gold pans at home, coming mainly to fish, or to hike in the beautiful valleys around Pemberton. **Visitor Information** can be obtained at the intersection of Portage and Cottonwood; open daily in summer only.

From Pemberton you can explore three valleys (expect some unpaved roads), or take the shortcut over the mountains to Lillooet—all are best traveled in summer unless you're familiar with the roads: one route takes you through Pemberton Meadows, over Hurley Pass, to the historic mining communities of **Bralorne** and **Gold Bridge** (several fancy resorts here). The second goes through **Mount Currie** along the Birkenhead River to **D'Arcy.** The third runs down to **Lillooet Lake.** If you're in a hurry to see more of B.C., go to Mount Currie, then take the mountain shortcut, Duffy Lake Rd. (the paved Gold Nugget Route) to **Lillooet** (see below).

Shortcut To Lillooet

Continuing toward Lillooet via Duffy Lake Rd. (suitable for travel only in summer), your path traces an ancient Indian trail through the mountains. If you happen to be in **Mount Currie** (an Indian reservation) in May you'll witness one of the largest rodeos in the province; see broncobusting, calf roping, and chuckwagon races. Between Mount Currie and Lillooet Lake the road follows part of the original gold-rush trail where fortune-seekers labored through untamed wilderness toward the Cariboo goldfields between 1862 and 1866.

From Mount Currie on, the road (96 km to Lillooet) zigzags steeply up the mountains to cross a high pass, where even in summer the weather can rapidly change and you can find yourself traveling through a sudden snow storm! Be prepared. However, the scenery makes the effort and risks worthwhile—beautiful lakes with steep mountains plunging down into them, B.C. Recreation sites and campsites in all the best locations, fast rivers, summer wildflowers, steep ravines with rivers in the bottom, deep-blue mountains, never-ending forests, and vistas in every shade of green imaginable! You'll eventually pass the deep-turquoise reservoir, **Seton Lake,** and shoreline **Seton Lake Recreation Area.** Go down the road to the recreation

Chiliwack Museum is housed in the historic 1911 City Hall building.

area. A trail leads from the parking lot down to a delightful wild rose- and grass-edged beach with picnic tables and pit toilets. Farther along the main highway is the turnoff to another recreation area on the lake, this one with campsites.

Lillooet

"B.C.'s Little Nugget," Lillooet in the early 1860s was one of the largest cities north of San Francisco and west of Chicago. At the junction of Cayoosh Creek and the Fraser River, it was "Mile 0" of the old Cariboo Rd., built in 1858, that led north to the Barkerville and Wells goldfields. Lillooet played an important part in the Cariboo gold rush of the last century as the major supply center for interior goldfields. Today it's just a small town with a busy railway station, surrounded by mountains, and loaded with history from a colorful past.

Saunter along Main St. and pretend you're back in the gold-rush days—if you happen to be there in June during **Only in Lillooet Days** this won't be hard. The town re-creates the Old West for one week, with all sorts of entertaining Western-style events. Visit **Lillooet and District Museum** on Main St. across from 8th Ave. (open daily from mid-May to mid-Oct.) for heapings of history, the old **hangman's tree,** and the cairn in Main St. that marks "Mile 0" of the old Cariboo Road. Rockhounders gravitate toward the Lillooet area—it's rich in semiprecious stones. Many a chunk of jade has been found in them thar hills. For more info, call in at the main **Travel InfoCentre** in the museum building on Main St., town center.

VANCOUVER TO HOPE VIA THE FRASER VALLEY

When you leave Vancouver and head due east, you travel through the most built-up and heavily populated area of British Columbia, skirting modern cities, residential suburbs, and zones of heavy industry. However, it's not an unattractive area—the main roads follow the mighty Fraser River through a fertile valley of rolling farmland dotted with historic villages, and in the distance in just about any direction are beautiful mountains.

You have a choice of two major routes: fast Trans-Canada Hwy. 1 on the south side of the Fraser which leads you out of southeast Vancouver through the cities of **Abbotsford** (an excellent International Airshow is held here in Aug.), or scenic **Chilliwack** to **Hope. Cultus Lake Provincial Park,** 11 km south of Chilliwack, with its warm-water lake surrounded by mountains, is a good spot for a swim and picnic, or campsite (open year-round, $12 per night March-October). For detailed info on Southwestern B.C., call in at the **Chilliwack Travel InfoCentre,** clearly marked off Hwy. 1.

Slower, more picturesque Hwy. 7 meanders along the north side of the Fraser River through **Mission,** named after a Roman Catholic Mission school built in 1861 and now known for its Benedictine monastery, which has a retreat center open to the public. Highway 7 then passes the road to **Harrison Hot Springs,** a resort at the base of Harrison Lake, and over the Fraser River to Hope. In summer you can pick and choose from an endless number of roadside stands selling fresh fruit at bargain prices—the raspberries in July are delectable!

This entire southern strip of Southwestern B.C., nicknamed "Rainbow Country," has several provincial parks that attract great numbers of Vancouver residents for weekends and day-trips, a couple of fascinating historic parks, numerous information centers (all signposted off Hwy. 1), and a fistful of commercial attractions designed to lure families into staying awhile ("Mum, Dad, pleeeease can we stop at the waterslides, fun park," etc., etc.). If you're in a hurry to explore the rest of the province or get off the beaten track, whiz on through!

Rainbow Country Highlights

To find out all about B.C.'s beginnings, make your first stop at **Fort Langley National Historic Park** on the south bank of the Fraser River, one km north off Hwy. 1 at Fort Langley (40 km from Vancouver). Fort Langley was the first European establishment in the Fraser Valley—a trading post, provisions and administrative center set up by the Hudson's Bay Company in 1827 that played a major role in the development of British Columbia. Out its gates have vamoosed Indian fur and salmon traders, adventurous explorers who opened up the interior, Company traders, and fortune seekers heading for the goldfields of the upper Fraser River. When B.C. became a crown colony in 1858, the official proclamation was uttered here in the "big house." Today the restored trading post springs to life as park interpreters in period costumes animate the fort's history. Located at 23433 Mavis St., tel. 888-4424; open daily 1000-1630 (extended hours in summer), admission adult $2.25, child (6-16) $1, senior and child under five free, family $5.50.

If you take the Hwy. 7 route out of Vancouver, **Kilby Museum Provincial Historic Park** between Dewdney and Harrison Mills (look for the inconspicuous sign close to Harrison Mills) is off the beaten track and often missed by those unfamiliar with the area. It's located on the shores of the Harrison River, tel. 796-9576. Visit the fascinating museum/country store which is fully stocked with all the old brands and types of goods that were commonplace in the 1920s and '30s (open weekends year-round, daily 1000-1600 in summer; admission by donation). Picnic, swim, fish, or use the boat launch in the park on Harrison Bay (around the corner and

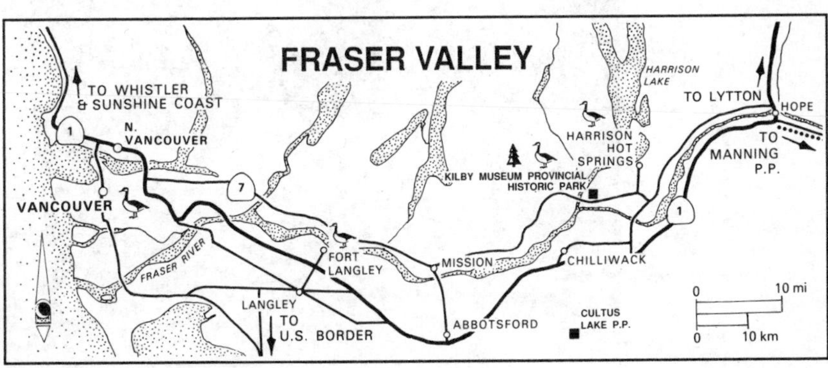

down the road from the museum), or stay awhile in the popular campground (campsites and toilets only); $6 per night March-Oct., open year-round—it can get crowded in summer. Be warned, Harrison Bay is "Sasquatch Country." If you see any extremely tall hairy giants running around in the area, it's best to keep this revelation to yourself!

Harrison Hot Springs on the sandy southern shores of large **Harrison Lake** is a popular resort self-described as "the Spa of Canada." One of the main attractions is the public hot pool: scalding mineral water is pumped from its source, cooled to a soothing 39° C, then pumped into the pool; open daily, on the corner of Harrison Hot Springs Rd. and Esplanade Avenue. The 70-km lake provides good swimming, fishing for trout and coho salmon, sailing, and canoeing. Try sailing lessons, rent sailboats or rowboats, or take a boat tour of the lake in summer from the elegant (and expensive) shoreside Harrison Hotel. To get to Harrison Hot Springs, follow Hwy. 9 from the Hwy. 7/9 junction for about six km.

HOPE

Locals smugly say "all roads lead to Hope"—and they're right! Located on the Fraser at the mouth of the Coquihalla River, 158 km from Vancouver, with Highways 1 and 7 (from Vancouver), 5 (to Kamloops), and 3 (to Princeton) meeting at Hope, it's truly a highway hub in the southeast corner of Southwestern British Columbia. Surrounded by magnificent mountains and rivers (the Fraser, Coquihalla, Nicolum, and Silver Creek), with lakes and provincial parks only a short drive away, it's also an outdoor activity and recreation center.

Simon Fraser, after whom the Fraser Canyon was obviously named, stopped in this area in 1808 after leading the first expedition through the canyon. By 1848 Fort Hope had been set up by the Hudson's Bay Company as a fur-trading post. With the discovery of gold in the canyon in 1858, Hope became a busy stopping point and meeting spot for adventurers and fortune seekers. How did Hope get its name? Well, the most popular (and most gloomy) of several educated theories is that this area was where many prospectors lived in hope but eventually died in despair.

Attractions

To find out more about the history of Hope, visit the **Hope Museum** in the same building as the **Travel InfoCentre** on Water Street. It has a comprehensive collection of pioneer artifacts displayed in real-life kitchen, bedroom, parlor, schoolroom, and blacksmith-

Hope Museum and Travel InfoCentre

shop settings, along with local Indian crafts, and artifacts from the original Fort Hope and gold-rush days. Outside, climb on the Home Gold Mill, a restored gold-ore concentrator from the Coquihalla area. The museum is open daily 0900-1700 in May and June, and 0800-2000 every day in July and Aug.; donation.

While you're discovering the downtown area, check out the authentic **Japanese garden** in Memorial Park beside Hope Town Hall. The garden was constructed to commemorate Tashme, a WW II Internment Camp for Japanese-Canadians that was located east of Hope. Also don't miss the tree stump art in Memorial Park. The eagle holding a salmon in its claws was created by a local chainsaw artist.

Five of the most unusual attractions in the area are the **Othello-Quintette Tunnels,** in a steep gorge of the **Coquihalla Canyon.** Kettle Valley Railway steam locomotives originally puffed through these huge tunnels, carved out of solid granite and opened in 1916, on their way to the Kootenays. But the line between Vancouver and Nelson was plagued by snow, rock slides, and washouts, and closed for repairs more often than it was open. It was eventually abandoned in 1961. By 1962 the tracks and four steel bridges linking the tunnels over the awesome Coquihalla River gorge had been removed.

Today a short, tree-shaded walk takes you down from the **Coquihalla Canyon Recreation Area** parking lot to these massive, dark tunnels—stroll through (if you get easily spooked, take a flashlight) and over the sturdy wooden bridges to admire the gorge and the power and the roar of the Coquihalla River below. The sandbar, cliff, and tunnels were all used in stunt scenes in the movie *First Blood,* but please, stifle any subconscious desires to be Rambo, and stay on the path! (Another movie, *Shoot To Kill,* was also filmed in the Hope area, heavily featuring the Fraser River.) To get to the tunnels from the InfoCentre, take Wallace (the main street downtown) to Sixth Ave. and turn right. Turn left on Kawkawa Lake Rd., crossing the Coquihalla River Bridge and railway tracks. At the first intersection take the right branch, Othello Rd., and continue until you see a sign to the right leading to the recreation area.

Kawkawa Lake Provincial Park is another delightful spot to relax, stroll along a beautiful lake backed by steep mountains, picnic on grassy banks, swim, boat, fish, or observe wildlife—especially all the Canada geese bringing up their families (lots of fluffy yellow goslings in May). To get there follow the same directions for the tunnels (see above) but turn left on Lakeview Road.

Outdoor Action

There are so many rivers, streams, creeks, and lakes around Hope that most outdoor activities revolve around water—most of *it* contains fish. An angler can virtually decide what fish he wants for dinner, buy a couple of lemons, whip up some camper's freeze-dried tartar sauce, and then go looking for that perfect little fishing hole: rainbow or cutthroat trout, kokanee salmon, spring and coho salmon, steelhead, or sturgeon, choose your *poisson*—but know the local regulations and be sure to get a license from a local sporting-goods store before your line hits the water.

For rip-roaring excitement and a healthy dose of adrenalin, spend a couple of hours, or a couple of days, rafting whitewater in the Fraser Canyon (several companies operate rafting trips from Boston Bar to Yale, north of Hope) and on the Thompson River (from Spences Bridge to Lytton). Pick up brochures on the various rafting companies and their river adventures at the Hope InfoCentre.

Canoeing is another sport popular in this district. Looking for a quiet, relaxing paddle? Go to **Kawkawa Lake** (in Hope) or **Silver Lake** (seven km upstream on Skagit Valley Rd.; campgrounds at the south and west ends). For more variety (look out for boils and eddies) canoe the **Fraser River** between Hope and New Westminster (225 km), and if you're an experienced paddler in search of whitewater excitement, put your canoe into the **Skagit River;** access is from Silver Creek, and it's canoeable from the 26 Mile Bridge for 18 km down to a lake. Rent canoes and all the necessary equipment at **Western**

Canoeing at 2142 West Riverside in Abbotsford, tel. 853-9320.

If you're feeling lucky, join the ranks of all the gold miners who've been panning the coarse sand and gravel along the banks of the Fraser River since 1858 and you may still find some color. All you need is a black plastic pan, a small trowel or shovel, and a bucket for your nuggets. Or just go and talk to the weekend prospectors working the gravel bars during low water (early spring, and Aug. through November). You may not score any gold, but you'll hear some darn good stories!

Accommodations, Food, And Entertainment

Hope has a large number of campgrounds (several in the Kawkawa Lake and Othello Tunnels vicinity on the east side of town), with sites ranging from $8-17 per night. Most of its multitude of motels are on old Hope-Princeton Way. Rooms range from $30-46 s, $35-58 d. Refer to the *Accommodations Guide* put out by the Ministry of Tourism, and the *Hope Hospitality Accommodations Guide* brochure, both free at the InfoCentre.

The Hope Chamber of Commerce can also provide you with a free *Dining Guide* brochure listing all the restaurants in town and their summer hours. Try the **Kan Yon Restaurant** (in the Mid Town Shopping Plaza) on Third Ave. for good Chinese dishes and daily specials (more than you can eat) for $5-9, or Canadian dishes $7.50-10 a plate. Other local recommendations include **Rainbow Country Kitchen, Lee's Kettle Valley Restaurant** at 293 Wallace St. (known for its smorgasbord breakfast served all day), or **The Home Restaurant** (large meals at reasonable prices) on Fraser Street.

Get all your entertainment during the day here—there's not much to do at night. **Hope Cinema** features new features each week (call for titles and times at 869-5616), and you can dance to live music on the weekends or play billiards or darts at the three downtown pubs—the **Hope Hotel, Silver Chalice Pub,** and **Hope Legion.** That's it, folks!

Information And Transportation

The **Hope And District Chamber Of Commerce Travel InfoCentre** is located at 919 Water Ave. in the same building as the museum; open daily 0900-1700 in May and June, daily 0800-2000 July and August. Transportation from Hope is via **VIA Rail** (station downtown) or Greyhound (the **bus depot** is on Third St. at the corner of Fort).

NORTH TO BOSTON BAR

Emory Provincial Park

Take Trans-Canada Hwy. 1 north and you'll be following the historic gold rush trail along the mighty Fraser River. The first place you may want to stop is Emory Creek Provincial Park where you can wander along riverside trails, try some fishing, or stay at one of the wooded campsites ($8 May to Oct., open April-November).

Yale

The small town of Yale has quite a history. It started off as one of the many Hudson's Bay Company posts, then it became a transportation center at the head of the navigable lower section of the Fraser River—terminus of one of the largest sternwheeler operations on the West Coast. Enormous Lady Franklin Rock blocked the upriver section to steamer traffic so all goods heading for the interior had to be carried from this point by wagon train along the famous Cariboo Wagon Road. In 1858 Yale flourished as a typical gold-rush town made up of tents, shacks, bars, gambling joints, and shops. After the gold rush ended, and the Canadian Pacific Railway was completed all the way to Vancouver (1886), Yale's population dwindled to the small forestry and service center that it has been for 100 years. If you want to find out more about Yale's historic past, the gold rush, Cariboo Wagon Rd., and CPR construction, visit the **Yale Museum** on Douglas St.; open daily in summer. **Yale Travel InfoCentre** is on the Trans-Canada Hwy.; open daily June-September.

Alexandra Bridge Provincial Park

Stretch your legs and check out the interpretive kiosk at this historic park, 22 km north of Yale, then wander down the remains of the original Cariboo Wagon Rd. to the abandoned **Alexandra Bridge** for a great view of the river rushing beneath your feet.

Between 1808 (when Simon Fraser first came through) and 1863, the treacherous Fraser Canyon posed a major transportation obstacle between the trails from the south and the interior. Several routes across the river were attempted, including the 1848 Anderson Bridge trail from Fort Yale to Spuzzum, a canoe crossing, and a cable ferry. The gold rush of the 1850s and the onslaught of gold miners and mule trains on the route increased the need for a safe river crossing, so finally in 1863 a bridge was completed. However, with the successful completion of the Canadian Pacific Railway through the canyon, the bridge and the Cariboo Wagon Rd. fell into disrepair. The popularity of the automobile forced engineers to construct a new suspension bridge in 1926 (using the original abutments), which lasted right up to 1962 when it was replaced by the bridge that is used today by Hwy. 1 traffic. When you stand on the old bridge, let your imagination take over for a few moments. If you listen very carefully, maybe you'll hear the miners and their mules clip-clopping and clanking across the bridge on the well-worn path to riches, or see Simon Fraser clinging to precarious ladders and hanging platforms made by Thompson Indians as he explored his way through the canyon.

Alexandra Bridge

Hell's Gate

Well-known Hell's Gate is where the Fraser River powers its way through a narrow, glacially carved, 34-meter-wide gorge. When Fraser saw this section of the gorge in 1808 he called it "the gates of Hell" and the name stuck. In 1914 a massive rock slide rocketed down into the gorge, blocking it even further and resulting in the almost-total obliteration of the sockeye salmon population. In 1944 giant concrete fishways were built to slow the waters and allow the spawning salmon to jump upstream—the river soon swarmed with salmon once again. Today you can whiz down into the canyon and over to the other side by the **Hell's Gate Airtram** ($6.75 adult, $3.75 child) to see the river close up, browse through landscaped gardens, learn more about the fishway and salmon, or sink your teeth into a fresh salmon at **The Salmon House Restaurant.**

Boston Bar

Another small town with a gold-rush history, Boston Bar is today a popular whitewater rafting mecca for those brave enough to roar down the Fraser River in large rafts with even larger floats, the guides narrating a variety of historic anecdotes between exciting rapid confrontations. **Fraser Rafting Expeditions** operates trips from Boston Bar to Yale, braving fearsome Hell's Gate, several times a week mid-April to mid-May, then mid-July to October. For the complete rundown and current rates, call 863-2336 (Yale) or 939-8840 (Vancouver).

Hope To Merritt

If you're heading northeast to Merritt or Kamloops, take the impressive, fast, four-lane **Coquihalla Hwy.**, ascending and descending through magnificent mountain and river scenery to dry semiarid grasslands. Cruise through the Lower Coquihalla River and Boston Bar Creek valleys, climb to the 1,240-meter summit of Coquihalla Pass near Coquihalla Lakes, descend along the Coldwater River, then climb the Coldwater's eastern valley slope to Merritt. From Merritt the highway climbs the Nicola River and Clapperton Creek valleys to join Hwy. 1 near Kamloops.

This highway should be driven for the scenery (115 km of interior grandeur) whether you want to go to Kamloops or not. However, you do have to pay to appreciate it. The toll gate is near the summit; $10 for cars and RVs, more for trucks. No gas stations are along the highway, so fuel up in Hope or Merritt. Along the way you can pull off at rest stops (the only exit is at Merritt) to enjoy the scenery, or efficiently whiz all the way to the end.

The Hope-Princeton Highway

On Hwy. 3, about a 15-minute drive southeast of Hope, the effects of one of nature's amazing forces can be seen. On Jan. 9, 1965, a minor earthquake caused a huge section of mountain to come crashing down, filling the bottom of the Nicolum Creek Valley and destroying about three km of the Hope-Princeton Highway. The highway, viewpoint, and parking area are built over the **Hope Slide,** but you can still see the slide's treeless boundaries along the south side of the valley. Read more about it in the parking area.

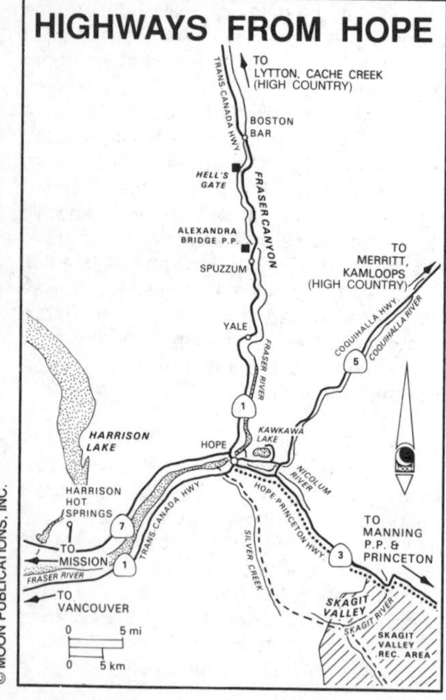

MANNING PROVINCIAL PARK

This spectacular 71,400-hectare park in the Cascades, about 224 km east of Vancouver, stretches down to the Canadian/U.S. border; Hwy. 3 makes a "U" through the park—from the northwest to south to northeast corners. You can drive through without stopping, drinking up the scenery from your vehicle—but don't! At least stop at all the short nature trails signposted off the highway. If you enjoy hiking wilderness trails or cross-country skiing through rugged forest-clad mountains, subalpine meadows, and deep valleys, around lakes, and along rivers (the Skagit and Similkameen rivers both rise within the park), seeing a great variety of vegetation and wildlife as you go, you're gonna love this place! Plan to stay awhile.

In Summer

Between July and Sept., the 15-km paved road to **Cascade Lookout** is a worthwhile side trip off the main highway for a wonderful view of the valley and surrounding peaks. Drivers can continue from the lookout via the six-km gravel road to the **Blackwall Peak**

subalpine meadows and the start of several trails. Take **Heather Trail** from Blackwall Peak to Three Brothers Mt. (10 km OW to Three Brothers, 21 km OW for the entire trail) between late July and mid-Aug. and you won't believe your eyes—a rich yellow, orange, and white carpet of wildflowers for as far as you can see.

Along the main highway are a number of short self-guided nature trails (don't miss **Rhododendron Flats** at the west end of the park), historic trails (built in the 1800s, they were major routes between the coast and the interior until the early 1900s), horse trails, a variety of day-hikes, and plenty of longer hikes.

During the summer months, you can fish in rivers, streams, and lakes (license required), or rent a canoe ($9.50 an hour) or rowboat ($10.50 an hour) at **Lightning Lakes,** or jump on a horse and go on a guided trail ride (from $13 an hour) from Manning Park Corral (next to Manning Park Resort); tel. 840-8844.

In Winter

Manning gets plenty of dry snow for good skiing conditions. At the **Gibson Pass Ski Area** skiers can choose from double chairlifts, a T-bar, or a beginner's rope tow to get some elevation; costs start at adult $23 full day, $16 half day, youth $14-18, child $9-12. Facilities include a cafeteria and ski school, and ski rentals (adult alpine $9 half day, $16 full day). The park is also a cross-country skier's paradise, providing 157 kilometers of ski trails and 30 kilometers of groomed and track-set trails; adult trail pass is $7 full day, $5 half day, youth $4-6, child $3-4; cross-country ski rental is available for adult $10 full day, $6 half day.

Manning Park Resort

In the heart of the park midway between Hope and Princeton on Hwy. 3, this full-facility resort provides comfortable hotel rooms, cabins, and triplexes, saunas, a TV room, an open fireside lounge, indoor recreational games, tennis courts, a self-serve cafeteria or full-serve licensed dining room, a small grocery store, coin-op washers and driers, and a gift shop—it's all here. Rates run $45-65 s, $54-70 d per night in the lodge, $74-79 s or d in the cabins, and $64-89 s, $109-149 d in a chalet with a kitchen. Rates change according to the season (winter is high season). For more details and reservations, call 840-8822.

Campgrounds

Within the park are many campgrounds, each with water, toilets, and firewood nearby: **Coldspring** ($8 per night, two km west of HQ), **Lightning Lake,** which has showers ($13 per night, two km south of HQ on Gibson Pass Rd.), **Hampton** ($8 per night, open as and when required, three km east of park HQ on Hwy. 3), and **Mule Deer** ($8 per night, 10 km east of HQ). All the above campgrounds are open April-Nov.; the overnight fee is charged May-October. Wilderness campgrounds are located at **Pacific Crest, Larch Grove, Poland Lake, Buckhorn, Mowich, Kicking Horse, Nicomen Lake,** and the south end of **Strike Lake.** Be aware of black bears, and don't approach or feed them—let's keep them wild, the way they're meant to be. For more info, call the Visitor Information Centre at tel. 840-8836.

Information

See natural, human history, and recreational displays, and collect detailed information and a map at the park **Visitor Information Centre,** one km east of Manning Park Resort, open weekdays 0830-1630, daily in summer. In July and Aug. park interpreters offer guided walks and interesting slide shows or talks in the evenings at the amphitheater on Gibson Pass Road. Scan info boards around the park and at the Visitor Information Centre to see what's on.

Skagit Valley Provincial Recreation Area

In the extremely unlikely event that you run out of places to explore in the park, you can always mosey over to the adjoining 32,570-hectare Skagit Valley Provincial Recreation Area on the west side; access by vehicle from Silver Creek via Silver Skagit Rd. (60 km of gravel road to Ross Lake), and on foot. It's another wilderness off-the-beaten-track retreat where you can enjoy hiking, camping (open year-round; $8 per night March-Oct.), canoeing, swimming, fishing, and cross-country skiing.

Similkameen Falls

Continuing east on Hwy. 3, between the eastern entrance to Manning Park and Princeton, look out for the sign to Similkameen Falls and a campground. The tree-shaded campground has a great location on the edge of the beautiful Similkameen River, a couple of minutes' walk from the small but powerful falls which are well worth seeing. Sites with fireplaces and wood provided are $8 per night; pit toilets, hot showers 1700-2200.

TODD CLARK

LOUISE FOOTE

OKANAGAN/ SIMILKAMEEN

INTRODUCTION

This small L-shaped region encompasses two major valleys and a great variety of landscapes, including the scenic **Similkameen River Valley** from the splendid white peaks of Manning Provincial Park in the west to the "pocket desert" around Osoyoos near the Canadian/U.S. border, and the warm sunny **Okanagan Valley** from the U.S. border up to Enderby in the north. Vast glittering lakes and sandy beaches, lakeside provincial parks, lush orchards (a perfumed spectacle in spring), fertile irrigated valleys, dry rolling hills, vineyards (if you give all 11 the taste test you'll really be staggering), ski mountains, tourist attractions, waterslides, great weather, and lots of people—in a nutshell, that's what you can expect to find in this part of British Columbia.

Although it's only a fraction of the overall province, the Okanagan has British Columbia's largest interior population concentration in its three main cities—**Penticton** at the south end of large **Lake Okanagan** (home of Ogopogo, the friendly lake monster), **Kelowna** midway up the lake, and **Vernon.** The Okanagan has been accurately described as "a land of beaches, peaches, sunshine, and wine." With its numerous lakeside communities doubling or tripling in size between May and Oct., it's really one long narrow resort attracting hordes of vacationers who return summer after summer—especially Canadians from cooler climates in search of guaranteed sunshine, lazy days on a beach, and a take-away tan.

All the credit for developing the Okanagan into Canada's fruit basket goes to the original planter, Father Charles Pandosy, a French oblate priest who established a mission in the

Kelowna area in 1859. Within a couple of years he had successfully introduced apple trees to the district. With the long 5½-month growing season, over 2,000 hours of sunshine a year, relatively mild winters, and the availability of water, the trees positively blossomed under his care. Soon fruit orchards of all types were springing up everywhere, and today the Okanagan/Similkameen region produces 30% of Canada's apples, 60% of its cherries, 20% of its peaches, half of its pears and prunes, and all the apricots in the country.

THE SIMILKAMEEN VALLEY

Princeton

At the convergence of the Similkameen and Tulameen rivers, surrounded by low tree-covered hills, lies the small friendly ranching town of Princeton, focused around its recently restored downtown triangle and park. The main attractions include fossil and crystal seeking, gold panning (though much of the river is staked), fishing in the more than 30 good trout lakes within an 80-km radius (locals smugly say you can fish "a lake a day as long as you stay"), river and lake kayaking, family downhill and cross-country skiing at **Snowpatch** off the road to Coalmont, and thoroughbred and quarter-horse racing events as well as rodeo events at the **Sunflower Downs** race track.

Princeton And District Pioneer Museum at 167 Vermilion Ave. features pioneer artifacts from Granite City (see below), Chinese and Interior Salish artifacts, and a good fossil display. Another local attraction is the 75-year-old stone and concrete ruins of a cement plant beside twinkling One Mile Creek at **Castle Park** on the northeast side of town. Around, through, and over these magnificent ruins grow trees, wild roses, lilacs, and lupines, luring any avid photographer into shooting an entire roll of film. (For safety's sake, keep some distance from the walls unless you happen to be wearing a suit of armor or hard hat.) Take a look at the concrete paths and steps leading down from the back of the administrative building to the ruins—the concrete is loaded with fossilized shells. The ruins are now part of an RV park and campground; $12 per vehicle (up to four people) per night, water and electricity included. To get there from Princeton, cross the bridge at the north end of Bridge St., turn right on Old Hedley Rd., and cross Hwy. 5. Turn left on 5 Mile Rd., then continue until the sign to the park leads you right, passing a small lake before coming to the park entrance.

If you're looking to stay indoors, try **Riverside Motel,** built in 1934 as a hunting and fishing lodge. Ask the owner, Mrs. Burke, to show you a photo of the place taken in 1937—the original cabins still look exactly the same! Each comfortable self-contained log cabin has a toilet and shower, and kitchen with fridge, stove, cooking utensils, crockery, and cutlery; reasonable rates: $26-28 s, $30-36 d. It's on Thomas St. at the north end of Bridge St., right beside the river (in the height of summer the river drops to expose a small beach and shallow swimming hole), a short stroll from downtown.

The main drag is Bridge St., with a post office, a bank, a good deli, a bakery (closed Mon.), a variety of shops, and an Overwaitea Supermarket. The **Princeton and District Chamber of Commerce Travel InfoCentre** is located at the west entrance to Princeton and is open during the summer months. If it's closed, go to the Chamber of Commerce office, which is located at 195 Bridge St., tel. 295-3103 (or write: P.O. Box 540, Princeton, B.C. V0X 1W0). Also go to the Provincial Government Building at 151 Vermilion Ave. and visit the **Ministry of Forests and Lands** office (weekdays 0830-1630) for a detailed map of the area marked with all the camping and recreation sites, and the **B.C. Government Agent** office (weekdays 0830-1630) where you can get brochures on the local area and the entire province. The **Grey-**

hound Bus Depot is at 301 Vermilion Ave., tel. 295-3939.

Laughing With Coalmont

If you want to see some impressive canyon scenery off the main tourist drag, cross the river at the north end of Bridge St. in Princeton and turn left, heading west toward Coalmont (about 18 km) and Granite City (20 km). Coalmont came to the forefront when gold-rush activity moved from Granite City (see below) to this village in 1911. Today, you can't help but notice that its residents have a sense of humor. The welcoming sign states that Coalmont has no industry but plenty of activity in the form of sleeping and daydreaming. It also claims Coalmont has a hot, cold, wet, and dry climate, warns traveling salesmen to stay away, and adivses single women that their safety is not guaranteed due to the predominance of bachelors here! The attractive old **Coalmont Hotel** (circa 1911) still stands, along with quite a number of homes—some with backyards crammed with unique ornaments (and we're not just talking pink plastic flamingoes!).

Ghostly Granite City

Continue straight ahead at the stop sign in Coalmont to Granite Creek, turn left on Hope St., right over the creek, then follow the road (that's if you get by the black dog that brazenly challenges all vehicles on his road) until you reach the remains of **Granite City,** a ghost town. After the discovery of a gold nugget back in 1885 in Granite Creek, a 13-saloon gold-rush city sprang to life in 1886 on this spot—third-largest city in the province at that time with a population of over 2,000. It's on the right just after the first road intersection, but it's easy to miss because there isn't much left—just a few fallen-down cabins amongst wild lilac bushes and trees, but there's plenty of atmosphere if you use your imagination. It's another place to take your camera and run wild!

If you continue along Rice Rd., you'll end up at **Granite Creek Recreation Site,** provided by the B.C. Forest Service—a gorgeous place to picnic or camp. Tree-shaded

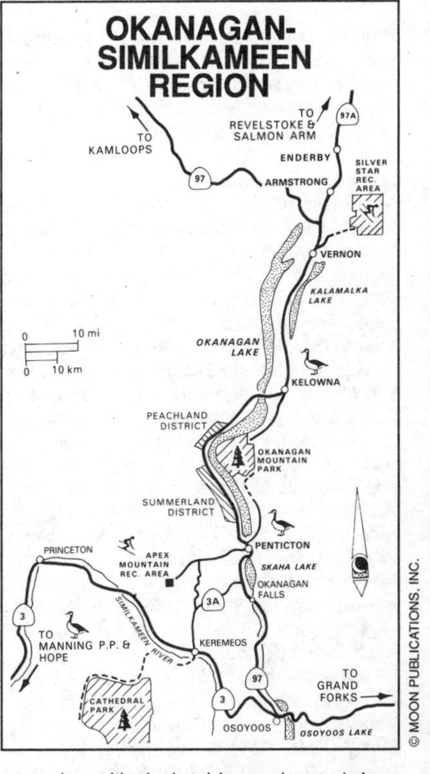

campsites with picnic tables are located along the creek in a large daisy-filled meadow (complete with cows) with pit toilets nearby; free.

Continuing East On Hwy. 3

From Princeton, Hwy. 3 takes you on a scenic route through the beautiful Similkameen River Valley, with lots of places to camp along the way, either in provincial parks or private camping grounds. Between Princeton and Keremeos the road follows the **Dewdney Trail,** a 468-km mule track used in the 1860s to connect Hope with the Kootenay goldfields. This stretch itself has also been a major mining area, supplying a fortune in gold, silver, nickel, and copper over the years. Notice the changes in vegetation as you progress east—from tall, tree-covered mountains between Hope and Princeton through rolling hills covered in sagebrush and lush irrigated orchards around Keremeos to desert (complete with lizards, cactus, rattlesnakes, etc.) around Osoyoos on the Canadian/U.S. border.

Cathedral Provincial Park

Wilderness hikers and mountaineers should not miss the turnoff to this spectacular 33,272-hectare park between Hedley and Keremeos (just west of Keremeos). A 21-km gravel road leads into the park, ending at the Cathedral Lakes Resort base camp. From here you have to drive one km to the parking lot, then hike uphill for about 16 km to the core, or catch a 4WD taxi up Jeep Rd. to privately owned **Cathedral Lakes Resort** (advance reservations have to be made for transportation). The resort provides accommodation in the main lodge, cabins, or tent sites, two meals a day, use of a recreation room and hot tub, and transportation from and to the base camp. July-Sept. the minimum stay is a two-day package; $90-140 per night. For current rates and reservations, call 499-5848. If you don't want to rough it while you explore this park, this is the way to go!

Hike more than 32 km of wilderness trails leading to a variety of striking and enticingly named rock formations including **Stone City, Giant Cleft, Devil's Woodpile, Macabre Tower, Grimface Mountain, Denture Ridge,** and **Smokey the Bear.** Wander through meadows waving with dainty alpine flowers, climb peaks for tremendous views, fish for trout in sparkling turquoise lakes, capture on film immense glacier-topped mountains, or camp by the Ashnola River. For more info on the park and its facilities, call 494-0321.

Keremeos

As you approach mountain-surrounded Keremeos from the west, the road is lined with lush irrigated orchards and fruit stands, one after another, which is probably what inspirerd the title, "Fruit Stand Capital Of Canada." Keremeos has one of the longest growing seasons in the provincial fruit basket. Try a tastebud-tingling fruit juice shake in summer from the second-to-last stand as you head east out of town. Harvest dates: mid-June to mid-July for cherries; mid-July to early Aug. for apricots; mid-July to early Sept. for peaches; mid-Aug. to mid-Sept. for pears; early Aug. to mid-Oct. for apples; early to mid-Sept. for prunes; early Sept. to early Oct. for grapes. And where you have fruit, you had flowers. The best time to see the valley clothed in a seething mass of blossoms is mid-April to mid-May, weather permitting.

Go through town on the main highway, turn north on 3A to Penticton, then right at the Historic Site sign on Upper Bench Rd. to the **Grist Mill,** a restored water-powered mill built in 1877, to see how pioneer Similkameen Valley settlers used to grind locally produced wheat into flour. Take a free guided tour of the mill any day of the week from mid-May to Oct. (closed the rest of the year), then try your hand at the many informative and entertaining hands-on displays in the museum and visitor center; admission by donation, tel. 499-2888.

Another local highlight is small **Keremeos Columns Provincial Park,** named after a 90-meter cliff of remarkable hexagonal basalt columns rising from a lava base just outside the park boundary. (A surveying accident, the columns were supposed to be in the park but actually stand on private land!) Access the viewpoint by a steep eight-km logging road off Hwy. 3 about four km north of town (turn right at the Keremeos cemetery), then take another steep eight-km hike (allow at least three hours OW) across private property; ask for permission and track details at the house at the end of the paved road.

In the mood for a bit of wine tasting? Head for **St. Laszlo Vineyards** on Hwy. 3 about one km east of Keremeos. They produce 18 varieties of wine from American and French hybrids and exotic vinifera grapes from their vineyard, and no preservatives or chemicals are used in the preparation. Tasters are welcome; call 499-5600 for current hours.

Osoyoos
If you continue along Hwy. 3 from Keremeos, you'll enter a surprisingly arid desert area (who imagines desert when thinking of British Columbia?) complete with sand, cacti, sagebrush, lizards, snakes, and other desert accompaniments. **Osoyoos,** the self-proclaimed "Spanish Capital of Canada" (the town's architecture has been Spanish-ed) is on the shores of **Osoyoos Lake,** the "warmest freshwater lake in Canada," which attracts hordes of boaters, waterskiers, anglers, and sailboarders onto its surface, and sun worshippers to its beaches. For more info, visit the **Osoyoos Chamber of Commerce** at the junction of Highways 3 and 97, tel. 495-7142; open year-round, Mon.-Fri. 0800-1700. From Osoyoos, Hwy. 3 continues east into the Kootenay/Boundary region, or Hwy. 97 leads north to Penticton, with several provincial parks and roadside tourist attractions along the way.

Shortcut From Keremeos To Penticton
Turn northeast on Hwy. 3A after passing through Keremeos for the shortcut route into the Okanagan. Along this stretch is the turn-off to **Apex Recreation Area** (27 km off the main road), described as the sunniest of Okanagan ski resorts. The slopes provide 550 vertical meters and 36 runs (four beginner, 18 intermediate, 14 expert), along with groomed Nordic ski trails. Facilities also include triple and double chairs, a T-bar and poma lift, a day lodge, a cafeteria, a grocery and liquor store, lounges, restaurants, free outdoor hot tubs, an ice rink, a ski school, and a ski shop with rentals. Day tickets for downhill skiing are around adult $29, youth (13-17) $24, junior (9-12) or senior $19, child $13. Ski lessons (1½ hours) start at adult $20. Skis, boots, and poles can all be rented. Nordic skiing starts at $5 a day for adults, or $3 a day for juniors (13-17). This is the closest ski area to Penticton (a 30-minute drive from downtown via the more direct east-west route; see map on p. 168).

Highway 3A joins Hwy. 97 north to Penticton (or south to Osoyoos). Head north and you'll pass **Okanagan Game Farm**, which contains 700 animals from around the world (open daily 0800-dusk; admission adult $8, child $6, under five free), and numerous lakeside campgrounds, getting good views of Penticton sandwiched between Skaha and Okanagan lakes.

PENTICTON

Penticton, or "Peach City," South Okanagan's major center (population 25,000), is located between the north end of Skaha Lake and the south end of Okanagan Lake, 390 km from Vancouver. As you approach the city (from "Pen-TAK-Tin," a "Place To Stay Forever" to nomadic Salish Indians), a roadside plaque honors pioneer Thomas Ellis, who arrived in the valley in 1886, then built a great cattle empire and planted the first orchard in this area. Today fruit orchards are everywhere! The annual **Penticton Peach Festival** celebrates the harvest in late July with a week of sailing races, parades, games, and entertainment, and in the second week of Sept. the **Penticton Harvest and Grape Fiesta** is another fruitful event.

As you enter Penticton from the south, the highway is lined with campgrounds, waterslide parks, motels, and restaurants. Follow the traffic down Main St. to come to the vast park- and beach-fringed **Okanagan Lake** (120 km long) at the north end of town, and attractive Lakeshore Drive.

Attractions
Wander west along the tree-shaded shores of Lake Okanagan to see the SS *Sicamous,* the last CPR sternwheeler to work on Okanagan Lake (1914-51) resting on the lakeshore at the end of the beach; now a museum, it's open Mon.-Sat. 0700-1500; admission is only $1. Then stroll to the back of the adjacent **rose garden** with its perfect blooms and

manicured lawns to see and read all the stats on **Okanagan Lake Dam** and flood-control system. Next to the rose gardens is a **miniature golf course** (open daily 1100-2000) and a bicycle-rental outfit and craft shop (see "Transportation," below).

If you wander east from the tourist center along Lakeshore Dr., you'll come to the art gallery (see below) at the bottom of Ellis Street. Then turn off down to the water and you'll arrive at the local **marina**—another enjoyable spot for a lakeside stroll and photograph possibilities.

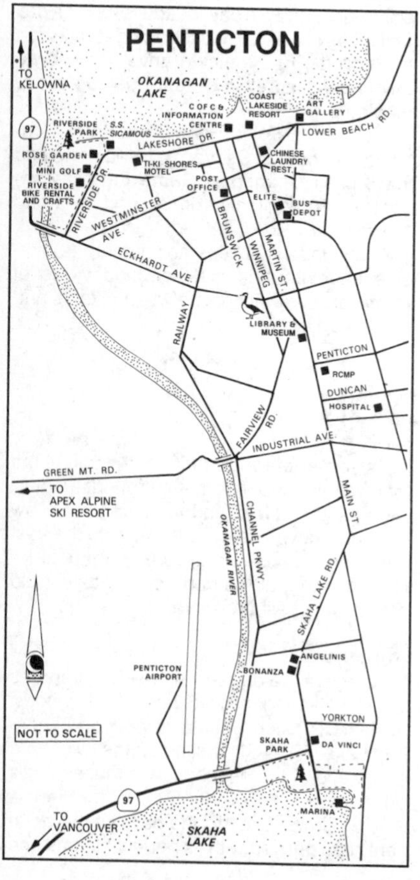

Penticton is quite the cultural center; many residents take enthusiastic interest in the arts. If you enjoy museums, don't miss **Penticton Museum** with its huge, excellent collection of Western Canadiana, covering natural history, local Indian history, fur-trading days, railways, early Chinese residents, militaria, and sternwheelers. This museum also features an enormous taxidermy section, and mining, ranching, and ghost-town artifacts and treasures—allow at least an hour or two in here. It's at 785 Main St., tel. 492-6025, open weekdays 1000-1700, in summer Mon.-Sat. 1000-1700; admission is free but donations are definitely in order. Another cultural must-see is the attractive **Art Gallery of the South Okanagan** on Okanagan lakefront at 11 Ellis St. (east of the Information Centre), tel. 493-2928; open Tues.-Fri. 1000-1700, weekends 1300-1700, admission is free but donations are suggested. The craft shop is a good place to pick up creative treasures (beautiful silk scarves) and handmade souvenirs. If you're visiting on a Sun. afternoon, you can participate in afternoon tea 1400-1600.

What would a trip to the fruit-laden Okanagan be without a tipple or two? Call in at the Penticton Chamber of Commerce on Lakeshore Dr. to find out if any local winery is offering a tour and/or wine tasting. (Don't forget to appoint a designated driver if you go!) **Cartier Wines** is open Tues.-Sat., with tours and tastings offered on the half-hour; get more details at the chamber.

From Penticton north you'll no doubt notice that waterslide mania has hit the Okanagan hard! Even the TraveLodge has an indoor waterslide in Penticton. If you're in the mood for a bit of slip slidin' away, try **Wonderful Waterworld** at 225 Yorkton Ave. at Skaha Lake Rd., tel. 493-8121 (open daily; adult $10.50, child $7 for the day). If you'd rather be skiing than sliding, head out and up to the **Apex Recreation Area,** a 30-minute drive west of town (from Channel Parkway, take Green Mountain Rd. over the Okanagan River and continue west). See p. 167 for more information.

Penticton Marina

Accommodations

Whether you're looking for a lakeside tent site, an RV site next to waterslides, a motel (pick a spot, any spot on the city map, and you'll find a motel within a stone's throw), a room at a bed and breakfast, or a hotel suite, you can find it in Penticton. Refer to the *Accommodations Guide* and collect the free *Okanagan/Similkameen Campground and RV Guide* and *Okanagan Valley Bed and Breakfast Network* brochures from the Information Centre to aid in narrowing down the possibilities.

The **Ti-ki Shores Motel** at 914 Lakeshore Dr., tel. 492-8769, is one of the more reasonable motels, and it has a good location directly across the road from Okanagan Lake; $45-50 s, $49-54 d, kitchen facilities for an extra $10. For a million-dollar lake view, head for the **Coast Lakeside Resort** at 21 Lakeshore Dr. W, tel. 493-8221, a full-service hotel on the shores of the lake, with indoor swimming pool, whirlpool, saunas, tennis courts, lounges and restaurant; $95-160 s or d. Another three-star hotel with health club, pub, and restaurants is the **Penticton Inn** at 333 Martin St., tel. 492-3600; rates start at $89 s or d.

Food

For tangy tastebud-tantalizing Greek dishes, head for **Angelinis** on Skaha Lake Rd. (across from Skaha Centre and next to the Bonanza Restaurant). Surrounded by picture and stained-glass windows, wood, and plants, or outside on a small patio, you can tuck into delicious Greek specialties starting at around $6 for a main course (small portions) at lunch, more expensive at dinner. It's fully licensed, open daily from 1100 to late, and always busy.

For home cooking at inexpensive prices, try the family-style **Elite** restaurant on Main St. (near Wade). They have good-value daily specials (soup or salad, main course, dessert, and coffee) for around $7-8; open seven days a week from early to 2400.

Other local recommendations include: **Galileo's** for Italian and seafood dishes on Skaha Lake Rd. and Yorktown Ave.; **Theo's Restaurant** at 687 Main St. for delicious Greek food and a comfortable atmosphere (very popular, reservations needed on weekends, tel. 492-4019); **Bonanza Restaurant** (family-style self-serve with a "fresh-tastic" salad bar; lunch from $6, dinner $7-12) on Skaha Lake Rd. just across from Skaha Centre between Waterford and Green Ave.; **Chinese Laundry** restaurant for Chinese food at 53 Front St. (between Main St. and Forbes); **Mr. Mike's** for steak and salad bar at 2150 Main St. across from Cherry Lane; and **Pizza Hut** for the obvious on the corner of Main and Duncan Ave. East.

Entertainment

Penticton seems to have festivals, parades, events, or competitions going on throughout the year. In Feb. the residents celebrate **Mid-Winter Break-Out,** in April or early May the **Blossom Festival,** in July the **Highland Games** and **Okanagan Summer School of the Arts,** at the end of July to early in Aug. the **Penticton Peach Festival,** in Aug. the **Ironman Canada Triathlon** and **B.C. Square Dance Jamboree,** and in Oct. the **Okanagan Wine Festival.** Get more info on all these events at the Information Centre.

Information And Services

You can't miss the **Penticton Visitor's Information Centre** at 185 Lakeshore Dr., tel. 493-4055. This is a large place to start your discovery of Penticton and the rest of the province; open weekdays 0900-1700, weekends 1000-1500, with extended hours, 0800-2000, in summer. If closed, orient yourself to local surroundings with the gigantic town map and directory outside the entrance. Public restrooms are also located in the pavilion, open when the center is open. Information centers are also located on Hwy. 97 at both the north and south ends of town (only open in summer).

The **hospital** is on Carmi Ave. (east off Main St.), tel. 492-4000. For an **ambulance** call 493-1020, for the **police** call 492-4300. The **post office** is on the corner of Winnipeg St. and Nanaimo Ave., tel. 492-5717.

Transportation

The **Greyhound Bus Depot** is on Robinson St., tel. 493-4101. **Canadian Airlines,** tel. 492-0614; **Air Canada,** tel. 492-2165; **Penticton Transit Bus,** tel. 492-5602; **Avis Car and Truck Rentals,** tel. 493-8133; **Budget Rent-a-Car,** tel. 493-0212; **Tilden Rent-a-Car,** tel. 493-7288. It's easy to get around Penticton by city bus—pick up a schedule at the Information Centre, or at Penticton Transit Service, 301 East Warren Avenue. At **Riverside Bike Rental and Crafts,** rent mountain bikes, six-speeds, or cruisers for $6 first hour, $4 second hour, or $20 a day. They also rent a variety of other two- or four-wheeled contraptions. Located on Riverside Dr. by Riverside Park at the west end of Okanagan lakefront, tel. 493-1188; open daily May-September. **Menzie's Sports Shop** at 1521 Main St. also rents mountain bikes and in-line skates; call for current rates at 493-0704.

PENTICTON TO KELOWNA

A secondary road (14 km) runs northwest out of Penticton along the east side of Okanagan Lake through the small community of **Naramata.** Two farm wineries off Naramata Rd. offer tasting and info on their private vineyards: **Hillside Cellars** just outside Penticton (tel. 493-4424), and **Lang Vineyards** near Naramata on Gammon Rd. (follow the signs from Naramata Rd., tel. 496-5987). Both reputedly offer their quality wines for sale, but they're only available by visiting the properties. Continue through Naramata and up into the mountains where the road fizzles out near the south border of undeveloped 10,461-hectare **Okanagan Mountain Park.** The only way to get into this piece of untouched wilderness is to walk (an access road from Kelowna also ends at the northern park boundary) or boat over. Hike in for the day taking a picnic (and warm clothes—it gets cold up here even when it's warm and balmy down in Penticton), go fishing, explore 24 km of trails across a high-country landscape covered in cactus and sagebrush, or make your own way-off-the-beaten-track campsite. Be prepared if you plan to stay overnight; no facilities.

Back on Hwy. 97 heading north from Penticton you'll pass a couple more lakeside provincial parks: **Kickininee Provincial Park** with lots of trees, picnic tables, and beaches (good swimming), and **Sun-Oka Beach Provincial Park** with much of the same, farther along.

As you enter **Summerland,** nestled between Giants Head Mountain (great view from the top) and the lake, you'll be amazed how the road is lined with orchards (and resulting fruit stands) and vineyards for as far as the eye can see. Whether you're a fruitologist, fruitcake, or wearing Fruit of the Loom, or you have a sweet tooth worth your fillings, pull off here for a free tour of the **Summerland Sweets** factory on Canyon View Rd. to see syrups, jams, and candy being made from fresh and frozen fruit, and (naturally) buy some. Call for current hours at 494-0377; from Hwy. 97 take the Dunn St. or Arkell Rd. exit west, right on Gartrell Rd., left on Happy Valley Rd., right on Hillborn St., then left on Canyon View Road.

One km north of Summerland, **Sumac Ridge Estate Winery and Golf and Country Club** offers tours, tastings, golf, and a whole lot more. Stagger out of the winery after a free tour and taste (May-Oct., seven days a week, at 1000, 1400, and 1600, tel. 494-0451) and onto the par-three golf course (open daily 1000-1400) for a game you (and no doubt others) will never forget—if you can remember it at all!

Continue toward Kelowna passing pretty **Okanagan Lake Provincial Park** (two entrances to this grassy, tree-shaded, beach-fringed park, providing picnic tables, tent and RV sites from $13 a night April-Oct., boating and swimming; busy in summer), **Antlers Beach Provincial Park** farther along, and the community of **Peachland.** Crammed between a rocky bluff and Okanagan Lake, Peachland was founded in 1808 by Manitoba entrepreneur and newspaperman John Robinson, who came to the Okanagan in search of mining prospects but turned his talents to developing the delicious locally grown dessert peaches. While you're in this neck of the woods, tour and taste the wines of local **Chateau St. Clair Winery,** which overlooks Summerland from its hilltop perch on Trepannier Bench Road. In summer they're open seven days a week 1000-1630, in winter hours vary; call for more info at 767-3113.

As you continue down to Kelowna you'll pass the road west to **Last Mountain** (good family skiing; see p. 175) just before entering the town of **Westbank,** virtually a suburb of Kelowna but on the other side of the lake, providing numerous beach campgrounds, RV parks, and lakeside resorts. **Bear Creek Provincial Park** (seven km off the highway to the west) has picnic tables, camping and RV sites from $13 a night April-Oct., 10 km of easy walks and hiking trails, and kokanee spawning in mid-September. More wine? Try **Cedar Creek Winery** for more tour and taste delights—hiccup!

KELOWNA

Located on the shores of Lake Okanagan, approximately halfway between Penticton in the south and Vernon in the north, the large city of Kelowna (the name originally came from an Indian word meaning "grizzly bear") has a population of 74,000 and is the center of the Okanagan fruit, vegetable, and vineyard region. Its scenic location—amongst mountains and low rolling hills; sparkling lakes providing all kinds of water sports, fishing, and sandy beaches; lush orchards of flowers and fruit; an abundance of vineyards and free-flowing wine; numerous lakeside provincial parks; and nearby **Last** and **Big White** mountains, with excellent skiing—lures visitors from near and afar. Kelowna also boasts the unbeatable combination of long, sunny summers and short, mild winters with snow from mid-Dec. to late Feb., and claims to be "Canada's Apple Capital" (also enthusiastically promoted by the chamber of commerce as the "City of Sunshine, Beaches and Smiles"). Visit any time of year and you will not be disappointed.

Enter the city via the 1,400-meter-long floating bridge which spans Okanagan Lake, connecting Westbank with Kelowna. This amazing drawbridge was built in 1958 on a series of pontoons so that it can float up and down with the lake level and allow large boats through. Tootle over the bridge then straight ahead for four blocks to the Info-Centre on the left, or after the bridge turn left on Abbot St., passing ever-so-green City Park, to start your personal discovery of lakeside Kelowna from . . . the lakeside.

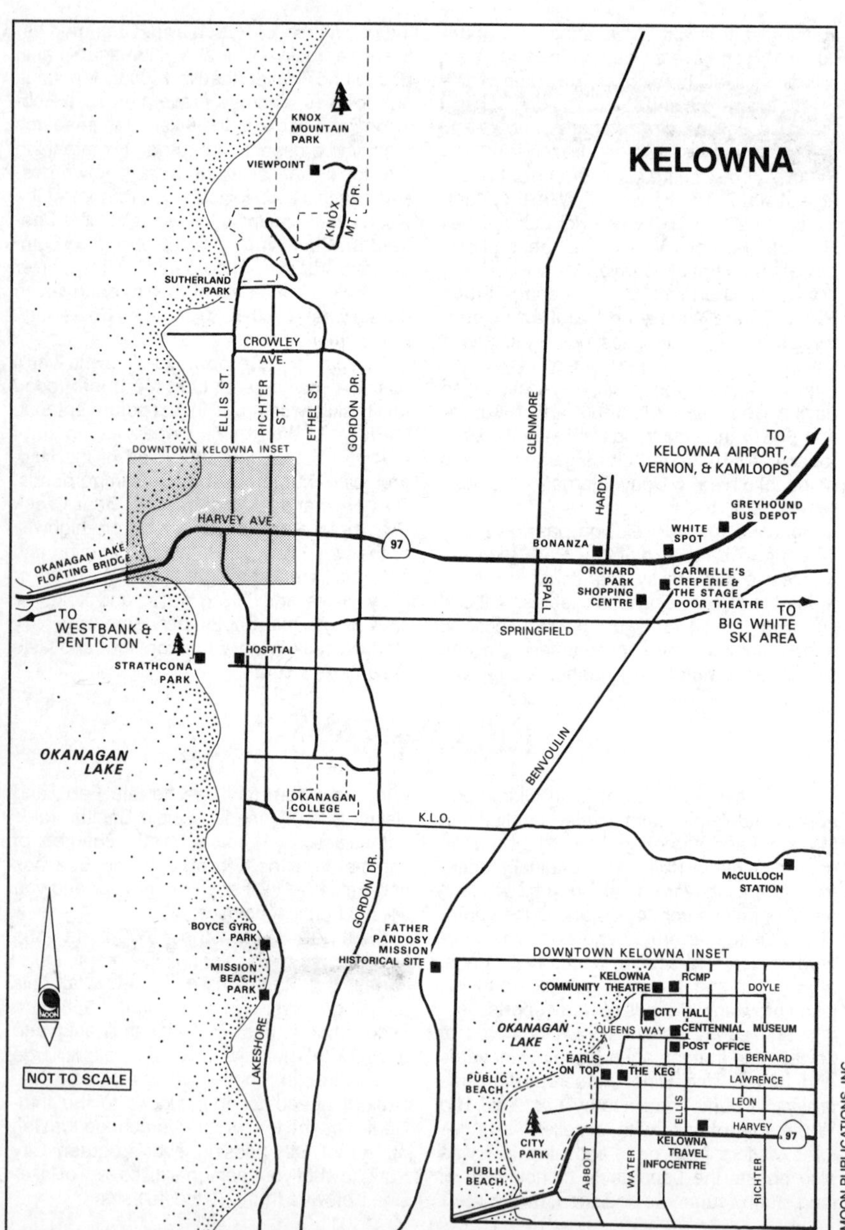
KELOWNA
KNOX MOUNTAIN PARK
VIEWPOINT
KNOX MT. DR.
SUTHERLAND PARK
CROWLEY AVE.
ELLIS ST.
RICHTER ST.
ETHEL ST.
GORDON DR.
GLENMORE
HARDY
TO KELOWNA AIRPORT, VERNON, & KAMLOOPS
GREYHOUND BUS DEPOT
WHITE SPOT
BONANZA
DOWNTOWN KELOWNA INSET
HARVEY AVE.
97
OKANAGAN LAKE FLOATING BRIDGE
TO WESTBANK & PENTICTON
ORCHARD PARK SHOPPING CENTRE
CARMELLE'S CREPERIE & THE STAGE DOOR THEATRE
SPALL
SPRINGFIELD
TO BIG WHITE SKI AREA
STRATHCONA PARK
HOSPITAL
OKANAGAN LAKE
BENVOULIN
OKANAGAN COLLEGE
K.L.O.
McCULLOCH STATION
BOYCE GYRO PARK
MISSION BEACH PARK
FATHER PANDOSY MISSION HISTORICAL SITE
LAKESHORE
MOON
NOT TO SCALE
DOWNTOWN KELOWNA INSET
KELOWNA COMMUNITY THEATRE
RCMP
DOYLE
CITY HALL
QUEENS WAY
CENTENNIAL MUSEUM
POST OFFICE
BERNARD
EARLS ON TOP
THE KEG
LAWRENCE
PUBLIC BEACH
LEON
ELLIS
HARVEY
CITY PARK
KELOWNA TRAVEL INFOCENTRE
ABBOTT
WATER
RICHTER
PUBLIC BEACH
© MOON PUBLICATIONS, INC.

ATTRACTIONS

Waterfront Wandering

Beautiful, 14-hectare, lakefront **City Park,** largest park in a city full of green spots, has large shady trees, flowers, grassy lawns, and a public beach. If you feel like taking to the water, several lakefront marinas offer boats, fishing equipment, houseboat rentals and charters, and the opportunity to do some water-skiing and parasailing. Sailboarding enthusiasts tend to head for **Gyro** and **Mission** beaches at the south end of town.

Near the entrance to the park is the large, sparkling-white, attention-grabbing Dow Reid sculpture, "Sails," and a replica of "Ogopogo," the friendly Loch-Ness-style sea serpent that lives on the bottom of "bottomless" Lake Okanagan. Local Indians told the first white men who came to live in the Okanagan Valley that a fast-swimming lake monster called N'ha-a-tik lived in a cave at Squally Pt., near present-day Kelowna. Whenever they had to canoe near that particular point, they unceremoniously threw an animal overboard as a sacrifice. (So that's where the rhinocerous bones on the beach came from!) Keep your eyes open and your camera at hand. In 1988 the best photo of Ogopogo was worth $2,000 (ask at the Kelowna Chamber of Commerce if the competition is still on, and pick up your "Ogopogo Info Pak"). Capture him alive and you receive a cool million in cash and prizes! Continue along the waterfront to Water St. and Queensway—and downtown Kelowna.

Do The Lake In Style

The paddlewheeler MV *Fintry Queen* is moored at the foot of Bernard Ave.—a fun and stylish way to see some of Lake Okanagan. Summertime Sun. afternoon cruises (two hours) depart 1400; adult $8, child $5. Evening cruises depart Mon.-Fri. at 1930 and Sun. at 1730; adult $8, child $5. If you like to eat 'n' cruise all in one go, try the smorgasbord in the fully licensed **Paddlewheeler Dining Lounge** on board. Evening buffet cruises depart Mon.-Fri. and Sun. at 1930 and 2130; adult $25, child $7-11. On Sat. a moonlight cruise runs from 2100-2400 for $10, or $25 including the buffet (dining from 1700). For more info, call 763-2780.

Centennial Museum And Art Gallery

This museum has a mish-mash of fascinating displays, including horse-drawn carriages; fossils found in the Princeton area; Indian arts, crafts, clothing, jewelry, beads, and furs; children's books and games; radio equipment; pioneer artifacts; John McDougall's fully stocked Trading Post (he was a Hudson's Bay Company trader in the 1840s who retired from active service and opened a small trad-

Ogopogo keeps a friendly eye on the MV Fintry Queen.

ing post here in 1861); a Chinese store; and a display of the interior of a Salish winter dwelling—to name just a few! Allow a couple of hours in here to see everything. At 470 Queensway Ave., opposite the post office, the entrance is marked by an attractive, brightly painted totem pole. Open Mon.-Sat. 1000-1700 July-Sept., Tues.-Sat. 1000-1700 the rest of the year, but closed on holidays, tel. 763-2417; admission by donation. **Kelowna Art Gallery** is housed in the same building as the museum, open Tues.-Sat. 1000-1700.

Knox Mountain

See Knox Mountain by hiking trail or drive up the paved road, along with enthusiastic bicycle riders working up a good sweat, to the viewpoint at the cacti-covered top for great lake and city views. To get there head north out of town along the lakeshore, passing pretty, lakeside **Sutherland Park** (good views of **Crown Forest Mill** and log rafts), then take Knox Mountain Dr. up to **Knox Mountain Park,** stopping at **Crown Viewpoint** on the way to the top. Walking trails lead off in all directions. In May the mountain swarms with activity as the cars and motorcycles of **Knox Mountain Hill Climb** zoom up the mountain.

Tours Galore

You could probably spend a couple of weeks taking one tour a day around Kelowna—orchard tours, vineyard tours, fruit factory tours, forestry tours, industrial tours, etc.—get the complete rundown at the Travel InfoCentre. One that all tour-lovers will enjoy is the free 30-minute tour of the **Sun-Rype Fruit-Processing Plant** in summer to see how apple juice, applesauce, and pie fillings are created. It's at 1165 Ethel St., open on weekdays 0900-1445 May-Sept., tel. 762-2604 (closed shoes required). Another popular tour is the **Fletcher Challenge Products** tour through **Fletcher Challenge Mill** at 820 Guy St., tel. 762-3411 (phone ahead for times). Or if you have your own transportation, take the self-guided **McCulloch Forest Tour** along a short forest route southeast of Kelowna; collect a brochure with a map to various points of interest at the InfoCentre.

A Step Back In Time

Drive south from downtown along Pandosy, turn left on K.L.O. Rd., then right on rural Benvoulin Rd., and you'll come to the provincial historic site of **Father Pandosy Mission.** The route meanders through obviously irrigated, very green farmland and orchards, passing large country homes with picture-perfect flower and vegetable gardens, fields of content, grass-munching horses, and nurseries. Father Pandosy, an oblate priest, established his mission with its church, school, and farm in 1859 on this site, ministering to natives and whites in widely separated areas of the province until his death in 1891. His mission claimed a lot of "firsts"—first white settlement in the Okanagan (and in the Interior, aside from Hudson's Bay Company forts), first Roman Catholic mission in B.C.'s interior, site of the first school and the first fruit and vine crops. It's open daily from 0800 to dark, and the $2 donation includes an informative tour of the buildings, grounds, and antique farming equipment.

Nectar From The Gods

The following wineries in or around Kelowna offer free tours and tastings. **Calona Wines** at 1125 Richter St. has tours every 30 minutes; open to Labor Day 0900-1600 (tel. 762-9144). **Gray Monk Cellars** in Okanagan Centre on Camp Rd. (22½ kilometers north via Hwy. 97) has daily tours on the hour 1100-1600, May-Dec., by appointment the rest of the year (tel. 766-3168), and a wine shop open daily 1000-1700. **Hiram Walker & Sons** in Winfield provides one-hour tours and tastings of Canadian Club whiskey, vodka, gin, rum, and liqueurs daily at 0930, 1000, 1200, 1300, 1400, and 1500. Phone ahead at 766-2431/4922; no one under 12 allowed; wear closed shoes; cameras not permitted. Take Hwy. 97 north, turn east on Beaver Lake Rd., then south on Jim Bailey Rd. and follow the signs. Also find out what's happening at **Hainle Wineries** (tastings Tues.-Sun. 1000-1700, tours through prior arrangement), **Cedar Creek Winery** (daily tours on the hour 1200-1600 until the end of Aug.), and **Mission Hill Winery** (daily tours on the hour 1000-1700, in July and Aug. also at 1900). Contact the InfoCentre for all the details.

The entire valley joins together to celebrate its wines during the **Okanagan Wine Festival** in Penticton in mid-October. It's held at the Penticton Trade and Convention Centre; for more info call 492-6893.

So What Happens In Winter?

Take Hwy. 33 to **Big White Ski Area,** 57 km east of Kelowna, for 49 runs; six lifts; 610-meter vertical; high-speed and regular quad, double, and triple chairs; a T-bar; a ski school with rentals; a ski shop; and over 25 km of cross-country trails. A complete on-mountain village with everything you need is within a snowball's throw of the slopes. It's also open for night skiing, and known for its annual **Snowfest** in late Jan., which features a parade, cross-country ski and snowmobile races, ice sculptures, the Frostbite Fishing Derby, casino, and dances. **Last Mountain** in Westbank (other side of the lake) is the closest local family ski area providing day and night skiing, 20 runs, 182-meter vertical, double chair and T-bars, a day lodge, a ski school with rentals, a ski shop, and reasonable prices. Cross-country skiers will find unlimited terrain in the high country around Kelowna.

Family Attractions

Wild 'N Wet Water Slide Park, three km northwest on Hwy. 97, tel. 768-5141, is open daily May-Sept.; adult $11, child (four to six) $7.50, under three free. **Flintstones Bedrock City,** 6½ km north on Hwy. 97 at 990 McCurdy Rd., is open daily May-Oct.; call for current rates at 765-3733. **Malibu Grand Prix** and all sorts of children's amusement parks line Hwy. 97 north as you head out of Kelowna. Five km north on Hwy. 97 at McCurdy Rd. is **Wild Waters Waterslide Park,** tel. 765-9453, open daily late May-Sept.; adults, seniors, and students $10, child (two to seven) $7.50. South of Kelowna (13 km) is **Old MacDonald's Farm** on Hwy. 97, tel. 768-5167; open daily May-Sept., adult $6.50, senior and child $5.

ACCOMMODATIONS

Outdoors

Most of the campgrounds and RV parks are located on the west shore of Lake Okanagan at Westbank, and a number of provincial parks have campsites along the lake between Westbank and Summerland. The closest private campground to Kelowna on the east side of the lake is **Hiawatha RV Park,** five km south at 3787 Lakeshore Rd., tel. 762-3412. It provides shady camping next to a sandy beach with a boat launch nearby, full and partial hookups, showers, laundromat, a games room, a playground, and a store; $18-21 d per site, electricity additional $2, sewer $1.

Indoors

The highway on the north side of Kelowna is lined with motels and fast-food restaurants. For large rooms, equipped kitchenettes, and reasonable rates try the **Wayside Motor Inn,** then the **Budget Western Inn**—both advertising the least-expensive rates in town (from as low as $25 s in the off-season). **Thrift Inn** at 2592 Hwy. 97 North, tel. 762-8222, also has cheap rates in the off-season, and regular rates, $35-45 s.

For bed-and-breakfast listings, ask at the chamber of commerce or call the Bed and Breakfast Network at 868-2700. They can put you in touch with a place in the area.

If you're looking for comfort and all the added extras, head for the **Capri Hotel** at 1171 Harvey Ave., tel. 860-6060, a full-service hotel with a heated pool, a hot tub and sauna, a coffee shop, and a licensed restaurant, pub, and night club; rates are $79-170 s, $92-170 d, $92-170 t. The **Lodge Motor Inn** at 2170 Harvey Ave., tel. 860-9711, has an indoor pool, a whirlpool, a sauna, a sundeck, and a pub and restaurant, and it's adjacent to the large Orchard Park Shopping Centre; rates are $69-140 s or d, $75-140 t, kitchen $6. Snazzy **Lake Okanagan Resort,** 17 km along Westside Rd., tel. 769-3511, has tennis courts, a par-three golf course, swimming pools, a full-service marina, and horseback riding; May-Oct., rates are $100-165 s or d (kitchen included).

FOOD AND ENTERTAINMENT

Trendy

Earl's On Top Restaurant does a booming business, deservedly. You get a wide variety of delicious meals, snacks, and cocktail concoctions served amongst an ultra-mod, shiny, black-and-white decor with flashy neon lighting (nothing beats a neon palm tree) and a mass of plants, with background '60s music. Grab a table on the rooftop garden patio and absorb the lake view, or pretend you're outside (not hard to do with all the plants). Soup, salads, gourmet burgers, chicken, seafood, pasta, *tapas*, steak—an average lunch is $6-9, dinner $6-20. Or pull up a seat at the Cappuccino Bar where you can get all kinds of coffee drinks with a punch for $1.25-2.75. For a quiet atmosphere, go for dinner 1630-1730—from 1730 on the place is mobbed! It's upstairs at 211 Bernard Ave. (corner of Abbott) opposite City Park, tel. 763-2777; open for lunch daily 1130-1400, and dinner every night 1630-2200, later on Fri. and Sat. nights.

And The Specialty Is Crepes

Carmelle's Creperie gives you the pleasing option of sitting in the bright nonsmokers' room with picture windows and a view of orchards and hills across the road, or the darker smokers' room with a large open fireplace. A relaxing atmosphere, plenty of candles, and low-hanging orange-tassled lampshades suspended over each table invite quiet conversation while you tuck in to a variety of tantalizing crepes for $9-15, other main dishes for $10-16, and sinful dessert crepes for $3-5. Three-course early dinner specials are served 1630-1830 for $8. At 1862 Benvoulin Rd., next to the Orchard Park Petrocan, tel. 762-6350.

Steak Or Salad

The Keg restaurant is open Mon.-Thurs. 1630-2300, Fri. 1630-2400, Sat. 1700-2400 and Sun. 1700-2200, with a 60-item salad bar, steaks, seafood, prime rib, and steak or chicken fajitas; expect to pay $6.95-18 for a main course. It's at 274 Lawrence Ave. between Water St. and City Park. **Bonanza Restaurant** is another good place for a variety of dishes in the $6-12 range, especially the salad bar, on the corner of Hardy and Harvey.

Greek

For tangy Greek food, locals recommend **Talos Greek Restaurant** at 1570 Water St. downtown, tel. 763-1656. You can expect fine cuisine in an authentic Greek atmosphere.

Familiar Standbys

White Spot Restaurant is on the corner of Harvey (Hwy. 97) and Dillworth Drive. Expect a variety of good standard Canadian dishes, specials of the day, and desserts to please even the sweetest tooth, all at prices that won't take you to the cleaners; $6-12 for a main course. If you're looking for fast food, Harvey Ave. will delight you—it's lined with fast-food restaurants and shopping malls.

Entertainment

Try one of Kelowna's friendly neighborhood pubs. For loads of atmosphere, pubbing, munching (full meals $5-8), and the opportunity to meet locals, visit **McCulloch Station,** surrounded by orchards. From Hwy. 97 take Gordon Dr. south to K.L.O. Rd. and turn west (left). Continue along this orchard- and vineyard-bordered road to the pub.

Sunshine Theatre puts on four to five plays throughout the summer; pick up a schedule at the InfoCentre, and get more details and book tickets at Towne Ticket Centre, 6/565 Bernard Ave., tel. 860-1470. Another fun way to eat and be entertained at the same time is to take a dinner cruise on the paddleboat MV *Fintry Queen* to see the city lights and dance the evening away. Or take in a concert by the prominent **Okanagan Symphony Orchestra**—more details at the InfoCentre. For movies, the **Paramount Theatre** is on Bernard St.; the **Uptown Cinema Centre** is on Lawrence and Water streets.

OTHER PRACTICALITIES

Information And Services

Kelowna Travel InfoCentre is at 544 Harvey Ave., tel. 861-1515; coming into town from the south on Hwy. 97, continue up Harvey for five blocks, then turn left on Richter at the traffic lights and go back one block (free parking). A good map for immediate orientation is posted outside the center and has a legend of motels and attractions. **North Park InfoCentre** is on Hwy. 97 North opposite Kelowna Airport (open May-Sept.), and another InfoCentre is located at 2565 Hwy. 97 South, Westbank.

Kelowna General Hospital is on the corner of Strathcona and Pandosy, between Strathcona and Rose (on the right side of Pandosy as you head south), tel. 862-4000. For an **ambulance,** call 374-5937. The **police** station is at 350 Doyle Ave., tel. 762-3300. Shop till you drop at downtown boutiques, **Orchard Park Mall** (largest mall in the Okanagan, next to Carmelle's Creperie), and six other major malls.

Transportation

The local buses are run by **Kelowna Transit,** at 1953 Windsor Rd.; office open Mon.-Fri. 0800-1200 and 1300-1630. For schedule and route info, call 860-8121. The downtown terminus is at Bernard and Ellis. If you buy your ticket on the bus, have exact change; one zone adult 65 cents, senior 60 cents, child 50 cents, or buy a day pass for adult $1.75, senior and child $1.25. **Greyhound Bus Lines** is at 2366 Leckie Rd., tel. 860-3835.

For a taxi, call **Kelowna Cabs** at 762-4444/5555, or call 762-5111 or 763-5000. **Budget** car and truck rental is at 1553 Harvey Ave., tel. 860-2464 (weekend specials, weekly rates, group rates available). **Hertz** is at 1171 Harvey Ave., tel. 860-7808, or at Kelowna Airport, tel. 765-3822. **Tilden Rent-A-Car** is at 1140 Harvey Ave. (across from Capri), tel. 861-5242, or at the airport, tel. 765-7202.

Kelowna Airport is on the north side of town (third-busiest in the province), about 20 km north on Hwy. 97, and served by **Canadian Airlines International,** tel. 763-6620; **Time Air,** tel. (800) 661-1484; and **Air B.C.,** tel. 861-4696; with daily flights to and from Vancouver, Calgary, and Edmonton, and flights to most places in western Canada.

Kelowna To Vernon

Between Kelowna and Vernon are several lake lookouts, resorts, provincial parks, viewpoints, and gorgeous **Kalamalka Lake.** Enthusiastic scuba divers should make a point of stopping at **Ellison Provincial Park,** about a 15-minute drive south of Vernon, to experience B.C.'s first freshwater marine "dive park." Enjoy shallow-water snorkeling and diving, weed beds full of life, underwater rock formations, a plastic bubble "communication center," a deep-water wreck, beach showers, and a number of campsites from $12 a night April-October. As you get close to Vernon, the highway climbs up through treeless grass-covered hills with the lake down below (good views). **Kalamalka Lake Viewpoint,** five km south of Vernon on Hwy. 97, is worth a stop to appreciate the continuously changing emerald and turquoise water of the "Lake of a Thousand Colors," the Coldstream Valley, and mountains, mountains, mountains.

VERNON

The city of Vernon (population 20,400) stands at the junction of four valleys between **Okanagan, Kalamalka,** and **Swan lakes** at the north end of the Okanagan. When gold was discovered at Cherry Creek (now Monashee Creek, east of Vernon), a mini-goldrush resulted. But some of the miners noticed the agricultural potential of the Vernon area and decided to plant instead of pan. Forbes George Vernon, after whom the town was named in 1887, was one of these early settlers. Cornelius O'Keefe, bound for the gold in the Cariboo, was another who noticed the lush growth of bunchgrass (cattle and horses thrive on it) in the area and established a ranch. Between the 1860s and '70s, a number of large ranches sprang up. By 1890 over 4,000 head of cattle were mowing the bunchgrass on the rangelands around Vernon.

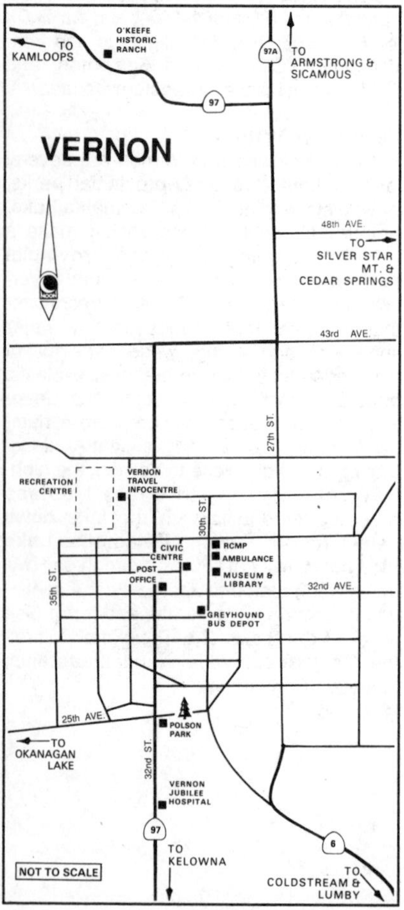

With the construction of the Shuswap and Okanagan Railroad connecting Vernon with the CPR mainline at Sicamous, Vernon grew from a sleepy little cattle community to a town of 500 residents by 1891, the year the first passenger train puffed into town. That same year, Lord Aberdeen bought the Coldstream Ranch from Forbes Vernon to sell in parcels of all sizes at affordable prices, and therefore encourage settlement. He also promoted the idea of growing trees in the area—another fruitful pioneer! Vernon became a city in 1892, which makes it the oldest city in the Interior and fifth-oldest in the province.

Today Vernon provides the vacationer with lots of public and provincial sandy beaches, fishing in over 100 lakes within an hour's drive of the city, spectacular views of Kalamalka Lake from the **Kal Lake Lookout** just south of Vernon, and plenty of heritage buildings (over 550, in fact)—enjoy the leisurely "Vernon, Past and Present" walking tour organized by Vernon Museum.

ATTRACTIONS

In Town

Vernon Museum and Archives has lots of info on Vernon's beginnings, photos from the early 1900s, displays covering natural history, recreation, period costumes, and steamships, and plenty of pioneer and Indian artifacts. It's at 3009 32nd Ave. (corner 31st St.) behind the clock tower and fountain, tel. 542- 3142. In the same building is the art gallery and library, open Mon.-Sat. 1000-1730, closed holidays, admission is free but a donation is welcome.

Polson Park, off Hwy. 97 just before 25th Ave., has a Chinese teahouse and Japanese garden, but most people go to stare at the spectacular floral clock—nine meters wide, made up of more than 3,500 plants, and the only one of its kind in western Canada.

Swoosh—It's Silver Star Mountain!

For winter or summer recreation, head up to **Silver Star Ski Resort** (22 km from town; take 48th off Hwy. 97). You pass the road that leads to a delightful campground amongst fragrant cedar trees (see "Accommodations," below). The views of Vernon as you climb the mountain are worth the fairly long, steep drive, and at the top is a resort with several hotels, cabins for rent, restaurants, and nightlife. Starting at the end of June, a summer chairlift runs to the top of Silver Star Mountain (1,915 meters) for terrific views of Vernon nestled between Kalamalka and Okanagan lakes, and good hiking in alpine meadows; it's in operation until Sept. daily 1000-1600; adult $7.50, child $4.25. Saunter back down the mountain via a trail. To take your mountain bike up the chair it costs $7.50 for an adult single ride or $15 for three rides, child $4.25 single ride.

Also in summer you can go horseback riding on beautiful trails adjacent to the village, or discover mountain biking on the "Mile High Descent Tour" with **Silver Star Mountain Bike Tours.** Their 2½-hour tour takes you down a 30-km, 1535-meter drop from Silver Star summit to Vernon, and the price includes the use of a mountain bike, helmet, safety vest, and gloves, a souvenir water bottle, a chairlift ride, guided descent, and return transportation, for only $33 pp (children must be at least 12 years old), or $25 pp if you have your own bike. The tour operates twice a day from July through September. They also provide quality mountain-bike rentals for adult $6.50 an hour, $12 a half-day, or $21 a full day, child $4.50 an hour, $8 per half-day, or $14 per day. For bookings and more info, call 542-0224. Another wheel alternative is to rent in-line skates from **Ferris & Co. Mercantile** at the resort, and try these in-line wheels in the parking lot. Safety padding is included with your rental, and instruction is also available.

From Nov. through April this resort is mobbed by downhill and cross-country skiers and snowmobilers. Silver Star Resort, 22 km up the mountain from Vernon, is shrouded in snow every winter (little falls in the valley, but plenty smothers the mountain), offering exceptional downhill and Nordic skiing, and backcountry skiing and ski touring can also be attempted in mountains nearby. Aside from skiing, snowmobiling and skating are also very popular local activities. Early in Feb., Vernon celebrates its **Winter Carnival,** with all sorts of fun-in-the-snow activities.

O'Keefe Ranch

To get to the historic ranch, one of the main local attractions, take Hwy. 97 north out of Vernon toward Kamloops (it's about 13 km from Vernon), through the rolling grass-covered hills and fields of cattle and horse country. On your way there you pass yet another waterslide, **Atlantis World of Water** (seven km north of Vernon at Pleasant Valley Rd.; open daily June-Sept. 1000-2000; adult $11.50, child $7.25, tel. 549-4121), and **Okanagan Bobslide** 8½ km north (open daily May-Oct. 1100-2000, extended hours July and Aug.; adult $3, child $2, tel. 542-0104). The O'Keefe Ranch was one of the earliest cattle ranches established in the Okanagan (1867). It's open daily mid-May to early Oct. 1000-2000 with extended hours in July and Aug.; admission adult $4.50, senior $3.50, child $2.50, which includes an interesting lower-floor tour of the opulent, fully furnished (circa early 1800s) O'Keefe Mansion (treat your ears—ask the guide to play the music box). After the tour, wander around the upper floor and the rest of the grounds at your own speed to see the furnished old log house (the O'Keefe's original home), a working blacksmith's shop, St. Ann's Church (the first service was held in 1889, and it's still used today), a fully stocked General Store (where you can buy postcards and old-fashioned candy), and the Chinese cook's bunkhouse. Allow at least two hours here, tel. 542-7868. After your self-guided tour, visit the **Homestead Restaurant,** open Mon. 0900-1700, Tues.-Fri. 0900-2000, Sat. 0900-2400 (with dancing and D.J. entertainment), and Sun. 0900-2000.

PRACTICALITIES

Accommodations

Cedar Falls Campground is on Tillicum Rd. (on the way to Silver Star Mountain; from Hwy. 97 north turn east on 48th Ave. then continue straight ahead on Silver Star Rd., right on Tillicum), tel. 545-2888. It provides attractive camping spots amongst cedar trees, each with a table, and washroom and laundry facilities in a large log cabin shaded by the trees. A short trail leads to Cedar Falls along the creek (a 15-minute walk); $10 per site for two, extra $1.50 for power, firewood $2. There's also a grocery store selling snacks, soft drinks, ice cream, etc.

If you've always wanted to stay in a windmill, now's your chance. Turn off on Hwy. 6 (a beautiful route, see it in daylight!) and continue to the small community of Coldstream. Turn right at Learmouth Rd. and keep on for at least 10 minutes until you eventually come to the **Windmill House.** It's at 5672 Learmouth Rd., tel. 549-2804. Aside from the intriguing angular rooms with rural views (nonsmoking environment), the delicious breakfasts (choose from four) include homemade preserves and jams, and you can purchase original artwork, crafts, and custom frames and enjoy the owners' purebred dairy goats (participate in the morning and night milkings if you like!); from $35 s, $39.95 d, senior and child rates also available. Call ahead and see if they have a room before you make the trek out there (in summer they're particularly busy), and ask for specific directions. If you have no transportation, collection can be arranged. If you don't want to spend the night, but want to see the (nonworking) windmill, tours are $1 adult, 50 cents child, or go for afternoon tea (1400-1600) and a tour. Call ahead and make a reservation.

For a full list of motel and hotel accommodations, refer to the free *Accommodations* guide put out by the Ministry of Tourism. And pick up a *Bed and Breakfast at the Top of the Okanagan* brochure from the Visitors Centre; it lists all the local B&Bs in Vernon and includes a map showing their location; rates range $28.50-35 s, $35-55 d.

Food And Entertainment

One of the local favorite restaurants is the **Sundowner** at 2501 53rd Ave., tel. 542-5142. Serving steak, seafood, pasta, with an extensive salad bar, main courses run $6.99-32.90 (they also offer child and senior menus), and the restaurant is open daily. Or go for the Sun. brunch 1030-1400 which costs adult $8.49, senior $6.49, child $3.99. Mon.-Sat. their noon luncheon buffet is adult $6.65, senior $5.65, child $3.95. On Thurs. nights the Sundowner puts on a seafood night buffet, and on Sun. nights it's the continental or Hawaiian buffet. This is one of the busiest restaurants in town.

Bonanza Family Restaurant at 5601 27th St., tel. 545-7877, open daily 1100-2100, also has an extensive salad bar, and steak, seafood, and chicken for $5-10. Another local recommendation is **Kelly O'Bryan's Restaurant** at 2905 29th St., tel. 549-2112. Tuck in to burgers, steak, seafood, salads, and pasta ($10-16); open daily 1100-2400. For more of a dinnertime splurge try **The Courtyard Restaurant** (or **Checkers Pub**) at **Vernon Lodge** for continental cuisine (nightly specials), open daily for dinner from 1700. The lodge coffee shop is open daily 0700-1700; at 3914 32nd St., tel. 545-3385.

If you're in search of all the usual fast-food standbys, you'll find **Wendys, Smittys,** and **McDonald's** on Hwy. 97 north of Vernon (near the 53rd Ave. intersection), and **Pizza Hut** just after 45th. Cooking your own food?

Don't miss **Vernon Farmers' Market** at the Recreation Centre Parking Lot at 33rd St. and 39th Ave. (parking in the Curling Club Parking Lot). It's held every Mon. and Thurs. spring to fall, "morning 'til noon" and features fresh fruit and vegies, farm produce, baked goods, eggs, honey, plants, and handicrafts.

The annual **Creative Chaos** craft fair held in early June in the Craft Centre (one street over from the Visitor Bureau) always has an impressive turnout of both craftspeople and customers; admission is free. For live theater, check out the **Powerhouse Theatre,** or enjoy dinner theater at **The Livingroom Supper Club** near the old train station. Vernon also has its share of festivals and events. In winter (early Feb.) the town springs to life to celebrate **Vernon Winter Carnival** with parades, sleigh rides, ice sculptures, stock car races on ice, the **Over The Hill Downhill** team ski race at Silver Star, and dances. Get all the event info and dates at the Visitor Bureau.

Information And Transportation

Greater Vernon Visitor and Convention Bureau is located at 6326 Hwy. 97 North, tel. 542-1415; open daily 0800-2100. Stock up on printed material on the entire area, or visit the seasonal InfoCentres on Hwy. 97 at the north and south ends of town (open May-September).

The Vernon **post office** is on the corner of 31st St. and 32nd Avenue. For local bus info and schedule, contact **KIA Transit** at 4210 24th Ave., tel. 545-7221. The **Greyhound Bus Station** is on the corner of 30th St. and 31st Ave., tel. 545-0527. For original works of art by Okanagan artists, including pottery, weaving, painting, silk, jewelry, sculpture, woodwork, graphics, tapestry, and cards, stop by **The Galloping Goose Gift Gallery** at 3316 30th Ave., tel. 545-7606.

For an emergency, call 911. For nonemergency **ambulance** call 374-5937, for **police** call 545-7171, for a **fire** call 542-5361, for the **poison control center** call 545-2211, in case of **marine and aircraft distress** call (800) 742-1313. **Pharmacies** are located at 3101 30th Ave., tel. 542-4181, and at 3417 31st Ave., tel. 542-9542.

Routes Out Of Vernon

Highway 97A leads you north through the small towns of Armstrong and Enderby to Sicamous in High Country, at the junction of Trans-Canada Hwy. 1. Just north of Vernon, Hwy. 97 branches away from 97A northwest through vast rolling rangeland toward Kamloops, also in High Country. The third alternative is to take Hwy. 6 east into the beautiful, majestic mountain-and-lake landscape of Kootenay country (see "Kootenay/Boundary," p. 182) and on toward the Rockies.

LOUISE FOOTE

KOOTENAY/BOUNDARY

NATURAL-HIGH COUNTRY

Steep snow-mantled mountains in all directions. Serene deep-blue lakes once churned by sternwheelers, now only stirred by the slap of a canoe paddle or the swirl and kerplop of a surface-breaking trout. Forest-covered hills and emerald valleys abounding with deer. Meandering streams, rollicking rivers, steaming hot springs, and ravenous rapids. Ghost towns, historic silver- and gold-mining towns, small, friendly cities combining the best of the old and the new, and tucked-away communities of inspired artists and outdoor adventurers. These are the crisp, clean images of beautiful Kootenay Country. Hike, canoe, ski, renew. Stay a couple of weeks and you may stay a lifetime!

The first settlers came to the Kootenays in the late 1800s in search of precious metals—silver, lead, and zinc, all of which they found in large quantities—but they stayed for the bountiful harvests and scenic beauty. Located west of the Rocky Mountain region in the southeast corner of B.C., Kootenay Country is separated into a couple of north-south valleys and small pockets of civilization by the mighty **Purcell, Selkirk,** and **Monashee** mountain ranges. In the lush green valleys lie long, narrow **Kootenay Lake,** equally long and even narrower **Upper** and **Lower Arrow** lakes, and several smaller lakes. With its almost completely mountainous terrain, this region certainly receives its share of annual precipitation, with plenty of snow (the skiing is terrific), plus a large diurnal temperature range. No boring, predictable weather on this part of the globe!

Almost all the outdoor activities in the Kootenays and Boundary Country include water in two out of its three forms. Fishing for trout, char, kokanee salmon, and freshwater cod and bass; canoeing; and skiing are the favorites. One of the most popular canoe routes

1. Whistler Village from Blackcomb Mountain (Jane King); **2.** hiking on the Athabasca Glacier (Jane King); **3.** Seely Lake, near New Hazelton (Jane King)

1 

3 

5 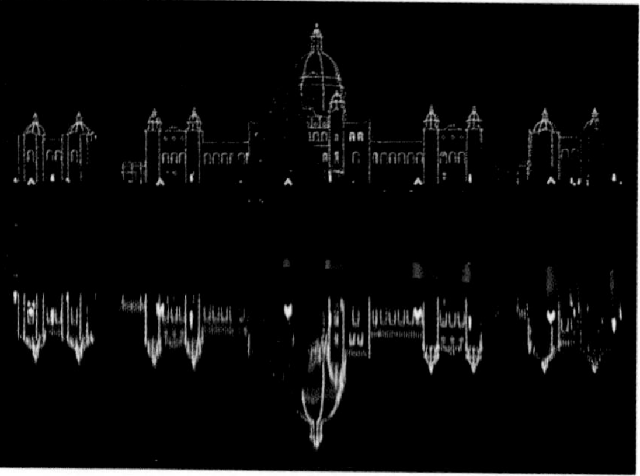

1. Kitsilano Beach, Vancouver (Province of British Columbia) (Jane King); 2. Thunderbird Park totem poles (Jane King); 3. Harbour Centre from the Price Waterhouse Centre (Jane King); 4. Legislative buildings, Victoria (Jane King); 5. Parliament buildings at right, Victoria (Jane King); 6. sunset at Victoria (Jane King)

focuses on Upper and Lower Arrow lakes, flanked by the Selkirk and Monashee mountains. Together these two interconnected lakes, lined with beaches and camping spots, stretch for a total of about 185 km (facilities are sparse—carry everything you need).

Travelers in a hurry to get to the Rockies zoom up Hwy. 97 through the Okanagan, then along Hwy. 1 east to the Alberta border. Others wind along Hwy. 3 just north of the Canadian/U.S. border, then ooh-and-ahh their way up Hwy. 93 to Lake Louise. Most head for the Rockies or Vancouver by one route and return by the other. Both of these routes are direct and scenic, but if you have the time and the yearning to putter through an especially pleasing chunk of B.C., consider taking Hwy. 6 from Vernon to Nakusp (200 km), then continue down the gentle Slocan Valley to Nelson (160 km)—or visit a ghost town and follow both shores of Kootenay Lake to Nelson (145 km)—and *then* continue east. You'll be glad you did.

VERNON TO NAKUSP

The Coldstream Valley

From Vernon, Hwy. 6 meanders east through the gentle Coldstream Valley, passing field crops, orchards, and low, rolling, tree-covered hills; paddocks where horses frolic in fluorescent-green grass; rustic old barns in various degrees of disrepair; and well-loved old homes. The valley was one of the earliest settled in the Okanagan. Just before Lumby, a turnoff leads to **Mabel Lake Provincial Park** (camping and picnicking) and the **Shuswap River Fish Hatchery** (15 km). In **Lumby,** stop at the **Travel InfoCentre** on the main highway, where enthusiastic students will give you the rundown on ghost towns, historic spots, and hot springs along the route ahead, and schedules for the free Needles-Fauquier and Balfour-Kootenay Bay ferries. Also check your fuel supply before continuing. Gas stations are few and far between, and Murphy will see to it that the one you finally reach—spluttering to a stop with your gauge on empty—is closed!

Between Lumby and Needles, craggy bare-rock mountains lie to the south and fields of yellow and purple wildflowers line the road as it winds through one gorgeous valley after another—so gorgeous it's hard to keep your eyes on the road at times! At the Shuswap River you can picnic and launch your canoe, or take the Sugar Lake Rd. turnoff to 7,513-hectare **Monashee Provincial Park** (35 km from the main road) at **Cherryville.** After a 12-km hike from the end of the road to the park boundary, choose from many wilderness trails through mountain, canyon, and lake scenery to alpine flower-filled meadows, waterfalls, and viewpoints; go for an exhilarating dip; or catch a fish for supper. Take everything you need with you—no facilities. A topographical map of the park is available from Map and Air Photo Sales (MAPS B.C.), Ministry of Lands and Parks, Parliament Buildings, Victoria, B.C. V8V 1X5.

Monashee Pass To Needles

This stretch of road is scenically stunning with the sudden appearance of high snowcapped mountains straight ahead. Don't do it in the dark. Your camera will never forgive you, and odds are you'll destroy at least one or two of the deer that play a particularly suicidal version of "now you see us, now you don't" with vehicles along here. There's never a dull moment, even in broad daylight. You'll probably notice several signs to **Arrow Lakes Provincial Park** between Needles and Burton (on the other side of Arrow Lake), but don't worry, you're not hallucinating—the 72-hectare park is split into three sites, one by Edgewood (east of Needles), one at Fauquier, and one at Burton, each providing perfect spots to swim, fish, and launch lakeworthy contraptions.

Needles To Nakusp

At Needles (just a ferry dock) cross Lower Arrow Lake to **Fauquier** on the free vehicular ferry which departs every half-hour 0615-2145, with shuttle service from 2215 to 0600. A telephone and restrooms are located by the ferry lineup. Ten cruising minutes later you're in **Fauquier** (56 km from Nakusp)

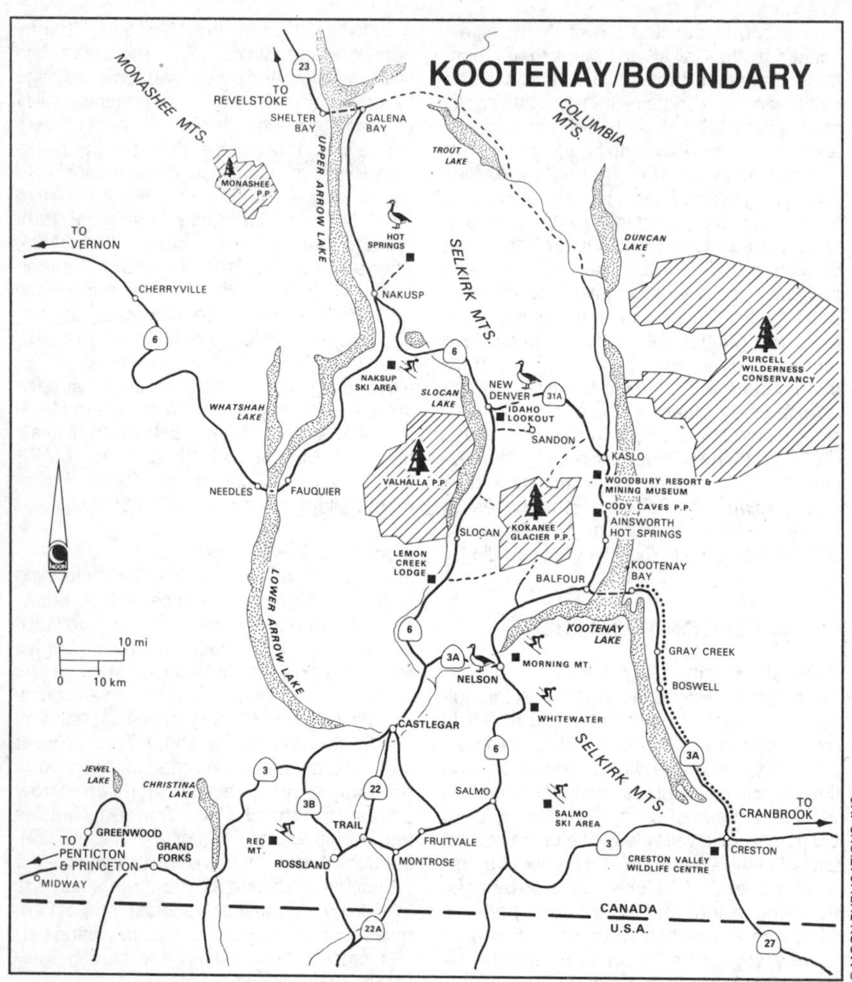

where there's a gas station, a motel, handfuls of homes, and a golf course. The highway follows the blue and jade **Upper Arrow Lake** into the mountains, and the mountains just seem to keep multiplying, growing larger, more magnificent, and more snow-covered as you continue north. Save plenty of film for this stretch of the road.

NAKUSP

This small town, established during the mining boom years, has a stunning location on **Upper Arrow Lake** (anglers swear the lake is three parts rainbow trout, Dolly Varden, and kokanee salmon, one part water!), surrounded by the snowcapped peaks of the Selkirk Mountain Range. If you get there on a dull day when the clouds are low, stay the night and keep your fingers crossed that the clouds lift by morning. Bod-soakers and campers will enjoy Nakusp's main local attraction, sizzling **Nakusp Hot Springs** and campground, just north in the Selkirk Mountains (see below).

Before heading up to the springs, stock up at the Overwaitea Store (open Mon.-Sat., daily in July and Aug.), or the deli (open daily), both on Broadway. Or order up some Canadian (around $5-7) or Chinese ($6-9) food at **The Manor** (also on Broadway, open daily 0630-2100), a favorite local hangout. The **Travel InfoCentre,** in the small building with a big yellow paddlewheel on 6th Ave. W is open Sept.-June Mon.-Fri. 0830-1630, in July and Aug. daily 0830-1830; go through town and turn north on 6th Ave. W (Hwy. 23) toward Galena Bay and you can't miss it. If you don't already have the Balfour-Kootenay Bay ferry schedule, collect it here.

The **Nakusp Museum** next to the InfoCentre has an odd but intriguing collection of items, such as an old barber's chair and pole; admission adult $1, child free. Other local attractions include **Summit Lake Ski Hill** (off the highway to Nelson), cross-country skiing on abandoned logging roads, **Kootenay Helicopter Skiing** from Jan. through April in the Selkirk and Monashee ranges (tel. 265-3121), **Nakusp Centennial Golf Course and Driving Range** off Hwy. 6 S, and houseboating on Arrow Lakes from **W-4 Park and Marina** on Waterfield Rd., tel. 265-3553.

Nakusp Hot Springs

Go through town on Broadway, turn right at the stop light on 6th Ave. West, continue north along Hwy. 23 for approximately one km, then turn up the road signposted to the springs (12 km). The springs are open 0930-2200 June-Sept., 1030-2100 Oct.-May (tel. 352-4033), and the surrounding park provides hiking and cross-country ski trails. Soak your cares away in the two outdoor pools, admission adult $3.75 or $5.35 for a day pass, seniors $2.75-4.30, child $2.50-4. Swimsuit rental is $1.10, towel 75 cents, locker 25 cents plus $2 deposit. Expect to share the pools with many other happy campers on summer weekends. To see the source of the springs, take a 10-minute stroll along a sandy trail (grab a raincoat) that starts behind the pools, crossing the river and clambering through damp rainforest crammed with ferns and mosses, until you come to an impressive waterfall where you can smell the sulphur from the springs and get dowsed in spray.

The campground is terrific—even if it *is* high density in summer. There's a flat grassy area for tents, wooded vehicle campsites beside roaring Kuskanax River (a soothing sound for campfire dining and sleeping) only a short stroll from the hot pools, and washroom facilities with a free shower; campsites are $6 per night (grab your spot early in the day in summer, especially on weekends). **Nakusp Hot Springs Cedar Chalets** are also available for $36-52 s, $41-52 d, which includes complete cooking facilities—supply your own food. Rent by the day or the week, but they're usually booked ahead in summer; check at 265-4505. Chalet patrons can buy basic groceries at the office—the less privileged campers have to provide their own.

From Nakusp, Hwy. 23 continues north paralleling Upper Arrow Lake to **Galena Bay** (with more hot springs along the route), where a ferry back across the lake connects to **Shelter Bay** and the highway north to **Revelstoke.**

THE SLOCAN VALLEY

New Denver

From Nakusp, take Hwy. 6 south to New Denver (48 km), passing grassy meadows full of summer wildflowers, large horse paddocks, nice homes, rolling hills, tree-covered mountains, several lakes with campsites, **Rosebery Lake Provincial Park** (camp and vehicle sites), and **Slocan Lake Golf**

Course. The historic village of New Denver, the 1892 western gateway to "Silver Country," was originally called Eldorado; renamed after Denver, Colorado, New Denver reached its mining peak in the 1890s and remained a thriving community for 20 years.

Follow the sign from the highway downtown to wander along the main street lined with funky false-fronted stores and pioneer-style heritage buildings left over from the prosperous silver days. Visit the **Silvery Slocan Museum** to find out all about New Denver's heyday as a silver center (corner of 6th St. and Marine Dr., open July to early Sept., tel. 358-2201). Stroll along the crystal-clear lake to appreciate the view of snow-covered peaks, or hike the steep trail to the top of 2,280-meter **Idaho Peak** for panoramic views.

More Almost-impossible Decisions

New Denver sits on the junction of Highways 6 and 31A. Highway 6 runs straight down the lush, gently rolling Slocan Valley to Castlegar (or Nelson); Hwy. 31A meanders past the road to Sandon, a ghost town, then southeast to picturesque Kaslo on Kootenay Lake, and Nelson. Both routes are hardly what anyone could describe as on the beaten track, and they both offer great scenery and access to provincial parks and lakes. But 31A, crossing the Selkirk Mountains to Kootenay Lake, is the lesser highway, attracting less traffic. The decision is yours!

Scenic Six

Ho hum—more gorgeous scenery! Highway 6 meanders down Slocan Lake between the snowcapped Selkirk Mountains in the east and the Monashee Mountains in the west, and eventually parallels the muted-green Slocan River between lush fields and tree-covered hills toward Castlegar. What's there to do along this stretch of the road aside from taking scenery shots every few minutes? Well, there's hiking, fishing, canoeing, swimming, cross-country skiing, horseriding, and golfing to start—then more wilderness hiking and mountaineering in undeveloped **Valhalla Provincial Park** to the west and **Kokanee Glacier Provincial Park** to the east—more than most people could accomplish on a several-year vacation. Get detailed info on your particular outdoor passion at New Denver or Slocan City if you're approaching from the north, Castlegar or Nelson from the south.

Valhalla Provincial Park

These 49,600 hectares of rugged, untouched mountain and lake wilderness (sandy beaches) on the west side of Slocan Lake are accessed by boat (lifejacket required) and hiking trail, or a trail from the village of **Slocan** that connects with the Evans Creek-Beatrice Lake Trail (park your vehicle south of the Slocan River bridge and walk about 200 meters along the residential road to the trailhead). Vehicular access is by 41 km of logging road at Slocan City or Passmore (not suitable for low-clearance or bus-type vehicles, or trailers), 10 km north of the Hwy. 6/3A junction. Vehicle and trail access is also possible from Hills on Hwy. 6, but the 28-km dirt road to the hiking trails leads right into extremely rugged terrain—for experienced hikers only.

Hiking trails in Valhalla range 3½-12½ km OW (two to six hours) and the condition of each trail varies. The park has no facilities, just a couple of beaches with pit toilets that are the most popular campsites, and two cabins (at Evans Lake and Cove Creek, each accommodating four, with no cooking facilities). You need to be totally self-sufficient and prepared for rugged terrain and possible bad weather (if the wind picks up and dark clouds form, immediately head for shore or shelter).

Before you explore Valhalla get your hands on topographic map sheets 82F/13, 82F/14, and 82K/3W (nominal fee for each) from MAPS BC, Ministry of Lands and Parks, Parliament Buildings, Victoria, B.C. V8V 1X5, and a copy of the *Trail Guide to Valhalla Provincial Park* ($4) from the Valhalla Wilderness Society, Box 224, New Denver, B.C. V0G 1S0. For the most current info on access and facilities, contact the **West Kootenay District Park Office,** Parks and Outdoor Recreation Div., R.R.3, Nelson, V1L 5P6.

Kokanee Glacier Provincial Park

This beautiful 25,600-hectare wilderness park is reached by two major roads from Hwy. 31A (see "The Kootenay Lake Route To Nelson," below, for details), but can also be approached by two dirt access roads to the west side of the park from Hwy. 6. The first is two km north of Enterprise Creek and 11 km south of Silverton via 13 km of dirt; the second is eight km south of Slocan City via 16 km of dirt along Lemon Creek.

Lemon Creek Lodge

If you're planning on staying in Slocan Valley awhile, this unique comfortable lodge is an easy way to do it. It's about seven km south of Slocan (1.6 km west off the main highway at the sign, on Kennedy Rd.), close to both Valhalla and Kokanee Glacier Provincial Park access roads. The entertaining owner (and builder of the lodge from the ground up), Keith Kessler, is a cross-country ski instructor and guide, knows the local backcountry better than the back of his hand, and is a creative cook. Activities in the immediate area include cross-country skiing, telemarking, and mountain touring.

Stay the night in the lodge for $35 s, $50 d (breakfast included) or $50 s, $80 d (three meals included), or in the antler cabin (sleeps six) for $50 d plus $5 each additional person. The rustic "museum" sleeps four for $50 d plus $5 each additional person, and the gingerbread cabin sleeps six for $80 d plus $5 each additional person. Or grab a grassy camp or RV site for $6-10 per night. In winter most guests go for one of the ski packages, which range from a day-trip (cross-country ski instruction, lunch, and sauna/hot tub) for $30 pp to the five-day Trekker (telemarking instruction, a trip to Nakusp Hot Springs, accommodations, all meals, and transportation) for $285 pp d or $325 single. Pickup from Castlegar bus depot or airport or Nelson bus depot can be arranged. For more details and reservations, call Keith at 355-2403.

THE KOOTENAY LAKE ROUTE TO NELSON

Sandon

Those with a fascination for ghost towns and a healthy imagination shouldn't miss taking Hwy. 31A toward Kaslo, then turning off to Sandon (13 km) along a good gravel road that parallels a bouncing rock-laden creek. The historically rich Slocan Valley, or "Silvery Slocan," sprang into the limelight in the 1890s when silver was discovered in the Kootenays. Sandon, near the top of Idaho Peak, briefly became a silver boomtown with 24 hotels, 23 saloons, general stores, mining brokers' offices, a newspaper, banking estab-

the Tin Cup Cafe, Sandon

lishments along its main street, and a population of 5,000 (1895-1900). The Kaslo-Slocan Railway was built in a hurry to connect the mines with paddlewheeler transportation on Kootenay Lake so that men and supplies could quickly reach the mines and ore could be carried out. Sandon was destroyed by fire in 1902, but quickly rebuilt on top of Carpenter Creek (the boardwalk covered the creek) and incorporated as a city in 1908. It thrived until the Great Depression of 1929 but remained the "soul of the Silvery Slocan" for over half a century. Finally in the spring of 1955 the creek flooded, sweeping away most of the city and leaving it as it remains today—a ghost town.

Only a few of the original buildings (now boarded up) still stand, but the atmosphere is unmistakable. A visit to **Sandon Museum** (cross the creek and turn left; sporadically open) brings the town back to life, and you can see traces of mine workings in the surrounding hills. Visit the intriguing **Tin Cup Cafe** (by Mountain Momma's House) at the far end of town and have a cuppa with a local. Or hike along the 5.6-km **KNS Historic Trail** (set off early and take a warm waterproof jacket), which follows the route taken by the old wood-burning engines of the Kaslo-Slocan Railway (built in 1855) as they carried rich silver ore from Sandon to Kaslo, until the railway was destroyed by fire in 1910. You pass several mining sites and get a fabulous view of the **New Denver Glacier** in **Valhalla Park,** then take a 1.4-km pack trail down to Three Forks. Read all about it on the info board at the start of the trail (lots of fascinating black-and-white photos of Sandon in the old days), and sign your name in the register.

SANDON TO BALFOUR

Kokanee Glacier Provincial Park

This 25,600-hectare mountain wilderness park lies west of Hwy. 31A, providing the modern-day explorer and outdoor enthusiast with plenty of magnificent scenery and wildlife, more than 30 lakes, many glaciers, hiking trails ranging from 3 to 11 km OW (one to eight hours), mountaineering ops for the experienced, and cross-country skiing (avalanche knowledge is a must here, and you need to be prepared to camp overnight in case the weather suddenly changes for the worse). There are no developed campgrounds (camp in designated areas only), but three cabins provide limited accommodation (reservations required Nov. to the end of May for Slocan Chief Cabin, no cooking facilities, $10 per night; the other two cabins are free). Two major access roads lead to the east side of the park from Hwy. 31A: five km north of Kaslo via 24 km of gravel to the Joker Millsite, and 21 km northeast of Nelson via 16 km of gravel along Kokanee Creek to Gibson Lake. (Two dirt access roads also lead to the west boundary of the park from Hwy. 6: two km north of Enterprise Creek and 11 km south of Silverton via 13 km of dirt, and eight km south of Slocan City via 16 km of dirt along Lemon Creek.) Before you explore the park, get topographic maps (nominal fee) from MAPS BC, Ministry of Lands and Parks, Parliament Buildings, Victoria, B.C. V8V 1X5, or from the Government Agent at 310 Ward St. in Nelson.

Kaslo

On the road to Kaslo (42 km from Sandon) it's easy to get nonchalant about the scenery. I mean, you can only rave about snowcapped peaks, dense fir forests, huge, snaking waterfalls, serene lakes, rollicking whitecapped rivers, and more waterfalls only so long before you drive yourself and/or your companions crazy! If you like to fish, pull over at **Fish Lake**—with a name like that you're bound to get a bite.

The small, quaint town of Kaslo lies on the west shore of Kootenay Lake. With its great number of elegant heritage homes, and fancy architecture from the late 1800s and early 1900s on just about every street, large shady trees and flower-filled gardens, and lake and mountain views, photo ops await capture on celluloid around every corner. Kaslo began as a sawmill community in 1889, but with silver strikes in 1893 it quickly became a

Kaslo City Hall

thriving city. City hall, built in 1898, is one of only two wooden buildings in the country that are still the seats of local government.

Drydocked by the lakefront stands the grand old red-and-white sternwheeler, the 50-meter SS *Moyie,* last CPR sternwheeler to splash up Kootenay Lake. Built in 1897 and launched the following year at Nelson, she was used for transportation and communication right up until retirement in 1957. Today the old sternwheeler contains a fine collection of photos, antiques, and artifacts of the region, and nearby is the local **Travel InfoCentre** (open daily 0900-1700 during July and August).

In winter, if you're a strong intermediate skier, get in some deep powder thrills at **Selkirk Wilderness Skiing** on Meadow Mountain at Meadow Creek, north of Kaslo on Hwy. 31. Specialized powder skis can be rented, and transportation up the slopes is by Sno-Cat. Ski packages include instruction, guides, accommodations, and all meals at **Meadow Mountain Lodge,** and transportation from Nelson; tel. 366-4424. If you need transportation to the ski area, call the above number to see if a carpool is being arranged.

Rock And Resort

On Hwy. 31A a few kilometers north of Ainsworth Hot Springs, **Woodbury Resort** consists of a marina with boat rentals and sales, fishing supplies, a heated swimming pool, a store, accommodations in housekeeping units (from $44 for four persons, $5 each additional person) or cabins (from $58 for four persons, $5 each additional person) or a campground (from $13-15 up to four persons, plus $1 each additional person), and a licensed restaurant and pub, all on the shores of Kootenay Lake. Opposite the resort is the **Woodbury Mining Museum** where you can take a half-hour tour (daily July to early Sept.) of the underground silver, lead, and zinc mine (began operating in 1896), learning about its history through rock and mineral displays, mining tools, and photos—or try your luck at a bit of gold panning.

Aaaaahhhhhh!

Cody Cave was first discovered by prospector Henry Cody in the 1880s. Made up of several large chambers and an underground creek that drops 11 meters over Cody Falls, the cave was designated **Cody Cave Provincial Park** in 1966. Turn off Hwy. 31A just north of Ainsworth Hot Springs along the narrow 15-km gravel road to the trailhead, then hike 20 minutes to the cave entrance, where you can explore about 800 meters of passages and the cave (you'll need a hardhat, a minimum of three spelunkers, and at least two lights per person). When you're done, head for the mineral-rich waters of **Ainsworth Hot Springs** where you can do some serious soaking in the main outdoor pool, Jacuzzi corner, Horseshoe Cave (steam bath), or cold plunge pool; open year-round, in summer daily 0830-2130, admission charge, suit and towel rental available.

The springs were first discovered in the early 1800s by local Indians who found that the hot, odorless water (high in magnesium sulphate, calcium sulphate, and sodium carbonate) helped heal their wounds and ease their aches and pains. If you want a bit more pampering, stay at the adjacent **Ainsworth Hot Springs Hotel** (on Hwy. 31A about 15 km north of Balfour, tel. 229-4212), with its exercise and massage rooms, or eat at **The Springs,** a licensed restaurant overlooking the main pool and beautiful Kootenay Lake. Several other accommodation choices are found in Ainsworth—check your *Accommodations Guide* for details.

Balfour

About 15 km south of the hot springs, this picturesque fishing village, with its many campgrounds, waterfront cafes by the ferry dock, community of partially tame Canada geese hanging out on the beach awaiting handouts, and lake views, lies at the junction of the north, south, and west arms of Kootenay Lake—the western terminus of the "longest free ferry ride in North America." Take the 45-minute trip across Kootenay Lake for the majestic and serene scenery, or for fun, whether you want to go to the other side or not (see "Sidetrip to Creston," below). The vehicular ferry leaves every two hours or so (fuel your vehicle and stock up on film before you leave Balfour). Back in the 1890s the lake used to be a-chop with sternwheelers dropping off passengers at isolated settlements and prospectors and supplies at mines. However, the completion of the railway (in the early 1900s) quickly dropped the demand for water transportation, putting many of the sternwheelers out of action. The last one, SS Moyie, now drydocked at Kaslo, continued to ply the lake until 1957.

Sidetrip To Creston

When you arrive by ferry at pretty **Kootenay Bay,** don't expect much in the way of facilities—there's a restaurant and store, and a small resort less than a kilometer off the main road. Highway 3A, lined with purple and yellow wildflowers in summer, follows the east shore of southern Kootenay Lake almost all the way to Creston, passing through one tiny community after another, with views of snow-capped-mountain reflections in the lake on a calm day. Before long you need to find imaginative synonyms for the monotonous "oohs" and "aahs," and a certain strength to resist the urge to snap photos around every bend. Hunger pangs? Stop at **Destiny Bay Resort Restaurant** (south of Gray Creek) for delicious meals (reservations needed for dinner) and wonderful lake views, but expect to pay for those views.

As you approach **Creston** (population 4,190), the road wanders through a large, open river valley and a sea of bright green grass. In Creston, "Apple of the Kootenays," the main attractions (as you head east on Hwy. 3) are **Creston Valley Museum** (on the right; open daily 1000-1600), the brightly painted wall mural on 11th St. claimed by locals to be "Canada's Best Mural," and tours of local ceramic and candle-making factories—get all the details at **Creston Chamber of Commerce and Tourist Information Centre,** on the main highway on the east side of town; open daily 0900-1700, in summer 0800-2000.

If you're heading west along Hwy. 3 between May and Oct., take the opportunity to visit **Creston Wildlife Centre** (11 km west of town, open daily 0900-1700, tel. 428-3259; donation), which provides naturalist-led walks, guided canoe rides ($2 pp, bookings advised), and evening talks and slide shows. See countless varieties of wildlife—from tiny hummingbirds to mighty moose! Stay less than a kilometer away at **Summit Creek Campground** (operated by the wildife center) during July and Aug. for $10 per site up to four persons, each additional person 75 cents; toilets and hot showers; tel. 428-3260.

Kokanee Creek Provincial Park

South of Balfour (19 km east of Nelson) is one of the access roads to **Kokanee Glacier Provincial Park** (16 km from the highway to the park) and a **Visitor Centre** (open daily in summer), both within the boundaries of beautiful 257-hectare Kokanee Creek Provincial Park. Walk the many short tree-shaded trails, launch your boat or canoe (good fishing in the lake), have a picnic, cross-country ski (groomed beginner's trail), or stay at Redfish or Sandspit campgrounds. Grassy, tree-shaded Sandspit has access to a beach on the West Arm of Kootenay Lake (toilets but no showers) for $10 per night May-Sept., open April-Oct. (see "Kokanee Glacier Provincial Park," p. 188).

NELSON

One glimpse of the elegant city of Nelson (population 8,134), nestled on the south shore of the West Arm of Kootenay Lake in the heart of the Selkirk Mountains, and you'll know why it's called the "Heritage Capital of the Kootenays." The hilly tree-lined streets abound with decorative turn-of-the-century architectural treasures (more than 350 have been officially designated as Heritage buildings), all used as homes, shops, or offices to this day, most with splendid lake and mountain views.

The discovery of copper and silver deposits on Toad Mountain in 1886 led to the development of the **Silver King Mine** and the further discovery of high-grade silver and iron pyrite in the area in 1887. Nelson started out as a small tent and shack camp along the banks of Ward Creek, but during the following decade the town expanded rapidly, and construction began on a smelter at the end of 1895 (it was burned down by an arsonist in 1911). Nelson was incorporated in March 1897 and quickly flourished as a commercial and cultural center of the B.C. Interior, with 23 hotels and six saloons. Wagon roads, railroads, and steamboats were developed to keep up with demand, and although operations at the mine waned by the turn of the century, silver had left a grand impact on yet another boomtown in the Kootenays. Nelson has retained its grandeur to this day.

The city has several claims to fame—first city in the province to operate an electric power plant, on Cottonwood Creek, smallest city in the country to have a streetcar system (1899 to 1949—the number 23 streetcar has been recently renovated to run along the lakeshore), and two movies were filmed here in 1986 and 1987—almost all of the 1987 movie *Roxanne* (starring Steve Martin), and *Housekeeping*!

Outdoor activities are abundant in this area. A number of lakes provide excellent fishing, sailing, canoeing, and water sports, the mountains support two popular ski hills only minutes from the city; there are heli-skiing opportunities, an abundance of cross-country skiing trails, hot springs within a short drive, hiking trails through stunning alpine scenery, and several nearby provincial parks, with some of the best scenery in the province. Nelson makes a great base from which to savor this outdoorsy paradise. Enjoy!

Entering From The Northeast

From Hwy. 3A, enter Nelson by the bridge over the West Arm of Kootenay Lake, passing several motels, fast-food outlets, and gas stations, and continue to the end of Nelson Ave. to the museum (corner of Nelson Ave. and Anderson Street). Turn right at the museum, continue along Front St., then make a left at any of the six streets after Cedar St. and you'll be smack in the heart of Nelson's historic commercial district. Baker St., running east-west, is the main street downtown.

SIGHTS

Heritage Hunting

This city has more heritage buildings per capita than any other city in B.C., save Victoria. The first thing to do in Nelson is to get rid of your vehicle and walk or cycle around

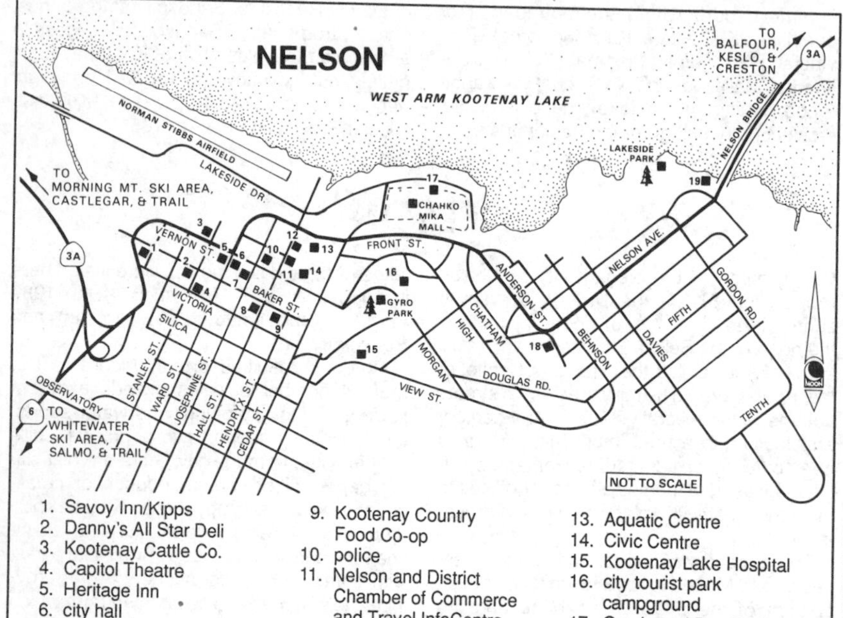

downtown to appreciate the architectural curiosities and perhaps visit some of the craft shops and art galleries—Nelson is home to many of B.C.'s finest artists and craftspeople. Pick up the detailed *Heritage Walking Tour* or *Heritage Motoring Tour* brochures from the InfoCentre. The stone and brick castle-like **City Hall,** built in 1902, is an attention-getter (on the corner of Vernon and Ward streets). Many other beautifully preserved and restored buildings (most built around 1912) are found along Ward and Baker streets. If you enjoy stickybeaking at people's homes from the anonymity of your car, drive out of Nelson along Hwy. 3A toward Balfour, passing several intriguing pieces of architecture, including a house resembling an old steamboat and a fabulous mansion. On weekends these suburbs are alive with lawn mowers.

Orient Yourself!

Gyro Park is a good place to orient yourself to your Nelson surroundings. Wander through a lovingly tended, flowering rock garden, watch all the toddlers toddle in the children's toddling pool on a hot summer's day, then mosey along the bush trail past all sorts of flowering plants, shrubs, and trees to a viewpoint for outstanding panoramic views of Nelson, the West Arm of Kootenay Lake, the airfield, and the bridge that links Nelson with the north shore. The entrance is on Gyro Park Street. Another pleasant green spot in which to meander and catch up on postcard writing is **Lakeside Park,** by the bridge. It has a large sandy beach, tennis courts, a picnic area, rose gardens, a boat launch, and plenty of live sailboarder entertainment.

Museums
To find out more about Nelson's colorful past, visit the two museums. **Nelson Museum** is at 402 Anderson St., open in summer daily 1300-1800, in winter Mon.-Sat. 1300-1600, closed holidays, tel. 352-9813; admission adult $1, child 50 cents. It concentrates on local history, with displays covering native peoples, explorers, miners, traders, early transportation, Nelson's contribution to WW I, and the Doukhobors (a religious group). It also contains the restored Kootenay Lakes *Ladybird,* a record-breaking speedboat prior to the more advanced designs of the 1950s hydroplane, and other boats from days gone by.

To absorb some of Nelson's mining history, cruise past the mining artifacts, mineral displays, and historic photos at the **Chamber of Mines of Eastern B.C. Museum** next to the chamber of commerce on Hall St. (tel. 352-5242).

Sensational Skiing
Skiing is one of the biggest activities in this area—many fanatics move to Nelson for the two outrageous ski hills nearby. **Whitewater Ski Area** (locals call it WH_2O), 19 km south of Nelson off Hwy. 6, has a long season (Nov.-May), heaps of snow (over 700 centimeters annual average), 18 runs suitable for all levels of skiers, and some of the "very best powder in the whole of Canada!" What more could any self-respecting ski bum want?! Facilities include chairlifts, a T-bar, a lodge, a cafeteria, a lounge, a ski rental shop, and a ski school; full-day lift ticket starts at adult $22, senior or student $19, under six free, half-day adult $17, senior or student $13. For more info call 354-4944 or the 24-hour reservation and info line, tel. 352-7669. Kilometers of groomed cross-country trails are also found in the Whitewater area. The steep windy road up to the ski area is worth driving at any time of year just for the heck of it (and of course the magnificent scenery in good weather), but watch out for more crazy kamikaze deer.

Morning Mountain Ski Area provides good family skiing, with runs geared to beginners and intermediate skiers, off Hwy. 3A West. Facilities include a T-bar, a lodge, food service, ski rental, and a ski school. It's open Sat., Sun., and Mon. 0900-1530, and Tues., Wed., and Thurs. nights 1830-2130; for more info call 352-9969. Several heli-skiing and wilderness skiing operations are also based in and around Nelson—get current details at the InfoCentre.

ACCOMMODATIONS

Campsites
The downtown campground is **City Tourist Park,** on the corner of High and Willow streets, open mid-May through Sept., tel. 352-9031; the rates are $8-10 per night (all hookups available, sewer $1), with washrooms (free shower if you're camping), a sink for cleaning cooking utensils, and a public telephone. At the office you can buy ice for $2. Noncampers can use the shower or RV sewer drop for $3.

Hotels And Motels
Nelson has a couple of downtown hotels on Vernon and Baker streets, and several motels (most are on Hwy. 31A at the northeast end of town, or over the bridge on the north side of the lake). For full listings, refer to the *Accommodations Guide.* If you enter Nelson on Hwy. 3A from the east, the **Duhamel Motel and Campground,** eight km from town, provides comfortable sleeping units with kitchenettes at very reasonable prices ($30-32 s, $34-46 d), just across the road from Kootenay Lake (the front units have lake and mountain views), with access to a private sandy beach. Coin-operated laundry facilities, a fully stocked grocery store, and a campground with full hookups ($10-12 per night, including all hookups); tel. 825-4645.

Heritage Inn
For bed and breakfast downtown, try the old-fashioned Heritage Inn at 422 Vernon St., tel. 352-5331, which provides attractive, recently refurbished rooms (no a/c), some with lake views, for $44-56 s or $48-66 d including

breakfast. If you can't stand any noise when you sleep, let them know at the front desk when you check in—some rooms are clearly within earshot of the disco, and you may find your bed bouncing to the beat when you're not! Love the friendly sign in the parking lot—"Customer Parking Only. All Other Cars Will Be Crushed And Melted."

Whitewater Inn

If you have your own transportation, this attractive and comfy lodge is the best place to stay in this area. It's on Hwy. 6 (look for the old boat and sign to the right at the base of the ski hill road), 11 km south of Nelson, 10 km from Whitewater Ski Hill, tel. 352-9150. (Note that it's closed in May, Oct., and November.) The big wooden lodge has bunk rooms and private rooms (with windows at eye level so you can wake up and see the trees or snow, depending on the season, without moving anything more than an eyelid), shared or private washrooms and showers, and a sauna. In the communal living area/gallery/restaurant you can get three meals a day, join in the après-ski scene with a drink and munchies, see movies (ask to see the *Whitewater Skiing* movie), and buy Carol's pottery creations, whimsical powder pigs and dragons, and handpainted silk scarves (treat yourself, or stock up on all your gifts here). Cross-country ski rental is also available—snap on your skis at the front door and step out onto a groomed trail (kilometers and kilometers).

Pat, Carol, Buster the dog, and Pouncer the cat at the Whitewater Inn

Rates at Whitewater Inn start at $15-50 s (minimum two nights at the $15 rate), $30-55 d (some have private baths, one has a kitchenette), $55 d for the honeymoon unit with brass bed, private bath, and hot tub, and all include a delicious healthy breakfast. Advance reservations are wise for winter weekends and holidays. Friendly owners Pat and Carol also operate a restaurant in the lodge, open for breakfast, lunch, and dinner (drop-ins welcome)—pull up a pew for a good homecooked meal using pottery crockery made by Carol. The Inn is open for the ski season—generally from the end of Nov./first of Dec. through April—and from June through Sept. caters to hikers, anglers, and travelers passing through.

OTHER PRACTICALITIES

Food

For sandwiches try **Danny's All Star Deli**, casual, very popular at lunchtime. It's at 358 Baker St., tel. 352-2828; open weekdays 0800-1730, Sat. 0800-1600. If you're just looking for a delectable bakery snack or a soup and sandwich lunch, try **Ione's Bakery and Deli** in the Chahko-Mika Mall, 1109 Lakeside—eat there in the small sit-down section or at the counter, or take your calories away. **Main Street Diner** is wonderful for Greek food, but they also have steaks, seafood, and burgers on the menu; at 616 Baker St., open Mon.-Sat. 1100-2000, Fri. 1100- 2200.

Kootenay Cattle Co., in the rustic Heritage Jam Factory building at 303 Vernon St., serves a chuckwagon full of salads, steaks, seafood—and prime rib on the weekends—in an Old West atmosphere. The large lunches cost around $6-8, and dinners are $9-29 (daily good-value specials); open Tues.-Fri. 1130-1400 and 1700-2200, Sat. 1700-2200, Sun. 1700-2100. The old-fashioned, tapestried, tassled **General Store** restaurant in the Heritage Inn at 422 Vernon St. is the place to go on Sun. between 1100 and 1400 for a smorgasbord brunch (as much as you want) serving eggs, meats, and a variety of salads for $8.50 pp. It's also open daily for lunch (buffet soup and salad bar $7) and dinner ($8-15), with inexpensive dinner specials offered on Fri. and Sat., 1700-2130.

Entertainment

Locals get their lively entertainment at the **Boiler Room**—a bar and disco (with pop videos) that's "Hot, hot, hot, and ready to rock"; open Wed.-Sat. 2000-0200. More in the mood for a quiet drink? Settle into one of the tapestried chairs by the fireplace, grab a book, and strike up a conversation with one of the bare-breasted maidens that so elegantly support the decadent, draped ceiling in **The Library.** Both bars are located in the **Heritage Inn** at 422 Vernon Street. For live bands on the weekends and disco during the week, **Kipps** in the Savoy Inn at 198 Baker St. is the place to be.

Live theater happens at **The Capitol** at 417 Victoria St., near the corner of Ward (drop in and find out what's playing, call 352-6363, or visit the InfoCentre); in winter you can attend one of the concert series. The **Aquatic Centre** at 800 Front St. (tel. 354-4044, open year-round) has a pool, a fitness center, a whirlpool, and saunas, and the **Civic Center** on the corner of Vernon and Hendryx streets puts on movies and theater, and has ice rinks, a badminton room, and tennis courts. And then there's always the **Savoy Lanes Bowling Alley** at 520 Falls St., open daily.

The major local celebration is the annual **Mid-Summer Bonspiel,** held in July, with local curling events and all sorts of fun activities. And **Canada Day** on July 1 is always a good time to be in Nelson—the locals celebrate it in a big way.

Information And Services

Nelson And District Chamber of Commerce Travel InfoCentre is at 225 Hall St., open year-round. In summer (June to the end of Aug.) it's open seven days 0830-1830, the rest of the year on weekdays only 0830-1630; tel. 352-3433. For free accommodation booking service, call 354-4944.

Kootenay Lake District Hospital has three good views from 3 View St., tel. 352-3111. The **post office** is at 514 Vernon Street. For quality arts and crafts, drop by **The Craft Connection,** a member-run co-op owned and operated by local artists and craftspersons, at 441 Baker St., tel. 352-3006; open Mon.-Wed. and Sat. 0930-1730, Thurs. and Fri. 0930-2100.

Transportation

Nelson has local bus transportation—pick up a schedule and info at the InfoCentre or call **Nelson Bus Service** at 352-3416. Auto rental can be arranged at **Whitewater Motors Ltd.** at 623 Railway St., tel. 352-7202, or **Rent-A-Wreck** at 301 Nelson Ave., tel. 352-5122. The only long-distance ground transportation is by bus; the **Greyhound Bus Station** is at the Chahko-Mika Mall on Lakeside Dr., running services southwest to Castlegar, or south to Salmo and then east to Creston and on into Alberta. **Norman Stubbs Airfield** lies along the lakeshore, walking distance from downtown, but no commercial airlines offer service out of Nelson—the closest commercial airport is at Castlegar.

PUSHING THE BOUNDARY

The Crowsnest Route

Highway 3, also known as the Crowsnest Hwy., wanders through Boundary Country (named after Boundary Creek, which joins the Kettle River just south of Midway at the Canada/U.S. border) along or just above the 49th parallel, passing through **Greenwood, Grand Forks, Castlegar, Salmo,** and **Creston.** The Crowsnest, one of the highest highways in Canada (the highest all-weather pass runs through Stagleap Provincial Park, east of Salmo), is the major route through the Kootenays for traffic zooming between the popular tourist regions of the Okanagan in the west and the Canadian Rockies in the east. This southernmost section of the Kootenay/Boundary region is an intriguing mixture of lakes, rivers, dams, steep ski hills, abandoned and still-active smelters, logging and mining communities, and several small industrial cities (Trail and Castlegar are the largest). If you travel the Crowsnest in either direction, even looping south from Castlegar to **Trail** and **Rossland** and back up to Salmo, you can easily cover this stretch of B.C. by car in a day, or in several days if you visit each city's main attractions, or in a week if you stop in at all the chamber of commerce Travel InfoCentres and innocently ask, "Is there anything to see and do around here?"

Greenwood

The tiny community of Greenwood has one large (or small) claim to fame—it's the smallest incorporated city in the province (some say in Canada, others doubt it). It's certainly had an up-and-down history, starting off as a silver- and gold-mining community in 1897, growing into a service-center boomtown with a population of more than 3,000 by the early 20th century, becoming a ghost town after WW I, a Japanese-Canadian internment camp in the 1940s, then finally stabilizing into the small logging and silver- and gold-mining community (pop. 700) that it is today.

See many restored historic buildings downtown, visit **Greenwood Museum** (on the highway) to find out more about Greenwood's mining mania, and follow trails to old mine sites (maps and details available at the **InfoCentre** in the museum; open daily May-September). Fish for trout at 49-hectare **Jewel Lake Provincial Park** (about 11 km northeast), or take your downhill or cross-country skis to **Phoenix Ski Hill** (continue along Hwy. 3 for about 20 km, then turn right on the 13-km gravel road to Ski Hill and Phoenix Mine Site). As you continue along the highway to Grand Forks, notice the attractive brick settlements (now abandoned) built by the Doukhobors, a Russian religious sect (see below).

Grand Forks

The small town of Grand Forks, perched at the confluence of the Granby and Kettle rivers, is the unofficial capital of Boundary Country. It started out as a trading district for the Hudson's Bay Company and became a mining town (prior to WW I, nearby Granby Mine operated the largest nonferrous smelter in the British Empire) made up of miners, Indians, ranchers, land developers, and Doukhobor immigrants. The Doukhobors, a religious sect that practices pacifism and vegetarianism, fled their Russian homeland in the late 1800s when they were persecuted for their beliefs (refusing to serve in the army got them in a lot of trouble), mass-migrating to Saskatchewan in 1898-99, then setting up communes in B.C. in the early 1900s. They kept a low profile, farming and making everything they needed. When their leader, Peter Verigin, died in 1924, the Doukhobor way of life began to change and deteriorate. Today Doukhobor descendants (many live in Grand Forks and Castlegar) still follow their beliefs and speak Russian (Russian is taught in local schools), but no longer live in the once-communal villages. Find out more about the

Doukhobor lifestyle at the **Mountain View Doukhobor Museum**—a 1912 Doukhobor communal farmhouse on Hardy Mountain Rd., tel. 442-8855.

Today Grand Forks is a mixture of historic turn-of-the-century homes, restored heritage buildings on tree-lined streets, and modern industry—predominantly logging, sawmill, and seed-growing companies. See all sorts of mining artifacts, photos from the past, historic pioneer artifacts, even hearse lamps, at the **Boundary Museum** on 5th St. (open daily May-Oct.), and pick up a *Take A Walk Through Historic Grand Forks* brochure at the **Chamber of Commerce InfoCentre** (tel. 442-2833) next door.

Nineteen-km-long, tree-lined **Christina Lake** (25 km east of Grand Forks) attracts droves of water-recreation lovers and anglers to its warm waters in summer. It's one of the warmest lakes in the province and has a reputation for good rainbow trout, bass, and kokanee fishing. Stay at one of the many commercial campgrounds nearby.

CASTLEGAR

Castlegar (pop. 7,200), the "Crossroads of the Kootenays," is a spread-out city with no obvious downtown core, at the junction of the Columbia and Kootenay rivers. Highways 3 (east and west), 3A (north), and 22 (south) all converge at Castlegar. The first residents of this area (1908) were the Doukhobors, living in villages between Castlegar and Brilliant—many of their descendants still live in the Castlegar area (see "Sights," below).

Today the local economy is based on forestry, mining (nonresidents sarcastically refer to the city as "Smellgar," but keep this less-than-friendly reference to yourself when you're within earshot of locals), and hydropower industries, along with tourism. Also

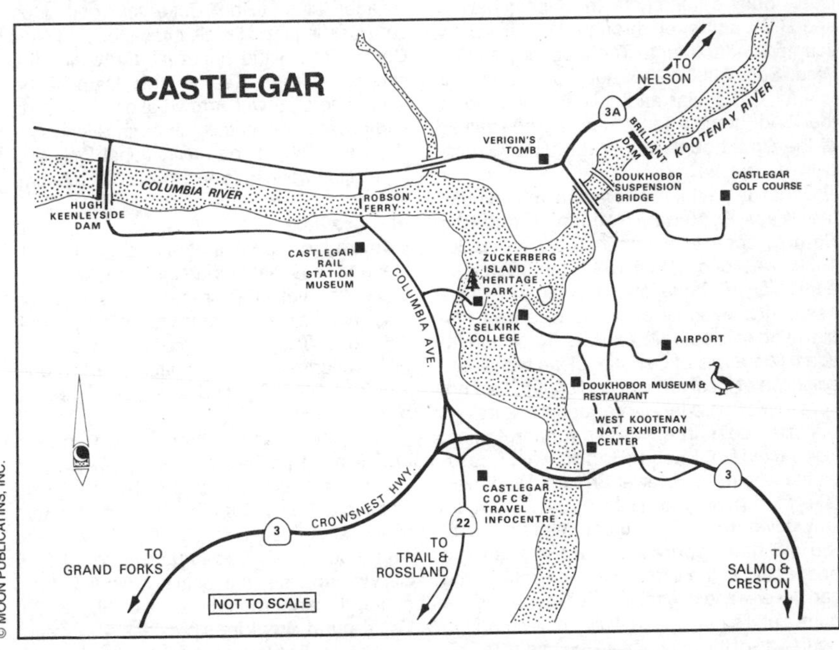

called the "Gateway to the Arrow Lakes," Castlegar lures waterbabies from afar to explore kilometer after kilometer of exceptional freshwater fishing and boating waters.

Sights

One of the local highlights is the **Doukhobor Historical Museum.** Take Hwy. 3A toward Nelson and head for Castlegar Airport; at the stoplight, cross the intersection away from the airport and turn left at the sign, noting all the antiquated pieces of farm machinery and equipment along the road as you approach the museum. Starting inside the main building, a Doukhobor descendent takes you on a lively tour through the simply furnished brick dwellings and outbuildings. See how they used to live (the rooms contain authentic artifacts, clothing, fine handwoven materials, crocheted bedspreads and shawls, carved wooden spoons and ladles); study the historic photo collection of the original Doukhobor settlements in Saskatchewan and B.C.; and stroll through the deliciously scented cedar sauna. The museum is open Wed.-Sun. 0900-1700; admission and tour is adult $4, senior and child $3. Just down the road, sample tasty Russian specialties at the **Doukhobor Restaurant** (see "Practicalities," below).

Continue past the village and you come to the **West Kootenay National Exhibition Centre,** open in summer Tues.-Fri. 1030-1630, weekends 1200-1630, tel. 365-3337; admission by donation. The center always has a good variety of works of art on display—often elaborate exhibits from the National Museums of Canada, along with a fine selection of local artwork and crafts. It's a hot spot to pick up a locally created treasure.

While you're in a Russian frame of mind, visit the old **Doukhobor Bridge,** which crosses the Kootenay River at Brilliant. When you take the highway (to Nelson) over the river, look down to the right to see the remains of the old hand-poured cement suspension bridge built in the first half of the century. You can get down to it by taking the first road to the right, but it's not safe to walk on. Also on the north side of the river, above the bridge at Brilliant, lies **Verigin's Tomb,** final resting place of the Doukhobors' spiritual leader, surrounded by an impressive floral display.

Before leaving Castlegar, meander around **Zuckerberg Island Park,** the island home of Russian immigrant Alexander Zuckerberg, who came to Castlegar to teach Doukhobor children in 1931. The island lies at the confluence of the Kootenay and Columbia rivers and is connected to the mainland by a creaking suspension bridge. You can walk right around the tree-covered island, passing a full-scale model of a *kukuli* (Indian winter pit house), a Hiroshima memorial, the Stump Lady, a Russian orthodox chapel house, a cemetery, a log house, a salmon-fishing river, and many other Zuckerberg creations and stops of natural- and human-historical interest relating to the island, in about 15-30 minutes. To get there, turn off Hwy. 22 at 9th St., turn left on 7th Ave., then immediately right (the road turns back on itself).

Other things to do? Take your golf clubs onto Castlegar's 18-hole championship **Golf Course,** one of the "finest in B.C.," or visit the enormous **Hugh Keenleyside Dam** at the south end of Lower Arrow Lake, where tugs and private boats cruise through a lock system—the only inland navigational lock system "in the world" (it's on the road to Robson).

Practicalities

If you're looking for a comfortable, hospitable, and reasonable motel, head straight for **Cozy Pines** at 2100 Crestview Crescent (on Hwy. 3 at the west entrance to Castlegar), tel. 365-5613. The spotless rooms with kitchenettes (courtesy tea and coffee) start at only $28-32 s, $32-38 d, and off-season rates are also available.

The **Castlegar Chamber of Commerce and Travel InfoCentre** is off the highway as you leave Castlegar toward Trail. Turn off Columbia Ave. at 20th St.—it's at the bottom of the street; open 0830-1930 daily, June-Aug. 0800-1900. **Castlegar Regional Bus Service** operates the local bus service; for a schedule and route info, call 365-3100. **Greyhound Bus Lines** provides service between Castlegar and Vancouver, Nelson,

Salmo, Creston, and on toward Alberta—get a current schedule at the InfoCentre. **Castlegar Airport,** the main airport for the region, serviced by **Canadian Airlines** (tel. 365-8488), **Air B.C.** (tel. 800-663-0522), and **Time Air** (tel. 800-663-3502), is about six km north of the city off Hwy. 3A.

TRAIL

Nestled in the Columbia River Valley, 27 km southwest of Castlegar, Trail (pop. 7,730) clings to both east and west banks of the Columbia River. Unlike most other mining towns in the region, Trail began as a Columbia River sternwheeler port in the early 1890s, servicing the miners as they followed the lure of gold, silver, and copper to Red Mountain near present-day Rossland. In 1896 a smelter was constructed in Trail. It's now the largest lead and zinc smelter "in the world," producing much of Canada's silver as a by-product of lead and zinc concentrate. A large population of Italian migrant workers, who originally came to the area to work the mines in the late 1800s and the railway in the early 1900s, stayed on to work at the smelter—today you can arrange to visit the **Italian Community Archives,** the "only" Italian Archives in North America, in the heart of the Italian section of town at 584 Rossland Ave., West Trail, tel. 364-2052 (tours run in July and August). Rossland Ave. is also a great place to sink your teeth into a bowl of spaghetti—a large percentage of Trail's population has lItalian heritage.

Today Trail is without a doubt an industrial town—approach it from the east and you'll understand why it's been described as "Cominco with a town built around it." Huge 120-meter-high smokestacks overshadow the entire city, belching thick plumes of smoke into the atmosphere. Guess what the main attraction is here? Why, touring the **Cominco complex,** of course. See where ores are melted and separated and hear how the company converts waste products into fertilizer and a number of other products. The factory is on Aldridge Ave. in West Trail. The tours are free (wear good walking shoes) and held daily in summer (meet at 1000 weekdays at the company's Main Gate, tel. 368-3144), in winter book through the InfoCentre (children under 12 don't get to go).

The **City of Trail Museum** is the place to go if you want to read up on the city's history; at 1051 Victoria, open weekdays 1000-1200 and 1300-1600 June to the end of Aug., free admission. While you're near city hall, check out the **City of Lead and Zinc frieze,** by Victorian artist George Norris, on one of the city hall windows.

Escape the smokestacks. Go hiking, swimming, fishing for rainbow trout, cross-country skiing, and snowshoeing, or see some wildlife (of the animal variety) at the 1,408-hectare **Champion Lakes Provincial Park.** Take Hwy. 3B east for about 22 km to the turnoff. The three Champion Lakes, connected by hiking trails, lie in the Bonnington Range. Within the park are campsites ($8 per night June-Sept.) and a sani station, and in summer visitor programs are put on by park staff.

Trail and District Chamber Of Commerce is at 843 Rossland Ave., tel. 368-3144; open weekdays 0900-1700, in summer weekdays 0900-1800 and weekends 0900-1700. Long-distance transportation is provided by **Greyhound Coach Lines** (on Bay Ave. off the highway on the west side of the Columbia River in West Trail, tel. 368-8400). The company provides three daily services to Vancouver and Calgary. The nearest major airport is at Castlegar.

ROSSLAND

Sitting in an extinct volcanic crater amongst the steep, tree-covered Monashee Mountains, Rossland, six km west of Trail, is promoted as "The Golden City." The precious yellow metal was discovered on 1,580-meter Red Mountain (now a skier's haven) in 1890 by prospectors following the nearby Dewdney Trail—a boom naturally followed. From the mineral-rich Rossland Mines came 6,000,000 tons of ore worth $125 million, along with the development of the enormous smelter at Trail, and the city of Rossland.

Many restored buildings (early 1900s) and old-fashioned street lamps line the streets of Rossland. Collect a *Heritage Walking Tour* pamphlet from the museum, library, or downtown shops, and hit the streets. Kick up your heels (or watch the cancan girls and singing gamblers kicking up theirs) at a "Gold-fever Follies" performance in the historic 1898 Miners Hall on Columbia Avenue. You can spend a couple of hours at the Le Roi Gold Mine and **Rossland Historical Museum** (junction of Highways 22 and 3B, open from mid-May to Sept. seven days a week 0900-1700, tel. 362-7722), where the lustrous geological and human history of the area is recaptured. In the "Ski Hall of Fame," see displays honoring world-class champion skier Nancy Greene, a local heroine who won a gold medal in the 1968 Olympics, and the wooden skis and trophies of Olaus Jeldness, the first person to introduce a passion for skiing to this area, in 1896. The museum is open daily 0900-1700, mid-May to Oct., tours at 1000, 1100, 1230, 1400, 1500, and 1600; museum admission adult $6, senior or student $5, child $3, under six free. The **Rossland Travel InfoCentre** and **Tearoom** (open daily 0900-1700) are in the same complex (light meals $4-7).

It's easier to imagine the day-to-day life of those early-1890s hardrock miners if you tour the restored underground tunnels of the **Le Roi Gold Mine,** next to the museum complex. A gigantic compressor, a simulated mine shaft, and large pieces of mining machinery stand outside, then up the path is the gold mine, where your introductory course in local geology begins. Mineral veins, dykes, faults, and old and new mining equipment are displayed. Impress your friends with detailed explanations of how ore is mined and trammed and drilled and blasted, and how to use explosives, then round out your education by learning the difference between igneous, metamorphic, and sedimentary rocks at the rock garden. Admission to the museum and gold mine tour is adult $4, senior $3, student and child $2.

White Magic At Red Mountain

Highway 3B toward Castlegar leads to Red Mountain (three km north of Rossland) for fabulous wintertime skiing on world-class slopes. The road to steep **Red Mountain Ski Area** takes you past **Red Mountain Motel and Restaurant**, with cabins and chalets, cross-country ski rentals, and the **Red Shutter Inn.** Skiing was first introduced to the area in 1896 by Olaus Jeldness—his wooden skis and trophies are housed in the Western Canada Ski Hall of Fame in Rossland Museum.

Snowfall at Red Mt. averages 1,300 centimeters a year and the season runs from mid-Nov. to mid-April. Three faces on two mountains provide excellent skiing opportunities for all levels: a vertical drop of 415 meters and triple chair on **Paradise,** a 920-meter vertical drop, double chair, 7½-km intermediate run, world-class downhill course, and powder fields on **Granite Mountain,** and a vertical drop of 415 meters, double chair, an intermediate area serviced by a T-bar, and night skiing on Wed. and Sat. at **Red Mountain.** Several world champions and Olympic skiers got their start here—in fact, the resort contributes a large number of members to Canada's National Ski Team each year. Services include a cafeteria, a licensed lounge, a ski school, and a ski shop with sales, rentals, and repairs. Cross-country skiers also take to the slopes in the Blackjack area next to Red Mountain to silently swoosh along more than 50 km of groomed tracks through a pristine winter wonderland.

At the intersection of Hwy. 3B and the access road to Red Mountain is **Ram's Head Inn,** a bed-and-breakfast lodge on 4½ acres adjacent to the ski area, only a slip and a slide from the bottom of the ski hill. Offering comfy rooms with private bathrooms, a spacious communal lounge with luxurious chairs and a large fireplace, a dining area, a games room, and a sauna, the lodge primarily caters to skiers (reservations usually necessary in winter), but it's also open in summer (much easier to get a room, reservations usually not necessary). In winter, guests tend to book in groups, taking several rooms for a week or so at a time, but if there's a room free, it's yours. The rates include breakfast (dinners available on the package rate); summer rates start at $40-70 s, $40-80 d. Call for info on their two-day winter packages and their longer package rates and make reservations at 362-9577.

Salmo

The small village of Salmo has pleasing old-fashioned wooden buildings, spacious verandas, and streets decorated in summer with huge hanging flower baskets bursting with brilliant color. It's called the "Hub of the Kootenays;" at the Hwy. 6/3 junction. **Salmo Ski Hill,** only two km east of town off Hwy. 3/6 south, provides good family skiing and night skiing, a 320-meter vertical drop, a 1,235-meter T-bar lift, a rope tow, a day lodge, a restaurant, and rental facilities.

Gastric rumblings are happily silenced at **Trapper John's Restaurant and Coffee Shop**, back along Hwy. 3 toward Trail by Motel Ave., tel. 357-2296. Open daily, 0900-2100 weekdays, 0700-2200 weekends, they serve good meal deals (lunch from around $5, dinner includes salad bar for $8-16), or a snack that's guaranteed to go straight to cellulite, but what the heck. Wrap your lips, if you can, around one of their monster-size sticky-sweet cinnamon rolls (large enough for two regular-sized monsters). Just across the road from Trapper John's, beside the Sal-Crest Motel, is the wooden "oldest phone booth in the world." The Salmo **Travel InfoCentre** booth is open mid-June to mid-Sept. on Hwy. 6 and Fourth St., tel. 832-5223. The **Greyhound Bus Depot** is at the Petro-Canada Station on the right side of Hwy. 6 as you enter Salmo from Nelson.

Salmo To Creston

Between Salmo and Creston, the Crowsnest Hwy. crosses the Selkirk Mountains over the 1,774-meter Kootenay Pass—the highest paved highway in the country. About 35 km east of Salmo lies 1,133-hectare **Stagleap Provincial Park,** where travelers can pause to picnic by Bridal Lake, go for a hike, cross-country ski, and visit the visitor centre for more info on the local area. For info on Creston (82 km east of Salmo), see p. 190.

TODD CLARK

LOUISE FOOTE

ROCKY MOUNTAINS

MAJESTIC PEAKS AND PERFECT PARKS

Splendid craggy mountains stained red and orange by the setting sun, topped by row upon row of white glaciated peaks jaggedly jutting into the horizon. Emerald lakes, alpine meadows tangled in masses of wildflowers, and crisp air. Rivers rushing through wide open valleys and tree-crowded canyons, meandering trout streams, and splashy silver waterfalls. Exhilarating ski hills and soothing hot springs. Fast highways bordered with scarlet Indian paintbush and brilliant yellow and white daisies, and wilderness parks abounding with more wildlife than you could hope to see in a lifetime. It's all here. One of the most beautiful landscapes on earth.

This stunning chunk of British Columbia lies between the mountainous Kootenay region in the west and the province of Alberta in the east, encompassing the Purcell Mountains, the Rocky Mountain Trench, and the Rocky Mountains. At the north end of this long, narrow strip lies Kinbasket Lake, at the south end the U.S. border. Wherever you travel within this area you see mountains—either the bare rock vertebrae of the **Canadian Rocky Mountains** (2,000-3,954 meters high) or the steep, tree-covered **Purcell Range** (2,000-3,162 meters high). Highway 93/95 snakes along the relatively wide Rocky Mountain Trench between the two ranges, following the mighty Columbia River much of the way, connecting the cities of **Cranbrook** and **Kimberley** in the southeast with **Lake Louise** (in Banff National Park) and **Golden** in the northwest.

No matter where you go in the Rocky Mountain region, expect scenery that makes other magnificent parts of the world pale in comparison, and an abundance of activities bound to keep any self-respecting outdoors enthusiast busy from dawn to dusk. Your eyes are in for a treat and your camera is in for a workout; take lots of film—a telephoto lens and tripod are handy for wildlife subjects.

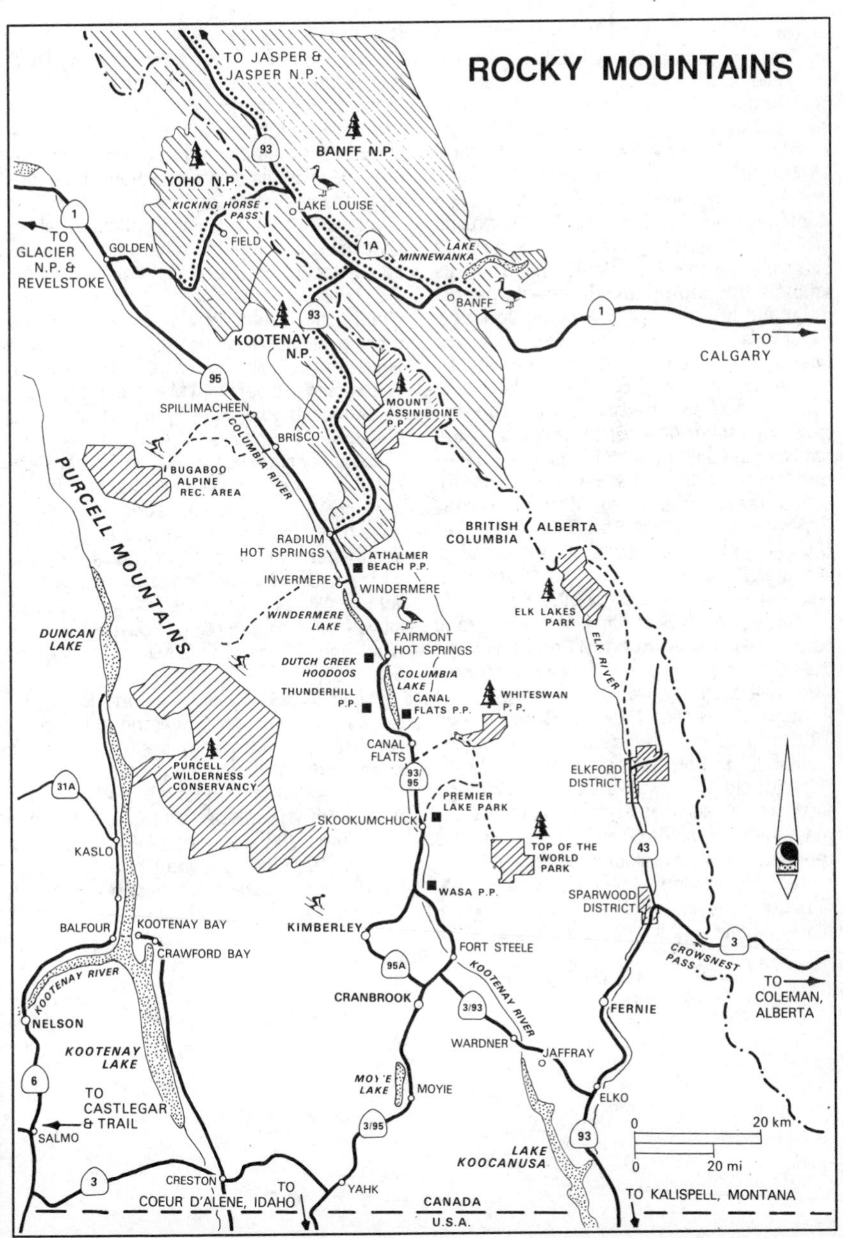
ROCKY MOUNTAINS
TO JASPER & JASPER N.P.
93
BANFF N.P.
YOHO N.P.
KICKING HORSE PASS
LAKE LOUISE
1
TO GLACIER N.P. & REVELSTOKE
FIELD
GOLDEN
1A
LAKE MINNEWANKA
BANFF
1
TO CALGARY
93
KOOTENAY N.P.
95
MOUNT ASSINIBOINE P.P.
SPILLIMACHEEN
COLUMBIA RIVER
BRISCO
BUGABOO ALPINE REC. AREA
PURCELL MOUNTAINS
BRITISH COLUMBIA
ALBERTA
RADIUM HOT SPRINGS
ATHALMER BEACH P.P.
INVERMERE
WINDERMERE
WINDERMERE LAKE
ELK LAKES PARK
ELK RIVER
DUNCAN LAKE
FAIRMONT HOT SPRINGS
DUTCH CREEK HOODOOS
COLUMBIA LAKE
COLUMBIA
THUNDERHILL P.P.
CANAL FLATS P.P.
WHITESWAN P.P.
CANAL FLATS
PURCELL WILDERNESS CONSERVANCY
93/95
ELKFORD DISTRICT
31A
PREMIER LAKE PARK
SKOOKUMCHUCK
TOP OF THE WORLD PARK
KASLO
43
WASA P.P.
SPARWOOD DISTRICT
BALFOUR
KOOTENAY BAY
KIMBERLEY
CRAWFORD BAY
FORT STEELE
3
CROWSNEST PASS
KOOTENAY RIVER
95A
KOOTENAY RIVER
CRANBROOK
TO COLEMAN, ALBERTA
NELSON
3/93
FERNIE
KOOTENAY LAKE
WARDNER
JAFFRAY
6
TO CASTLEGAR & TRAIL
MOYIE LAKE
MOYIE
ELKO
SALMO
3/95
93
0
20 km
0
20 mi
LAKE KOOCANUSA
3
CRESTON
TO COEUR D'ALENE, IDAHO
YAHK
CANADA
U.S.A.
TO KALISPELL, MONTANA

History

The Kootenay Indians have lived in this beautiful valley for the last 2,000 years, hunting, gathering, and making horseback trips over the Rockies to hunt buffalo on the Albertan plains. In 1807 David Thompson, an explorer for the fur-trading North West Company, found his way over Howse Pass and set up Kootenay House trading post at the north end of **Lake Windermere.** During the next 50 years the region was explored and mined, its animals trapped by fur traders, its people preached to and baptized by missionaries. But it wasn't until 1863 that settlers showed much interest in the rugged, mountainous terrain. At the shout of "Gold!" along Wild Horse Creek, miners swarmed into the area, and the town of **Fisherville** sprang up along the banks of the gold-bearing creek. Later a second town, **Galbraith's Ferry,** was established nearby on the edge of the Kootenay River—renamed **Fort Steele** in 1888 after Superintendent Sam Steele of the North West Mounted Police who built the first NWMP post west of the Rockies at Galbraith's Ferry.

In 1893 North Star Mine (lead, zinc, and silver) opened in **Kimberley.** Fort Steele was the commercial center of the region for several years, until the CPR railway, built through Crowsnest Pass to Cranbrook in 1898, completely bypassed it. Cranbrook flourished as Fort Steele diminished. Today Fort Steele is a well-preserved Heritage Park, worth visiting at any time of the year but most fun in summer when its vivid history is reenacted in the saloons, hotels, general store, barber's shop, jail, etc., by park staff. Cranbrook became the major city in the region—a position it still holds today.

Creston To Cranbrook

The first community you come to along Hwy. 3/95 is **Yahk,** a small but thriving lumber town in the 1920s, abandoned by the 1930s. Today many empty houses and hotels line the streets, but the pioneer **museum** keeps history alive with its displays of household artifacts and costumes from the past. Stop for a bite to eat at the popular **Fiddlers Restaurant** as you approach Yahk from the west, add a local "I've been to Yahk and Back" T-shirt to your collection, or pull off at tiny nine-hectare **Yahk Provincial Park** on the rushing Moyie River east of town for some good trout or Dolly Varden fishing, picnicking, or camping ($8 per night May-Oct.); be aware of curious bears—keep your distance and never offer them food.

If you continue east of Yahk between April and mid-Autumn (daylight savings time), you pass into the next time zone—everything goes dark for a few moments, a tingling sensation starts at the base of your spine, and you're suddenly surrounded by pinpoints of light in all the colors of the rainbow. Actually, all you do is enter mountain daylight savings time, and you need to advance your watch one hour!

Highway 3/95 winds back and forth over the Moyie River until you come to the small community of **Moyie** (gas station, general store, Tudor-style pub, 1907 Moyie Fire Hall, and a handful of homes). **Moyie Lake Provincial Park** (north on Munro Lake Rd.) has campsites ($8 per night, May-Oct.) and shower facilities, a sandy beach, a boat launch, good fishing for rainbow and cutthroat trout, and a sani station.

CRANBROOK

At the south end of the Rocky Mountain Trench, Cranbrook was originally a campsite for Kootenay Indians. The Galbraiths, who ran the ferry across Kootenay River at Galbraith's Ferry (later known as Fort Steele), were the first European landowners here. They sold the land to Colonel James Baker in the 1880s; he tried to establish a townsite here with little success until the CPR railway bypassed well-established Fort Steele and trains began chugging into the small settlement of Cranbrook. Fort Steele dwindled to nothing as Cranbrook rapidly grew, and in 1905 the city of Cranbrook was incorporated. Today this service and transportation center is the major city in the Rocky Mountain region, with a population of 16,500 and an economy based on forestry, mining, ranching, and tourism.

One of the best things about Cranbrook is the ever-present view of marvelous mountains at the east end of what seems like every street. The town itself has few tourist attractions (though plenty of motels and restaurants), but with all that stunning scenery nearby, who cares? Within 100 km are more than 100 lakes and 100 mountains.

On the southern outskirts of Cranbrook is a **Travel InfoCentre** (open May-Sept.) on the right side of the highway, and Cross Rd. on the left side leading west to 12-hectare **Jimsmith Lake Provincial Park** (four km). The Park has wooded campsites ($8 per night, May to Oct.) with picnic tables and firewood, and pit toilets (no showers), a short stroll from the lake. Many locals swim, canoe (canoe launching area, no power boats allowed), fish, or catch a tan on the sandy beach or grassy banks in summer, or ice-skate, ice fish, or cross-country ski in winter.

As you enter town on Hwy. 3/95 from the south, you come in on Van Horne St. passing several of the less-expensive motels. Van Horne becomes Cranbrook St., also known as "the Strip," where many motels, inns, restaurants, and fast-food places are located. To get to the older, downtown section of Cranbrook turn right off Van Horne St. onto Baker Street.

SIGHTS

Cranbrook Railway Museum

This is the main local attraction, featuring the only surviving and restored set of special railway cars from the Trans-Canada Limited, a luxury train (also called "The Millionaire's Train") built in Canada for the Canadian Pacific Railway in 1929. The dining, sleeping, and solarium lounge cars sport inlaid mahogany and walnut paneling, plush upholsteries, and brass fixtures. Restoration displays, viewing corridor, a model railway display, and a slide show are included

Cranbrook Railway Museum

CRANBROOK

1. Heritage Estate Motel
2. Heritage Rose DIning House
3. federal building/post office
4. movie theater
5. RCMP
6. Baker Park/city campground
7. hospital
8. library
9. Cranbrook Mall
10. Kootenay Cattle Co.
11. Jug and Platter Restaurant
12. Apollo Ristorante
13. Mr. Mike's
14. Greyhound Bus Depot
15. Tamarack Mall
16. Bonanza Restaurant

TO KIMBERLY AIRPORT & SKI HILL
OLD AIRPORT RD.
95A
TO ST. EUGENE MISSION
TO FORT STEELE, RADIUM, FERNIE, & SPARWOOD
3/95
22 ST. N
CRANBROOK C OF C & TRAVEL INFOCENTRE
THEATRE RD.
CRANBROOK ST.
6 ST. NW
("THE STRIP")
KOOTENAY ST.
6 ST. N
4 ST. N
2 ST. N
VICTORIA AVE.
RAILWAY MUSEUM
VAN HORNE ST.
BAKER ST.
1 ST. S
2 ST. S
3 ST. S
24 AVE.
CRANBROOK GOLF CLUB
5 AVE. S
14 AVE. S
TOURIST INFORMATION
11 ST. S
TO JIM SMITH LAKE P.P.
JIM SMITH LAKE RD.
ELIZABETH LAKE BIRD SANCTUARY
VICTORIA DR.
NOT TO SCALE
TO CRESTON & VANCOUVER

in the price of a coach-class ticket; $2.25 adult, $1.75 senior, $1.25 student, under six free, or $4.50 family. Buy your ticket at the restored **Elko Station** (circa 1900). The first-class ticket (an extra $1.50 adult, $1.25 senior, 75 cents student) gets you all of the above plus a 25-minute guided tour (every half hour) of the interiors of the cars. The museum is on Van Horne St. (Hwy. 3/95), open daily in winter 1200-1700, in summer (May-Sept.) 1000-1800, tel. 489-3918. Finish off your tour with scones and a cup of tea in the **Dining Car Tearoom** (open daily for morning and afternoon tea), where you can also see, but not use, the railway silver, china, and glassware collection.

At one end of the viewing corridor is the entrance to **Cranbrook Public Art Gallery** (you don't have to tour the museum to enter the gallery), which has changing exhibitions throughout the year featuring local artists—and Cranbrook has some mighty fine local artists. Open in summer 0900-2000, varying hours in winter (tel. 426-8324); admission by donation.

Heritage Treasures

The locals are proud of their heritage buildings downtown—leftovers from the early days as "Joseph's Prairie" in the 1880s and the age of rapid development after 1898 when the railway came to town. See them for yourself by picking up the handy *Cranbrook Heritage Tour* brochure from InfoCentres or the railway museum (number one on the tour) and taking a self-guided tour. Start at the Rotary Clock Tower in Cranbrook Square—the tower is an exact replica of the old post office tower that stood across Baker St. at the corner of 10th Ave., demolished in 1971 much to the dismay of Cranbrook preservationists. The clock from the old tower was reincorporated in the new tower. You can still see Colonel Baker's home (he was the original Cranbrook developer—the main street downtown is named after him) in Baker Park off 1st St. S; the Interpretation Room is open weekdays 0900-1700. Many of the heritage homes are found in the block between 10th and 13th avenues and 1st St. S and 4th St. South.

If you're still in a heritage mood and heading for Kimberley, take Old Airport Rd. (a continuation of Theatre Rd.) north to **St. Eugene's Mission Church** (between Cranbrook and Kimberley). This is the finest Gothic-style mission church (built in 1897 and restored in 1983) in B.C.—beautiful, hand-painted Italian stained-glass windows. The imposing residential school, built in 1912, is the largest heritage building in the region. Tours can be arranged by calling Kootenay Indian Area Council (in charge of restoration) at 489-2464.

Wildlife Museum

This is the place to go to appreciate wildlife of the East Kootenay region. Enjoy life-size displays in settings that are as natural as possible and photographic displays while you read up on all the biological details on the exhibits. It's operated by the East Kootenay Hunters' Association, whose main goals and objectives are conservation and preservation of wildlife habitat. The museum is in the Cranbrook Chamber of Commerce building at 2279 Cranbrook St. North. Open Sept.-April on weekdays 1000-1200 and 1300-1600, in May and June weekdays 0900-1600, and in July and Aug. seven days a week 0900-1900; admission is $2 adults, $1 seniors and 12 and under, or $5 for the whole family.

Farther Afield

The main out-of-town attraction in this area is **Fort Steele Heritage Park** (see p. 210), 16 km northeast of town on Hwy. 93/95—keep in the left lane heading toward Invermere, Radium, and Fernie, cross under the overpass, then get in the right lane.

PRACTICALITIES

Accommodations

One of the area's most attractive campgrounds is in **Jimsmith Lake Provincial**

Park, four km off the main highway at the southern outskirts of the city. It has wooded campsites and everything you need (except showers); $8 per night, May-October. If you'd rather be downtown with the hot showers, **Cranbrook Municipal Tourist Park,** open in summer (May 15-Sept. 10), provides grassy tent sites and full hookups in park surroundings with a stream and waterfall flowing nearby. Sites are $8.75-10.75 (shower extra $2.50!); in Baker Park at 14th Ave. and 1st St. S, tel. 426-2162.

The flower basket-adorned **Heritage Estate Motel** has roomy rooms at reasonable rates, and it's usually busy—nab your room before you explore the town or go out to dinner. It's at 362 Van Horne St. SW (the main highway) between 2nd St. S and 1st St. S (next to the Heritage Rose Dining House), tel. 426-3862; $27-32 s, $33-38 d. Many other motels, hotels, and inns are located along both Van Horne and Cranbrook streets. Cruise The Strip and you're bound to find a place that appeals. If you're looking for deluxe rooms and an indoor pool, Jacuzzi, sauna, dining room, cocktail lounge, and nightclub all in one spot, try **Inn Of The South** at 803 Cranbrook St., tel. 489-4301; from $62-65 s, $69-72 d.

Heritage Rose Dining House

Food

All the plants inside the **Jug And Platter** restaurant on the Strip (611 Cranbrook St. next to Cranbrook Motor Inn) more than make up for the lack of greenery outside. This is the place for breakfast (specialty of the house served all day for $3-5), and they also whip up a variety of sandwiches ($4-6) and Ukrainian specials (borscht, pirogies, and other delicacies for around $6-7), along with Canadian fare for the less exotic taste; open daily 0630-2230, tel. 489-5515.

Kootenay Cattle Co. steakhouse is at 40 Van Horne St. N, tel. 489-5811, just along the road from Cranbrook Railway Museum; open Tues.-Fri. 1130-1400, Mon.-Sat. 1700-2200, Sun. 1700-2100. For steak dinners, a variety of other dishes, and excellent salad bar (from $1.49 with meals), expect to pay around $5-8 for lunch, $14-18 for dinner. Another reliable place for reasonable steak, chicken, seafood, and salad bar is **Bonanza** restaurant on The Strip, tel. 489-1888. **Apollo Ristorante and Steak House** at 1012 Cranbrook St. gets high marks from Cranbrookites, tel. 426-3721. Go for the salad bar, steaks, seafood, combos, and Italian dishes (25 varieties of pizza); expect to pay around $5.25 at lunch, from $10.75 for dinner, or go for one of the daily specials; open every day 1100-0100, except Sat. 1600-2200. Another familiar standby is **Mr. Mike's** at 1225 Cranbrook St. North (corner of Victoria), tel. 426-8313, serving steaks, their "megalicious" salad bar, burgers, and an assortment of dinners; lunch costs around $3.50-8, dinner $4-9.

Fancy a bit of a splurge? The **Heritage Rose Dining House** (a restored 1907 home) creates culinary delights in a stunning whitewashed heritage home. Tuck in to excellent steak, seafood, or duck à l'orange; $9.95-26 per main dish, lunch dishes average $6, dinner dishes $15. It's at 356 Van Horne St. S (on the main highway as you enter Cranbrook from the southwest), open Mon.-Sat. from 1700. Usually busy, reservations (tel. 426-3454) are a good idea. Dress up and slap everything on your credit card!

Entertainment

For top-40 music, go to the **Cactus Parrot Nightclub** in the **Inn of the South** on Cranbrook St. (no cover charge). For live bands try **Jughead's.** Other popular nightspots are **Misty's** on Thurs.-Sat. nights in the **Town and Country Motor Inn** on Cranbrook St., the **York Hotel,** the **Mt. Baker Hotel,** and for comedy on Fri. and Sat. nights take your funny bone to **Yuk Yuk's Comedy Club.** Country-music lovers congregate at the **Byng Hotel** on Cranbrook Street. Find out who's playing what, where, and when at the chamber of commerce, tel. 426-5914. The **movie theater** is on 10th Ave. South, near the post office; the **drive-in** is at 2315 Theatre Rd., tel. 426-7617. The annual four-day **Sam Steele Days** festival is held on the third weekend in June and honors the commander of the first North West Mounted Police post in this region (1887). Expect a huge parade, the Sweetheart Pageant, loggers' sports, bicycle and wheelchair races, a truck rodeo, a variety of sporting events, live theater, and whatever else the Sam Steele society comes up with each year. Find out all the details at 426-4161.

Information And Services

The main **Cranbrook Chamber of Commerce Travel InfoCentre** is at 2279 Cranbrook St. N (off the highway by 22nd St. North at the north end of town); open year-round Mon.-Fri: 0900-1630, in summer seven days a week 0900-1630 (longer hours if they have staff available), tel. 426-5914. The summer **Travel InfoCentre** (tel. 489-5261) is beside **Elizabeth Lake Bird Sanctuary,** a large marsh that attracts large numbers of waterfowl and wildlife and an important nesting area for Canada geese, teal, ringneck, scaup, redhead, bufflehead, goldeneye, and ruddy ducks. You can also see coots, grebes, black terns, songbirds, muskrats, white-tailed deer, and moose here if you're lucky. The InfoCentre is open May-September.

The local **hospital** is off 2nd St. North (and Victoria Ave.) by Cranbrook Golf Club. The **post office** is on the corner of 10th Ave. S and 1st St. S right across the road from the **Rotary International Park.** Emergency Service Numbers: **hospital,** tel. 426-5281; **ambulance,** tel. 426-8944; **police,** tel. 426-8422.

Transportation

The **Greyhound Bus Depot** is on the corner of Victoria and Cranbrook streets, tel. 426-3331; open year-round Mon.-Fri. 0700-1730, Sat. 0700-1630, and Sun. 1030-2230, providing services twice a day in each direction east to Fernie, Sparwood, and into Alberta; west to Creston and Castlegar; or north to Kimberley, Radium Hot Springs, Kootenay National Park, Banff National Park, and on to Calgary. **Dewdney Coach Lines** runs daily service (except Sun.) between Cranbrook and Golden, tel. 426-4662. **Budget** is at 1024 Cranbrook St. N, tel. 489-4371; **Hertz Rent-a-Car,** tel. (800) 263-060; **Rent-A-Wreck,** tel. 426-3004; **Sears Rent-a-Car,** tel. 426-5414; **Tilden Rent-a-Car,** tel. (800) 387-4747. **Star Taxi,** tel. 426-5511. The **airport** is on the north side of town off Hwy. 95A, served by **Canadian Airlines,** tel. 489-4393; **Time Air,** tel. 489-4393; and **Air B.C.,** tel. 489-1114, from Vancouver and Calgary.

VICINITY OF CRANBROOK

FORT STEELE HERITAGE PARK

Gold miners first poured into this area in the 1860s, crossing the Kootenay River by ferry at the settlement that became known as Galbraith's Ferry to get to the ore-rich banks of Wild Horse Creek. From 1864 throughout the peak gold rush period, the miners had to fork out $10 per loaded pack animal and $5 per man to take that ferry to the other side (the first bridge was constructed in 1888). In 1887 the North West Mounted Police established a post here, building well-constructed shake-roofed log houses from yellow pine. Superintendent Sam Steele and his 75 men settled the tensions that quickly developed between local Indians and new ranchers over land ownership, easing friction and maintaining order without firing a shot—quite an accomplishment in those days! When silver-lead discoveries were made in East Kootenay in the 1890s, Fort Steele surged onto the scene, rapidly becoming a social, administrative, and supply center for the region, and a busy river-traffic hub for sternwheelers carrying ore and supplies to American refineries. However, the glory and bustle were short-lived. When the railway bypassed the town in 1898, putting Cranbrook on the map instead, Fort Steele's population plummeted—to a miserable 500 people by 1905. Another boomtown faded into oblivion.

Today, however, Fort Steele lives again. See over 60 restored, reconstructed, fully furnished buildings, including log barracks (amazingly cool inside on a hot summer day), a courthouse, a jail, hotels, a museum (open daily 1000-1700 1 May to mid-June and 3 Sept.-31 Oct., daily 0930-2000 mid-June-early Sept.), a general store crammed to the rafters with intriguing items from the past, a dentist's office (the sign advertises "painless dentistry," but the equipment on display looks ominous, to say the least!), a ferry office, a printing office, and a water tower. Notice all the old clocks ticking away in just about every building—the park must have a full-time clock winder.

In midsummer, park staff brings Fort Steele back to life—with appropriately costumed working blacksmiths, carpenters, quilters, weavers, bakers, and ice-cream makers, and many others. Hop on a stagecoach or a steam train, heckle a street politician, witness a crime and testify at a trial, and attend one of the professional 1880s live theater performances at the **Wild Horse Theatre;** showtimes are daily (end of June-Sept.) at 1400 ($6.50 adult, senior $5, youth $3.50, child 6-12 $2) and 2000 ($7.50 adult, senior $6, youth $4.50, child 6-12 $2.50). Silent movies are shown daily at 1100, 1230, and 1600; adult $3, senior $2.50, youth $2, child 6-12 $1. Free operatic performances are presented on Mondays in the Opera House. You can easily spend a good portion of a day out here, particularly in summer when all the events are going on. For munchies there's a snack bar at the entrance to the park, but if you want a light sit-down meal head for the **Tearoom** on the upper floor of the cheerful white-and-red museum building in the center of the park. Help yourself to breakfast (from $4), sandwiches and salads (from $5), baked goods, refreshments, and ice cream; open daily May-Oct. 1000-1700, till 2000 from mid-June to September.

Fort Steele is 16 km northeast of Cranbrook. Take Hwy. 95 north toward Invermere and Radium, passing **Fort Steele Campground** (one km off Kelly Rd. with recreation hall, TV lounge, pool, hot tub, some groceries, tel. 426-5117; from $11 per night, plus electricity $2, sewer $2), and **Norbury Lake Provincial Park** (campsites $6 per night May-October). Cross over Kootenay River, passing a **Travel InfoCentre** on the left, then turn left into the park. Fort Steele Park grounds are open year-round. From mid-June to early Sept. the park is open daily 0930-1730, and an admission charge of $5 adult, $3 senior or youth, $1 child, or $10 per family is good for two days (season passes at good savings can also be purchased). For more info call 426-6923 (taped message); Wildhorse Theater, tel. 426-5682; Tearoom, tel. 426-5195; Fort Steele Bakery, tel. 426-3474; Kershaw Store, tel. 489-3122; Snack Bar, tel. 426-6344.

Another Stroll Back In Time

Continue along the highway to Radium Hot Springs then turn right at the campground to follow the logging road to Bull River and Kootenay Trout Hatchery (open 0900-1600). Park at the **Wild Horse Graveyard** (about 5½ km from the main road). From this point you can hike a section of Wild Horse Creek, visiting the old graveyard, the Chinese burial ground, the site of the Wild Horse post office, the site of Fisherville (first town in the East Kootenays, 1864-65), the diggings, and several other historic sites. It only takes about two hours to do the trail, even if you stop at all the plaques along the way. Or walk the last 2½ km of the Dewdney Trail (Hope to Wild Horse Creek), imagining all the men and packhorses, loaded to the hilt, that struggled along the path ahead of you more than a century ago. Before you set out, grab an informative pamphlet with map from the Travel InfoCentre on the main highway near Fort Steele Heritage Park.

FORT STEELE TO SPARWOOD

This is another one of those stretches of British Columbia highway worth seeing whether you're Alberta-bound or not. From **Elko** all the way to **Sparwood,** the highway meanders through the magnificent **Elk Valley** between steep mountain ranges—keep checking your rearview mirror for glorious scenery or you may miss seeing some got-to-get-that-on-film views from a different angle, and watch out for elk (and bighorn sheep)—they didn't name this area Elk-this and Elk-that for nothing!

About 14 km west of Fernie, 1½ km off the main highway, lies **Snow Valley Ski Hill,** Fernie's ski resort, hosting skiers from Nov. to late April, with 640 meters vertical, runs up to five km long, chairs, T-bars, rope tow, day lodge with cafeteria and bar, ski rentals and repairs, luxurious accommodations at **The Griz Inn** (rooms $90-238 s or d; off-season summer rates; tel. 423-9221) at the base of the slopes, and cross-country ski trails. Just east of the ski hill, 259-hectare **Mount Fernie Provincial Park** has hiking trails, Lizard Creek and waterfall, picnic spots, and campsites ($8 per night May-September). For hotel/motel accommodation, continue into Fernie.

Fernie, a coal-mining and forestry town (93 km from Fort Steele) established at the turn of the century, nestles in a bowl of impressive steep mountains, with lakes and rivers close by and an 18-hole golf course. It covers all the outdoor bases, including whitewater rafting (get more info on your outdoor passion at the InfoCentre). Wander downtown to appreciate many heritage buildings (collect a map to historic buildings from the **Fernie Chamber of Commerce and Travel InfoCentre** on the north side of town by the enormous oil derrick, Hwy. 3 and Dicken Rd., tel. 423-6868.), and don't miss the impressive red brick Courthouse (and Provincial Government offices) on the corner of Fourth St. and Fourth Avenue.

Sparwood And Elkford

The next town along Hwy. 3 is **Sparwood,** another coal-mining town. On weekdays June-Aug., tour **Balmer Mine,** largest open-pit mine in the country; for more info and reservations, contact the **Sparwood Travel InfoCentre** (the building with a larger-than-life statue of a miner in front) on Aspen Dr., tel. 425-2423. From Sparwood, Hwy. 3 continues for another 18 km to the Alberta border, and Hwy. 43 heads north along the Elk River for another 30 km or so to the small mining town of **Elkford.** Don't miss **Josephine Falls** (park off Fording Mine Rd. and follow the nature trail to the falls), a spectacle in summer *or* winter.

Continue north of Elkford (collect a map first from the **InfoCentre** at the junction of the highway and Michel Rd., tel. 865-4362), and you'll end up at either the Alberta border or the 17,245-hectare subalpine **Elk Lakes Provincial Park** and adjacent **Recreation Area** (87-km gravel road from Elkford—find out current conditions before you leave town). The park provides hiking trails, good fishing, plentiful wildlife, and walk-in campsites amongst lake, mountain, and glacier scenery. Take *everything* you need because there's nothing up there but unbeatable scenery and kilometers of wilderness. Get contour map 82J11, *Kananaskis Lakes,* for a nominal fee from MAPS B.C., Ministry of Lands and Parks, Parliament Buildings, Victoria, B.C. V8V 1X5.

KIMBERLEY

Kimberley, 32 km north of Cranbrook, is the "Bavarian City of the Canadian Rockies." Standing 1,117 meters above sea level in the Purcell Mountains, on the slopes of Sullivan and North Star hills, it's the highest city in Canada. The town is surrounded by steep, permanently snow-covered peaks—hike up to the snow at any time of year. Wandering downtown you'll discover that most of the shops and businesses, and many of Kimberley's homes, have been "Bavarianized"—decorated Bavarian-style with dark wood finish and flowery trim, steep triangular roofs, fancy balconies, brightly painted window shutters with flower-filled window boxes in summer, even a pedestrian-only shopping plaza downtown called The Bavarian Platzl, complete with the largest operating cuckoo clock in the world! It's like you've just driven into a village high in the Swiss Alps—even the local car dealership looks like a chalet where you'd expect to find a bunch of bell-wearing cows and brightly dressed braided-hair milkmaids rather than cars.

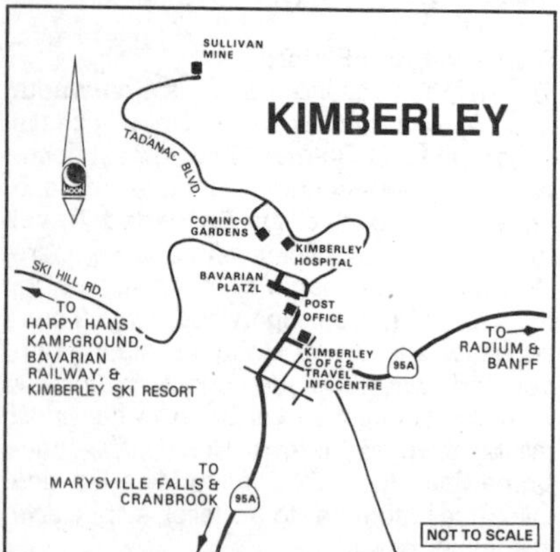

The Bavarianization occurred in the 1970s when a group of local businessmen devised the idea as a way to attract tourists and keep the town alive when the mine eventually fizzled out—the mine continues to produce, and the tourists continue to saunter in! They did such a good job of luring visitors that many Europeans found Kimberley appealing and joined the town's resident population of 7,000—the European-style delis and restaurants you see downtown are mostly authentic.

Kimberley has always been a mining town. With the discovery of silver and lead at North Star and Sullivan mines in 1892, the town sprang onto the map of B.C. The Sullivan Mine changed hands several times before being taken over by the Consolidated Mining and Smelting Company, still in operation today.

Sights

On the southern outskirts of Kimberley (entering from Hwy. 95A) is the community of **Marysville.** Be sure to stop and stretch your legs at **Marysville Waterfalls,** several kilometers from downtown Kimberley. Park your vehicle in the lot by the bridge, then walk downstream through the woods, passing masses of wild rosebushes and assorted wildflowers (everything abloom and a-smelling in June) along the boardwalk and gravel **Al Fabro Mark Creek Walk** (a five-minute walk—15 minutes if you stop and smell the flowers). It takes you to a series of small waterfalls and one large falls.

Follow signs to Kimberley City Centre and **The Bavarian Platzl** on Spokane St., the focus of downtown; park behind the **Kimberley Chamber of Commerce Travel InfoCentre** (open 0900-1700 daily in summer, Mon.-Sat. in winter) or in the Platzl Parking Lot. The Plaztl is a cheerful, red brick, pedestrian-only plaza complete with babbling brook, ornamental bridges, and the "World's Largest Cuckoo Clock" ("Happy Hans" pops out and yodels on the hour), lined with shops and many German restaurants and delis selling European specialties (see "Food," below).

At the far end of the Platzl at 105 Spokane St. is the **library** and **Kimberley Heritage Museum** (open May.-Sept. Mon.-Sat. 0900-1630, in winter Mon.-Sat. 1300-1600, tel. 427-7510). Local history is the main emphasis, but you can also see a stuffed grizzly bear, Cominco mining history displays and equipment, a hodgepodge of artifacts, and displays of all the popular outdoor sports in this area—honoring Kimberley's local champion Gerry Sorensen, world's fastest downhill skier in 1982. **Kimberley International Art School And Centre** is one block north of the Platzl at 49 Deer Park (tel. 427-5160), presenting sculptures and carvings of famous international artists; open seven days 1100-1800.

Another local attraction is the superb **Kimberley Gardens,** also known as **Cominco Gardens,** a green-thumber's delight next to the hospital on Fourth Ave.; admission $2 adult, $5 family. After a stroll through the flower garden, refresh yourself at **Greenhouse Tea Garden** next door (see "Food," below).

The **Sullivan Mine,** owned and operated by **Cominco,** is one of the largest lead and zinc mines in the world. You can view operations from the Ski and Summer Resort and see the original 1902 portal from the Bavarian City Mining Railway route. The **Bavarian City Mining Railway** was constructed using the original rails previously used in the H.B. Mine in Salmo. Jump on the train for a 2½-km scenic ride, stopping to appreciate mountain views, the original Townsite and Sullivan mine entrance, mining artifacts, views of the ski hill and the alpine slide, and the railway station's photos of early mining days and the railway. It's located in the **Happy Hans Kampground** (see "Accommodations," below), two km from downtown on Gerry Sorensen Way, and operates on weekends till 25 June, daily throughout the summer; $2 adult.

Whether it's summer or winter, the **Kimberley Ski and Summer Resort** (four km from the Platzl via Gerry Sorensen Way and Ski Hill Rd.) has something for everyone—good hiking, skiing, chairlifting, sliding, bumper boats, go-carts, and miniature golf. Take the summertime **chairlift** to the top of North Star Mt. and come back down on the alpine slide. The resort operates weekends till 25 June, then daily during peak season. In winter the resort provides excellent downhill skiing, 701 meters vertical, the longest T-bar ski lift (1,800 meters) in North America, lots of runs including one 6½ km, a double chair, triple chairs, a T-bar, rope tows, a ski school, cross-country skiing, ski rentals, and indoor and outdoor tennis courts. For more info, call 427-4881.

Accommodations

Vast **Happy Hans Kampground,** two km north of city center on the way to the Ski Hill, has a swimming pool, miniature golf, and the Kimberley Bavarian City Mining Railway within the grounds, attractive campsites amongst the trees, plenty of powered sites, and spotlessly clean bathrooms. Rates are $13-15 per vehicle; Gerry Sorenson Way, tel. 427-2929. Kimberley has quite a few lodges, resorts, and inns at the base of the ski hill, catering to the skiing brigade that descends on the area each winter (many have off-season summer rates). The city also has a number of motels, inns, and condo resort hotels; these rooms start at $26-50 s, $32-55 d. For campground and accommodation reservations, call the InfoCentre at 427-3666.

Food And Entertainment

When in Kimberley, sample all the European specialties (predominantly German) available around town. A good place to wander when you're feeling peckish is the Platzl. At lunch, do as the locals do—crowd into **Kimberley City Bakery,** a Swiss bakery, tearoom, and sidewalk cafe in the Platzl; open seven days a week in summer. Or try the **Gasthaus am Platzl,** in the Platzl, open Oct.-Apr. daily 1130-1400 and 1630-2200, May-Sept. daily 1130-2200. Soup and salad bar and German lunches start at $5, German dinner specialties such as **bratwurst, rheinischer sauerbraten, wienerschnitzel,** and **kassler rippchen** (try saying these quickly after several glasses of wine!) go for $9-14, steak and seafood from $14.

The **Greenhouse Tea Garden** next to Kimberley Gardens (follow "H" to the Hospital) is a great spot to go for your classic afternoon tea (delicious fresh-baked scones with jam, and tea, of course dahling), salads, open sandwiches, and fresh home-baked desserts at very reasonable prices. You enjoy all this inside a real greenhouse, surrounded by hanging plants, flowery tablecloths, and a stunning pink-and-green decor, with views of the distant mountains and gardens; open daily May, June, and Sept. 1100-1700, July and Aug. 1100-1900, tel. 427-4885.

For fine dining, including sandwiches, salad bar, hamburgers, pizza, pasta, steaks, seafood, barbecued chicken, and continental dishes, locals point the way to downtown **Alpenrose,** off the Platzl; open daily June-Sept., closed on Mondays Oct.-May. Another local recommendation for Bavarian specialties and plenty of atmosphere is **The Old Baurenhaus** at 280 Norton Ave. (Ski Hill Rd.), tel. 427-5133; open seasonally. The post-and-beam building housing the restaurant was originally constructed about 350 years ago in Southern Bavaria. Taken apart, shipped to Canada, and painstakingly rebuilt, the building has quite a history of its own!

Kimberley has several annual events to draw in the crowds: in mid-Feb. a Winterfest, in the second week of July an **International Accordion Championship,** and the following week, **Julyfest** (soccer, arm wrestling, horseshoe throwing, and a parade). In Aug. there's **B.C. Days,** and on the long Labour Day weekend, Kimberley kicks up its heels at the **Alpine Folk Dance Festival.** Get the complete rundown from the Travel InfoCentre.

Information

For all the info you could possibly need to enjoy Kimberley and the surrounding area, drop by **Kimberley Chamber of Commerce Travel InfoCentre** at 350 Ross St., tel. 427-3666. For accommodation and campground reservations, call 427-2929.

KIMBERLEY TO RADIUM

Highway 95A from Kimberley to Wasa Junction, then Hwy. 93/95 to Radium (and the entrance to Kootenay National Park), takes you along the Rocky Mountain Trench between the Purcell and Rocky Mountain ranges. As you'd expect by looking at the map, the scenery is great! The craggy bare Rockies get closer and closer as the road winds through grassy hills and meadows full of horses, passing turnoffs to many provincial parks—always worth exploring if you have the time or are in search of a perfect campsite.

The first park along the route is 144-hectare **Wasa Provincial Park,** with campsites (from $8 per night May-Oct.), picnic tables, a nature trail, and swimming and water sports (not a fishing hot spot though). Highway 93/95 then follows the beautiful Kootenay River through more green hectares dotted with horses to the turnoff to 662-hectare **Premier Lake Provincial Park,** just north of the small settlement of **Skookumchuck** (a pulp mill town). The park is 16 km off the main highway and has one large lake and four small lakes (the fishing is supposed to be good year-round—ice fishing in winter) with swimming, hiking, and cross-country skiing, and a picnic area and campsites (from $8 per night May-October).

As the Rockies close in, the scenery is unbelievably beautiful. The next signposted turnoff is to 994-hectare **Whiteswan Provin-**

cial Park and 8,791-hectare **Top Of The World Park.** The rough gravel logging road leads to six campgrounds (from $8 per night May-Oct.) and numerous lakes and creeks with excellent trout fishing (drive defensively and keep your eyes open for logging trucks—they always have the right-of-way). Off-the-beaten-track Top Of The World Park is another 30 km or so beyond Alces Lake in Whiteswan Park, offering the adventurer splendid alpine wilderness, hiking trails, trout and Dolly Varden fishing, cross-country skiing, and walk-in camping (you need to be totally self-sufficient and prepared for sudden weather changes—there are no supplies or equipment up there). A large cabin on Fish Lake sleeps up to 24 people (small charge). Get a contour map (Quinn Creek 82G/14W) for a nominal fee from MAPS BC, Ministry of Lands and Parks, Parliament Buildings, Victoria, B.C. V8V 1X5.

The next turnoff is to **Canal Flats Provincial Park** on the east side of Columbia Lake (four km, day use only). The small community of **Canal Flats,** a lumber and sawmill town, lies between the Kootenay River and Columbia Lake. David Thompson, the first European explorer in this neck of the woods, named this flat McGillivray's Portage in 1808 as he crossed from Columbia Lake to the Kootenay River. In 1889 the two waterways were connected by a canal with a single lock, but the passage was so narrow and dangerous that only two steamboats ever got through, one in 1894 and the other in 1902. The next place to definitely pull off the highway is **Thunder Hill Provincial Park,** a very pretty spot up on a hill overlooking the multihued turquoise and blue Columbia Lake, with campsites (from $6 per night May-Oct.) and pit toilets amongst the fields and trees.

As you get closer to Fairmont Hot Springs the scenery gets more magnificent, with ever-changing views and colors of the steep, craggy Rockies on the far side of Columbia Lake. The road leaves the lake then approaches and passes by the steep, vertical, weird-shaped **Dutch Creek Hoodoos,** very photogenic earth formations carved over time by ice, water, and wind.

FAIRMONT HOT SPRINGS

As you approach Fairmont Hot Springs from the south, the highway takes you past the enormous runway of **Fairmont-Panorama Airport.** Although it's used by **CAIR** jets (from Vancouver and Calgary), charter, and private planes at present, a Boeing 737 *could* land here if one ever needed to. To catch a bird's-eye view of this superb landscape, scenic flights are offered in summer by **Adventure Glacier Sightseeing**—call in at the airport office for details and current prices.

Fairmont Hot Springs was established in 1922 (though the Kootenay Indians had naturally used these springs as a healing source for eons prior to European "discovery"). Entering from the south, **Spruce Grove Resort** on the right side of the highway provides alluring grassy, tree-shaded tent sites along the banks of the Columbia River (best spot in the entire resort for tent camping), RV sites, several cabins, a restaurant, an outdoor pool, a store, and a gas station, only a short two-km walk from the hot springs. Open March-Nov., campsites are $9-13 per night plus $2 electricity, $1 sewer, $1 water, and units are $35-45 s, $45-58 d; tel. 345-6561.

Fairmont Hot Springs Resort and **Fairmont Hot Springs Ski Area** are both off the highway to the east. Just up the resort road is a gas station, a cafe, a small shopping plaza with a laundromat, a grocery store (open seven days), superb golf courses (Riverside and Mountainside), a lodge, a livery (you can rent horses by the hour for trail riding), tennis courts, and a variety of accommodations. Take a drive up the ski hill in winter to ski and sightsee, in summer to hike and sightsee—it's truly beautiful. The road up is good gravel most of the way. The **Ski Area** is a family ski hill with 304 meters vertical, a school, rentals, a triple chair and platter, and cross-country ski trails, all amongst incredible Rocky Mountain scenery.

Fairmont Hot Springs (fed by healthy calcium springs with no sulphurous smell) is the local highlight—and quite a magical experience on a glorious evening. Lazily swim or float around in the large warm pool, dive into the cool pool, or sit 'n' sizzle in the hot pool and watch the setting sun color those vertical Rocky Mountains immediately behind the resort—an unbeatable combination of sight and sensation that sets all your senses a-tingling. There's nothing quite like it. The pools are open daily 0800-2200; admission is adult $4, student $3.50, child $3, and day passes are also available. If you go between 2100 and 2200 (the best time for summertime sunsets), it's only $2 adult.

Stay the night (or the week!) in the large, tree-shaded resort campground, a one-minute stroll from the hot pools, in the shadow of the mountains. Rates start at $12 for an unserviced campsite in summer (peak period is July and Aug.), $16-18 per night for full hookups. In winter you can camp there for less—the water is turned off but the electricity is still on for RVs. Resort sleeping units (some with lofts and kitchens) are $105-115 s, $108-145 d, kitchen extra $12. For more info on the resort and to make reservations, call 345-6311.

Windermere And Invermere

The next area to lure travelers off Hwy. 93/95 is **Windermere Lake,** a popular spot for swimming and water sports. The small community of **Windermere** is off the highway to the left, with a pub, a campground, a couple of gas stations, and cafes. The road to the thriving town of **Invermere,** the original site of the Kootenay House trading post set up by explorer David Thompson in 1807, also leads to small **James Chabot Provincial Park** (picnic sites, swimming, day use only), and **Panorama Alpine Resort** about 18 km from the main highway. **Invermere,** the business and commercial center of the valley, has a pub, a campground, a motel, a hotel, a gas station, a number of cafes and fine restaurants, grocery stores, bakeries, coin-op laundries, a bus depot, marinas, tourist shops, a hospital (tel. 342-9201), and an airfield. In winter take to Panorama's slopes for some good downhill skiing with 1,158 meters vertical, runs up to 3.4 km long, chairlifts, T-bars, a platter lift, and rope tow, or go heli-skiing or cross-country skiing. In summer go hiking, horseback riding, or rafting. Panorama Alpine Resort offers the visitor a number of accommodations (hotel rooms and condos) and restaurants. For more info and reservations, call 342-6941.

If you take the road to Panorama but continue straight ahead instead of branching off to the resort, you end up at the boundary of **Purcell Wilderness Conservancy,** a vast area of wilderness with a 61-km hiking trail crossing the Purcell Mountains over 2,256-meter Earl Grey Pass.

RADIUM HOT SPRINGS

A Veritable Outdoor Smorgy

This small town lies at the foot of the Canadian Rockies, at the junction of highways 95 and 93, 72 km north of Cranbrook, 134 km west of Banff. The actual hot springs are on the east side of town, just inside the southwest boundary of Kootenay National Park, a World Heritage Site. On first appearances Radium is just a small logging town with an abundance of motels, surrounded by stunning scenery. But for outdoor enthusiasts it's a year-round resort with exciting outdoor activities to suit *almost* everybody—sorry, no camel racing yet!

In summer the lush beauty of adjacent **Kootenay National Park** can be experienced by road, by canoe, or on foot; the more remote wilderness of nearby **Mount Assiniboine Provincial Park** awaits the ardent adventurer (access by hiking trail only). Splash down rivers in your own canoe, or raft the Kootenay, Vermilion, and Kicking Horse rivers (call **Kootenay River Runners** at 347-9210; from $49 for a half-day trip to $189 for an overnighter), or just swim or fish in the warm water of **Lake Windermere** to the south. Jump on a horse and gallop with the wind (call **Radium Valley Stables** at 347-9755), or whack a ball down one of five local golf courses (try **Radium Hot Springs Resort** at 347-9311, or **The Springs Golf and Country Club** at 347-6444).

In winter, the white powdered slopes at **Panorama** (tel. 342-6941) lure expert downhill skiers and heli-skiers, and cross-country skiers and snowshoers can simply step outside, snap on their equipment, and go. And to finish off your day in soothing comfort, lower your tired but happy bod into **Radium Hot Springs** (see "Kootenay National Park," below)—aaahhh!

Accommodations And Food

Radium has plenty of places to stay—from campgrounds and RV resorts to motels, condos, and luxury lodges. Many are located along Hwy. 95 at the south end of town and at the Hwy. 95/93 junction. Even more line Hwy. 93 as you head toward the park. Expect to pay anywhere from $30 to $100 per night for a motel room (more in the lodges and resorts). **Canyon Camp** has creekside sites and all the facilities you need, close to all the shops and stores, $10.50-16 per night; on Sinclair Creek Loop Rd., tel. 347-9564. **Skyview Motel and Campground** on Hwy. 95, just north of Radium Junction, is open for camping March-Oct. (from $8 per night plus $2 for electricity) and has small but comfy rooms with coffee- and tea-making facilities starting at a very reasonable $20 s or d in the off-season; tel. 347-9698. At the other end of the scale **Radium Hot Springs Resort** offers rooms in Radium Inn starting at $80-130 s, $95-145 d, and in Radium Condominiums/Villas (one to three bedrooms) from $125 s, $140-170 d, and both golf and ski accommodations packages are offered seasonally; for info and reservations phone 347-9311, or toll-free in North America (800) 665-3585. The resort can arrange air/heli tours, whitewater rafting, fly-fishing tours, mountain-bike tours, backcountry tours, boat and jet-ski rentals, sightseeing tours, trail rides; just call 347-9311 and tell them what you want to do and how much you can afford!

Busy **Husky House Restaurant** on Hwy. 93 (at the highway junction) gets you fueled and back out on the road with homestyle cooking and baking at family prices (senior discounts); it's at the Hwy. 93/95 junction, tel. 347-9811; open daily 0700-2300. Another busy place whipping up breakfasts from $3.50, hamburgers and sandwiches from $4, or dinners from $7 is **Karp's Kountry Kitchen** on Hwy. 93/95. Tired of typical Canadian fare? The one place to go is **Silver Springs Restaurant** on Hwy. 93 (left side on your way to the park). The chefs tantalize your taste buds with their many excellent Chinese dishes from $6 (lots of variety, large portions), or you can order the usual hamburger and sandwiches from $4, steaks and other main dishes from $8. It's open year-round, seven days a week 1000-2200, in midsummer 0800-2200. For fine dining, continental cuisine from around the world, and an appetizing decor, head for the **Radium Hot Springs Resort** dining room. Make reservations at 347-9311.

Information

On the west side of the Hwy. 93/95 junction is the **Radium Hot Springs Travel Info-Centre,** open varying hours May-Sept., 0900-2100 in July and August. (If it's closed, call Kootenay National Park Visitors Information at tel. 347-9505.) Get all your local info here, and pick up the handy *Columbia Valley Visitor's Guide* (free) which has all sorts of useful info on the entire valley. Maps showing hiking and fishing in Kootenay National Park can also be purchased here (get the most current, detailed park info at the west entrance to the park). For an **ambulance** call 1-374-5937 (no charge to caller); for **police** dial 347-9393.

Radium Hot Springs To Golden

Highway 95 from Radium Hot Springs north to Golden (107 km north at the junction of Hwy. 1) runs between the Rocky Mountains and the Columbia River, passing Christmas-tree farms, wildlife refuges (lots of ospreys and bald eagles build their nests in the poplars near **Harrogate**), and a handful of tiny communities as you follow the route established by the CPR in 1884.

At **Brisco** and **Spillimacheen** are gravel roads (open spring through fall—avoid tangling with logging trucks) leading 45 km west to the glaciated wilderness beauty of 25,274-

hectare **Bugaboo Glacier Provincial Park and Alpine Recreation Area** in the ancient Purcell Mountain Ranges—formed long before the Rockies. This park is best suited to experienced mountaineers and hikers (limited number of trails), and campers willing to walk in with all their gear. The only facilities are two alpine huts open in summer. One has propane stoves for cooking, and you're charged a small overnight fee; the other has walls and a roof. Carry everything you need. Before heading into the wilderness it's wise to equip yourself with map sheets 82K/10 and K/15, available for a nominal fee from MAPS BC, Ministry of Lands and Parks, Parliament Buildings, Victoria, B.C. V8V 1X5.

The closest commercial facilities are at **Bugaboo Lodge** (run by Canadian Mountain Holidays; H.Q. tel. 403-346-3366), near the entrance to the park. If you're exploring the park on your own, leave your vehicle in the public lot, not the Lodge parking area, unless you have prior permission. Wire mesh, logs, and heavy branches are provided by park staff to protect your vehicle against local rubber-eating porcupines! A reader (thanks Klaus Horenburg!) informed me that the porcupines enjoy attacking anything made of rubber, including tires and water hoses. So wrap the lower section of your vehicle with wire before you leave it.

KOOTENAY NATIONAL PARK

MARVELOUS MOUNTAINS AND MEADOWS

Many first-time visitors to the Canadian Rockies have heard the word "Banff" uttered in the same sentence as just about all the scenic superlatives in the thesaurus, and therefore they make Banff their ultimate destination. But when they approach the Rockies from the west via Kootenay National Park, they're often surprised to find that Kootenay is in every way just as splendid. Once you've been through Kootenay, certain images jump to mind. Majestic mountains, marbled canyons carved by the splashy Kootenay, Vermilion, and Simpson rivers, frothy rapids and waterfalls, icy lakes and bathwater-warm hot springs, incredibly green alpine meadows waving with summertime wildflowers, wild critters big and small—mountain goats, bighorn sheep, and moose mowing the roadsides, and cheeky ground squirrels that invade picnic areas the moment the food's on the table. Winding through all of this beauty is the spectacular, 105-km Kootenay Parkway—Hwy. 93.

As you would expect, the initial explorers and settlers of this region were the Kootenai Indians. The hot springs area (the mineral-rich waters were used for therapeutic and, no doubt, sensory purposes) was a meeting place for mountain and Plains bands. They collected the ochre or iron oxide from the Paint Pots area and used it for ceremonial painting purposes and made their way over the pass to the flat Alberta plains for a bit of bison hunting. In the 1800s, explorers and fur traders came through in search of transportation routes through the mountains. David Thompson, first European to explore this mountainous region, used the already well-traveled corridor that was to remain a major transportation route in the 20th century.

In 1905 Randolph Bruce, an Invermere businessman, persuaded the Canadian government and Canadian Pacific Railway to build a road between Banff and Windermere so that western produce could get to the prairies. Construction of the difficult Banff-Windermere Rd. (across three mountain ranges and fast, deep rivers, to name a few obstacles) was begun in 1911 by the province, but the money for the project ran out after the completion of only 22 kilometers. The first pool and bathhouse were built the same year at Radium Hot Springs. In order to get the highway project going again, B.C. agreed to hand over a section of land (eight

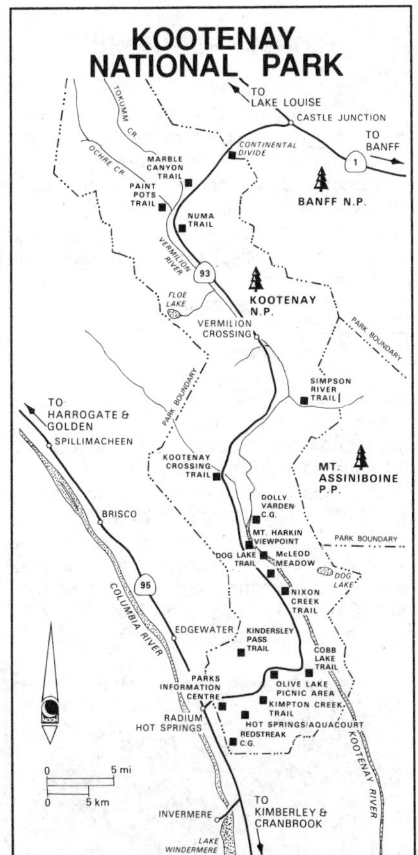

km) along both sides of the proposed highway to the federal government in 1919—this land became Kootenay National Park (then known as "the Highway Park") the following year. The road was finally finished in 1922—the official ribbon-cutting ceremony was held at Kootenay Crossing in 1923 (a plaque marks the spot).

These 140,600 hectares lie along the western slopes of the Canadian Rocky Mountains, sandwiched between **Mount Assiniboine Provincial Park** to the south, **Banff National Park** to the east, and **Yoho National Park** to the north. Its eastern border is the summit of the **Continental Divide,** below which all rivers run either east to the Arctic Ocean or Hudson Bay or west to the Pacific. The park highway allows the less energetic to enjoy the spectacular mountain scenery from the car, providing ample stretch-your-legs spots at perfect picnic havens, always-interesting roadside interpretive exhibits, places of historic and scenic interest, and viewpoints with the best views imaginable. Short, easy-to-follow trails lead to several of the most popular highlights.

Drive the highway early in the morning or just before dusk and you'll probably see more than your share of wildlife, especially mountain goats, deer, elk, and bighorn sheep. Try to avoid driving the road at night—it's a real scenic deprivation, and you have to keep your eyes peeled and your feet ready for sudden wildlife-collision-avoidance procedures. To truly experience the park's beauty and wildlife, leave your vehicle in the parking areas and walk the many backcountry hiking trails (park use permit required for overnight camping trips) to hanging glaciers, deep canyons, and high alpine lakes—get all the details on longer trails and a topographical map from park information centers.

Information

On entering the park, all visitors in vehicles have to stop at the booth and buy a permit; day permit $4.25, four-day permit $9.50, annual permit valid in all national parks $26.75. Those on foot, horseback, bicycle, or camel do not require permits—they're just waved on by.

The **West Gate Information Centre** just past the ticket booth is an essential first stop. Collect a free map with descriptions of all trails on the back, along with park regulations, info on camping, mountain weather, horse use, and cycling and mountain biking routes—or buy a topographical map for $9. Ask about specialized info on flora and fauna, backcountry hiking trails, and cross-country trails; eight easy ski trails are marked with the skier symbol, and there are ski mountaineering trails requiring specialized equipment, avalanche awareness, and voluntary registration. Also reel in the hottest fishing spots from the staff—buy a seven-day license ($5.25) or annual license ($10.75) at the information centers, main gate booths, campgrounds, or Aquacourt, and collect a *Fishing Regulations Summary* brochure. Keep in mind that you're in bear country—read the brochure before entering any of the national parks and report any bear sightings to park staff. For detailed geological, historical, or flora and fauna info on the Rockies, refer to the *Handbook of the Canadian Rockies* by Ben Gadd (Corax Press).

West Gate Information Centre is open weekends 18 May-16 June; from mid-June to early Sept. it's open daily 0800-2000. In the peak summer season free one-hour slide shows and talks are presented by park naturalists at **Redstreak, McLeod Meadows,** and **Marble Canyon Campground and Day Use Area,** usually starting around dusk. Guided group hikes and other activities are also frequently scheduled. All the program details are posted at campgrounds and information centers (tel. 347-9615/9505). The **Marble Canyon Information Centre** at the eastern end of the park is open daily mid-June-Sept. 0800-1700. For more detailed park info, write to The Superintendent, Kootenay National Park, Box 220, Radium Hot Springs, B.C. V0A 1M0, or phone 347-9615.

Campgrounds

Redstreak (vehicle access from Hwy. 93/95 on the south side of Radium Hot Springs township) has full hookups and showers and costs $11.75-16 May-September. From the campground, several trails lead to the Aquacourt pools (you can do the loop trail in three hours RT), to a couple of viewpoints, to the village, or along Valley View Trail. **McLeod Meadows** and **Marble Canyon** (mid-June-early Sept.) have no individual hookups or showers, and each costs $9.50 per night. Many backcountry campsites with pit toilets and firewood are located throughout the park, most at the northern end. Backcountry campgrounds are free, but you need to get a park use permit (also free) from information centers to camp overnight and longer.

HIGHWAY HIGHLIGHTS

Radium Hot Springs

Forty-five-degree-centigrade odorless mineral water gushes out at the foot of Redstreak Mountain and is then diverted into the **Aquacourt** pools. Kootenai Indians valued the springs—once called Kootemik, or "Places of Hot Water"—for their soothing, therapeutic qualities. Steep cliffs tower directly above the hot pool, where calcium, magnesium, and sodium sulfates, plus calcium bicarbonate, are the principal salts in the milky blue waters. The hot pool is particularly stimulating in winter when it's edged by snow and covered in steam—your head is almost cold in the chilling atmosphere, but your submerged body melts into oblivion from the neck down.

The pools are open year-round, daily 0830-2300 in summer with extended hours on holidays, shorter hours the rest of the year; admission to the outdoor 40° C hot pool and 27° C swimming pool is adult $2 (day pass $4), child $1.25 (day pass $2.50), and if you need a swimsuit it's only an extra $1; 75

cheeky Columbian ground squirrel

cents for a towel; and 25 cents for a locker. The restaurant is open in summer (May-Oct.) during pool hours serving breakfasts for $3-5, burgers and sandwiches from $4, and daily specials. **Radium Hot Springs Lodge** overlooks the hot pools (rooms from $50-64 s, $50-75 d). A number of short trails lead from the springs to Redstreak Campground—**Redstreak Campground Trail** (the most direct), **Juniper Trail,** and **Sinclair Canyon Trail.** Keep one eye on the road and one eye on the surrounding scenery when you continue along the highway from the hot springs to Kindersley Pass—in summer mountain goats and bighorn sheep are often seen along the edge of the road.

Sinclair Canyon

The first signposted trail along the highway is two-km **Redstreak Hiking Trail,** which wanders along Redstreak Creek. The highway parallels pretty Kimpton Creek for a distance, bordered in summer by banks of wildflowers with views of tree-covered mountains and distant rocky peaks. **Kimpton Creek Trail** leads 5½ km off the highway following the creek. At **Sinclair Creek** you can have a picnic at one of the tables or walk the 10.1-km trail to **Kindersley Pass.** To do the loop route back to the highway north of where you started, continue onto 6.4-km **Sinclair Creek Trail.** Beautiful, appropriately named **Olive Lake,** with its banks crammed with bright yellow wildflowers in summer, is another nice place to spread out a picnic. The next hiking opportunity is the 3.7-km trail to **Cobb Lake.**

Kootenay Valley Viewpoint

This viewpoint gives a splendid view of the wild Kootenay River Valley, the "Valley of National Parks," and the mountains—get out your camera! Beyond the viewpoint the highway meanders through some incredible scenery—omnipresent focal-point mountain peaks covered in snow, even in the middle of summer.

Look out for moose as you continue along the highway—it's not uncommon to drive around a bend in the road to find a cow and a calf grazing right beside the road, along with five cars, a couple of cyclists, and two RVs loaded with camera-toting visitors determined to get that perfect moose shot, even if it means chasing the animals back into the wild. Please stay in your vehicles when you get the chance to view wildlife. Apart from being safer (cows with calves are *especially* unpredictable), this causes less harassment for wildlife and allows everyone else the same opportunity to enjoy the view. The meadows in the **Nixon Creek** area are alive in summer with small, fat, furry Columbian ground squirrels that pop their heads out of earth mounds and holes in the ground, utter high-pitched squeaks, then disappear.

At **McLeod Meadows Campground** you can camp (no hookups or showers) for $9.50 per night and take the 3.4-km trail to **Dog Lake.** Gorgeous scenery and good views of **Mt. Harkin** are easily appreciated from the highway in this neck of the mountains, but if you stop and hike some of the trails as you go your experience of Kootenay National Park will be much more fulfilling. Not much farther along the highway is **Dolly Varden Picnic Site.**

Kootenay Crossing

Kootenay Crossing was where the official ribbon-cutting ceremony opening the Banff-Windermere Rd. took place in 1923. You'll find a historic roadside exhibit, a number of signposted hiking and cross-country ski trails, and a warden's station. As you cross the pretty Kootenay River and pass small, green **Kootenay Pond,** look out for mountain goats while your eyes revel in views of milky-green rivers, lush grassy meadows, tree-covered hills, and craggy, snowcapped peaks.

Wardle Creek To Vermilion Crossing

Wardle Creek picnic stop is a particularly nice picnic spot beside the creek—if you like being mobbed by Columbian ground squirrels or want a good close-up of these friendly critters. Please resist the almost overwhelming urge to feed them. In summer, mountain goats also tend to cluster around the **Mt. Wardle** area. At the **Animal Lick,** a creekside clay bank rich in tasty minerals, you may see deer, elk, or moose licking if you're lucky.

The **Simpson monument** honors Sir George Simpson, another one of those Hudson's Bay Company men who explored this area in the early 1840s. Under his direction the company took a lead in exploration.

Access To Mount Assiniboine Provincial Park

Thirty-two-km **Simpson River Hiking Trail and Cross-Country Ski Trail** leads to 39,052-hectare Mt. Assiniboine Provincial Park. It starts at the junction of the Vermilion and Simpson rivers and follows the Simpson to Surprise Creek (8.2 km, about 2-2½ hours OW). Then two separate trails (one 20 km long, taking just over five hours OW, the other 32 km, taking eight hours OW) both lead to **Lake Magog.** This spectacular mountainous park, named after 3,618-meter, pyramid-shaped **Mt. Assiniboine**, lies between Banff and Kootenay national parks and attracts experienced mountaineers, backcountry hikers (trails vary from easy day-hikes to strenuous routes), and cross-country skiers (be aware of avalanche danger). Limited primitive facilities are provided—campsites, four alpine cabin shelters on the south side of Magog Creek (by reservation only Dec.-May, tel. 422-3212; small overnight fee), and a climbing shelter. The only commercial facilities are at **Mount Assiniboine Lodge** near Lake Magog, but advance reservations are required to stay overnight or have meals. Before you head off into the park, get hold of map sheets 82J/13 and 820/4 from MAPS BC, Ministry of Lands and Parks, Parliament Buildings, Victoria, B.C. V8V 1X5.

Vermilion Crossing

The tiny summertime community of Vermilion Crossing has a gas station, a store, cabins, a signposted 11.6-km trail to **Verdant Creek** by the bridge over Vermilion River, and a 3.9-km trail along **Verendrye Creek.** On the other side and just up the road, stop for a fantastic view of snow-covered rocky crags with the Vermilion River in the foreground, then continue along the highway to the starting points for several lengthy backcountry hiking trails along creeks to glaciers and lakes. For an amazing array of tiny plants, many flowering in summer, stroll down from the highway to the Vermilion River.

Paint Pots

The **Paint Pots** hiking trail is well worth a stop and a stroll. The scenic one-km, 30-minute trail over the river through a very green moss-draped forest gives you stunning views of snow-crowned peaks on the way to three circular ponds stained red, orange, and mustard-yellow by oxide-bearing springs (Indians claim animal and thunder spirits reside in the springs). Take your camera and plenty of film. The Indians collected their ochre here, mixing it with animal fat or fish oil then using it for ceremonial body and rock painting (ochre had spiritual association to the Indians and was used in important rituals). Europeans, seeing an opportunity to "add to the growing economy of the nation," mined the ochre in the early 1900s and shipped it to paint manufacturers in Calgary. Several much longer hiking trails lead off the Paint Pots trail to **Goodsir** and **Ottertail** passes and **Tumbling** and **Helmet** creeks, as well as a number of backcountry campgrounds.

Marble Canyon

Be sure to stop at Marble Canyon to walk the enjoyable self-guided one-km trail that leads you along the ice-carved, limestone and dolomite, marble-streaked canyon. It only takes about 30 minutes or so, yet as one of several interpretive plaques says, it takes you back over 500 million years! The trail leads along the pale-green water of Vermilion River, crossing the canyon several times by log bridges, following a fault in the limestone and marble bedrock which has been eroded to depths of 37 meters by noisy **Tokumm Creek.** As the canyon gets narrow, narrower, then narrows even further, the water roars down a series of falls far below the viewpoints. The trail ends at a natural rock arch across the gorge and a splendid viewpoint. At this point 21-meter Tokumm Creek powers its way through the narrowest portion of the canyon with a deafening roar, and the ground trembles beneath your feet—the combined sensations set off an adrenalin rush that lasts the rest of the day! Other trails lead to **Kaufmann Lake** and **Tokumm Creek. Marble Canyon Campground** is about seven km east of Vermilion Pass and the east park entrance.

The Northeast Entrance

As you approach the northeast entrance to Kootenay National Park, you pass the 4.8-km **Stanley Glacier Trail** by the **Vermilion Pass Burn** area (1,651 meters). From the road everything seems pretty dead, but if you stop to stroll along the short 0.8-km **Fireweed Trail** through the burn area and back to the parking lot, you'll see the growth of a new forest on the floor of the old. Lightning started the fire that roared through this area in 1968, destroying thousands of hectares of trees. Lodgepole pines, which require the heat of a fire to release their seeds, were the first trees to colonize the site, along with fireweed, the most dominant plant on the burn. Birds and small mammals rapidly moved into the area to feed on the new food supply. The summit of the Continental Divide is the geographical border between **Kootenay National Park** on the west and **Banff National Park** in the province of Alberta on the east.

BANFF NATIONAL PARK

Beautiful Banff. A place so endowed with natural picture-postcard perfection in all seasons that one visit is never enough—it's just the beginning of a love affair with nature at its finest. No matter which direction you look, unforgettable jaw-dropping scenery and magnificent wild creatures overwhelm your visual cortex (stop, I can't take any more), and Mr. Kodak and Mr. Fuji rub their hands together with glee. Don't show up in Banff without oodles of film (and mosquito repellent in summer).

The arrival of the transcontinental railway in western Alberta marked the beginning of the national parks system in Canada. As early as 1883 Canadian Pacific Railway officials, realizing the increased passenger volume tourism would bring, suggested that certain areas be preserved as national parks. That year three railway surveyors who stumbled across Cave and Basin Hot Springs envisioned the creation of a fabulous super-profitable resort—one that would rival the most well-known European spas. Arguments over ownership prevented their fantasy from being realized, and eventually the Canadian government stepped in, taking over the springs in 1885 and making them the focal point of a small reserve for all to enjoy. Two years later the reserve became **Rocky Mountains Park,** Canada's first national park, later renamed **Banff National Park.**

The folded, jagged, bare-rock Canadian Rockies are the result of tremendous upheaval, faulting, and erosion. Running through Banff National Park are the Main and Front ranges. The limestone, sandstone, and shale **Main Ranges,** uplifted in the Pre-Cambrian era roughly 200 million years ago, include the oldest rock and the highest mountains in the Rockies, forming the Continental Divide; massive, turreted, 2,728-meter **Castle Mountain,** northwest of Castle Junction, is perhaps the most dramatic Main Range peak in the park. The limestone and shale **Front Ranges** have a tilted, folded appearance—2,949-meter **Mt. Rundle,** southeast of Banff, is a characteristic Front Range peak. Amongst the rock pinnacles nestle many turquoise, sapphire-blue, or pea-green lakes, their color depending on the amount of glacial silt suspended in the water. In the major watersheds of the park the angling enthusiast can catch cutthroat, rainbow, lake, and brook trout, Dolly Varden, northern pike, and lake and mountain whitefish (you need a fishing permit—$5.25 for seven days or $10.75 annual—from information centers or sporting-goods stores).

When it comes to flora and fauna you'll notice three distinct vegetation zones. In the lowest valleys the montane zone is made up of grassy meadows and forests of Douglas fir, white spruce, quaking aspen, and lodgepole pine. In the subalpine zone at lower elevations lie coniferous forests of Engelmann spruce, subalpine fir, and lodgepole pine, along with open meadows; at higher elevations are mature forests with subalpine fir, krummholz, and Engelmann spruce, and meadows carpeted in wildflowers. Above timberline in the alpine zone are beautiful grassy meadows backed by jagged peaks—drive to Bow Summit, near Lake Louise, to see some of the prettiest. The park is home to a varied wildlife population including 56 species of mammals. Elk, mountain goat, bighorn sheep, moose, white-tailed deer, and mule deer can frequently be sighted if you're in the right place at the right time, and less frequently black bears, grizzly bears, cougars, and timber wolves. More than 263 species of birds, including golden and bald eagles, also live here. Please don't feed, entice, or molest any wildlife in the park, and keep your distance. You are in *their* territory.

Today the park boundary has grown to 6,641 square kilometers of marvelous mountains, multicolored lakes, alpine meadows, rivers, forests, and hot springs. Even though more than three million visitors cruise through Banff each year, it retains its vast, untouched-wilderness radiance. You can admire earth's architecture, flora, and fauna from the main highway without taking a step from your vehicle, though there's no replacing the thrill of escaping into the beckoning beyond where mountain goats and bighorn sheep may be your only company. When you've reached your backcountry limits, it's easy to soak away your hiking aches and pains at mineral-rich **Cave and Basin Hot Springs** or **Upper Hot Springs** at Banff. Or day-trip to the tall columnar **Hoodoos** by the Bow River, **Johnston Canyon,** or the **Ink Pots** (seven springs of different colors). Live it up in the friendly, bustling town of **Banff** or the small community of **Lake Louise.** Endless outdoor activities here include hiking on 1,500 km of trails, backpacking, bicycling (many designated trails), horseback riding, canoeing, sailing, rafting, fishing, cross-country skiing, downhill skiing (at nearby **Mt. Norquay, Sunshine,** or **Lake Louise**), golfing, and playing tennis, to name but a handful.

Information

For detailed info visit the **Park Information Centre** on Banff Ave., downtown Banff, where you can collect free maps and printed info on everything you could possibly need to know, pick the brains of park staff, and buy topographical maps. Or write to Superintendent, Banff National Park, Box 900, Banff, Alberta T0L 0C0; tel. (403) 762-3324.

Hostels

Seven hostels, ranging from small, cozy log cabins to large, impressive Banff Hostel, are operated by the Southern Alberta Hostelling Association in Banff National Park. They're open to everyone (any age) and cost up to $14 per night for YH adult members, $9 youth, $19 for nonmembers (you'll need your own sleeping bag in most). For more info and reservations call in at Banff International Hostel on Tunnel Mountain Rd., Banff, tel. 762-4122. (Also see "Accommodations," below.)

BANFF

Banff is a sparkling little town made up of wide streets with names like Bear, Buffalo, Muskrat, and Moose, rustic log and stone buildings, and groomed tree- and flower-filled parks dwarfed by surrounding bare-rock mountain peaks. Around it lies one of the most beautiful parks in the world, and it's all only a 1½-hour drive from big-city Calgary. If money burns a hole in your pocket, beware—Banff has more than its share of tourist shops! And its one long main street positively crawls with international visitors in summer (the shops along Banff Ave. are great places to brush up on your Japanese).

Start your discovery of Banff at **Central Park** by the Bow River at the south end of Banff Ave. (the main street), a popular summer gathering place where local families picnic at the many tables or in the gazebo, hippies from psychedelic painted vans sit cross-legged on the grass playing guitars, workers stretch out and relax during their lunch breaks, backpackers rest their loads and make plans, and tired visitors regroup after a frantic day of shopping.

SIGHTS

Downtown

There's no excuse for getting bored in downtown Banff, even if the weather isn't cooperating. Banff has more than its share of intriguing museums—not the stuffy, boring kind either. At the south end of Banff Ave., next to the bridge you'll find **Banff National Park Museum,** crammed with stuffed wildlife and artifacts. Even if taxidermy isn't your bag, this museum is worth visiting so you can recognize some of the wildlife you're bound to see while you're exploring the park; open daily 1000-1800, admission is free.

The **Natural History Museum** on Banff Ave., just up from the Park Museum, explores the geological evolution of the Canadian Rockies with all sorts of displays. Learn about forests of the mountain parks, flowers of the valleys and forests, the legend of Bigfoot, gemstones, and fossils; and there's also a riveting 20-minute movie on the volcanic eruption of Mt. St. Helens; open daily 1000-1800 in winter, 1000-2000 in summer (July and Aug. to 2200), admission adult $2, child and senior $1.

Whyte Museum of the Canadian Rockies is on Bear St., just up the street from Central Park. Inside are displays on the history of modern exploration and tourism, a heritage art collection and changing exhibitions, and archives. Tours of nearby historic buildings are also offered by museum staff. It's open daily in winter 1300-1700, in summer 1000-1800; admission adult $2, seniors and students $1.

If you're interested in learning more about Banff National Park, stop in at the **Parks Canada Information** building on Banff Ave., between Caribou and Wolf streets. Aside from helpful park staff on hand to answer all your questions and fill your day pack with maps and brochures, there's a good slide show presentation on the park. The **Banff/ Lake Louise Chamber of Commerce** office is also in this building (see "Information," below).

For those tired of walking or trying to find somewhere to park, why not see Banff by **horse-drawn carriage?** Catch one from 132 Banff Ave.; from $5 for 15 minutes (minimum $10 per ride).

On The South Side

Go over the Bow River Bridge at the south end of Banff Ave. to find plenty more attractions. Fancy a horseback ride? From the Bow River Bridge, take Cave Ave. west toward the Cave and Basin Hot Springs, and at the Recreation Grounds turn right, following the signs to horse stables. **Martins Stables** on Birch Ave. across from the Recreation Grounds provides one-hour ($18), two-hour ($28), and three-hour rides ($34), Mountain Morning Breakfast rides ($40), all-day rides ($85) including a steak lunch, or evening rides ($40) including a steak dinner, and overnight pack trips. For current prices, call 762-4551.

At the end of Cave Ave. is **Cave and Basin Hot Springs,** discovered in 1883, the birthplace of Canada's national parks in 1885. This unique cave has a steaming pool fed by natural sulphur springs (not for soaking, only for viewing). An exhibit room houses computer games testing your knowledge of national parks and Canadian Pacific Railway info (open daily 1000-1700; free admission). The 34° C turquoise waters of the restored open-air hot pool (admission adult $2, child under 16 $1.25, swimsuit rental $1, towel 75 cents, locker 25 cents) are open daily, mid-June-Sept., 1000-1600.

Get High!

One way to get right to the heart of this area and see the mountaintops from a mountaintop without hiking for hours is to cruise up **Sulphur Mountain** on a **gondola.** From the south side of the Bow River Bridge, turn left on Spray Ave., right on Mountain Ave., and continue all the way to the gondola parking lot. The gondola is open year-round, daily in summer 0830-2000 (last car leaves the summit at 2000), elevating you almost to the top (2,450 meters) in eight minutes; adult $8, child $3.50. Around the upper terminal in summer are large numbers of semitame (some extremely friendly) bighorn sheep just dying to lick your salty skin and chew up your sweatshirt (if you're at all worried about being covered in sheep slobber, keep some distance!). It's also a great spot to get close-ups of baby bighorns. Hike up the short 0.8-km, well-trodden trail to the top—the fabulous views are well worth the few extra steps, then satisfy your appetite in the restaurant (open daily 0900-1930 with early-bird breakfast specials for $3.45 served to 1000, excellent food at surprisingly reasonable prices, and a view you just can't buy!). Don't forget to load film in your camera, and bring something warm to wear at the top, even in summer. You can also hike up a trail from the parking lot and ride down for free.

When your feet are back down at parking-lot level, a stone's throw from the gondola, get a different type of high—soak your tired but exhilarated bod in the highest and hottest of the springs (40° C) on Sulphur Mountain at **Upper Hot Springs;** adult $2, child under 16 $1.25, suit rental $1, towel 75 cents, locker 25 cents.

Banff Springs Hotel

It's worthwhile taking a gander at grandeur by touring the elegant, gray stone, green-roofed **Banff Springs Hotel,** which is visible from just about everywhere. From the south side of the Bow River Bridge turn east on Spray Ave. and continue to the end of the road. The original hotel opened on this site in June 1888. You can easily spend an hour or more browsing through the main lobby (at most times of the day a-bustle with Japanese honeymooners and package tourists by the busload), the numerous delis, cafes, restaurants (many feature live evening entertainment), nightclubs, the ski store (rentals and repairs), and fancy shops selling upper-echelon souvenirs at fancy prices. Around the back are lovely views of the Bow Valley, mountains, and **Banff Springs Hotel Golf Course.** The hotel also has a sauna and indoor and outdoor pools (for guests).

Just down the road from the hotel, horses can be hired May-Sept. from **Banff Springs Corral;** daily rides for $18 an hour (hourly rides every hour on the hour 0900-1700 daily), $28 for two hours (at 1000 and 1400), $34 for three hours (at 0900, 1300, and 1400 daily). For more info, phone 762-4551. Down from the corral toward the Bow River is fast, wide, oft-photographed **Bow Falls.**

Pick A View, Any View

Back on the north side of the river, take Buffalo St. east to the first viewpoint for excellent views of the Bow River, Bow Falls, and the Banff Springs Hotel, then continue along Tunnel Mountain Dr. to the next viewpoint (passing the turnoff to the Banff Centre) to see the town of Banff in all its scenic glory.

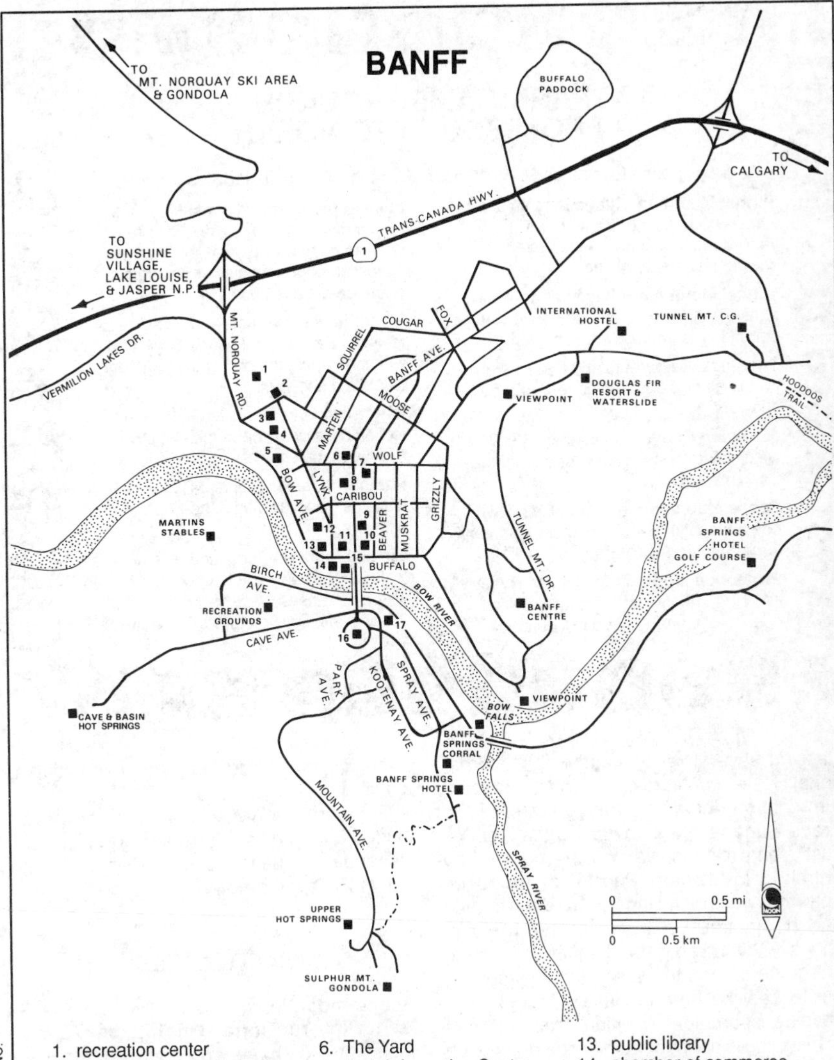

1. recreation center
2. The Caboose Steak & Lobster Restaurant & Train Station
3. RCMP
4. bus stop
5. hospital
6. The Yard
7. Park Information Centre
8. Giorgios
9. Balkan Restaurant
10. Natural History Museum
11. post office
12. Whyte Museum
13. public library
14. chamber of commerce
15. Banff National Park Museum
16. Park Administration Building
17. YWCA

PARK CAMPGROUNDS FROM SOUTH TO NORTH

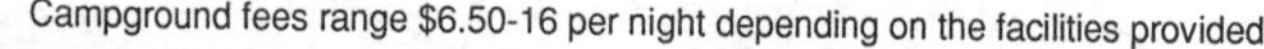

Campground fees range $6.50-16 per night depending on the facilities provided.

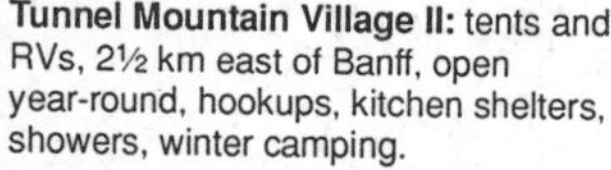

Tunnel Mountain Village II: tents and RVs, 2½ km east of Banff, open year-round, hookups, kitchen shelters, showers, winter camping.

Tunnel Mountain Village I and Trailer: tents, RVs, trailers, four km east of Banff, open May to end of Sept., showers.

Two Jack Main: tents and RVs, 13 km northeast of Banff, mid-June-Sept., no showers.

Johnston Canyon: tents and RVs, 26 km west of Banff on Hwy. 1A, open mid-May-Sept., no showers.

Castle Mountain: tents and RVs, Hwy. 1A, one km east of Castle Junction, open early June-Sept., no showers.

Protection Mountain: tents and RVs, Hwy. 1A, 11 km northwest of Castle Junction, open mid-June-Sept., no showers.

Lake Louise: tent sites mid-May-Oct. (depending on snow cover), RV sites year-round, showers available nearby. Follow campground signs from highway entrance to Lake Louise.

Mosquito Creek: tents and RVs, km 24 Icefields Parkway, mid-June-Sept. and for winter camping the rest of the year, dry toilets, no showers.

Waterfowl Lake: tents and RVs, km 57 Icefields Parkway, open mid-June to mid-Sept., no showers.

Rampart Creek: tents and RVs, km 88 Icefields Parkway, mid-June-Sept., no showers.

Cirrus Mountain: tents and RVs, on the Icefields Parkway 102 km from the junction with the Trans-Canada Hwy., open late June to late Aug., pit toilets, no showers.

Passing several resorts and Banff International Hostel, continue to the end of the road, turn right on Banff Ave., then go west on the Trans-Canada Hwy. toward Lake Louise. Just along the highway on the right is the entrance to **Buffalo Paddocks** (entrance only from westbound lane). There are cycling and hiking trails in this area (and lots of cheeky Columbian ground squirrels popping out of the ground to squeak and disappear), but to see the herd of buffalo you have to have transportation—walking through on foot or bicycling is not permitted as the buffalo are wild and unpredictable; admission is free.

For more fabulous expansive views of Banff, 2,949-meter Mt. Rundle, and the Bow River Valley, head up the six-km road that climbs **Mt. Norquay,** the local ski hill, stopping at several of the viewpoints as you climb. On the way up, keep your eyes peeled for wildlife.

Get there via Trans-Canada Hwy. 1 West toward Lake Louise; turn north on Norquay Rd. and continue to the top—a bicycle workout you'll never forget!

PRACTICALITIES

Accommodations

Banff International Hostel, on Tunnel Mountain Rd., three km north of downtown, provides kitchen and laundry facilities, a large, comfy lounge area, a recreation room with TV, a ski and bike workshop (you'll need your own tools), and a self-serve cafe where you can help yourself to a healthy meal at a good price (guests only); $14 per night for YH members, $19 for Canadian nonmembers, $9 youth; use your own sleeping bag or rent linen for $1. If you're not a member or you're not Canadian and you still want to stay at the hostel, purchase a membership. It's open (and staffed) all day, and everyone is welcome; tel. (403) 762-4122. To get there from town, catch a Happy Bus (happy because it saves you from dragging your pack up the steep hill) from any of the downtown hotels on Banff Ave. and get off at Douglas Fir Resort, $2 OW, or take a taxi for about $5 from the bus depot or station. Grocery, laundromat, and bicycle-rental facilities (discount on proof of YH membership) are located across the road from the hostel. The info board is a good place to leave or collect messages and find a lift or share transportation, and it has a really good park display with all sorts of useful information.

Tunnel Mountain Campground and Trailer Park, run by the national park administration, is just up the road from the International Hostel and has splendid views of Mt. Rundle; hot showers, hookups are $14-16. In **Two Jack Campground** farther up the road (toward Calgary), tent sites and vehicle sites without hookups are $9.50 per night. No showers.

Aside from the hostel, the next most reasonable place to stay (and most convenient if you don't have transportation) is the **YWCA** at 102 Spray Ave. (south side of town, just across the river, first building on the left) for women and men, tel. (403) 762-3560. Bunk rooms (provide your own sleeping bag) start at $16 pp, and group rates are available. Private rooms with sinks (linen provided, towels can be rented for $1 apiece) start at $35 per night. Some rooms have private toilets for a few dollars extra per night; otherwise, the bathrooms are shared by all. Family rooms start at $60 per night. Reservations recommended. It also has coin-op laundry facilities, and the **Spray Cafe** downstairs, open 0700-2100, serving good inexpensive meals and snacks. If you haven't made a reservation, grab a room as soon as you arrive in Banff—by late afternoon you'll be out of luck.

Castle Mountain and Bow River from Highway 1

The chamber of commerce has a complete accommodations listing which includes private homes that rent out rooms at rates much lower than most hotels and motels. Make reservations or grab a room as early in the day as possible. For something luxurious, Banff has plenty of hotels, inns, and resorts to suit your line of credit. The most grand is the impressive old **Banff Springs Hotel,** but expect to pay from $200 d a night for the privilege and the views!

Food And Entertainment

Accommodations are expensive in Banff, but food is reasonable and you'll find a large variety of eating places—from cheap cafes and bistros to gourmet establishments with prices to match the names of the dishes. **The Yard Restaurant** is a local favorite, serving burgers, seafood, steak, and Texas-style

Mexican dishes (lunch $4-6, dinner $8-16). It's at 137 Banff Ave. (third floor, with a patio), open 1100-2300. **Balkan Restaurant** at 120 Banff Ave. has delicious Greek specialties. It's open 1100-2300 for lunch (the Balkan House Salad is gigantic for $4.95, other dishes $5-9) and dinner ($8-16). The white-washed walls with blue trim, background Greek music, ouzo, retsina, metaxa, and rich, sticky baklava will soon have you convinced you're really on a Greek island! **Giorgio's** at 219 Banff Ave. is two restaurants in one—with good pasta and pizza for the budget-conscious and fine Northern Italian cuisine for the gourmet fancier. The **Caboose Steak and Lobster Restaurant** is located in Banff's historic railway depot. Enjoy salads and sourdough bread from the porter's cart, soup and salad for $7.95, steak and lobster for $24.95. Don your better duds and make a night of it.

For entertainment, take an evening stroll downtown and follow the crowds. Many of the pubs have live music, particularly on weekends. You can also have a good time at the **Banff Springs Hotel** bars, lounges, and nightclub. The park staff program materializes in the evenings at the **Park Information Centre** on Banff Avenue. For all sorts of cultural activities—plays, concerts, operas, dance presentations, visiting performers and celebrities, cinema first-screenings—visit the **Banff Centre** on St. Julien Rd. (off Tunnel Mountain Rd.), tel. 762-6300. The **indoor water slide** at Douglas Fir Resort on Tunnel Mountain Rd. is open to the public; $6 to 1800, $4.50 after 1800 (free if you're staying at the resort). **Banff Recreation Area** off Norquay Rd. has a cafeteria, a skating rink (speed skating, ice-skating, curling, and hockey), and tennis courts.

Banff has several annual events: in late Jan. and early Feb., the **Banff Winter Festival;** in June, the **Banff Television Festival** is held at The Banff Park Lodge; June-Sept., the **Banff Festival of the Arts** offers an extensive assortment of performances and exhibits at the Banff Centre; on 1 July the town puts on its own **Canada Day Parade;** and in early Nov., the **Mountain Film Festival** is held at the Banff Centre.

Information

For all your local info, maps, and several tons of brochures, call in at the **Banff/Lake Louise Chamber of Commerce** in the Parks Canada Building at 224 Banff Ave.; open daily 1000-1800 in winter, 0800-2200 in summer. Ask for the free *Campground Guide, Guide To Accommodations in Banff,* and *Dining in Banff* handouts. For detailed info on Banff National Park, the **Park Information Centre,** also at 224 Banff Ave., is open daily 1000-1800, June-Sept. 0800-2200, tel. 762-4256. Spend a little time in the Information Centre learning about the park (free slide show and displays), ask the knowledgeable staff everything you want to know about the park and collect detailed maps, and pick up some of the pamphlets on your way out. Also ask for one of their Banff and Vicinity Drives and Walks brochures, which describe a number of strolls, walks, and day-hikes around Banff.

If you plan an overnight trip, a **park use permit** is required; safety register (optional; even a good idea for longer day-trips) at the Information Centre or any warden office. Anglers need a fishing license. The *Backcountry Visitor's Guide* lists all rules and regulations to protect you and the park on overnight trips. Mountain bikers should ask for the brochure on mountain biking, which lists all the designated trails in the park and offers many useful hints. And for those planning horseback trips, ask for the *Horse Users Guide*.

Services

The **Mineral Springs Hospital** is just across from the bus depot, access from Lynx St., tel. 762-2222. For an **ambulance** call 762-4333; **police,** tel. 762-2226. The **post office** is at the intersection of Bear and Buffalo streets. For **currency exchange** transactions, head for banks, which give you the going rate. After hours, most major currencies are available (slightly lower rates) at the Foreign Exchange offices in the Banff Springs Hotel on Spray Ave., and Freya's in the Clock Tower Village

Mall off Banff Ave., and at Bank of America Canada at 124 Banff Avenue. **Banff Public Library** is on Bear Street.

Bicycles can easily be rented in Banff. Try **Park 'N Pedal** at 226 Bear St.; mountain bikes start at $6 an hour or $24 a day. **Performance Ski and Sport,** just up the street, offers the same, as well as rental equipment for an extensive variety of sports.

Transportation

The **Bus Depot** is behind the police station and just across the road from the **VIA Station** on Railway Avenue. Within are both **Greyhound** long-distance services and **Brewster Transportation and Tours** info booths (pick up your schedules and buy tickets here), and a cafeteria. Greyhound runs east to Calgary several times a day for $11.90 OW, and west to Lake Louise for $5.20 OW. Brewster runs a tour bus to Lake Louise for $23.50 OW, to Jasper for $55 OW, or an express bus direct to Jasper for $32.75 OW.

The **Rocky Mountaineer** offers a scenic two-day daylight train journey (includes hotel accommodation in Kamloops) between Vancouver and Banff. For info and reservations call (800) 661-1152. At the historic railway depot you can devour a first-class meal at the Caboose Steak and Lobster Restaurant, relax with a drink in the dark, old-fashioned lounge, and read all the train info in the corridor. If you need books or film, the Whistlestop shop has all the paraphernalia to make a long train trip more enjoyable—that is, once you get used to the scenery! For railway schedules and fares, visit the chamber of commerce downtown.

Pacific Western Transportation provides daily service from Banff to Lake Louise and to Calgary Airport (courtesy pickups can be arranged with a reservation at 762-4558). The company also operates the local "Happy Bus," which does the rounds of the hotels and resorts ($2 OW). For more info or pickup, dial 762-4558.

For car rental, contact **Avis Rent-a-Car** at 209 Bear St., tel. 762-3222 (out of town reservations, 800-268-2310). At **Avis, Hertz,** and **Budget,** expect to pay around $35 per day (usually the first 100 or so kilometers are free), plus up to 25 cents per kilometer. Taxis can be flagged down around town for $2, then it's $1 per kilometer.

Banff To Lake Louise

Those traveling to Lake Louise have a choice of taking either the main Trans-Canada Hwy. 1, on the west side of the glassy, emerald-green Bow River, or the slower and quieter secondary (less traffic) Bow Valley Parkway, on the east side of the river. Either way it's just under 60 km to Lake Louise, and both routes offer outstanding scenery—what else would you expect?! Along the Bow Valley Parkway you'll discover walking trails, scenic viewpoints, interpretive displays, and fishing spots. Great numbers of elk and deer can be seen, especially early in the morning and again around dusk—another spot where you need to be ready for snappy wildlife-avoidance driving techniques.

LAKE LOUISE

In a dramatic mountain and glacier setting, intense blue-green Lake Louise, nicknamed the "Gem of the Rockies," was discovered in 1882 by Tom Wilson, a Canadian Pacific Railway workman. He was guided there by a local Indian and was the first European to set eyes on its beauty. Wilson appropriately named it "Emerald Lake," but this was later changed by the Geographic Board to honor Princess Louise, wife of the then-governor-general of Canada. The original Chateau was built by the CPR in 1890, but was sadly destroyed by fire in 1924. It was rebuilt and today still stands as **Chateau Lake Louise**—a magnificent architectural masterpiece that looks like it fell right out of the pages of a book of fairy tales.

Small **Lake Louise Village** started out as a railway depot in the Bow Valley. It's still small, and still has a railway station, but now it has a post office, gas stations, a small shopping mall, a handful of hotels and motels, and a visitor center. A 4½-km winding road, 2.7-km **Louise Creek Trail,** and 4½-km **Tramline Trail** provide access from the village on the valley floor to Lake Louise.

Activities

Along the northwest shore of the lake is three-km **Louise Lakeshore Trail** which skirts below the high cliffs (popular with rock climbers) at the far end leading to the flat, muddy, delta plains. From here you can continue upward via the **Plain of Six Glaciers Trail** for views of **Victoria Glacier, Abbot Pass,** and the **Death Trap,** an enormous glacier-filled gorge. Hiking trails of varying length and difficulty crisscross the landscape around Lake Louise. For more info pick up a handy *Drives and Walks Lake Louise and Vicinity* brochure from the Parks Canada Information Centre.

The main reasons to spend time in this area are to revel in truly outstanding scenery, to meander around (or stay at) the Chateau, to hike the myriad of trails in summer, to go horseback riding, or to swoosh down the slopes or along cross-country ski trails in winter. In summer (from mid-June on) you can glide and splash through the frigid blue-green waters of Lake Louise in canoes from the Lake Louise Boathouse, or be entertained by watching first-time canoeists as they get swept in the wind toward the outflow (rescues are common!).

For outrageous views of ice-age glaciers, the rugged peaks of the Continental Divide, and distant Lake Louise, climb aboard the **Lake Louise Gondola,** one of the longest gondola rides in Canada. It takes about 20 minutes to soar up the face of **Mount Whitehorn** to an elevation of over 2,000 meters, one of the best vantage points you could imagine. At the top are alpine meadows. In Whitehorn Lodge or on the outdoor sundeck, you can replenish the calories you burnt snapping photos every couple of minutes all the way up. The gondola runs daily from early June through mid-Sept. 0900-1800; adult $7.50 RT, $5 OW "hiker's special," child $3.75, "lift and lunch" (up to a $6.50 meal) adult $12.95, child $6.95. In winter this spot turns into a pure white wonderland, the largest ski area in Canada, with three mountain faces, 44 named runs, and an enormous area of bowl skiing. The runs suit everyone from beginner to expert.

Practicalities

The **Parks Canada Information Centre** is on Village Rd. near Samson Mall; from the Trans-Canada Hwy. take the exit into Lake Louise Village and follow the "question marks." It's open year-round; hours vary season by season; tel. 522-3833.

Most of the places to stay in this area are in the village—and they're expensive, unless you're camping or traveling in your own RV. The **campground** (for tents) at Lake Louise is a wonderful spot between the Bow River

Chateau Lake Louise

and Louise Creek, with flat grassy sites and lots of trees, kitchen shelters, plenty of free already-gathered firewood, running water, and flush toilets; $10.50 per night. (For a hot shower head for the laundry in Sampson Mall; $2.50.) It's open June-Sept., for winter camping Nov.-April. Turn off Lake Louise Dr. onto Fairview Rd. following the camping signs. The **RV campground** is a little farther along Fairview Rd. and provides electrical hookups; open year-round. Ask at the information center about the **Canadian Alpine Centre and International Hostel at Lake Louise,** a 100-bed hostel with cafe, offering reduced rates for hostel and Alpine Club members.

If you really want to throw money to the wind (and have a darn good time doing it), stay at the prestigious **Chateau Lake Louise** on the shores of the lake, but check the limit on your credit card in advance, make reservations way ahead of time if you can, and expect to pay anything from $150 to $550 for a double!

Other village facilities are concentrated in **Samson Mall** off Whitehorn Rd. (on the right as you head up the road to the lake); the sumptuous **Laggan's Mountain Bakery and Delicatessen** ("scrumptious muffins, date and cherry squares, meat pies, cookies, sandwiches, and coffee, and fast, friendly service" says reader Brian Bourassa—thanks for the tip!), an ice-cream parlor, a liquor store, a laundry, public showers ($2.50; open 0800-2000 May-Sept., varying hours Nov.-April), a photographic store, a gift/souvenir shop, a grocery store, a sports/rental store, and lockers. For fine dining, local suggestions include **Deer Lodge** and the **Post Hotel,** and for delicious meals with a million-dollar view, head up to **Chateau Lake Louise**—but expect to pay for that incredible view! Foreign currency exchange is also available at the Chateau.

Greyhound provides service from Samson Mall east to Banff ($5.20 OW). **Pacific Western Transportation** provides service to Calgary Airport; for info and reservations, call 762-4558. Local transportation within the village is provided by taxi; tel. 522-2020.

DECISIONS, DECISIONS

Just northwest of Lake Louise is the Hwy. 1/93 intersection. Trans-Canada Hwy. 1 runs west through **Yoho National Park** for 72 km to **Golden,** then on to **Revelstoke** in High Country. Highway 93, the Icefields Parkway, leads northwest through **Jasper National Park** (see below) 230 km to **Jasper.** Both routes offer outstanding scenery and plenty of wildlife, short walkways to highway highlights, lengthy hiking trails, roadside interpretive displays, and scenic viewpoints. If you have to choose, Yoho has densely forested mountains with distant snow-covered peaks, rushing rivers, lakes, and waterfalls, and in summer it's very green. Jasper has much of the same beauty plus spectacular roadside glaciers—it's more of an ice-dominated landscape. You can do either route in a day if you're traveling by car and only stopping at roadside highlights, but to experience each park takes much longer. If you have plenty of time to meander through the Rockies, explore both!

JASPER NATIONAL PARK

It wasn't until the early 1800s that explorers and fur traders of the Hudson's Bay and North West companies, and French-Canadian *voyageurs* (lots of names *en francais* in this area), came seeking a route through the mountains to the Pacific Ocean. Over the years they were followed by geologists, railroad surveyors, prospectors, mountaineers, and naturalists. In 1807 David Thompson, famous surveyor and mapmaker for the North West Company, located the more southerly route through the Rockies (today's Hwy. 11) along the North Saskatchewan and Howse rivers, but encountered trouble from B.C. Piegan Indian tribes, who closed Howse Pass. Thompson turned around to look for another path to the Columbia River and the rich fur resources of the Pacific Coast. Following the Athabasca River from Fort Edmonton into the mountains (today's Hwy. 16 East), he and his men rested in the large valley where the Miette River flows into the Athabasca, building the first supply depot in the winter of 1810-11. This was the beginning of the town of Jasper, named after long-time North West Company clerk and trapper Jasper Hawes.

Thompson's gang continued up the Athabasca then branched off along the Whirlpool River, which took them across a low point of the Continental Divide into British Columbia. This became the main canoe, horse, and foot route through the Rockies for the North West and Hudson's Bay companies' fur brigades for the next 50 years. After 1850 fur trading declined; apart from a few handfuls of adventurers and mountaineers in the 1860-90s (some coming from as far away as Europe to conquer the highest peaks), few travelers passed through the area until Grand Trunk Pacific Railway trains chugged through the Yellowhead Pass in 1907. "Jasper Forest Park," as it was then called, was set aside as a reserve that same year. By 1915 there were two railways through Jasper—in 1922 they joined together to become the Canadian National Railway, and the spectacular Columbia Icefields to the south were added to the park. Despite the development of the railways and highways, Jasper's wilderness splendor has been well preserved—the area still looks pretty much the same as it did when David Thompson first saw it almost two centuries ago.

Jasper National Park, northernmost and largest of the Rocky Mountain Parks, encompasses 10,878 square km of rugged mountains, massive icefields and cascading glaciers, wide valleys, mirror-perfect turquoise lakes, rivers, forests, and flower-filled alpine meadows along the eastern slopes of the Canadian Rockies. Home to large numbers of elk, mule deer, bighorn sheep, mountain goats, black and grizzly bears, and endangered wildlife such as the bison and whooping crane, the park is also considered one of the last great wildlife ecosystems in the Rocky Mountains. (For your safety and the preservation of these wonderful creatures, please don't feed the wildlife.)

Jasper has some pretty impressive geological facts and figures. The limestone, sandstone, and shale **Main Ranges** that run through Jasper include the oldest rock and the highest mountains (**Mt. Edith Cavell** at 3,363 meters is one of the most dramatic peaks) in the Rockies, and the mountains are

CAMPGROUNDS FROM SOUTH TO NORTH

Wilcox Creek: Kilometer 111 South Icefields Parkway, open mid-June to Sept., tent and RV sites, kitchen shelter, pit toilets, no showers; $6.50. Gorgeous views of the Athabasca Glacier. Watch out for cheeky birds swooping down from the trees and swiping your bacon right out of the frying pan (not quite a remake of *The Birds*)!

Columbia Icefield: Kilometer 109 South Icefields Parkway, open late June to late Aug., tentsites, kitchen shelter, pit toilets, no showers; $6.50.

Jonas Creek: Kilometer 77 South Icefields Parkway, open mid-May-Nov., tent and RV sites, kitchen shelter, pit toilets, no showers; $6.50.

Honeymoon Lake: Kilometer 52 Icefields Parkway, open mid-June to mid-Oct., tent and RV sites, kitchen shelter, pit toilets, no showers; $6.50.

Mount Kerkeslin: Kilometer 36 South Icefields Parkway, open mid-May-Sept., tent and RV sites, kitchen shelter, pit toilets, no showers; $6.50.

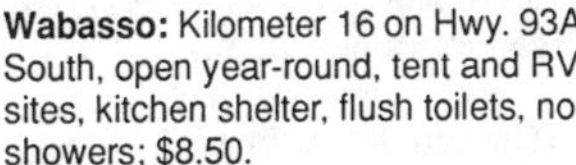

Wabasso: Kilometer 16 on Hwy. 93A South, open year-round, tent and RV sites, kitchen shelter, flush toilets, no showers; $8.50.

Wapiti: Kilometer 3 South Icefields Parkway, open mid-May-Sept., tent and RV sites, kitchen shelter, flush toilets, showers; $11.75-12.75.

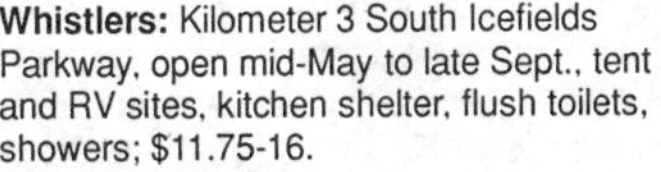

Whistlers: Kilometer 3 South Icefields Parkway, open mid-May to late Sept., tent and RV sites, kitchen shelter, flush toilets, showers; $11.75-16.

Snaring River: Kilometer 11 on Hwy. 16 North to Snaring Rd., open mid-May-Sept., tent and RV sites, kitchen shelter, pit toilets, no showers; $6.50.

Pocahontas: Kilometer 43 on Hwy. 16, north of the junction, three km on Miette Rd., open mid-May-Sept., tent and RV sites, no showers; $8.50.

ceremoniously draped with icefields and active glaciers (the last major glacial advance ended about 10,000 years ago). The 325-square-kilometer **Columbia Icefield** spanning the Continental Divide along the boundary between Banff and Jasper national parks is the largest icefield in North America's subarctic interior. **Athabasca Glacier** adjacent to the Icefields Parkway is the most accessible of dozens of local ice rivers—hike it with experienced glacier guides, or take a "snocoach" from Columbia Icefield Centre right up onto the ice. The tilted, tooth-like limestone and shale mountains on the northeast side of the park are part of the **Front Ranges.** The rounded, rolling **foothills** in the southeast portion of Jasper form the easternmost extension of the Rockies.

Jasper Highlights

Aside from kilometer after kilometer of spectacular scenery (any shutterbug can expect callused fingertips), Jasper has more than 1,000 km of hiking and cross-country ski trails, lakes with plenty of smiling anglers, and many striking features accessible by road: **Athabasca Glacier, Sunwapta** and **Athabasca falls,** a soak in the hot sulphur pool at **Miette Hotsprings** (open daily mid-May-early Sept. 1030-1800 with extended hours in peak season), glacier-clad **Mt. Edith Cavell, Maligne Canyon,** and the serene, mountain-surrounded, deep-blue **Maligne Lake** where you can paddle your own canoe or catch a commercial boat ride. From the town of Jasper, ride the tramway to the top of **The Whistlers** for an incredible view of surrounding mountain peaks and the lakes that dot the wide Athabasca Valley; go horseback riding, or mountain biking, or take one of the many commercial tours available.

Heading Into The Backcountry?

Before venturing out overnight (hikers, campers, and skiers), pick up a free **park use permit** at the Townsite Information Centre in Jasper (open year-round 0900-1700, with extended hours mid-June-Sept.) or the Columbia Icefield Centre (open mid-May to mid-June 0900-1700, and early June-Sept. 0900-1900), or warden stations, signposted from the highway, after the Icefield Centre closes for the winter—it's a way of keeping backcountry campsites uncrowded and undamaged. If you're on horseback, a grazing permit (free) is also required. Along with the permits, park personnel provide info on recent bear sightings, trail conditions, wildlife to look for, and seasonal hazards. Fill out a voluntary safety registration slip if you're planning a hazardous activity, but remember to return it after your trip, otherwise wardens will needlessly be out in the wilderness tracking you down.

Fires may only be lit in the metal fireboxes provided in campgrounds and picnic areas (wood is scarce in many backcountry locations and fire restrictions apply on some trails); carry a stove if you're planning an overnighter. Anglers need a national parks **fishing permit** ($5.25 for seven days or $10.75 annually), available from information centers or sporting-goods stores in Jasper; pick up the fishing regulations at the same time. Rowboats, canoes, and kayaks are permitted on most lakes and rivers in the park, powerboats on Pyramid Lake.

Tents, RVs, And Hostels

Camping facilities range from primitive hike-in sites to campgrounds providing full trailer hookups, and winter camping is also available. A number of YHs are also located along the highway; $8-16 per night (nonmembers pay slightly more per night than members). Provide your own gear.

Information

Two main sources provide all the info and maps of the park. **Jasper Townsite Information Centre** is open year-round and has movies on national parks and wildlife, displays of horns and antlers, special programs, and free guided one- to four-hour walks with park interpreters, June-September. **Columbia Icefield Centre** is open June-Oct. with info, exhibits, slide shows, and guided walks. For more info, write to The Superintendent, Jasper National Park, Box 10, Jasper, Alberta T0E 1E0, or call (403) 852-6161.

Campfire talks with hot spiced tea (bring a cup) happen at **Wabasso, Honeymoon, Wilcox,** and **Pocahontas** campgrounds in summer. Evening talks about the park's human and natural history (a different interpretive program is held each evening) are held at **Whistlers Campground Theatre.**

THE ICEFIELDS PARKWAY

The strikingly tall and craggy Main Ranges, with their chain of massive icefields straddling the Continental Divide, form part of the backbone of the continent. The magnificent 230-km Icefields Parkway (Hwy. 93)—connecting the towns of Lake Louise and Jasper—runs in their shadow. In the early 1800s native people and fur traders followed sections of this route through the mountains—it's no wonder the early pack-train travelers called it the "Wonder Trail." But it wasn't until the 1930s that the first Banff-Jasper road was built—a relief-work project during the Depression. The Icefields Parkway of today was finished in the early 1960s. Descriptive Indian words and the names of fur traders, packers, explorers, and mountaineers along the way commemorate the cultures and individuals who have marveled at the same towering, icy peaks, impressive glaciers and waterfalls, and fragrant pine forests that lie adjacent to the highway.

It used to take pack trains two weeks to travel the same route that today you can superficially see in four to five hours—but why rush? Many signposted trails ranging in length from short walks to long routes leading deep into the backcountry start at the Parkway. In winter, cross-country skiers silently swoosh off into a white winter paradise. All vehicle travelers are required to have a **park use permit** (available from information centers) to motor through the park (the highway is open year-round but can get tricky in winter). Before you set off from Lake Louise, pick up a free *Icefields Parkway* brochure from the park information center, fill up on gas, and keep in mind that gas, accommodations, and other services are available in only a few places along the highway. Be prepared for varied weather conditions—even in midsummer the highest passes can suddenly become white and slippery with snow.

Natural Marvels And Marvelous Nature

Keep your eyes peeled for signs leading to points of interest along short walking trails; they're all worthwhile stops—you can bank on it. **Bow Summit** at 2,088 meters above sea level is the highest point on the parkway. A short trail leads up from the lower parking area to a lookout, then hiking trails lead up through subalpine meadows (incredibly colorful with wildflowers in July and Aug.) to a high viewpoint overlooking beautiful, emerald-green **Peyto Lake**—the lake changes colors with the seasons, depending on the amount of glacial sediment in the water. **Mistaya Canyon,** about 71 km north of Lake Louise, has been sculpted by the Mistaya River—take the 10-minute trail from the parking area to the small-yet-spectacular limestone gorge. At **Saskatchewan River Crossing**, where the David Thompson Hwy. (Hwy. 11) meets Hwy. 93, motel rooms, a cafeteria, a dining room, a grocery store, and a gas station are open March to mid-November. Watch for bighorn sheep.

The most popular attractions along the highway are the three (out of 12) large glaciers visible from the Parkway—the **Athabasca, Dome,** and **Stutfield** that spill down from the **Columbia Icefield,** one of the largest accumulations (325 square km, no less) of snow and ice in the Northern Hemisphere south of the Arctic Circle. Water from the Columbia Icefield finds its way into the Arctic, Pacific, and Atlantic oceans. The **Icefields Centre** (open May-Oct.) presents an informative slide show, an exhibit about **Castlegar Caves** (largest cave system in Canada), which tunnel many kilometers under the ice from the Icefields' southern extremity, and frontline park rangers to answer all your iciest

Elk are often seen when you're hiking along backcountry trails.

questions. Naturalists give guided hikes and evening programs in the area in summer; check out the current schedule. Mountaineering info and advice and voluntary safety registration are available at the Centre in summer, at the Sunwapta Warden Station in winter. The adjoining **Columbia Icefield Chalet** offers accommodations, meals, souvenirs (great bulky sweaters if you have a spare $100 or more!), and gas.

The Columbia Icefield is only accessible to experienced mountaineers. However, many alpine trails in the area provide excellent hiking and walking opportunities; get details at Icefields Centre. You can actually go up the toe of the **Athabasca Glacier** by special ice road, and onto the ice as far as the jumbled ice headwall, by **Snocoach Tours'** "Happy Bus" and "Snocoach" (with an entertaining commentary as you go). It's a fun 1½-hour trip (if you have another $16.50 to spare!). An alternative way to see the glacier close up is to go on one of the **Athabasca Glacier Icewalks** led by an experienced guide/naturalist (from the end of June through early September). Peer into mill wells and crevasses and run your eyes over seracs and stunning alpine vistas. The three-hour "Ice Cubed" walk on the Athabasca Glacier is offered daily (except Thurs. and Sun.) at 1100 and costs adult $16, child 8-17 $7. The five-hour "Icewalk Deluxe" (destinations vary) goes out on Sun. and Thurs. at 1100, adult $21, child $10. Groups meet in the Toe of the Glacier Parking Lot (wear layers of warm clothes, sturdy hiking boots, sunglasses, and sunscreen, and take a lunch and a camera for the five-hour walk) across from the Columbia Icefields Centre; buy tickets at the front desk in the Icefields Chalet, or in advance at Jasper Central Reservations at 218 Connaught Ave. in Jasper, tel. (403) 852-5665.

experiencing the Athabasca Glacier close up

The next place for leg stretching is turbulent **Sunwapta Falls.** A short access road leads to a footbridge for thrilling views of the Sunwapta River changing course through a deep right-angled canyon in a spectacular waterfall. Another short hiking trail follows the riverbank to more falls and rapids downstream. **Athabasca Falls,** 20 km farther along the Parkway, is another impressive sight worth capturing on film. With your camera on a tripod, set to one-fifteenth of a second or slower, shoot the enormously wide, frothy Athabasca River as it thunders through a narrow gorge; from one of several viewpoints you can get a dreamy "soft" shot. If you take the Hwy. 93A route to Jasper (lots of wildlife), be sure to drive up the switchback Cavell Rd. to the base of dramatic, glacier-covered **Mt. Edith Cavell,** one of the highest peaks in the area.

JASPER

Lying at 1,063 meters above sea level in a wide valley where the Miette and Maligne rivers flow into the Athabasca River, Jasper is the center of Jasper National Park. It's surrounded by beautiful lakes and forests, and peaks with elevations almost three times higher than the town's. There are so many outdoorsy things to do in the nearby wilderness (hiking, horseback riding, fishing, skiing, and rafting) that the town has become a thriving year-round resort with a population of more than 4,000. Still, Jasper has retained its small-town identity—everything is within walking distance. It does not have the "resort" appearance or atmosphere that Banff has, with a surprising lack of souvenir shops, and it's not as jammed with tourists in summer. It's also not unusual to see elk and deer taking an early-morning or late-evening stroll through town.

Is There Anything To Do Here?

There's not much to do in town—visit the museum, shop for a souvenir, play tennis or golf, or swim. But there's plenty to do in the park, and plenty of ways to see it: by bicycle, raft, horseback, foot, cross-country skiing, or tour bus. For a list of all the best sights, a week's worth of hiking trails, and limitless outdoor activities nearby, stop in at the **Park Information Centre** on Connaught Dr.—ask for the free *Day Hikes in Jasper National Park, Backcountry Users' Guide,* and *Cross-country Skiing in Jasper National Park* brochures. To find out what local tours are being offered (plenty of these too—from day-trips to multiday tours), collect a bagful of brochures at **Jasper Park Chamber of Commerce** on the same street, or take a self-guided interpretive tour of the park at your own pace with a guide-on-tape cassette for your car.

One of the most enjoyable ways to part with a few dollars is to take the 10-minute **Jasper Tramway** up **Whistlers Mountain** to an elevation of 2,277 meters (commentary on the way up) and the interpretive area and restaurant. Look for the hoary marmots (mountain groundhogs) that can often be seen scurrying around the buildings at the top. Whistlers Mountain got its name from these chunky, nervous critters—they make a hoarse, piercing whistle when alarmed. The mountain and valley views are incredible! Hike the steep trail to the top (up to one hour OW; take a jacket if it's windy) for even better views—well worth some inevitable huffing and puffing. The tram terminal is seven km south of Jasper and operates daily 0800-2100 from mid-April/May through mid-Oct. (longer hours midsummer); adult $9.50 RT, child (5-14) $4.50. To get there, turn off Hwy. 93 onto Whistlers Mountain Rd. for three km, or take the Jasper Tramway bus from Jasper Park Lodge, Marmot, Chateau Jasper, Jasper Inn, Astoria, or Mt. Robson hotels, or Whistler campground (ask for the current schedule at the information center).

One of the best day-trips from Jasper is to stunning **Maligne Canyon** where the Maligne River plummets 23 meters between sheer rock walls, and on to beautiful **Maligne Lake,** the largest and deepest glacier-fed lake (22 km long and 97 meters deep) in the park, surrounded by the towering peaks (most over 3,000 meters high) of the Queen Elizabeth Ranges. The lake is 48 km southeast of Jasper (take Hwy. 16E, turn off on Maligne Rd.) and can be explored by canoe, rowboat (rentals available), or commercial tour boat (June-Sept.; 1½-hour tour $22 per adult). Reel in a tasty rainbow trout so big it could pull a canoe underwater, or walk or cross-country glide along local trails (3½ to 12-km loop trails). And if you didn't bring a picnic, a meal from the cafeteria or dining room in the lakeside Chalet should satisfy any rumbling stomach. The lake is a day-use area only; no camping. Another good day-trip from Jasper is to **Miette Hotsprings,** 61 km northeast of Jasper near the northeastern park boundary, where you can melt away after a long day's hiking in the hot mineral-springs pool.

The closest ski mountain to Jasper is **Marmot,** 19 km southwest of town on Hwy. 93A, where both downhill and cross-country skiers can get their wintertime adrenalin rush—though the weather can be pretty harsh. Open early Dec.-late April, the basin is serviced by four chairlifts and three T-bars, has groomed runs, open bowls, and tree skiing to suit beginner to expert—even a "Never Skied

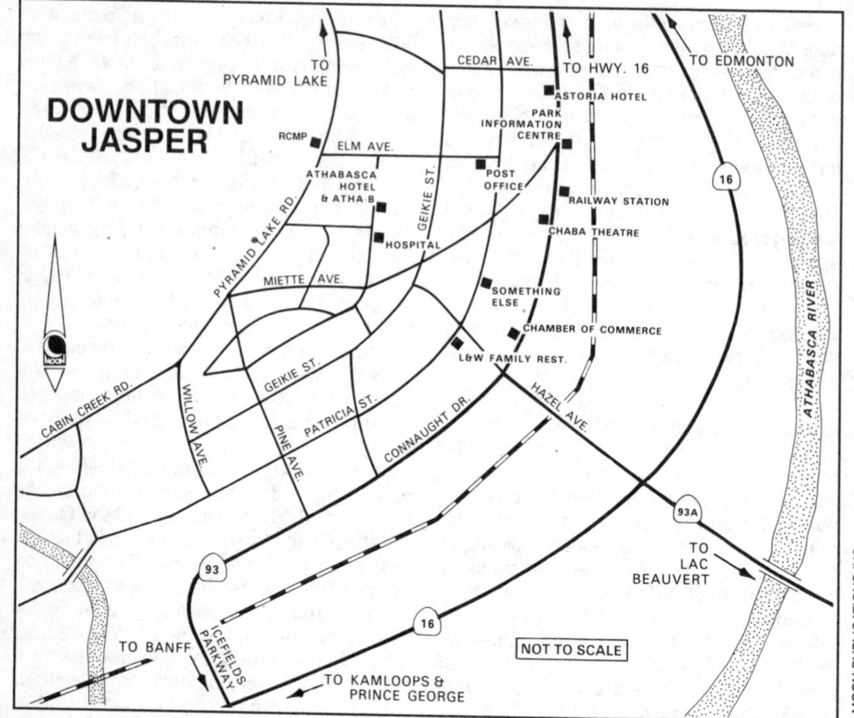

Before" program. Get more info at (403) 852-3316, or find out what ski packages are available from the **Rocky Mountain Holiday Reservation and Tours** office at 218 Connaught Dr., tel. (403) 852-4242.

Accommodations

Closest of the many park campgrounds is **Whistlers,** only a couple of kilometers south of Jasper on the Icefields Parkway at Whistlers Mountain Rd., and they have hot showers! Sites range $11.75-16. Nab your site early in the afternoon in midsummer because they go quickly. Maligne Tours Limited operates a **campground shuttle bus** service between the campground and Jasper several times a day; $2 OW. Looking for a YH? Comfortable **Whistlers Hostel** is open 1700-2300, providing bunk rooms, communal kitchen, and living room; $6 members and $10 for nonmembers. It's two km south of town (off Hwy. 93 A) on Whistler Rd. (the road to Whistlers Tramway) and three km uphill from the highway, tel. (403) 439-3089. Hike, hitch, or catch the daytime bus from town to the tramway and walk downhill to the hostel.

To locate a motel, hotel, lodge, or homestay, the chamber of commerce (Connaught Dr.) *Summer Accommodation Rates* handout lists all the places to stay and their prices (expect to pay at least $50 d), and park campgrounds. Another way to go is to stay at one of the locals' homes—quite a number rent out rooms for $20 d, and it's a great way to make new friends; get the listings at the chamber of commerce and check them out. For something more luxurious, **Jasper Park Lodge** (open Feb. to mid-Oct.) is on the edge of green, sapphire-blue, and turquoise Lac

Beauvert, where the cedar chalets and log cabins (and we're not talking rustic at more than $250 d per night!) are surrounded by trees and mountains. Facilities include a swimming pool, rec center, 18-hole golf course, horseback riding, cycling, skating, and cross-country skiing. It's on the east side of the Athabasca River: take Hwy. 16 East, turn off toward Maligne Canyon but turn right after crossing the river and continue to the end of the road; reservations tel. (403) 852-3301.

Food And Entertainment

The handy *Jasper Dining Guide* handout, available at the chamber of commerce, lists all the restaurants, their hours, and the kind of food served *and* tells you the "average cheque" (a great service!).

For tastebud-tantalizing Greek specialties, **Something Else Greek Taverna** at 621 Patricia St. is the place to go. Appetizers start at $4, Italian dishes are around $9, steaks are $12-14, and pizza is $8-12; open 1100-0100. Another good place for Greek food and pasta, seafood, and salads is the very popular **L & W Family Restaurant** at Hazel and Patricia St., open 1100-0100. It's fairly expensive (main dishes $8-18), but the good food in the garden-like interior or on the outdoor patio is worth it. For good vegetarian food try **Mountain Foods Cafe** on Connaught Dr.—always crammed with patrons.

The **Atha-B** nightclub is *the* place to go for live music, dancing into the wee hours, drinking, and socializing. Just follow the crowds and the beat to the Athabasca Hotel on Patricia Street. The **Astoria Hotel** on Connaught has a tavern where you can listen to music or throw darts. The **Chaba Theatre** is on Connaught Dr. across from the depot; adult $6 (less on Tuesdays). Special showings (like adventure films) during the peak summer months are usually less expensive. Call for info at (403) 852-4728.

Information And Services

Travel Alberta Information Centre and Jasper Park Chamber Of Commerce is at 632 Connaught Dr., open daily 0800-2000, tel. (403) 852-4919. Stock up on local info and brochures and find out what tours are currently being offered. Pick up the free accommodations and dining handouts (they don't book accommodations). **Jasper Experience Central Reservation** at 622 Connaught Dr., tel. (403) 852-4242, books adventure tours, Brewster tour bus reservations, and accommodations. A $10.70 fee is charged for Jasper bookings and a $12.84 fee for other locations. Reservations are necessary by April if you want to stay in a Jasper motel or hotel during July or August.

Detailed Jasper National Park info is available at the **Park Information Centre** at 500 Connaught Dr., tel. (403) 852-6176. Aside from friendly park staff ready and willing to answer every question you can come up with, they provide detailed maps (topographical maps are available for a few dollars), trail maps and info, camping info, weather forecasts, bear sighting info, wildlife info, and a riveting slide-show presentation on the history of the park. The center is open daily 0900-1700, 0800-2100 June-Sept., daily 0900-1700 Sept.-May, and daily 0800-1700 May-June.

The **post office** is on Patricia Street. The **RCMP** is off Pyramid Lake Rd., tel. (403) 852-4848. The **hospital** is at 518 Robson St., tel. (403) 852-3344. **Coin-Op Laundry and Showers** on Patricia St. is open daily 0700-2300; you can take a 10-minute shower for $1 while you do your washing for $1.75 per load.

Transportation

Both the **VIA Railway** and **Greyhound Bus** stations are on Connaught Dr. (the main road into Jasper). The train station is open daily Mon.-Sat. 0730-2230, Sun. 0730-1100 and 1830-2230, and inside is **National Tilden Car Rentals** (closed Nov.-April), and lockers (75 cents). **VIA Rail** runs train service west to Prince Rupert ($107 OW), east to Edmonton ($67.41 OW), and southwest to Vancouver ($115.56 OW). **Brewster Transportation And Tours** operates bus tours (all depart in the morning) to Lake Louise, Banff, and Maligne Lake, express bus service to Lake

Louise, Banff, and Calgary, and raft tours on the Athabasca River (half day $26 adult, full day $60). **Greyhound** has daily departures to Vancouver ($73.65 OW), Prince George ($34.85 OW), and Edmonton ($34.80 OW), with connections to Calgary.

Avis Rent-a-Car is at 300 Connaught Dr., tel. 852-3970. **Budget Rent-a-Car** is at 638 Connaught Dr., tel. 852-3330 ("guaranteed lowest rates in town," and half-day rates). **Jasper Taxi** costs $2 to start, then $1.30 per *mile;* tel. 852-3146. **The Sports Shop** on Connaught Dr. is the place to go if you fancy renting a mountain bike: $4 an hour or $20 a day with an imprint of your credit card or an ID card and deposit of $100; open year-round, daily 0900-2130 in summer. **Home Hardware** on Patricia St. also has bike rentals for $4 per hour or $12 per day.

YOHO NATIONAL PARK

The Kootenay and Shuswap Indian tribes living in central B.C. were the first users of Yoho's valleys. The men are believed to have hidden their families in them while they crossed over the mountains into what is now Alberta to hunt buffalo and to trade. On their return they set up seasonal camps in the river valleys to dry the buffalo meat and hides. However, this lifestyle changed with the arrival of the white man, and trading posts were set up in B.C. during the early 19th century. By 1880 the buffalo herds had been eradicated.

The first European to explore the Kicking Horse River valley, now the main route through the park, was geologist Dr. James Hector. Accompanying the Palliser Expedition of 1858 in search of transportation routes through the Rockies, Hector inadvertently contributed to the naming of the Kicking Horse River when his horse bucked and kicked him into the land of unconsciousness for two hours at the confluence of two rivers—one named Beaverfoot, the other unnamed.

The coming of the railway opened up the park—along with the rest of Western Canada. In 1884 the Canadian Pacific Railway built a line across Kicking Horse Pass, necessitating an incredibly steep grade down the Kicking Horse gorge (huge "pusher" steam locomotives were required to assist passenger and freight trains up the four-mile "Big Hill" to the top of Kicking Horse Pass). And there were many runaway trains over the years—a problem solved by building spiral tunnels inside mountains—an engineering feat. The segment of road that later became part of the Trans-Canada Hwy. was built in 1927 and followed the railway's route. On completion of the track in 1886, 26 square km of land around the base of **Mt. Stephen** (a dramatic Main Range peak near **Field**) was set aside as a mountain park in 1886 by the federal government, but managed by the provincial government. Today Yoho National Park covers 1,313 square km on the western slopes of the Rocky Mountains, bordered by Banff National Park on the east and Kootenay National Park on the south.

In 1909 Charles Walcott, an expert in rocks and fossils of the Cambrian period, led a pack train along the Highline Trail near Burgess Pass and discovered the **Burgess Shale,** loaded with some of the world's best marine fossils (more than 120 species), dating back 530 million years. Between 1910 and 1917 Walcott and friends excavated an estimated 65,000 specimens from the fossil beds, sending them to the Smithsonian Institute in Washington, D.C. Today the Burgess Shale fossil beds are protected and recognized as one of the special resources included in the Canadian Rockies World Heritage Site, designated in 1981. Only qualified researchers with permission may remove fossils from the site or split rocks in search of fossils; fossilized remains of creatures never before known to have existed have been found. Mineral extraction (lead, zinc, and sil-

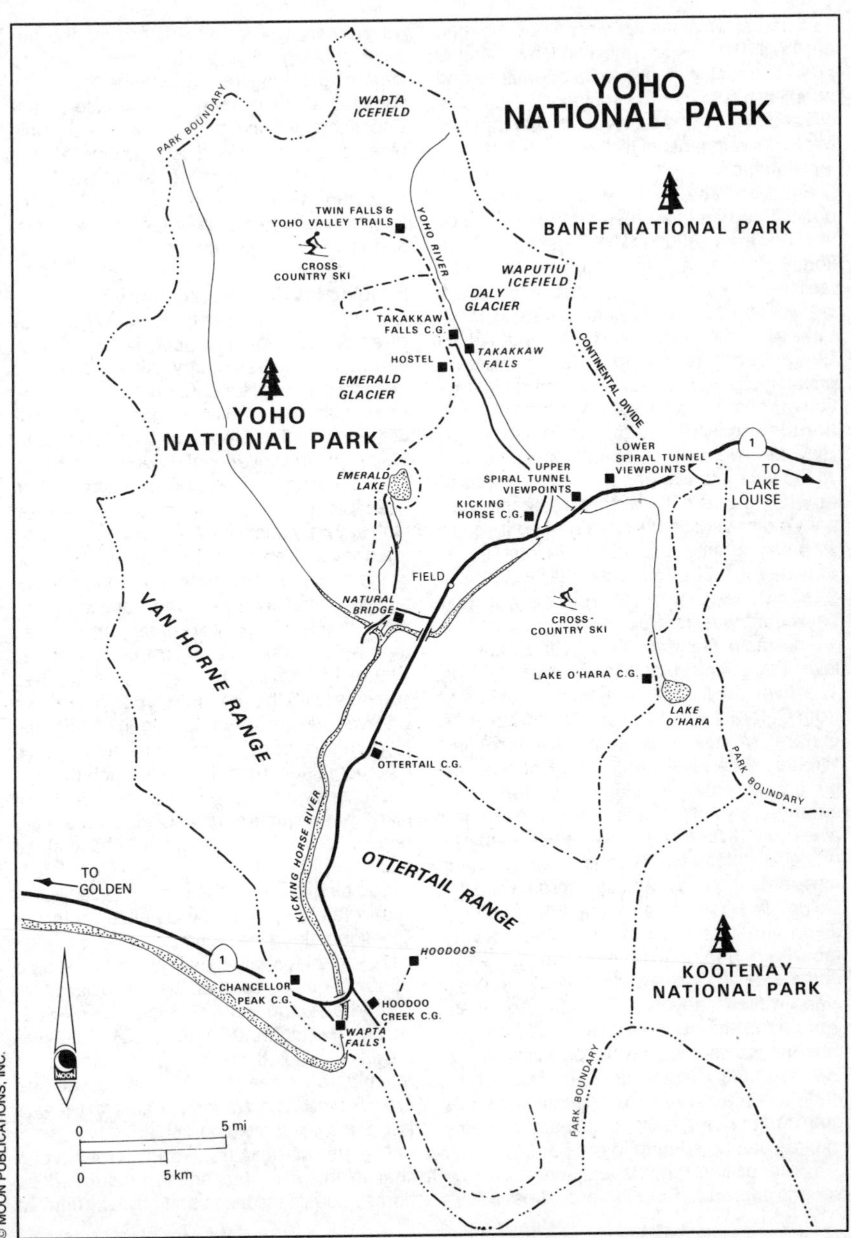
YOHO
NATIONAL PARK
WAPTA
ICEFIELD
PARK BOUNDARY
TWIN FALLS &
YOHO VALLEY TRAILS
YOHO RIVER
CROSS
COUNTRY SKI
BANFF NATIONAL PARK
WAPUTIU
ICEFIELD
DALY
GLACIER
TAKAKKAW
FALLS C.G.
TAKAKKAW
FALLS
HOSTEL
EMERALD
GLACIER
CONTINENTAL DIVIDE
YOHO
NATIONAL PARK
1
LOWER
SPIRAL TUNNEL
VIEWPOINTS
TO
LAKE
LOUISE
UPPER
SPIRAL TUNNEL
VIEWPOINTS
EMERALD
LAKE
KICKING
HORSE C.G.
FIELD
NATURAL
BRIDGE
CROSS-
COUNTRY SKI
VAN HORNE RANGE
LAKE O'HARA C.G.
LAKE
O'HARA
OTTERTAIL C.G.
PARK
BOUNDARY
KICKING HORSE RIVER
OTTERTAIL RANGE
TO
GOLDEN
HOODOOS
1
KOOTENAY
NATIONAL PARK
CHANCELLOR
PEAK C.G.
HOODOO
CREEK C.G.
WAPTA
FALLS
MOON
PARK BOUNDARY
0
5 mi
0
5 km

ver) and sawmill leases were freely handed out until 1911, when the two governments agreed to restrict commercial operations and adopt fish and game regulations—you can still see holes in the faces of Mt. Stephen and Mt. Field, remnants of the Monarch and Kicking Horse mines.

Field became a railway maintenance depot, with a hotel and restaurant operated by the CPR from 1886 to 1918 (leveled in 1963). Today it's a small railway town with limited facilities for the visitor. To encourage tourism the CPR built **Emerald Lake Lodge** in 1902, **Lake O'Hara Lodge** in 1913, and **Wapta Lodge Bungalow Camp** in 1921 (now all are privately owned) at several natural attractions. Yoho National Park **Visitor Information Centre** is located on the Trans-Canada Hwy. at Field, and it's open year-round. Get all the park info you need, plus road and trail reports, the latest weather forecast, your park motor-vehicle permit (required if you're stopping in any Canadian National Park; one-day $4.25, four-day $9.50, annual $26.75), and a park-use permit (for backcountry users; free) here.

The main highway through the park follows the spectacular Kicking Horse River. The river originates from Wapta Lake (fed from Cataract Brook, which flows from Lake O'Hara), romps through the **Eastern** and **Western Main Ranges** of the Rockies, fed by small, colorful lakes and meltwater streams, then splashes west through the awesome **Kicking Horse River Canyon** (the Cree Indian word "Yoho" means awe or amazement) to eventually merge with the Columbia River. If you were a leaf floating down the river you'd slip between lofty mountain peaks with massive icefields, bounce down rapids and waterfalls through steep-walled canyons and narrow gorges, and glide past dense silent forests and alpine meadows ablaze with colorful wildflowers in summer. Moose, deer, elk, bears, coyotes, mountain goats (this is well known as goat country), marmots, pikas, and a variety of birds can be spotted in the park.

Three distinct vegetation zones can be seen in the park: the montane zone in low-lying areas, with grassy meadows and forests of Douglas fir, white spruce, quaking aspen, and lodgepole pine; the subalpine zone higher up the mountains, with forests of Engelmann spruce, alpine fir, and lodgepole pine (and plentiful wildlife); and the above-timberline alpine zone just below the bare-rock and snow-covered peaks, with plants that have adapted to short growing seasons and extreme temperatures.

Heading Into The Backcountry?

Getting into the backcountry is the best way to enjoy Yoho, be it on foot, horse, bicycle, snowshoes, cross-country skis, or by canoe or kayak. Hiking trails (more than 400 km) range from short walks to lengthy routes; ask at the Information Centre for the *Backcountry Guide to Yoho National Park,* which has a map showing the location of the trails and descriptions. If you're getting off the main highway in winter, it's best to check at the Information Centre at Field on the condition of the trails, the forecasted weather, and avalanche conditions. Anyone camping overnight needs a free **park-use permit,** also available from the Information Centre. Campfires are allowed only in established fireplaces; it's best to take your own stove with you (cutting wood is illegal). And if you plan on doing any hazardous activities such as mountaineering or hiking through the wild backcountry areas, you may register your plans at the Information Centre (voluntary registration); make sure to report back at the end of your trip.

Climbing is one of the most popular activities in this area; pick up detailed route descriptions at the information center, and discuss your plans with a park warden. To find a climbing guide, contact the Association of Canadian Mountain Guides, Box 1537, Banff, Alberta T0L 0C0, tel. (403) 762-3761. Bicylists will find several designated trails ranging from three to 40 km; ask for the free *Trail Bicycling in National Parks in Alberta and British Columbia* pamphlet.

Anglers will find trout and Dolly Varden char in the river, but nothing worth writing home about in the lakes and glacially derived

PARK CAMPGROUNDS FROM EAST TO WEST

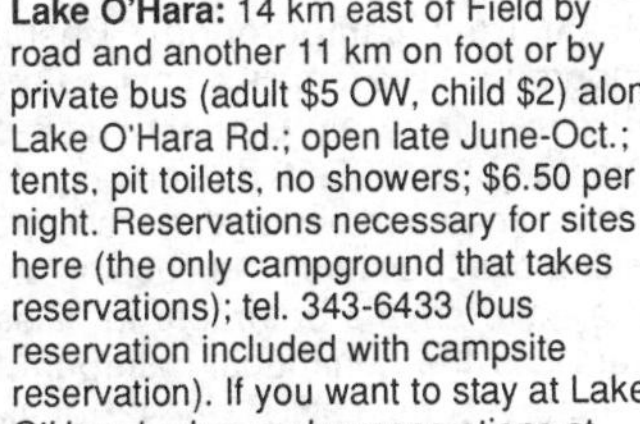

Lake O'Hara: 14 km east of Field by road and another 11 km on foot or by private bus (adult $5 OW, child $2) along Lake O'Hara Rd.; open late June-Oct.; tents, pit toilets, no showers; $6.50 per night. Reservations necessary for sites here (the only campground that takes reservations); tel. 343-6433 (bus reservation included with campsite reservation). If you want to stay at Lake O'Hara Lodge, make reservations at 343-6418 (mid-June to late Sept.) or 762-2118 (Oct.-June).

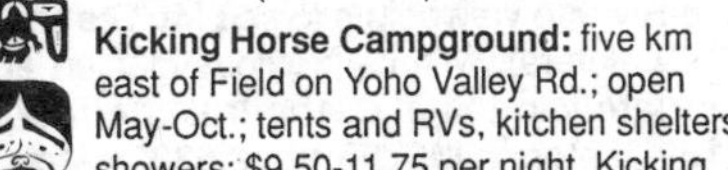

Kicking Horse Campground: five km east of Field on Yoho Valley Rd.; open May-Oct.; tents and RVs, kitchen shelters, showers; $9.50-11.75 per night. Kicking Horse Campground Overflow available for off-season camping; kitchen shelter, pit toilet; free late Oct.-April.

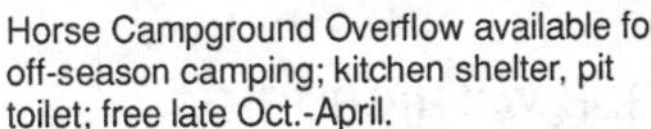

Takakkaw Falls: 16 km along Yoho Valley Rd.; open June-Sept.; tents, pit toilets, no showers. Camping equipment must be packed in a short distance from the parking lot (carts provided); $6.50 per night.

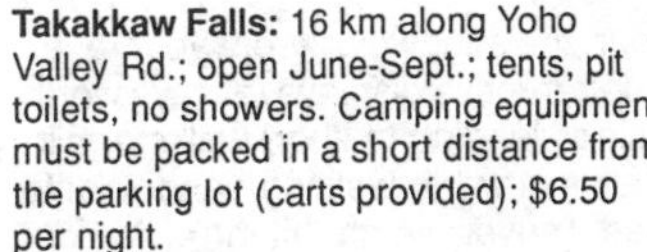

Hoodoo Creek: 23 km west of Field; open late June-Sept.; tents and RVs, no showers; $9 per night.

Chancellor Peak: 28 km west of Field; open May-Oct.; tents and RVs, kitchen shelters, pit toilets, no showers; $6.50 per night.

streams. A national parks **fishing permit** is required (seven-day permit $5.25, annual permit $10.75); also find out the local fishing regulations. Those with canoes or kayaks can paddle anywhere their hearts desire; power boats are not allowed on park waters. If you're heading for water, consider purchasing a *Kicking Horse River Guide* from the Friends of Yoho sales outlet at the Information Centre (navigable sections of the Kicking Horse River, gradient, portages, rapids and their grades). Water levels are adequate from June (peak water level) to mid-September. Flat-water paddling is also popular on Emerald Lake (rentals available) and Wapta Lake. The park is at its busiest from late June through early September. It's fairly quiet in winter but attracts ice-climbers and cross-country skiers who happily slide along the Yoho Valley and Lake O'Hara trails.

Campgrounds

Campground fees range from $6.50 per night for an unserviced site to $11.75 for a site with hookups and showers. Primitive wilderness campsites in backcountry areas are free, but users must obtain a park use permit from the Information Centre.

Information

Collect maps and trail info and ask questions at the **Visitor Information Centre** on the Trans-Canada Hwy. at Field; open year-round (Oct. to mid-May 0800-1600, mid-May to mid-June 0800-1800, mid-June to Sept. 0800-2000, Sept.-Oct. 0800-1600). For more info write to the Superintendent, Yoho National Park, Box 99, Field, B.C. V0A 1G0, or call (604) 343-6324. Although the park is open year-round, most facilities and services are provided only in the summer. The park interpreters offer guided walks and presentations (slide shows, lectures, and fireside talks) throughout July and Aug.; check at the Information Centre for the current schedule of events and locations. Also available are topographical maps of three parks (Yoho, Kootenay, and Banff) for $9, a detailed map of the Yoho Valley area for $2, and a Lake O'Hara trail map for $2, all from the Friends of Yoho sales outlet in the Information Centre.

Emergency Numbers: RCMP 343-6316; ambulance 374-5937; warden office 343-6326 or 343-6324; hospital (Golden) 344-2411 or 344-5271; fire 343-6316.

HIGHWAY HIGHLIGHTS

As you tour the highway, keep your eyes peeled for interpretive displays (always worth reading), signs leading to short walks or hiking trails (always worth walking), and wildlife in the road (never worth hitting). A *Four Mountain Park* brochure is also handy to feed you extra info on what you're experiencing.

On Hwy. 1A is a sign at the Continental Divide where a stream splits into two—one branch heads west for the Pacific Ocean and the other heads east for Hudson Bay. The Continental Divide separates the east and west watersheds of North America.

Engineering Feat Extraordinaire

If you're any kind of a railway enthusiast or engineering fanatic, the **Spiral Tunnel Viewpoint** is a must-stop-and-read-all-the-signs spot. Interpretive displays tell the fascinating history of "Big Hill" tortuous grades, runaway trains, crashes and other disasters (a trail from the Kicking Horse Campground takes you past the remains of one of those doomed trains), and how the railway engineers and builders solved the problem. By building two spiral tunnels (through Cathedral Mt. and Mt. Ogden) they were able to successfully slow descending trains on the steep western side of Kicking Horse Pass. If you happen to be at the viewpoint when a train enters the tunnel, you'll see the front end disappear and then reappear before the last car enters at the top—the trains are *that* long!

Yoho Valley

The next area to explore is north of the main highway along Yoho Valley Road. Follow the signs to the **Kicking Horse Campground,** a forested campground (noisy at night when the trains chug through) with hot showers (and separate overflow area without showers where you may end up if you get there in the evening during peak season); from $9.50 per night in off-season, $5.25 in overflow area. Nab your campsite early in the day from June through August—this place hums. Continue along the road toward **Takakkaw Falls** (13 km from campground). Beside the campground is a small grocery store and **Cathedral Mountain Chalets'** rustic cabins (from $30-50 s, $35-60 d per night). All cabins have linen and bedding, towels, propane cooking plate, dishes, and cooking utensils; some have private bathroom facilities, and others use the communal bathroom block. For reservations, call 343-6442 (off-season tel. 343-6385).

Continue along the road and across the Yoho River to viewpoints to see **Mt. Stephen** (3,199 meters), with its fabulous glacier; appropriately named **Cathedral Mountain** (3,189 meters); **Mt. Field** (2,638 meters); **Upper Spiral Tunnel** through Cathedral Mountain; and the merging of milky Yoho River and clear, green Kicking Horse River.

The road parallels the bounding Yoho River, zigzagging up through avalanche zones and glacier-covered mountains, until you spot the distant falls—"ooooh" escapes before you know what's happening. Try to resist taking photos here unless you have oodles of film to spare—you'll be taking more later. **Whiskey Jack Hostel** just off the road to the left has a good view of Takakkaw Falls, and another lovely waterfall is not far from its front veranda. The hostel has an excellent location amongst beautiful glacier-covered peaks and tree-covered hills, with nearby hiking trails to **Hidden Lakes** (1.4 km), **Iceline** (a hiking experience second to none taking you into an incredibly beautiful glaciated piece of the planet), **Yoho Lake** (4.1 km), **Emerald Lake** (12.1 km), and **Field** (18.4 km); check trail conditions at the self-registration box. The hostel has shower and cooking facilities and is open from 1700 to 0900; anyone can stay here, but YH members get lower rates.

Takakkaw Falls

At the end of the road is the parking lot for Takakkaw Falls. If you're heading for the

You can get right to the bottom of 380-meter Takakkaw Falls by a short trail.

walk-in tent sites at **Takakkaw Falls Campground**, park in the farthest lot and use the carts for transporting your gear. The campsites are 400 meters along the trail, which also leads through Yoho Valley to the junction of **Point Lace Falls** (2.7 km), the junction of **Angel Staircase Falls** (2.7 km), **Laughing Falls** (4.8 km), **Twin Falls Lookout** (8½ km), and the **Yoho Glacier Lookout** (9.2 km). Spectacular 380-meter Takakkaw Falls (a Cree word, it means "Magnificent"), one of the highest waterfalls in Canada, is well worth the sidetrack off the main highway. You can clearly see the falls from the parking lot, but for outrageous views, stroll past the interpretive displays and scale model of the area (glaciers, lakes, hiking trails, and campsites) and take the well-trodden 10-minute trail over the Yoho River to the bottom of the falls—so close you get drenched in spray (take a raincoat!). **Daly Glacier,** fed by the Waputik Icefields, is 350 meters from the brink and feeds the falls. In summer the falls are a massive torrent, in winter a ribbon of ice.

Field

Back on the main highway heading west, you pass the turnoff to the small town of Field, on the other side of the Kicking Horse River. It provides essential services, a gas station, an RCMP station, parks administration and post offices, a general store, a school, a church, and the park **Information Centre** (open Oct. to mid-May 0800-1600, mid-May to mid-June 0800-1800, mid-June to Sept. 0800-2000, Sept.-Oct. 0800-1800). **Accommodations:** self-contained suites in private homes (on Kicking Horse Ave. and 1st Ave., Field) are available; expect to pay from around $50 per night. Get the addresses and telephone numbers from the information center.

Water Wonder

Natural Bridge, the next attraction well worth seeing, is reached via Emerald Lake Rd. (three km west of Field), which leads to translucent Emerald Lake. Two km along this road the Kicking Horse River has worn a hole through the middle of a wall of rock, creating a bridge. Several viewpoints allow you to get just the right angle for that award-winning photo!

Emerald Lake

Continue along the road for another six km or so to pass **Emerald Lake Stables** (rent horses for a one-hour trip around Emerald Lake for $18, two-hour rides $28, three-hour rides $34, lunch rides $54 pp, all-day rides with dinner $85 pp) and end up in the **Emerald Lake** (elevation 1,302 meters) parking lot. From here trails lead to **Emerald Basin Junction** (2.1 km), **Emerald Lake Circuit** (5.3 km), **Yoho Pass** (7.3 km), and **Yoho Lake** (eight km).

Walk down to this beautiful green lake and over the bridge to the **Emerald Lake Trading Company** (food and gifts, open May-Oct.), and elegant **Emerald Lake Lodge,** Yoho's answer to Chateau Lake Louise and the

Banff Springs Hotel. Made up of luxurious cabins with verandas and lake views and a main lodge built in 1902 by the Canadian Pacific Railway, the hotel provides guests with the use of a hot tub, a sauna, an exercise and games room, a formal dining room (reservations necessary), and the less formal **Kicking Horse Bar** (lunch and light meals 1200-2100, to 2200 with entertainment on Fri. and Sat. nights). Rooms (European Plan) in the lodge range $200-265 s or d (off-season rates available); tel. 343-6321, or toll-free in Canada and the U.S. (800) 663-6336. One of the most delicious things to do here on a rainy day is to settle into one of the comfy chairs by the open fire and appreciate the wall wildlife, or nab a picture-window seat and gaze at the lake from **Emerald Lake Lounge** (ground floor, main building). Satisfy your cravings for tasty savories, hearty meals, sinful desserts, or just a pot of tea, and the prices are surprizingly reasonable for the surroundings.

When the weather is cooperating, a hike around the lake reveals heritage sites, geological formations, and in summer, masses of wildflowers. You can also jump on a horse, take to the water, or in winter, go cross-country skiing. Canoe or rowboat rental is available from the boatshed: $13.50 first hour, $9 for the second. They also rent fishing equipment—and the little splashes or surface stirrings every now and again prove that this lake *does* have trout! The angling season opens around the beginning of July; opening day the lake is a mass of bobbing anglers. If you're looking for the true get-away-from-it-all fly-in wilderness fishing adventure from a comfortable base camp, wander down to the canoe rental place and pick up one of the brochures.

The West End

Back on the main highway you pass tree-covered mountains with waterfalls winding down from snowpacks at the top, picnic areas, viewpoints, and sapphire **Faeder Lake**, which reflects the surrounding peaks on a still day—a good spot for a picnic and a picture.

The next attraction is the **Hoodoos,** intriguingly shaped pillars of glacial silt topped by precariously balanced boulders (accessed by a short but steep trail). **Hoodoo Creek Campground** provides sheltered private spots amongst the trees, no showers; $9 per night. Several other short trails in this neck of the park lead to an avalanche slope and the first warden cabin erected in the park.

Continue along the main highway past the road north to **Chancellor Peak Camp-**

On a still day. Faeder Lake is a good spot to take reflection shots.

ground (just after the Kicking Horse River bridge) and take two-km Wapta Falls Rd. to the most westerly park attraction, wide **Wapta Falls.** An easy 30-minute stroll along a 2.3-km (OW) trail leads to the biggest waterfall on the Kicking Horse River, where the water drops 30 meters (best vista from the lower viewpoint). Remember you're in bear country (park staff recommend yelling a periodic, loud "Yahoo!" to scare bears away), and bug country.

GOLDEN

The highway from the western boundary of Yoho National Park to the small town of Golden meanders down a beautiful tree-filled valley to the ever-present river and railway lines at the bottom. On the far side of the river the trees lie like a rich, green shag carpet. The **Golden and District Chamber of Commerce and Travel InfoCentre** is in downtown Golden and is open year-round; tel. 344-7125. A seasonal satellite **Travel InfoCentre** is on Trans-Canada Hwy. 1 (open mid-May to Sept. 1; look for the teepee-shaped building beside the Esso Gas Station at the north end of town). All sorts of outdoor recreational activities are available in the surrounding area; call in at the InfoCentre for details.

Golden has a number of food stores, a **museum** on 14th St. S (free admission), a **wildlife museum** (small admission charge), about 20 motels, hotels, and lodges, riverside **Golden Community Park** and **swimming pool,** and the very pleasing **Golden Municipal Campground** on 9th St. S (turn east at the one traffic light in town). The campsites are in a park setting by the river—and if you like to count cars on kilometer-long trains it's a great place to watch them chugging slowly by on the other side of the river. The campground has coin-op hot showers for 25 cents, and charges from $9 for an unserviced site (add an extra $1 for electricity).

Many food outlets—from fast food to fine dining—are located in and around town. Local recommendations for good meals at reasonable prices include the **Peking Inn** in the Golden Arms Hotel on Station Ave., slightly expensive **Pillars Family Restaurant** on Trans-Canada Hwy. 1 (on the right heading for Revelstoke), and the **Sawmill Restaurant** also on the main highway. The big event in Golden is the **rodeo** held on Labour Day weekend in September. During the weekend you can participate in the Fri. night barbecue and street dance or enjoy a two-day rodeo and sporting events. The **bus depot** (serviced by **Greyhound**) is on Trans-Canada Hwy. 1 at the north end of town.

HIGH COUNTRY

WHERE SALMON RUN, GRIZZLIES ROAM, AND PEOPLE PLAY

This region of British Columbia is a naturalist's paradise. Tour it from east to west or south to north—it doesn't matter which way. You'll be struck by so many different kinds of scenery it's enough to boggle your mind! National and provincial parks provide hiking and climbing trail access to steep mountain peaks, spectacular glaciers, dense forests, and flower-filled alpine meadows, and the opportunity to appreciate all kinds of wildlife—don't miss **Glacier** and **Mount Revelstoke** national parks in the east. For excellent fishing, houseboating, sternwheeler cruising, and just relaxing in the sun, gigantic **Shuswap Lake** and the many other surrounding lakes can't fail to satisfy. In the middle of southern High Country is the city of **Kamloops,** hub of the high and dry interior at the junction of the north and south branches of the Thompson River. Northward, the Yellowhead Hwy. meanders along the North Thompson River through plenty of ooh-and-aah scenery to the vast wilderness and thundering waterfall magic of **Wells Gray Park,** and on to impressive **Mount Robson Park** amongst the splendid, craggy Canadian Rockies.

As you travel through High Country you can't help but admire the explorers, fur traders, settlers, and railway and highway engineers and builders who struggled to develop this rugged land over the last two centuries. Their endeavors and persistence have allowed today's travelers to enjoy a good taste of the scenery from highway or railway comfort. For the more adventurous backcountry enthusiast there's plenty of hiking, climbing, and cross-country ski trails, canoe routes, lake and river fishing, whitewater rafting down the Thompson, and skiing in the **Monashee, Selkirk,** and **Cariboo** ranges. Wildlife watching is terrific if you're willing to wander away from signs of civilization—**Glacier National Park** is noted for its grizzly bear population. The mid-Oct. sockeye salmon run in the **Adams River** between Shuswap and Adams lakes is likely to impress even those who were born with silver lure in mouth. Finally, this region provides enough photographic opportunities to wear out even the newest camera, forcing those determined to capture every scene on film to replenish celluloid supplies as often as food, water, and sleep.

GLACIER NATIONAL PARK

Covering 1,350 square km of the rugged **Columbia Mountains** just west of the Rockies, impressive Glacier National Park was established in 1886. Trans-Canada Hwy. 1 meanders through the middle of the park via spectacular **Rogers Pass.** Ranging in elevation from the **Beaver River Valley** at 853 meters to 3,390-meter **Mt. Dawson** and containing more than 400 glaciers, 14% of the landscape is permanently mantled in snow and ice.

If you happen to visit on a fine day, you'll see steep craggy mountains topped with glaciers and thundering waterfalls snaking down rocky cliffs through deep-green rainforests to lush, wet, densely vegetated valleys. With the enormous amount of snowfall, thousands of avalanches crash down the steep slopes each year, evidenced by many light-green, treeless paths left behind. Chances are it'll be snowing, raining, or about to when you pass through—in which case you can still hope for the offending clouds to part for a moment and tease you with fleeting glimpses of grandeur. This is, after all, B.C.'s interior wet belt—they say it rains four days out of every three! On a dull day everything becomes a gray and green blur except for floral splashes of orange, red, pink, yellow, and white all along the road in summer. Keep your raincoat ready in summer and your cross-country skis waxed in winter.

History

Discovered in 1881 by Major A.B. Rogers, chief engineer of the Canadian Pacific Railway mountain division, **Rogers Pass** is the only route through the central Columbia Mountains, and one of the most beautiful passes through the Columbia and Selkirk ranges. Approaching the pass from the west, Rogers traced the Illecillewaet River to its source (the Illecillewaet Glacier), but ran out of supplies and had to turn back. In 1882 he was back—approaching the pass from the east this time. The first people to battle through this mountainous terrain with picks and shovels were the CPR workers who completed the railway line in 1885. It quickly became a major transportation corridor. From 1886 to 1916 the CPR operated a passenger service over the pass, delighting thousands of pioneer passengers. Unfortunately, despite railway engineering ingenuity, frequent and devastating avalanches forced the CPR to tunnel under Mount Macdonald and the pass in 1916. The number of visitors to the park dropped dramatically. Early in the 1950s Rogers Pass was again chosen as the best route through the mountains, and by 1962 the Trans-Canada Highway had been completed—this time with the addition of concrete snowsheds and the creation of a mobile avalanche control program (largest in the world). Experts constantly monitor the weather and snow conditions so that they can accurately predict when and where avalanches will occur, then stabilize conditions by closing the highway and dislodging potential slides with mobile howitzers (the movie on this in the information center is particularly intriguing).

Flora And Fauna

Three distinct vegetation zones can be seen within the park—Columbia forest (600-1,300 meters), interior subalpine forest (1,300-1,900 meters), and alpine tundra (1,900 to 3,000-plus meters). Within the forests are

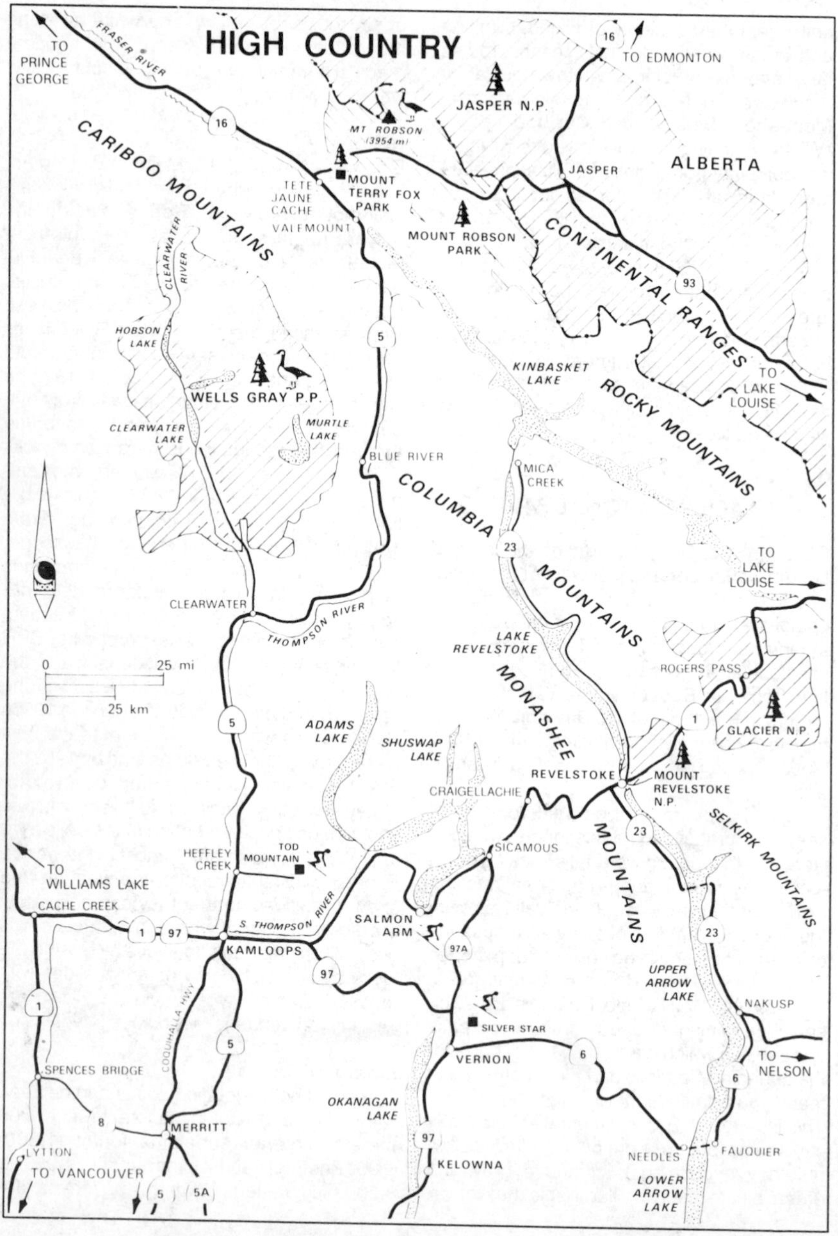

HIGH COUNTRY

TO PRINCE GEORGE
FRASER RIVER
16
CARIBOO MOUNTAINS
MT ROBSON (3954 m)
JASPER N.P.
16
TO EDMONTON
JASPER
ALBERTA
TETE JAUNE CACHE
MOUNT TERRY FOX PARK
VALEMOUNT
MOUNT ROBSON PARK
CONTINENTAL RANGES
93
CLEARWATER RIVER
HOBSON LAKE
5
KINBASKET LAKE
TO LAKE LOUISE
ROCKY MOUNTAINS
WELLS GRAY P.P.
CLEARWATER LAKE
MURTLE LAKE
BLUE RIVER
MICA CREEK
COLUMBIA MOUNTAINS
23
TO LAKE LOUISE
CLEARWATER
THOMPSON RIVER
LAKE REVELSTOKE
0 25 mi
0 25 km
ROGERS PASS
MONASHEE MOUNTAINS
1
GLACIER N.P.
5
ADAMS LAKE
SHUSWAP LAKE
REVELSTOKE
MOUNT REVELSTOKE N.P.
CRAIGELLACHIE
23
SELKIRK MOUNTAINS
TOD MOUNTAIN
HEFFLEY CREEK
SICAMOUS
TO WILLIAMS LAKE
CACHE CREEK
SALMON ARM
1
97
S. THOMPSON RIVER
KAMLOOPS
97A
23
UPPER ARROW LAKE
97
COQUIHALLA HWY
1
SILVER STAR
NAKUSP
5
VERNON
6
TO NELSON
SPENCES BRIDGE
6
OKANAGAN LAKE
8
MERRITT
97
LYTTON
NEEDLES
FAUQUIER
KELOWNA
TO VANCOUVER
LOWER ARROW LAKE
5
5A

found mountain hemlock, subalpine fir, Engelmann spruce, western red cedar, western hemlock, lodgepole, white bark, western white pine, black cottonwood, Douglas maple, quaking aspen, and white birch. For the flower lover, a mere 600 species of flowering plants have been identified within the park! The best time to see wildflowers in the high meadows and forests is early August, though starting in May an amazing profusion of color sweeps through the lower elevation forests, and in July the edge of the highway and avalanche paths turn bright yellow with wild lilies.

The tough terrain, long hard winters, and deep snow in winter mean that the resident animals are a tough and hardy bunch. If you're hoping to see some wildlife, look for bare rocky cliffs where mountain goats like to scramble and forage for food; keep an eye out for moose in **Beaver River Valley;** and expect to see Columbia ground squirrels and hoary marmots near Illecillewaet Campground. Also black and grizzly bears are frequently seen in the park—take noisemakers with you when you hike or climb in the backcountry so they know you're coming (pick up the free *Hiking In Bear Country* pamphlet). Unlike the parks to the east, bighorn sheep do not live around here—there's no winter range. In summer the park attracts a large variety of birds (176 species) but in winter they sensibly leave for gentler climates. Two species of reptile make the park their home, as do five species of fish—rainbow and cutthroat trout, Rocky Mountain whitefish, Dolly Varden, and slimy sculpin. The fishing season is generally open July-Oct. (fishing permit required; seven-day permit $5.25, annual $10.75, buy one at the information center). All vehicles stopping in the national park require a permit; one-day permit (valid from day of purchase to noon the next day) $4.25, four-day permit (valid to midnight of the fourth day) $9.50, Canadian seniors free (with proof of age, citizenship, and vehicle registration).

Let's Get Physical!

To stay dry, sightsee from your vehicle and stop at viewpoints such as **Summit Monument** (1,330 meters; 1.2 km south of the information center) to see several of the glaciers. If you drive through the park you can see the **Illecillewaet Glacier** névé from the highway, and the **Illecillewaet, Asulkan,** and **Swiss** glaciers from the front lawn of the information center. The best place to start your discovery of this park is at **Rogers Pass Information Centre,** where you can collect a *Footloose in the Columbias* hiker's guide to the trails of both Glacier and Mount Revelstoke national parks (trail length, hiking time,

Daisies carpet Glacier National Park lower elevations in summer.

elevation range, trailhead, and description), a brochure on ski-touring in the park, maps, and all other pertinent information. If you're planning an overnight trip you must register and report back on return.

Twenty-one hiking trails in the park cover 140 km and range from short and easy (and wet) to long, steep, and difficult (and wet). Two of the easiest are the **Abandoned Rails Trail,** which starts at the information center walkway (30 minutes), and the **Meeting of the Waters Trail,** which starts behind Illecillewaet Campground (four km west of the center; a 30-minute walk). If you plan on doing any of the day-hikes, pick up a copy of the park's *Hiker's Guide.* For great glacier views, do the one-day **Abbot Ridge** or **Avalanche Crest** trails. Abbot Ridge features the Illecillewaet, Bonney, and Asulkan glaciers, Avalanche Crest features the Asulkan and Illecillewaet glaciers. For overnight backpacking trips, park staff suggest the trails in the Purcell Mountains along the eastern boundary. The 16-km (OW) **Copper Stain Trail** takes you up to alpine tundra and the meadows of **Bald Mountain.** From here the backpacking and backcountry camping opportunities are endless. The trailhead is at the Beaver River gravel pit, 12 km east of Rogers Pass Centre. **Warning:** if you find a strange metal object while you're exploring the park, *leave it alone!* It may well be an unexploded howitzer shell (used to stabilize avalanches) and touching it could blow your vacation plans to smithereens. Let a park warden know where you found it.

One trail is open to mountain bikers—the first 20 km of **Beaver River Trail** starting on the east side of the Beaver Valley near the Beaver gravel pit (watch out for horseback riders); register at the Warden Office. Mountaineering, cross-country skiing, and ski-touring are other popular sports in the park; however, all require skill and knowledge, and avalanches add a very real element of danger to these activities. With the avalanche control program it is especially necessary to discuss your plans and register with park wardens (office located across the highway from the information center). Pick up the free *Skiing in Glacier National Park* brochure. If you're an experienced caver, special permits may be obtained to explore caves within the park, but they are not open for general exploration.

Information

The **Rogers Pass Information Centre** resembles the old snowsheds that protected the railroad from avalanches. It's 1.2 km east of Rogers Pass Summit, a fascinating place to stop whether you plan on exploring the park or are just driving through. Displays feature natural and human history. Videotapes on various aspects of the park are shown on the TV (the comfy viewing area by the fireplace is a great spot to snuggle up and read, or watch the gogglebox on wet, dull days), and the award-winning documentary on avalanche protection, *Snow War,* is shown in the theater. The center is also the HQ for interpretive programs. Park staff offer guided hikes featuring history, wildflowers, wildlife, and glaciers July-August: usually four to six hours and fairly strenuous, wear sturdy hiking shoes and take a rainjacket and lunch.

In summer the center is open daily 0800-2000, in autumn daily 0900-1600, in winter Mon.-Fri. 0900-1600, and in spring daily 0900-1600. For 24-hour info, or in case of an emergency, call 837-6274 or contact the warden station directly across the highway from the information center. Registration is required for all overnight climbing or hiking trips. Next-door is a gas station, **Best Western Glacier Park Lodge,** a cafe, and a souvenir gift shop.

Campgrounds

Two park campgrounds are open in summer—**Illecillewaet** and **Loop Brook.** They operate on a first-come, first-served basis, and a daily use fee of $9.50 per night is charged. Loop Brook, 6.4 km west of Rogers Pass Information Centre, has a kitchen shelter, flush toilets, firewood, and a trailer limit of 3.7 meters. Although the road through the park is open year-round, only **Illecillewaet Campground,** 3.4 km west of the information center, remains open in winter (popular with cross-country skiers)—but the snow is not cleared; access by snowshoe or skis. It has kitchen shelters, flush toilets, firewood, and a trailer limit of 3.7 meters. In summer, interpreters lead three- to five-hour hikes several times a week from the campground.

Backcountry camping: you can camp anywhere, provided you're at least three km from the highway and have registered with the warden. Open fires are discouraged in the backcountry—take a stove. Copper Stain Trail offers excellent backcountry camping potential. Aside from the campgrounds, the Best Western **Glacier Park Lodge** at the summit of Rogers Pass provides accommodations, a licensed dining room, a coffee shop, a lounge, a gift shop, a gas station, and a convenience store. Rooms from $90 s, $95 d, and off-season rates are available from Oct.; for more info and reservations, phone 837-2126.

If camping by mineral hot springs sounds appealing, continue west along the highway for about 40 km and stop at **Canyon Hot Springs** (35 km east of Revelstoke) for some sizzling in the 40° C hot pool or soothing laps in the 26° C pool. Grab a bite to eat in the licensed restaurant, and camp in a natural forest setting in the Selkirk Mountains. The campsites have picnic tables and fire pits (wood provided), free showers, sani-dump, and water station, and there's also a convenience store. The pools are open daily in May, June, and Sept 0900-2100, in July and Aug. 0900-2200; single swim adult $4, day pass $6, senior $3.50 or day pass $5, child $3 or day pass $4.50, family of four $11 or day pass $16. The springs are on the Trans-Canada Hwy. at Albert Canyon (watch for the red umbrella sign); for more info call 837-2420.

MOUNT REVELSTOKE NATIONAL PARK

Mount Revelstoke National Park (established in 1914) covers 260 square km of the rugged **Clachnacudainn Range** in the steep **Columbia Mountains.** It's bordered on the east by the Rockies and on the west by the Interior Plateau. Dominating the center of the park is the impressive **Clachnacudainn Icefield**, with its many glaciers. Elevation ranges from the **Columbia River Valley** at 460 meters to 2,646-meter **Mt. Coursier,** highest peak in the park.

The Trans-Canada Hwy. skirts the southernmost section of Mount Revelstoke National Park—its heart is accessed by a road on the northeast side of Revelstoke. Drive through the park in good weather (if you're lucky) and you'll see steep craggy peaks permanently covered in ice and snow, subalpine forest of fir and Engelmann spruce, brilliant flower-filled meadows, lush valleys crowded with giant cedar and hemlock rainforest, and silver waterfalls snaking down from icy peaks through dense greenery. This park, like neighboring Glacier National Park, has a high rainfall in summer and heavy snowfall in winter, complete with frequent snowslides and dangerous avalanches that limit habitation of this area by large animals or man.

You can cruise through the southeast fringe of the park via the highway, stopping at viewpoints, interpretive signs, picnic areas, and short hiking trails (don't miss the short Giant Cedars Trail; see below), but if you really want to appreciate the scenery from your vehicle and on foot, drive on into the city of Revelstoke, then take the 26-km hairpin-bend Summit Rd. to the summit of (surprise, surprise!) Mount Revelstoke (1,938 meters). By cruising up this mountain you not only get the chance to appreciate landscape changes from lowland forest to flowery meadows to high-country tundra, but you also get views of the city, the Columbia and Illecillewaet river valleys, and the Monashee Mountains as you climb. Several trails lead off Summit Rd., and many more, both short and long, start at the parking lot at the summit. The park is open year-round, but buried in snow from Oct. to mid-June.

Physical Fun

The best way to get to know the park is along the more than 65 km of hiking trails. Before you start exploration, pick up a topographical map and trail guide at the Government Agent office located in the Court House in Revelstoke, or get the handy *Footloose In The Columbias* booklet at Rogers Pass Information Centre in Glacier National Park. It's a good idea to discuss your backcountry plans with wardens—registration is required for overnight hiking, climbing, and camping trips.

Thirteen diverse trails cover a variety of landscapes. Whether you're looking for a level stroll through a scented cedar forest or an alpine scramble through wildflowers in almost every color of the rainbow (at their best in early August), there's a trail to suit you. The first short trail you come to at the western end of the park is ½-km (RT) **Giant Cedars Trail**—a delicious trail through an ancient cedar forest in the Columbias. Watch for the sign off the main highway. Starting at a picnic area (with restrooms) in a meadow full of Kodak wildflowers, a boardwalk lures you along a sparkling creek through the fragrant Columbia forest, carpeted in lush ferns, lichens, and mosses, to towering, spiky cedars that make you feel as inconspicuous as you really are. It's a lush tropical jungle minus the heat! Other short walks start from Summit Rd. in the southwestern section. If you visit the park in July, Aug., or Sept., the trail system at the summit of **Mt. Revelstoke** is recommended. For overnight backpacking trips, head for the **Jade Lake** area off Summit Road.

Skiing: Two cross-country trails (two- and five-km) are packed and groomed at the base of Mt. Revelstoke. If you're sliding off into the backcountry, be sure to check on trail conditions and avalanche hazards with a warden beforehand. **Mountain biking:** The five-km cross-country trail is open to mountain biking in summer. This 40-minute ride loops through dense cedar and hemlock forest, passing giant boulders and tumbling brooks (numerous short hills, expect a vigorous workout), starting near the Mt. Revelstoke Ski Chalet.

Practicalities

There are no campgrounds or facilities in Mount Revelstoke National Park. Backcountry camping is free (take a stove). For safety, registration is required at the park administration office in Revelstoke. Private campgrounds are operated along the Trans-Canada Hwy. both east and west of the park. The city of Revelstoke has all the amenities; read on. For more info, a topographical map, and a trail guide, drop by the **Park HQ** at 313 3rd St. West in Revelstoke (open weekdays 0900-1700), or visit **Rogers Pass Information Centre** in nearby Glacier National Park, where you can also join a guided hike in the Columbia Mountains with a park naturalist.

REVELSTOKE

The city of Revelstoke dates back to the mid-1800s and the Columbia River goldrush days. It nestles between the western end of Rogers Pass and the eastern end of Eagle Pass in the Selkirk Mountains where the Illecillewaet River joins the Columbia River. Surrounded by tree-covered hills and distant snowcapped mountains, the historic downtown area has been rejuvenated with an appealing, all-brick **Grizzly Plaza,** good-looking shops, and buckets of flowers in summer—but it still has an old-fashioned feeling. Wander from downtown along Mackenzie Ave. to the Columbia River and **Riverside, Centennial,** and **Queen Elizabeth** parks. Farther along is the local swimming pool.

Sights

The big attractions in this area are Revelstoke National Park, Revelstoke Dam, and Mt. Mackenzie Ski Hill. But while you're downtown, the **Revelstoke Museum** in the old Revelstoke post office building on the corner of Boyle Ave. and First St. has plenty to see (a good place to hang out on a rainy day). Along with lots of historic black-and-white photos, it's the place to learn about Lord Revelstoke (who provided the funding to complete construction of the CPR—the town was named after him in 1866), local industries from days gone by, the Chinese mining population (1865-66), and skiing at Mt. Mackenzie. See a furnished kitchen com-

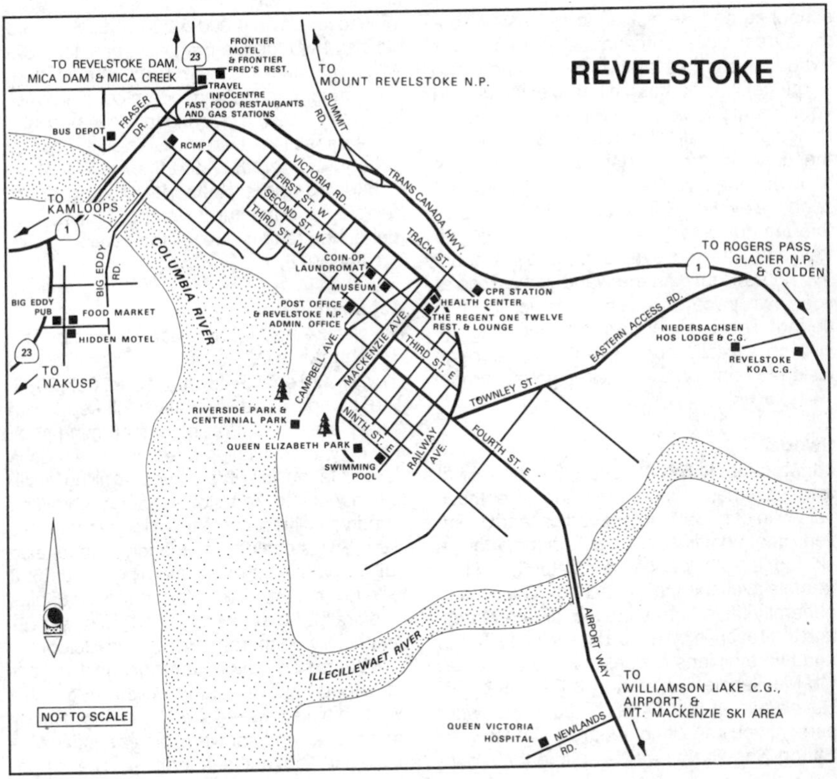

REVELSTOKE

TO REVELSTOKE DAM, MICA DAM & MICA CREEK
FRONTIER MOTEL & FRONTIER FRED'S REST.
TRAVEL INFOCENTRE
FAST FOOD RESTAURANTS AND GAS STATIONS
TO MOUNT REVELSTOKE N.P.
SUMMIT RD.
BUS DEPOT
FRASER DR.
RCMP
VICTORIA RD.
FIRST ST. W
SECOND ST. W
THIRD ST. W
TRANS CANADA HWY.
TO KAMLOOPS
TRACK ST.
COLUMBIA RIVER
BIG EDDY RD.
COIN-OP LAUNDROMAT
MUSEUM
CPR STATION
HEALTH CENTER
THE REGENT ONE TWELVE REST. & LOUNGE
POST OFFICE & REVELSTOKE N.P. ADMIN. OFFICE
TO ROGERS PASS, GLACIER N.P. & GOLDEN
EASTERN ACCESS RD.
NIEDERSACHSEN HOS LODGE & C.G.
REVELSTOKE KOA C.G.
BIG EDDY PUB
FOOD MARKET
HIDDEN MOTEL
TO NAKUSP
CAMPBELL AVE.
MACKENZIE AVE.
THIRD ST. E
TOWNLEY ST.
RIVERSIDE PARK & CENTENNIAL PARK
NINTH ST. E
RAILWAY AVE.
FOURTH ST. E
QUEEN ELIZABETH PARK
SWIMMING POOL
ILLECILLEWAET RIVER
AIRPORT WAY
TO WILLIAMSON LAKE C.G., AIRPORT, & MT. MACKENZIE SKI AREA
NOT TO SCALE
QUEEN VICTORIA HOSPITAL
NEWLANDS RD.

plete with old stove and gadgets from the 1890s to early 1900s, an 1890s school room, old telephones, and some extraordinary and rather gruesome doctor's office equipment. Upstairs is the local **art gallery** (changing exhibits). The museum and art gallery are open in June weekdays 1300-2100, in Sept. and Oct. weekdays 1300-1630, and Nov.-April on Mon., Wed., and Fri. 1300-1630; admission is by donation.

To get to the number-one local sight, **Revelstoke National Park,** take the 26-km Summit Rd. turnoff from the Trans-Canada Highway to the spectacular top of **Mount Revelstoke**. You can also get up there by 10-km **Summit Trail** (four to five hours OW), starting at the edge of the parking lot marked for trailer drop-offs at the base of Summit Road. The views on the way up are worth the effort, and at the top are many more hiking trails of varying lengths. For more info see "Revelstoke National Park," above.

The next most popular attraction is **Revelstoke Dam** on the mighty Columbia River, which provides hydroelectric power and flood control. Take Hwy. 23 north (beside the InfoCentre) toward Mica Creek (139 km, Mica Dam 149 km). Revelstoke Dam is about eight km up this road—in summer lined with purple, white, pink, orange, red, and yellow wildflowers. Follow the signs to the **Revelstoke Dam Visitor Centre,** open weekdays 0900-1700 throughout the year, June-Sept. 0800-2000. The dam is interesting—even if you think you visited enough damn dams during your school career. Admission to the visitor center is free. Upon entry you're given a clever "wand" (looks like a streamlined telephone earpiece). Walk past all the exhibits and your magic wand activates a recording, bringing to life all the displays and models of the dam. In the theater, dam movies are shown. When you're through, let the high-speed elevator whisk you up to the top of the dam for an excellent view. If you do the tour and listen to everything it takes about 1½ hours—but with the wand you can go at your own pace and skip anything you find boring! The center is a refreshing place to visit on a really hot day—it's cold enough inside to bring on an attack of goosebumps!

Swoosh!

Mt. Mackenzie Ski Area, six km from downtown, is a major resort, providing ski enthusiasts with over 600 meters vertical and unlimited runs, chairlifts, a T-bar, a handle tow, a ski lodge with lounge, a cafeteria, a shop (rentals available), and a school. The season generally lasts from mid-Dec. to late March, and the resort is open six days (closed Tues.) and two evenings a week; for more info call Mt. Mackenzie Ski Area at 837-5268 or Ski Revelstoke at 837-9489. If you're a powder person, you can climb aboard a **Cat Powder Skiing** Sno-Cat for a ride up into the mountains to ski down 4,000-5,000 vertical meters per day (two- or five-day packages; tel. 837-9489), or take a course in mountaineering, ski touring, telemarking, or rock or ice climbing in the Selkirks, staying in a comfy chalet at the base of the Durrand Glacier (access by helicopter; tel. 837-9489 or 837-2381). **Selkirk Tangiers Helicopter Skiing** offers heli-skiing adventures in the Selkirk and Monashee ranges. Get all the details by calling 344-5016.

Accommodation

Revelstoke has many places to camp. The **Revelstoke KOA** is off the Trans-Canada Hwy. six km east of downtown, tel. 837-2085. The campground is really well-kept, with grassy sites, lots of trees, a swimming pool, a pond with multicolored feathered friends, a dump station for RVs, propane filling facilities, a well-stocked store, free hot showers, laundry facilities, and a main lodge that looks like a Swiss chalet. The friendly owners also put on pancakes every morning 0700-1000 for a few dollars. Sites start at $15.50 d, plus an extra $2.50 for electricity, $1.50 sewer, $1 water; only open from May to mid-October.

Williamson Lake Campground is another quiet spot to camp on the edge of a warm alpine lake—good swimming. Shady grassy sites, hot showers, picnic shelter, firepits, just above the shoreline. The camp-

Revelstoke Dam

ground is about seven km south of town on Airport Way, tel. 837-5512. Sites start at $13 for three persons, electricity, sewer, and water all included.

If a good cheap motel is your preference, try the quiet **Hidden Motel** where the cabin-style rooms (complete with bright red doors and brown window shutters decorated with hearts) are reasonable at $27-37 s or d, and a kitchen is available. It's at 1855 Big Eddy Rd. (off Hwy. 23 South), tel. 837-4240, opposite a market and just down the road from Big Eddy Pub. **Frontier Motel,** behind the InfoCentre at the junction of the Trans-Canada Hwy. and Hwy. 23 N, also has reasonable prices at $29-32 s, $32-35 d, and a convenient location with a good restaurant adjacent; tel. 837-5119.

Food And Entertainment

Frontier Fred's Restaurant, open daily 0600-2100, is just behind the InfoCentre. Its atmosphere lives up to its name: wood interior decorated with cowboy boots, hats, horns, and red-and-white checkered curtains, frilly-bloused jean-clad waitresses, and a sign outside that says "Y'all come back, y'hear!" And Fred's food is good. Huge breakfasts are around $4.85 (includes everything), lunch is around $5-6, dinner (the usual Canadian fare) is around $11-14 with all the trimmin's and a visit to the chuckwagon salad bar. On the corner of Hwy. 1 and Hwy. 23 N, tel. 837-5119.

The **One Twelve Restaurant** at the Regent Inn at 112 Victoria Rd. is a popular place to go if you're in the mood for a bit of a splurge (open Mon.-Sat. for lunch and dinner, tel. 837-2107), and the **One Twelve Lounge and Regent Pub** is the favorite town pub, dance spot, and meeting place.

In July and Aug. a variety of live entertainment (singing, dancing, comedy, magic shows, etc.) is put on at Grizzly Plaza **Bandshell** most evenings—and it's free! For music and dancing, the young crowd heads for **Big Eddy Inn** at 2108 Big Eddy Rd., **Speeders Pub** in McGregors at 201 West Second, and **Dapper Dan's** in the Regent Inn at 112 First St. East. For country music and dancing, it's the **King Edward Hotel Pub** at 112 East Second Street. For a quieter evening's entertainment head for the poolside lounge at the **Sandman Inn** on the Trans-Canada Highway. The **Roxy Theatre** in Grizzly Plaza is the place to go for the latest movies. For something different, take a 19-km drive west of Revelstoke along the Trans-Canada Hwy. to **Three Valley Gap** where you can hear Sky Floyd Drew, an authentic Canadian cowboy, tell stories, sing, yodel, and do a bit of trick and fancy roping in the **Walter Moberly Theatre;** for more info call 837-2109 (open mid-March through October).

Information And Services

The **Revelstoke Chamber of Commerce and Travel InfoCentre** is on the Trans-Canada Hwy. by the Hwy. 23 N turnoff, tel. 837-5345; open May to the end of June 1000-1800, July to the end of Aug daily 0800-2000. The **Chamber of Commerce** is open weekdays year-round on the corner of Second and Campbell avenues, downtown. **Revelstoke National Park Administration office** is in the **post office** building at 313 Third St. West, tel. 837-5155. **Queen Victoria Hospital** is on Newlands Rd. (off Airport Way), on the east side of town. The **CPR station** is off Track Street. The **Greyhound bus depot** is at the west side of town on Fraser Drive. Greyhound runs four trips east and seven trips west daily. For more info, call 837-5874.

ON TO SALMON ARM

Continuing west along Trans-Canada Hwy. 1 toward Salmon Arm, several campgrounds and gas stations lie along the highway as you leave Revelstoke. From the outskirts of the city to the small community of Sicamous the road meanders through a heavily forested ravine to pass intriguing black **Summit Lake** with its tree-covered cliffs and its waterfall plummeting down into the lake. Equally black **Victor Lake** has another photo-perfect waterfall, and shoreside **Victor Lake Provincial Park** is a good spot for a picnic.

The well-marked tourist attraction, **Three Valley Gap** ghost town, a rebuilt pioneer community, has more than 20 historic buildings, which were moved here from around B.C., on the edge of dark-green **Three Valley Lake.** It's open daily 0800-dusk, mid-March through Oct.; there's an admission charge to see the ghost town. Three Valley Gap is also a lakeside resort with a motor inn, a restaurant, a cafeteria, an indoor swimming pool, and gardens. For more info or reservations, call 837-2109. The next commercial tourist attraction is the **Enchanted Forest,** where a wooded trail meanders past more than 250 handcrafted figurines amongst the trees to fairyland buildings. It's open mid-May to mid-Sept. 0800 to half an hour before dusk, tel. 837-9477 or 837-9655; admission charged. **Beardale Castle Miniatureland,** the next venture along the highway, takes miniature appreciators through several European towns and villages, into the world of nursery rhymes and fairy tales, and on into the world of trains. It's open daily May through Sept. from 0900 to dusk, tel. 836-2268; admission charged.

At **Craigellachie** signs point off the highway to the **Last Spike Site**, open daily. It was here on Nov. 7, 1885, that a plain iron spike welded the Canadian Pacific Rail line east to west—the last section completed, Canada was finally linked from sea to sea. A cairn with a plaque and a piece of railway line marks the spot, along with picnic tables and a seasonal Travel InfoCentre (open May-Oct.) in the **Craigellachie Station,** and a gift shop selling train paraphernalia and souvenirs.

As you approach the small community of **Sicamous** from the east, note the signs! The first says "Turn Left. So Much More To See In The Okanagan." The next sign says "Go Straight. The Direct Way To Vancouver. So Much To See In Kamloops." Sicamous, unchallenged "Houseboat Capital of Canada" (some say of the world!), is at the junction of Trans-Canada Hwy. 1 and Hwy. 97A. The signs are proof of the considerable rivalry between Kamloops and the cities of the Okanagan for tourist trade—especially since the fast Coquihalla Hwy. was built, bypassing the Okanagan. From Sicamous the highway wanders along the edge of enormous, deep

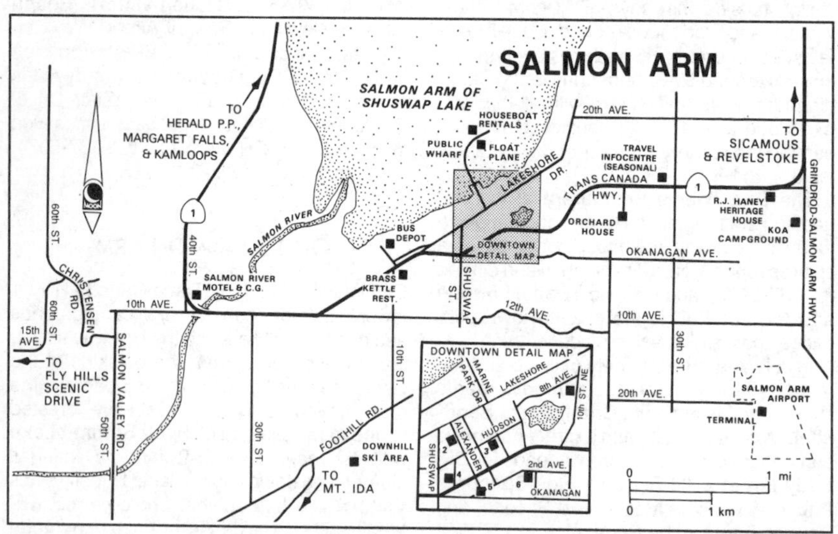

blue-green **Shuswap Lake.** With more than 1,000 km of placid navigable waterways, secluded beaches, marine parks, and distant forest-covered hills, this stunning lake takes its name from the Shuswap Indians, northernmost of the great Salishan family and the largest tribe in British Columbia. All kinds of water sports are popular on the lake, especially parasailing and self-propelled waterskiing, but houseboating seems to be the number-one activity. You can rent houseboats from many of the lakeshore resorts.

SALMON ARM

The "gem of the Shuswap," Salmon Arm lies along the Salmon Arm of Shuswap Lake at the northern end of the Okanagan, surrounded by lush farmland and forest-covered hills. Locals claim that the name of the town came from the days when the rivers were chockablock with salmon and farmers used to spear them with pitchforks and use the fish for fertilizer! You'll find plenty of campgrounds, RV and trailer parks, and motels here, and if you want to just kick back and relax in the sun by the lake, this is another place to do just that. On entering town from the east, the highway passes motel after motel, parks, several malls (the Greyhound bus depot is at Village West Mall), restaurants, and a waterslide.

Sights

From downtown, follow the Salmon Arm wharf signs to sparkling **Marine Park** with its grassy lawns, picnic tables, and an abundance of flowering plants hanging from all the lampposts in summer. The attractive **Salmon Arm Wharf,** longest curved wharf and marina structure in interior B.C., lures you out over the water, past a boat-launching area, to the end where you can rent a houseboat for a close-up view of the lake. The marina can accommodate houseboats, pleasure boats, and cruisers, and has a gas barge, a portable water supply, a sanitary dump, restrooms, telephones, and a snack bar.

The **R.J. Haney Heritage House** is a turn-of-the-century farmhouse set amongst beautiful, park-like surroundings. It's next to the KOA Campground, two km east of Salmon Arm off Hwy. 97 B (to Vernon), open June and Sept. daily 1000-1800, in July and Aug. daily 1000-2000; admission adult $2, student under 12 $1, children under five free. For more info call 832-5243. The **Salmon Arm Museum and Heritage Society** relates the town's early history through a slide show and photo albums, and you can pick up pamphlets describing self-guided tours of Salmon Arm's historic sites and buildings. The museum is open Mon.-Sat. 1000-2000, on 3rd St. Southeast.

For excellent views of the **Salmon Valley,** take the **Fly Hills Scenic Drive** along a forest road starting almost opposite the Salmon River Motel on the Trans-Canada Hwy. (east end of town). Turn off the highway on 40th St., following scenic route signs, turn right on 10th Ave., left on Salmon Valley Rd., right on Christensen Rd., left on 5th Ave., left on 60th St., right on 15th Ave., then continue up the forest service road to Fly Hills, following snowmobile signs. The road gets pretty rough (dirt and gravel with deep potholes) in sections—definitely unsuitable for Ferraris, but neither is 4WD necessary in summer. The higher you go, the better the valley and lake views become. In winter there's lots of deep snow up here, attracting hordes of snowmobilers and cross-country skiers.

Outdoor Action

In summer this region offers plentiful hiking (ask for the handy *Hiking in the Shuswap* pamphlet put out by the chamber of commerce), and fly and lure fishing in so many lakes it could take you a lifetime to discover them all. The chamber also produces an equally handy *Fishing in the Shuswap District* pamphlet.

The main thing to do here in winter is to don cross-country skis and silently glide along the groomed woodland trails of large **Larch Hills Cross-Country Ski Area,** a 20-minute drive from downtown. At the end of

Salmon Arm's week-long Winter Festival, Larch Hills hosts the annual Reino Keski-Salmi Loppet, a cross-country ski marathon (first of nine) sanctioned by Cross Country Canada as part of the Canadian Ski Odyssey Series. To get there take Hwy. 97B for 12 km, then turn left on Edgar Rd. and continue for another six kilometers.

One of the most enjoyable short walks is at the end of a short drive along the north side of the Salmon Arm of Shuswap Lake. Take the Trans-Canada Hwy. northwest to Kamloops but turn right just past the Tappen Co-op toward **Sunnybrae Recreation Area** and **Herald Provincial Park** (about seven km along a twisty, scenic lakeside road). The park has good picnicking, swimming from a grass and sand beach, and camping (May-Sept.) for $13 per night. Just a little way up the road from the park campground is a gorgeous 15-minute walk to **Margaret Falls**—don't miss it! The level, well-made trail meanders along Reinecker Creek through a deep, fragrant canyon full of leaning cedar trees (deliciously cool on a hot summer day) and finishes at a wide, splashy waterfall. As a couple encountered on the trail said, "You couldn't ask for a better falls at the end of a better walk."

Practicalities

The landscaped **Salmon Arm KOA** has free hot showers, laundry, a heated pool and hot tub, a store, miniature golf, a playground, small farm animals that little (and big!) kids enjoy, and tractor-drawn hay rides that are offered around the camp. Tentsites start at $15-16 d, plus $2.50 for electricity, $1.50 for sewer, water included. It's on Hwy. 97B, tel. 832-6489, next to the R.J. Haney Heritage House. **Salmon River Motel and Campground** has shady tent and RV sites beside the river (a couple of salmon do mosey by), behind the motel, starting at $10 per night, plus $2 electricity, $1 water, sewer included. Free showers and laundry facilities. Rooms with kitchenettes range from $32 s, $39 d, plus an extra $3 to use the stove unless you're just making a cup of tea or coffee. Just down the road a store sells fresh fruit and tasty apple cider. It's at 910 40th St. Southwest, tel. 832-3065.

The Eatery, on Alexander St. NE, downtown, does a brisk soup-and-sandwich business. Eat in or outside on the small patio. For Canadian fare with a delicious salad bar and family prices, the **Brass Kettle** on the Trans-Canada Hwy. (west end of town) is a safe bet. The **Orchard House** on 22nd St. off the Trans-Canada Hwy. on the eastern outskirts of town is where the locals splurge—main courses start at $12; dressy. The **Shuswap Lake Estates** Golf Club is another local favorite for fine dining—try the **Log 'N Hearth Restaurant,** which overlooks the golf course. It's at Blind Bay on the Trans-Canada Hwy. (a 15-minute drive west of Salmon Arm); for reservations phone 675-4433.

The **Salmon Arm Chamber of Commerce and Travel InfoCentre** on the Trans-Canada Hwy. is open year-round Mon.-Fri. 0830-1700. The seasonal Travel InfoCentre is on the Trans-Canada Hwy. east of downtown, open daily in summer 0830-2000. The **Greyhound bus depot** is at the Village West Mall on the main highway. **Salmon Arm Airport** is at 4402 20th Ave. Southeast. **Shuswap Air** offers scenic flights, charters, and scheduled flights to Kelowna and Vancouver; for more info, dial 832-8830.

Salmon Arm To Kamloops

The Trans-Canada Hwy. winds along pretty, sparkling **Shuswap Lake,** passing the turnoff (48 km west of Salmon Arm) at Squilax Bridge to **Haig-Brown Park** and **Adams Lake.** One of the best reasons to sidetrack here, aside from exploring the north side of Shuswap Lake, is to visit the gravel beds of the **Adams River,** protected spawning ground of the sockeye salmon. Every four years like clockwork, the dominant Adams sockeye return here. In intervening years you can see other species of sockeye—but the dominant run (1994, 1998, etc.) is most spectacular. Wear sturdy footwear and walk the network of paths and platforms to see the red and green salmon laying thousands of pale orange eggs, fertilizing them, and then dying. The life cycle of this magnificent fish is colorfully depicted on display boards. The most exciting time to see all the salmon is during the second and third weeks of October.

After the community of **Chase,** the hills of the Thompson Plateau get drier and browner, the road closely follows the railway lines and the sapphire-blue South Thompson River, and there are fewer and fewer trees—welcome to sprinkler country! Not far beyond the Hwy. 1/97 (to Vernon) intersection, 27 km east of Kamloops, is **Kamloops Vacationland, Waterslide, RV Park, and Wildlife Park,** tel. 573-3789 or 374-7446. The waterslide is open on weekends in May, daily to Sept.; the RV Park is open May-Oct.; the Wildlife Park is open Oct.-June 0800-1600 and July-Sept. 0800-2000. Admission is adult $5, senior and child $2.50.

KAMLOOPS

HOT AND BROWN, COLD AND WHITE

The Shuswap Indians were the first people to live in this region, basing their life-style on hunting and salmon fishing. Founded in 1812 as a fur-trading depot of the North West Company, Kamloops sprang into being at the junction of the north and south branches of the Thompson River where the water then flows westward into long, narrow **Kamloops Lake.** Named after the Shuswap Indian word for "Confluence" or "Meeting of the Waters," Kamloops is certainly appropriately named. Aside from the merging of the rivers, the Canadian Pacific and Canadian National railways converge here, and major highways meet from all directions of the compass. Today Kamloops is the largest city in the southern interior (pop. 65,000), and fifth largest in the province—a vital transportation and commercial center for the region.

Over the years all kinds of colorful characters have passed through or lived here—fur traders, explorers, gold miners (from the Cariboo and Kootenay gold rushes of the 1860s), cattle ranchers, railway builders, and farmers. Sternwheelers plied the inland waters dropping off passengers and collecting lumber, but the arrival of the railway in Kamloops contributed the most to the development of the region. The Canadian Pacific Railway line was completed in 1885. Settlers flocked in on the trains; lumber and cattle were chugged out. The Canadian Northern Railway (now the Canadian National Railway) was completed in 1915, and Kamloops became a major transportation center. Today most of the residents are in some way involved with the forest industry (logging or pulp, paper, plywood, or lumber production), copper mining, cattle or sheep ranching, or tourism.

Touted as "Canada's Sunshine Capital," Kamloops is known for its sunny, dry climate. It's hot and dry in summer when river rafting on the Thompson is at its best, and anglers come to catch Kamloops trout in more than 200 regional lakes and streams. It's cold, with plenty of snow, in winter; skiers come to swoosh down the slopes of 2,131-meter **Tod Mountain** (53 km north) or nearby **Harper Mountain,** or go cross-country skiing or ice fishing at **Lac Le Jeune** to the south (access from the Coquihalla Highway).

As you enter the city from the east, the highway zips through a bare, parched landscape of gently rolling hills—semi-desert land kept bearable by the presence of the mighty Thompson River. The brown hills of summer really set off the deep-blue river and lush green parks of Kamloops. Passing **Kamloops Wildlife Park** (over 150 animals) and adjacent **Waterslide** and **RV Park,** a large number of motels, stores, fast-food restaurants, shopping centers, and gas stations, take the Battle St. exit (becomes Lansdowne; stay south of the river) to downtown. City center lies along the south side of the Thompson River junction, with suburbs spread out and sprawling up the hills to the immediate south and the equally hilly north

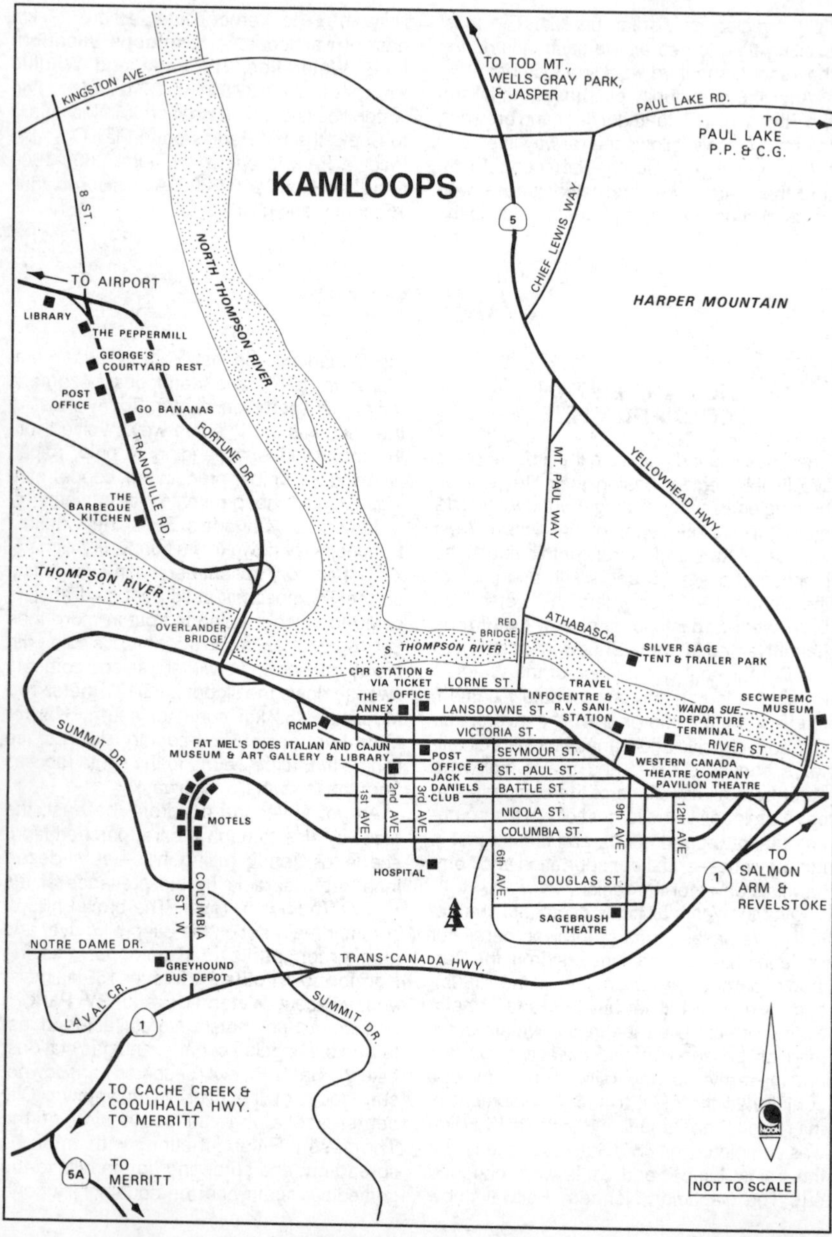

KAMLOOPS

KINGSTON AVE.
TO TOD MT., WELLS GRAY PARK, & JASPER
PAUL LAKE RD.
TO PAUL LAKE P.P. & C.G.
8 ST.
5
CHIEF LEWIS WAY
NORTH THOMPSON RIVER
TO AIRPORT
HARPER MOUNTAIN
LIBRARY
THE PEPPERMILL
GEORGE'S COURTYARD REST.
POST OFFICE
GO BANANAS
FORTUNE DR.
TRANQUILLE RD.
MT. PAUL WAY
YELLOWHEAD HWY.
THE BARBEQUE KITCHEN
THOMPSON RIVER
OVERLANDER BRIDGE
RED BRIDGE
ATHABASCA
S. THOMPSON RIVER
SILVER SAGE TENT & TRAILER PARK
CPR STATION & VIA TICKET OFFICE
LORNE ST.
TRAVEL INFOCENTRE & R.V. SANI STATION
THE ANNEX
LANSDOWNE ST.
SECWEPEMC MUSEUM
RCMP
VICTORIA ST.
WANDA SUE DEPARTURE TERMINAL
RIVER ST.
FAT MEL'S DOES ITALIAN AND CAJUN
MUSEUM & ART GALLERY & LIBRARY
POST OFFICE & JACK DANIELS CLUB
SEYMOUR ST.
ST. PAUL ST.
BATTLE ST.
WESTERN CANADA THEATRE COMPANY PAVILION THEATRE
SUMMIT DR.
MOTELS
1st AVE.
2nd AVE.
3rd AVE.
NICOLA ST.
COLUMBIA ST.
9th AVE.
12th AVE.
HOSPITAL
6th AVE.
DOUGLAS ST.
TO SALMON ARM & REVELSTOKE
1
COLUMBIA ST. W
SAGEBRUSH THEATRE
NOTRE DAME DR.
GREYHOUND BUS DEPOT
TRANS-CANADA HWY.
LAVAL CR.
1
SUMMIT DR.
TO CACHE CREEK & COQUIHALLA HWY. TO MERRITT
5A
TO MERRITT
NOT TO SCALE

side of the river (access by Overlander Bridge). Turn right on 10th Ave. to start your exploration of this region at the **Kamloops Chamber of Commerce and Travel Info-Centre** (no. 10, far end).

SIGHTS

Kamloops Museum

This museum is another nonstuffy one, well worth a visit; allow an hour or two. See everything there is to see (and there's plenty) and you may feel as though you've just completed a crash course in Kamloop's Past 101. The displays cover local Indian culture, the fur trade (peek in the reconstructed fur trader's cabin), pioneer days, natural history (more taxidermied critters), industry, and transportation. There's also a furnished turn-of-the-century living area, a stable complete with horse gear and carriage, a blacksmith shop, paddlewheels, old wall clocks and cameras, and a 15-minute slide presentation on the history of the city. Kamloops Art Gallery in the same building has modern works of art in all sorts of media by contemporary artists—quite a contrast to the museum, with its items from the past! Both are at 207 Seymour St.; open daily in summer 1000-2100, Tues.-Sat. 1000-1700 the rest of the year, tel. 828-3576. Admission free but donations accepted.

Hit The Water In Old-fashioned Style

One of the best ways to appreciate the city and some of its history is to take to the water the way they did in the late 1860s—by cruising on the Thompson River in a reconstructed sternwheeler, the *Wanda Sue*. The boat departs several times a day May-Sept. (get your ticket from the wharf ticket office up to one hour before sailing) for a two-hour cruise, and light meals and alcoholic beverages are available onboard; from adult $9, senior $8, child $5. For current times and more info, call 374-1505 or 374-7447. The *Wanda Sue* departs from the terminal at the **Old Yacht Club Public Wharf** on River St. (from the Info-Centre on 10th, head toward the river and you'll come to it).

Secwepemc Museum

To find out more about the Shuswap Indians, their history and rich mythology, and to see archaeological treasures found on local reserves and a model of a traditional summer shelter, take Hwy. 5 North across the river (via the Yellowhead Bridge) and turn right immediately after the bridge at the sign, **Kamloops Indian Band.** The museum is in the historic Kamloops Indian Residential School Building on the Kamloops Indian Reserve at 345 Yellowhead Highway. It's open Mon.-Fri. 0830-1630; admission is free but donations are accepted. For more info, phone 374-0616.

Paul Lake Provincial Park

This small 402-hectare provincial park northeast of Kamloops is a relaxing, grassy, tree-shaded spot to take a picnic, go swimming in warm Paul Lake, or camp (see "Accommodations," below). And the drive out there, following Paul Creek through scrub-covered rolling hills and flower-filled meadows is an enjoyable ramble through the countryside (watch out for cows making suicidal saunters onto the road). This is also the way to **Harper Mountain Ski Area.** At the picnic area and beach (separate from the campground but connected by trail or road), edged by grassy, tree-shaded banks, are picnic tables, toilets, and changing rooms. The picnic area attracts its fair share of locals on a hot summer's day.

PRACTICALITIES

Accommodations

The campground closest to downtown is **Silver Sage Tent and Trailer Park** at 771 East Athabasca, tel. 372-9644. Shady river-frontage campsites, hookups, showers, and laundromat; open May-November. If it's really hot and staying by a waterslide grabs your attention, **Kamloops Waterslide and RV Park,** about 26 km east of town on the Trans-Canada Hwy., may be just what the doctor ordered. It has full hookups, hot metered showers, laundry facilities, sani-dump, handi-

George's Courtyard Restaurant

capped facilities, and barbecue pits. It's open May-Oct., tel. 573-3789; expect to pay from $8-12 d, plus $1.50 for electricity, $1.50 for sewer, and $1 for water.

The most scenic campground in the area (if you don't mind the lack of a shower and a bit of a drive) is **Paul Lake Provincial Park Campground** (see "Sights," above). Tree-shaded campsites are $8 per night, seniors $4. Drinking water and toilets are provided. Trails lead from the campground down to Paul Lake, the beach, and the picnic area. This is a popular camping spot in summer, especially on weekends.

Kamloops has a large number of motels, hotels, and inns. Most of them flank the Trans-Canada Hwy. at the eastern outskirts of town, and another handful flank Columbia St. West (the western access to downtown). Cruise past and see which appeals. Prices generally start out around $30 s, $35 d and go all the way up! **Thrift Inn** at 2459 East Trans-Canada Hwy. (on the eastern outskirts of town) has a heated pool and reasonable room rates—from $22.95-35.95 s (depending on the season) and $25.95-37.95 d. For full listings refer to the free *Accommodations Guide* put out by the Ministry of Tourism.

Food And Entertainment

For a quick sandwich downtown, locals head for the **Annex Sidewalk Cafe** on the corner of 3rd and Lansdowne. Whether you munch inside or out on the patio, it's usually busy. Those with larger appetites should head for **Fat Mel's Does Italian and Cajun** on Seymour St. between 2nd and 3rd, across from the museum. Settle into one of the cane chairs amongst the plants, stuffed birds, and antler ornaments, and spend the next 15 minutes laughing at the menu. Daily soup and sandwich specials start at around $4, pasta dishes at $5, and they have many tasty salads ranging $5.55-9.99. Dinners—veal, chicken, steak, ribs, pasta, and spaghetti—range $7-15. The specialty of the house is "Fat Mel's moo bones," spicy Louisiana fare, and Italian dishes. It's open Tues.-Sat. from 1100-2300—"you never tasted anythin' like it!"

One of the best places to eat is the **Peppermill Restaurant**, on the north side of town at 755 Tranquille St. at the corner of Renfrew Ave., open daily from 0630, tel. 376-7344. Specializing in "buffet extravaganzas" for $9.95, you can also get tasty sandwiches for $4-7, a sandwich special and salad bar at lunch for $4.95, and main dishes for $6-11. For an eye-popping, attention-getting, extremely filling dinner, order the Peppermill Gourmet for $6.75! It's a real conversation-starter.

George's Courtyard Restaurant at 501 Tranquille Rd. (tel. 376-1500) is another good place to try. Choose from a variety of Mediterranean foods, but the Greek is especially good. The cool pink-and-gray decor is soothing on a hot summer day; outdoor dining on the patio is also an option. Greek lunches are $5.50-8.50, sandwiches $4.50-6.50. At dinner, salads are $5-7.50, Greek dishes $9-13, Italian dishes $6.50-10.50, steak and lobster $13-18. Leave some room for one of their sinful desserts—the huge portion of deep-fried ice cream covered in whipped cream and strawberries is something to write home about! Open daily 1100-1430 and 1630-2300.

The **Barbecue Kitchen** at 273 Tranquille Rd. is noted locally for its particularly good traditional Chinese fare. Dishes range $4.50-10 and you get ample portions for the price, specialties $6-10. Take-out is also available; tel. 376-0333. It's open Tues.-Sat. 1200-2100, Sun. 1700-2100.

Go Bananas nightclub at 348 Tranquille Rd. is popular with the college crowd, featuring comedy or other live entertainment in the evenings, dancing, and drinking ("proper dress" required); tel. 376-1292. **Jack Daniels Club** is another bar with a dance floor and plenty of local color! Feeling loony? Join Aussies in a sing-along or tuck in to some good finger food, sandwiches, salads, or burgers at **Loonies Pub** in The Place Inn, 1285 West Trans-Canada Highway. For classic and pop performances by the **Kamloops Symphony Orchestra** (amateurs and professionals), the **Sagebrush Theatre** is the place to check out. It's in the Senior High School on 10th Avenue. The **Western Canada Theatre Company** in the Pavilion Theatre just across 10th Ave. from the Travel InfoCentre has live theater productions by top Canadian actors, producers, and designers. If you're looking for a movie theater, Kamloops has plenty (six within three blocks downtown)—pick up a free city map at the Travel InfoCentre, marked with all of their locations.

Information And Services

Kamloops Chamber of Commerce and Travel InfoCentre at 10 10th Ave. is open in winter Mon.-Fri. 0900-1700, in summer daily 0800-2000, tel. 374-3377. There is also another seasonal InfoCentre on the outskirts of the city—in a cattle car and caboose on the Yellowhead Hwy. N off Halston Avenue. Both provide visitors with a detailed map of the city, brochures, and info (all free). The **Royal Inland Hospital** is at the south end of 3rd St. at 311 Columbia St., tel. 374-5111. For an **ambulance** in an emergency, call 911; non-emergency, call 374-4411. The **RCMP** is at 455 Columbia St., tel. 372-5511. The **post office** is at 301 Seymour St., tel. 374-2444.

Transportation

The **VIA Rail office** is at 95 3rd Ave. behind Lansdowne. VIA Rail (tel. 800-561-8630) runs train service northeast to Clearwater, Blue River, Valemount, and on to Jasper, and west to Ashcroft, North Bend, Yale, Agassiz, Mission, Port Coquitlam, and Vancouver. The **Greyhound Bus Station** is at 725 Notre Dame Dr. (off the Columbia St. W exit from the Trans-Canada Hwy. at the west end of town), tel. (800) 661-8747; Greyhound provides daily service to most parts of the province. **Kamloops Airport** is on Airport Rd., seven km northwest of city center (go through North Shore on Tranquille Rd. until you come to Airport Rd. on the left); serviced by **Air B.C.** and **Time Air.** Local bus transportation is provided by **Kamloops Transit Service;** adult fare $1, student 80 cents, senior 65 cents, adult day pass (ride anywhere all day long) $2.50, student $2, senior $1.65. For a schedule and route info, call in at 1550 Ord Rd., Mon.-Fri. 0830-1630, or phone 376-1216. For 24-hour airport limo and taxi service call **Kami Cabs** at 374-5151.

Highways From Kamloops

From Kamloops highways lead in all directions. Choose between Hwy. 5 northeast to stunning **Wells Gray Park** (you may want to stock up on groceries and supplies in Kamloops, though most necessities are available in Clearwater) and on to **Mount Robson Park** and **Jasper** (six hours away) in the Canadian Rockies, the Trans-Canada Hwy.

west to **Cache Creek** and into the Cariboo. If you're heading south to Vancouver, Hwy. 5 to **Merritt** and the Coquihalla Hwy. is the most direct route (3½ hours), Hwy. 1 to **Cache Creek**, then down the Thompson and Fraser rivers to Vancouver, is longer (five hours) but gives you the opportunity to raft the Thompson from several places along the way. Both routes are scenic, and hot and dry in summer—take something cool to drink.

FABULOUS FIVE— THE YELLOWHEAD HIGHWAY NORTH

Kamloops To Clearwater

The magnificent Yellowhead Hwy., named after a light-haired Iroquois trapper who guided many of the Hudson's Bay Company men through a pass (later named Yellowhead) in the late 1800s and early 1900s, closely follows the North Thompson River to **Tete Jaune Cache.** Passing the Heffley Station Rd. turnoff to **Tod Mountain Ski Area** at **Heffley Creek,** the Thompson River winds through lush green pastures (a mass of sprinklers showering the land with spray in summer) and forested areas, then through a steep ravine with the ever-present railway tracks running along the edge. As you continue north, the wide, glassy Thompson winds through rolling emerald-green meadows and swathed fields scattered with giant pinwheels of hay, and up and down low, tree-covered hills, giving pleasing snapshot opportunities at frequent intervals.

Clearwater

The small town of Clearwater is rather spread out—a few motels, restaurants, gas stations, services, and an InfoCentre are on the highway, the rest of the community is off the highway to the south. For those exploring nearby **Wells Gray Provincial Park** (if you have at least half a day to spare, don't miss it!), the town is a good base. Several campgrounds lie within the park, but for hot showers and other pleasures, Clearwater has what you need. The best and most reasonable place to stay is **Jasper Way Inn** on the shores of beautiful **Dutch Lake.** Wake up to a view of a wildflower-edged, glassy lake with tree-covered hills on the far side and small snow-covered mountains in the distance (great reflection shots on a still day). Beside it is a public lakeside park with a picnic area and lots of semitame feathered friends waiting for handouts, a public beach, an offshore pontoon, and restrooms. Motel rooms start at $28-33 s, $32-38 d, $34-40 t, kitchen available for an extra $4; it's at 57 East Old Thompson Hwy. (get there by turning north off the main highway onto the Old North Thompson Hwy. and continue about two blocks), tel. 674-3345. Several other motels, lodges, and inns in the Clearwater area provide rooms for $32-89 s, $44-89 d, a bed and breakfast has rooms $28-35 per night, and two campgrounds have sites ranging $10-16 a night. Get all the details at the InfoCentre.

At the highway junction in summer there's an ice-cream booth called **Ice Cream Adventure** (enormous cones are $1), and across the highway a booth where you can arrange a whitewater rafting trip through **Clearwater Raft Trip,** tel. 674-3354. A half-day trip (three to four hours) on the Clearwater River (grade two to four) starts around $30 pp, and wetsuits can be hired for an extra $10 pp (if you feel the cold this is a very good investment!). In winter this area attracts a good number of cross-country skiers. Continue east along Hwy. 5 and you come to the turnoff to Wells Gray Provincial Park, a gas station/store/Greyhound bus station, and **Clearwater and District Chamber of Commerce and Business InfoCentre.** Hungry? Take rumbling stomachs to the **Caboose Restaurant** on the other side of the main highway. At the takeaway window, sandwiches, meals, and drinks can be quickly obtained and enjoyed outside at the picnic tables—or go inside for a sit-down hamburger, sandwich, salad, or main meal for $6-14.

WELLS GRAY PROVINCIAL PARK

Before you venture into this 5,200-square-km wilderness park, call in at the excellent **Info-Centre** on the corner of the access road and Hwy. 5 (across from the gas station)—just look for the life-size steel moose that solemnly faces Hwy. 5 (and the eye of many a camera). Staff members enthusiastically produce brochures on local activities, detailed park info and models of the park, topographical maps (a must if you're getting off the beaten track), trail maps and descriptions, self-guided tour sheets for 50 cents each, geological info, and weather conditions. Pick up a free *Wells Gray Provincial Park and Recreation Area* brochure, put out by the Ministry of Lands and Parks, which shows all the trails, lakes, campsites, roadside attractions, and picnic areas. The center is open Sept. through May Mon.-Sat. 0900-1700 and Sun. 1000-1700, daily in June and Oct. 0900-1800, and daily in July and Aug. 0800-2000. If you really want to get to know this park, the book *Exploring Wells Gray Park,* by Roland Neave, has detailed coverage; available at the InfoCentre gift shop for $6.95. Also check out *Nature Wells Gray* for $9.95.

Helmcken Falls

Imagine snow-clad peaks, extinct volcanoes and ancient lava flows, amazing waterfalls—so many the park is often referred to as the "Waterfall Park"—icy mineral springs, subalpine forest and flower-filled meadows, and an abundance of lakes and rivers where canoeists can make a 102-km roundtrip and anglers can fish to their heart's content for rainbow trout and Dolly Varden. This is Wells Gray Park! You can take a half-day drive up Wells Gray Park Rd., stopping to do short walks to all the waterfalls and signposted roadway attractions (best to allow a leisurely day and take a picnic), or hike off into the wilderness and not see anyone else for as long you wish. The road is paved for 47 km from Clearwater to Helmcken Falls, then gravel for 16 km to the end. It's a good road, but dusty in summer; slushy in winter but usually cleared of snow as far as Helmcken Falls. Stock up on supplies (including insect repellent and film), and buy your fishing license and gas before you leave Clearwater—there are no services (aside from a couple of lodges) along the access road once you leave town.

Highlights On The Road To The Park

The road follows the Clearwater River for about 10 km to the first attraction outside the park, **Spahats Creek Provincial Park.** A short trail from the parking lot leads you along the creek-carved, 122-meter-deep, red and gray lava canyon to gaze in awe at 61-meter **Spahats Creek Falls** from an observation platform. The red, orange, yellow, and brown

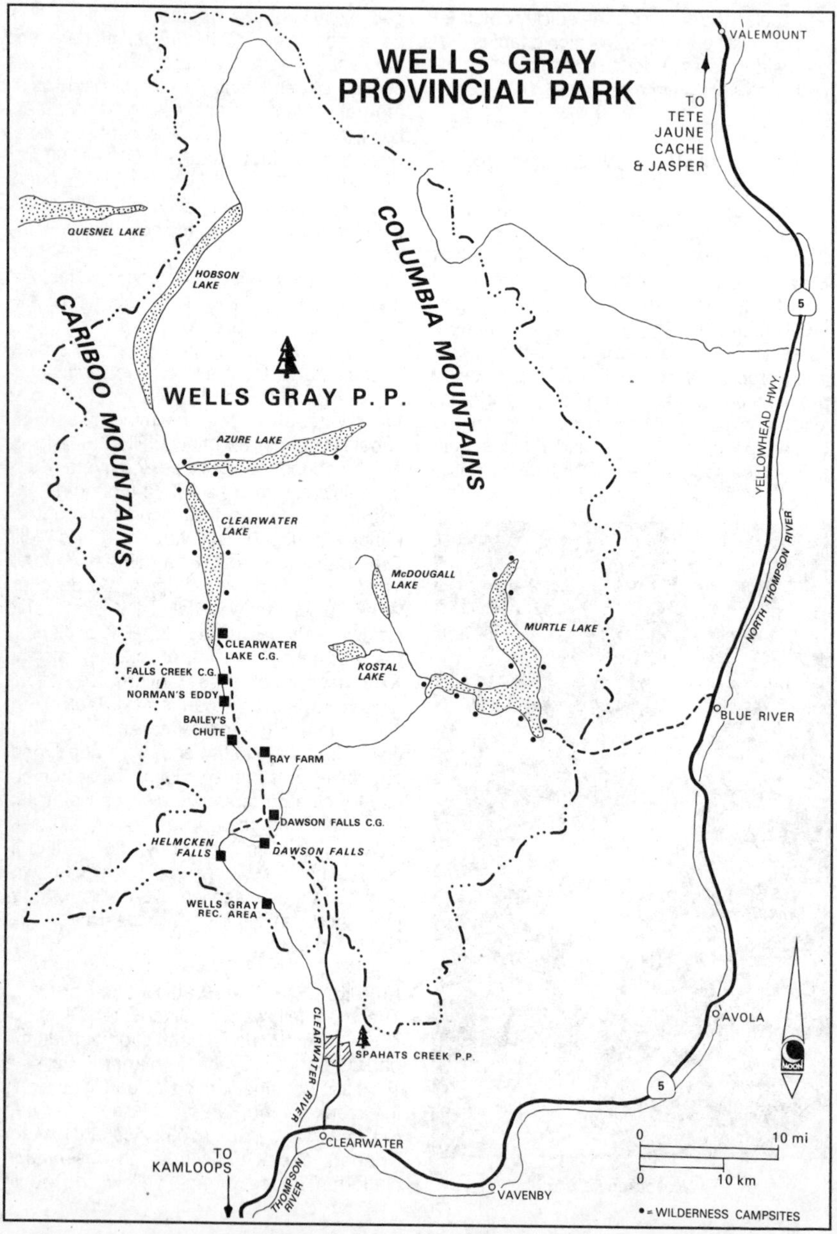

WELLS GRAY PROVINCIAL PARK

VALEMOUNT
TO TETE JAUNE CACHE & JASPER
QUESNEL LAKE
HOBSON LAKE
CARIBOO MOUNTAINS
COLUMBIA MOUNTAINS
WELLS GRAY P. P.
AZURE LAKE
CLEARWATER LAKE
McDOUGALL LAKE
MURTLE LAKE
KOSTAL LAKE
CLEARWATER LAKE C.G.
FALLS CREEK C.G.
NORMAN'S EDDY
BAILEY'S CHUTE
RAY FARM
DAWSON FALLS C.G.
HELMCKEN FALLS
DAWSON FALLS
WELLS GRAY REC. AREA
SPAHATS CREEK P.P.
CLEARWATER RIVER
CLEARWATER
TO KAMLOOPS
THOMPSON RIVER
VAVENBY
AVOLA
BLUE RIVER
NORTH THOMPSON RIVER
YELLOWHEAD HWY.
5
5
MOON
0 10 mi
0 10 km
• = WILDERNESS CAMPSITES

colorations of the cliff are highlighted just before sunset. The water plummets down the cliff in a narrow silver ribbon into a wide pool before merging with the Clearwater River. Back on the road, a 15-km gravel road to the right and a 1½-km hike, or a 45-minute cross-country ski trip, leads you to the **Trophy Mountain Wells Gray Recreation Area** where, in summer, the wildflowers put on a spectacular display and grizzly bears are sometimes seen (take a noisemaker so that any bears hear you coming).

Continuing toward the park, gorgeous views of the Clearwater canyon are seen from the road where in summer the shoulders are intensely white with daisies—if you didn't know better you'd swear it had just snowed! **Wells Gray Guest Ranch,** surrounded by grassy meadows full of wildflowers and grazing horses, provides unserviced campsites for $10 per site, toilets, picnic tables, fire pits and wood, cabins from $20-60 s or twin, optional hayrides and barbecues, one- to two-week canoe or trail-riding trips, boat trips, and whitewater rafting on the Clearwater; free pick-up or drop-off in Clearwater. For more info and reservations call **Stoney Mountain Wilderness Adventures** at 674-2774/2792. At the park boundary, **Helmcken Falls Lodge** (32 km from Clearwater) has a great view of meadows, tree-covered mountains, and distant peaks. Campsites and full hookups (hot showers) are $10-14 per night. Motel units are $59-89 s or d, and the lodge provides licensed dining, a store, a gift shop, horseback riding, canoes, and guides. For more info, call 674-3657.

Park Attractions

Thirty-six km from the InfoCentre, 10-meter-high **Green Viewing Tower** stands atop **Green Mountain.** This towering viewpoint allows appreciation of many spectacular, rugged peaks, including Pyramid Mountain, a volcanic cone, and Garnet Peak, highest in the park and covered with snow most of the year. Interpretive panels provide plenty of informative reading. After entering Wells Gray Park, take the first gravel road to the left—this winding road leads to the top of the mountain.

Of the park's numerous trailheads (all well marked and described in the park brochure), be sure to stop at **Dawson Falls** (38 km from Clearwater). Here the **Murtle River** turns into a miniature but still spectacular Niagara Falls, 91 meters wide and 18 meters high. A short path leads to several viewpoints—go armed with insect repellent in summer. **Dawson Falls Campground** (water, toilets, firewood; $8 per night May-Oct.) is also located here. A little farther along the main road is the **Mush Bowl** (or Devil's Punchbowl), where the river has carved huge holes in the riverbed rock. The next place to stop is incredible **Helmcken Falls** (47 km from Clearwater), fourth-highest falls in the province. The Murtle River cascades off the edge of Murtle Plateau in a 137-meter sparkling torrent to join the Clearwater River. It's just as spectacular in winter when an enormous ice cone (equal in size to a 20-story building) rises up from the plunge pool base. Several viewpoints allow the photo buff to go hog wild! This is also a popular spot with prewedding photographers and bridal parties in full regalia.

Ray Farm Trail is an enjoyable 15-minute trail to the historic abandoned farm of John Bunyon Ray, the first pioneer to homestead in this area. He cleared his farm out of the wilderness in 1912 and he and his wife raised a family in this almost completely isolated spot. The picturesque abandoned farm buildings are amongst rolling meadows full of wildflowers, but douse yourself in insect repellent before you set off in summer or you'll be doing the "Aussie wave" to ward off large divebombing flies, mosquitos, and bees. Some years the insects are so bad (the biting no-see-ums are the worst—they go for your hairline, neck, and behind your ears and leave large, itchy lumps) that a head-to-toe beekeeper's outfit or spacesuit should be required trailwear! Another short trail leads from the farm to Ray's Mineral Springs.

The next short 10-minute trail (look for the info board describing salmon) leads through one of the remaining stands of cedar trees (most cedars were destroyed in an enormous fire in the 1920s) to **Bailey's Chute.** At the river are two water chutes where, in fall, great numbers of chinook salmon battle the torrent. This is, however, as far as they get—after a number of valiant attempts (great photos from the viewing platform early morning or late afternoon in Aug. and Sept.), they're washed back downstream to the gravel beds where they spawn and die. Farther up the road, mountain-surrounded **Shadow Lake,** with its small stream and lilies, provides yet another great photo opportunity. To the left is the 20-minute trail to **Norman's Eddy,** where the Clearwater River temporarily reverses its direction in a quiet pool only a few meters from the main flow (look for animal tracks). **Falls Creek Campground** (water, toilets, firewood) has spacious riverside sites for $8 pp per night (May-October).

Clearwater Lake Campground, almost at the end of the road, has water, toilets, sani-dump facilities, firewood, and naturalist talks in summer. It's also particularly popular with canoeists, boaters, and anglers, as it's right on the edge of the lake and has boat-launching facilities; $8 pp per night, May-October. In summer **Clearwater Lake Tours** runs a four-hour trip from Clearwater Lake Campground (departing at 1000) to **Azure Lake** for adult $32, senior $27, child 8-16 years $22, up to eight years $5. They also provide canoe rentals for $25 a day or $125 a week, and a water taxi service; tel. 674-3052 or 674-2121.

Several lengthy trails lead to lakes, lava beds, and a volcanic cone. The road dead-ends at 25-km-long, tree-edged **Clearwater Lake** (64 km from the town of Clearwater) and a boat launch (fishing info here). This lake, one of six major ones in the park, was created when an ancient lava flow blocked the valley. Several wilderness campsites are located around the lake; $5 per night per vessel site is charged June through September. One of the most popular things to do here, aside from hiking off into the wilderness, is to boat from Clearwater Lake to 24-km-long **Azure Lake** (to see **Rainbow Falls**) and back, making a 102-km RT—rainbow trout fishing as you go! Canoeists: portage of one-half km is required due to swift, rough water, and during June and July canoe portage is accessible only to experienced paddlers. Boats with 9.9 HP motors or over have no trouble navigating the Azure River between Clearwater and Azure lakes. Wilderness campsites are also located around Azure Lake; $5 per night per vessel site. Be aware that the water temperature of these lakes is very cold, and sudden, violent storms can blow up seemingly from nowhere—go prepared!

The central and rugged northern area of Wells Gray Park is a vast wilderness of tall peaks, dense forests, and lakes and rivers—it can only be reached on foot. It's also the part of the park where the animals like to hang out—mountain goats, caribou, moose, mule deer, and brown and grizzly bears. Access into the east side of the park is by a 24-km gravel road off Hwy. 5 just north of the community of **Blue River,** then a 2½-km hike (half an hour) to the eastern shoreline of **Murtle Lake,** largest freshwater lake in the park—it's a canoeist's paradise (restricted to canoes only) offering the added bonuses of sandy beaches and excellent fishing. Many wilderness campsites are located around Murtle Lake; $5 per night per vessel site.

AND THE BEAUTY CONTINUES

Continuing northeast along Hwy. 5, the road meanders through beautiful forest-covered hills and lush green meadows following the North Thompson River and the railway tracks, passing through a few small communities with a motel and gas station here and there. In summer a mass of wildflowers adds splashes of glorious color to the landscape. Just north of **Blue River** is the eastern access road (24 km of gravel) to Wells Gray Park. The road finishes before you reach the park boundary, then it's a short walk to **Murtle Lake** and several wilderness campsites (see above). North of Blue River the road winds through high mountains, then open valleys—in some areas the countryside is carpeted in yellow wildflowers. The mountains get higher and higher as you approach the town of **Valemount,** a cross-country skier's paradise in winter (turn right at the

entrance to Mount Robson Provincial Park

Tourist InfoCentre; open daily 0800-2000). Continuing north, if you're peckish stop at **Tete Jaune Cache** and grab a bite at the **Tete Jaune Motel Restaurant** beside the peaceful Fraser River. You'll get real homestyle cooking (delicious apple pie) for $4-7, and equally delicious river views.

Turn east on beautiful, daisy-edged Hwy. 16, following the milky-blue Fraser River through forested hills with a background of jagged mountains (you'll be scrambling for your camera around every bend) toward Jasper (100 km), and you come to the **Mount Terry Fox Viewpoint** and park. The mountain was named after Terry Fox, a 22-year-old British Columbian who lost his leg to cancer but courageously ran 5,375 km across a section of Canada on an artificial limb to raise funds for cancer research.

MOUNT ROBSON PROVINCIAL PARK

Cross the Robson River and you cross the western boundary of spectacular Mount Robson Provincial Park in the Canadian Rocky Mountains—217,200 hectares of rugged mountain peaks permanently blanketed in snow and ice, steep canyons and wide forested valleys, icy lakes, rivers, and streams, bordered on the east by Jasper National Park. The impressive focal point is magnificent 3,954-meter **Mt. Robson,** highest peak in the Canadian Rockies, towering over the western entrance of the park. The Indians used to call it Yuh-Hai-Has-Hun, "Mountain Of The Spiral Road." Today it's referred to as the Monarch of the Rockies (no one knows for sure how the mountain became known as Mt. Robson). Within the park spruce, fir, cedar, balsam, alder, lodgepole pine, and birch trees can all be found growing up to the tree line—above are jagged rocks and rugged snowcapped peaks. All sorts of wildlife can be seen off the beaten track—marmot, pika, chipmunks, mule deer, black bear, mountain goat, caribou, moose, and grizzly bear, along with more than 170 species of birds.

The south face of Mt. Robson can easily be admired from the west end of the park, but try and save some film for the view from the Visitor Centre, where the mountain towers above. Running through the middle of the park is the Yellowhead Hwy. (open year-round), making access easy. This park can be enjoyed from the highway or by trail, and it attracts outdoor enthusiasts in search of wilderness hiking, backcountry camping, demanding mountain climbing (particularly difficult because the mountain makes its own bad weather), canoeing, horseback riding—and adventure.

A number of lengthy trails lead from the highway along rivers to waterfalls, lakes, and high mountain glaciers, joining other extensive trail networks. One of the most popular is **Berg Lake Trail,** which climbs 22 km along the Robson River into the high country, passing **Kinney Lake,** entering the aptly named **Valley of the Thousand Falls** and the **Whitehorn Valley** to arrive at beautiful **Berg Lake** (allow up to two days OW). Above the lake towers Mt. Robson, with its stunning icy-blue **Berg Glacier** mantle which sheds large ice chunks into the water at fairly regular intervals—hence the name Berg Lake. A seasonal ranger station, several wilderness campsites, and cooking shelters are located along the lake, and you can do several dayhikes from this point or join other lengthy trail networks. Get all the details and maps at the Visitor Centre.

Information And Services

Start your discovery of the park at the **Mt. Robson Visitor Centre,** lying in the shadow of mighty Mt. Robson. The view of the large, daisy-filled meadow, dark green forest, and mighty mountain above is outrageous on a clear sunny day—if it's raining or obscured by clouds, you'll just *have* to come back! The center is open daily in summer 0800-1600, 0800-2000 in the peak summer months, closed from the end of Sept. to June.

The free *Mount Robson Provincial Park* brochure put out by the Ministry of Lands and Parks is handy if you're only driving through, but hikers and climbers need to collect the free trail maps and descriptions and buy a topographical map (essential if you're heading into the backcountry). The nature house (0800-1800) has informative slide shows on the natural history of the area; in summer evening programs are held behind the Visitor Centre at 2000, and guided walks are led by park interpreters—check out the current schedule. Across the parking lot from the Visitor Centre is a gas station and popular **Cafe Mount Robson,** with awe-inspiring views.

Park Campgrounds And Commercial Facilities

Just down the road from the center are several campgrounds along the Fraser River. The three park campgrounds are **Robson Meadows** and **Robson River** near the western boundary (west of the Visitor Centre), and **Lucerne** 10 km west of the eastern park boundary. All provide water, toilets, and firewood, and showers are available at Meadows and Rivers campgrounds, but no hook-

Mount Fitzwilliam (2,911 m) can be appreciated from the highway.

ups (Robson Meadows has a sani station); from $8 per night.

Mount Robson Ranch, off the highway to the south on Hargreaves Rd., provides campsites for $10, units for $50-60 s, $59-69 d, and horse riding; for more info and reservations, phone 566-4370. **Robson Shadows Campground** five km west of the park on Hwy. 16 has campsites with partial hookups for $10-13, a store, and a coffee shop; for more info and reservations, call 566-4821. **Emperor Ridge Campground** has heated washrooms and showers; $10 per night, tel. 566-4714. Contact **Mount Robson Adventure Holidays** at 566-4351 for guided canoeing/backpacking trips and equipment rentals.

Highway Scenics

Heading east from the Visitor Centre, the highway meanders past the trailhead for pretty **Overlander Falls** (15 minutes RT), and then sapphire, emerald, and turquoise five-km-long **Moose Lake,** with waterfalls on the far side—a lovely spot to put in a canoe. If you're lucky you may see a moose moosing around in Moose Lake, one of their favorite places to frolic (have your camera ready). The road, edged with white daisies, blood-red Indian paintbrush, and pale-pink wild roses in summer, continues past **Moose Marsh** where the Moose River joins the Fraser. The marsh is loaded with waterfowl (pull off the highway and sit quietly, telephoto lens in hand, and you'll be surprised how many birds you will see) and everywhere you look are amazingly bright green, grassy marshes. Eventually the highway crosses the Fraser River (look out for deer).

Narrow **Yellowhead Lake**, lying adjacent to the highway and below 2,458-meter **Yellowhead Mountain,** is another popular canoe stop. A trail from the other side of the lake climbs the mountain; another trail from the opposite side of the highway leads to the base of 2,911-meter **Mount Fitzwilliam.** From the western boundary of the park and the eastern border of Jasper National Park (see "Jasper National Park," p. 234) the highway runs through **Yellowhead Pass** to Jasper. Don't miss stretching your legs at border **Portal Lake,** covered in yellow waterlilies in summer. A short trail leads along the east side of the lake allowing you to savor the perfume of hundreds of blooming wild pink roses before continuing into Alberta—and they call Alberta "wild rose country!"

LOUISE FOOTE

CARIBOO

GOLD PANNING, FISHING, AND THE WILD WEST

The wild, untamed Cariboo-Chilcotin region stretches from east to west almost clear across the province. Starting from the lush western base of the **Cariboo Mountains,** a landscape of forests and a myriad of excellent fishing lakes, it covers the Fraser River's deep twisted canyons, the high **Fraser** and **Interior plateaus,** the lakes and rolling grass-covered hills of Chilcotin ranchland, and the mighty **Coast Mountains,** all the way to the deeply indented fiordland area of the central west coast. The Cariboo Hwy. (Hwy. 97) runs north-south along the Fraser River, along which most people have made their homes. The two main cities are **Williams Lake** and **Quesnel.** Highway 20 meanders for 490 km from Williams Lake to **Bella Coola,** passing an abundance of fish-filled lakes and resorts on the rugged Chilcotin Plateau, through the southern section of vast **Tweedsmuir Provincial Park,** to the lush Bella Coola Valley. Forestry (logging and sawmilling), cattle ranching, and mining are the mainstays of the region.

Think of the Cariboo and images jump to mind of rolling hills, ranches, endless lodgepole pine fences, forests, fish-filled lakes, frisky horses, cowboys with big hats and coiled ropes, rodeos, restored gold towns, museums full of gold-mining paraphernalia, abandoned ghost towns, and hardy pioneers. Tune your radio to a country and western station, scream "yeeeeha," and ride off into the Cariboo sunset!

HISTORY

"Gold!" was the cry that lured thousands of miners and fortune seekers into the Cariboo in 1858 to explore the Fraser River and its tributaries for color. The resulting overload of the Hudson's Bay Company fur brigadc trails forced the Royal Engineers to come up with a new transportation route. They decided on the Lake Trail route between the lower Fraser River and Anderson and Seton lakes, just west of **Lillooet,** which was surveyed for a townsite in 1860. The new River Trail began at Lillooet, paralleling the east side of the Fraser north to **Williams Lake.**

The next waterway to turn golden was **Williams Creek** (east of Quesnel) in 1861. The following year prospector Billy Barker struck gold-rich gravel in the creek, and the area leaped onto all gold miners' maps. Barker's find was the beginning of **Barkerville,** the "largest town west of Chicago and north of San Francisco"—one of several at the time. In the meantime the Royal Engineers were busy surveying a wagon road between **Yale** and **Lytton** in 1861, constructing it through the rugged lower Fraser Canyon the next year. By the end of 1863 a toll road had been completed between Yale and **Soda Creek**—a mammoth undertaking.

Sternwheelers, Stagecoaches, Pony Express

From Soda Creek, a booming freighter and stagecoach terminus crowded with miners, the sternwheelers plied the upper Fraser River as far as **Quesnel.** The first sternwheeler was the *Enterprise* in 1863, joined by another 11 boats that cruised the Fraser until 1921. A

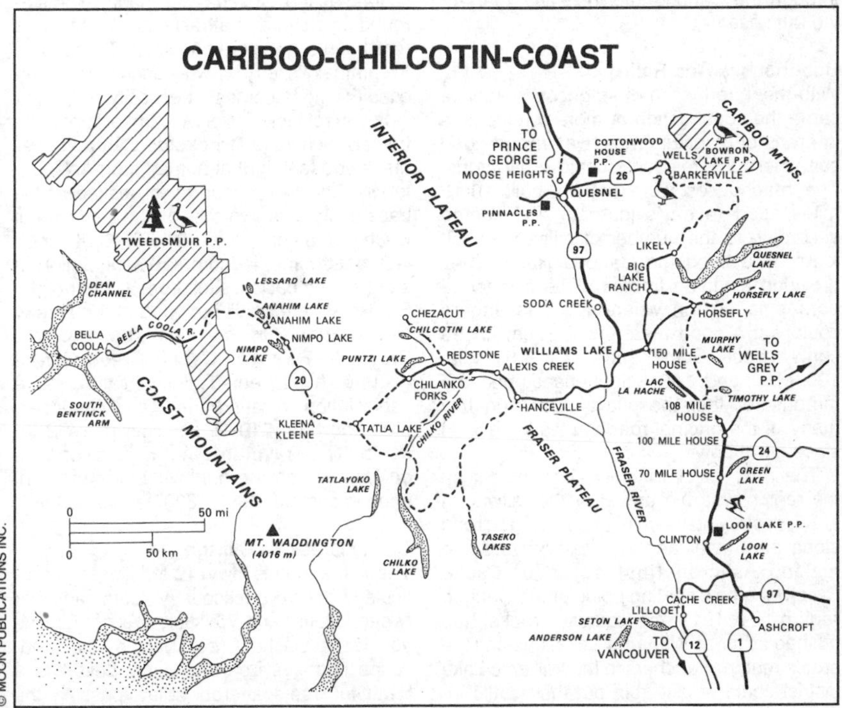

trail then connected Quesnel to Barkerville. The freight load and demand on the paddle-wheelers was so intense in those early golden years that a wagon road between Soda Creek and Barkerville became a necessity—it was finished in 1865. The stagecoach became the fastest and most practical form of transportation on the **Cariboo Wagon Road,** and stagecoach drivers became invaluable and trusted members of the community. Their expertise allowed the safe carriage of passengers and mail from Yale to Barkerville in all sorts of weather in an amazing 48 hours. Francis Jones Barnard, the first expressman, started carrying the mail on foot to the goldfields in 1858. By 1862 he had his own horses and started a pony express, and two years later he put together the first stagecoach service, the B.C. Express Company—locals called it the BX. This company trotted through the Cariboo into the early years of the 20th century.

Roadhouses And Railroads

With the introduction of stagecoach service came the construction of more roadhouses in areas of plentiful grass, water, and good soil where the residents could grow crops. The roadhouses were usually built 10-15 miles apart (a day's journey) and named according to the number of miles from Lillooet, Mile 0 on the Cariboo Road. They provided anything from a place to change horses to an inn where the passengers could get a good meal and a room for 50 cents apiece. Some, such as the 83 Mile, 100 Mile, and 150 Mile houses, became famous for their hospitality. Unfortunately many of the original roadhouses have long since burnt down.

The next major transportation impact on the region was the arrival of the railway in 1885, destroying much of the old wagon road along the Fraser and Thompson rivers and making **Ashcroft** (just south of **Cache Creek**) the new starting point for the Cariboo region. By 1919 the railway tracks had pushed as far as **Williams Lake,** causing the area's rebirth. Ranchers in the Williams Lake district could at last train out their cattle instead of trail driving them all the way to Ashcroft, and Williams Lake became a major transportation center in the middle of the region.

DOWN SOUTH

Cache Creek

A town born with the fur trade, here traders made a cache for their furs, food supplies, and trade goods. Today it's a stopping place (plenty of motels, campgrounds, restaurants, and gas stations) at the junction of Hwy. 1 from Vancouver in the south, Hwy. 1/97 from Kamloops in the east, and Hwy. 97 from Prince George in the north. With its desert climate, bare volcanic landscape, sagebrush, cacti, and tumbleweeds blowing through town, Cache Creek is often described as the "Arizona of Canada." The surrounding mountains attract rock climbers and rock hounds (jade is a popular find) from afar. In summer it's very brown—and very hot! Air-conditioning becomes a necessity.

If you're looking for a campground, the friendly owners of **Brookside Campsite** will make you feel right at home (open April-October). The campground lies nestled at the base of steep brown cliffs on the east side of Cache Creek on Hwy. 1, tel. 457-6633; spotless bathrooms, laundromat, sani station, a store selling basics, sites from $11 per night. Breakfasts are small but good at the **Husky Gas Station.** On the north side of Cache Creek on Hwy. 97, **Cache Creek Campgrounds** has a heated pool, miniature golf, a sani station, a laundromat, and coin-operated showers; $10-15 per site, plus $2 for sewer. The **Travel InfoCentre** (seasonal) is on Hwy. 97 on the northwest side of town; open in summer 0900-1800, tel. 457-5306.

Cache Creek To Clinton

The first turnoff is Hwy. 12 to Lillooet (a particularly scenic backcountry route runs between Lillooet and Whistler; see p. 153). As you leave Cache Creek behind, the landscape changes from the dusty desert to a beautiful tree-scattered valley, passing the turnoff to long, narrow **Loon Lake,** 17 km from the highway. The lake has excellent trout fishing, **Loon Creek Hatchery,** public campsites, and a large number of plush lakeside resorts. At the end of the road (26 km from the main highway) is **Loon Lake Provincial Park** with picnic facilities and campsites ($6 per night May-October).

Approaching the historic town of Clinton, the highway twists and turns past open fields full of happy horses, trees, ponds, a lake, and the **Clinton Ski Area** turnoff. **Clinton,** originally called 47 Mile House on the old Wagon Rd. at the junction of the gold-rush trails, is an old-fashioned town with a number of heritage buildings. It has the comfortable atmosphere of a bygone era—you wouldn't be surprised to see a packtrain loaded with gold pans, picks, and supplies making its way through the streets.

The huge log structure on the main street (one of the largest commercial log buildings in the province), **Cariboo Lodge** has a pub, a coffee shop, a dining room, and accommodations, tel. 459-7992. **Clinton Museum,** originally a schoolhouse of handmade bricks fired locally in the 1890s, contains pioneer belongings, guns, old photos, Indian and Chinese artifacts, freight wagons, and all sorts of items from the gold-rush days, giving you a good peek into the past. It's on the main highway, open weekdays May-Aug. 1000-1800, tel. 459-2442. **Clinton Travel InfoCentre** is housed in a beautiful old house (built in 1910) on the main street of town, tel. 459-2640; open daily May through Aug. 0900-1800. Several guest ranches in the area provide visitors with comfortable accommodations, good meals, and just about every outdoor activity you could imagine; pick up brochures at the InfoCentre.

The original 47 Mile House burned down in 1958. They used to hold the **Clinton Ball** there in May, attracting people from all over the area wearing their best finery. The ball continues to this day but in other locations. Not far north of Clinton is the turnoff to 141-hectare **Chasm Provincial Park** and **Painted Chasm,** a 120-meter-deep, three-sided box canyon cut by glacial meltwater in volcanic bedrock full of mineral-laden rocks—quite a spectacle when the sunlight brings out the color and sparkle of the minerals.

Clinton To 100 Mile House

The next turnoff to the west is a gravel backroad leading into ranch country, and 332-hectare **Big Bar Lake Provincial Park** (campsites $6 per night May-Sept., picnic facilities, swimming, and fishing; open May-Oct.) on the Fraser Plateau. Also in the vicinity is the enormous **Gang Ranch;** started in the 1860s, it was at one time the largest ranch in North America. Stop by for a visit.

Highway 97 winds through the desert following the Thompson River and the railway tracks south of Cache Creek.

Back on the main highway between the communities of **70 Mile House** (the original roadhouse burned down here also) and **100 Mile House** are several turnoffs to hundreds of Cariboo lakes, big and small, and the usual accompanying resorts catering to fishermen and hunters. Ask at InfoCentres for the invaluable *Cariboo-Chilcotin Fishing Guide* booklet—it's updated every year, costs $2 (plus tax), and has fishing info (where, when, and with what) for many of the lakes, plus maps, camping info, and even recipes for the fighters that didn't get away! Thirty-two-km **Green Lake** (19 km from the highway) lies along an old Hudson's Bay fur brigade trail (you can see traces of the trail along the shores) and has a number of parks suitable for picnicking and day use, and overnight camping at **Green Lake Provincial Park** ($8 per night May-September). Anglers are usually seen heading east for the Interlakes District at this point!

Around **100 Mile House** (a well-known stopping place on the Cariboo Rd. from 1861—and yes, the original roadhouse burned down in 1937), you pass the turnoff to **99 Mile Ski Area** to the west, and **Horse Lake Resort Area** to the east (access to more good fishing lakes). The local **Travel InfoCentre** is in a log cabin on the main highway (look for the two huge skis outside), just before the intersection of Airport Rd., tel. 395-5353; open year-round.

100 Mile House To Williams Lake

North of 100 Mile House is the turnoff to several more lakes and natural attractions to the east—**Ruth Lake** (30 km), **Canim Beach Provincial Park** (40 km; drive-in and walk-in campsites are $6 per night May-Sept. but the camp area is open April-Oct.), **Manhood Falls** between **Canim** and **Manhood** lakes, and the eastern border of **Wells Gray Provincial Park** (wilderness campsite at the end of the road; see p. 270). At **108 Mile House** you'll discover **108 Resort, 108 Mall, 108 Golf Course,** and **108 Mile Recreational Ranch,** which offers cross-country ski trails in winter and horse riding and golf in summer. If your ambition here is to snap 108 photos, don't miss **108 Lake Heritage Site** (the sign on the highway points to a rest area) where there's a photogenic old barn which used to house Clydesdale horses (to the right) and under restoration down the road (to the left)—tours are offered through the main house.

Along the highway is the turnoff to **Mount Timothy Ski Area** (23½ km; alpine and Nordic skiing, T-bar, set cross-country ski tracks, cafe, ski shop and rentals). The community of **Lac La Hache** stands at the south end of the 19-km lake of the same name with a tiny tree-covered island in the middle. The **Travel InfoCentre** (seasonal; tel. 396-7620) and **Lac La Hache Museum** are housed in the small log building on the highway. **Lac La Hache Provincial Park** has picnicking facilities and campsites ($8 per night May-September). All along this stretch of the highway are ranches with imposing self-standing arches marking their entrances, fields scattered with pinwheels of hay, meandering creeks, and a swampy lake chockablock with bright yellow waterlilies near 132 Mile House.

The next main turnoff at **150 Mile House** takes you on a scenic drive to **Horsefly Lake** (65 km; good swimming and fishing), **Horsefly Lake Provincial Park** (picnicking, and campsites from $8 per night May-Sept.), and **Quesnel Lake.** As you approach the city of **Williams Lake,** the highway parallels the watery version of Williams Lake—a long and narrow body of water, very popular with boaters and waterskiers, surrounded by forested hills and pockets of development.

WILLIAMS LAKE

Gold seekers poured into the Cariboo in 1860, and Williams Lake (initially just a roadhouse, a courthouse, and a jail) became the HQ for the gold commissioner and the regional postal center. It should have become a busy center, hub of the region, but in 1863 the Cariboo Road contractors decided to link 150 Mile House with the sternwheeler terminus of Soda Creek, thus bypassing Williams Lake and terminating the small community's reason for being. William Pinchbeck, one of the first settlers in Williams Lake, decided to stay in the valley, and with William Lyne created a mighty farm that supplied the gold camps and Barkerville miners with bacon, ham, fresh vegetables, flour, and white wheat whiskey from their own distillery. Pinchbeck was not only a farmer, he also acted as the judge, lawyer, and doctor for the area! Today's Stampede Ground is built on some of his old ranch (his grave can still be seen behind the Stampede Ground).

In September 1919 the Pacific Great Eastern Railway (now B.C. Rail) pushed its iron track around the lake, and surveyors started laying out the streets for the new town of Williams Lake. To celebrate the event that put Williams Lake back on the map, a large picnic and rodeo was held—the first Williams Lake Stampede. By 1920 the town had hotels, stores, and homes, and ranchers were thrilled to be able to put their cattle on the train instead of trail driving them to Ashcroft.

No one knows for sure how Williams Lake got its name, but the most popular theory is that it was named after Shuswap Indian Chief Williams (Will-yum) who kept the peace as best he could between the Indians and the early white settlers of the valley. Prior to Chief Williams' time, the lake had been called Col-

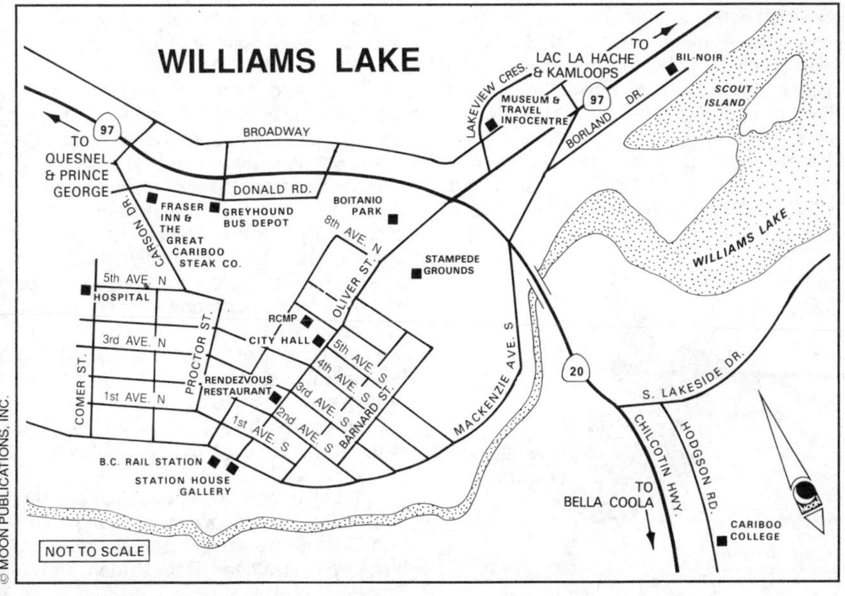

umneetza, an Athabascan word meaning "Meeting Place of the Princely People." Today Williams Lake is a ranching and forest industry center, the business hub of the Cariboo, and self-proclaimed "Stampede Capital of British Columbia."

ATTRACTIONS AND ACTIVITIES

Indoor

Make your first stop the excellent **Williams Lake InfoCentre** at 1148 South Broadway (off Hwy. 97 on the south side of town), tel. 392-5025. The office is shared by the **Williams Lake District Chamber of Commerce.** The InfoCentre staff are some of the best—if you ask a question they can't answer, they'll enthusiastically try to find out as much as they can. It's open year-round 0900-1700, from May-Sept. daily 0800-1800.

The large **Williams Lake Historic Museum** at 113 N. 4th Ave. across from the Fire Hall is well worth a visit. Step back into the past via the black-and-white photo displays, remains of the Chinese settlement at Quesnel Forks, and all kinds of picks, pans, and axes from gold-mining days. There's also plenty of good reading matter on the ghost town of Quesnel Forks, the gold-rush town of Barkerville, the building of the Cariboo Wagon Rd., exciting gold-rush days, sternwheelers, ranching, and roadhouses.

At the foot of Oliver St. is the **Station House Gallery** in the historic PGE Railway depot—a good place for pottery, weaving, photos, paintings, jewelry, and other local crafts, and to appreciate the works of art in the gallery (exhibitions changed every month). The gallery is open in summer Mon.-Sat. 1000-1700, Tues.-Sat. 1000-1700 the rest of the year; at 1 Mackenzie Ave. N, tel. 392-6113. Another place to see art and pick up locally made crafts is the **Image Gallery** at 3-85 S. 3rd Ave. (across from Paradise Twin Theatres), tel. 392-6360; open Tues.-Sat. 1000-1700.

TODD CLARK

Outdoor

This region has plenty to suit the outdoors lover—year-round. First collect all sorts of brochures to cover just about any activity you can come up with at the Travel InfoCentre. In summer you can puff up any of the nearest hills for great views, huff into the backcountry (be well-equipped for weather changes and go in a group), or just saunter around the **Scout Island Ecological Conservancy** near town. The nature center explains the wetlands ecosystem, the observation tower provides a bird's-eye view of the birds and wildlife, and marshlife can be experienced close-up from a number of trails; open Mon.-Fri. 0900-1700, Sun. 1330-1630, at the southeast end of the city—take Hwy. 97 south, turn right on Mackenzie Ave., then left on Scout Island Road. Any of the whitewater rivers, streams, and serene lakes in the region (hundreds!) can make a perfect spot for canoe and kayak discovery trips into the backcountry, and the Fraser River provides opportunities for exciting rafting trips. Another fun way to explore the Cariboo is to get in the Western mode and leap on a horse! Ask at the InfoCentre if any of the local ranches currently offers trail rides—**Springhouse Trails Ranch,** about 20 km southwest of town along Hwy. 20 on the Dog Creek Rd., will put you on horseback for $12 an hour (May-Sept.); check availability of horses at 392-4780.

One of the most popular outdoor activities is the excellent and rewarding fishing in Cariboo-Chilcotin lakes for rainbow, lake, and brook trout, steelhead, Dolly Varden, and kokanee. At Williams Lake you need your own boat and trolling equipment—early in summer you can catch rainbow trout, but the more isolated fly-in lakes have by far the best fishing. For the most complete guide to fishing in the region, ask for the invaluable *Cariboo-Chilcotin Fishing Guide* booklet ($2 plus tax) at the InfoCentre. It covers many of the region's best lakes, the necessary equipment and hot tips, fly-selection tips, the best times to fish, a fishing diary (so you can accurately brag about your catch later with written proof); camping info—even how to cook your catch. The booklet is updated each year.

In winter the most popular local activity is cross-country skiing in perfect conditions on perfect terrain—just strap them on and go, or follow the 30 km of color-coded (all levels) wooded trails on **Bull Mountain,** about 20 km north on Hwy. 97 up Bull Mountain Rd. (pick up a map at the InfoCentre). The closest downhill ski resort is **Mt. Timothy,** 25 km east of Lac La Hache, with 18 runs and almost 300 meters of vertical, a T-bar, a day lodge, a ski-rental shop, and washrooms. Snowboarding has also emerged on the slopes, and snowmobiling and icefishing are also popular winter activities in the surrounding region, but you need to be properly equipped with layers of warm clothing.

PRACTICALITIES

Accommodations

The **Wildwood Mobile Home and R.V. Park** is the best campground in the area, even though it's at the north end of town about 13 km from city center. Tent and RV sites, full hookups, washrooms and showers, laundry facilities, sanistation, tel. 989-4711; $11-14 per site. **Chief Will-yum Campsite** is on the south side of Williams Lake, operated by the Williams Lake Indian Band, tel. 296-4544. Pitch your tent or RV, or rent an authentic teepee for the night. Facilities include full hookups, shower house, camp store, picnic tables, and playground; $12 per night, full hookups. The most central campground is at the Stampede Grounds, catering to self-contained RVs: water, portable washrooms, picnic tables, and firepit.

The least expensive motels are located along the Cariboo Hwy. as you enter the city from the south, or along the highway on the north side. **Slumber Lodge** has a more central location downtown at 27 7th Ave. S (tel. 392-7116), and provides an indoor pool, saunas, a recreation room, a restaurant, and sleeping or housekeeping units from $44 s, $49 d, kitchen extra $5. Off the highway at the northern end of town is the **Fraser Inn,** a full-service hotel with whirlpool, saunas, a gym, a gift shop, a busy pub, a good licensed restaurant (the Great Cariboo Steak Co.; see below), and rooms from $50-57 s, $50-62 d, kitchen extra $10; at 285 Donald Rd., tel. 398-7055.

If a ranching vacation is more your style, call the **Springhouse Trails Ranch** at 392-4780 for room availability. The ranch offers campsites starting at $12 a night, rooms from $45 s or $49 d, horseback riding at $12 an hour, or package deals including accommodations, all meals, horseback riding, and ranch facilities from $86 pp per day, children 3-11 20% off.

Food And Entertainment

Rendezvous restaurant at 240 Oliver St., tel. 398-8312, is open for lunch serving soup and salad bar for $4.95, burgers, sandwiches, pizza, and Mexican dishes for around $3.50-7. At dinner the main dishes (fish, chicken, steak, etc.) all include a delicious salad from the salad bar and range $8.50-14, with nightly specials for around $8-9; open Mon.-Thurs. 1100-2200, Fri. and Sat. 1100-2230, and Sun. 1630-2200.

The Great Cariboo Steak Company in the Fraser Inn Hotel at 285 Donald Rd. is open for breakfast from 0600 on weekdays, from 0700 on Sat., from 0800 on Sun., and breakfast ranges $3.95-6. All-you-can-eat lunch buffets are around $7, sandwiches, croissants, and burgers are $5-8. Dinner prices start around $7.50 for all-you-can-eat salad (good salad bar) and bread; expect to pay $8-18 for steak, prime rib, chicken, seafood, pasta, etc. For good Chinese food try

One of the largest rodeos in the country, the Williams Lake Stampede is held here on the first weekend of July each year.

the **Bil-Nor Restaurant** on Hwy. 97 S (south of the InfoCentre)—locals say it's the best Chinese place in town. You can also tuck in to steak, seafood salads, burgers, and sandwiches; open seven days a week 0700-2300, tel. 392-4221/4223. **Pizza Hut** is located at the intersection of 8th Ave. and Oliver St., tel. 392-4331. A number of fast-food restaurants are situated along the highway at the southern end of town.

See what's happening in the way of live plays at the **Cariboo College Studio Theatre** where the Williams Lake Players Club is featured; access to the college is off Hwy. 20. One of the most lively pubs is the **Billy Miner Pub** with **Billy's Lookout** (patio with view of the city) in the Fraser Inn Hotel; 285 Donald Rd. (off the highway at the north end of town). For exercise, the **Sam Ketcham Memorial Pool** at the northwest corner of Boitanio Park has a 25-meter indoor pool, a hot pool, a sauna, and an exercise room; open daily, for current schedule phone 398-7665. The two local movie theaters are the **Alston Theatre** at 178 Oliver St. and **Paradise Twins** at 78 South 3rd Ave.; tel. 392-4722 for movie information.

Williams Lake Stampede, one of the largest rodeos in the country, is usually held at the end of June/beginning of July and attracts people from afar. If you're in Williams Lake at the right time, you'll soon realize that something big is going on! The locals wear more-Western-than-usual garb, the stores acquire 19th-century Western decor and false fronts, and cowboys and cowgirls ride in from throughout Canada and the U.S. to participate in professional bucking-bronc riding, bull riding, calf-roping, and cow-milking contests. Barrel racing, tractor pulls, chariot races, raft races, a parade, barn dances, Stampede breakfasts and steak-outs, and a host of other decidedly Western-flavored activities round out the fun. If you can't make it to this rodeo, plenty of much smaller rodeos are held throughout the region from May to September—just ask the staff at the InfoCentre to point you in the right direction for a bit of country-and-western action!

Services And Transportation

Emergency numbers: **hospital** tel. 392-4411; **ambulance** tel. 392-5402; **RCMP** tel. 392-6211. For all your information needs head for the **Travel InfoCentre** and **Williams Lake and District Chamber of Commerce** at 1148 South Broadway, tel. 392-5025; open daily.

The **Greyhound Bus Depot** is on Donald Rd. (left side of the highway going north); regular bus service north and south. **Chilcotin Stage Lines** operates bus service twice a week west to Bella Coola. Train service north and south is provided by **B.C. Rail;** the railway station is on Mackenzie Ave., for reservations call 392-7182. **Budget Rent-a-Car** is at 497 N. 11th Ave., tel. 398-7522. **Tilden Rent-a-Car** is at 84-A N. Broadway, tel. 392-2976. **Williams Lake Airport,** serviced by **Air B.C.** and **Aviair,** is on the northern outskirts of town (13 km from city center)—flights to Prince George, Bella Coola, Vancouver, Kamloops, Kelowna, Penticton, and other major destinations.

HIGHWAY 20 TO BELLA COOLA

Highway 20 west of Williams Lake is a partly paved (170 km), but mostly all-weather, gravel road across the **Chilcotin Plateau** for a full 464 km to Bella Coola, passing numerous roadside fishing resorts and a multitude of access roads to isolated lakeside resorts. The highway is also called the "Route to the Valley of the Thunderbird" because the lush Bella Coola valley is home to the Thunderbird in coastal Indian mythology. A well-traveled road in summer, it's still a good idea to get your vehicle checked out before you set off from Williams Lake, and carry spare tires, tools, and water. If you want to get right off the beaten track you need a 4WD vehicle. You can also get to Bella Coola from Williams Lake on a **Chilcotin Stage Lines** bus (twice a week service), but to explore the road at leisure (and fish to your heart's content) you really need your own form of transportation.

Along the road you can expect to see vast plains splattered with boulders, large ranches, falling-down abandoned cabins, one-horse communities with limited services, and majestic snowcapped peaks, passing turnoffs to lakes, more lakes, and even more lakes, with some of the best angling opportunities on the continent (you need 4WD to get to many). As you explore you're likely to meet fellow anglers, canoeists, hikers, cross- country skiers in winter, and hardy outdoor enthusiasts heading for the wilds of **Tweedsmuir Provincial Park.** Stay at forest service recreation sites, the provincial park **Atnarko River Campground** (pit toilets, no showers; $6 per night), lodge (reasonable rates, tel. 982-2402), or lakeside camping areas (often limited space). Or try the many lodges, guest ranches, or plush resorts along the way. Some lodges also offer campsites with washroom facilities (around $8-14 per site), some have cabins or units from as little as $25 s, $35 d (at the luxurious lodges the sky's the limit!), others work on the American plan (includes meals and activities in the cost). For details and prices on each lodge and resort along the way, refer to the ever-useful *Accommodations Guide.* Most of the resorts have basic stores (best to stock up on your gear and necessities in Williams Lake), and offer fishing and hunting opportunities, boat and tackle rental, canoe rentals, horseback riding, etc. Some have fly-in facilities.

Tweedsmuir Provincial Park is the largest provincial park in British Columbia, covering an amazing 981,000 hectares of the **Rainbow** and **Coastal ranges,** glaciers, alpine meadows, and deep river valleys. Highway 20 meanders through only a small portion of Tweedsmuir Park South. The untouched wilderness of this park attracts hardy hikers, campers, anglers, hunters, and canoeists—but all visitors need to be experienced outdoorsmen and totally self-sufficient or should hire a professional guide before venturing into the backcountry. We're talking real wilderness here, with real grizzly bears (especially along the Atnarko and Dean rivers where they fish in fall). Most of the trails are only suitable for experienced backcountry hikers with stamina—many are not maintained. Angling for steelhead and salmon is excellent in the Bella Coola and Atnarko rivers, the fly-fishing is good in the Dean River, and you can catch trout, whitefish, and Dolly Varden in most of the lakes in the park. Campgrounds are located along the Atnarko River (near Park HQ) and at the Fisheries Pool (near Stuie), providing toilets, water, and wood (no showers or hookups) for around $8 a night. Get detailed info and maps from **Park HQ,** 34 km west of the park entrance. For topographical maps (small charge) write to MAPS B.C., Ministry of Lands and Parks, Parliament Building, Victoria, B.C. V8V 1X5.

Many people drive this scenic highway just to see what's at the end! The town of **Bella Coola** (population under 1,000) lies at the head of the **North Bentinck Arm** of the Pacific Ocean—it's the stepping-stone to the islands of the Inside Passage and the Central Coast, though not connected by ferry (charter boats only). This village of the Bella Coola Indians was visited by Alex Mackenzie, first non-Native explorer, in July 1793 after he traveled overland from the Fraser River. You can see **Mackenzie Rock,** on which he inscribed his name and date of arrival, in the Dean Channel—take a charter boat from Bella Coola. The Hudson's Bay Company established a post at Bella Coola in 1869, but it wasn't until 1894 and the arrival of a Norwegian reverend and his flock that settlement of Bella Coola Valley began in earnest.

At Bella Coola are all the tourist facilities you need including a hospital, a seasonal **Travel InfoCentre** (tel. 799-5919), a store, fishing charters and outfitters, equipment rentals and fishing licenses, an airport (regular air service and charters), even car rental. The **Bella Coola Museum** downtown is housed in a schoolhouse and surveyor's cabin, featuring artifacts of early Norwegian settlers and the Hudson's Bay Company; open June-September. **Thorsen Creek Campsite** (five km from town) is open May-Nov., with tent sites, partial hookups, coin-operated showers and laundromat, pit toilets, and a store; $6-10 per site, tel. 799-5659. Bella Coola also has a motel and inn downtown, and a motor hotel, motel, and campground are located 14 km east at Hagensborg.

QUESNEL

Williams Lake To Quesnel

Between Williams Lake and Quesnel Hwy. 97 continues north along the Fraser River valley, passing turnoffs to fishing lakes in the east, to the community of **Soda Creek** at the head of the upper Fraser Canyon, through large open meadows, rolling hills, and lush green fields where contented horses frolic and pinwheels of hay dry in the sun. As you get closer to Quesnel the highway is decorated by wagon wheels, black Arabian stallion stables, and Alamo-this and Alamo-that. The Western atmosphere lives on! **Quesnel River Fish Hatchery** is 72 km off the highway along Beaver Lake Rd., not far south of Quesnel.

Let's Relive The Past

With its roots firmly entrenched in the gold-rush days of the 1860s, the small city of Quesnel (Kwuh-NELL) sits at the junction of the Fraser and Quesnel rivers—at a point where gold miners used to either get off the paddle wheelers and head east for Barkerville, or continue north up the Fraser River. On the southern outskirts of Quesnel is the exit to the **North Star Road Pulp Mill and Plywood Plant** (tours available; info at the Travel InfoCentre) and **Quesnel And District Recreation Centre and Pool,** then the highway crosses the deep-green Quesnel River into town. Follow the signs to city center.

If you wander around town you'll notice pioneer buildings here and there (Quesnel was first incorporated in 1928), and if you want to transport yourself back to the historic gold rush and the days of Billy Barker (who first found gold in the Barkerville area), or go farther back to the days of explorer Alexander Mackenzie, spend at least an hour in **Quesnel and District Museum** on Hwy. 97 at the south end of town; open May to mid-June daily 1000-1700, mid-June to the end of Aug. daily 1000-1900, and Sept. daily 1000-1700, tel. 992-9580, admission free. Today Quesnel (population 8,300) thrives around the lumber, pulp, and plywood mill, cattle ranching, mining, and tourism—which thrives on reliving the past.

The main drawing cards downtown are the museum, gold panning in the Quesnel River (where it meets the Fraser—everywhere else is staked!), and **Heritage Corner** at Carson and Front streets, where you can see the Old Fraser Bridge, the remains of the *Enterprise* steamer, a Cornish waterwheel used by the gold miners, and the original **Hudson's Bay Store.** Take a refreshment break at **Grampa's Place,** a coffee shop and bistro. One

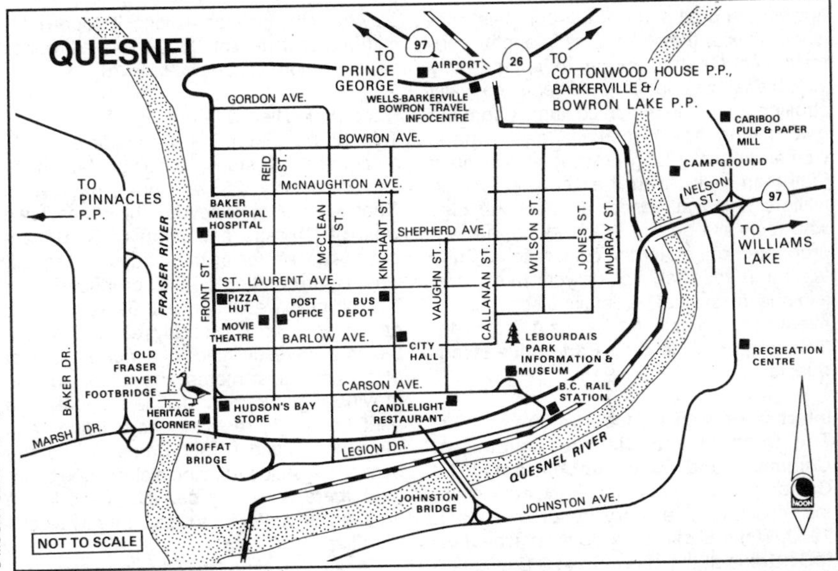

way to enjoy the downtown area is to follow the 4½-km **Riverfront Walk** along the Fraser and Quesnel rivers and back along Bowron Avenue. An eight-km drive west on Baker Dr. brings you to the geologically intriguing, glacially eroded **Hoodoos** in **Pinnacles Provincial Park** (good photo ops—dazzle the folks back home). The most popular out-of-town attractions are all on Hwy. 26, east of Quesnel (see below).

Sleeping, Eating, And Merrymaking

The best places to head are the nearby provincial parks, such as **Ten Mile Lake,** off Hwy. 97 north of town, where campsites are $8 a night May-September. Or try **Robert's Roost Campground** on the west side of Dragon Lake (safe swimming beach, boat rentals) with a view of Dragon Mountain, tel. 747-2015. It's at 3121 Gook Rd. (take Hwy. 97 south, turn east on Gook Rd. and go to the end); from $12 a night d, plus $1-2 for electricity, $1 for sewer, and $1 for water. **Quesnel Airport Inn, Motel, and RV Park** on the north side of town, about one km south of Barkerville and Airport Junction, also has campsites for $8-12 per night, hookups included, and motel rooms from $30-36 s, $32-38 d; tel. 992-5942. Quesnel has a number of motels in the city center, several on Front St., with prices ranging $30-49 s, $34-48 d. Some have handy kitchen units—to cook up all those fish you've been catching!

If you're in one of those just-got-to-have-a-pizza moods, **Pizza Hut** on the corner of Front St. (the main road) and St. Laurent does a roaring trade—their pizza is excellent (a small supreme starts at $11.25) and the salad bar has a fairly large selection. **Savala's Steak House** at 240 Reid St. (tel. 992-9453) has an extensive salad bar, and house specialties include steaks, spareribs, pizza, and a variety of Italian dishes. Expect to pay from $6.95 (salad bar alone), $10-18 (steaks), and $11-19 (seafood). Quesnel has a fairly large variety of good restaurants—one to meet everyone's tastebuds and pocketbook.

The main event here in summer is the **Billy Barker Days** celebration (third full weekend in July), when some of the downtown streets are closed off to traffic in favor of an outdoor crafts fair, along with dances, a rodeo, and all sorts of fun activities—finished off with fireworks. This is another entertaining Cariboo event to accidentally stumble across to find residents casually strolling around in period costumes from the gold-mining days—men in cowboy hats, women in slinky long dresses with brightly feathered hats, even the shop assistants, waiters and waitresses, and anyone else who feels like getting in the mood, are appropriately attired for the celebrations. Put a feather in your hat, kick up your heels, and join the festivities! A detailed schedule of events is available at the main Travel InfoCentre, or at the **Billy Barkerville Headquarters.**

Information And Transportation

The **Quesnel and District Chamber of Commerce and Travel InfoCentre** is at 703 Carson Ave. by Lebourdais Park, adjacent to the museum, open daily in summer 0800-1900. **Wells Barkerville Bowron Travel InfoCentre** is at the Hwy. 97 N/26 E intersection on the northern outskirts of Quesnel; open in summer 1000-1800.

Transportation in and out of Quesnel is via **Greyhound Lines** (bus depot on the corner of St. Laurent Ave. and Kinchant St.), with three northbound and three southbound coaches a day. **B.C. Rail** (train station is at the east end of Carson Ave. across from the museum and InfoCentre) has passenger service daily (in summer) to Prince George and Vancouver. **Air B.C.** (the airport is off Hwy. 97 N on the northern outskirts of Quesnel) operates a daily service to and from Vancouver and other destinations.

HIGHWAY 26 HIGHLIGHTS

Cottonwood House Provincial Historic Park

About 28 km east of Quesnel on Hwy. 26, this park features a former roadhouse, built in 1864, with a guesthouse, a barn, a stable, old buildings and farming equipment, and an interpretation center. In summer carriage rides are one of the main attractions. It's open daily mid-May to mid-Sept. 0800-2000, admission free. For more info, call 992-8716.

Barkerville Historic Park

This 1870s gold-rush town made up of 75 authentically restored buildings (about 89 km along Hwy. 26, an hour's drive from Quesnel) was, in its heyday, the largest town west of Chicago and north of San Francisco—the center of the gold-rich Cariboo, where surrounding creeks produced over $40 million in wealth. In 1916 Barkerville was destroyed by fire but quickly rebuilt, however the gold gravel dwindled to a trickle and a lot of the miners lost interest and moved on. The provincial government decided to make it a heritage site by restoring the buildings and atmosphere, and in 1958 Barkerville sprang back to life. Aside from the picturesque buildings, there are many beautiful trails in the area, and in winter it's a cross-country skier's paradise.

On all the countless brochures it's described as a "walking, talking, singing, dancing museum of the 1870s"—and rightfully so! It's open year-round (admission free in winter), but in summer historic reenactments are in full swing and the shops, stores, restaurants, bakery (some of the most mouth-watering baked goods in the province), and theater are run the way they were many years ago. Visit Barkerville to stroll back into the past, dine at wonderful restaurants, and take an active part in all the fun street activities; admission adult $5, senior or child $3, under 12 $1. Try to time your visit to coincide with one of the musical comedy performances at the theater (daily except Fri. at 1300 or 1600; adult $7.50). On Sat. and Sun. nights at 2000 a different performance is put on, so you can go back and enjoy it all over again. Reservations are not taken for any of the shows—buy your ticket in Barkerville at Barnard's Express, available 30 minutes before each performance. A large number of provincial campsites (some providing flush toilets and showers) are also available in the park for $8-10 per night.

Bowron Lakes Provincial Park
Outdoor enthusiasts, in particular canoeists, should take the Bowron Lakes Rd. to gorgeous 123,117-hectare **Bowron Lakes Provincial Park** in the Cariboo Mountains (112 km east of Quesnel) where a chain of wilderness lakes can be canoed between June and October. This route consists of six major lakes—**Bowron, Indianpoint, Isaac, Lanezi, Sandy,** and **Spectacle**—and some smaller lakes and waterways, making a 116-km circuit—reputedly one of the best in the province. Some portaging is required between lakes, and those attempting the route should be extremely well-prepared, physically fit, and experienced for the seven- to 10-day trip. July and Aug. are the most popular months (avoid departing on a weekend when it gets very busy), but Sept. is one of the most colorful months to enjoy the circuit and see the trees dressed in their fall regalia.

Pick up a *Bowron Lakes Provincial Park* brochure at any InfoCentre, and get all the details and register (required on departure and return for safety purposes) at the Registration Centre next to the main parking lot. In order to protect the park's wilderness qualities, groups of six or more are required to make reservations by writing to the Ministry of Parks, 540 Borland St., Williams Lake, B.C. V2G 1R8; phone 398-4414. To do the circuit costs $40 (plus tax) per canoe; west side only is $20 (plus tax) per canoe. Campsites, cabins, and cooking shelters are located at strategic distances along the circuit. All water should be boiled for at least one minute before drinking or brushing teeth to kill off Giardia lamblia, a common parasite in the mountainous regions of Canada. A campground providing water, pit toilets, and firewood (no showers) is located on the north shore of Bowron Lake, 1.6 km from the park entrance; $8 per site, open June to the end of September. Two privately owned lodges are also located on the northwest shore of Bowron Lake, providing accommodations, meals, supplies, and boat and canoe rentals.

Quesnel To Prince George
Between Quesnel and Prince George, Hwy. 97 meanders through gentle agricultural scenery with lots of trees and masses of wildflowers in summer splashing the roadsides with all colors of the rainbow. The highway passes 241-hectare **Ten Mile Lake Provincial Park,** which has picnic sites, campsites (toilets, no showers; $8 per site May through Oct.), a beach, boating and fishing, and hiking and cross-country ski trails.

TODD CLARK

LOUISE FOOTE

NORTH BY NORTHWEST

The vast, L-shaped North By Northwest region of B.C., originally named New Caledonia, encompasses more than 300,000 square kilometers of mountains and forests. It stretches from the Rockies in the east to the Pacific Ocean and the Queen Charlotte Islands in the west, from interior Cariboo Country in the south all the way to the Yukon border in the north. Within North By Northwest's boundaries lies some of Canada's most outstanding wilderness scenery—towering white-capped mountains, sky-blue glaciers, kilometer after kilometer of fragrant pine, fir, spruce, and cedar forests, pristine provincial parks, untamed rivers and icy-cold streams, and thousands of lakes alive with fighting steelhead, rainbow trout, salmon, char, Dolly Varden, and whitefish. Throughout this glorious landscape lives abundant wildlife—so plentiful you can see deer, moose, and bear without even stepping out of your vehicle, and along many stretches of highway you're more likely to see wildlife than other human beings. The region offers all sorts of summer and winter outdoor recreational activities to suit even the most ardent adventurer, ancient Indian villages where many original totem poles still stand, a handful of towns with all the comforts of home, and two major cities—interior Prince George and coastal Prince Rupert.

Looking at the map it's fairly easy to imagine how difficult it must have been for pioneer explorers to find routes through this wild and harsh land inhabited by Carrier, Tsimshian, Tlingit, and Haida Indians. The first European discoveries in B.C. were made by sea in the early 18th century by Russian and Spanish explorers, followed in 1778 by the English ships *Resolution* and *Discovery* under Capt. James Cook. Cook traded with the native Indians for a variety of their goods, including luxurious sea otter furs which he was later able to sell for a small fortune in China. (When this became known in Europe, a fur rush began.) In the meantime, the Rockies were crossed by traders and explorers working for the North West Company, including Alexander Mackenzie, Simon Fraser, and David Thompson, three of its most famous frontiersmen. The fur-trading empire in central B.C. became known as New Caledonia—Simon Fraser's name for an area that reminded him of his native Scotland. Trading posts were established in the northern interior beginning in 1805, and Fort St. James became the capital of the region. But it wasn't until after the Cariboo gold rush of the 1860s that settlement began in earnest in the region. Getting to Fort George, an outpost at the junction of the Fraser and Nechako rivers, by sternwheeler or Cariboo Wagon Road with all the necessities and a few luxuries of life was quite an arduous task. The arrival of the Grand Trunk Pacific Railroad in early 1914 finally linked the northwest coast with the rest of Canada, heralding the development of the interior northwest.

The major road running through the region is Highway 16, also known as the Yellowhead, which parallels the CNR railway tracks and mighty Fraser, Nechako, Bulkley, and Skeena rivers from Tete Jaune Cache to Prince Rupert. It runs between the Rocky and Cariboo mountains, across the Interior Plateau, then through the Hazelton and Coast mountains—1,073 magnificent kilometers from the Alberta border to the ocean. Branching off Hwy. 16 west of New Hazelton is Hwy. 37, the Stewart-Cassiar, which leads northwest between the Coast and Skeena mountains to Stewart on the Alaska border, or north through the Stikine Ranges and Cassiar Mountains to the Yukon—746 km from Kitwanga to Watson Lake. Bus or train along the Yellowhead Hwy. is fast, efficient, and spectacular. Major airlines fly into Prince George and Prince Rupert, and Prince Rupert is also serviced by ferry from Vancouver Island and Alaska. Where you can't get by road you can easily reach by bush- or floatplane, or helicopter if you don't mind returning home to an enormous credit card bill. Floatplanes moored at lakes are a common sight in the north, and many a ranch has a helicopter perkily parked in the homestead's backyard. The rest of the roads in the region are gravel or dirt, with gas and service stations few and far between.

To get the most out of a visit to this region you need your own reliable car and tent, a camper, or an RV. In addition to spare parts and essential supplies, bring a camera and year's supply of film, a fishing rod, an adventurous spirit—and time to see it all. It's entirely possible to drive the Yellowhead east to west in several days—but to absorb the scenery and enjoy the various communities and activities along the way, allow at least a week. The same goes for the Stewart-Cassiar and Alaska highways.

The Rockies To Prince George

Both the Yellowhead Highway and Tete Jaune Cache (pronounced Tee-Jon-Cash), easternmost community in the North By Northwest region, were named after a blond-haired, Iroquois trapper from Quebec who was nicknamed Tete Jaune, or Yellow Head. He was lured west to work for fur-trading companies and remained in the area after his contract expired, hunting, trapping, and guiding fur traders through the Rocky Mountains via the Yellowhead Pass in the 1820s. Tete Jaune became most well-known for his famous cache of furs which he concealed somewhere in the area. The exact location of the cache remains a mystery to this day.

From the intersection of Highways 5 and 16, Prince George is 278 km along an excellent highway—one very long scenic drive. As you leave the jagged peaks of the Rockies behind, the landscape becomes gentler. The highway runs through a flat, meadow-filled valley splattered with stands of trees between low forest-covered hills. As you pass large ranches where cows and horses contentedly chew fluorescent-green grass and fields are dotted with triangular and circular haystacks, the occasional roadside sign advertises the availability of bed and breakfast. As you wind back and forth over the Fraser River and a number of small streams, more snowcapped mountains in the distance lure you onward.

The only small town interrupting the wilderness is **McBride,** "Cedar Pole Capital of the

Country." Serving the agricultural, lumbering, and ranching district of Robson Valley, McBride has off-highway stores, gas stations, restaurants, motels, campgrounds, and a caboosed Travel InfoCentre on the highway. In all directions are rolling green meadows and high white peaks. If you're continuing west and you enjoy getting off the beaten track, stop at the InfoCentre for directions to the **Boulder Mountain Trail** (32 km west of town, past the West Twin Creek highway sign) for a day-hike to the 2,100-meter summit and some inspirational views. The staff can also suggest a number of other short walks to waterfalls (and good fishing spots) or longer scrambles to alpine lakes. In winter McBride becomes a white wonderland for cross-country skiers and snowmobilers, and in Jan. the locals celebrate Cabin Fever Days. Before leaving town, fill up with gas—no regular services for the next 144 kilometers.

Westward, Hwy. 16 meanders through forests, up over mountains, then down a steep grade to eventually cross the Goat River. The next stretch takes you through beautiful forested ravines and contrasting barren logged areas before coming to a private resort (store, gas) at Purden Lake, and then **Purden Lake Provincial Park,** with a campground ($8 per site May-Sept.), a picnic area, and boat-launching facilities. As you approach Prince George, the seemingly endless arrow-straight highway climbs up and down grass-covered hills giving equally endless rural views in all directions. **Tabor Mountain Ski Area,** with chairlifts visible from the road, is signposted off the highway to the left.

PRINCE GEORGE

THE CENTER OF IT ALL

Prince George, B.C.'s northern capital, is located at the junction of the Fraser and Nechako rivers. The Fraser is the longest river in B.C., flowing from near Jasper for 1,360 km to the sea, and the Nechako River is the Fraser's third-largest tributary, flowing from the west for 260 kilometers. Together the two rivers flow for 50 km within the boundaries of the city, which is almost slap in the center of the province. Sprawled around the junctions of Highways 16 and 97 and the Canadian National and B.C. railways, Prince George is a central transportation hub for traffic traveling both north-south and east-west.

The history of the Prince George area focuses on its two rivers. Trappers and explorers used the rivers as transportation routes into the northern reaches of the province. When they discovered that the region was rich in wolf, fox, linx, mink, wolverine, otter, and muskrat furs, forts and trading posts were quickly established by rivers and lakes so that furs could be sent out and supplies could be brought in. In 1807 the first spruce logs were cut by Fraser's men near the junction of the two rivers for the construction of Fort George, named after then-reigning King George III of England. The local, semi-nomadic Carrier Sekani Indians had summer and winter village sites in the area (they moved from camp to camp following the animals and fish upon which their existence depended), but with the establishment of Fort George set up a permanent village just north of the post.

In 1821 the two major fur-trading companies, North West and Hudson's Bay, amalgamated and Fort George was operated as a Hudson's Bay Company post until 1915. The Carrier sold their reserve to the Grand Trunk Railway, moving upriver to Shelley, and Fort George became a major divisional point for the railway in 1908. The original Fort George, along with South Fort George, a second townsite eight km south on the Fraser River, were soon flooded with new settlers. The railroad finally arrived in 1914, and the following year the GTR built a third town site, Prince George, between the other two. It

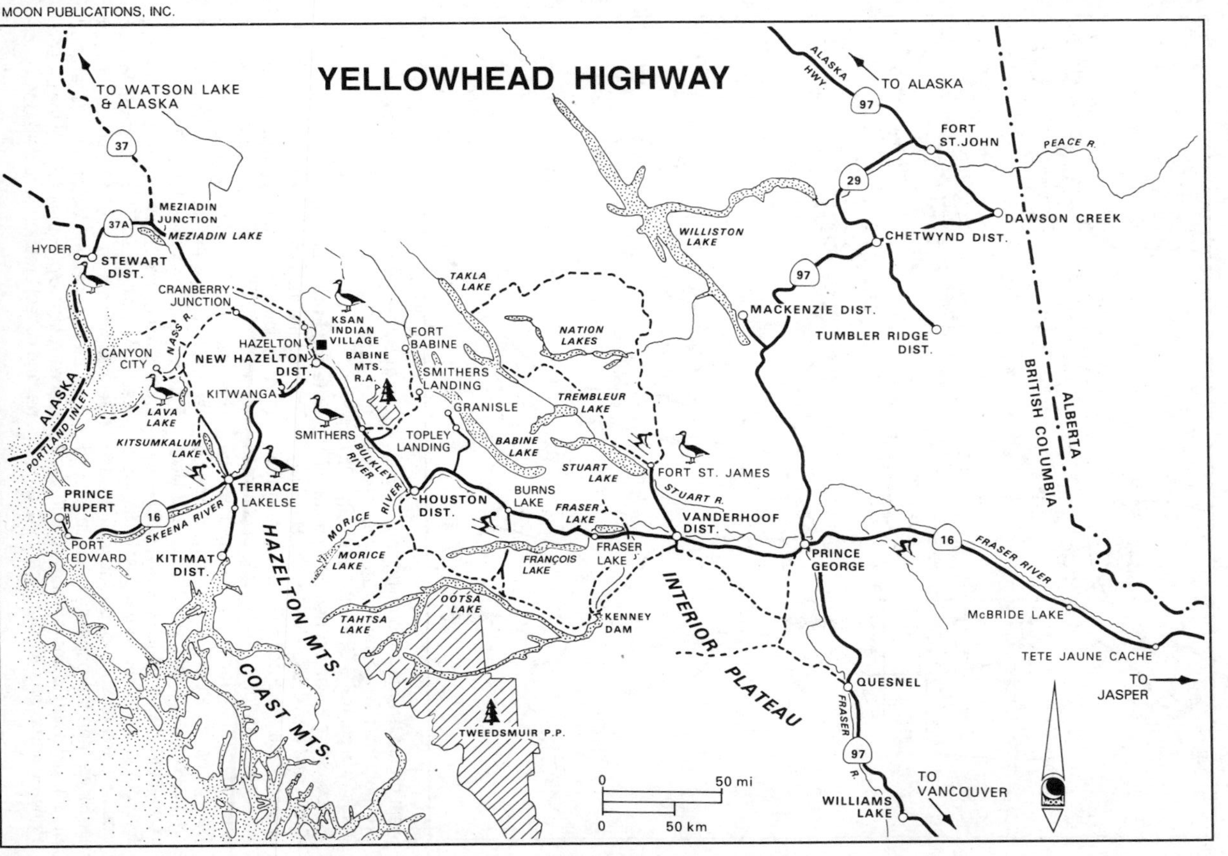
YELLOWHEAD HIGHWAY
TO WATSON LAKE & ALASKA
37
37A
HYDER
STEWART DIST.
MEZIADIN JUNCTION
MEZIADIN LAKE
CRANBERRY JUNCTION
NASS R.
CANYON CITY
LAVA LAKE
ALASKA
PORTLAND INLET
KITSUMKALUM LAKE
HAZELTON
NEW HAZELTON DIST.
KITWANGA
KSAN INDIAN VILLAGE
BABINE MTS. R.A.
FORT BABINE
SMITHERS LANDING
SMITHERS
BULKLEY RIVER
TOPLEY LANDING
GRANISLE
TAKLA LAKE
NATION LAKES
TREMBLEUR LAKE
BABINE LAKE
STUART LAKE
FORT ST. JAMES
STUART R.
WILLISTON LAKE
ALASKA HWY.
TO ALASKA
97
FORT ST. JOHN
PEACE R.
29
DAWSON CREEK
CHETWYND DIST.
MACKENZIE DIST.
TUMBLER RIDGE DIST.
BRITISH COLUMBIA
ALBERTA
PRINCE RUPERT
16
SKEENA RIVER
PORT EDWARD
TERRACE
LAKELSE
KITIMAT DIST.
HOUSTON DIST.
MORICE RIVER
MORICE LAKE
BURNS LAKE
FRASER LAKE
FRANÇOIS LAKE
FRASER LAKE
VANDERHOOF DIST.
PRINCE GEORGE
FRASER RIVER
McBRIDE LAKE
TETE JAUNE CACHE
TO JASPER
HAZELTON MTS.
COAST MTS.
OOTSA LAKE
TAHTSA LAKE
KENNEY DAM
INTERIOR PLATEAU
TWEEDSMUIR P.P.
QUESNEL
FRASER R.
97
WILLIAMS LAKE
TO VANCOUVER
0
50 mi
0
50 km

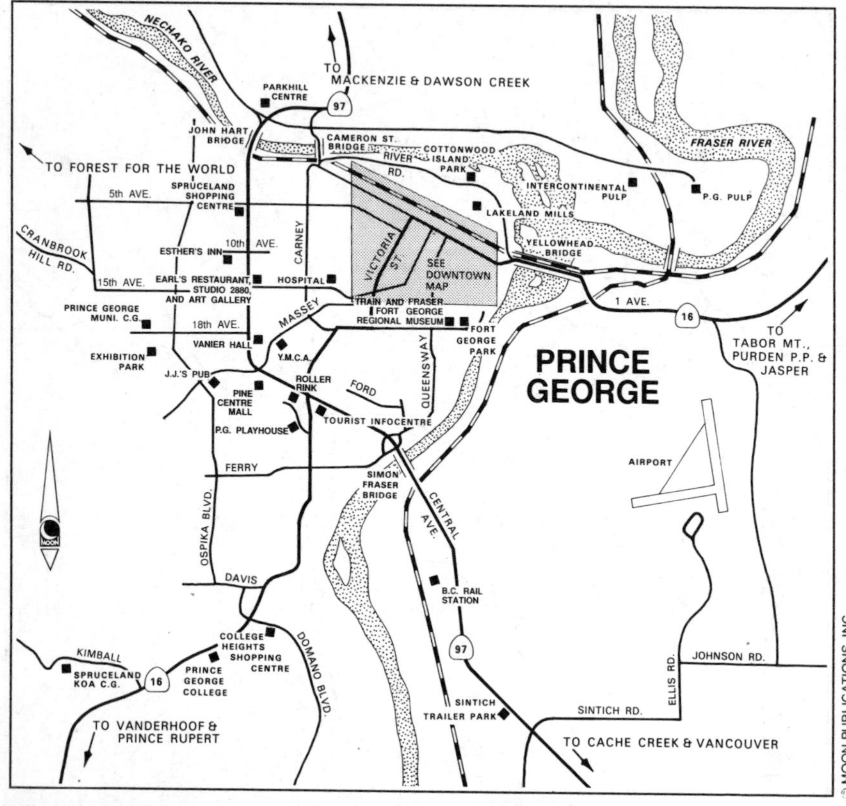

went on to become a major logging, sawmill, and pulp mill town, center of the white spruce industry in central B.C. in the 1940s. By 1951 Prince George was connected with Dawson Creek and the Alaska Hwy. by the Hart Hwy., and in 1958 the Pacific Great Eastern Railway reached town. Hundreds of sawmills started cutting local timber, and Prince George became the self-proclaimed "Spruce Capital of the World." The Yellowhead Hwy. connected the city to Tete Jaune Cache and Edmonton in 1968, three pulp mills were opened, and all sorts of businesses flooded in. Since then the population has increased at a rapid rate to more than 70,000, and Prince George has become the third-largest city in B.C.—the economic, social, and cultural center of the north.

Entering From The East

Passing the intersection with Hwy. 97 South (Old Cariboo Highway), continue down the hill for views of the mighty Fraser River, the city, and a number of large pulp mills on the far side. Cross the river via Yellowhead Bridge, pass the exit to River Rd., and continue straight on 1st Ave.; signs to the left lead to city center. The **Tourism Prince George** office is at 1198 Victoria St., across from the Connaught Motor Inn. It's a good place to start, to pick the brains of the personnel and collect brochures, and it's open year-round on weekdays 0830-1700. Another seasonal InfoCentre stands at the intersection of Highways 97 South and 16 West.

SIGHTS

Fraser Fort George Regional Museum

Fraser Fort George Museum is an excellent place to discover the fascinating natural history of Prince George, and the lifestyle and culture of local Carrier Indians. (Some experts think they were called Carrier because wives carried the charred bones of their deceased husbands on their backs to show their grief.) The self-guided tour pamphlet (pick one up at the main entrance) gives you the opportunity to explore the museum at your own pace; allow at least 30 minutes—though you'll probably want to take longer. Some of the items on display include taxidermied specimens of wild animals and birds native to British Columbia, fine crafts of the Carrier Indians, an impressive sternwheeler anchor, snowshoes, guns, horrific animal traps and other relics of the fur trade, artifacts from early saw-milling days, an old buggy, and mock-ups of early business establishments (don't miss the gruesome dental equipment!). The museum is at the end of 20th Ave. (off Gorse St.) in riverside Fort George Park, tel. 562-1612; open mid-May to mid-Sept. on Mon., Wed., and Sun. 1000-1700 and Tues. 1000-2000; mid-Sept. to mid-May on Tues. 1200-2000 and Wed.-Sun. 1200-1700; admission adult $1, senior and child 50 cents.

Outside the museum, 36-hectare, grassy, tree-shaded Fort George Park is the site of Fraser's original North West Company fort. Trails lead through the park, along the river, and to the Indian Burial Grounds. Just across from the museum is the original **Fort George Railway Station** where on weekends and holidays 1300-1600, weather permitting, a miniature steam train provides rides along a kilometer or so of track; adult $1.25, senior or child 75 cents. Next to the rail station is an old schoolhouse—if locked, peek in through the window at row after row of old-fashioned desks. In summer, Fort George Park is the setting for the July **Folk Fest** celebrations and **Simon Fraser Days** in July/August.

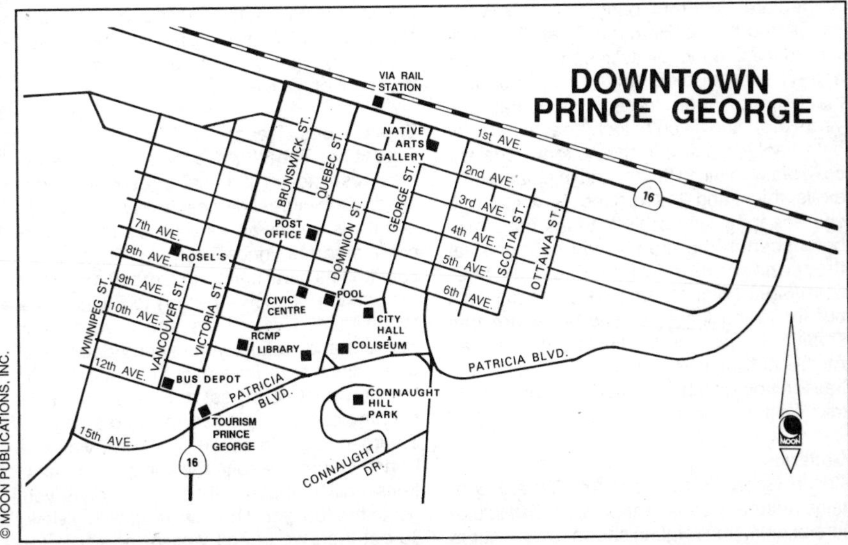

Prince George Railway And Forestry Museum

Here's one railway buffs shouldn't miss. Take a self-guided tour through some of the antiquated railway cars and buildings, clamber on retired railway equipment, and chug back in time via the black-and-white photo displays and assorted memorabilia. The museum has all sorts of railway equipment, and some waiting to be restored when the B.C. Railroad Preservation and Museum Society can assemble the funds. The museum sells bookends and paperweights made from vintage 1910-1914 rail, and railway-related caps, books, crests, tapes, videos, and calendars. It's on River Rd., open May-Sept. daily 1000-1700, tel. 563-7351; admission is free but donations are gladly accepted. From town, take the River Rd. exit to the left just before the Yellowhead Bridge over the Fraser.

Cottonwood Island Nature Park

Just along River Rd. from the Railroad Museum is the entrance to beautiful Cottonwood Island Nature Park—one of Prince George's 116 city parks, and a beautiful spot for a quiet stroll or picnic. In this peaceful 33-hectare riverfront park, one of several connected by the Heritage River Trail System (see "Outdoor Activities," below), you'll see all sorts of birds, many large northern black cottonwood trees (some over 300 years old), and if you're lucky, beaver, fox, or bald eagles. In spring the cottonwoods are covered with sticky buds, and in summer the air is thick and the ground is white with seed-bearing tufts of fluff. Bears have also been seen in the area (if you spot one, let the conservation office know at 565-6140/6290). Signs warn park users to watch out for falling limbs, and to be aware that some trails flood during times of high water. At the entrance is a map showing all the trails. If you only have time for a quick stroll, take Cottonwood Trail to the river.

Galleries

Prince George's two-floor **Art Gallery** contains a large, permanent painting and sculpture exhibit, and rotating shows (every four to five weeks). High-quality artwork—paintings, sculpture, pottery, beadwork, woven and painted silk items, and jewelry—by local artists is also for sale. It's a good spot to pick up a handcrafted treasure at a reasonable price. The gallery is at 2840 15th Ave. (bus stop outside), next to Studio 2880 (where you can catch artists in the act of creation), open Mon.-Sat. 1000-1700, Sun. 1300-1700, tel. 563-6447; admission by donation.

To see and buy all sorts of native arts and crafts, head for the **Native Art Gallery** at 144 George St., between 1st and 2nd avenues, tel. 562-7385. It's open Tues.-Sat. year-round 1000-1800. Admission is free, and in summer you can see crafts being demonstrated. Sweatshirts with Indian designs, moccasins, jewelry, carvings, and hand-printed cards are all for sale.

Views, Views, Views

For a 360-degree view of the city and surrounding landscape, walk or drive up the small but fairly steep hill to **Connaught Hill Park** in the center of the city. At the summit are several well-kept rock gardens crammed with color in summer, grassy tree-shaded lawns, picnic spots, and viewpoints. Get there from downtown by taking Queensway St. south, then turn right on Connaught Dr. and right on Caine Drive.

Trees, Trees, Trees

Forest For The World, a forested, motor-vehicle-restricted, 106-hectare recreation area set aside for forest demos, hiking, and cross-country skiing, was established in 1986 to commemorate Prince George's 75th anniversary and its participation in Expo86. A map at the parking lot shows the way to Shane Lake (10 minutes), where it's fun to watch the beavers and waterfowl (in spring ducks and geese flock here for a migratory rest), a hilltop viewpoint northwest of Shane Lake (15-minute hike), plus picnic spots and a shelter. The road to the forest does not give views of Prince George despite the climb—too many trees—but if you're willing to hike once you get to the top, you'll be rewarded with a view. To get there you need your own vehicle (or bicycle if you've got plenty of calories to burn). Cruise to the west end of the city via 15th Ave., continue onto Foothills Blvd., and turn left on Cranbrook Hill Rd., which steeply climbs Cranbrook Hill. At the signs for Forest Of The World, turn left on gravel Kueng Rd. and continue to the end.

Tours

Forestry is the heart and soul of Prince George's economy. If you want to get more of an idea of what goes on in a forest-products company, or a lumber or pulp mill, call in at one of the Tourist InfoCentres and book one of their three- to four-hour tours. **Northwood Pulp and Timber Tours** (May-Sept.) will guide you through the nursery where thousands of seedlings grow in a climate-controlled atmosphere, the sawmill where logs are processed into dimension lumber, and the pulp mill where high-quality pulp is produced for paper manufacturers around the world. The tour is free, but visitors are required to wear long pants and closed-toe shoes for safety. Visitors with heart or respiratory problems should avoid this tour, as it involves climbing up and down lots of stairs. Tours depart from the Tourism Prince George office every afternoon—they're very popular, so book ahead at 562-3700 to avoid disappointment. Northwood also provides free tours through **North Central Plywood** to see plywood being made with the latest technology—from lathe to shipping.

The Tourism Prince George staff conducts a variety of other three- to four-hour city tours of the parks, galleries, museums, etc., for a nominal fee. Or on request they'll design a tour to include special interests. Again, these are popular in summer so book a day or so ahead at 562-3700. They generally depart from the Tourism Prince George office in the morning. If you'd rather take a self-guided tour, ask the staff for suggestions to suit your schedule and interests.

Outdoor Activities

Prince George is a convenient central base for a wide range of outdoor pursuits—from lake and river fishing for trout, char, salmon, steelhead, Dolly Varden, whitefish, sturgeon, and grayling, to canoeing or boating on nearby lakes, to wildlife watching for black and grizzly bear, elk, mountain goats and sheep, caribou, wolves, deer, and moose. In spring, autumn, and winter, visit the unique **Moose Viewing Area** near Tabor Mountain to see these enormous wild vegetarians in their natural habitat. Anglers must have a license and follow the rules (catch and possession limits are strictly enforced), and non-B.C. resident hunters must be accompanied by a licensed guide. Several guiding outfits also offer a number of outdoor activities, from a day-trip rafting the Bowron River (from $55 pp) to guided hunting and fishing trips from remote backcountry lodges (credit card time)—peruse all the brochures in the InfoCentre for the complete picture.

Hikers can follow the **Heritage River Trails** through the city, appreciating the local natural history through a number of interpretive signs. The clearly marked gravel trail, which can be used by hikers, joggers, cyclists, and cross-country skiers, runs between the Cameron St. Overpass and Carrie Jane Gray Park (a total of 11 km if you complete the circuit by following Carney Street). Ask for the "Heritage River Trails" pamphlet at the InfoCentre. The staff will also provide you with many other free pamphlets and brochures describing trails in the Prince George area and surrounds. If you want to get off the beaten track, request the **Fort George Canyon Trail** booklet (and map), which describes the 4½-km trail through the canyon (striking in autumn) east of **West Lake Provincial Park.** To get there go west along Hwy. 16, turn south on Blackwater Rd. S, then left on West Lake Road. Continue to the winter parking area, and a summer parking area farther along at the end of a narrow gravel road.

Downhill skiers head for **Purden Ski Village** and **Tabor Mountain** (east of the city) where lessons and rentals are available, or **Powder King** (international level) in the Pine Pass. Within a few hours' drive from Prince George are the well-known **Hudson Bay Mountain** ski area at Smithers and **Marmot**

Basin at Jasper. Cross-country skiers can find beautiful spots to ski just about anywhere in the area—**Fort George Park** or **Cottonwood Island Park** downtown, a day ski along abandoned logging roads, or an overnight ski to **Raven Lake.** Get more details at the InfoCentres.

ACCOMMODATIONS

Camping Out

Spruceland KOA is a popular campground (crowded in summer—grab a site by mid-afternoon) on the west side of town; open April 1-Oct. 31. Away from the main highway, it's quiet and many of the sites are partially separated by trees. Each site has a picnic table and a barbecue grate, and the facilities include spotlessly clean heated bathrooms, coin-operated laundry, swimming pool, dump station, and playground. Sites from $13-14, additional $2 each for electricity and sewer hookups. A pancake breakfast is up for grabs 0700-0900 every day. The KOA is on Kimball Rd., off Hwy. 16 (about five km west of the Hwy. 16/97 junction), tel. 964-7272.

The closest campground to city center is the treeless **Prince George Municipal Campground and Trailer Park** across from Exhibition Park at 4188 18th Ave. (entrance on 18th Ave. and Ospika Blvd.), tel. 563-2313. It's open May-Sept., has hot showers, a sanistation, a playground, and limited electrical hookups. Sites start at $9.50 d, plus an additional $2 for electricity. On the south side of Prince George (five km south, off Hwy. 97), **Sintich RV Park** is an adult-only park with landscaped lots for RVs, washrooms, showers, laundry, store, service station, and RV storage. Sites range $9-15; tel. 963-9862.

Bed And Breakfast

Usually several homes in the area provide B&B for guests, but hosts and homes come and go. Expect to pay from $30 s, $35 d per night. Check out the current listings and make reservations at one of the InfoCentres.

Motels And Hotels

Prince George has plenty of motels, most of them downtown or along the Hwy. 97 bypass. Singles are $28-45, doubles $30-55. Expect to pay slightly more at one of the several motor inns. For a comfortable room and a load of extras at a reasonable price, try **Esther's Inn.** The interior is a sight for sore eyes and weary bodies—a lush tropical oasis of palms and philodendrons, waterfalls, Polynesian artifacts from Hawaii and Tahiti, Jacuzzis, and pools, with a waterslide next door if the pool and Jacuzzis don't provide enough zing! Rooms range from $40-56 s, $43-62 d, $52-62 twin. For an extra $5 you can have a room with a kitchen—or try the thatched-roof Papaya Grove restaurant for a filling breakfast or buffet lunch (see "Food," below). The inn is at 1151 Commercial Dr. (one block off Hwy 97 North and 10th Ave.), tel. 562-4131.

Holiday Inn downtown has all the full-service hotel facilities you'd exect, plus a restaurant, a lounge, a pub, an indoor pool, a sauna and whirlpool, a casino, a gift shop, and free covered parking. Rooms are $91-107 s, $107-122 d, $91-96 twin. It's at 444 George St., tel. 563-0055.

FOOD

Great Lunches

At **Earl's,** the servings are small, the prices are average, but the *food* is . . . mm-mm-good. You may have to wait for a table (the outdoor patio is in demand), but there's plenty to look at in the meantime. From the mirrored ceiling hangs a mass of papier-mâché parrots on bird stands in all sorts of poses, white tables and chairs lurk amongst plenty of foliage, and everything is green or white. Sandwiches, croissants, burgers, salads, and daily specials are $5-9, main meals $8 and up, with an enormous selection of wines and beers from around the world. Their Djakarta Chicken with peanut sauce is particularly tasty, but order a side salad (it's large for the price) and french fries or bread to make it a meal. It's open daily 1100 to 2400, at 1440 East Central (by 15th), tel. 562-1527.

Another excellent place for lunch is the poolside **Papaya Grove** in Esther's Inn, open weekdays 0630-2200, weekends from around 0900. They serve filling breakfasts (from $3), Sunday brunch 1100-1400 for around $9 per adult, $5 child. Monday-Sat. 1100-1400 don't miss the eat-all-you-can luncheon buffet (salad bar, hot dishes, vegetables, and desserts, with a different theme each day of the week—Thurs. is generally Chinese, Fri. seafood, etc.); around $6 adult, $4 child. For dinner expect to pay $8-28 for a main course of seafood, steak, or island specialties. The other restaurant in the inn also has a salad bar, sandwiches and hamburgers, salads, and dinners (more expensive). The inn is at 1151 Commercial Dr., tel. 562-4131.

Great Dinners

Niner's Diner at 508 George St. has an intriguing green-and-gray 1950s diner decor, and all the waiters and waitresses are garbed in shiny shirts and small green aprons. Chicken dishes are $6-10 (the stir fry is huge), sandwiches and burgers from $5, pasta, seafood, steaks, and prime rib range $9-16, and desserts are $2-5. It's open Sun.-Thurs. 1130-2300, Fri. and Sat. 1130-2330, tel. 562-1299. **The Keg** at 582 George St. (corner of 6th Ave.) has "more than an appetizer but less than a meal" snacks for $7-10, steak for $11-18, seafood $13-20, chicken, ribs, prime rib, and a tantalizing salad bar (a meal in itself). It's impossible to leave here hungry! It's open Mon.-Thurs. 1600-2300, Fri. and Sat. 1600-2400, Sun. 1600-2230, tel. 563-1768.

Bonanza Restaurant at 2757 Spruce St., tel. 562-9025, also features a huge salad bar, steak and seafood, and reasonable prices. Another popular spot with locals is **Cariboo Steak and Seafood Restaurant** at 1165 5th Ave. (between George and Dominion streets), open Mon.-Sat. for lunch and dinner, on Sun. for dinner only. Salads and sandwiches at lunchtime start at around $5, charbroiled hamburgers and steaks around $7, and chicken, veal, and seafood specialties are $5.50-8. At dinner you can expect to pay $12-22 for a main course; tel. 564-1220.

When locals feel like dressing up and splashing out a little, they head for **Rosel's.** Located in a heritage house (with an outdoor patio), Rosel's serves daily lunch specials such as soup in a bowl of bread or summer salads for $5-8, main courses (veal, prawns, cabbage rolls, Viennese schnitzel, pasta, European sausages, and sandwiches) for $7-9. Dinners are $8-18, and with all the main dishes you have the option of selecting small or regular portions—handy for the diet-conscious. It's on the corner of Vancouver and 7th Ave., tel. 562-4972, open Mon.-Sat. 1100-1500 and daily from 1700. For more restaurant suggestions, refer to the very handy *Visitor's Guide to Prince George* pamphlet, free from Tourism Prince George.

ENTERTAINMENT

Sit Down And Listen

Prince George offers as much to do in the evening as it does during the day. For live theater (excellent Prince George Theatre workshop productions), check out the schedule at the **Prince George Playhouse** on Hwy. 16 W across from the Hwy. 97 junction and the InfoCentre, tel. 563-8401. **Studio 2880** is the local arts center, operated by the Community Arts Council. It hosts many of the cultural activities in the area (acts as a ticket office for events) and organizes the two major craft markets each year, workshops, art classes, special events, concerts, and ballets. Drop by and see what's happening at 2880 15th Ave., or tel. 562-4526. In 800-seat **Vanier Hall,** you can take in a performance by the **Prince George Symphony, Friends of the Opera,** and many visiting performers. Even larger events (such as Octoberfest, sporting and recreational meets including rodeos, lacrosse tournaments, and shows) are held in the 2,500-seat **Coliseum,** between the library and Four Seasons Pool on the other side of Dominion. Find out what's going on in the local newspaper and at the InfoCentres. Prince George also has four movie theaters—refer to the local newspaper for showings.

Get Up And Boogie

Of the city's many pubs and nightclubs, two of the most popular are **Steamers** at 2595 Queensway (tel. 562-6654), and **J.J.'s** at 3601 Massey (tel. 562-0001). **Overdrive Cabaret** at 1192 5th Ave. (tel. 564-3773) has a DJ playing top-40 hits, as does the **770 Club** in the Coast Inn of the North at 770 Brunswick (tel. 563-0121), while the **Rockpit** at 1380 2nd Ave. (tel. 563-7720) features live bands—usually heavy metal. If you're just looking for a friendly pub and a quiet drink, try **Coach's Corner Pub** in the Holiday Inn at 444 George Street.

Burn Off Those Calories

If entertainment for you means doing something active, the **Four Seasons Pool** at 700 Dominion (the corner of 7th Ave.) is open daily 0630-2200/2300; admission allows use of the pools, saunas, Jacuzzi, waterslide, snackbar, and several daily aquafit classes. Waterslide fanatics may want to hurl their bods down the **Fantasy North Waterslide** next to Esther's Inn (entrance in the inn); call for current hours at 562-4131. Prince George also has a large number of recreational facilities, including bowling alleys, roller and curling rinks, and golf courses.

Festivals And Wacky Events

Prince George is certainly not short on year-round celebrations and goofy seasonal events. In spring, **Elks May Days** and the biennial **Forestry Exhibition** start the festival ball rolling. In May, Prince George holds its **Canadian Northern Childrens Festival,** in June and Nov. two major craft shows. **Simon Fraser Days** is a 10-day citywide summer celebration, held around the beginning of Aug., that coincides with the Prince George Exhibition. During this week and a half of madness, you'll witness just about everything: sandblasting (skiing down gravel cutbanks), mudbowl volleyball, raft races, rodeo, triathlon. There's also the **Folkfest** in Fort George Park early in July, when the city celebrates its ethnic heritage through song, dance, food, and dress, and **Octoberfest** wails for days with Bavarian oom-pah-pah at the Coliseum. In Jan. the **Prince George Winter Carnival** features logging sports, scuba diving, and dogsled and car races on the ice at nearby Tabor Lake. Mid-Feb. the city goes berserk with a 10-day **Mardi Gras,** featuring snoball and snogolf in bright crazy costumes, knurdling (jousting using padded poles), bed races on ice and other hog-wild events, and it's all finished off with a fireworks display. Several other music, dance, and theater festivals are held during the rest of the year—ask at the InfoCentre for a free calendar of events. There's no excuse for being bored here!

INFORMATION AND SERVICES

The main InfoCentre is **Tourism Prince George** at the corner of Victoria St. and Patricia Blvd., tel. 562-3700. The helpful staff arranges three- to four-hour city, special-interest, and industrial tours, and they have a wide assortment of brochures and pamphlets. It's open Mon.-Fri. 0830-1700 year-round. The seasonal **Travel Infocentre** (open May-Sept.) is on the southwest side of the city at the intersection of Highways 16 W and 97, tel. 563-5493; open daily 0900-2000. The staff here will also arrange and book city and industrial tours, but they depart from Tourism Prince George downtown.

The **hospital** is at 2000 15th Ave.; tel. 565-2000, or 565-2444 in an emergency. For an **ambulance** phone 564-4558. A **health clinic** deals with walk-in problems; turn off 15th Ave. on Edmonton by the hospital. The **RCMP** is on the corner of Brunswick and 10th Ave. (behind the library); tel. 562-3371, or 563-1111 in an emergency. The main **post office** is on the corner of 5th Ave. and Quebec St. (open weekdays 0830-1700). **Prince George Public Libary** is at 887 Dominion (tel. 563-9251), and it has a good display of Indian art and artifacts; open Mon.-Thurs. 1000-2100, Fri. and Sat. 1000-1730, Sun. 1300- 1700. Public **showers** are available for a nominal fee at the YMCA off Massey, tel. 562-9341, and at the Municipal Campground, tel. 563-2313.

Prince George shops, even the large supermarkets, close at 1800 except on Fri., when they're open until 2100. **Pine Centre Mall** is at 3117 Massey Dr., off Hwy. 97 N, and has a Sears store along with a cavalcade of other shops. The **Overwaitea** store in the **Spruceland Shopping Centre** on Rear Central St. (northwest side of town) has a fantastic selection of bulk foods, salads, pizzas, take-home meals, and a fresh juice bar, along with the usual groceries. **Parkwood Shopping Centre** is at 1602 15th Avenue.

TRANSPORTATION

By Bus

To get around Prince George by city bus (no service on Sun. or holidays; have plenty of coins at the ready), pick up a current *Prince George Rider's Guide* from the InfoCentre or stop in at 1039 Great St., tel. 563-0011. Prince George **handyDART** provides door-to-door transportation for the disabled unable to use the regular bus service; for info or to request a trip, call 562-1394 weekdays 0900-1700. For **Airporter** service call 563-2220.

The Greyhound **Bus Depot** is at 1566 12th Ave. (corner of Victoria), just across from the InfoCentre, tel. 564-5454. Inside is a waiting room and a restaurant. **Greyhound** provides bus services south to the Okanagan and to Vancouver via Williams Lake and Quesnel, west to Vanderhoof, Fort St. James, Smithers, Terrace, and Prince Rupert, north to Chetwynd, Mackenzie, Dawson Creek, and Fort St. John, and east to McBride, Jasper, and Edmonton.

By Train

The **VIA Rail station** is on 1st Ave. between Brunswick and Quebec streets, tel. 564-5233 (departures and arrivals) or (800) 561-8630 (within B.C.); passenger trains travel east-west, servicing Prince Rupert and Jasper, Edmonton and Eastern Canada. Prince George to Prince Rupert (14 hours) departs Tues., Thurs., and Sat. at 0615; Prince George to Edmonton (16 hours with a two-hour wait in Jasper) departs Mon., Wed., and Fri. at 1110; students with ID card and seniors get one-third off regular fares. All trains have dining cars; sleeping berths cost extra. If you arrive in Prince George after dark, don't wander around the station area as there are lots of bars nearby—phone for a taxi.

The **B.C. Rail Passenger Station** is on the southeast side of the city, off Terminal Blvd. (go to the end and cross the first set of railway tracks—the station is on the left before the next set of tracks), tel. 564-9081. B.C. Rail provides north-south passenger service between Prince Rupert and North Vancouver, taking about 13 hours, with daily service June-September. Costs $71.50 OW or $128.50 RT coach class (food available), $108 OW or $194.50 RT Cariboo class (includes three meals; book tickets in advance), specials for seniors and children. Their schedule has a handy guide to attractions you can see from the track. Buy tickets at the station Mon.-Fri. 0700-1530, Sat. and Sun. mornings from around 0700. For more info and a current schedule, phone 564-9080. A bus meets the train in North Vancouver, taking passengers to the city bus depot on Dunsmuir Street.

By Air

The **airport** is about 18 km east of town, with a licensed lounge/bar and cafeteria. Get there by airporter bus for adult $8, child $2.68 OW; call 563-2220. In summer the road to the airport is edged by a wildflower carpet of every color imaginable—predominantly white daisies, pink clover, and bright orange-red Indian paintbrush. **Air B.C.** (tel. 561-2905) and **Canadian Airlines International** (tel. 563-0521) are represented at the airport, both with scheduled flights to most centers in British Columbia. For **Aviair Aviation** flight info or reservations, call (800) 482-3598 (in Kamloops 554-3161). Charter flights are also available.

By Car

For a **taxi,** dial 563-3333 or 564-4444. For car rental, expect to pay at least $40 a day plus 15 cents a kilometer for an economy car—considerably less if you rent by the week or longer. Rental car agencies: **Budget Rent-a-Car,** 125 Victoria St., tel. 564-8395, airport tel. 963-9339; **Hertz Rent-a-Car,** 600 Quebec St., tel. 561-1846, airport tel. 963-7454; **Sears Rent-a-Car,** 125 Victoria St., tel. 564-6767; **Tilden Rent-a-Car,** 1350 7th Ave., tel. 564-4847, airport tel. 963-7473; **Tweedsmuir Rent-a-Car,** 1331 Central St., tel. 562-3388, airport tel. 563-5123; **Rent-A-Wreck,** 1956 3rd Ave., tel. 563-7336; **Canuck Truck Rental,** 40-1839 1st Ave., tel. 563-3675; **Ryder Truck Rental,** 1755 1st Ave., tel. 564-4515.

PRINCE GEORGE TO SMITHERS

The First Stretch

As you leave Prince George, stock up on insect repellent (in summer you'll need it) and film. As you continue west orange, yellow, and white wildflowers brilliantly splash the grassy borders. In some areas the wildflowers are so dense you'd swear two wide strips of top-quality multicolored shag carpet had been laid along either side of the road for kilometer after kilometer—especially in early July when the shag is fresh out of the store! Highway 16 takes you past many lakes (and turnoffs to many more), then to **Bednesti Lake Resort** (50 km west of Prince George, tel. 441-3313). This resort has a beach, boat-launching facilities, units from $25-30 s, $27-32 d, campsites from $8 per night, showers, laundry facilities, licensed dining room and lounge, and a service station. Continue up and down low tree-covered hills for many kilometers, and you'll be continuously delighted by ponds choked with waterlilies, the occasional open meadow, more ponds and small lakes, well-kept farms, and endless wildflowers.

VANDERHOOF

The first town you come to west of Prince George is Vanderhoof, a small farming and logging community and the service center for the Nechako Valley. It also claims to be the geographical center of B.C. (the actual spot is marked by a cairn five km east of Vanderhoof). If you're tootling through this neck of the woods in search of good fishing opportunities, pick up an invaluable copy of the latest *North Central Fishing Guide* for $4.50 from the local InfoCentre. Rivers and lakes dot the region, many well-known for their excellent fishing—ask locals for advice and directions to the hottest spots. Another must-have for those who want to escape the main highway is the free *Forest Service Recreation Sites* brochure and map for Vanderhoof-Kluskus. It shows the Nechako River watershed south of Vanderhoof and Engen, including forest roads, trails, recreation sites, campsites, and facilities. If you're going on to Fort St. James, also collect the free Forest Service brochure and map for Stuart Lake.

Sights

The 1914 building at the corner of Hwy. 16 and Pine Ave. houses **Vanderhoof Community Museum** and is headquarters for **Heritage Village.** Amongst 11 heritage buildings, the museum displays taxidermied birds and animals, pioneer equipment, blacksmithing tools, a rock collection, and plenty of local history from gold-rush and pioneer days; open daily 1000-1700, admission by donation. Behind the museum is the **OK Cafe,** where you can tuck in to hearty homemade soup and rolls, salads, and tasty pie and ice cream inside this heritage-style building with its interior decorated with old-fashioned wallpaper and frilly curtains; open daily 1000-1700.

Vanderhoof's striking town sign is adorned with a Canada goose. You can see 50,001 (but who's counting?) of these beautiful birds and a variety of other waterfowl in spring and autumn at their transient home, **Nechako Bird Sanctuary,** along the banks of the Nechako River. Access is via the wooden bridge at the north end of Burrard Ave., the main street. If you want to get away from the main highway for a couple of hours, take a 100-km detour south along a good gravel road (Nechako Ave., then Kenney Dam Rd.) to the Alcan reservoir and **Kenney Dam.** It was once the largest earth-filled dam in the world—now surpassed by other dams in B.C. A 20-minute walk to 18-meter **Cheslatta Falls** is worth the effort (cross the dam, then turn back up the river to the falls and picnic area).

If you happen to be in town in July, you may also happen to notice 20,000 people—instead of the usual 3,000-4,000 milling around—in Vanderhoof to enjoy the spectacular three-day **Vanderhoof International Airshow,** one of the largest camping airshows in North America. Planes putt and zoom in from just about everywhere to see Canadian and U.S. military jet aerobatic displays, antique fighters and warbirds, static displays, and some of the best dancing in the sky—don't miss it! Admission is $11 adult, $7 senior or child ($9 and $6 if bought ahead); campsites are $9 per night. For more info write to Box 1248, Vanderhoof, B.C. V0J 3A0, or call 567-3144.

Practicalities

At **Vanderhoof Municipal Campground** on Stony Creek (follow Hwy. 16 through town and look for the sign on the left), tel. 567-9393, shaded campsites are only $4 per night, water included, but no hookups or showers. RV hookups are available at the **Buena Vista Motel and RV Park** on Hwy. 16 at the west end of town, tel. 567-2296; campsites are $8-15 per night, motel units are $36-40 s, $42-45 d, and cooking facilities are available for an extra $5. The main street downtown is Burrard Ave., which turns north off First St. (Hwy. 16). For delicious food at reasonable prices locals recommend the comfortable log-cabin **North Country Inn** on Burrard Ave. (almost opposite Connaught). At lunch burgers and sandwiches are $3.50-8, soup and salad bar is around $6; dinners start around $8 (soup and salad bar). Try the delicious chicken lasagne; steak or seafood dinners $9-25. For more of a splash, try **Tachick Lake Lodge**—take Nechako Ave. out of town toward Kenney Dam.

St. John Hospital is on Hospital Rd. on the north side of town; the **post office** is on Stewart St. (corner of Church); the **public library** is on Stewart St. by Creasey Avenue. Vanderhoof doesn't have a local bus system, but the **Greyhound depot** is in the **Co-op Mall** on Stewart Street. To get to the airport follow the highway west through town, continue for several kilometers, then turn right at the weigh scales toward Fort St. James.

FORT ST. JAMES

Before you head for Fort St. James (or any northwestern community, for that matter) in summer, check your supply of insect repellent. Continuing along Hwy. 16 W, look out for the turnoff to Fort St. James via Hwy. 27 N, a few kilometers west of Vanderhoof. If you have several hours to spend exploring this area, it's a worthwhile 64-km detour to see the first settlement on the Pacific Slope of B.C. The community boasts a National Historic Park housing the restored fort that used to be the capital of New Caledonia—the name originally given to central B.C. by Simon Fraser.

The Road To Fort St. James

Highway 27 takes you through gentle agricultural scenery, over the wide, glassy Nechako River, and through enormous rolling meadows with open vistas in all directions to wilderness forests that surround Fort St. James. In the distance lies a low range of deep-blue forest-covered hills. As you approach Fort St. James (residents refer to it as "the Fort"), you pass the turnoffs to **Paarens Beach Provincial Park** (11 km off the main road) and **Sowchea Bay Provincial Park,** both offering lakeside tent and vehicle camping, boat launch facilities, washrooms, and picnic areas; open May-Sept. with a $6 nightly fee for campers. Cross Stuart River where many floatplanes are moored; **Stuart River Campground** on Roberts Rd., tel. 996-8690, is open May-Oct., providing moorage, river fishing, boat launch and rentals, showers, and a laundromat; sites $10 per night plus $1 for electricity. Finally you come to **Stuart Lake,** seventh largest in the province: more than 90 km long, up to 13 km wide, and known to produce rainbow trout up to 17 pounds, lake char up to 30 pounds—not bad stats! You can also catch lake trout, whitefish, and kokanee (trolling is the accepted fishing method), and go sailing, waterskiing, and windsurfing. Note that the lake is not a safe place for small boats—it can get very rough very quickly. Small boats are particularly discouraged from using the main channel of the lake.

Town And Out-of-town Attractions

The village of Fort St. James has several attractions aside from the national historic park that everyone traveling the Yellowhead Hwy. hears about (see "The Park," below). Cruise the scenic lakefront (Stuart Dr. West, then Lakeshore Dr.) past Our Lady of Good Hope Catholic church, built in 1873, and the Russ Baker Memorial (Baker was a local bush pilot who founded Pacific Western Airlines). Find out more about the role bush pilots played in the early days of mining, fur trapping, and forestry in this area at the InfoCentre. Indian pictographs are found along the north shore but can only be seen by boat.

Many good hiking trails (details at the InfoCentre) wander away from the local area—three-km **Mt. Pope trail** northwest of town takes you to the summit for outrageous views of Stuart Lake and surrounding mountains and lakes; the **Mt. Shass trail** (four to five hours) takes you from the far end of Grassham Lake up the mountain, past pools and through meadows that one hiker claimed could have been the Scottish highlands—Simon Fraser must have done this hike! Be prepared for sudden weather changes. In winter, the local **Murray Ridge Ski Hill,** just 20 minutes north of Fort St. James, has 19 major downhill runs on a 1700-meter vertical hill, a T-bar, a day lodge, a ski rental shop, instruction (ski lesson packages), a ski patrol, a lunch counter, and a season that lasts from mid-Dec. to mid-April (Feb. is best). Cross-country skiing, snowmobiling, ice fishing, ice hockey, and curling are other popular winter activities.

North of Fort St. James, well-maintained gravel Germanson Landing North Rd. leads to the **Takla-Nation Lakes** region—a favorite with recreationists in search of untouched wilderness for great hiking and camping, and anglers desiring dozens of lakes crammed with grayling, char, rainbow trout, and Dolly Varden. Others canoe or boat along waterways used by pioneer explorers. Locals say it's possible, using a small motor boat, to putt 290 km through the lakes system from Fort St. James, taking 7-10 days. However, you need experience handling rough water and weather and should contact the local forest service office for advice about natural land and water hazards, weather patterns, and other pertinent conditions. Canoeists often travel the 100-km route through the Nation Lakes chain. The third very popular way of getting into the backcountry is by floatplane—to rustic lodges and remote fishing camps.

To get the scoop on the entire area and a community map, stop at the **Fort St. James Travel InfoCentre** on Douglas Ave., tel. 996-7023; open May, June, and Sept., Mon.-Fri. 0800-1630, in July and Aug. weekdays 0800-2000 and weekends 0900-1630.

The Park

Fort St. James, chief fur-trading post and capital of the large and prosperous district of New Caledonia in the early 1800s, is today a beautifully restored historic park at the west end of Stuart Lake. When Simon Fraser of the North West Company first arrived at Stuart Lake he was expanding the fur trade west of the Rockies and trying to find a water route to the Pacific. He established the fort among cooperative local Carrier Indians in 1806. The Indians did not fear the white man—they desired his iron, tools, weapons, and exotic jewelry—though their lifestyle was never the same again after the establishment of the fort. In 1821, after the amalgamation of the two major trading companies, the fort became a Hudson's Bay Company Fur Trading Post.

Enter the fort through the **Visitor Reception Centre** and, in May, June, and Sept., join one of the lively, fully guided walking tours—a great way to immerse yourself in British Columbia's adventurous past. In July and Aug. you're actively encouraged to get into the spirit of things and relive a bit of 1896 history. Appropriately dressed characters lurk in the log-constructed general store, the fish cache, the single men's bunkhouse, the main house, and the vegie garden. Play along! Tell them you've just arrived by canoe, want to stay the night in the men's house, and need a good horse and some provisions, and see what happens! These tours start at the reception area, and they're free.

The InfoCentre features displays on pioneer explorers, fur traders, and Carrier Indians (with moccasins, a bag for carrying bait, and other artifacts). An audio recording and a map trace the route of the early explorers, and a slide show fills you in on the restoration of the fort's original buildings. The park is open daily mid-May-June and Sept. 1000-1700, featuring the scheduled guided tours. In July and Aug. the hours are 0930-1730 seven days a week, with guided tours every 1½ hours. Although the restored trading post buildings are closed during the winter, the Visitor Reception Centre (tel. 996-7191) is open for visitors Mon.-Fri. 0800-1630; closed holidays. Admission is free.

ON TO BURNS LAKE

Pretty meadows, rolling hills, large trees, white daisies and psychedelic-orange Indian paintbrush along the road—the great scenery continues! Considering the number of stuffed critters that adorn restaurants and front porches in B.C., it's amazing how many wild animals, such as moose and deer, you can still admire from the highway. If you're hungry, pull off at the **Wagon Wheel Inn** for a quick bite; open 0600-2100. Ask the owners about their wilderness fishing trips and lodge in the mountains, accessible only by plane.

After passing through **Fort Fraser,** a former fur-trading post established by John Stuart in 1806 (one of the oldest communities in B.C.), you travel through a hilly forested area where the roadside carpet changes to white daisies splashed with bright-purple lupine. Cross the wide, deep-green Nechako River, passing the turnoff to **Beaumont Provincial Park** with its boating, and campsites, open May-Oct.; $8 per site May-September. Notice all the vehicles with canoes and kayaks atop, or towing boats, and RVs loaded to the hilt with canoes *and* kayaks *and* boats traveling this stretch of the highway in summer. Obviously, the area between Fort Fraser and Houston is a favorite boating and fishing destination. Most of the hundreds of lakes contain rainbow trout and char. The **Stellako River** (four km west of Fraser Lake) lures spin casters and fly-fishermen from afar, salmon enthusiasts for the annual salmon run between **Fraser** and **Francois** lakes, and canoeists to sample either beginner or expert rapids. In winter the ice-fishermen return to try their luck on Fraser and Francois lakes, and the area attracts its quota of cross-country skiers, skaters, and snowmobilers.

Between Fraser Lake and the forested hills lies a resort with a grassy, tree-shaded, lakeshore camping area (hookups and showers), more lakes, and another campground and motel. The small community of **Fraser Lake,** established on the south shore with the arrival of the Grand Trunk Pacific Railway, has a Travel InfoCentre on the highway as you enter town—call in for detailed fishing information. In the winter this area is aflutter with Canada geese, swans, and ducks.

After crossing the river a turnoff leads to **Francois Lake,** another fishy spot, and **Glenannan Tourist Area** at the east end, where a handful of resorts provide everything an angler could possibly desire. Also on the shores of Francois Lake is the **Darter Ranch,** where the annual three-day **Burns Lake Bluegrass Music Festival** is held early in July (free "rough" campsites). After **Endako,** you're in moose country for the next 17 km—drive with care. The highway crosses the Endako River, weaving back and forth across the railway tracks, through dense forest, passing distant lakes that sparkle through the trees, and more lakes—many jet black, their surfaces patterned with sunshine-yellow waterlilies.

BURNS LAKE

The first thing that strikes you when you enter this town is the welcoming sign with enormous chainsaw-carved trout and the inscription "Three Thousand Miles of Fishing!" That pretty much sums up what people like to do around here. Scenic Burns Lake, with its winding streets and heritage buildings, lies along the north shore of its namesake—another of those towns that jumped onto the map with the arrival of the Grand Trunk Pacific Railway in 1914-15.

Sights

Some of the town is off the highway, but continue along the main road through town for about one kilometer until you come to the green and white **Heritage Centre.** In the center is the **Burns Lake and District Travel InfoCentre**, open weekdays year-round, tel. 692-3773. Next door to the InfoCentre is the local museum. Its furnished rooms contain an odd assortment of articles, including a collection of foreign currency, memorabilia from an old ship viewed through a porthole, and a number of typewriters that have seen better days. Open daily 1300-1700; small admission charge. Ask at the InfoCentre for a pamphlet and map showing the location of all the heritage buildings around town, and the historic fur-trading depot and gambling den, **Bucket of Blood,** where a murder occurred during a poker game (Hwy. 16 and 5th Avenue). You'll also discover many gift shops where paintings and beadwork by the local Carrier Indian bands are on display.

For a wonderful view of the district, follow 5th Ave. up the hill out of town, then take the turnoff to the **Boer Mountain Forestry Lookout. Eagle Creek Agate Opal Site,** about 6½ km south of Burns Lake, is another local highlight for rock hounds. It's one of a few known areas in the province where precious opal can be found. Trails lead to picnic sites and campsites, Hoodoos, Opal Creek, and a collecting area (walking time about 1½ hours). Guided tours are available in July, leaving from the InfoCentre every Thurs. at 0900. Preregistration is required at tel. 692-3773 between 1000 and 1500. Provide your own transportation to the reserve, wear sturdy shoes or hiking boots, take your own rockhounding equipment, and don't forget the insect repellent.

Fish Fantasies

Burns Lake is in the heart of what is locally known as the Lakes District. More than 300 lakes dot the high country between the Fraser and Skeena river watersheds, and all are renowned fishing spots. To even mention all the lakes and their fishing possibilities would take another book! Ask at the InfoCentre for their free Burns Lake 3,000 Miles of Fishing map and info sheet, and the brochures on local fishing resorts, boat rental, floatplane adventures, and fishing and hunting guides. Fishing licenses are available at the resorts, sporting-goods stores, and B.C. government agent's office (ask how much the six-day and yearly licenses are; if you're fishing for several weeks it may be less expensive to buy the license for a year). Topographical maps of the Lakes District are available for $4 at the government agent's office. Burns Lake offers excellent fishing for rainbow, eastern brook, and cutthroat trout, kokanee, chinook, steelhead, and lake char, to name just a few.

Practicalities

Freeport KOA is off Hwy. 16 on Freeport Rd., about seven km east of Burns Lake, tel. 692-3105. It has picturesque tentsites up in a forested area where wild pink roses grow with abandon, and each site has a picnic table. The large RV section below, out in the open, has full hookups. Free showers, laundromat, store and gift shop. Tentsites from $12-16 d, plus electricity $2, sewer $1. **Burns Lake Motor Inn** has nonsmoking rooms, kitchenettes (add $6), and a sauna and fitness center; from $37 s, $47 d. On Hwy. 16 East, tel. 692-7545.

A local recommendation for eating out: **Panhandle Restaurant** at 710 Yellowhead serves good Chinese at reasonable prices; open Mon.-Thurs. 0700-2100, Fri. and Sat. to 2200, tel. 692-3316. For fast food try **The San-Bar** in **Lakeview Mall** by the highway; open Mon.-Sat. 0900-1800, Fri. till 2100, tel. 692-7538. **Burns Lake and District Hospital** is at 741 Centre St., tel. 692-3181. The **RCMP** is at 4th and Government St., tel. 692-7171. The **post office** is on Government Street. **Greyhound Bus Lines** is at Balmoral Plaza, Hwy. 16 and 35, tel. 692-3338. For **VIA Rail** call toll-free (800) 665-8630. For a **taxi** 24 hours a day, call 692-3333.

TWEEDSMUIR PROVINCIAL PARK (NORTH)

The town of Burns Lake is not only near the smallest provincial park in B.C. (Deadman's I. in Burns Lake), it also happens to be the northern gateway to the largest provincial park, Tweedsmuir. The northern boundary of this spectacular 981,000-hectare wilderness park is the **Ootsa-Whitesail Lakes Reservoir.** Most of the northern section of the park is made up of the forested or bare-rock **Quanchus Mountain Range,** with many peaks over 1,900 meters high, and the lake- and waterway-riddled **Nechako Plateau.** Wildlife abounds. If you're in the right place at the right time you can see caribou, mountain goats, moose, black and grizzly bear, mule deer, wolves, smaller mammals such as hoary marmots and wolverines in alpine meadows, and many birds. The lakes abound with fish—rainbow trout, kokanee, mountain whitefish, and burbot. Boating, fishing, hiking, horseback riding, photography, and camping are the main reasons people visit this spectacular park.

Touring By Water

The most popular thing to do in the northern section of Tweedsmuir, aside from fishing, is to boat, canoe, or kayak through **Ootsa, Whitesail, Eutsuk, Tetachuck,** and **Natalkuz** lakes in a circular route, with some portaging required. However, before attempting this route get all the info, brochures, and maps from the Ministry of Lands and Parks District Manager, Parks and Outdoor Recreation Division, Bag 5000, Smithers, B.C. V0J 2N0 (tel. 847-7322), or the same outfit at 1011 4th Ave., Prince George, B.C. V2L 3H9 (tel. 565-6270). For maps and air photos (nominal fee), contact MAPS B.C., Ministry of Lands and Parks, Parliament Buildings, Victoria, B.C. V8V 1X5.

The reservoir is the main access to the park but the shoreline has been described as a forest of drowned trees and floating hazards—very dangerous, with few places to land when the frequent strong winds funnel through the lakes. Some channels have been cut (follow the large yellow diamond signs) through the dead trees to emergency landing areas. Because of the strong winds (May is usually the worst month), keep as close to the shoreline as possible. Wilderness campsites are located at some of the lakes, and vehicle camping facilities are found on the north shore of the Nechako Reservoir at **Wistaria Provincial Park** ($6 per night) and at forest recreation sites (free). Keep in mind

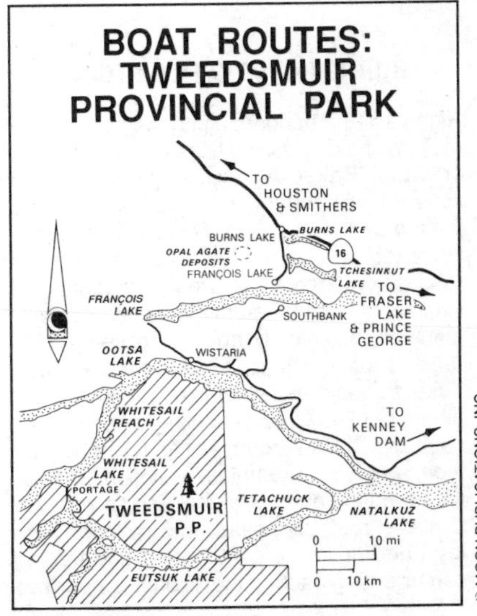

that this park is a wilderness area without *any* facilities. You need to be completely self-contained and an experienced outdoorsperson, or you should hire a guide to get the most enjoyment out of a visit to Tweedsmuir—ask at the InfoCentre for available guides.

Access

A road at the west end of town leads to the park, but to get *into* it you need a canoe, kayak, or motorboat, or to be willing to charter a floatplane. Access to the park is by secondary road (65 km) south of Burns Lake, then by free vehicle-ferry across Francois Lake to the settlement of Ootsa Lake (on the north shore of the Nechako Reservoir). Alternatively, two local floatplane operators provide service into the park: **Lakes District Air Services** on Francois Lake Rd. (tel. 692-3229) flies year-round—on floats in summer and skis in winter. It costs from $260 plus GST per hour to rent the three-passenger Cessna 185, $330 plus GST per hour to rent the six-passenger Beaver. Many resorts and rustic lodges are located in the area between Burns Lake and Tweedsmuir Park, most catering primarily to anglers and hunters—see their brochures in the Burns Lake InfoCentre.

BURNS LAKE TO HOUSTON

Highway 16 meanders along the north shore of Burns Lake, passing Burns Lake Air Tanker Base, **Baker Airport,** a jet-black pond covered with bright-yellow waterlilies, and the turnoff to Ross Lake. Steep hills, bushes, flowering shrubs, and wildflowers line the road as you continue west through small clusters of houses—sometimes named communities, but mostly not. At **Topley** a side road leads north to 177-km-long **Babine Lake,** largest freshwater lake in B.C, yet another spot known for producing trophy fish—rainbow, Dolly Varden, kokanee, coho salmon, and Rocky Mountain whitefish. The rivers flowing in and out of the lake splash with rainbow trout, steelhead, and salmon. **Topley Landing,** a former trapping and trading center dating back to the 1700s, is near two provincial parks. Continue past Topley Landing and the road terminates at **Granisle,** a small community best known for holding five fishing derbies each year.

As you approach Houston you get your first views of high mountains, either peeking out of clouds, sprinkled with snow in midsummer, or completely snow-clad in winter—magnificent. Along this stretch of the highway you can also expect to meet weather with a "yuck factor" of eight or higher on a scale of 1-10 at some time or another!

Houston

Houston also proudly bears a carved fish on its welcoming sign, this time a steelhead. Houston calls itself "Steelhead Country." With a backdrop of the suddenly high, snowcapped mountains of the **Telkwa** and **Babine** ranges, this sawmill, pulp mill, and paper mill town is situated at the confluence of the Bulkley and Morice rivers in the stunning Bulkley Valley. The main tourist activity here? Start rummaging through your fly box! In the surrounding countryside are *more* lakes and rivers and superb fishing. Pick up a *Northwood Pulp and Timber Limited Forest Operations* recreation map at the InfoCentre, which shows all the rivers and lakes in the Houston-Burns Lake-Topley Landing area on one side and the Prince George area on the other.

Some of the most excellent steelhead fishing is found in the Morice River—take the highway west toward Smithers, then turn left at the Northwood Pulp Mill sign and continue about 1.6 km to the end. At the dirt road turn right (at the bridge). Both bait fishing and fly-fishing are popular here. The prize? The fighting steelhead. Other big draws in the area are hiking trails (keep your eyes peeled for deer, bear, and the fierce wolverine) and mountaineering routes in the adjacent rugged terrain. **Houston Chamber of Commerce and Travel InfoCentre** is on the highway just before Benson Ave., tel. 845-7640. It's open year-round, but if you arrive after hours a handy sign outside lists telephone numbers for all kinds of services, urgent and general, and the map makes it easy to locate everything you need. The InfoCentre staff also hands out a free local map with everything marked on—including local campgrounds, motels, restaurants, laundromats, entertainment spots, and the bus depot (off Tweedie Avenue).

Telkwa

As you continue west, the scenery just keeps on getting better—through open fields and contrasting wooded areas, up and down tree-covered hills, surrounded by snowcapped mountains tantalizingly peeking out of clouds. Ever higher peaks lure you on. The small village of Telkwa, situated at the confluence of the Bulkley and Telkwa rivers, is a popular destination for spring salmon in late June, cohos from Aug., and steelhead from autumn to "freeze-up." It also appeals to river canoeists, with stretches of water to suit novices through intermediates. Many of the buildings in the village were put up between 1908 and 1924; the Telkwa Museum Society puts out a Walking Tour Through Historic Telkwa brochure, with descriptions of each of the buildings. Nearby **Tyhee Provincial Park** has a good swimming beach on the shores of Tyhee Lake, picnic facilities, toilets and water available, and in winter moose (and cross-country skiers) are often seen camping there; open April-Oct., $8 campsite fee May-September.

SMITHERS

Crossing the wide, green Bulkley River you enter the town of Smithers, surrounded by the Coast Mountains, with splendid 2,560-meter **Hudson Bay Mountain** towering directly above. The fur trade and two telegraph lines (the Collins Overland line and the Yukon Telegraph branch of the Dominion Telegraph System) brought the first white settlement to the Bulkley Valley. With the discovery of gold in the Omineca and Klondike regions, some prospectors stayed in the valley to try their hand at mining or farming. The first settlement was Aldermere in 1900 (now gone), then Telkwa in 1907. Traders used the same canoes and routes as the native Indians to get around the area, but by the late 19th century sternwheelers were battling the Skeena as far as Hazelton. Goods were then delivered to outposts such as Aldermere by pack train. Smithers was chosen as the main site for the Grand Trunk Pacific Railway's yards and station house in 1913—a picturesque spot at the base of Hudson Bay Mountain that was unfortunately a partially dried-up swamp—the first settlers quickly nicknamed the area the "Slough of Despond!"

Today Smithers calls itself "Northern B.C.'s Recreation Center," but it still salutes its historic past during the **Bulkley Valley Fall Fair and Exhibition** every year during the last weekend of Aug.—a three-day agricultural fair with lots of family events (admission adult $5, senior or child $2, three-day passes adult $12, senior or child $5). On the last weekend of Feb. Smithers celebrates its **Winter Festival,** with dog sledding, snowmobile rides, an ice sculpture contest, parades, and fireworks.

Main Street has a backdrop of magnificent towering mountains and an accompanying Bavarian theme, complete with "Alpine Man" statue and colorful "Ski Smithers" flags flapping from every lamppost—even in midsummer. Visitors shop here for Indian crafts and tourist paraphernalia—that is, in spare moments, when they're not busy experiencing the surrounding landscape.

SIGHTS

No Time To Dither In Smithers

Commence your discovery tour at the **InfoCentre.** It's in the railway club car behind the heritage Central Park building that now houses **Bulkley Valley Museum and Art Gallery.** Then wander through the museum (Hwy. 16 and Main St., tel. 847-5322), which features the history of the Bulkley Valley with plenty of black-and-white photos and pioneer equipment—allow at least an hour. It's open daily 1000-1700 in summer, Tues.-Sat. 1300-1700 in winter, and admission is by donation.

Outdoor activities abound around here—hiking, mountaineering, rockhounding, fishing, hunting, river rafting, swimming, canoeing, swooshing down Hudson Bay Mountain on skis, dogsledding, golfing, and trail riding to start! **Hudson Bay Mountain Lookout,** about eight km west of Smithers, provides jaw-dropping views of the mountain and **Kathlyn Glacier. Kathlyn Lake** sits at the base of Hudson Bay Mountain and offers good photographic opportunities (turn south off Hwy. 16 at Lake Kathlyn Road). Continue along Lake Kathlyn Rd. following signs for hikes to **Glacier Gulch** and dramatic **Twin Falls,** the former an easy half-km, 15-minute walk (rocky; wear sturdy shoes) to the base of the south falls, the latter a half-day (RT) hike from the south side of the falls to the glacier above.

Another local highlight is **Driftwood Canyon Provincial Park,** where you can see plant, insect, and fish fossils between 10 and 20 million years old. The most common plant specimens found are fernlike Meta Skoya (metasequoia), which is a type of California redwood. The park is 17 km northeast of town; from town take Babine Lake Rd., turn left on High Rd., then right on Driftwood Road. Excellent hiking trails are also located in the **Silver King Basin,** taking you through open meadows, around glaciers, and high into mountain country. To get to the trailhead continue along the road beyond the fossil beds onto the homemade log bridge which is the start of the trail—more detailed info available at the InfoCentre.

Hudson Bay Mountain Recreation Area

Excellent downhill and cross-country skiing and summertime hiking through flower-filled alpine meadows can be found on **Hudson Bay Mountain. Ski Smithers** boasts a sea-

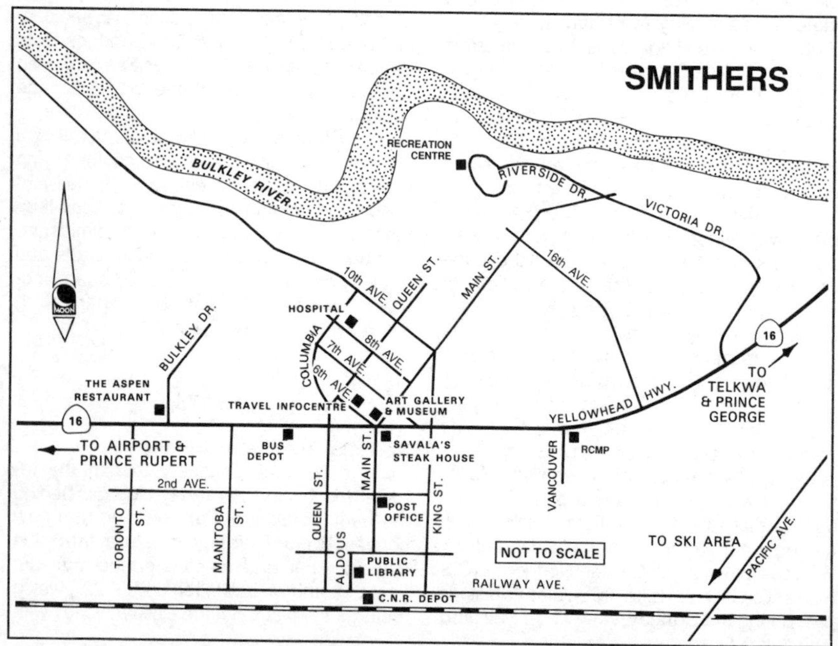

Moricetown Canyon was named after Father Morice, a pioneer missionary.

son from mid-Nov. to early May, a 2,000-meter triple chair, T-bars, 532 meters vertical with runs to suit beginners to experts, two day lodges, and a ski school with rentals and an accessory shop. Rates start around $27 adult for a day pass, $13 child, senior and child under eight free, $19 half-day pass from 1300, child $10—save money by buying a three- or five-day consecutive pass. For more info call 847-2058, or within B.C. toll-free at (800) 665-4299. Cross-country skiers can choose from a 2½-km marked trail on the mountain, or open alpine skiing accessible by T-bar, or the 10-km **Pine Creek Loop** on the road to the ski area. The local golf course and private properties also attract a good number of cross-country skiers. Ask for the free brochure available from the Info-Centre for more details. A cross-country ski marathon is held in Smithers every year. To get to the mountain from town take either Main St. or King St. south onto Railway Ave. and turn left. It's about 22½ km (30 minutes) from downtown.

PRACTICALITIES

Accommodation

Riverside Recreation Centre is beside the Bulkley River on Hwy. 16 E (tel. 847-3229), open May-Oct., providing shaded sites, hookups, and river fishing, only minutes from downtown. From $10 d per night, plus $2 for electricity, $2 for water. **Slumber Lodge Motel** has rooms (complimentary coffee) and the use of a sauna for $40 s, $44 d, $49 twin. At 1515 Main St., tel. 847-2208, or toll-free (800) 663-2831. If you're looking for somewhere really comfortable, try the Tudor-style **Hudson Bay Lodge** at 3251 East Hwy. 16, tel. 847-4581. It's a full-service hotel with whirlpool, saunas, a fireplace lounge, a restaurant and licensed dining room, nightly entertainment, and complimentary limo service to the airport or seaplane base. Rooms start at $55 s, $61 d, $65 twin.

Food

At busy **SavaLa's Steakhouse** at 138 Main St. (tel. 847-4567) you'll find pizza (a large "small" starts at around $10), a good salad bar (try the tangy house dressing), an assortment of tasty Italian dishes, ribs, steak cooked to perfection, and seafood. Main courses average $10. Finish it off with gourmet Italian ice cream. It's open daily 1100-2300, Sun. and holidays 1600-2200. The **Tyee Dining Room** in the Tyee Motor Inn at 1485 Main St. (corner of 8th Ave., one block from the InfoCentre), tel. 847-2201, is the place to go for Chinese at reasonable prices, particularly on Sun. nights when you can help yourself to the smorgasbord. **Aspen Restaurant,** in the Aspen Motor Inn on Hwy. 16 (west end of town), also comes highly recommended by locals if you're clamoring for some food from the sea or a salad bar. Go on a Wed., Thurs., or Fri. (sea-to-Smithers fresh), but expect to pay

$12-15 or more to satisfy your craving. It's open daily 0630-2200, tel. 847-4672.

Services

Smithers' unique **InfoCentre** is situated inside the upper-class bar car of an old train (tel. 847-9854 or 847-5072) next to the museum, and has comfy chairs to unwind in while you find out everything you need to know about the area. However, it's open only early June-Sept. 0800-1800 (extended to 1900 on demand). The rest of the year you have to go to the **Chamber of Commerce** above the museum, open Mon.-Fri. 0900-1700, for the complete rundown.

Several shopping centers are located along the main highway through town. The **hospital** is on 8th Ave. at Columbia Street. The **post office** is on the corner of Main St. and 2nd Avenue. The **Greyhound depot** is on Hwy. 16 west of the InfoCentre, next to the Bread and Butter Stop. The **railway station** is on Railway Avenue. **Smithers Airport** is right beside Hwy. 16, four km west of town, serviced by **Air B.C., Time Air,** and **Central Mountain Air.**

SMITHERS TO NEW HAZELTON

On the western outskirts of Smithers lies the local golf club, the airport, and the turnoff (Lake Kathlyn Rd.) to **Glacier Gulch** and **Twin Falls. Adam's Igloo Wildlife Museum,** another Smithers attraction, is on the left side of the highway about 10 km from town. Inside the igloo are a large number of taxidermied North American animals and birds exhibited in natural habitats. It's open daily 0900-1800 June-Sept., tel. 847-3188; admission charge, discount for Automobile Association members.

The Yellowhead Hwy. offers so much ooh-and-aah scenery from Smithers to Terrace, in fact all the way to Prince Rupert, that Mr. Kodak should be beaming from ear to ear. Year-round it's just plain gorgeous, but in summer it's particularly colorful. The highway, with its white, yellow, and scarlet wildflower-shoulders wanders through open fields and forested hills, with towering vertical mountains constantly on the left and lower bush-covered mountains on the right. Try to do this stretch on a fine day; otherwise, it's more likely than not that the mountains will be cloaked in dense low clouds and you won't even know what you're missing. A lot of award-winning photo ops jump out along here. Even the houses and cabins along the highway are pleasing to the eye, with their steep roofs and verandas loaded in summer with flower-filled hanging baskets. Several small creeks cross under the road and join the Bulkley River, which parallels the highway all the way to New Hazelton.

Moricetown Canyon

The next place to stop and stretch your legs is the viewpoint at Moricetown Canyon, where the ½-km-wide Bulkley River roars down through a 15-meter narrow canyon on **Moricetown Indian Reserve.** This area has been a Carrier Indian village site for more than 5,000 years. Salmon desperately hurl themselves up these spectacular rapids in autumn. Below the canyon the river pours into a large pool, one of the best fishing spots in the area. To fish on the reserve, pay the fee at the small cabin near the viewpoint where souvenirs and native crafts are for sale. **Moricetown Canyon Campground** (tel. 847-2133) is situated a short walk above the canyon (road access from the highway), with fully serviced sites, toilets, and coin-operated showers; from $7 per vehicle.

Ross Lake Provincial Park

About 20 km east of Hazelton the scenery abruptly changes. Suddenly pine trees line the Bulkley River and cover the hills and mountains. In fact, everywhere you look are trees. If you're in search of an excellent picnic spot (no campsites), take the Ross Lake Provincial Park turnoff to the right (four-km gravel road). Ross Lake is one of those wonderful discoveries you'll always remember. It has good swimming, crystal-clear waters where trout, salmon, and Dolly Varden congregate, and if you canoe around it (no power boats) you discover that it's surrounded by forested hills and a couple of spectacular white-capped peaks. Facilities include a boat-launching area, barbecue pits, picnic tables, and pit toilets. In the early mornings you can hear loon; in the evenings beaver slide into the water, slapping their tails. If you're lucky you may see a moose, though moose hunting is unfortunately popular in this area.

THE HAZELTONS

ALL THREE OF THEM

It's easy to be confused by the three "Hazeltons"—**Hazelton, New Hazelton,** and **South Hazelton**—situated at the most northerly point on the Yellowhead Highway. As usual, the arrival of the Grand Trunk Pacific Railway caused the confusion. The original Hazelton (called Old Town) was established 50 years or so before the railway; the other two Hazeltons were started because their landowners/promoters thought they each owned a better spot for a new railway town. Today the largest of the three small communities is New Hazelton, a service center overshadowed by spectacular **Mount Rocher Deboule.** Pull off at the **Travel InfoCentre** at the intersection of Highways 16 and 62 to find out more about all three Hazeltons; open daily June-Sept. 0900-1700, tel. 842-6071.

Don't Pass This Up!

Lakes and rivers with excellent fishing dot the region (many resorts catering to anglers are situated off the road to Kispiox), and a large number of hiking trails wander through splendid mountain scenery. The staff at the InfoCentre happily provides all the details and directions, along with a handy *Forest Service Recreation Sites* map for the Smithers and Hazelton area on request. Don't miss the eight-km detour to Hazelton, one of the smallest incorporated villages in B.C., and 'Ksan Indian Village (see below). The adjacent campground is one of the best places to pitch a tent or park an RV between Smithers and Prince Rupert.

Eeek, Mmmm, And Aaah To Hazelton

To head toward Hazelton and its Indian village, turn off Hwy. 16, following signs to Kispiox. First you have to cross the one-lane **Hagwilget Suspension Bridge** 79 meters above the turbulent Bulkley River—read the plaque about the original Indian footbridge made from poles and cedar rope that once spanned the gorge and you'll be glad you live in modern times!

Farther along the road on the left is the log **Hummingbird Restaurant**—a delicious place to eat in the Hazeltons. Amongst an all-wood interior decorated with etched glass and hanging lamps, you'll be dazzled by the million-dollar picture-window view of Mount Rocher Deboule (named by a French priest, it means "Mountain of Rolling Rocks"; the Indian name means "Guests Falling To Their Deaths"). Tiny hummingbirds flit back and forth between the feeders outside the windows. At lunch, expect to pay around $5-8 for sandwiches, hamburgers, or a huge taco salad. At dinner choose from steaks, chicken, and the usual, all for around $12. It's open daily 1100-2200, later on Sat. nights, tel. 842-5628. New Hazelton has several restaurants offering Canadian and Chinese cuisine, Old Hazelton has three, and South Hazelton boasts a fully licensed inn with complete menu.

Hazelton, about eight km northwest of New Hazelton, lies at the junction of the Bulkley and Skeena rivers. It has retained its unique 1890s-style architecture and pioneer settlement atmosphere. The main local attraction is 'Ksan Village.

'Ksan Historic Indian Village

'Ksan, which means "Between the Banks," is an authentic reconstructed Gitksan Indian village. To best appreciate the history and culture of the village, join one of the fascinating guided tours; admission to the grounds is free but tours are $4.50 adult, $3 senior,

$2.50 student (13-18), $1.50 child (6-12); allow 30 minutes to an hour. From 0900 on they leave every hour on the hour, visiting the burial house, food cache, smokehouse, community houses, and the 'Ksan artists' carving shop and studio, where works of art take shape before your eyes.

Each of the Fireweed, Wolf, and Frog houses is decorated with traditional northwest coast carved interiors, paintings, and painted screens, and contains fine examples of Indian artifacts, arts and crafts, implements, tools, and personal possessions. Hear how the Indians lived, their beliefs and legends, while you tour each building. Along the fronts of the buildings are a large number of magnificent totem poles—a photographer's delight (especially early in the morning when it's misty and no one's around). Finish up in the **Northwestern National Exhibition Centre and Museum,** which features cedar bark mats, woven and button blankets, masks, coppers (the most valuable single object a chief possessed), bent boxes of red cedar, rattles used by shamans as a direct link with the supernatural, and an art gallery with changing exhibitions. In the gift shop are the works of on-site artists. The village is open daily May to mid-Oct. 0900-1800, tel. 842-5544.

'Ksan Campground

Stay at the adjacent, well-designed, riverside 'Ksan Campground, which has outstanding views of the **Babine Range** (particularly on misty mornings). It's also very popular with fishermen—dangle a line from the back of your tent site, or join the others on an early-morning or late-evening trek along the riverside trail to the best spots. Tent sites are grassy, and large vehicle campsites are separated by trees and bushes; $9 per night. RV sites have less privacy but full hookups are available; $12 per night. Showers for two people are included in the camp rates, otherwise they're $1 extra (hot in the evening or early in the morning, lukewarm if you sleep in!)—pay when you check in; tel. 842-5940.

Kispiox

Kispiox, farther along the road, is a small traditional Gitksan village, 14 km from Hazelton. The residents (from original Frog, Wolf, and Fireweed clans) continue their practices of feasting, dancing, and food preparation. Visit the large collection of red cedar **totem poles** (15 old and new) near the confluence of the Skeena and Kispiox rivers, and the locally operated, log-constructed **Kispiox Salmon Hatchery** (it has the capacity to rear 500,000 fry per year);

Burial house at 'Ksan Historic Indian Village

open daily 0800-1200 and 1300-1630. This area is another fishy one—mainly for steelhead in the Kispiox Sept.-Nov., but also for coho in Aug. and September. **Kitseguecla** (between the Kitwanga turnoff and Usk, on Hwy. 16), **Kitwanga,** and **Kitwancool** (on Hwy. 37 North) also have striking stands of totem poles—Kitwancool has the oldest totem in North America.

WESTWARD HO

The next not-to-be-missed place along the Yellowhead is **Seeley Lake Provincial Park.** It's situated just above the edge of beautiful Seeley Lake, which on a still day reflects the vertical snowcapped mountains towering directly above—the best campground around if you don't mind going without a shower; pit toilets and water are the only facilities. On a fine day, this spot is magical, especially in winter when everything is thickly coated with snow. Open April-Oct., $8 per night from May-Sept.—in summer nab your site early in the day because by late afternoon all the sites are taken.

The mountains all along this stretch of the highway are incredible—straight up (it's easy to get a neckache around here) and snowcapped year-round, with waterfalls cascading down here and there. The highway now parallels the mighty Skeena River (which gets progressively mightier as you approach the coast) through a forested canyon, then crosses the river, still heading toward more majestic mountains.

At the intersection of Highways 16 and 37 North you have three choices: northwest to Stewart, which lies on the B.C./Alaska border (237 km), then over the border into the Alaskan town of Hyder (another three km; no customs or immigration checks); due north along the mostly paved Cassiar Hwy. to join the Alaska Hwy. in the Yukon (728 km with about 200 km of dirt road); or continuing west to Prince Rupert (239 km), but don't do this spectacular section of the highway in the dark. If you don't have the time or the inclination to follow Hwy. 37 all the way to the Yukon but do like the idea of seeing incredible glaciers and waterfalls, take a day-trip to Stewart, Hyder, and back. It's 201 km along a good paved road to the **Bear Glacier** just before Stewart—well worth the drive. Fuel up before you leave the Hazeltons—gas stations are few and relatively far between (there's a PetroCanada station at Kitwanga and at Meziadin Junction, and a number of small communities provide a variety of services), and the price of gassing up is considerably higher up north.

STEWART-CASSIAR HIGHWAY

THE 237 SCENIC KILOMETERS TO STEWART

Totems

Admirers of totem poles should pull off to the right less than one kilometer from the highway intersection and visit the **Gitwangak Reserve.** Opposite the community's splendid stand of totems is St. Paul's Anglican Church, built in 1893. The road rejoins Hwy. 37 a few kilometers farther north so you don't need to backtrack.

Kitwanga

The first community on Hwy. 37 is **Kitwanga,** a small sawmill town best known for its historic site, **Battle Hill,** overlooking the Kitwanga River. Nekt, an Indian warrior, used the 13-meter-high hill 200 years ago to fend off attacks from hostile neighbors. It's the first national historic site commemorating Native culture in Western Canada. A trail leads from the parking lot down to the flat area around the bottom of the hill, where you can read display panels describing the hill's history. The site is on Kitwanga Valley Rd. (open year-round; admission free) not far past the **Travel InfoCentre** in the video store (open June-early Sept., tel. 849-5760).

Kitwancool Totem Poles

Continuing north, you're paralleling what was commonly called the Grease Trail, the route Coastal Indians took to the interior to trade their greasy oolichans (miniscule fish) with other tribes. The next spot to pull off the highway is Kitwancool, where you can see an outstanding group of totem poles, most more than 100 years old. The oldest, "Hole in the Ice," is approximately 140 years old and still standing in its original location. It represents the story of a man preventing his people from starving by chopping a hole in the ice and doing a spot of ice fishing—hence the name. They say it's the oldest standing totem pole in the world.

North To Meziadin Junction

Tree-covered hills, dense patches of snow-white daisies, craggy mountains, beautiful lakes covered in yellow water lilies, banks of pink and white clover, purple lupine, distant peaks, and lots of logging trucks flying along the road—these are images of the highway to **Meziadin Lake Provincial Park.** The park lies along the northeast shores of Meziadin Lake, two km from the highway. It's open June-Oct. and has a boat launch, pit toilets, and campsites ($8 per night May-September). At **Meziadin Junction** the road to the left leads 67 km to Stewart, the road to the right 600 km to Watson Lake. Pick up info on the Cassiar Hwy. and check road conditions at the intersection **Travel InfoCentre;** open June-Sept., tel. 636-2763.

Glacial Glory

From the highway junction all the way to Stewart the scenery is just plain old spectacular—tall snowcapped **Coast Mountains,** pine forests, lakes, waterfalls, and then a string of glaciers sitting like thick icy slabs on the tops of the almost-vertical mountains to the left of the highway. Suddenly, and quite unexpectedly, you round a corner and there in front of you is magnificent, eggshell-blue **Bear Glacier,** tumbling down into deep-blue **Strohn Lake** where large icebergs sail across the surface in the breeze—and it's right beside the highway! To get a really good look at it, turn around and go back to the rest and picnic area (easy to miss in the excitement of spotting the glacier), where tables and pit toilets are provided. Nothing enhances the flavor of a sandwich like such a view! As you continue toward Stewart, keep an eye out for three mighty waterfalls on the right (easier to see on the return trip), one after another. One plummets down into a

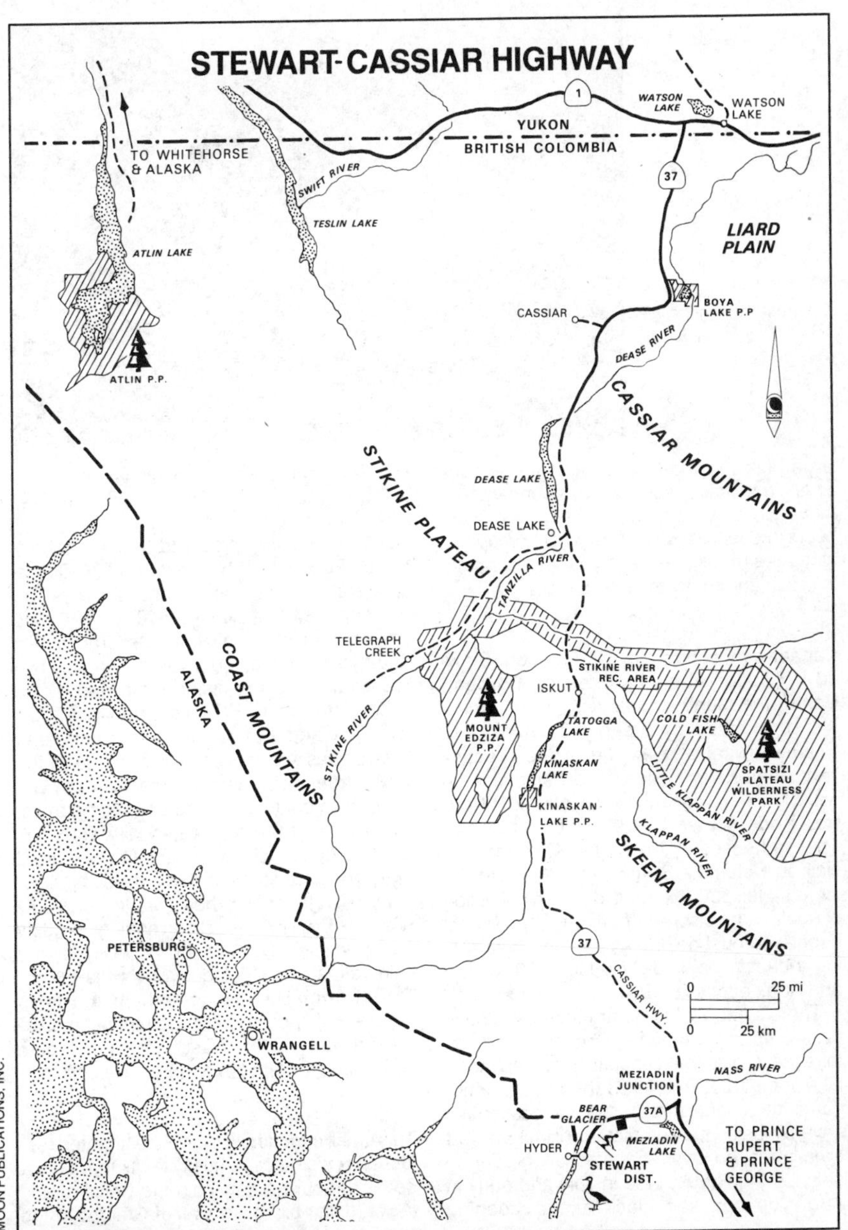
STEWART-CASSIAR HIGHWAY
1
WATSON LAKE
WATSON LAKE
YUKON
BRITISH COLOMBIA
TO WHITEHORSE & ALASKA
SWIFT RIVER
TESLIN LAKE
37
LIARD PLAIN
ATLIN LAKE
BOYA LAKE P.P
CASSIAR
DEASE RIVER
ATLIN P.P.
CASSIAR MOUNTAINS
STIKINE PLATEAU
DEASE LAKE
DEASE LAKE
TANZILLA RIVER
TELEGRAPH CREEK
COAST MOUNTAINS
ALASKA
STIKINE RIVER REC. AREA
ISKUT
TATOGGA LAKE
COLD FISH LAKE
STIKINE RIVER
MOUNT EDZIZA P.P.
KINASKAN LAKE
SPATSIZI PLATEAU WILDERNESS PARK
LITTLE KLAPPAN RIVER
KINASKAN LAKE P.P.
KLAPPAN RIVER
SKEENA MOUNTAINS
PETERSBURG
37
CASSIAR HWY.
0
25 mi
0
25 km
WRANGELL
NASS RIVER
MEZIADIN JUNCTION
BEAR GLACIER
37A
TO PRINCE RUPERT & PRINCE GEORGE
HYDER
MEZIADIN LAKE
STEWART DIST.

The stunning Bear Glacier is right beside the highway.

large buildup of ice, complete with blue ice cave. You may also spot an abundance of mountain goats on the hillsides, and black bears (keep your distance) and porcupines along the roadside—have your camera within reach and ready to shoot!

Stewart

Canada's most northerly ice-free port, Stewart is situated at the north end of **Portland Canal,** the fourth-longest fiord in the world. It's surrounded by steep mountains—Mt. Rainey towers above, one of the greatest vertical rises from sea level, also "in the world." Follow signs for the **Travel InfoCentre** and **Stewart Historical Museum.** They're housed in the original City and Fire Hall on Columbia St. (between 6th and 7th streets), tel. 636-2568. Inside are a collection of tools and displays featuring the town's boom-and-bust gold, copper, and silver mining industry; open daily 0900-1800 in July and Aug., admission $2.

There's not a lot to do around here—soak up the splendid mountain scenery and admire the wildlife (bald eagles, bears, salmon), hike some trails (the InfoCentre has a handout on three local hikes), see the locations of several major movies filmed in the Stewart area, then go over the Alaskan border to neighboring **Hyder.** Late in July and early in Aug. you can see black bears scooping spawning salmon out of local rivers—an enjoyable spectacle, but keep a respectful distance! Get directions from the InfoCentre.

The local **campground** is at **Rainey Creek Park,** which has tent and RV sites, a sani station, washrooms, and showers; $6 per night for tent sites, $9-12 for RV sites (electric hookup available). Several motels and hotels are located in town. The only two restaurants are the dining room and coffee shop at the **King Edward Hotel** (the local favorite) and **Fongs** Chinese restaurant. Stewart has two gas stations. The one on the main street also has diesel service, but you have to go out to their card-operated pumps, taking one of the attendants with you. The other station provides propane fillups. Locals brag about celebrating the longest birthday party in North America here. Starting on 1 July (Canada Day) in Stewart and ending on 4 July (Independence Day in the U.S.) in Hyder, the celebration's most intriguing event is the **International Bed Race**—which starts in Alaska and ends in British Columbia! In summer Stewart is on the Alaska State Ferry route (May through Sept.) to and from Ketchikan.

Hyder

This small community (only 70 estimated residents) is well known mostly for its three bars, open 23 hours a day. Join the tradition and tack a dollar bill to the wall of **Glacier Inn** to ensure that you won't return broke, then throw down a shot glass of pure grain alcohol in one swallow to qualify for your "I've been Hyderized" card before you stagger outside. To get there from Stewart, continue along the main road by Portland Canal, passing the small fishing fleet at Stewart Hyder Marina. The saltwater fishing for cod, halibut, red snapper, crab, shrimp, prawns, mussels, steelhead, and salmon here is reportedly excellent, but you need separate licenses for the Canadian and U.S. sides of the canal. Waterfalls tumble down from high glaciers on the other side of the water, and the surface is covered with floating logs—very photogenic in any kind of weather.

Next thing you know, you're in Alaska—and without all the formalities and checkpoints you'd expect at a border. But read the signs—the RCMP carries out spot checks every now and again to make sure everyone is obeying the rules. The road terminates in Hyder, though there's really nowhere to go. It's certainly not what you'd call a tourist town. It's rather ramshackle, but it has plenty of atmosphere, and it's at the end of the road—a good enough reason to visit. You can see more black bear fishing and feasting on spawning salmon in late July and early Aug. at **Fish Creek,** several kilometers beyond town—but keep your distance. Hyder has an inn and a lodge, an RV park, several restaurants (one has a sign saying "Sorry, We're Open!"), a grocery store, a couple of gift shops, a church, and a library.

NORTH TO THE YUKON

Gas Up And Carry Spares

This highway is another superb scenic drive from beginning to end, passing through some of the best of British Columbia's—and Canada's—vast wilderness scenery. From the highway you can admire magnificent glaciers, rivers such as the Iskut and Tanzilla where most fishermen just can't resist pulling off and trying their luck, and numerous lakes where anglers leave with a good catch and a smile.

The highway north from **Meziadin Junction** is mainly improved gravel, with a paved section for about 80 km before and after Iskut and toward the end. Gas stations and services can be found along the highway, however it's not a bad idea to fill up with gas wherever and whenever you get the opportunity, and take spare tires, belts, hoses, bailing wire, a strong adhesive, and parts to be on the safe side. In summer many visitors (lots of RVs) and logging trucks take this route, so if you do get stranded it shouldn't (though it can) be too long before someone comes along. One of the worst factors in dry weather is the dust. Use caution when approaching and crossing the many very narrow, one-lane bridges.

Kinaskan Lake Provincial Park

The first park you come to, roughly 200 km from Meziadin Junction, is 1,800-hectare Kinaskan Lake Provincial Park, known for its rainbow trout fishing, camping at the south end, and **Mowdade Trail** (trailhead accessed by boat), which leads east into Mount Edziza Provincial Park. It's open May-Oct. with an $8 per night fee for camping (limited facilities) May-September. About 25 km farther north is a resort, gas, and food at **Tatogga Lake.** Also check here on the conditions of the road ahead. Access to trailheads leading into Spatsizi Plateau Wilderness Park (see below) via an abandoned railway line bed (not suitable for all vehicles and can be impassable in bad weather) starts at Tatogga Lake—ask local advice before attempting it, and get detailed directions. The rail bed runs down the southwest boundary of the park for 60 km, paralleling the **Klappan River.**

Spatsizi Plateau Wilderness Park

This wilderness park is just that—656,785 hectares of total wilderness. Access is by foot from trailheads that start at the western boundary, by canoe, or by floatplane. It's not a suitable park for inexperienced, unfit, or ill-equipped adventurers. It covers a section of the **Stikine Plateau,** the rolling **Spatsizi Plateau,** and the **Skeena Mountains,** with their stunning peaks, glaciers, rivers, and lakes. Its beauty cannot be described in a few words—see it to believe it. Wildlife abounds—grizzly bears, moose, mountain goats, caribou, birds, and fish. It has wilderness camping, eight cabins with cooking facilities, and a sauna at **Cold Fish Lake.** Get detailed info on the park at Iskut.

Iskut To Dease Lake

Closest community to Spatsizi Plateau and Mount Edziza provincial parks, **Iskut** provides gas stations, stores, resorts, and outfitters who run fishing, rafting, and horseback-riding trips in the local area. Get info at the Iskut Band Administration Office. Between Iskut and Dease Lake the highway runs through the **Stikine River Recreation Area,** which borders the Stikine River on both sides, linking the two wilderness parks on either side of the highway. The Stikine River is used as a pull-out point for canoe trips that start in Spatsizi—from the bridge down, the river flows through the **Grand Canyon,** a 100-km-long canyon with vertical rock walls towering more than 300 meters above—don't let your canoe go down this one!

Dease Lake To Telegraph Creek

The small community of **Dease Lake,** on the shores of its namesake, provides all the services you need, plus guides and outfitters for the two provincial parks and air service to Terrace. Get more info in the stores. At Dease Lake a road leads 119 km west along the **Tanzilla River,** down an incredibly steep (in parts quite scary) road through the Stikine River Recreation Area to **Telegraph Creek,** a community of 300 people living on a terraced hill overlooking the Stikine. It has gorgeous scenery, friendly people, heritage buildings dating back to the 1860s gold rush, accommodations, food, gas, and riverboat and aircraft services. It's also the gateway to Mount Edziza Provincial Park.

Mount Edziza Provincial Park

This 232,698-hectare park is known for its moonscape volcanic cone and craters, several major lakes, and **Spectrum Range,** which has rocks with many colors of the spectrum. You can get into the park by hiking trail (see moose, stone sheep, mountain goats, caribou, and plenty of birds), and guided hiking and horseback trips can be arranged in Telegraph Creek. Again, there are no facilities, and the park is not suitable for casual or unprepared outdoor enthusiasts.

Dease Lake To The End Of The Road

As you continue north along Hwy. 37 the road parallels the eastern shores of **Dease Lake.** Good campsites are found by the lake, along with the occasional chunk of jade along the lakeshore—the area has been called the jade capital "of the world." From Dease Lake to the border it's clear sailing on pavement through spectacular countryside. From Dease Lake town it's 117 km to the cutoff for Cassiar, a small mining settlement eight km from the highway; the gas station workers can fix tires and make minor repairs—excellent in a pinch. Natural highlights include the **Dease River, Pyramid Mountain,** and 4,597-hectare **Boya Lake Provincial Park,** with its clear, icy-cold lake, good fishing (not productive on a clear day due to the clarity of the water) and swimming (if you're brave—or desperate), and white clay-like beaches. The park is open May-Oct., with an $8 per site camping fee June-Sept.; limited facilities. From here the highway runs through the high **Liard Plain** to the B.C./Yukon boundary. From the boundary it's another four km to the junction of the Alaska Hwy., and another 25 km east to Watson Lake.

THE NORTHWESTERN CORNER

Atlin

If you want to visit the stunningly beautiful area around glacier-fed **Atlin Lake** (largest natural lake in the province), 271,410-hectare glaciated **Atlin Park,** and the town of Atlin in the *far* northwestern corner of British Columbia, the only road access is from the Yukon. After crossing into the Yukon, go west on the Alaska Hwy. 347 km to Jake's Corner, then turn left on Hwy. 7 to travel along 98 km of gravel south to Atlin.

Atlin was a boomtown with more than 5,000 people during the 1898 Klondike goldrush—today they're still finding some color, but the town population has dwindled to about 500. Start your discovery at the **Travel InfoCentre** in the museum at 3rd and Trainor; open from the end of June through early September.

Town Sights

Atlin Historical Museum, housed in a 1902 schoolhouse, lets you relive the excitement of the gold rush and Atlin's early days and view the display of Tlingit Indian artifacts. It's on 3rd and Trainor, tel. 651-7522. Open daily 0900-1730 July-Sept., make an appointment the rest of the year; adult $1.50, senior or child 75 cents. If you stroll through town following the walking tour in the visitor's guide (available at the InfoCentre), you'll see many historic buildings and artifacts pretty much untouched from the gold rush era, then a trip to the **Pioneer Cemetery** (less than two km east of town) reveals Atlin's pioneer history through stories and tales on weathered grave markers. Visit the spots where the wonderful movie *Never Cry Wolf* was filmed, or just wander along the lakeshore to admire the MV *Tarahne,* built in 1916, which plied the lake for 20 years, providing freight and transportation services—and outrageous views of sparkling peaks, glaciers, waterfalls, and mountain streams. You can also rent a boat (small runabout from $80 for eight hours; houseboats too) and cruise Atlin Lake yourself, through **Norseman Adventures,** tel. 651-7535 (there's also a campground, where sites including water and electric hookups are $10 per vehicle per night), or visit **Atlin Warm Springs,** where 29° C mineral water bubbles up at Warm Bay, about 25 km south of Atlin.

Outdoor Paradise

This area has much to interest the avid outdoorsperson: hiking, mountain climbing, fishing (trolling or fly-in fishing for salmon, steelhead, and rainbow trout), canoeing, houseboating, and horseback riding. Or try gold panning on Spruce Creek (one of the largest nuggets found on Spruce Creek was 30 ounces)—maybe you'll be lucky and be able to pay for your entire vacation with what you find! It's also a photographer's haven. Get all the details at the InfoCentre downtown.

Practicalities

There's plenty to do here, and Atlin provides the necessities: a campground and RV park (from $10 per night), hotel/motel rooms (from around $52 s, $63 d), cottages (from $63 s, $75 d), a grocery store, fishing tackle and gift shops, a laundromat, a post office, and aircraft and helicopter service. If you want to stay in the inn (tel. 651-7546) or cottages (tel. 651-7500), reservations ahead of time are essential.

TERRACE

Terrace, the next city along the Yellowhead Hwy., is built on a series of steep terraces along the beautiful **Skeena River**, second-largest river system in the province, completely surrounded by the spectacular peaks of the **Hazelton** and **Coast** mountains. It's visually stunning. There's not a lot to do *in* town, but who cares? The scenery's great, the air is fresh and clean, and many outdoor attractions are found within the immediate region. It's the kind of place you might plan to stay a day but end up staying four.

SIGHTS AND ACTIVITIES

Heritage Park Museum

At this outdoor-indoor museum, a one-hour guided tour takes you through an old, beautifully furnished log hotel, a dance hall, a barn, and six authentic log cabins dating from 1910-55. These structures, from around the area, have been dismantled and reconstructed on this site. Some of the cabins are furnished, others contain objects and artifacts from the past or collections of antique farming and mining equipment. While you tour the cabins the guide fills you in on the early history of Terrace—covering gold, copper, and lead mining, fur trading, construction of the telegraph line, logging, and the homesteaders of the late 1800s and early 1900s. The museum is on Kerby St. (locals call this upper terraced area "The Bench"), tel. 567-2991, open seven days a week in summer 1000-1800; admission adult $1.50, student and senior $1, family $4.

Galleries

At 4820 Halliwell St., **Northern Lights Studio** is an art studio, gallery, and shop featuring custom framing, stained glass, Native art, B.C. jade, fine silver jewelry, and original paintings. Whether you're "just looking" or buying, spend a little time in here and go prepared to part with some extra pocket money. Open Mon.-Sat. 0930-1730, closed Sunday, tel. 638-1403. Bus no. 2 Halliwell stops just outside the studio. The local **Art Gallery** is on the basement floor of **Terrace Public Library.** It has changing exhibitions each month; open Tues.-Sat. 1200-1500, Tues.-Thurs. 1900-2100, Sun. 1300-1600, closed Monday. Extended hours in summer.

Hiking Trails

Terrace has many excellent hiking trails, from short strolls at **Lakelse Lake** (south of town off Hwy. 37) to major overnight treks. One of the local favorites is the scenic **Clearwater Lakes Trail,** which is only 3.6 km RT to the first lake, Little Clearwater, and five km RT to the second lake, Big Clearwater. The trail also follows a creek between the lakes, with many spots to picnic and pick berries along the way. To get there go south along Hwy. 37 toward Kitimat and stop at the easy **Onion Lake** trail which leads off the highway to a lookout (3.6 km RT) for outstanding views of Lakelse Lake. Where the Onion Lake trail branches right, keep to the left and continue to the Clearwater lakes.

The **Terrace Mountain Nature Trail** is a five-km semicircular trail which gives great views of the city and surrounds. It takes about two to three hours to cover because much of it is uphill (wear sturdy footwear or hiking boots), and starts at the intersection of Halliwell and Anderson, finishing at the end of Johnstone St. (or vice versa). Complete the circle by walking along Johnstone to the end, turning right on Park Ave., right on Kalum, then continuing straight onto Skeenaview back to Halliwell. To get the rundown on all the best hikes in the area, ask for the handy *Terrace Hiking Trails* handout at the InfoCentre.

More Fishing!

The Skeena River is abundant with trout, chinook, spring salmon (May, July, and Aug.), coho salmon (Aug.-Oct.), and steelhead

(April-May and Aug.-October). Fishermen claim that sportfishing around Terrace is excellent almost year-round—the rivers usually freeze up in Jan., but in Feb. they're fishable again. Be sure to get a license and read up on the latest rules and regulations. If you require the services of a guide or wish to charter a boat or floatplane to get you into those pristine backcountry areas where enormous fish just about throw themselves out of the water at your feet screaming "take me, I'm yours," Terrace has many guides and outfitters just waiting for your call. Call in at the InfoCentre and pick up all the guiding companies' free brochures. And if you catch that monster, you can even have it videotaped and fiberglassed in Terrace through **Northwest Fishing Guides,** tel. 635-5295.

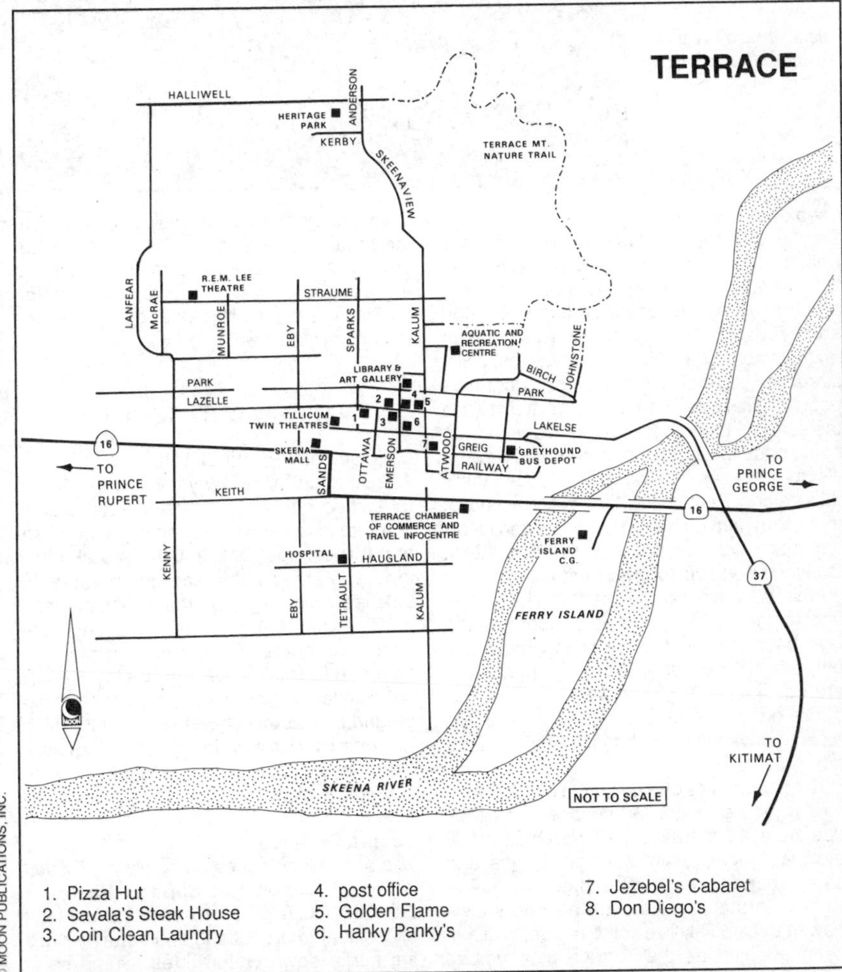

sandy beach at Lakelse Lake Provincial Park

Tseax Lava Beds
Another attraction, 78 km north of Terrace via Kalum Lake Dr., is Canada's youngest lava flow, about 18 km long and three km wide, which experts think occurred between 1650 and 1750. You can see all different types of lava, and bare rock chunks, crevasses, spiky pinnacles, sinkholes, craters, and bright-blue pools where underground rivers have risen to the surface. Explore the lava with caution—in some parts the surface may be unstable, and it's treacherous on footgear. To get there drive along Hwy. 16 to the western end of town, turn right on Kalum Lake Dr., and follow the road north beyond Kitsumkalum Lake. Continue north via logging roads (it's about a 90-minute drive from Terrace). The Travel InfoCentre has a very good handout on the lava beds. It's best to travel logging roads only after 1600 or on weekends, when trucks are not likely to be flying through here. The trucks have right of way at all times—if you have to drive into a ditch to avoid a head-on, do!

Keep your eyes peeled for the elusive, very rare white kermodei (pronounced kerr-MO-dee) bear, a separate and distinct member of the black bear family with small eyes and small rounded ears. The bear has been sighted in this area, though no one knows how many actually live in the region, and has been adopted as the Terrace city symbol.

Continue beyond the lava flow and turn left at the road paralleling the Nass River to **Canyon City.** This unique community can be entered only by pedestrian suspension bridge. The scenic **Nass Valley** also makes the drive worthwhile.

HIGHWAY 37 SOUTH

Lakelse Lake Provincial Park
A drive south along Hwy. 37 toward Kitimat (branches off Hwy. 16 at the east end of Terrace) is rewarding. Passing **Terrace Kitimat Airport,** you come to **Lakelse Lake Provincial Park** on the shores of beautiful Lakelse Lake. Hiking trails, picnic areas, good swimming beaches, boating, and campsites are all here. You also pass the right-hand turnoff to **Waterlily Bay Resort,** an excellent place to stay in a small campground or in comfy cabins, and the turnoff to **Furlong Bay Provincial Park Campground** (see "Accommodations," below, for the resort and both parks).

Soothe Or Scream!
The next place to stop along Hwy. 37 South is **Mount Layton Hot Springs Resort** on Lakelse Lake (about a 15-minute drive south of Terrace) for a soothing swim or a hair-raising hurtle down **waterslides.** Stand below

them on the outside of the complex to see silhouetted bodies hurtling down the enclosed vertical tubes issuing bloodcurdling screams—then decide if you want to join in! Hot springs have been channeled into a large swimming pool, down five waterslides, and into a separate therapeutic pool; admission is $5 for a two-hour session for all pools and slides, $3 for the pools and smallest slide, seniors $2. It's open year-round. The resort also provides a restaurant (0730-2300) and lounge (Sun.-Thurs. 1100-2400, Fri. and Sat. 1100-0100) open to the public, and accommodations (see below).

Kitimat

Start your discovery of the planned industrial community of Kitimat at the **Travel InfoCentre** on Hwy. 37 as you enter town from the north. Located at the northern end of the Kitimat Arm of the **Douglas Channel,** Kitimat calls itself B.C.'s "Aluminum City." Here you can choose from a number of conducted industrial tours in summer—**Ocelot Ammonia's Methanol Plant** (the town's newest major industry and the first petrochemical plant in northern B.C., tel. 639-9292; bearded men are not admitted), **Eurocan's Pulp and Paper Complex** (tel. 632-6111) or **Alcan's Kitimat Works Aluminum Smelter** (tel. 639-8259). All the tours are free but reservations ahead of time are necessary.

Bodies hurtle down these slides with hair-raising screams.

Get back to nature at the **Kitimat River Fish Hatchery** (open weekdays, May-Aug., for a conducted tour by prior arrangement at tel. 639-9616), in **Radley Park** along the Kitimat River, and see B.C.'s largest living tree, a 500-year-old giant Sitka spruce (behind the Riverlodge Recreation Centre). The **Centennial Museum** at 293 City Centre displays historic and native artifacts, and the gallery features locally produced artwork; open mid-May to Sept., Tues.-Sat. 1000-1700 and Fri. to 2000, the rest of the year from 1100, tel. 632-7022. The fishing around Kitimat is excellent; ask at the InfoCentre for the brochure *Fishing in Kitimat,* and info on the many fresh- and saltwater charters and guiding services available in Kitimat.

ACCOMMODATIONS

Camping

Terrace has quite a choice when it comes to campsites. **Ferry Island Municipal Campground** has sheltered sites amongst birch and cottonwood trees, berry bushes, and wildflowers, on an island in the Skeena River, just over three km east of downtown. It's at 5/3215 Eby St., tel. 638-1174. Some of the sites have excellent views of the river and mountains, and a hiking trail runs through the woods and along the Skeena around the island. Water, picnic tables, fire grates, free firewood, picnic shelters, and pit toilets. A few sites have electrical hookups. No showers. Unserviced sites are $7 per night, serviced sites are $9, and there's no time limit. **Lakelse Lake Provincial Park** is signposted off Hwy. 37 S toward Kitimat. Aside from hiking trails, picnic areas, and good swimming and boating, it has a large campground open May-Oct., with water and pit toilets provided; $10 per night May-September.

Waterlily Bay Resort is off Hwy. 37 S on Waterlily Bay Rd., between Terrace and Furlong Bay, tel. 798-2267. The campsites are amongst trees (drinking water and pit toilets provided), a short stroll from a small protected beach, marina, and air station. You can rent a canoe or small boat, but you need your own fishing equipment for trout and salmon fishing in the lake—the salmon run starts early in July. A floatplane moored at the marina is available for flightseeing and charters. Campsites are $10 per night, hot showers near the office are $1 (take an extra four quarters or be prepared to exit the shower seminaked, still covered in shampoo). Lakeshore cabins (rustic ones with woodstoves and outside toilets, you pack in your water; modern ones with inside toilet and shower) range $38-58 per night Sept.-June (they're usually booked way ahead; pets allowed). All cabins have covered verandas (they get a lot of rain) and glorious views of the lake and marina.

Furlong Bay Provincial Park Campground on Lakelse Lake has a yellow-sand beach, safe swimming, boat-launching facilities, a great playground, and an interpretive amphitheatre, but it's nearly always busy (can get a little noisy during summer). Water and flush toilets are provided; the wooded campsites are $10 per night. The gates close between 2300 and 0700.

Motels, Trailer Parks, and Resorts

Another popular place (judging by the large number of fishing boats) is the **The Reel In Motel and Trailer Park** at 5508 Hwy. 16 W, tel. 635-2803. Housekeeping units are $34 s, $36 d, $38 twin, and trailer hookups are $12, including electricity, sewer, and water—in midsummer just about every trailer and RV here has a boat. The **Copper River Motel** is the least expensive in town, on the east side. It's clean and has coffee- and tea-making facilities, friendly owners, a store, and everything you need—but paper-thin walls! From $26-30 s, $28-32 d, $32-38 twin; kitchen available for an extra $4. At 4113 Hwy. 16 E, tel. 635-6124.

Mount Layton Hotsprings Resort off Hwy. 37 S (a 15-minute drive south of Terrace), tel. 798-2214, has hot pools, waterslides, a therapeutic pool, a restaurant, and a lounge. Very comfortable rooms start at $55 s or $61 d, which includes admission to the pools (though you have to fork out an extra couple of dollars to have a go on the waterslides).

Food And Entertainment

For breakfast one of the most popular places to go is the **Northern Motor Inn,** next to the Chevron Gas Station on Hwy. 16 just east of Terrace. Large omelettes, hash browns, toast, and coffee run around $7. At 4741 Kalum St. downtown is **Don Diegos** Mexican restaurant, a small, bright cafe with lots of plants, Mexican wall hangings, and delicious food, but trendy small portions. Lunch $5.50-7 (the shrimp crepes are superb). Dinners start at around $8 per plate. It's always busy so you may have to wait for a table. It's open Tues.-Sat. 1100-2200, Sun. 1600-2000, tel. 635-2307. **Pizza Hut** at 4665 Lazelle and the corner of Sparks is also popular, particularly at lunchtime; open Mon.-Thurs. 1100-2200, Fri. and Sat. 1200-2400, tel. 638-8086.

Another good restaurant, especially if your tastebuds are clamoring for excellent Canadian Greek, is **The Golden Flame** at 4606 Lazelle Street. They have all sorts of Greek specialties, but to give you an idea: a house salad (tangy house dressing), a large portion of marinated chicken or moussaka, rice, vegies, more salad, and garlic bread will cost you less than $12! The food is excellent, the service is friendly, and the bright interior has plenty of Greek artifacts to stare at while you wait. Open daily 1100-2300, tel. 635-7229. **Savala's Steak House,** also on Lazelle, has steak, seafood, pizza, and pasta, and a good salad bar. Expect to pay around $9-14 for a main course, and more. It's open Mon.-Thurs. 1100-2300, Fri. and Sat. 1100-2400, Sun. 1600-2200, tel. 635-5944.

For entertainment, **R.E.M. Lee Theatre** on Straume presents everything from live theater, music, bands, and musicals to local talent and art shows. For the nightclub atmosphere try **Hanky Panky's** in the Inn of the West on Lakelse. A popular local pub where you can kick up your heels to country and soft rock music (light meals also available) is the **Thornhill Pub** off Lake Dr. on the east side of town. **Tillicum Twin Theatres** is on Lakelse. If you're not already exhausted from hiking and fishing all day, finish yourself off with a few laps at the **Aquatic and Recreation Centre** on Paul Clark, off Kalum.

Information And Services

The **Terrace Chamber of Commerce and Travel InfoCentre** is on Hwy. 16 on the east side of town, at 4511 Keith Ave., tel. 635-2063. It's open from the end of June to Sept., seven days a week 0900-2000, the rest of the year Mon.-Fri. 0900-1700. The helpful staff will happily load you down with brochures and pamphlets and tell you everything there is to do in the area with little prompting.

Mills Memorial Hospital is on Tetrault. For an **ambulance,** call 638-1102. The **post office** is on the corner of Lazelle and Emerson. **Coin Clean Laundry** is located on the other corner of Lazelle and Emerson. **Skeena Mall** (Overwaitea Foods, Northern Drugs, K mart, and others) is between Lakelse and Greig streets (turn off Hwy. 16 at the light, cross the railway lines, and the back of the mall is facing you).

Transportation

Farwest Bus Lines is the local bus company. Call in at their office on Hwy. 16 W for a current timetable (no service on Sun. or public holidays), or tel. 635-6617. All local buses depart from **Skeena Mall,** just off the main highway between Greig and Lakelse streets. The **Greyhound Bus Depot** is on the corner of Greig and Apsley streets (entrance on Apsley), with daily services east and west. To travel by **VIA Rail** (service three times a week), go to **Elan Travel** at 4741 Lakelse for info and tickets, tel. 635-6181. There's no actual train station—just a small building on Railway Rd. that opens only when a train arrives or leaves. Get more info on long-distance service by calling (800) 665-8630. Tickets must be purchased through local travel agents in advance.

If it's summer and you're traveling west to catch a **B.C. Ferry** from Prince Rupert, be sure to call ahead at 624-9627 (P.R.) to make a booking. It's easy—just give them your name, home address, and phone number, and they give you a reservation number and tell you the cost of your ticket. Go to the ticket office (at the end of Hwy. 16) at least one hour before sailing to pay for and collect your ticket. All the usual **car rental companies** are represented in Terrace. **Terrace and Kitimat Airport** is off Hwy. 37 to Kitimat, about eight km south of Terrace, with scheduled jet service by **Canadian Airlines International** and **Air B.C.** (daily multiflight service to Vancouver), charter and flightseeing flights with **Lakelse Air,** charters with **Trans Provincial Airlines,** and helicopter services.

TERRACE TO PRINCE RUPERT

Continuing west along Hwy. 16 toward Prince Rupert (144 km, approximately 1½ hours), the beautiful Skeena ("River Of Mists") is on the left side of the road and the railway tracks are on the right, all the way. If you can travel this section of road on a fine day, it's stunning—snowcapped mountains, trees, ponds covered in yellow water lilies, and vertical cliffs with waterfalls like narrow ribbons of silver snaking down from the snow high above. **Exchamsiks River Provincial Park** off the highway to the right has a grassy picnic area on the edge of deep green Exchamsiks River (good fishing). Not far beyond a beautiful waterfall (the first of many) plummets down almost-vertical tree-covered mountains on the right, and on the far side of the river are more forest- and snow-covered peaks.

As you get closer to the coast, the river expands until eventually it becomes a very wide tidal estuary. Sandbars and marshes, exposed at low tide, are a mass of colorful mosses and wading birds looking for a tasty tidbit. In some stretches the highway shrinks down to two extremely narrow lanes neatly sandwiched between the railway tracks and the water—cross your fingers and hope that you don't meet a train and a logging truck and have to squeeze between them! About 20 km from Port Edward (32 km from Prince Rupert), the road leaves the river and meanders inland through high forested cliffs, passing **Prudhomme Lake** with its forested islands on the left. **Prudhomme Lake Provincial Park** on the right has campsites (open April-Nov.; $8 per night May-Sept.)—busy in summer. At Diana Creek a gravel road leads left off the highway for 16 km, passing a rust-colored stream and lots of anglers, to **Diana Lake Provincial Park** on the sandy shores of Diana Lake. On a hot muggy summer's day plenty of families are found here picnicking and paddling.

As you approach Prince Rupert, you pass the turnoff to the pulp mill (that's what you've been smelling!) and Port Edward (see "Sights," under "Prince Rupert," below), the turnoff to Ridley Island, and another turnoff to the Butze Rapids viewpoint—worth a quick look. The churning water of these reversing tidal rapids produces lots of floating foam called Kaien by local Tsimshian Indians—hence the name, Kaien Island, upon which the city of Prince Rupert stands.

PRINCE RUPERT

CITY OF RAINBOWS

Prince Rupert, just south of the Alaska Panhandle, lies at the end of the road, the end of the railway line, the northern end of British Columbia's ferry system, the southern end of the Alaska Marine Highway, and more often than not, the end of the rainbow! Perched along the shores of an ice-free harbor, Prince Rupert is an odd but intriguing mixture of old buildings decorated with English coats of arms, a few high-rise hotels, an architecturally modern civic center, streets with British names, and Pacific Northwest Indian totem poles, all crammed together on hilly **Kaien Island.** The atmosphere is transient Western frontier—many are just passing through. Since WW I, fishing has been the mainstay of the economy, with up to 2,000 fishing vessels cruising off in search of salmon, herring, lingcod, sole, and halibut; averaging an annual catch of some 7,000 tons, it's the self-proclaimed "Halibut Capital of the World." Today Prince Rupert's population of 17,000 supports large fishing fleets and four fish-processing plants, extensive deepwater-port facilities, grain and coal terminals, and a thriving wood-products industry.

"Rupert" is another of those places that looks quite different in good and bad weather—chances are, you won't see it at its best. It's well-known for being miserable and wet ("City of Rainbows" sounds much nicer!), but when the sun does shine, everything is clean and fresh, and the city positively sparkles. Ask the locals how they cope with all the rain and they'll tell you they get up in the morning, put on their raingear, *then* look outside. Activities go on regardless. They also look at rain in a somewhat different way—one fisherman patiently explained to me, "It's sunny above all those clouds and this wet damp stuff is actually liquid sunshine!"

Five Thousand Years Of History

For at least 5,000 years Prince Rupert Harbour and Venn Passage have been inhabited by the ancestors of the Coast Tsimshian, their lives dominated by food gathering and the sea. They followed the spring and summer salmon and oolichan runs, returning every season to the same village sites. Trade networks were established, artistic traditions emerged, and a class system evolved. Before 1790 Prince Rupert Harbour and Venn Passage were among the most heavily populated areas on the B.C. coast, and many petroglyphs, rock carvings, and paintings have been discovered (and are now protected). When Europeans arrived on the northwest coast, the Tsimshian of Prince Rupert Harbour moved to **Fort Simpson,** a Hudson's Bay Company post north of Prince Rupert, eager to cash in on fur trading. They still held potlatches, with feasting, story-telling, and dancing in elaborate costumes and masks that lasted several days, a crucial part of their economic, trade, and social systems. However, the government, swayed by church lobbyists who claimed the practice was evil, banned potlatching in 1884, and this millenia-old structure effectively collapsed.

Port Essington, originally a Tsimshian site called Spokeshute, was established as a shipping settlement (with a hotel and trading post) to supply Hudson's Bay Company brigades and ports. Although the fur trade declined, the salmon industry thrived, and in the early 19th century 12 canneries were started in the area—mainly staffed by Chinese, Japanese, and Indian laborers. Port Essington flourished during fishing seasons and boasted hotels, restaurants, stores, and a red-light district. In the 1890s, miners stopped in on their way to northern Canadian goldfields, and the inevitable missionaries tried to enforce Christianity. The port was supplied by sternwheelers and river boats; however, with the arrival of the Grand Trunk Pacific Railway, engine-powered fishing boats, and canneries built near the railhead at Prince Rupert, Port Essington was abandoned. Today only charred fragments remain.

Prince Rupert was the idea of Charles M. Hays, general manager of the Grand Trunk Pacific Railway (now CN) who in 1902 wanted to build a railway line from North Bay, Ontario, to Port Simpson (after surveys, Kaien I.) on the Pacific Coast. He hoped the new port would rival Vancouver and become *the* Pacific port for Canada. His dream partially came true in 1914 on the completion of the railway, though Hays never saw it—he went down with the Titanic in 1912. The new city was named after a pioneer business magnate and adventurer, Prince Rupert, cousin of Charles II. After WW I, fishing and fish processing became important parts of the city's industrial base, and during WW II Prince Rupert became a shipbuilding center and American army base. Tourism started in the '60s with the commencement of B.C. and Alaska ferry services.

SIGHTS

Soar With The Eagles

Take the one-km gravel road off the main highway to 732-meter **Mount Hays.** Along the road is the Prince Rupert Salmonid Enhancement Society's **Oldfield Creek Hatchery,** which is open for tours. Jumping on the gondola (adult $6, child $4) is worthwhile if it's a clear or at least partially clear day. You get excellent views of Prince Rupert, the sound, and Southeastern Alaska and see plenty of bald eagles soaring through updrafts and practicing finely tuned aerobatics. Short boardwalk trails lead through beautiful alpine flora to several lookouts. In winter, if it gets enough snow, the recreation area becomes a ski slope. A cafeteria and restaurant lie above the gondola terminal—skip the food, just go for the views! The gondola is

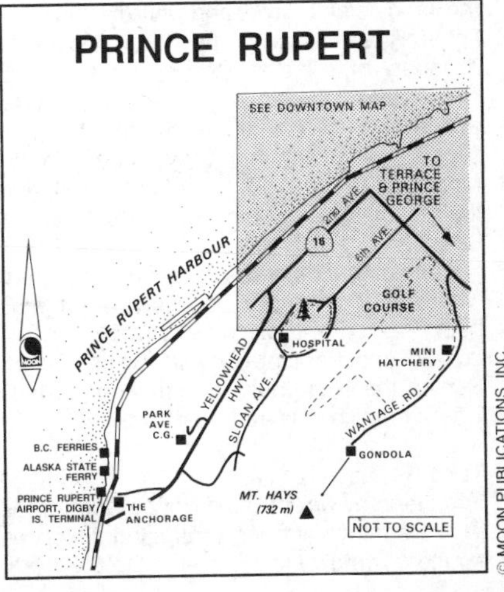

open (summer hours) 1200-2145 every day. You can also climb the hill, but as a couple of enthusiastic hikers said, "it's hard work!"

Museum Of Northern British Columbia And Prince Rupert Art Gallery
You can easily spend several hours in this small but fascinating museum on 1st Ave. and McBride Street. It traces the history of Prince Rupert from 5,000-year-old Tsimshian settlements through fur-trading days to the founding of P.R. as the western terminus of the Grand Trunk Pacific Railroad in 1914. See taxidermied birds, household items and treasures from 1912-14, a furnished pioneer room, and info on the early missionaries and fishing and canning industries. Many of the most fascinating displays feature the Coast Tsimshian Indians—their history, culture and traditions, trade networks, and potlatches. Appreciate their totem poles, pots, masks, beautiful bent boxes, a striking chilkat blanket (made from the wool of three mountain goats and cedar bark fibers), baskets, black shiny argillite carvings and sculptures, weapons, and petroglyphs, including a replica of *The Man Who Fell From Heaven*.

In another room is the art gallery (changing exhibitions), and Indian artifacts, including the intricate black, red, and white button blanket of "Raven Stealing The Moon." Videos on a variety of subjects, and an excellent gift shop (books, Indian prints, arts and crafts, and jewelry) complete the picture. The complex is open in summer (May 15-early Sept.) Mon.-Sat. 0900-2100, Sun. 0900-1700, and the rest of the year Mon.-Sat. 1000-1700, tel. 624-3207.

Behind the museum is a **carving shed** where, if you're lucky, you may see totems being carved and pieces of silver being engraved and transformed into wearable art. Behind the courthouse are sunken gardens where munitions were once stored.

Take A Hike!
For a lengthy walk around Prince Rupert, call in at the InfoCentre for a map and directions for the downtown tour, passing the **City Hall,** decorated with Indian designs, and the memorial to William Hays, founder of Prince Rupert. Also ask for a map, directions, and trail descriptions for **Kinsmen's Linear Park East Section.** One trail (there are several) is about nine km long (including public roads). It starts at McClymont Park, just across Hwy. 16 from the Civic Centre, and finishes at Chamberlin Avenue. If you find buildings interesting, you may want to walk around the modern **Civic Centre** with its three brightly painted totem poles—Grizzly Bear of Tow Hill pole, Eagle and Grizzly pole, Grizzly Bear of the Sea pole—at the front. The ultramodern **Prince Rupert Performing Arts Centre** is also worth a visit—you can take a guided tour through its muted-purple and orange interior, by appointment. For a walk with an outstanding view of Prince Rupert Harbour at the end, hike up the hill to the viewpoint in **Roosevelt Park** (picnic tables, totem pole, and map of the harbor) on Summit Dr. (near the hospital).

Industrial Tours
Prince Rupert's main industrial terminals, a **Grain Terminal** and a **Coal Terminal,** are located on 455-hectare **Ridley Island,** a small island south of Kaien Island; access off Hwy. 16 via Ridley Island Industrial Road. Tours (approximately 1½ hours) of both fully automated terminals are offered in summer; make arrangements through the Prince Rupert Information Centre.

Take To The Water
To find out the names and telephone numbers of all the local charter operators, their vessels, tours, and rates, and more info on fishing harbor adventure tours, call 627-7777. Brochures listing all the operators are also available at the InfoCentre.

Adventurers longing to get out on the water for a few hours may want to try a yacht trip or spend a day looking for eagles, waterfowl, seals, otters, porpoises, and killer whales. Beachcomb, visit historic canneries, or fish for salmon, halibut, or cod (with gear and bait supplied). All kinds of custom tours can be arranged ($600-700 per day, four to six people) by calling 627-7777. **Rupert Pelican**

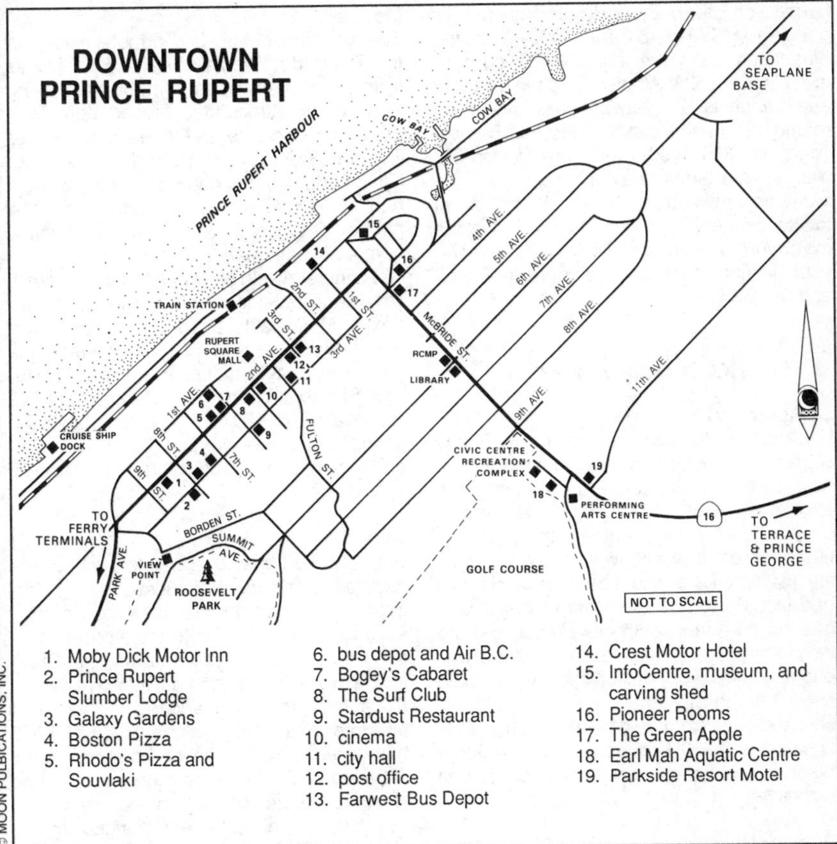

Charters provides a variety of tours on a unique coastal schooner, from a four-hour tour of the harbor from $200 (max. 12) to all-inclusive weekly adventure tours for a small fortune. Get all the details at 627-7777.

Port Edward

The main attraction within the village is **The North Pacific Cannery,** built in 1889. It's the oldest salmon cannery remaining from more than 200 such plants in B.C., and it's now classified as a historic site. Here you can find out everything you've ever wanted to know about fish, the fishing industry, canning (from handmade to fully automated)—even what is considered to be the best-tasting fish: locals claim the prize goes to red snapper every time.

From the Port Edward (and pulp mill) turn-off on Hwy. 16 all the way to the cannery (keep going till you see the signs), it's an enjoyable scenic drive along curvy roads. On entering, a guide takes you on a tour of the museum (you may grow a few scales by the end of it!), and then you're free to stroll at your own pace along the boardwalk through the riverside cannery settlement with buildings dating back to the 1890s. The cannery store has film and souvenirs, and in the mess house you can buy snacks and drinks. It's open daily 15 May-15 Sept., 1000-1700, and off-season tours are available by appointment at 628-3538. Admission to the museum and village is $5 (season pass available), refundable in the cannery stores. Farwest Tours (tel. 624-6400) runs a bus to Port Edward several times a day on weekdays, twice a day on weekends for $1.25 OW, but to get to the cannery (another 6½ km down the road) you have to specifically tell the driver your destination when you board in Rupert and pay $2 OW.

ACCOMMODATIONS

Campground

Finding budget accommodations in Prince Rupert can be difficult in summer if you haven't reserved ahead—the campground and most reasonable lodgings fill and empty on a daily basis with the arrival and departure of the ferries. If you know when you're arriving in the city, phone ahead to avoid any hassles. **Park Avenue Campground** is a one-km hike from both city center and the ferry terminals. Hot showers, sani-dump, pay phones, mail drop, visitor info, and a slide show on the city and area. Tent and unserviced sites from $9-11, full hookups $15. Located at 1750 Park Ave., tel. 624-5861; reservations accepted with deposit of one night's fee.

Pioneer Rooms

The bright blue and green Pioneer Rooms is mostly full of "steadies" in winter, but in summer the manager makes available plenty of daily or weekly accommodations. Outside yard with barbecue (barbecues are often put on for guests in summer), small clean rooms, shared bathrooms, living room with TV and guest use of a microwave and fridge; $15-20 s, $25 d. If you're just looking for a hot shower, it's $3 for nonresidents. Rooms rapidly fill with ferry arrivals and departures, but reservations can be made over the phone a day or two ahead. It's at 167 3rd Ave. E, tel. 624-2334.

Motels

The most reasonably priced motel in town is the **Parkside Resort Motel,** seven blocks from city center across from the Performing Arts Centre. Large old-fashioned rooms with optional kitchenette and fridge, and satellite TV; from $49 s, $54 d, $58 twin, extra $6 for kitchenette. Rooms go quickly in summer—nab one early in the day or reserve ahead by phone. The motel also provides a limited number of camper hookups (no campsites—just concrete) with shower and laundry facilities in the parking lot around the back. It's next to McDonalds, at 101 11th Ave. E (corner of Hwy. 16), tel. 624-9131. Another of the more reasonable motels is the **Prince Rupert Slumber Lodge** (one of a chain) at 909 3rd Ave. W tel. 627-1711. It has cable TV, sauna, lounge, restaurant (good breakfasts), and a games room; rooms start at $49 s, $55 d, $59 twin.

Hotel

Prince Rupert has several hotels with all the facilities you'd expect—it's just a case of picking the one with the best views or the most suitable location. Refer to the *Accommodations Guide* for all the details. The **Crest Motor Hotel** has a good downtown location. It's within strolling distance of the museum and InfoCentre, and most of its rooms have harbor views. A full-service hotel, the Crest provides cable TV, a dining room, a coffee shop, a lounge with nightly entertainment, free local phone calls, and parking; rooms start at $75-95 s, $85-105 d, $90-110 twin. Located at 222 1st Ave. W tel. 624-6771.

FOOD

A Breakfast Steal Of A Deal

The restaurant of the **Moby Dick Motor Inn** is well known among locals for its substantial and inexpensive breakfasts. You can order anything from a bowl of fruit and a muffin for $3 to eggs, bacon, and toast for under $5; at 935 2nd Ave. (on the main drag to the ferry terminal), tel. 624-6961. Other local suggestions for breakfast include **Slumber Lodge**

Restaurant on 3rd Ave. W or **Raffles Inn,** also on 3rd Avenue.

Seafood

Ask anyone where to go for good seafood and the answer, with a smile, is invariably **Smile's Seafood Cafe.** The diner-style cafe, decorated with black-and-white fishing photos and colored-glass floats, has been serving seafood since 1934 and it's always busy. It doesn't seem to matter what time of day it is, it's mobbed by local fishermen, residents, and visitors, and the atmosphere is distinctly casual. The extensive menu includes seafood salads, burgers (oyster burgers—mmm!), a large variety of seafood and other sandwiches, fish (pick your fish, any fish) and chips, shellfish, and seafood specialties. Prices range $4-22 per plate. At 113 George Hills Way, Cow Bay (tel. 624-3072), Smile's is open year-round 1000-2100, in July and Aug. 0800-2200. To get there follow 3rd Ave. E onto Cow Bay Rd. and continue down to the waterfront. Next door to Smile's is **Breakers Pub,** a popular local pub with plenty of atmosphere, an outdoor deck with harbor view at the back, and **The Breakers Galley,** serving deli/fast food at reasonable prices.

Another notable place for fresh seafood is the casual **Anchorage Restaurant,** at the end of the Yellowhead Hwy. beside the Alaska Ferry Terminal. Open Mon.-Fri. 0700-2200, weekends and holidays 1000-2200. For delicious fish and chips, or burgers, try **The Green Apple** on the corner of Hwy. 16 and 3rd Ave.—expect a short wait as it does a perpetually roaring trade. For a gourmet seafood bash (at gourmet prices), try the dining room at the **Crest Motor Hotel,** 222 1st Ave. West. The hotel also has a coffee shop, a lounge, and nightly entertainment.

Chinese

Stardust Restaurant serves large helpings of good Chinese food at reasonable prices. The average price for one dish is $8, combo plates are $7-10, and it's fairly difficult to walk away hungry! They also do take-out orders and provide free delivery. It's open (summer hours) Mon.-Sat. 0900-2300, Sun. 1000-2200, at 627 3rd Ave. (between 5th and 6th streets), tel. 627-1221. **Galaxy Gardens** at 844 W 3rd Ave. has a flashier decor with lots of wicker and bamboo, and tasty chow meins, prawn and chicken dishes, special combos (all average prices), and Cantonese dishes which are a little pricier; open 1100-2400 year-round, tel. 624-3122. They also do take-out orders and free home delivery.

Continental

Rodho's Pizza and Souvlaki is another popular eating-out destination for pizza (take-out and free delivery), steak, and delicious Greek specialties (from $9). On the walls are Greek plates and artifacts, and the background music is, you guessed it, Greek! Patrons seem to outnumber waitpeople six to one—expect a wait. At 716 2nd Ave. W beside the Prince Rupert Hotel, tel. 624-9797.

Another place to go for pizza, pasta, sandwiches, and salads (mainly lettuce) at average prices is **Boston Pizza** at 812 3rd Ave. W tel. 624-2121. It's comfy, popular, and smells delicious when you enter. Open Mon.-Thurs. 1130-0300, Fri. and Sat. 1130-0400, Sun. till late.

ENTERTAINMENT

Mental

All within one block are the Performing Arts Centre, the Civic Centre with its three brightly colored totem poles, the Arena, and the Recreation Complex, at 1000-1100 McBride St. (Hwy. 16) at the east end of town. Inside the ultramodern muted-orange and purple **Prince Rupert Performing Arts Centre** (corner of Wantage Rd.) just about anything could be happening—a symphony concert, a play, a lecture, a big band, or an opera. In summer on weekends at 1930 attend a performance in which actors and native dancers in authentic costumes humorously bring the history of Prince Rupert to life (call ahead and check if it's still on). Buy tickets at the door; expect to pay from adult $6, child under 12

$3.50. If there's nothing happening, you can still take a guided tour of the center, by appointment. Drop in to find out what's on, and buy tickets.

Kick Up Your Heels

Breakers Pub, with its outdoor deck and harbor view, is one of the popular local pubs, at Cow Bay. And **Breakers Galley** provides peckish drinkers with deli/fast food at reasonable prices. Many rowdy bars can be found downtown—just follow your nose and ears. For the cabaret atmosphere and dancing into the wee hours, try **Bogey's Cabaret** on 2nd Ave. (between 6th and 7th streets), or **The Surf Club** on 2nd Ave. (between 5th and 6th streets), tel. 624-3050. Most of the hotels also have licensed lounges with some form of entertainment, particularly on weekends. **Prince Rupert Cinemas** provides three theaters, each film shown twice each evening, with some Sat. matinees. It's at 525 2nd Ave. W tel. 624-6770. Check the schedule in the daily newspaper or give them a call.

Grizzly Bear of the Sea Pole, Eagle and Grizzly Pole, and Grizzly Bear Pole of Tow Hill outside the Civic Centre

Physical

Prince Rupert has an extraordinary number of physical recreation venues. For recreation info (swimming, skating, and casual activity schedules) call 624-9000. In the **Civic Centre** building you can have a game of squash, or watch badminton, basketball, or volleyball in action; tel. 624-6707 for a schedule. In the **Arena** is a roller-skating rink in summer and an ice-skating rink in winter; skate rental is available. Phone 624-9000 for schedule. Visitors are welcome next door at the **Recreation Complex** and **Earl Mah Aquatic Centre,** which has two pools (one with diving board), lap lanes, a sizzling whirlpool, two saunas, and a fitness area; admission is adult $3, student $1.30, child $1, family $6, senior free. Phone for current schedule at 627-7946 or 624-9000. **Totem Lanes Bowling Centre** has 16 lanes of five-pin bowling, a lounge, a cafeteria, a playroom for the kids, locker and shoe rental. Open Fri. and Sat. 1800-2300, and Sun. 1200-2200 (summer hours), at 1241 Prince George St., tel. 624-3291. The entrance to the local 18-hole **golf course** and clubhouse, pro shop (rentals available), and restaurant is on 9th Ave. West.

Celebrations

The major annual celebration here is **Seafest,** held in June. All sorts of wacky events involving the sea are always scheduled—a canoe dunking event (and the water's icy so no one wants to lose!), bathtub races, and fish filleting competitions to name but three. Ask at the InfoCentre for a schedule of events. Another event held in June is the authentic Native Indian **Culture Days,** featuring a **Salmon Festival** and plenty of singing, dancing, and feasting.

INFORMATION AND SERVICES

Prince Rupert InfoCentre is at the corner of 1st Ave. and McBride St., tel. 624-5637. It's one of the best InfoCentres around, with knowledgeable staff and lots of printed info on Prince Rupert sights, walking tours, restaurants, services, and ferry schedules; open mid-May-early Sept. Mon.-Sat. 0900-2100, Sun. 0900-1700, and the rest of the year Mon.-Sat. 1000-1700. Ask for a visitor's information pack which has a map, a booklet on Prince Rupert, and a variety of brochures. Both indoor and outdoor vehicle storage is available for those traveling as foot passengers on the Alaska Marine Highway System; ask for locations and rates.

The **hospital** is on Summit Ave. in Roosevelt Park. The **RCMP** is on the corner of McBride St. and 6th Ave. West. The **post office** is on 2nd Ave. (corner 3rd Street). The **public library** is on McBride St., between 6th and 7th avenues. If you're looking for books, especially on B.C. Native art or history, spend some time at **Star of the West Books and Gallery**. A gallery in the back of the store features local wildlife, Native art, and photography. It's on 518 3rd Ave. W tel. 624-9053; open weekdays 0900-2100, Sat. 0900-1700. **Rupert Square Shopping Mall** is at 500 2nd Ave. W providing 35 stores, all amenities, and parking. If you need a babysitter, go to **The Growing Space** in the **Pride O' The North Mall** (2nd and 2nd), tel. 624-9777. In July and Aug. they're open weekdays 0900-1700, winter hours Mon., Wed, and Fri. 0900-1200.

TRANSPORTATION

Prince Rupert is the "Gateway to the North," a jumping-off place for those who want to continue north (or south) by jet, small plane, or ferry, and the western terminus of the Canadian railway system and the Yellowhead Highway for those wanting to drive or bus east. All the major long-distance companies are represented, and car rental is also easily arranged. It's truly a transportation hub!

By Bus

Local bus service is provided by **Coastal Bus Lines,** 225 West 2nd Ave., tel. 624-3343. Adult fare starts around 75 cents, senior 45 cents, student/child 55 cents, child under five free if accompanied by an adult. All-day passes (ride anywhere, all day) are available for $2 from the driver. Have exact fare ready—drivers don't carry change. For transit info, tel. 624-3343.

The **Greyhound terminal** is on 6th St., tel. 624-5090. Reservations are not taken—just turn up and buy your ticket on the day you want to go. Sample OW fares (including GST): Prince Rupert to Terrace is $14.02, Smithers $33.54 (a popular skiing day-trip), Prince George $64.44, Jasper $106.73, Whitehorse $250.38 (special three day in advance purchase, nonrefundable fare to Whitehorse is $151.94 OW), and Vancouver $142.10. Long-distance excursion fares are available to a number of locations (these vary throughout the year; contact Greyhound and ask if your destination is "on special") are available if bought three or fourteen days in advance. Discounts: seniors 10%, child 5-11 half fare, under five free if accompanied by an adult (one child per adult), and YHA members get 25% off all regular fares on proof of membership. Outbound buses depart at 1115 and 2000; inbound arrive at 0925 and 1845. Office hours for buying tickets are Mon.-Fri. 0800-2000, Sat. 0800-1200 and 1600-2000, Sun. and holidays 0900-1115 and 1800-2000. No smoking on all buses. For **bus tour** information, contact **Farwest Tours Inc.** at 225 2nd Ave. W tel. 624-6400.

By Train

The station is at 211-1150 Station St., along the waterfront in town; open Mon., Wed., Fri. 0700-1500, Tues. and Thurs. 0800-1600 and 1800-2100, Sat. 1200-1600, closed Sunday. For train info, reservations, or tickets by mail, contact **VIA Rail Canada** at (800) 561-8640 (toll-free within B.C.). Hours of operation:

Tues.-Fri. and Sun. 1000-1600. The VIA passenger train departs from Platform 6.

By B.C. Ferry

Both the Prince Rupert B.C. and Alaska Marine Highway ferry terminals are about two km from downtown. A bus meets all ferry arrivals: $2 OW from town. A taxi is approximately $5 into town.

To the Queen Charlotte Islands: The MV *Queen of Prince Rupert* cruises to Skidegate Landing several times a week in summer (less often in winter), taking approximately 6½ hours. One-way fares start at: driver or passenger $16, child 5-11 $6.40, child under five free, vehicle/camper under seven feet high $61, vehicle/camper over seven feet high $80, motorcycle $30.50, motorcycle with sidecar or trailer $61, bicycle/kayak/canoe $5.50, vehicle over 5,500 kilograms $8.75 per foot. B.C. seniors must provide two pieces of ID to travel at a special fare (seven days a week), but can travel free Mon.-Thurs. (except statutory holidays).

To get a ticket (particularly if you're taking a vehicle over), it's essential to book ahead in summer: Prince Rupert tel. 624-9627, Victoria tel. 386-3431. You must give your name and address, the number of passengers, your destination, and the length of your vehicle. If you want a cabin, noisy lower-deck two-berth cabins with shared washrooms are $20 a day (overnight $25) and four-berth cabins are $30 a day (overnight $45), not-as-noisy prom-deck cabins with private toilet and sink are $32 (overnight $40), and relatively quiet bridge-deck cabins with private toilet, sink, and shower are $38 (overnight $46), plus passenger and vehicle fare. Make cabin reservations as you reserve tickets—sometimes you can get a cabin once you're onboard, but don't count on it. It is possible to sleep fairly comfortably on the chairs, or you can take the detachable cushions off and make a bed on the floor. Check the return ferry schedule before you go exploring!

To Vancouver Island: In summer (June-Sept.) don't expect to arrive at Prince Rupert and just drive on. Bookings are necessary at least two months ahead of the date you wish to go, and if you want a cabin, book that at the same time. In winter you also need to book ahead because there may only be one sailing a week—check well ahead and then book. It's easy to make a reservation—just call ahead and give them all the info they require.

The ferry trip between Prince Rupert and Port Hardy (15-18 hours) is a beautiful ride on a well-equipped boat. One-way fares start at: driver/passenger $80, child five to eleven $33.60, child under five free, vehicle/camper under seven feet high $165, vehicle/camper over seven feet high $250, motorcycle $82.50, motorcycle with sidecar or trailer $165, bicycle/kayak/canoe $6, vehicle over 5,500 kilograms $10 per foot. You can sleep on the chairs, or get a sleeping berth for two days and one night for $49 (two-berth) to $117. Dayrooms range from $22 (two-berth) to $43. Showers are available. The good onboard cafeteria serves soup and salad bar, large meals at inexpensive prices (under $10), and a variety of desserts. The day cruise in summer leaves on even-numbered days at 0730 and takes approximately 15 hours to Port Hardy. In winter the services are less often and may take up to 18 hours, depending on whether you stop at Bella Bella en route, the weather, and the time of year. For reservations write to B.C. Ferry, 1112 Fort St., Victoria, B.C. V8V 4V2, or call 386-3431.

By Alaska Marine Highway Ferry

The American **Alaska Marine Highway** operates the ferries north from Prince Rupert (to Ketchikan it's six hours). All fares are quoted in American dollars. The one-way fare for an adult passenger from Prince Rupert to Ketchikan is $32, child 6-11 $16, vehicle up to 10 feet $35—and more the longer your vehicle is. A two-berth inside cabin with complete facilities is $36, outside $41, a four-berth inside cabin is $48, outside $55, outside with sitting room $60. All cabins have their own toilet, sink, and shower—see the current schedule for rates—they vary according to your destination. If you don't want a cabin, sleeping is possible, if somewhat uncomfortable, in reclining chairs (the cushions are not detachable so you can't put them on the floor!). Or roll out your Thermalite pad and fiber-filled bag up in the solarium; depending on how crowded it is, tents can also be put up in the solarium. Check-in time is three hours ahead of sailing time—it takes up to two hours to go through Customs and one hour to load up. Foot passengers must be there one hour ahead of sailing.

To make the trip in summer, reserve three—that's right, three—months ahead. In winter call ahead to see how busy they are because there are only two sailings a week. If you cancel up to two weeks before sailing in summer (May 15 to the end of Sept.) a 10% penalty ($10 minimum) is enforced. You can go on a standby list if you show up in person at the Prince Rupert reservations/ticketing office, but then you're given a number and you may have to wait several days. If you're taking an RV or trailer home onboard, all propane must be turned off. Don't stock up on perishables—no electrical hookups are provided on board. No fruit is allowed on unless it's marked "Sunkist." Pets are permitted but must be kept in cages or cars; they need proof of vaccinations, etc., and must be exercised periodically during the day.

The ferry stops at most of the ports for approximately one hour (Sitka one to three hours, depending on tides) and passengers are permitted to disembark during this time. If you want to stop for longer at any port, you must let them know your plans when you originally buy the ticket (vehicle *or* foot passengers). To stop longer requires a port-to-port ticket which only costs around $4-18 more for several stopovers. Otherwise, you can't change ferries on your way north, and your vehicle will remain onboard the original ferry all the way to its destination.

If you call the Juneau reservation office, toll-free at (800) 544-2251, you can pay for tickets over the phone by credit card; open daily in summer 0800-1900, in winter Mon.-Fri. 0900-1700. In the Prince Rupert reservation/ticketing office you must pay in person (no over-the-phone reservations or payments). Written reservations are accepted up to one year ahead of sailing. If you know the exact departure date you want and whether you want a cabin, book and pay as far ahead as possible. The Prince Rupert Terminal and Ticket Office is open May-Sept. 0500-1200 for info, reservations, and ticketing, and the rest of the year it's open Mon., Wed., and Thurs. 0930-1600, Tues. and Fri. 0500-1200, and on arrival and departure of vessels; tel. 627-1744 or 627-1745. For more info, write to Alaska Marine Highway, Box R, Juneau, AK 99811, or call outside Alaska (800) 544-2251, within Alaska (800) 551-7185.

By Air

Prince Rupert Airport is west of Prince Rupert on Digby I., connected by airport ferry. Take a bus from **Canadian Airlines** in Rupert Square (2nd Ave. W), provided free by the airline if you're a passenger. It goes out to meet all incoming and departing flights. The ferry is $9 OW. No cars are allowed on the ferry, only buses and foot passengers. Canadian Airlines provides daily service to Sandspit (Queen Charlotte Islands) and Vancouver. **CP Air** is at 201-500 2nd Ave. W, tel. 624-9181. **Air B.C.** is located on 6th St., next to the Greyhound Bus Depot.

Seal Cove Air Base, developed by the RCAF in 1941, lies at the east end of town and serves as the seaplane base for Prince Rupert. **Trans-Provincial Airlines** is based at the Seal Cove Floatplane Terminal—a scenic spot to visit at sunset if you have a love for aviation. The company provides a scheduled flight to Sandspit or Queen Charlotte City for $94 plus GST, to Masset for $76, and to Ketchikan for $110. You can also charter a Beaver (carries six) for $402.32 an hour, a Cessna (three) for $309.23 an hour, an Otter (nine) for $479 an hour, and the Goose (nine) for $665 an hour. On a nice day quite a few people turn up at the terminal to charter one of the planes for a half-hour scenic flight. Buy your ticket just before you board. For more info, phone 627-1341. For more charter (same routes) and flightseeing tour info, contact **North Coast Airlines,** also based at Seal Cove, at 627-1359, or **Vancouver Island Helicopters** at 624-2792, located farther along the road.

QUEEN CHARLOTTE ISLANDS

THE MISTY ISLES

Wild. Quiet. Mysterious. Primordial. The Queen Charlotte Islands lie like a large upside-down triangle approximately 102 km (as the crow flies) off the northwest coast of mainland British Columbia, 48 km south of Alaska. Of the chain's 150 mountainous and densely forested islands and islets, the main ones are **Graham I.** to the north and **Moresby I.** to the south, separated by **Skidegate Channel.** The islands stretch 270 km from north to south between 52° and 54° latitude, up to 85 km across at the widest spot. Running down the west side of the islands are the rugged **Queen Charlotte** and **San Christoval** ranges, which effectively protect the east side from Pacific battering, although the east coast, where most of the villages are located, still receives a wet 125 cm of rain a year.

Wildlife abounds on and around these islands, often called the "Galapagos of the North." Come to the Charlottes and you can expect to see plenty of deer, bald eagles, Peale's peregrine falcons (more abundant here than anywhere else in the world), and if you're lucky, American black bear (reportedly enormous but rarely seen). No grizzlies live on the islands. Stare out to sea to spot killer whales, dolphins, seals, sea lions, otters, and tufted puffins; around the islands, in addition, swim fish galore. If you visit between late April and June, gray whales may be seen pausing to feed in Hecate Strait on their way from Mexico to Alaska. The best places to whalewatch are along Skidegate Inlet near the museum (whales are often seen from the ferry, then everyone rushes to one side, the ferry tilts, and people slide off the upper deck!), or on the beach at Skidegate village, or at the northernmost tip of Rose Spit.

A Brief History

Haida Indians have lived on the Queen Charlottes since time immemorial. Fearless warriors, expert hunters and fishermen, and skilled woodcarvers, they believed in owning slaves and throwing lavish potlatches. They had no written language. The totem, which could be from three to 104 meters high, was the only way they recorded tribal history, legends, and important events. Living in villages scattered throughout the islands, they hunted sea otters for their luxuriant furs, fished for halibut and Pacific salmon, and collected chiton, clams, and seaweed from tidal pools.

The first European contact occurred in 1774 when Juan Perez discovered the Charlottes. The islands weren't given a European name until 1787 when British Capt. George Dixon, an officer on Capt. James Cook's third voyage, arrived and began trading with the Haida. He named the islands after his queen, wife of George III, and his ship *The Queen Charlotte.* The Haida were keen to receive goods, liquor, tools, blankets, and firearms in return for their sea otter furs (over a 40-year period the otters were hunted almost to extinction). However, with contact with the white man also came European diseases that ravaged and greatly depleted the Haida.

White settlers began moving over to the Charlottes to live along the low flat east coast and the protected shores of Masset Inlet north of Graham Island. The Haida started using their woodcarving skills to turn argillite, a soft, slate-like stone discovered in the 1820s at Slatechuck Mountain on Graham I., into beautiful mythological sculptures. But by the 1830s the traditional lifestyle of the Haida was coming to an end. The governments on the mainland banned the owning of slaves and the throwing of potlatches (an important social and economic part of their culture), and instructed that all children attend missionary schools. The Haida abandoned their village sites on many of the islands and moved onto reserves at Skidegate Mission and Haida on Graham Island. Some of their abandoned village sites can still be seen along the shores of Moresby Island.

Today totem poles are rising once again on the Queen Charlottes, as a renewed interest in Haida art and culture is compelling skilled elders to pass their knowledge on to the younger generation. The first totem pole to be erected in 90 years was put up in 1969 in Masset, followed by one in 1978 at Skidegate. In 1986 a 50-foot dugout canoe, created out of a single huge cedar log, was commissioned for Expo86—now used by a Native tour company, Haida Gwaii—and a second canoe was launched in Haida. For many years now the Haida have struggled alongside the Island Protection Society to preserve South Moresby. Their longtime efforts paid off when **South Moresby National Park Reserve,** Canada's newest, came into being in 1988.

Much of the islands' population of 5,000 base their living on fishing (many for only a certain number of months each year, though you can successfully fish year-round), logging, and other kinds of work. Some now cater to the growing tourism industry as more and more people discover the elusive Queen Charlottes.

Read This Before You Go!

The best time to visit the islands is late summer (July through Sept.), when you're less likely to come face to face with bad storms—but take a heavy raincoat, a hat, and waterproof boots anyway. Part of the islands' charm and mystery is due to their erratic weather—sunny and calm one moment, howling wind and a downpour the next. Mist and fog seem to enshroud one area or another at any given time. The residents are so used to rain that many don't even own a raincoat or umbrella. It's a common sight to see people just walking along in the rain, drenched from head to toe, seemingly oblivious!

The most inexpensive way to discover the Queen Charlottes, as anywhere, is to bring over your own basic supplies from the mainland, and be prepared to camp out (from $8 a night plus extra for showers) or stay in your own RV, cook for yourself, and use your own car or hitchhike. If you prefer to do the islands in real comfort, be prepared to pay an arm and a leg—for accommodations, restaurants, tours, and/or car rental. Visitors either fly to **Sandspit** on Moresby I., then catch a bus to Alliford Bay and the interisland ferry over to Graham I., or come by ferry from Prince Rupert. Both ferries arrive at **Skidegate Landing** between Skidegate (northeast) and Queen Charlotte City (west). Unless you're immediately heading south to **South Moresby National Park Reserve** to

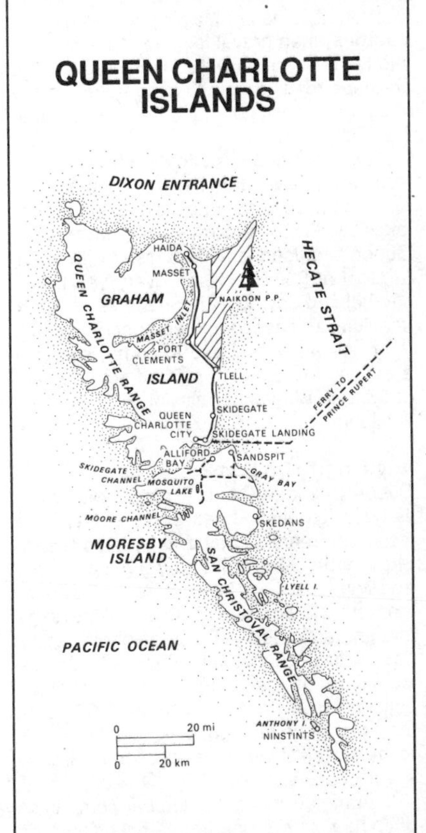

join a tour, start your discovery of the Charlottes at Queen Charlotte City, southernmost community on Graham I. and administrative center for the islands. Once you're off the ferry, follow the signs for Queen Charlotte City.

QUEEN CHARLOTTE CITY

Perched along the shores of Bearskin Bay, Queen Charlotte City (population 1,000) has the distinctly laid-back *mañana* atmosphere of a fishing village. If you continue through town the paved road terminates at the Queen Charlotte Division of **MacMillan Bloedel Industries,** then gravel logging roads lead off into the bush (permission is required to drive on these roads during logging hours) to the interior of the island and to the west coast at Rennell Sound.

Make your first stop **Joy's Island Jewellers and Travel InfoCentre** on the main road on the eastern outskirts of Queen Charlotte City. Pick up the invaluable Guide to the Queen Charlotte Islands booklet with maps (a steal at $3.95; revised every year), and say hello to Joy, Queen Charlotte's friendly unofficial ambassador. If you get off the late ferry and have nowhere to camp, she may allow you to stay on her lawn for $5 per tent or $8 per RV. Ask permission first! Water is available.

Anything To Do Here?

Queen Charlotte City is a picturesque spot, its buildings nestled between the deep-blue waters of Bearskin Bay and forested **Sleeping Beauty Mountain** (a rough trail runs from the turnoff on Crown Forest roads near the Honna River to the south end of the range for panoramic views). For good photographic possibilities, wander out onto the marina and look back at the village. Several heritage buildings in town date back to 1909-1910, most along the main road—check the *Guide to the Queen Charlotte Islands* for details and exact locations.

In summer one of the lumber companies often runs a "four-hour" forestry bus tour (up to six hours depending on the enthusiasm of the guide and/or group; take your own lunch and drinks) through all the stages of logging. It's a good way to see some of Moresby I. if you don't have your own transportation. The tour departs from the Fletcher Challenge Tourist Information Centre, Sandspit, on Wed. and Fri. at noon, and it's free, but reservations ahead of time are necessary; book through the Queen Charlotte City InfoCentre. MacMillan Bloedel also offers tours (take your own food and drinks), departing from Queen Charlotte City and Port Clements. Pick up a free brochure with amap showing logging roads on both Graham and Moresby Islands; points of interest, hiking trails, and picnic spots have been identified along the way.

Tours Galore

You can also go on all kinds of island tours from here if you have the time *and* the money—you pay for the isolation, and for supplies coming from the mainland. At the InfoCentre find out all the latest. Sea-kayaking tours are one of the most popular ways to discover the quiet beauty of the islands. **Moresby Mountain Sports** rents out kayaks and paddles, lifejackets, splash skirts—everything the happy kayaker needs! A single kayak starts at $40 a day or $180 a week, a double $50 a day or $310 a week. For more info call 559-8234. For fishing charters contact **Misty Island Charters** at 559-4588. They provide fishing gear, onboard lunch, coffee, and tea, and will even prepare your catch for shipment; from $250 pp per day based on a party of four. Spring salmon run March-Oct., coho Sept. and Oct., steelhead Nov.-March, and the bottom fish they go after are halibut and snapper in season.

For eight-hour ($800 for six to eight people) to six-day ($160 pp per day) trips, or custom charters sailing around the islands in a comfortable cabin cruiser with fresh seafood meals and refreshments included, contact **Husband Charters** at 559-4582. **South Moresby Air Charters's** floatplanes cost $260 an hour, or $2.40 a mile, plus $40 an hour waiting time. Certain destinations have set prices, such as $259.20 RT (maximum three passengers) to a South Moresby I. beach where you can walk over a hill to hot springs, or $148.80 RT to Skedans, an abandoned Haida village, plus $40 an hour waiting time. Contact Marvin Boyd at 559-4222.

If you have a particular type of tour in mind for your visit to the Queen Charlottes and prefer to have it all arranged for you ahead of time, contact Mary Morris at **Kallahin Expeditions,** a booking service, tel. 559-4746. To give you a rough estimate of booking service prices, a day tour of the islands by boat starts at $100-160 pp per day (includes picnic lunch and fully guided tour), a land-based day tour starts around $80 pp per day (minimum four), and flightseeing tours by floatplane or helicopter start at around $100 pp for a one-hour flight. Budget accordingly! You can also rent kayaks by the day or week (from $180), go on fishing trips for around $200-250 pp per day, rent bikes, or have your accommodations and car rental prearranged through the service.

Accommodations

Accommodations are expensive on the islands unless you're willing to camp out or stay in a hostel or bed and breakfast. Rustic **Gracie's Place** is delightful lodging in Queen Charlotte City. Decorated with sea treasures and flowering plants, two cozy guest rooms downstairs each have their own toilet, shower, and entrance. The smaller costs $40 s or $45 d, the larger $45 s or $50 d. It's on 3rd Ave. just past Alder St.; make reservations as far ahead as possible at 559-4262. Furnished **Cedar Springs Cottages** have their own bathroom and kitchen facilities, spectacular ocean views, and they're less than two km from the ferry terminal; $50 s or d, $10 each additional person. On Relax Rd., tel. 559-8356 (in July tel. 559-4245). **Spruce Point Lodging** has a great downtown location with superb water views and offers the choice of a hostel bed for $15 per night, or bed-and-breakfast lodging for $40-45 s, $50-65 d or twin. It's at 609 6th Ave., tel. 559-8234. The centrally located **Premier Hotel,** built in 1910, offers budget "sleeping rooms" or rooms with fridge (some with a kitchenette), free coffee, TV, and balcony with view from $25-52 s or $45-60 d; reservations recommended at 559-8415. **Hecate Inn** is five km from the ferry terminal and provides sleeping rooms with private bathroom facilities and communal kitchens; from $50 s, $55 d or twin, on the corner of 3rd Ave. and 4th St., tel. 559-4543.

Gracie's Place in Queen Charlotte City

Food And Entertainment

The place to go for breakfast is **Margaret's Cafe** (as you enter the village take the left branch and it's right there). All the locals congregate here. The restaurant has plenty of atmosphere, and the food is good and plentiful for the price (average breakfast $4). It's open Mon.-Fri. 0600-1330, Sat. and holidays 0700-1000. Another local favorite is **Laudette's Place** but don't go here if you're starving—you may have to wait until your growling stomach gets the attention of the waitress (it's always busy)! However, the food is usually worth waiting for, though on the pricey side with most main dinner dishes in the $10-17 range. It's open daily 1000-2200 (take-out also available, tel. 559-4543) at the corner of 3rd Ave. and 3rd Street. For evening entertainment there's not much going on anywhere on the island—just drinking (and dancing on weekends) in the local pub. Check in at the InfoCentre—Joy always knows what's going on. Most people who come to the islands are outdoorsy types—and the outdoors is the main source of entertainment.

Information And Services

On the main road as you enter Queen Charlotte City, stop at **Joy's Island Jewellers and Travel InfoCentre.** Inside you'll meet Joy (who's a joy!) and find a wide variety of brochures and info on everything that's going on around the islands. Don't leave without buying a copy of the latest edition of the *Guide to the Queen Charlotte Islands,* booklet which has maps and detailed info on all the villages (plus more) for $3.95.

For an emergency **doctor,** call 559-4447; **Queen Charlotte General Hospital,** emergency tel. 559-4506, general tel. 559-8466, pharmacy tel. 559-8315 (downstairs in the hospital, open weekdays 1030-1230 and 1330-1715, closed Wed. mornings); **RCMP,** tel. 559-4421. The **post office** (open weekdays 0830-1730, Sat. 0830-1230) and a **laundromat** are located in the City Center Building off 2nd Avenue.

Transportation

There's no public transportation, but hitching a ride is fairly easy. Car rental is also available. Give **Rustic Car Rentals** a call at 559-4641 (after hours 559-4586), located at Charlotte Island Tire Ltd., 605 Hwy. 33. They have the most reasonable rates on the island—from $37 a day plus 10 cents a kilometer. The closest ferry service is at Skidegate Landing. **Trans-Provincial Airlines** provides seaplane service between Queen Charlotte City, Masset, Sandspit, and Prince Rupert each day; tel. 637-5355 (Sandspit) or 626-3944 (Masset) for more information. **South Moresby Air Charters** provides floatplane charters; contact Marvin Boyd at Box 346, Queen Charlotte City, B.C. V0T 1S0, tel. 559-4222.

SKIDEGATE LANDING AND SKIDEGATE

Queen Charlotte Islands Museum

The main attraction in Skidegate is the Queen Charlotte Islands Museum, built on a rocky point at Second Beach at the north end of Skidegate Landing (signposted off the main road). It's open Mon.-Fri. 0900-1700 and weekends 1300-1700 throughout summer (for winter hours call 559-4643); admission is adult $2, seniors and students free. Inside are striking Haida wood and argillite carvings, pioneer artifacts, a beautiful woven blanket, historic black-and-white photos, stunning black, white, and red prints by Haida artist Robert Davidson, ancient totems from Tanu and Skedans dating to 1878, the skull of a humpback whale, shells galore, and a collection of stuffed birds. When you leave the museum, be sure to wander up the road and visit the cedar **carving shed** where the fantastic 80-meter-long canoe *Loo Taas,* with its striking red-and-black painted designs, is housed, awaiting due admiration. It was commissioned for Expo86 and carved from just one enormous cedar log (see below).

Haida Village Permits
To visit abandoned Haida villages on the remote islands in the south, you must first call in at the Skidegate Band office (tel. 559-4496) and apply for a permit (fill out a form and pay $10); for more info phone 559-8225.

An Eye And Tastebud Feast
At **Skidegate Mission,** a Haida reserve farther along the road, a 100-year-old, weathered totem pole still stands. The Haida longhouse facing the beach, home of the Skidegate Haida Band Council House, is fronted by a new tall totem carved by Haida artist Bill Reid, and inside local craftsmen fashion miniature totem poles, argillite ornaments, and jewelry in traditional designs. In summer in the **Old Skidegate Hall** on Thurs. nights a **Haida Gwaii Dinner** is held 1700-1800, and everyone with $20 (or $10 per child) is welcome to participate.

CONTINUING NORTH

Continuing north, the road, edged by yellow buttercups and other tiny wildflowers in summer, follows the shoreline, passing an attractive old graveyard on the left. The first stop of interest is **Balance Rock,** one km north of Skidegate village. Look for the highway sign, park at the pullout, then walk down the short trail to the shore—you'll know this rock when you see it. The gray-sand beach is a beachcomber's delight, with shells crammed in the rocks, and crabs, dead and alive, everywhere you look. Bald eagles soar around above. As you continue along the road, be prepared for a sudden swerve—this stretch has a large population of suicidal deer, ready to end it all, lurking behind trees. There's nothing quite so heartrending as the sight of a small young deer lying crumpled and bleeding beside the road—please watch out for them.

As you continue through gentle rural scenery, the beaches become more rocky and strewn with driftwood, and if you take the time to wander out onto the beach every now and again, you often find rock pools swarming with tiny crabs. At the next bulldozed pullout, notice the tree stumps which have been roughly carved in the shapes of animals and birds. Keep your eyes peeled for **St. Mary's Spring,** farther along on the left, marked by a small carved statue of St. Mary. Rumor has it, if you drink the spring water you'll return to the islands someday (resist the urge unless you know the water is good). Across from the spring is another rocky beach littered with gray, orange, and pink boulders. **Halibut's Bite Rest Area** is an excellent spot for a picnic at the tables, and has pit toilets.

Tlell
This small ranching community is the northernmost settlement on the east coast before the road swings inland toward Port Clements and Masset. In the blink of an eye you pass attractive **Tlell River Lodge** on the left (rooms with bathrooms, family-style meals; from $85 pp per day, tel. 559-4569), **Tlell Weavers,** then **Richardson Ranch** feed store, animal hospital, and kennels. The working Richardson Ranch was started in 1919 and has been in the family for four generations—one of the oldest properties in the area. If you spot a "Pottery" sign pointing off the main road, follow it! It leads to a small store where the owners make a variety of artistic and functional ceramic creations and sell them directly to the public at very reasonable prices. From just up the road northwest almost to Port Clements, you travel parallel to the southern border of Naikoon Provincial Park.

Just beyond **Naikoon Provincial Park Headquarters** (see below), the road curves inland, crossing pretty Tlell River, where **Tlell River Provincial Park Picnic Ground** is located—a forested river- and beachside trail leads north from here for 10 km to the **wreck of the *Pezuta,*** a wooden log barge that ran aground in 1928. Across the road from the picnic ground is the entrance to **Bellis Lodge and Hostel,** a particularly neat place to stay if you're a backpacker in search of a friendly place to lay your head (tel. 557-4434). A dorm bed is $17 pp or $12 if you're a hosteller, a shower is $2, laundry facilities are $2, and you can use the communal kitchen and relax in the comfy living area with TV. Hunting and fishing licenses are also available.

Naikoon Provincial Park
This spectacular park lies along the eastern shore of Hecate Strait, encompassing some 72,640 hectares of the Queen Charlotte Lowlands at the northeast tip of Graham Island. Within the park you find great hiking, fishing, camping, and swimming. *Naikoon* is the Haida word for "Long Nose," in reference to the five-km point of land at the northern tip of the park (Card Island), jutting between Dixon Entrance and Hecate Strait. Within the park are almost 97 km of sandy beaches with driftwood zones and dunes, low boglands surrounded by stunted lodgepole pine, red and yellow cedar, western hemlock, and sitka spruce. Wildlife is abundant: sitka blacktail deer, black bear, marten, river otter, raccoons, red squirrels, beaver, muskrat, small herds of wild cattle, and various species of birds. Offshore are found dolphins, harbor porpoise, and hair seals, and coho salmon and steelhead swim in the Tlell River. If you're in the neighborhood during May and June, scan the water for northern fur seals and California gray whales migrating north.

Stop in at **Naikoon Park HQ** (tel. 557-4390) in Tlell for a number of brochures on the park (with maps) and more information. A pay phone and water are available outside. To stay at noncrowded **Misty Meadows Picnic Ground and Campground** just down the road costs only $8 per site, $4 for seniors, and it has a picnic area, scenic campsites with firewood supplied, pit toilets, and beach trails.

Tlell To Port Clements
It's only 24 km from Tlell to Port Clements by road. Be sure to stop at **Mayer Lake Provincial Park** about halfway. The lake is completely covered at one end with green-leafed bright-yellow water lilies in summer—a beautiful spot to launch your canoe. Don't forget to take your camera down the short trail. The park has a lovely lakeside picnic area with tables, and a campground with firewood and pit toilets.

PORT CLEMENTS

At the road intersection turn left into the logging and fishing community of **Port Clements.** This village, with many of its weather-beaten houses decorated with driftwood, shells, Japanese glass fishing floats, and other seawashed treasures, snuggles along the eastern shores of the south side of Masset Inlet (an inland sea) at the mouth of the Yakoun River. Residents just call it "Port." On Bayview Dr. you pass **Bayview Market** (closes at 1800; has some of the most delicious in-season hothouse tomatoes on the planet), **The Loft** licensed restaurant (good view, but small portions and expensive), **Yakoun River Inn Pub** (good food, plenty of it, reasonable prices), and the community hall. The road then runs along the inlet with its spectacular lime-green mosses and lichens on the rocks, clear blue water, long red government wharf, and deep-blue cloud-wreathed mountains on the far side. Very colorful, no matter what the weather is doing!

Sights
Port Clements Museum on the main road houses an intriguing selection of pioneer artifacts and relics from the village, and black-and-white photos of logging camps and early village life (don't miss the old albums); open daily 1400-1600 in summer, admission by donation. Continue along Bayview Dr. (becomes gravel) and eventually you come to **Juskatla**, an old logging camp established in the 1940s in reaction to the demand for Queen Charlottes spruce for WW II airplanes. Today the main office for the MacMillan Bloedel logging company is located there. Don't do the road unless it's after 1600 on a weekday or on a weekend, and drive with your headlights on at all times—it's a logging road and, as usual, logging trucks always have the right of way (they're bigger!).

Two highlights lie along the logging road to Juskatla (both are signposted). The first (about six km from Port) is the **Golden Spruce,** an outstanding, 50-meter-tall, more than 300 years old, bright yellow Sitka spruce that really stands out from all the other green trees surrounding it (it produces only green-boughed seedlings so it's quite a mystery to foresters). To get to it, follow a beautiful five-minute trail through the lush, moist, almost-dripping forest full of tweeting birds to the oil-black, totally still Yakoun River (great reflection shots). The golden spruce lies on the opposite bank of the river and it's quite stunning—particularly before noon when the sun shines on it. The second highlight, much farther along the road, is an unfinished **Haida canoe** lying in a shelter in the forest, reached by a short trail. Many unfinished canoes lie in the bush, but this is the only one that can be easily reached. If you don't want to walk through the undergrowth to see one, look behind the museum in Old Massett.

On To Masset

The road, sandwiched between grassy shoulders and forests, crosses more jet-black or dark rust-colored rivers. Stretch your legs along the five-minute trail starting at the parking lot for **Pure Lake.** This is another gorgeous lake, with very dark, dense, reddish-brown waters that reflect everything around it. Picnic tables have been located along the shore, and hiking trails lead off around the lake. From here the road follows the inlet, passing a lumber mill, before reaching the town of Masset.

MASSET

Masset is the largest settlement on Graham I. and the gateway to Naikoon Provincial Park. It was first surveyed in 1909 for the Graham Steamship, Coal, and Lumber Company and was named Graham City, but when the village began managing the post office of the Haida community of Masset, the Haida village became known as **Old Masset** (or **Haida**) and the new town was called New Masset. In 1961 the village was incorporated as Masset, first town on the Queen Charlottes. About half the population of 1,600 is connected with the Department of National Defense station (built in 1971) and lives on the base. The other half is involved in the fishing industry—either as fishermen or as workers in the crab cannery or the fish-freezing plant.

As you first enter town, stop at the **InfoCentre** in the small van on the right. At the first road junction, turn left over the bridge and into Masset. On the right is the Canadian Forces Station at Masset. If you turn left on Delkatla Rd., passing the government wharf where a mass of fishing boats cluster in **Delkatla Inlet,** then take a right on Collison Ave., you're on the main street.

Town Sights

Masset is a good base from which to explore the beauty of the surrounding area and Naikoon Provincial Park. There's not actually

beautiful Pure Lake

much to do in town, aside from strolling around to see the heritage buildings (the Old Schoolhouse and the Old Hospital, both on Collison Avenue). Along **government wharf** some interesting activity is almost always going on: boats coming and going, fishermen loading up supplies or unloading their catch.

Another attraction in town is the **Delkatla Wildlife Sanctuary,** where you can see Canada geese, sandhill cranes, trumpeter swans, and other waterfowl resting during migration. After crossing Delkatla Inlet into town, continue along Hodges Ave. then turn right on Trumpeter Drive. The road follows the inlet, and several short walking trails meander along the shore. The other way to see more of the sanctuary is to drive along Tow Hill Rd. toward Naikoon Provincial Park, turning left at the sanctuary sign on Masset Cemetery Road. **Bird Walk** trail is signposted off the road, then farther along, stop at **Simpson Viewing Tower.** A trail leads through a wide open meadow and marshes dotted with wildflowers to the tower where you may see trumpeter swans, many varieties of ducks, birds of prey such as the bald eagle and peregrine falcon, wading birds such as the sandhill crane and great blue heron, and marsh animals such as the muskrat, raccoon, and black bear.

Continue along the road and you eventually come to a parking area and a trail to the beach. Just across from the parking area, behind the fence, is beautiful **Masset Cemetery** where the graves are marked by large aboveground mounds of moss planted with flowering bulbs and bushes amongst trees—a peaceful place to ponder the beauty of the Charlottes.

Haida

If you're in search of Haida treasures, take the coastal road from Masset to the Indian village of Haida, also known as **Old Masset,** a five-minute drive from Masset or about $2.50 by taxi. Go as far as the road takes you and you'll end up at a blue building, the **Haida Museum.** Inside are a large collection of fascinating old photographs showing how the villages used to look, Haida art and prints, and some of the original totems from around the Queen Charlottes; open daily, admission by donation. Continue up behind the museum to **Adams Family House of Silver** to view or buy carved-wood items (decorative and useful) and silver jewelry directly from the artist. He also has a fantastic Haida print collection. Open 1000-1200 and 1300-1800, or phone ahead for an appointment at 626-3215.

Next door, the impressive weathered building with tall totem pole at the front is **Claude and Sarah Davidson's Haida Arts and Jewellery** shop. Officially open 0900-1800, someone is usually there at all hours in summer. Here you can buy custom argillite carvings, silk-screened prints, handcrafted silver and abalone jewelry, books on Indian culture, printed sweatshirts, and greeting cards. Claude also operates **Haida Boat Charters.** Chartering the *Haida Myth* and skipper from $40 per hour (seats four to six), you can fish, dive, hunt, or sightsee. Take suitable clothing and your own food and drinks. For reservations call 626-5560. Only a few totems (though they're working on more) stand in Haida—the one outside the Davidsons', two in the field in front of the Davidsons', and one farther along the road; the originals have been snapped up by museums. The place to go to see a number of authentic poles still standing in their original spots is South Moresby I., but the only way to get there is by charter boat or on a tour (by sea kayak, raft, yacht, boat, floatplane, or helicopter), and permits are required from the Band Office in Masset ($15) to visit ancient Haida village sites.

Accommodations

The most scenic campsite in the local area, but also the farthest away, is **Agate Beach Campground** near Tow Hill, about 20 km from Masset. The campsites lie along the back of the beach (outstanding views), and are only $8 per night. A shelter and pit toilets are provided, but no showers. In summer you need to nab a spot early in the day—by late afternoon they're all taken! For a deliciously protected spot, perch your tent on the sand between the large pieces of driftwood above high-water line. (See below for more info.) **Masset-Haida Lions RV Site and Campground** is the closest to town (two km north, opposite the Delkatla Wildlife Sanctuary), and it has large, fairly private campsites with tables amongst the trees, communal washrooms with coin-operated hot showers (50-cent pieces; takes two for a decent length). It's on the right side of Tow Hill Rd., just up the road from the bridge into town; $8 per night, plus $2 for electricity.

The closest motel to the beach is **Naikoon Park Motel,** on Tow Hill Rd. (tel. 626-5187) near the entrance to Naikoon Provincial Park (walking distance from the beach). Sleeping units with showers are from $35 s or d (slightly lower rates in winter; 10% discount on stays of seven days and longer), and guests can use the courtesy coffee room (0700-1030), and microwave oven, bar, and barbecue area.

The best places to stay in town are the various bed and breakfasts. Most either offer good views or locations or are rustic in appearance and have a charm all their own! Stroll around town and look for the B&B signs hanging outside, and expect to pay at least $35 s, $40 d (some share bathrooms with owners and/or other guests). **Harbourview Lodging** at 1608 Delkatla St. is run by hospitable Vladimir Suna and Carol Sharpe, providing pleasant rooms (one with a view of the fishing pier), shared bathroom, and optional breakfast. Rates start at $45 s, $53 d, $62 family. They're busy year-round so if you want to stay here reserve ahead at 626-5109. Another popular bed and breakfast is David Phillip's **Copper Beech House** next to the fishing pier—rustic, decorated with sea treasures, and with a beautiful flower garden. It's at 1590 Delkatla, tel. 626-3225; from $40 pp. **Alaska View Lodge** is 12.6 km from Masset on Tow Hill Rd., tel. 626-3653, but has an excellent beachside location. A room with balcony and ocean and beach views, and breakfast (when you want it) starts at $45 s, $55 double. The owners also speak French.

Food And Entertainment

You may presume that it would be easy to get fresh seafood at a fishing village on the Queen Charlottes—but it's not. And when it is available it's expensive. Why? Because the fishermen can make a far more substantial living by selling all their fish by the pound to the canneries than to local restaurant owners who can't afford to pay the same high price. Restaurant owners therefore buy it from the mainland, or pay exorbitant prices that are, in turn, passed on to you. If you see seafood on the menu, ask if it's fresh.

Cafe Gallery on the corner of Collison Ave. and Orr St. has good food, but it's on the pricey side. They offer steak, seafood, chateaubriand, and pasta dishes; expect to pay from $9 for the least-expensive item on the menu. Daily specials, such as smoked Alaska cod with rice, vegies, and salad bar (lots of choices), run around $13.50; at noon each day they lay out a smorgasbord. Don't venture here if you're in a hurry—the meal may take several hours! Open Mon.-Sat. 1000-2200. Masset has two Chinese restaurants—**The Villager** (inexpensive) and **Pearl's Dining Room** on the corner of Main St. and Collison Ave. (next to Schooners General Store). Both Chinese and Canadian cuisine are on the menu, but go for the dee-licious Chinese. For under $10 you can get an enormous helping of chicken and vegetables in black bean sauce with a large bowl of steamed rice, tea, and the mandatory fortune cookie. Most of the good-value Chinese dishes start around $9. Even though the pink tablecloths are covered in plastic, this is obviously one of the better restaurants in town; open Mon.-Thurs. 1130-2100, Fri. and Sat. 1130-2200, Sun. closes early, tel. 626-3223.

For entertainment, a local suggested you "look out of your window!" There's not much to do in the evening unless you care to drink at **Daddy Cool's Neighbourhood Pub** on the corner of Collison Ave. and Main St. (open Mon.-Sat. 1200-0200, Sun. 1200-2400), or the often-rowdy **Singing Surf Inn** on Old Beach Rd. (as you enter Masset from the south), or head out to the **Base Recreation Centre** on Hodges Ave. and see if they'll let you use the gym or pool or attend their cinema.

Information And Services
The **Masset InfoCentre** on Tow Hill Rd., just as you approach the town of Masset from the south, is open seven days a week till 1600 in summer only. Pick up your brochures here.

The **hospital** is on Hodges Ave. by the Base Administration Building, tel. 626-3636. A **dental clinic** is at 1890 Harrison Ave., tel. 626-3238. The **RCMP** is on Collison Ave., tel. 626-3991. **Canada Post** is on Main St., tel. 626-5155; open weekdays 0830-1730 and Sat. 0830-1230. **Masset Travel** on Collison Ave. is the place to go for all your ongoing travel needs. See Louise Lamorie on weekdays 0930-1630 or Sat. 1000-1500, or phone 626-3604.

Transportation
There's no form of public transportation in Masset—just your thumb (it's fairly easy to get a ride, even in pouring rain), taxi (tel. 626-5017 or 626-5445), or car rental. **Budget Car Rental** on Collison Ave. rents everything from compact economy cars to 4WD trucks. Small cars start around $50 a day plus 25 cents per kilometer, plus a substantial drop-off charge if you don't return it to Masset. You need only a driver's license, and you can buy optional insurance. June-Aug. it's often necessary to reserve a car. Reserve up to a week ahead to ensure a vehicle for Sept. and Oct. when Masset is flooded with salmon fishermen.

Trans-Provincial Airlines floatplanes fly from their terminal off Old Beach Rd. (as you enter Masset from the south) between Masset and Prince Rupert twice a day in summer; $76 OW. Stop by for a current schedule or call 626-3944, or write to Box 280, Prince Rupert, B.C. V8J 3P6. The office opens only for arrivals or departures. **Wag Air** also flies from Masset to Port Hardy, Bella Bella, and Vancouver every day, tel. (800) 663-2875. **Tilden** cars are also available at the office; phone 626-3225.

THE ROAD TO TOW HILL

From Masset, one of the most beautiful areas to visit is Agate Beach (about 15-20 km east) and Tow Hill. The trip out there along Tow Hill Rd. is superb—through kilometer after kilometer of moss-draped trees. On the way you pass the municipal campground, the site of Masset Municipal Airport (not completed), the Dixon Entrance Golf and Country Club (18 holes), the Canadian Forces Station at Masset Operations Site, and Naikoon Park Motel. Then you enter **Naikoon Provincial Park** (it's another 14½ km from here to the beach campground).

Not far along is the start of a beach strewn with pebbles and driftwood, separated from the road by the Chown River. After crossing the Sangan River, you travel on gravel the rest of the way. Striking cabins and large private homes, all with forest and sea views, lie along the left side of the road, and on the right are forests heavily mantled with moss.

TODD CLARK

Tow Hill and the north end of Agate Beach

In **Tow Hill Ecological Reserve** the ground and most of the trees are completely cushioned in spongy yellow moss, and birds tweet from the treetops—it's a goblin forest of great beauty. Several beach access points for 4WD vehicles are marked along the road, as is a private Indian Reserve.

Agate Beach

This long, sandy beach strewn with shiny, smooth, sea-worn pebbles of every color under the sun, shells, and driftwood is a beachcomber's delight. Walk along the shores of **McIntyre Bay** and scramble over the rocks at the base of 109-meter **Tow Hill** to find more treasures and small sea creatures in the rock pools at low tide. Bald eagles soar on upcurrents by the almost-vertical cliffs, and the beach and Tow Hill from below make excellent photographic subjects. **Agate Beach Campground** is set along the back of the beach (see "Accommodations," above)—an excellent location and therefore always busy in summer. Swimmers need to beware possible strong undertows along the beaches and at river mouths, and vehicle operators can use their noggins by finding out where the soft sand is along the beach before driving out.

The road continues beyond the campground to **Tow Hill Provincial Park Picnic Ground,** where a walk along the short **Hiellen** riverside trail leads through the woods to the picnic ground and on to where the river joins the bay. A footpath also leads to the top of Tow Hill for splendid views. If you're fishing, walk down the opposite side of the river to join other keen anglers (catch and release is preferred for steelhead). At the far end of the parking lot is a bridge over dark reddish-brown Hiellen River to the start of several lengthy trails and 4WD vehicle routes. Using these, well-equipped adventurers can do an almost-circular route all the way up to **Rose Point** at the northeastern tip of the Charlottes (you may spot killer and gray whales, seals, and sea lions), then down the east coast to finish at Park HQ at Tlell. This has become a popular hike—take your time along with adequate rations and really enjoy it.

If you're going to do the four- to eight-day **East Beach Hike** (park staff suggests it be done from south to north) read all about it at the trailhead parking lot. Make sure you're suitably equipped, know the tides, take a stove to boil the brown but drinkable water found along the route (10 minutes will purify it), and expect to frequently meet 4WD enthusiasts along the beach. And carry water between Cape Fife and Tow Hill. A map and chart shows the distances along the hiking trail. The closest doctor to this point is at the

CFS Hospital in Masset, tel. 626-3772; the **RCMP** is also in Masset, tel. 626-3991.

MORESBY ISLAND

Moresby is a large wilderness island, basically untouched except for ancient abandoned Haida village sites and a few logging roads. **South Moresby I.** has recently been designated a **National Park Reserve,** much to the joy of resident Haida and white naturalists, and environmentalists around the world, and to the disgust of the resident logging companies. The only settlement on the island is **Sandspit,** where the main airport for the Queen Charlottes is located. Many fly in and catch a bus to Alliford Bay then the interisland ferry to Graham I. to start their discovery of the paved section of the Queen Charlottes. Others join a variety of tours to discover the natural beauty of the south.

You can drive on rough gravel logging roads to the northern interior and east and west coasts of Moresby I. in a circular route, but you need a good map before attempting it. However, note that during working hours (weekdays till 1800) you must get prior permission to use these roads from the Fletcher Challenge office in Sandspit, tel. 637-5323. If you don't stop along the way, the route takes about two hours to drive. To make the effort worthwhile, beautiful secluded campsites are located at **Gray Bay** on a long, curved, sandy beach (a hiking trail leads south along the beach to Cumshewa Head), and **Mosquito Lake,** which was named after the mosquito airplane, not the pesky insects (lakeside campsites and a small boat launch).

Off the southern tip of South Moresby I. lies **Anthony I.,** a provincial park that in 1982 became a UNESCO World Cultural Heritage Site to protect **Ninstints,** the best-preserved totem village in the world. It's a remarkable place—ancient brooding totems and remnants of mighty Haida longhouses in a stand against a backdrop of lush wilderness: dense trees, thick spongy moss, and rock-strewn beaches with incredibly clear water. Colonies of nesting seabirds, and an abundance of marinelife—killer and minke whales, sea lions, tufted puffins—all add to the atmosphere. It can only be reached if you have your own boat, join a wilderness tour group, or charter an aircraft, and you must get permits from both the Skidegate Band Council Office and the Masset Band Council before stepping ashore—the island is tended by a Haida Gwaii watchman.

Sandspit

Gateway to South Moresby, Sandspit (pop. 500) is primarily a small logging community with one main road. Facilities include a small variety of accommodations, a restaurant, a couple of grocery stores, a post office, several tour operators and fishing tackle stores, and 18-hole **Willows Golf Course,** with pro shop, coffee shop, and lounge. Try staying at the friendly **Moresby Island Guest House** at 385 Alliford Bay Rd., tel. 637-5305. It's a popular kayakers' hangout offering rooms with shared baths and kitchens, and laundry; a light breakfast is included in the rate of $40 s, $50 d. Sandspit also has several other bed-and-breakfast establishments (look for the signs). The comfortable (and more expensive) **Sandspit Inn** provides hotel and motel rooms starting at $55, a lounge, a restaurant, and a gift shop, and it's near the airport, tel. 637-5334. Get all your info about South Moresby I., its sights and facilities, and detailed directions on the logging roads to the interior at the **Tourist Information Centre** on Beach Rd., tel. 637-5436.

Sandspit Airport, only airport for the Queen Charlottes, is located here. **Canadian Airlines International** operates a twice-daily jet service from Vancouver or Prince Rupert to Sandspit (tel. 637-5388); **Trans-Provincial Airlines** (tel. 637-5355, Sandspit) provides seaplane flights several times a day from Prince Rupert to Sandspit (and to Masset and Queen Charlotte City). **Budget Rent-a-Car** (and truck) rentals can be arranged in Sandspit Airport terminal daily 0900-1300, and after-hours at tel. 637-5688. Their main office is in Masset, tel. 626- 5571.

Tour Operators

There are many ways to see the new park, and many more are springing up even as you read this! Here are just a few that have been recommended:

South Moresby Charters (based in Queen Charlotte City) offers everything from a kayaker drop-off and pick-up service to rental of their boat and crew to go wherever you like; tel. 559-8383. If you didn't bring a kayak and it's sounding awfully enticing, **Moresby Mountain Sports** (in Queen Charlotte City) rents them out along with paddles, lifejackets, splash skirts—you name it! A single kayak starts at $40 a day or $180 a week, a double $50 a day or $310 a week; tel. 559-8234.

Vancouver Island Helicopters' exciting tours are expensive but probably unforgettable. They'll go anywhere you want to go, weather permitting; based at Sandspit, tel. 637-5344. For more info on local charters and tour companies, drop by one of the InfoCentres.

A company based in Vancouver also specializes in Queen Charlotte Islands adventure discovery tours, but they obviously need to be prearranged: call **Ecosummer** at 669-7741 and ask for info on their 8- to 15-day sea kayaking/camping trips. Everything is included, but you must provide your own sleeping bag; rates start at around $1200 for eight days.

LOUISE FOOTE

PEACE RIVER/ ALASKA HIGHWAY

The vast area of wilderness that makes up the Peace River/Alaska Highway region still attracts adventurers and those wanting to escape the beaten track, as it has for the last 200 years or more. Native people have lived in the area for 10,000 years. As usual, the fur traders were the first white men to wander through the countryside. However, Alexander Mackenzie was the first to really explore the region in detail in the late 18th century, after which settlement began. The first white colony in the province was a trading post established in 1792 on the spot where the city of Fort St. John now sits. In 1861 the cry of "Gold!" brought miners to the Peace River, and then again in 1898 to the city of Dawson Creek, perched on the edge of the Klondike Gold Rush trail.

The double name of the region comes from the enormous Peace River that slices through the Rocky Mountains like a rapid highway—legend says the Beaver Indians made peace with their enemy on a point of land where the Smoky joins the river—and from the Alaska Hwy., an engineering and construction feat that stretches like a crooked finger 2,450 km north from Dawson Creek to De Ha Junction, Alaska. If you explore the region you'll travel through the Rockies, see enormous lakes and dams, follow major rivers, and visit the few major population centers, all in the south. Then blast off like a modern pioneer into the northern wilderness for hundreds of kilometers, stopping for wildlife, camping in beautiful provincial parks, fishing in icy streams, and perhaps soaking away the dust in natural hot springs along the way. The adventure is just beginning!

PRINCE GEORGE TO DAWSON CREEK

Provincial Park Paradise
Prince George to Dawson Creek is 409 km via the John Hart Hwy. (Hwy. 97 N)—a good road, but tedious if you get stuck behind a particularly slow vehicle or a string of RVs. For the first 160 km the highway runs through lush, rolling fields where you'll see horses and cows, and farmers on tractors, then up and down tree-covered hills passing lakes, turnoffs to lakes, and ponds chockablock with water lilies. In summer the roadside is ablaze with red-orange Indian paintbrush and purple lupine. At **Bear Lake, Crooked River Provincial Park** has camping and vehicle sites, picnic tables, and swimming; popular in summer. Watch out for the occasional moose strolling across the highway! The next large roadside lake, complete with tree-covered islands in the middle and surrounded by low forest-covered hills in all directions, is **McLeod Lake.**

Large 19,344-hectare **Carp Lake Provincial Park** (32 km off the highway along a rough road) has vehicle and campsites (open May-Oct.; $8 fee May-Sept.), picnic sites, walk-in wilderness campsites, and good swimming, fishing, and hiking trails. They say Carp Lake was Simon Fraser's favorite fishing hole! McLeod Lake has the first real signs of life along the highway since Prince

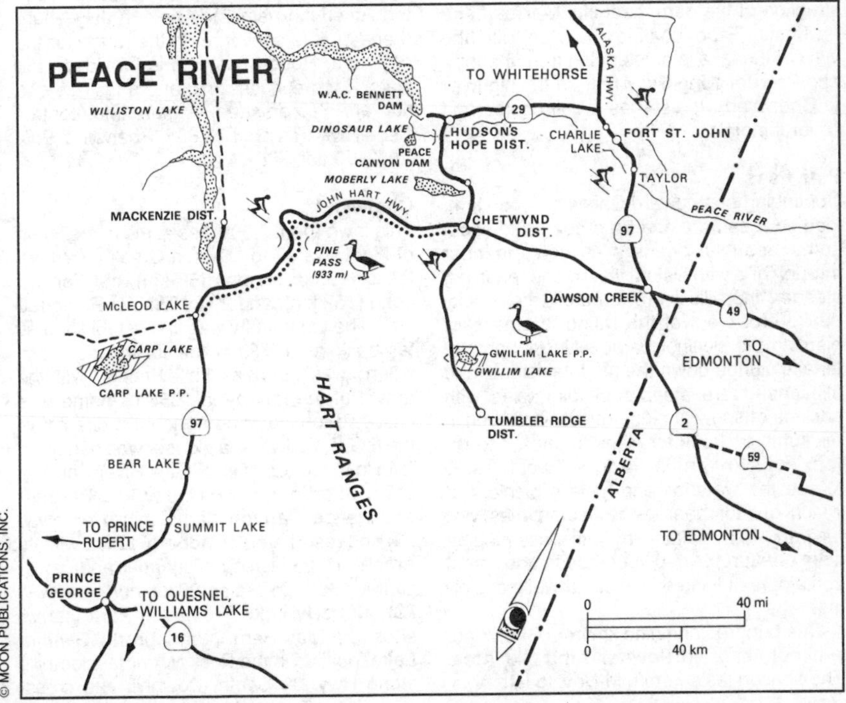

George, with a motel, a general store, funky log cabins with red doors, a post office, a gas station, and a restaurant. The next provincial park along the highway is **Tudyah Lake,** with a campground, picnic sites, a boat launch, and swimming and fishing. It's open May-Oct.; $6 per night May-September.

Mackenzie

At the junction of Hwy. 39 to **Mackenzie** is a **Travel InfoCentre.** Mackenzie (population 5,542) is 30 km north, sitting at the southern end of enormous **Williston Lake.** Built during the construction of the **W.A.C. Bennett Dam** near Hudson's Hope (which supplies almost one-third of British Columbia's power), Mackenzie is the gateway to lake recreation of all sorts. Local attractions include **Williston Lake Reservoir,** biggest manmade reservoir in North America, the "World's Largest Tree Crusher" which was used during the construction of the dam, beautiful **Morfee Lake** (swimming and boating), Morfee Hill (the view of the lake is outstanding from the top), and **Powder King Ski Area** (on the highway to Chetwynd). It also has a golf course and several motels.

Pine Pass

Continuing east toward Chetwynd (150 km), load your camera and be prepared to shoot some beautiful scenery as you meander through hills with distant views. The roads get steeper, the hills more forested, then rocky peaks break out of the range, dramatically piercing the skyline. Large silver-ribbon waterfalls plunge down the mountainsides, and still ahead are steep rock pinnacles with pockets of snow at higher elevations even in midsummer. Look for signs to the left to **Bijoux Falls Provincial Park,** well worth a stop to see the waterfall and have a picnic. But watch out for bears—they sometimes visit the park. To avoid tangling with these magnificent creatures, keep your food in odor-proof containers or locked in your car while exploring.

One hundred and nine km from Chetwynd, a turnoff leads to **Powder King Ski Area.** The season lasts from mid-Nov. to late April, and skiers are provided with a vertical rise of 630 meters, a 2,607-meter run, a ski school with rentals available, a shop, a cafeteria, and a village resort with a hotel, restaurants, and a tavern. For more info, phone 561-1776. From there the highway meanders over one of its most scenic stretches—933-meter Pine Pass—with excellent views of the Rockies. The emerald Pine River runs along the left side of the highway, through forested areas alternating with open bright-green paddocks. Photo fanatics are bound to use up a lot of film through here! Look out for moose.

As you approach Chetwynd, a wide river valley lies to the right side of the road and the hills are flattopped as though someone had just given them one of the latest punk hair-dos—with a chainsaw! On the right, 25 km from Chetwynd, is the huge **Bend River Ranch,** where every year a large three-day **Bluegrass Country Music Festival** (with top American names) is held in July—hundreds of RVs converge on the ranch for the occasion. Rough camping is provided, and water, food concessions, and a first-aid station are also on-site. For more info, contact Bend River Ranch, Box 684, Chetwynd, B.C. V0C 1J0, tel. 788-2471.

Chetwynd

This town (pop. 2,800) lies at the intersection of highways 97 to Dawson Creek (102 km), 29 to Hudson's Hope (68 km) and Fort St. John (152 km), and 29 to Tumbler Ridge (90 km). The community was first established as far back as 1778, in the fur-trading days, when it was known as "Little Prairie." With the arrival of the railway in 1958 its name was changed to Chetwynd to honor a director of the P.G.E. Railway—a pioneer who had great faith in the future of the Peace River Country. Local attractions include the **W.A.C. Bennett** and **Peace Canyon dams** (north on Hwy. 29), the resort area of **Moberly Lake,** with its excellent trout fishing in summer and cross-country skiing in winter (29 km north on Hwy. 29), **Moberly Lake Provincial Park** (campsites $8 May-Sept.), and pretty **Gwillim Lake,** nestled in the Rocky Mountain foothills along Hwy. 29 South. Downhill and cross-country skiers head for local **Wrecking Bar Mountain.** The one main road through town is lined with inns, restaurants, and gas stations, and the **Travel InfoCentre** is in a caboose beside the highway, tel. 788-3655; open 0800-2000.

If you're continuing north up to the Alaska Highway, you have the choice of two routes at Chetwynd—both worthwhile. Continue east to Dawson Creek then north to Fort St. John; or head due north to Hudson's Hope then east to Fort St. John (the shorter of the two routes). As both routes link up to make one circular route, take one way north and the other way south and you'll get the best of both worlds!

Tumbler Ridge

The first major road off Hwy. 97 to the right leads 90 km to Tumbler Ridge, a new coal town in the Rocky Mountain foothills that sprung up the same way gold-rush towns did a hundred years ago. It was created virtually overnight to allow the employees of the northeast coal project to settle in quickly and comfortably—with all the creature comforts, services, and recreational facilities you'd expect in a long-established town. The **Travel InfoCentre** is in the center of downtown. The main regional attractions include the forested and mountainous, 32,000-hectare wilderness **Monkman Provincial Park,** 88 km south of Tumbler Ridge. See the impressive 70-meter-high **Kinuseo Falls,** which can only be described as spectacular, and find out for yourself if the fishing is as excellent as they claim; wilderness walk-in campsites, no roads, accessible only by plane. Also visit **Gwillam Lake** for more excellent fishing, or go on the free tours of the largest computerized mines in the world—Quintette Coal and Mullmoose Mining Corporation—from mid-June to mid-Sept.; more details at the InfoCentre.

Chetwynd To Dawson Creek

This stretch of the highway takes you past **East Pine Provincial Park,** a good spot for a picnic, down a steep hill into a bush-filled valley, across the wide Pine River, and up the other side into vast open meadows. From then on, kilometer after kilometer of slightly rolling fields is all you'll see—another facet of British Columbia—and then you're into flat, flat prairie country. The next amazing change as you approach the city of Dawson Creek in summer (particularly in late June) is the bright yellow and green checkerboard landscape stretching out as far as you can see in all directions. Vast meadows of blossoming rape (Brossica napis), used in obtaining different types of oil similar to linseed or whale oil (far-reaching and varied uses), is grown all over Peace Country as a short-season cash crop. One-quarter of the total Canadian production comes from Peace Country, alternating well with the huge honey industry for which the region is world famous.

DAWSON CREEK

Dawson Creek was named after Dr. George Mercer Dawson, a Canadian geologist and scientist whose survey of the prairie in 1879 told of its fertility, assisted in its settlement, and prompted the later discovery of gas and oil fields. Most of the first settlers came to the area in 1912, but the arrival of the Northern Alberta Railway in 1931 put Dawson Creek on the map as an agricultural service center—and established it as the starting point of the Alaska Highway in 1942. Agriculture is still the main basis of Dawson Creek's economy: wheat, oats, barley, canola, vegetables, specialty crops, cattle, dairy, hog, sheep, and poultry. Honey is an important cash crop in the district. Oil and gas rigs stand in the Elmsworth Basin south of the city, and pipelines and processing plants are located to the east. Dawson Creek (pop. 10,473) stands at the junction of Hwy. 97 and the world-famous Alaska Highway.

On entering the city from the west, pass the highway intersection to Fort St. John and Whitehorse and continue along Alaska Ave. past a myriad of motels, restaurants, and gas stations. Turn right at 10th St. to city center (one block along 10th is the infamous Mile "0" sign), or continue along Alaska Ave. for half a block to the **Dawson Creek Tourist InfoCentre** in N.A.R. Park on the left.

SIGHTS

Northern Alberta Railway (N.A.R.) Park

The first place to visit is this park, in which you'll find the historic **Station Museum,** an **Art Gallery,** and the **Dawson Creek Tourist InfoCentre.** Start off in the restored original Northern Alberta Railway station, built in 1931, crammed with black-and-white photos of trains and railway memorabilia, a telegram office, and info on the city's founder, G.M. Dawson. The old station has a kitchen complete with antique stove, cooking utensils, and tea and coffee tins, a parlor with a spinning wheel, and two furnished bedrooms upstairs.

It's easy to spend at least an hour in the main rooms of the museum, studying black-and-white photos of the building of the Alaska Highway in 1942-43, display cases crowded with memorabilia from 1910 through the '60s, furs, snowshoes, and antlers that are estimated to be several thousand years old. Then there are predatory birds of northern North America, seed grains from Peace River country, old farming equipment, a gas pump from the 1920s, rattlesnake skin, African elephant tusks, and an alligator skull. And there's a 1941 Massey-Harris cream separator, old irons and washing machines and typewriters, stuffed critters, and B.C. bones—including one of the largest mammoth tusks found in western Canada and a dinosaur leg! If you're not mind-boggled by all this, rest your feet by viewing videos on all sorts of local items from the past and the present—make your selection at the desk. Admission to this marvelous and curious museum, open June-Sept. daily 0800-2000, is only $1 adult or $2 per family.

Art Gallery

The art gallery is just along from the museum, housed inside the Alberta Pool Elevators building. It's a fascinating old grain elevator that was saved from demolition and redesigned with a sloping walkway around the interior walls to make the most of the height of the building. Inside are high-quality paintings and locally made arts and crafts—for viewing and buying. It's open daily in summer 0900-1700, Sun. 0900-1300 and 1400-1700; admission free but donations accepted with a large smile.

Walter Wright Pioneer Village

At the Hart and Alaska highways junction, next to Mile Zero Campground, this village was started in 1969 when the city donated property to contain local pioneer buildings located by a Mr. Wright. Today you can see two pioneer churches, a furnished log house, a general store, the Napoleon Loiselle Blacksmith Shop, containing many of his inventions, a trapper's cabin with handmade furniture, and two schools, all of which stand in a village setting. Scattered around are pieces of old farm machinery, tools, and equipment that were used by the first homesteaders in the area. It's open July-Sept. 1000-2000; adult $1, family $2.

The Infamous Alaska Highway And Mile "0" Sign

The 2,450-km Alaska Canada Military Highway (also known as the Alaska Hwy. and the Alcan) was a road-construction feat unsurpassed in modern time. Its Mile "0" sign on 10th St. is probably one of the most photographed signs in the province. The original sign, only a one-meter-high post situated at the corner of 8th St. and Alaska Ave. to mark the beginning of the newly constructed Alaska Highway, was mowed down by a car in the 1940s. It was replaced in 1946 by a larger wooden post in the center of 102nd Ave. and 10th St. (not the exact geographical beginning of the highway but the center of the city). That post was moved by pranksters—locals claim that on Halloween one year the sign was taken, replaced by a porta-potty, and put under a bridge! Today the metal sign is slightly bigger, and it's firmly chained to the ground. A cairn marking the geographic beginning of the Alaska Highway stands in the corner of the N.A.R. Park. Above it, a sign reading "You are now entering the world-famous Alaska Highway" builds excitement as you do a last-minute check on essential supplies before starting your trek to the Yukon and Alaska.

In 1992 the Alaska Highway celebrates its 50th anniversary with all kinds of fun and entertaining events throughout the year. For info contact the Dawson Creek Rendezvous '92 Committee at 782-9595.

Dawson Creek Ski Hill

Four km south of the city on **Bear Mountain,** the ski hill provides skiers with a 124-meter vertical drop, a T-bar serving five runs, three runs with lights for night skiing, ski rental and lessons, and a modern-day lodge with lounge and catering service. To get there take 17th St. south out of the city. Cross-country skiing and snowmobiling are also popular pursuits in the neighboring region.

PRACTICALITIES

Accommodations

Dawson has three campgrounds: **Alahart,** near the junction of the Alaska and Hart high-

Dawson Creek Art Gallery

ways (mostly gravel campsites); **Tubby's,** on the Hart Hwy. (some grass and trees, full hookups); and **Mile Zero City Campground,** along the Alaska Hwy., by far the best for tenting and the most attractive. It's next to Dawson Creek Golf Course and has plenty of grass and trees. Each site has a picnic table. Bathroom blocks with hot showers, a shelter (very handy when the wind is blowing at 50 km/hour and you're trying to light your stove), and coin-operated washers and dryers are provided. Sites are $8 per night. It's less than a kilometer along the Alaska Hwy. from the Hwy. 97 junction, tel. 782-2590.

Econo Lodge at 632 103rd Ave., tel. 782-9181, is in the center of the city, east of Co-op Mall. The lodge has housekeeping and sleeping units, complimentary coffee, and prices ranging $25-28 s, $26-29 d, $30-39 twin. The **George Dawson Inn** is a full-service hotel, with licensed dining, pub, lounge, and winter plug-ins. Rooms from $49-55 s, $55-61 d or twin. Located at 11705 8th St., tel. 782-9151.

Food And Entertainment

The best place to eat in town is **Alaska Cafe,** with its old-fashioned wood decor and atmosphere, at 10213 10th St., tel. 782-7040. At lunch they serve tasty hamburgers, sandwiches, and croissants for $5-9; at dinner, steak, chicken, seafood, and pork dishes (lamb on Fri. and Sat.) start at around $9, but most are in the $12-16 range. Finish it off with a yummy dessert. It's always busy, and open seven days a week 1100-2300. **Boston Pizza** is another popular spot. Nibble your steaming hot pizza amongst all the greenery; gourmet pan pizzas start at $6 for a small. Or sample the pasta (half-orders also available) for $5-8, sandwiches for $4-6, or salads for around $4.50-6. Located at 1525 Alaska Ave., tel. 782-8585. Dawson Creek has several Chinese restaurants, but the one you hear the most about is **Dynasty** at 1009 102nd Ave., tel. 782-3138. It features Chinese cuisine, steak and seafood, and a salad bar, and offers a smorgasbord at lunch, and daily specials.

Dawson Creek Golf Course and Country Club has 18 challenging holes, next to the Mile Zero City Campground on the Alaska Highway west of town, tel. 782-7882. **Centennial Swimming Pool** is located on the corner of 10th St. and 105th Ave., tel. 782-7946, and provides a junior Olympic-size pool, a weight room, saunas, a Jacuzzi, and a tanning bed. Local performers and touring groups play at 600-seat **Unchagah Hall.** For a current schedule of events, call the InfoCentre at 782-9595. For evening entertainment see what's happening at **George's Lounge** in the George Dawson Inn at 11705 8th St., tel. 782-9151. **Center Cinema** is at 648 103rd Ave., next to the Co-op Mall, tel. 782-7117. **Hypertension Escape Bowling Lanes** (great name!) is at 1501 102nd Ave., tel. 782-8161.

Extravaganzas: This community certainly has plenty of celebrations and events going on throughout the year: in Feb. the **Mile Zero Mardi Gras** is held, in March the **Peace Country Arts Festival,** in April the **Kiwanis Trade and Sports Show,** and in May you can take part in the popular **Mile "0" Days,** during which you could attend a craft show, a parade, pig races, a fiddler's contest, a horse show, pancake breakfasts and cookouts, and a dart tournament. Schedules are available at the InfoCentre. In July the **Pouce Coupe Barbecue** is held. In Aug., the city holds its **Fall Fair Days and Rodeo,** in Oct. is the **Octoberfest,** and in Dec. is the **Rotary Carol Fest.**

Information And Services

Dawson Creek Tourist InfoCentre is at 900 Alaska Ave., tel. 782-9595. **Dawson Creek and District Chamber of Commerce** is at 816 Alaska Ave., no. 102, tel. 782-4868.

Dawson Creek and District Hospital is at 11100 13th St., tel. 782-8501. For an **ambulance,** call 782-2211; **RCMP,** tel. 782-5211. **Dawson Creek Farmers Market** is open on Sat. 0830-1500. The main **post office** is at 10401 10th St., tel. 782-2322. The **library** is at 1001 McKellar Ave., tel. 782-4661; open Tues., Wed., and Thurs. 1000-2100, Fri. and

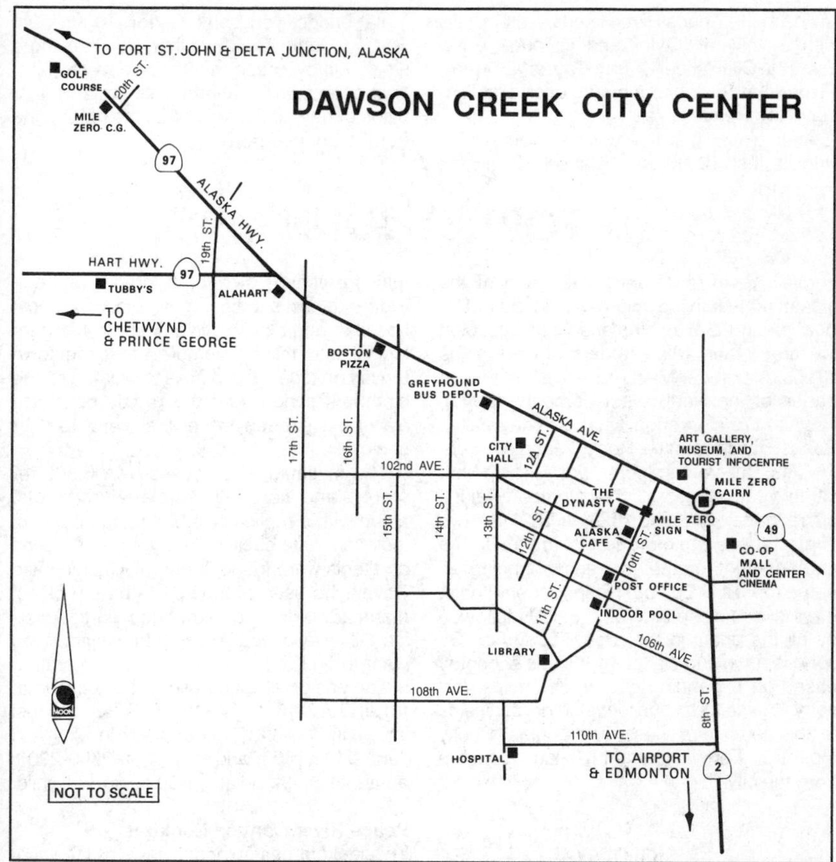

Sat. 1400-1730, and Sun. (Sept.-June) 1400-1730.

Transportation

The **Greyhound bus depot** is on Alaska Ave. between 12A and 14th streets. Railway lines run through Dawson Creek and trains stop at the station, but for freight only—no passenger service. At the **Dawson Creek Municipal Airport** south of town (take 8th St. south onto Hwy. 2), daily jet service is provided by **Air B.C.**

DAWSON CREEK TO FORT ST. JOHN

The Alaska Hwy. runs for 72 km north to Fort St. John, passing through almost-flat fields of crops, flowering rape, and wildflowers in summer for as far as you can see. **Kiskatinaw Provincial Park** is four km off the highway and has campsites, picnic tables, and fishing. Sites are $6 per night May-Sept., free in October. Watch out for deer in this area. The road then runs down through a steep ravine to the Peace River, lined by lumpy hills with a view of Taylor and its huge Petro Canada Oil Refinery. Tiny **Taylor Landing Provincial Park** has a boat launch and fishing in the Peace River.

After crossing the very wide Peace River, with its lush banks and islands, via a long metal bridge, you enter **Taylor,** 18 km from Fort St. John. On the other side are more small, lumpy, grass- and bush-covered hills, then open fields scattered with large circular bales of hay, and a sign off to the right to the Fort St. John Airport.

FORT ST. JOHN

Fort St. John is thought to be one of the oldest non-Native settlements in B.C. The Beaver and Sekani Indians both occupied the area when white traders arrived in the 1790s. Alexander Mackenzie was the first fur trader for the North West Company to venture, in 1793, through what is today called Peace River Country. Rocky Mountain Fort, the first fur-trading post, was set up that same year. Hudson's Bay Company didn't arrive in the area until 1820. In 1821 the two rival companies merged, taking over the management of the fort and changing its name to Fort D'Epinett. No longer profitable, the fort was closed in 1823, quickly followed by all the posts in the area. Today Fort St. John is a thriving city of 14,000, its economy based on expanding gas and oil fields, forestry, agriculture, and developing coalfields to the south and west. The original Rocky Mountain Fort lies about 10 km upstream from the city.

SIGHTS

Fort St. John/North Peace Museum

The museum is in the same building as the District Chamber of Commerce office. You can't miss the complex—outside the museum is restored **Holy Cross Chapel,** which was built in 1934, **Pump Jack** (a mechanical device attached to a submersible pump used to bring oil to the surface), and a skyscraping **oil derrick,** which came from Mile 143 on the Alaska Highway. In the museum local history springs to life—from the original Rocky Mountain Fort and fur-trading days with a trapper's cabin, through pioneer days with fully furnished kitchen, bedroom, schoolroom, dentist's office, post office, outpost hospital, and blacksmith's shop, to the geological and mining ventures that the town thrives on today. Don't miss the fur press, the birchbark canoe, and the grizzly bear with claws big enough to send shivers up your spine.

The museum also houses over 6,000 restored and carefully cataloged artifacts, along with a replica of a bead and photos of tools that date back 10,500 years—the bead and tools were found in nearby Charlie Lake Cave. The bead is thought to be the oldest manmade artifact unearthed in North America. Allow at least an hour for browsing. If you want to find out even more, ask the staff to put on one of the videos about the local area. It's at 9323 100th St., tel. 787-0430 (tourist info, call 785-3033); open daily in May and June 0800-1800, and July-Sept. 0800-2000; admission is $2 adult, $1.50 senior, $1 child.

Peace River Canyon Lookout

This lookout has splendid views of the wide, deep-green Peace River, lush fields, and the bush and rock canyon in both directions. Take your camera. It's well worth the short drive along a gravel road. From the Info-Centre, continue along 100th St. onto the gravel road at the end, and keep going—the road runs out at the edge of the canyon.

Charlie Lake

More than 10,500 years ago, Charlie Lake was part of a large ice-dammed lake formed from meltwater, which covered this area and northern Alberta. It has been named Lake Peace. At Charlie Lake Caves, artifacts such as stone tools, the bones of several animals, a fluted spear point, and a handmade stone bead (earliest found in North America) were discovered, leading archaeologists to believe that this area is possibly one of the earliest sites occupied by human beings. Charlie Lake is several kilometers north of Fort St. John. Today the lake is a popular recreation area known for its good trout, Arctic grayling, walleye, and northern pike fishing (not so good for swimming as the lake can clog with algae at times). Floatplanes can be chartered here to fly you into remote wilderness areas around the region.

At forested 92-hectare **Charlie Lake Provincial Park,** campsites and a sani station have been provided, along with boat-launching facilities, hiking trails, and good fishing. In winter the park's a lovely spot to strap on your cross-country skis and go. It's at the junction of highways 97 and 29; open May-Oct., with an $8 camp fee May-September.

Beatton Provincial Park is also located along Charlie Lake, but on the east side, six km north of Fort St. John. It features beautiful aspen-lined trails, a lakeside beach, boating, fishing, swimming, cross-country skiing, snowmobiling, ice-fishing (with warm-up huts), and campsites within its 312-hectare boundary. It's open May-Oct., $8 camp fee May-September. To get there from Fort St. John take Hwy. 97 N then turn right at the sign and continue approximately eight km along the gravel road.

Other recreational activities around the Fort St. John area include canoeing the rapids of the Peace River, skiing at **Big Bam,** and hunting for black bear, mountain caribou, and goat in the Rocky Mountain foothills.

PRACTICALITIES

Accommodations

Aside from lovely camping spots in the two provincial parks mentioned above, campsites can be found at **Fort St. John Centennial RV Park** which is open May-September. It provides tent sites, a sani station, showers, and laundry facilities, and it's between two

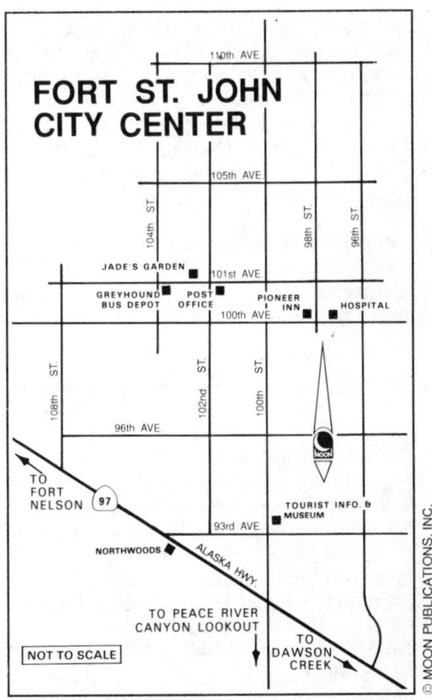

major shopping centers. Sites are $8-15 per night. At 9323 100th St., tel. 785-3033.

Most of the motels are located along Alaska Rd. or 100th St.; expect to pay from $30-35 s, $32-45 d. **Pioneer Inn** has a coffee shop, a dining room, lounges with evening entertainment, an indoor pool, a whirlpool and a sauna, and parking with hookups, and weekly rates are available. From $69 s, $78 d or t. At 9830 100th Ave., tel. 787-0521.

Food And Entertainment

Wilson Pizza has the best pizza in town and good lasagne at 9119 99th Ave., tel. 785-8969. If you're in the mood for some tasty Chinese, try the smorgasbord at **Jade's Garden** for under $10 pp. In fact, all their dishes are very reasonably priced. At 10108 101st Ave., tel. 787-2585; open daily from 1100.

For country and western music, locals flock to **Sidedoor** in the Pioneer Inn (free admission). For rock 'n' roll try the cabaret **Northwoods** on the Alaska Hwy. north of town (you hear locals saying they're heading for "The Woods,"), where you can expect to pay a couple of bucks to get in on Fri. or Sat. nights. **Casey's Neighborhood Pub** at 8163 100th Ave. is one of the most popular local meeting spots.

Information And Services

The **Fort St. John and District Travel InfoCentre** is at 9323 100th St. in the same building as the museum, tel. 785-3033; open daily 0800-1800 in May and June, daily 0800-2000 July-Sept., and on weekdays only 0800-1700 the rest of the year. The **hospital** is on 100th Ave. between 96th and 98th streets; the **post office** is on the corner of 101st Ave. and 102nd St.; the **library** is on 100th St. between 106th and 107th avenues.

Fort St. John has a local bus service; call in at the InfoCentre and pick up the current schedule. The **Greyhound bus depot** is on 101st Avenue. The airport is about nine km south of town off Hwy. 97, and is serviced by **Time Air, Air B.C.,** and charter companies.

HIGHWAY 29

Complete The Circle

Highway 29 is one of the most scenic roads in the region—and only 80 km between Fort St. John and Hudson's Hope. If you're not doing the Alaska Hwy., this is the route to take to return south! After leaving Fort St. John on the Alaska Hwy., you pass the turnoff to **Beatton Provincial Park** on the way to **Charlie Lake,** and the **Mukluk Trading Post** on the right side of the highway where you can admire and buy a wide variety of Indian crafts. Pass the appropriately named **Red Barn Pub** and then a large lake on the right before turning west on Hwy. 29 toward Hudson's Hope.

The road climbs up a hill then descends into the lush Peace River valley, providing highway travelers with delightul views most of the way down. In summer the route is perfumed by masses of wild roses that grow throughout the valley. At the bottom the highway meanders through a swampy area before climbing once again to drop back down to follow the river's path very closely—a beautiful, very wide, green, and unusually glassy river, despite the wind that whistles through the valley. **Dunlevy Recreation Area,** just before you enter Hudson's Hope, has good fishing, boat-launching facilities, and picnic sites.

HUDSON'S HOPE

This attractive small town (population 1,500) describes itself as the "Playground of the Peace" and the "Land of Dinosaurs and Dams." First discovered in 1793 by Alexander Mackenzie, the area was the site of a fur-trading post established in 1805. The post was moved in 1900 to the present townsite of Hudson's Hope on the north side of the beautiful Peace River—it's one of the oldest settlements in the province. Today it supports two nearby dams that generate almost 40% of the hydroelectricity used in the province—dams that have also created opportunities for all kinds of watersports and recreational activities.

Sights

Start off at the **Travel InfoCentre** on the main road, then wander across the street to **Hudson's Hope Museum,** which is crammed with geological rock specimens, bones and teeth from prehistoric animals (discovered when they were building the dams), and historic artifacts that belonged to trappers, miners, and early homesteaders. Beside the museum, on the north bank of the Peace River overlooking the spot where Simon Fraser wintered in 1805-1806, are a log replica of a 1900 Hudson's Bay trading post, a trapper's cabin, a fur cache, a furnished home from 1935, and the tiny log **St. Peter's Church**—peek inside, it's exquisite! The museum is open seven days a week 0930-1730 May-Sept., then on weekends up to Oct., admission free.

The main attractions, aside from the historic town itself, are the **Peace Canyon Dam** five km south at the outlet of the Peace River Canyon, downstream from the **W.A.C. Bennett Dam** (24 km south), one of the largest earth-fill structures in existence, built to harness hydroelectric power. Behind the dam lies 164,600-hectare **Williston Lake,** largest lake in British Columbia. You can take a self-guided tour of the Peace Dam (which reuses water that has generated electricity at the Bennett Dam) and find out all about it in the **Visitor Centre** adjacent to the powerhouse. Get there by taking 105th Ave. through town and continue toward Chetwynd. The center focuses on the fascinating natural history, exploration, and pioneers of the area, and the building of the Peace Canyon Project. You can also see the central control system, powerhouse, and switchgear station. Don't miss a trip up to the outside observation deck. Guided tours are also available for groups of eight or more; open daily 0800-1600 in summer, weekdays 0800-1600 the rest of the year, admission free. To view the dam structure from farther away, continue along the highway toward Chetwynd and cross the Peace River suspension bridge—good views from here.

You can also visit the **Bennett Dam Visitor Centre** on the top floor of the central control building. To get there take 107th Ave. onto Canyon Drive and continue west. See the photographic display of early Hudson's Hope, the construction of the dam, and the shocking displays featuring electricity. Guided underground tours (free) are also available at 1100, 1330, and 1430 year-round; open daily 0800-1600 in summer, weekdays 0800-1600 the rest of the year, admission free.

Practicalities

The **Travel InfoCentre** is beside **Beattie Park;** open in summer Fri.-Mon. 0800-2000, Tues.-Thurs. 0800-1800, tel. 788-3655. Pick up brochures on the local attractions, and the hiking trail guides—enjoyable walks but they aren't well marked and can be hard to follow (get more info before you set off). Hudson's Hope has several campgrounds and a couple of motel/hotels, a few restaurants and stores, a post office, and gas stations.

Hudson's Hope To Chetwynd

On your way back to Chetwynd you pass **Moberly Lake.** Just along the road is the **Moberly Lake and District Golf Club** on the left, where you can camp out, stay in a cabin, launch a boat, take a shower, stock up on supplies and gas at the store, or eat at the cafe. Several resorts are located along the highway, from which you can get glimpses of the enormous lake through the trees. The turnoff to **Moberly Lake Provincial Park** is to the right, with picnic sites, a boat launch, good swimming and fishing, and a campground (very popular with RV travelers in summer); open May-Oct., $8 camp fee May-September. Then it's down the hill and back into Chetwynd (see p.354).

THE ALASKA HIGHWAY

Travelers who had been along the infamous Alaska Hwy. years ago used to come back with tales of endless dust and mud holes, washed-out bridges, flat tires, broken windshields and smashed headlights, wildlife dashing out into the road, mosquitoes the "size of hummin'birds," few and crowded campgrounds, and sparse facilities. But they also sported "I drove the Alaska Hwy." bumper-stickers as though they had won a prize! Nowadays it can't be approached with quite the bravado—it's paved most of the way, has roadside lodges fairly frequently, and can easily be driven in three to four days, or two days and an all-nighter. What hasn't changed is the scenery—kilometer after kilometer of unspoiled wilderness: lush green hay fields, forests of spruce and aspen, the majestic, snow-dusted peaks of the Rockies, turquoise rivers and transparent streams, a deep-blue lake, even hot springs as you approach the Yukon border.

The 2,450-km Alaska Highway was built in nine months in 1942, connecting Dawson Creek with Delta Junction, Alaska, in response to a threatened Japanese invasion of Canada and the U.S. during WW II. It's infamous for being the longest strictly military road ever constructed in North America—an unsurpassed road-construction feat. At a cost of more than $140 million the highway was the major contributing factor in the 1940s to the growth of the Peace River region.

Read the brochures on the highway before you set off and you'll discover tips to make the route more enjoyable and less hazardous. Make sure your vehicle is dependable and has *five* good tires, stay well behind any vehicle in front of you to avoid flying gravel, approach construction work and repair areas with caution, slow down for bridges, bends in the road, pothole areas, and places where visibility is limited, and drive with your headlights on low beam. Be sure to carry spare essentials like tires, extra belts and hoses, and plenty of water. Also stock up on insect repellent in summer! The highway is maintained and can be driven year-round. Watch out for wildlife. From Fort St. John, Watson Lake (just over the Yukon border) is 532 kilometers. Information booths are located at Fort Nelson (tel. 774-2956) and Watson Lake (tel. 403-536-7496).

FORT ST. JOHN TO FORT NELSON

From One Fort To Another

After leaving Fort St. John, you pass **Beatton Provincial Park, Charlie Lake Provincial Park,** and the Hwy. 29 turnoff, which leads west to Hudson's Hope (75 km—see above). Passing through flat, forested countryside that progressively becomes more mountainous, the first small town is **Wonowan** (visitor services), about 80 km from Fort St. John. Not far north of **Pink Mountain** (visitor services) you enter the next time zone—in summer set your clock back one hour. At **Buckinghorse River Park,** located in the Rocky Mountain foothills, you'll find campsites, and some good river fishing. The park is open May-Oct. but a $6 fee is charged May-September. From here north, a new and scenic stretch of the highway runs through the **Minaker River Valley. Prophet River Recreation Area** overlooks the Prophet River (campsites $6 May-Sept.) and a hiking trail leads down to the river—watch out for bears and bison. Farther along is the tiny community of **Prophet River** (visitor services). The next place worth a detour, 12 km south of the highway along a dirt road, is 174-hectare **Andy Bailey Provincial Recreation Area.** Along Jackfish Creek you'll discover a sandy (yes, sandy) beach with good swimming and a boat launch, and the creek reportedly has good pike fishing. Oh, and the sand was brought in from elsewhere because most beaches up here are stony! The park is open

May-Oct.; campsites are $6 May-September. About 30 km from the park turnoff you enter Fort Nelson.

Fort Nelson

Fort Nelson (population 4,000) is the largest town between Fort St. John and the Yukon, lying on the site of many trading posts since 1800—each destroyed by either Indians, fire, or flood. It also lies at the meeting point of the **Muskwa, Prophet,** and **Sikanni Chief** rivers, all flowing together to create the large Fort Nelson River, which flows into the even larger **Liard River.** Fort Nelson's economy is based on forestry, oil, and gas—it has the second-largest gas-processing plant in North America, and the world's largest chopstick-manufacturing company.

The **Fort Nelson Historical Museum** contains more Alaska Highway construction items, and Indian and pioneer artifacts; open May-Sept. on Hwy. 9, at the north end of town, tel. 774-3536. Next door is the **Travel InfoCentre,** tel. 774-6400; open May-September. Throughout the rest of the year call 774-2541 for information. In summer the town puts on a Welcome Visitor Program—entertaining talks on local subjects for visitors or anyone who's interested. They take place in the Town Square; find out what the subject is at the InfoCentre. Fort Nelson has all the facilities visitors need. It also has an airport with scheduled and charter air services.

To get into remote 167,540-hectare **Kwadacha Wilderness Provincial Park** you need to hike or charter an airplane from Fort Nelson; no road access. The park, about 150 km southwest as the crow flies, offers spectacular glaciers, limestone peaks, hoodoos, forests, bright-blue lakes, and crystal-clear streams. It's a remote wilderness, abounding with wildlife (lots of grizzly bears), with good rainbow and lake trout fishing, hiking (make your own trails) and climbing, and wilderness walk-in campsites. Talk about getting off the beaten track! This is it.

FORT NELSON TO WATSON LAKE

Four hundred and eighty-three kilometers of Rocky Mountain peaks, glacial lakes, mountain streams, provincial parks with some of the best scenery, and the mighty Liard River. That's what awaits the traveler for the second half of the B.C. portion of the Alaska Highway. Branching off Hwy. 97 is the gravel **Liard Hwy.** (occasional facilities), which runs north to Fort Liard in Northwest Territories—this road makes the Alaska Highway look like a freeway! The next place with visitor services is the thriving community of **Steamboat Mountain,** population three! Nearby 1,067-meter Steamboat Mountain offers tremendous views from the top, accessible by a rough road branching off the highway about a kilometer or so north of the community. **Testa River** is another community of three. **Testa River Provincial Park** is accessed by a dirt road west off Hwy. 97. It offers grayling

KAREN WHITE

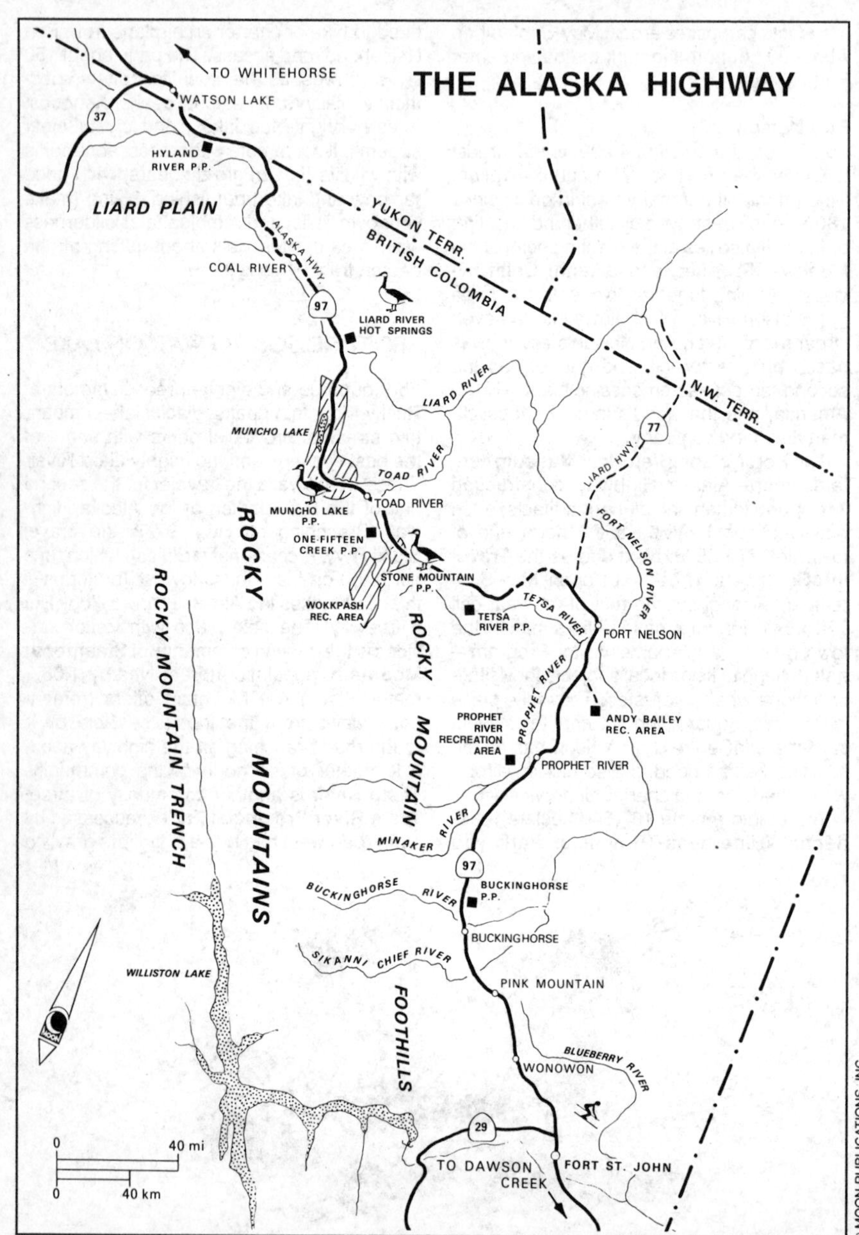

THE ALASKA HIGHWAY
TO WHITEHORSE
WATSON LAKE
37
HYLAND RIVER P.P.
LIARD PLAIN
YUKON TERR.
BRITISH COLOMBIA
ALASKA HWY.
COAL RIVER
97
LIARD RIVER HOT SPRINGS
LIARD RIVER
N.W. TERR.
77
LIARD HWY.
MUNCHO LAKE
TOAD RIVER
MUNCHO LAKE P.P.
TOAD RIVER
ONE-FIFTEEN CREEK P.P.
STONE MOUNTAIN P.P.
WOKKPASH REC. AREA
TETSA RIVER P.P.
TETSA RIVER
FORT NELSON RIVER
FORT NELSON
ROCKY MOUNTAIN TRENCH
ROCKY MOUNTAINS
ROCKY MOUNTAIN
PROPHET RIVER
PROPHET RIVER RECREATION AREA
ANDY BAILEY REC. AREA
PROPHET RIVER
MINAKER RIVER
97
BUCKINGHORSE RIVER
BUCKINGHORSE P.P.
BUCKINGHORSE
SIKANNI CHIEF RIVER
WILLISTON LAKE
PINK MOUNTAIN
FOOTHILLS
BLUEBERRY RIVER
WONOWON
29
TO DAWSON CREEK
FORT ST. JOHN
0
40 mi
0
40 km
MOON

fishing in the river, and short riverside hiking trails; open May-Oct., campsites are $8 per night May-September.

These provincial parks contain some of the most outstanding scenery and wildlife in northern B.C. The first, **Stone Mountain Provincial Park,** is 25,691 hectares of hoodoos, Rocky Mountain peaks, lakes, and rivers—a geological wonderland. The highway runs through the northernmost section of the park; within its boundaries are endless hiking and fishing, and walk-in wilderness campsites. Several trails lead to **Summit Lake** and to the summit of **Summit Peak. Wokkpash Provincial Recreation Area,** 37,800 hectares of wilderness suitable only for very experienced hikers and outdoorsmen, adjoins the southern boundary of Stone Mountain Park. The highway crosses **Summit Pass,** at 1,267 meters the highest point along the Alaska Highway. Just beyond is **Rocky Mountain Lodge** (visitor services).

One-fifteen Creek Provincial Park offers a few free campsites, and a short walk to ponds and huge beaver dams. At **Toad River** are visitor services and charter air service at the local airstrip. Look out for deer and stone sheep making mad dashes across the highway. **Muncho Lake Provincial Park** is another of the highway highlights—88,416 hectares around stunning, 12-km-long, blue-green **Muncho Lake.** Lying amongst mountains and forested valleys, with hoodoos, waterfalls, and plentiful wildlife attracted to its natural mineral licks, it's a naturalist's haven and a photographer's cloud nine. The highway winds right through the middle of the park for 80 km or so. The community of Muncho Lake, lying along the lakeshore, has visitor services.

One of the most wonderful places to stop on the whole Alcan is 668-hectare **Liard River Hot Springs Provincial Park,** where you can soak tired, dusty limbs in the Alpha and Beta hot pools (no soap or shampoo allowed), and while you relax, admire all the plants (they say there are 80 species not found anywhere else in northern B.C.) around the pools. Don't forget to remove your rings before stepping into the water. If you're lucky you'll see black bears, deer, and moose nearby. Below **Smith River Falls,** 30 km or so north of the hot pools, the fishing is good for grayling. More visitor services can be found at **Coal River.**

The next places to pull off for a few minutes are the viewpoint at **Whirlpool Canyon** to see both the canyon and the Liard River, then **Alan's Lookout** for more views of the Liard. You'll find visitor services at **Contact Creek** and **Iron Creek,** and riverside campsites and fishing at **Hyland River Provincial Park.** About 40 km beyond Hyland River Park is the B.C./Yukon border, where the Alaska Highway crosses the 60th parallel. The next town is **Watson Lake,** about 12 km northeast of the border.

Watson Lake, Yukon

The town of Watson Lake is famous for its highway-sign forest at the north end of town by the Hwy. 97 and Campbell Hwy. junction. It has an excellent **Alaska Highway Interpretive Centre,** which provides visitors with historic info on the highway through extensive displays and an audiovisual presentation, along with all the info you could possibly want on the Yukon. The staff can also provide you with info on road conditions and weather. The center is at the junction of the Alaska Hwy. and the Campbell Hwy., tel. 536-7469; open 0900-2100. The town has campgrounds, several restaurants, and all the services a traveler requires. In an emergency, an ambulance can be reached at 536-7355; the hospital at 536-7355; and the police at 536-7443, or dial 0 and ask for Zenith 5000.

BOOKLIST

HISTORY

Akrigg, G.V.P. and Helen B. Akrigg. *B.C./1847-1871 Chronicle.*

Duff, Wilson. *The Indian History of British Columbia: Vol. 1. The Impact Of The White Man.* Victoria: British Columbia Provincial Museum, 1987.

Elliot, Gordon R. *Parkerville. Quesnel, And The Cariboo Gold Rush.* Vancouver: Douglas and McIntrye, 1978.

Gold And Colonists. Discovery Press, 1977.

It Happened In British Columbia—A Pictorial Review 1871-1971. B.C. Centennial '71 Committee, 1970.

Pethick, Derek and Susan Im Baumgarten. *British Columbia Recalled: A Picture History 1741-1871.* Surrey: Hancock House Publishers Ltd., 1974.

Touchie, Rodger. *Vancouver Island: Portrait Of A Past.* Vancouver: J.J. Douglas Ltd., 1974.

GEOGRAPHY

Farley, A.L. *Atlas Of British Columbia: People, Environment, And Resource Use.* The University of British Columbia Press, 1979.

PEOPLE

Ashwell, Reg. *Indian Tribes Of The Northwest.* Surrey: Hancock House Publishers, 1977.

Malcolm, Andrew H. *The Canadians.* New York: Times Books, 1985.

Rogers, Edward S. *Indians Of The North Pacific Coast.* Toronto: Royal Ontario Museum, 1970.

Tanner, Ogden. *The Canadians.* Alexandria, Va.: Time-Life Books, 1977.

The Illustrated Library Of The World And Its Peoples. Greystone Press, 1967.

ARTS AND CRAFTS

Allen, D. *Totem Poles Of The Northwest.* Hancock House Publishers, 1977.

Kew, Della and P.E. Goddard. *Indian Art And Culture Of The Northwest Coast..* Surrey: Hancock House Publishers, 1974.

Knapp, Marilyn R. *Carved History.* Alaska Natural History Association, 1980.

FLORA AND FAUNA

Hunter, Tom. *Wildlife Of Western Canada.* Heritage House, 1986.

Kunelius, Rick. *Animals Of The Rockies.* Banff, Alberta: Altitude Publishing, 1983.

Langshaw, Rick. *Flowers Of The Canadian Rockies.* Summerthought Ltd., 1985.

Lyons, C.P. *Trees, Shrubs, And Flowers To Know In British Columbia.* T.M. Dent and Sons (Canada) Limited, 1976.

PARKS

Baird, D.M. *Banff National Park.* Edmunton: Hurtig Publishers, 1977.

Stephenson, Marylee. *Canada's National Parks: A Visitor's Guide.* Scarborough, Ontario: Prentice-Hall Canada, Inc., 1984.

TRAVEL

British Columbia's Coast: The Canadian Inside Passage. Alaska Geographic Society, 1985.

Brook, Paula. *Vancouver Rainy Day Guide.* San Francisco: Chronicle Books (in association with Solstice Press), 1984.

Bryan, Liz, and Jack Bryan. *Backroads Of British Columbia.* Vancouver: Sunflower Books, 1975.

Canadian Book Of The Road: A Complete Motoring Guide To Canada. Westmont, Quebec: Reader's Digest Books (in conjunction with the Canadian Auto Association), 1979.

Evans, Ginny, and Beth Evans. *The Vancouver Guide Book.* San Francisco: Chronicle Books, 1986.

Hazlitt, William Carew. *British Columbia And Vancouver Island.* S.R. Publishers Ltd., 1953, 1966.

Historic Fraser And Thompson River Canyons. Heritage House, 1986.

Macaree, Mary, and David Macaree. *103 Hikes In Southwestern British Columbia.* Seattle: The Mountaineers, 1987.

Magnificent Yellowhead Highway Vol. 2. Heritage House, 1980.

Searby, Ellen. *The Inside Passage Traveler: Getting Around In Southeastern Alaska.* Juneau: Windham Bay Press, 1986.

Shewchuk, Murphy. *Thompson Cariboo.* B.C. Backroads Explorer Vol. 1.

Stanley, David, and Deke Castleman,. *Alaska-Yukon Handbook.* Chico: Moon Publications, 1988.

ACCOMMODATIONS

B.C. Ministry of Tourism, Recreation, and Culture. *Accommodations.* Key Pacific Publishers Company Ltd. Printed every Jan., this free booklet is available at Travel InfoCentres throughout B.C.

Canadian Automobile Association. *Tour Book: Western Canada And Alaska.* Another free booklet available to members.

Pantel, Gerda. *The Canadian Bed And Breakfast Guide.* Markham, Ontario: Fitzhenry and Whiteside, 1987.

INDEX

Page numbers in **boldface** indicate the primary reference. *Italicized* page numbers indicate information in captions, callouts, charts, illustrations, or maps.

Jane King

ABOUT THE AUTHOR

Born in Scotland and raised in England, Jane King moved with her family to Sydney, Australia, in 1969. After attending secretarial college and nursing school in Sydney, she worked as a registered nurse in a small private surgical hospital farther north. A passion to see more of the world lured her away, and an exciting year of backpacking through Europe, with shorter trips to New Zealand, the U.S., and Canada, followed. Her love of travel was born! She met her American husband-to-be, Bruce, while exploring New Zealand in 1974. Since King enjoys outdoor adventures, such activities play a major part in this handbook. A person who "likes a good adrenalin rush," King also enjoys flying her 1942 Piper J-3 Cub, attending fly-ins and airshows, camping, hiking, cross-country skiing, river rafting, photography, spoiling her dogs and cats, and discovering more of the world with Bruce and their two-year-old daughter, Rachael.

FIJI ISLANDS HANDBOOK by David Stanley
The first and still the best source of information on travel around this 322-island archipelago. 8 color pages, 35 b/w photos, 78 illustrations, 26 maps, 3 charts, Fijian glossary, booklist, index. 198 pages. **$8.95**

INDONESIA HANDBOOK by Bill Dalton
This one-volume encyclopedia explores island by island the many facets of this sprawling, kaleidoscopic island nation. 30 b/w photos, 143 illustrations, 250 maps, 17 charts, booklist, extensive Indonesian vocabulary, index. 1,000 pages. **$19.95**

MICRONESIA HANDBOOK:
Guide to the Caroline, Gilbert, Mariana, and Marshall Islands by David Stanley
Micronesia Handbook guides you on a real Pacific adventure all your own. 8 color pages, 77 b/w photos, 68 illustrations, 69 maps, 18 tables and charts, index. 300 pages. **$11.95**

NEW ZEALAND HANDBOOK by Jane King
Introduces you to the people, places, history, and culture of this extraordinary land. 8 color pages, 99 b/w photos, 146 illustrations, 82 maps, booklist, index. 546 pages. **$14.95**

OUTBACK AUSTRALIA HANDBOOK by Marael Johnson
Australia is an endlessly fascinating, vast land, and *Outback Australia Handbook* explores the cities and towns, sheep stations, and wilderness areas of the Northern Territory, Western, and South Australia. Full of travel tips and cultural information for adventuring, relaxing, or just getting away from it all. 8 color pages, 39 b/w photos, 63 illustrations, 51 maps, booklist, index. 355 pages. **$15.95**

PHILIPPINES HANDBOOK by Peter Harper and Evelyn Peplow
Crammed with detailed information, *Philippines Handbook* equips the escapist, hedonist, or business traveler with thorough coverage of the Philippines's colorful history, landscapes, and culture. 8 color pages, 2 b/w photos, 60 illustrations, 93 maps, 30 charts, index. 587 pages. **$12.95**

SOUTHEAST ASIA HANDBOOK by Carl Parkes
Helps the enlightened traveler discover the real Southeast Asia. 16 color pages, 75 b/w photos, 11 illustrations, 169 maps, 140 charts, vocabulary and suggested reading, index. 873 pages. **$16.95**

SOUTH KOREA HANDBOOK by Robert Nilsen
Whether you're visiting on business or searching for adventure, *South Korea Handbook* is an invaluable companion. 8 color pages, 78 b/w photos, 93 illustrations, 109 maps, 10 charts, Korean glossary with useful notes on speaking and reading the language, booklist, index. 548 pages. **$14.95**

SOUTH PACIFIC HANDBOOK by David Stanley
The original comprehensive guide to the 16 territories in the South Pacific. 20 color pages, 195 b/w photos, 121 illustrations, 35 charts, 138 maps, booklist, glossary, index. 740 pages. **$15.95**

TAHITI-POLYNESIA HANDBOOK by David Stanley
All five French-Polynesian archipelagoes are covered in this comprehensive guide by Oceania's best-known travel writer. 12 color pages, 45 b/w photos, 64 illustrations, 33 maps, 7 charts, booklist, glossary, index. 235 pages. **$11.95**

THAILAND HANDBOOK by Carl Parkes
Presents the richest source of information on travel in Thailand. Color and b/w photos, illustrations, maps, charts, booklist, glossary, index. 600 pages **$16.95**

TIBET HANDBOOK by Victor Chan
This remarkable book is both a comprehensive trekking guide and a pilgrimage guide that draws on Tibetan literature and religious history. Color and b/w photos, illustrations, maps, charts, booklist, glossary, index. 1,200 pages. **$24.95**

The Hawaiian Series

BIG ISLAND OF HAWAII HANDBOOK by J.D. Bisignani
An entertaining yet informative text packed with insider tips on accommodations, dining, sports and outdoor activities, natural attractions, and must-see sights. 12 color pages, 72 b/w photos, 73 illustrations, 22 maps, 5 charts, booklist, glossary, index. 347 pages. **$11.95**

HAWAII HANDBOOK by J.D. Bisignani
Winner of the 1989 Hawaii Visitors Bureau's Best Guide Book Award and the Grand Award for Excellence in Travel Journalism, this guide takes you beyond the glitz and high-priced hype and leads you to a genuine Hawaiian experience. 12 color pages, 86 b/w photos, 132 illustrations, 86 maps, 44 graphs and charts, Hawaiian and pidgin glossaries, appendix, booklist, index. 879 pages. **$15.95**

KAUAI HANDBOOK by J.D. Bisignani
Kauai Handbook is the perfect antidote to the workaday world. 8 color pages, 36 b/w photos, 48 illustrations, 19 maps, 10 tables and charts, Hawaiian and pidgin glossaries, booklist, index. 236 pages. **$9.95**

MAUI HANDBOOK: Including Molokai and Lanai by J.D. Bisignani
"No fool-'round" advice on accommodations, eateries, and recreation, plus a comprehensive introduction to island ways, geography, and history. 8 color pages, 60 b/w photos, 72 illustrations, 34 maps, 19 charts, booklist, glossary, index. 350 pages. **$11.95**

OAHU HANDBOOK by J.D. Bisignani
A handy guide to Honolulu, renowned surfing beaches, and Oahu's countless other diversions. 12 color pages, 93 b/w photos, 67 illustrations, 18 maps, 8 charts, booklist, glossary, index. 354 pages. **$11.95**

The Americas Series

ALASKA-YUKON HANDBOOK by Deke Castleman and Don Pitcher
Get the inside story, with plenty of well-seasoned advice to help you cover more miles on less money. 8 color pages, 26 b/w photos, 95 illustrations, 92 maps, 10 charts, booklist, glossary, index. 384 pages. **$13.95**

ARIZONA TRAVELER'S HANDBOOK by Bill Weir
This meticulously researched guide contains everything necessary to make Arizona accessible and enjoyable. 8 color pages, 194 b/w photos, 74 illustrations, 53 maps, 6 charts, booklist, index. 505 pages. **$14.95**

BAJA HANDBOOK by Joe Cummings
A comprehensive guide with all the travel information and background on the land, history, and culture of this untamed thousand-mile-long peninsula. 8 color pages, 40 b/w photos, 28 illustrations, 41 maps, 29 charts, booklist, index. 356 pages. **$13.95**

BELIZE HANDBOOK by Chicki Mallan
Complete with detailed maps, practical information, and an overview of the area's flamboyant history, culture, and geographical features, *Belize Handbook* is the only comprehensive guide of its kind to this spectacular region. 8 color pages, 65 b/w photos, 43 illustrations, 25 maps, 30 charts, booklist, index. 212 pages. **$11.95**

BRITISH COLUMBIA HANDBOOK by Jane King
With an emphasis on outdoor adventures, this guide covers mainland British Columbia, Vancouver Island, the Queen Charlotte Islands, and the Canadian Rockies. 8 color pages, 56 b/w photos, 45 illustrations, 66 maps, 4 charts, booklist, index. 381 pages. **$13.95**

CANCUN HANDBOOK and Mexico's Caribbean Coast by Chicki Mallan
Covers the city's luxury scene as well as more modest attractions, plus many side trips to unspoiled beaches and Mayan ruins. 12 color pages, 76 b/w photos, 25 illustrations, 24 maps, 12 charts, Spanish glossary, booklist, index. 257 pages. **$10.95**

CATALINA ISLAND HANDBOOK: A Guide to California's Channel Islands
by Chicki Mallan
A complete guide to these remarkable islands, from the windy solitude of the Channel Islands National Marine Sanctuary to bustling Avalon. 8 color pages, 105 b/w photos, 65 illustrations, 40 maps, 32 charts, booklist, index. 245 pages. **$10.95**

COLORADO HANDBOOK by Stephen Metzger
Essential details to the all-season possibilities in Colorado fill this guide. Practical travel tips combine with recreation—skiing, nightlife, and wilderness exploration—plus entertaining essays. 8 color pages, 92 b/w photos, 15 illustrations, 57 maps, 10 charts, booklist, index. 422 pages. **$15.95**

IDAHO HANDBOOK by Bill Loftus
A year-round guide to everything in this outdoor wonderland, from whitewater adventures to rural hideaways. 8 color pages, 35 b/w photos, 21 illustrations, 42 maps, booklist, index. 275 pages. **$12.95**

JAMAICA HANDBOOK by Karl Luntta
From the sun and surf of Montego Bay and Ocho Rios to the cool slopes of the Blue Mountains, author Karl Luntta offers island-seekers a perceptive, personal view of Jamaica. 8 color pages, 21 b/w photos, 35 illustrations, 16 maps, 7 charts, booklist, glossary, index. 213 pages. **$12.95**

MONTANA HANDBOOK by W.C. McRae and Judy Jewell
The wild West is yours with this extensive guide to the Treasure State, complete with travel practicalities, history, and lively essays on Montana life. 8 color pages, 62 b/w photos, 43 illustrations, 49 maps, 10 charts, booklist, index. 393 pages. **$13.95**

NEVADA HANDBOOK by Deke Castleman
Nevada Handbook puts the Silver State into perspective and makes it manageable and affordable. 34 b/w photos, 43 illustrations, 37 maps, 17 charts, booklist, index. 400 pages. **$12.95**

NEW MEXICO HANDBOOK by Stephen Metzger
A close-up and complete look at every aspect of this wondrous state. 8 color pages, 85 b/w photos, 63 illustrations, 50 maps, 10 charts, booklist, index. 375 pages. **$13.95**

NORTHERN CALIFORNIA HANDBOOK by Kim Weir
An outstanding companion for imaginative travel in the territory north of the Tehachapis. 12 color pages, 200 b/w photos, 54 maps, 36 illustrations, booklist, index. 759 pages. **$16.95**

OREGON HANDBOOK by Stuart Warren and Ted Long Ishikawa
Brimming with travel practicalities and insider views on Oregon's history, culture, arts, and activities. 8 color pages, 113 b/w photos, 26 illustrations, 28 maps, 20 charts, booklist, index. 422 pages. **$12.95**

TEXAS HANDBOOK by Joe Cummings
Seasoned travel writer Joe Cummings brings an insider's perspective to his home state. 8 color pages, 79 b/w photos, 60 maps, 45 illustrations, 18 charts, booklist, index. 483 pages. **$13.95**

UTAH HANDBOOK by Bill Weir
Weir gives you all the carefully researched facts and background to make your visit a success. 8 color pages, 102 b/w photos, 61 illustrations, 30 maps, 9 charts, booklist, index. 452 pages. **$12.95**

WASHINGTON HANDBOOK by Dianne J. Boulerice Lyons and Archie Satterfield
Covers sights, shopping, services, transportation, and outdoor recreation, with complete listings for restaurants and accommodations. 8 color pages, 92 b/w photos, 24 illustrations, 81 maps, 8 charts, booklist, index. 433 pages. **$13.95**

WYOMING HANDBOOK by Don Pitcher
All you need to know to open the doors to this wide and wild state. 16 color pages, 30 b/w photos, 42 illustrations, 64 maps, 19 charts, booklist, index. 427 pages. **$12.95**

YUCATAN HANDBOOK by Chicki Mallan
All the information you'll need to guide you into every corner of this exotic land. 8 color pages, 154 b/w photos, 55 illustrations, 57 maps, 70 charts, appendix, booklist, Mayan and Spanish glossaries, index. 391 pages. **$12.95**

The International Series

EGYPT HANDBOOK by Kathy Hansen
An invaluable resource for intelligent travel in Egypt. 8 color pages, 20 b/w photos, 150 illustrations, 80 detailed maps and plans to museums and archaeological sites, Arabic glossary, booklist, index. 510 pages. **$14.95**

MOSCOW-LENINGRAD HANDBOOK by Masha Nordbye
Provides the visitor with an extensive introduction to the history, culture, and people of these two great cities, as well as practical information on where to stay, eat, and shop. 8 color pages, 36 b/w photos, 20 illustrations, 16 maps, 9 charts, booklist, index. 205 pages. **$12.95**

NEPAL HANDBOOK by Kerry Moran
Whether you're planning a week in Kathmandu or months out on the trail, *Nepal Handbook* will take you into the heart of this Himalayan jewel. 16 color pages, 76 b/w photos, 45 illustrations, 46 maps, 9 charts, booklist, glossary, index. 378 pages. **$12.95**

NEPALI AAMA by Broughton Coburn
A delightful photo-journey into the life of a Gurung tribeswoman of Central Nepal. Having lived with Aama (translated, "mother") for two years, first as an outsider and later as an adopted member of the family, Coburn presents an intimate glimpse into a culture alive with humor, folklore, religion, and ancient rituals. 67 b/w photos. 165 pages. **$13.95**

PAKISTAN HANDBOOK by Isobel Shaw
For armchair travelers and trekkers alike, the most detailed and authoritative guide to Pakistan ever published. 28 color pages, 86 maps, appendices, Urdu glossary, booklist, index. 478 pages. **$15.95**

Moonbelts

Made of heavy-duty Cordura nylon, the Moonbelt offers maximum protection for your money and important papers. This all-weather pouch slips under your shirt or waistband, rendering it virtually undetectable and inaccessible to pickpockets. One-inch-wide nylon webbing, heavy-duty zipper, one-inch quick release buckle. Accommodates traveler's checks, passport, cash, photos. Size 5 x 9 inches. Black. **$8.95**

New travel handbooks may be available that are not on this list.
To find out more about current or upcoming titles,
call us toll-free at (800) 345-5473.

IMPORTANT ORDERING INFORMATION

FOR FASTER SERVICE: Call to locate the bookstore nearest you that carries Moon Travel Handbooks or order directly from Moon Publications:

(800) 345-5473 · Monday-Friday · 9 a.m.-5 p.m. PST · fax (916) 345-6751

PRICES: All prices are subject to change. We always ship the most current edition. We will let you know if there is a price increase on the book you ordered.

SHIPPING & HANDLING OPTIONS:

1) Domestic UPS or USPS first class (allow 10 working days for delivery): $3.50 for the first item, 50 cents for each additional item.

Exceptions:

- **Moonbelt** shipping is $1.50 for one, 50 cents for each additional belt.
- Add $2.00 for same-day handling.

2) UPS 2nd Day Air or Printed Airmail requires a special quote.

3) International Surface Bookrate (8-12 weeks delivery): $3.00 for the first item, $1.00 for each additional item. Note: Moon Publications cannot guarantee international surface bookrate shipping.

FOREIGN ORDERS: All orders which originate outside the U.S.A. must be paid for with either an International Money Order or a check in U.S. currency drawn on a major U.S. bank based in the U.S.A.

TELEPHONE ORDERS: We accept Visa or MasterCard payments. Minimum order is US $15.00. Call in your order: 1 (800) 345-5473. 9 a.m.-5 p.m. Pacific Standard Time.

ORDER FORM

Be sure to call (800) 345-5473 for current prices and editions or for the name of the bookstore nearest you that carries Moon Travel Handbooks · 9 a.m.-5 p.m. PST (See important ordering information on preceding page)

Name:______________________________Date:______________

Street:____

City:________________________Daytime Phone:______________

State or Country:______________________Zip Code:____________

Quantity	Title	Price

Taxable Total	
Sales Tax (7.25%) for California Residents	
Shipping & Handling	
TOTAL	

Ship: ☐ 1st class ☐ UPS (no P.O. Boxes) ☐ International Surface

Ship to: ☐ address above ☐ other____________________________

____

____

Make checks payable to:

Moon Publications Inc., 722 Wall Street, Chico, California 95928 U.S.A.

We Accept Visa and MasterCard

To Order: Call in your Visa or MasterCard number, or send a written order with your Visa or MasterCard number and expiration date clearly written.

Card Number: ☐ **Visa** ☐ **MasterCard**

☐☐☐☐ ☐☐☐☐ ☐☐☐☐ ☐☐☐☐

Exact Name on Card: ☐ same as above expiration date:______________

☐ other____

signature____

3-77-8

WHERE TO BUY THIS BOOK

Bookstores and Libraries:
Moon Publications Handbooks are sold worldwide. Please write our sales manager for a list of wholesalers and distributors in your area that stock our travel handbooks.

Travelers:
We would like to have Moon Publications Handbooks available throughout the world. Please ask your bookstore to write or call us for ordering information. If your bookstore will not order our guides for you, please write or call for a free catalog.

MEASUREMENTS

British Columbia uses the metric system of measuring weights and distances, and the Celsius system for temperatures. The following conversion charts should be useful to those unfamiliar with these system.

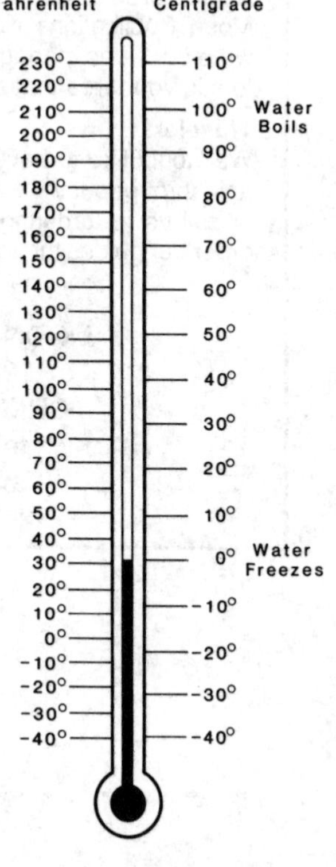

1 inch = 2.54 centimeters (cm)
1 foot = .304 meters (m)
1 mile = 1.6093 kilometers (km)
1 km = .6214 miles
1 fathom = 1.8288 m
1 chain = 20.1168 m
1 furlong = 201.168
1 acre = .4047 hectares (ha)
1 sq km = 100 ha
1 sq mile = 2.59 sq km
1 ounce = 28.35 grams
1 pound = .4536 kilograms (kg)
1 short ton = .90718 metric ton
1 short ton = 2000 pounds
1 long ton = 1.016 metric tons
1 long ton = 2240 pounds
1 metric ton = 1000 kg
1 quart = .94635 liters
1 US gallon = 3.7854 liters
1 Imperial gallon = 4.5459 liters
1 nautical mile = 1.852 km

To compute Centigrade temperatures, subtract 32 from Fahrenheit and divide by 1.8. To go the other way, multiply Centigrade by 1.8 and add 32.

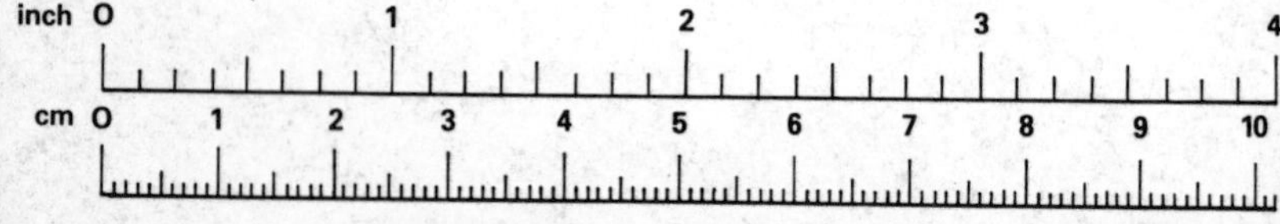